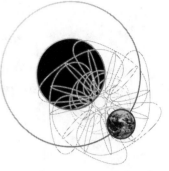

# Real World
# Adobe InDesign 2

*by*
Olav Martin Kvern
&
David Blatner

D0572510

Adobe

PEACHPIT PRESS

*for Max and Gabriel*

*& in memory of*
*Stanley Fleming Kvern, 1931-2002*

REAL WORLD ADOBE INDESIGN 2
Olav Martin Kvern and David Blatner

Copyright © 2003 by Olav Martin Kvern and David Blatner

PEACHPIT PRESS
1249 Eighth Street
Berkeley, California 94710
(800) 283-9444
(510) 524-2178
(510) 524-2221(fax)

Find us on the World Wide Web at: http://www.peachpit.com
Peachpit Press is a division of Pearson Education
*Real World Adobe InDesign 2* is published in association with Adobe Press

Editor: Nancy Davis
Indexer: Caroline Parks
Cover design: Gee + Chung Design
Cover illustration: Bud Peen
Cover Production: George Mattingly, GMD
Interior design, illustration, and production: Olav Martin Kvern, David Blatner, and Carl Juarez

ISBN 0-201-77317-1
9 8 7 6 5 4 3 2 1

Printed and bound in the United States of America

# CONTENTS

We're desktop publishers—just like you. We've been through the long shifts (some of them longer than 70 hours), entering and editing text, setting type, drawing paths, importing images, and trying to get files to print. On most of those late nights and early mornings, we could have been home in bed if we had known just one key piece of information. But we weren't. There was no one there to tell us.

We're here to tell you.

If some piece of information in this book saves you one late night, one early morning, or gets your document to print on the first pass through the imagesetter instead of the second or third, we will have succeeded in our purpose.

InDesign is a watershed of new technologies that have, until now, been at the edge of our page layout "radar": support for OpenType and Unicode, direct export of prepress-quality PDF files, integral PostScript/PDF screen rendering, multi-line composition, built-in font management, optical kerning, and solid scripting support, to name just a few of them. Adobe has always said that InDesign is "the future of page layout"—but we think they're selling themselves a bit short. With InDesign, the future is here.

And, to our eyes, at least, it looks pretty cool.

## How This Book Was Produced

To answer the question we've been asked so many times: Yes, we produced this book in InDesign 2. Chapters were written in Microsoft Word, saved as Rich Text Format (RTF) files, and imported into InDesign templates. Screen captures were produced using Snapz Pro (for Mac OS X) and SnagIt (for Windows). Other graphics were produced using either InDesign's drawing tools, Adobe Photoshop, or Adobe Illustrator.

David laid out chapters using a Macintosh Powerbook G4 (Titanium) running Mac OS X. Olav laid out chapters on a (now ancient) Silicon Graphics SGI 320 workstation running Windows 2000 and on a Macintosh Powerbook G3, also running Mac OS X.

The book is set entirely in Minion Pro (an Adobe OpenType face, which was particularly useful when moving files from Windows to Macintosh, and *vice versa*), except for a few symbol characters set in ITC Zapf Dingbats.

## Acknowledgments

Thanks to Adobe's InDesign team and all the other folks at Adobe who helped support this book—including Bruce Chizen, Will Eisley, Mark Niemann-Ross, David Cohen, Tim Cole, Thomas Phinney, Lonn Lorenz, Maria Yap, Eliot Harper, Mordy Golding, Eric Menninga, Zak Williamson, Priscilla Knoble, Roey Horns, Paul Sorrick, Michael Wallen, and Christine Yarrow. Special thanks, too, to David Evans, ex(traordinary)-InDesign evangelist for Adobe, who wrote the foreword to the first edition of this book.

Thanks to the Seattle Gilbert and Sullivan Society and their photographer, Ray O. Welch, for giving us permission to use some of their archival photographs as example images. Special thanks to Ed Poole for the free use and abuse of his moustache.

Thanks to Caroline Parks for our index, and thanks to all our friends at Peachpit Press for their patience, support, patience, professionalism, patience, and understanding (and did we mention patience?), including Nancy Ruenzel, our amazing editor Nancy Davis, Serena Herr, Mimi Heft, and Lisa Brazieal.

DAVID: "Thanks to all my officemates—Glenn Fleishman, Steve Roth, Jeff Carlson, Jeff Tolbert, and Larry Chen—and to my friends and family who have listened to me grouse about this book for too many months. Special thanks to my wife, Debbie Carlson, and to Gabriel Carl Blatner, who isn't quite old enough to help lay out pages (but sure would like to gum the keyboard)."

OLE: "Thanks to Max Olav Kvern, for covering my back when the brain-sucking undead Elmore zombies attack, and to the Anime Night gang for keeping me something like sane."

Olav Martin Kvern
ole@desktopscience.com

David Blatner
david@moo.com

Seattle, 2002

# Workspace

## CHAPTER 1

Come on in! Let us show you around. We'll be your tour guides to the world of InDesign. We're here to tell you what's what, what's where, and how it all fits together. This chapter is all about InDesign's user interface—the myriad windows, palettes, menus, and other gadgets InDesign displays on your screen. It tells you what they all are, and what we call them (this is important, because not everything in InDesign is clearly labeled—as you read through the techniques in this book, you need to know that we mean this button *over here*, and not that button *over there*).

This chapter also contains lots of tips and tricks for working with InDesign's user interface. These are the "little things" that make all the difference between enjoying and hating the time you spend working with InDesign (or any other program, for that matter). The point is to get you up to speed with all of these new tools so that you can get on with your work.

Ready? Let's start the tour.

**A Note About Keyboard Shortcuts:** Throughout this book, we will refer to keyboard shortcuts using the formatMac OS/Windows, as in "Command-Z/Ctrl-Z" (this is not necessarily in our order of platform preference, but it is in alphabetical order).

**Another Note About Keyboard Shortcuts:** Since you can redefine most of the keyboard shortcuts in InDesign, we can't guarantee that your keyboard shortcuts will match ours. And we can't follow every keyboard shortcut in the text with the disclaimer, "...or the shortcut you've defined for this action." So, as you read this, bear in mind that we're using the shortcuts from the default keyboard shortcut set. If you want to return to InDesign's default keyboard shortcuts, see "Customizing Keyboard Shortcuts," later in this chapter.

**Yet Another Note About Keyboard Shortcuts:** A few of InDesign's default keyboard shortcuts—especially those for selecting tools—do not use a modifier key (by "modifier key," we mean Command, Control, Option, Ctrl, Alt, Shift, and so on). If you're editing text, you can't use these keyboard shortcuts. If you do, you'll end up entering characters in the text.

The keyboard shortcut to switch to the Pen tool, for example, is "P." If you press the shortcut while the cursor is in text, you'll enter the character "P." If you use InDesign to set type (as most of us do), you'll almost certainly want to add a modifier key to the unmodified keyboard shortcuts you use most often.

Unfortunately, you can't modify the "hide all palettes" shortcut. It's hardwired to the Tab key. You also can't switch to the Selection tool (press Command/Ctrl) and then use the shortcut.

## Publication Windows

When you open or create an InDesign publication, you view and work on the publication in one or more publication windows (see Figure 1-1). Each publication window gives you a view on a page, spread, or pasteboard area in an InDesign publication. You can have multiple publication windows open on a single publication, and you can have multiple open publications.

The view of the publication you see in a publication window can be magnified or reduced to show more or less detail. Each publication window can be set to a different magnification. Since magnification is primarily a way of moving around in your publication, we'll cover it later in this chapter, in "Publication Navigation."

**Title Bar**   At the top of a publication window you'll see the title bar. The appearance of the title bar differs slightly between the Windows and Macintosh versions of InDesign (and between Mac OS X and previous Macintosh operating systems). In Windows, you'll see the title,

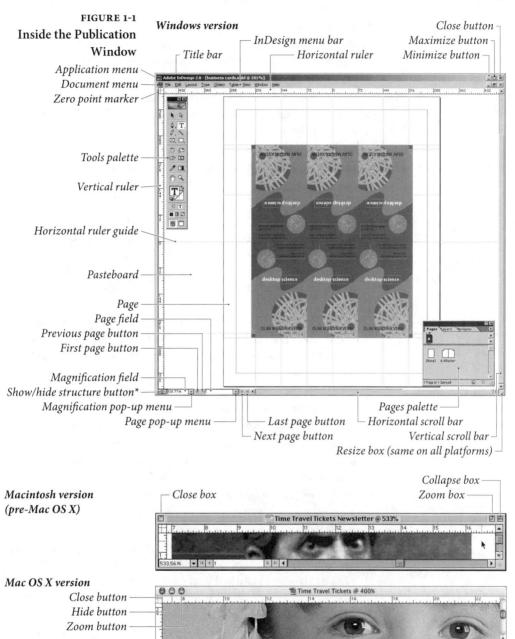

**FIGURE 1-1**
**Inside the Publication**
**Window**

*Windows version*

*Close button*
*Maximize button*
*Minimize button*

*InDesign menu bar*
*Horizontal ruler*

*Title bar*

*Application menu*
*Document menu*
*Zero point marker*

*Tools palette*

*Vertical ruler*

*Horizontal ruler guide*

*Pasteboard*

*Page*
*Page field*
*Previous page button*
*First page button*

*Magnification field*
*Show/hide structure button**
*Magnification pop-up menu*
*Page pop-up menu*

*Pages palette*
*Last page button*    *Horizontal scroll bar*
*Next page button*
*Vertical scroll bar*
*Resize box (same on all platforms)*

*Macintosh version*
*(pre-Mac OS X)*

*Close box*

*Collapse box*
*Zoom box*

Time Travel Tickets Newsletter @ 533%

533.56%

*Mac OS X version*
*Close button*
*Hide button*
*Zoom button*

Time Travel Tickets @ 400%

400%

control menu, and close/minimize/maximize buttons (click them to close, hide, or enlarge a publication window, respectively). On the Macintosh, you'll see the title (the name of your publication file), close box (click it to close the window), and zoom box (click it to expand the publication window to the size of the screen; click it again to return the publication window to its previous size). In Mac OS X, the close box, zoom box, and collapse box are replaced by the close button, zoom button, and hide button (respectively), which do pretty much the same things (with the addition of annoying animation).

To close a publication window, press Command-W/Ctrl-W (or Ctrl-F4). To close all publication windows, press Command-Option-Shift-W/Ctrl-Alt-Shift-W.

### Pasteboard and Page

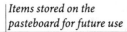

*Items stored on the pasteboard for future use*

*Document pages*
*Pasteboard*

Like most other page layout programs, InDesign is built around the concept of the pasteboard—an area on which you place pages and graphic elements. The pasteboard is not a fixed size, as it is in FreeHand or PageMaker, and it's not shared between spreads—each spread has its own pasteboard (as in QuarkXPress). You can use areas of the pasteboard for temporary storage of the elements you're working with—just drag the elements off the page, and they'll stay on the pasteboard until you need them (again, this is just like an old-fashioned layout board).

When objects can extend past the edge of the page, into the pasteboard, they create a "bleed." The objects will be clipped off at the edge of the paper when your commercial printer cuts your printed pages, but sometimes, that's just the design effect you want.

The size of the bleed, the page size, and the size of the paper (that is, the paper size you want to use when you print your final copy) all affect each other. In InDesign, the page size you define in the Document Setup dialog box should be the same as the final size of the document's page after it's been printed and trimmed by a commercial printer. You define the paper size in the Print dialog box (Macintosh) or Printer Properties dialog box (Windows) when it's time to print your publication. When you're printing to an imagesetter, the paper size is a defined area on the imagesetter's film roll (or sheet).

If your publication's page size (without the bleed) is the same as the paper size you've chosen in the Print Options dialog box, you can expect InDesign to neatly clip off any elements that extend beyond the edge of the page. Choose a larger paper size than your publication's page size when you want to print bleeds (choose Letter.Extra when you're printing a letter-size publication with a bleed, for example). If you want to learn how to create new paper sizes for imagesetters (we don't know of any laser printer that can handle custom paper sizes).

**Increasing the size of the pasteboard.** If you prefer a larger pasteboard (similar to the one found in PageMaker, for example), follow these steps.

1. Choose Document Setup from the File menu. InDesign displays the Document Setup dialog box.

2. Choose (or create) a page size larger than your current page size, then click OK to close the dialog box.

3. Zoom out and draw a rectangle that is at least the height of your new page size.

4. Return to the Document Setup dialog box and reinstate your original page size. InDesign applies the page size, but leaves the pasteboard at the larger size. You can delete the rectangle.

**Scroll Bars**

*The enemy of productivity*

The most obvious, least convenient, and slowest way to change your view of your publication is to use a scroll bar (that is, to click in a scroll bar, drag a scroll handle, or click the scroll arrows). For more on better ways to get around, see "Publication Navigation," later in this chapter.

**Page Field and Page Buttons**

The Page field/pop-up menu and its attached navigation buttons give you a way to get from one page to another. Click the Previous Page button to move to the previous page in your publication, or click the Next Page button to move to the next page. Alternatively, you can click the First Page button to go to the first page in the publication, or the Last Page button to go to the last one.

If you know exactly which page you want to go to, choose the page number from the Page pop-up menu or enter the page number in the Page field.

**Magnification Field**

Enter a magnification percentage in this field, or choose one from the attached pop-up menu, and InDesign magnifies or reduces the view of the publication you see in the publication window. There are better ways to do this, as shown in "Publication Navigation," later in this chapter.

To make the cursor "jump" into the Magnification field, press Command-Option-5/Ctrl-Alt-5. Enter a percentage and press Enter to change the publication window's magnification.

These views aren't the only magnifications available—if you use the Zoom tool, you can achieve any magnification you want. For more on using the Zoom tool, see "Zooming," later in this chapter.

**Rulers**

Pressing Command-R/Ctrl-R displays or hides InDesign's rulers—handy measuring tools that appear along the top and left sides of a publication window (see Figure 1-2). The rulers are marked off in the units of measurement specified in the Units & Increments Preferences dialog box. The actual increments shown on the rulers vary somewhat with the current magnification; in general, you'll see finer increments and more ruler tick marks at 800% size than you'll see at 12% size.

As you move the cursor, lines in the rulers (called shadow cursors) display the cursor's position on the rulers (see Figure 1-3).

To change the units of measurement used by a ruler, Control-click/Right-click the ruler to display the Context menu. Choose a new measurement system from the menu, or choose Custom to enter a custom measurement increment (if you do this, InDesign displays the Custom Measurement Unit dialog box, where you can enter the measurement unit you want to use).

**FIGURE 1-2**
**Rulers**

*The Context menu is the quickest way to change measurement units.*

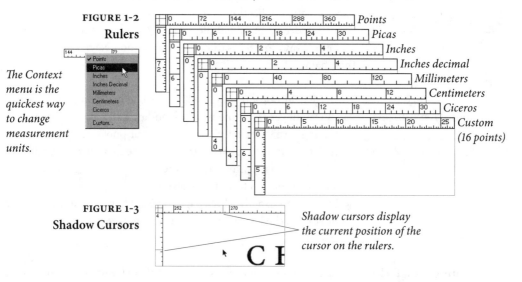

**FIGURE 1-3**
**Shadow Cursors**

*Shadow cursors display the current position of the cursor on the rulers.*

**Zero Point**   The intersection of the zero measurement on both rulers is called the zero point. In InDesign, the default location of the zero point is at the upper-left corner of the spread, page, or binding spine (it's an option in the Grids Preferences dialog box). To control the location of the zero point, use the zero point marker (see Figure 1-4).

To move the zero point, drag the zero point marker to a new position. As you drag, intersecting dotted lines show you the position of the zero point. Stop dragging, and the rulers will mark off their increments based on the new position of the zero point marker.

To reset the zero point to the default location, double-click the zero-point marker.

To lock the position of the zero point, use the Context menu. Point at the zero point, then hold down Control and click (Macintosh) or click the right mouse button (Windows). Choose Lock Zero Point from the Context menu (see Figure 1-5). To unlock the zero point, display the Context menu and choose Unlock Zero Point.

**FIGURE 1-4**
**Moving the Zero Point**

*Position the cursor over the zero point marker.*

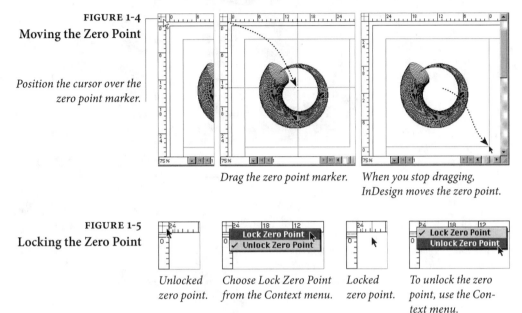

*Drag the zero point marker.*    *When you stop dragging, InDesign moves the zero point.*

**FIGURE 1-5**
**Locking the Zero Point**

*Unlocked zero point.*    *Choose Lock Zero Point from the Context menu.*    *Locked zero point.*    *To unlock the zero point, use the Context menu.*

---

## Managing Multiple Windows

*InDesign displays a list of open publication windows at the bottom of the Window menu.*

If you want to open more than one window on a publication, choose "New Window" from the Window menu. The new window covers the original window, so you'll have to drag and resize windows to see both views at once, or choose Tile Windows from the Window menu (see Figure 1-6). Choose Cascade from the Window menu to stack the open publication windows on top of each other.

To get from an active publication window to an inactive publication window, you can click any part of the inactive window, or you can choose a window name from the listing of open windows at the bottom of the Window menu.

Sometimes it's easier to display pages in multiple windows than it is to scroll or zoom from page to page. Think about using use multiple windows in the following situations:

◆ When you find yourself jumping back and forth between two or more locations in a publication.

◆ When you need to copy an object or objects from one page to another page that's several pages away. Dragging the objects

FIGURE 1-6
**Window Views**

*When you choose Cascade from the Window menu, InDesign stacks up the open publication windows. To bring any window to the front, click its title bar.*

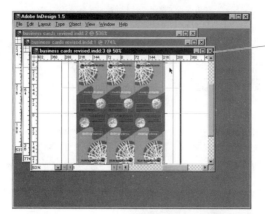

*InDesign highlights the title bar of the active publication window.*

*In either view, you can rearrange and resize windows to create custom views.*

*When you choose Tile from the Window menu, InDesign arranges the open publication windows to fill the screen (Macintosh) or the InDesign application window (Windows).*

*Use the Tile view when you want to drag objects from one window to another or from one publication to another.*

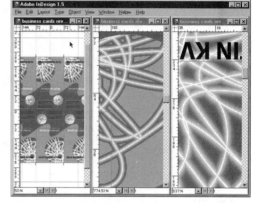

from one publication window to another is faster than scrolling and dragging or cutting and pasting.

◆ When you're trying to fit copy into a story that spans several pages. You can make one publication window focus on the end of the story, and, as you edit and format text, you can see exactly when the last line of the copy appears at the end of the last text frame (see Figure 1-7).

There's no trick to removing a view—simply close the window, and the view disappears from your Windows menu.

You can have as many different publications open as you like. You switch from one publication to another by choosing a window name from the bottom of the Window menu, or by clicking on their windows, just as you'd switch among applications.

To close all open windows, hold down Option as you click the Close box (Macintosh) or hold down Shift as you click the Close button (Windows). Or press Command-Option-Shift-W/Ctrl-Alt-Shift-W to close all of the open windows.

**FIGURE 1-7**
**Using Views**
**for Copyfitting**

*This window shows you the
text at the beginning of the
story.*

*With these two windows
open, you can quickly see
whether deleting these words
will make the story fit.*

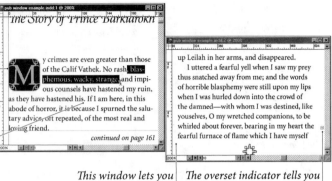

*This window lets you
"spy" on the end of the
story as you edit text.*

*The overset indicator tells you
that there's still more text in
the story to fit onto the page.*

*When you delete the
text in this window...*

*...you can see that the
story fits (the overset text
indicator disappears).*

## InDesign's Palettes

Can you see your page? If not, it's probably due to InDesign's omni-present palettes—there are plenty of them (see Figure 1-8). Don't rush out to buy a larger screen—you don't have to have all of the palettes open all of the time. The best way to work with InDesign's palettes is to have the minimum number of them open at once, to combine palettes into functional groups, and to learn and master the keyboard shortcuts for working with and navigating through palettes. That's what this part of the book is about.

InDesign's palettes work two ways—they display information about the publication or the selected object or objects, and they provide controls for changing the publication and the objects in it. The palettes are an integral part of InDesign's user interface and are the key to doing almost everything you can do in the program.

**FIGURE 1-8**
**InDesign Palettes**

You find tools in—where else—the Tools palette.

Why do we include pictures of the palettes? So you can take the book away from your computer and still be able to see what we're talking about. It's an attempt at creating a kind of virtual reality—on paper.

*Use the Pages palette to add, delete, and arrange document pages and apply master pages.*

*The Navigator palette gives you another way to change your view of a publication.*

Use the Library palette (or any number of Library palettes) to store text and graphics for future use.

*Want to work with objects "by the numbers?" If so, the Transform palette is for you.*

The Character palette controls character formatting.

*Use the Paragraph palette to set paragraph indents, alignment, and other paragraph formatting attributes.*

*When you import text or graphics, you create a link to the original file on disk. InDesign's Links palette helps you manage these connections.*

InDesign 2 adds indexing features—and the Index palette is where you work with index topics and cross-references.

*Use the Align palette to align and distribute objects.*

*When you want text to avoid a graphic, use the options in the Text Wrap palette.*

**FIGURE 1-8**
**InDesign Palettes**
**(Continued)**

Paragraph styles and Character styles can save you lots of time and trouble. These two palettes are the key to working with styles.

*Use the Tables palette to avoid lengthy trips to the table-related dialog boxes.*

Want to set a tab stop? You'll have to talk to the Tabs palette.

*Store, edit, and apply named colors, tints, and gradients using the Swatches palette.*

Use the Find/Change palette to find and change text in your InDesign publications.

*You can also define and apply unnamed colors and tints using the Color palette.*

*Use the Gradient palette to control the gradient ramp and angle of gradient fills and strokes.*

You've heard the rumor, and it's true: InDesign pushes the boundaries of user interface design (and possibly common sense) by providing the Check Spelling palette.

*Use the Stroke palette to set the stroke width, stroke type, and other stroke attributes.*

The options in the Attributes palette control the overprinting/knockout qualities of the fill or stroke of an object.

FIGURE 1-8
**InDesign Palettes**
**(Continued)**

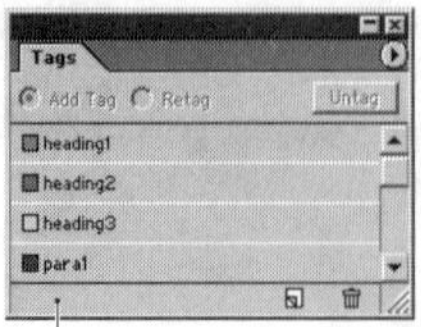

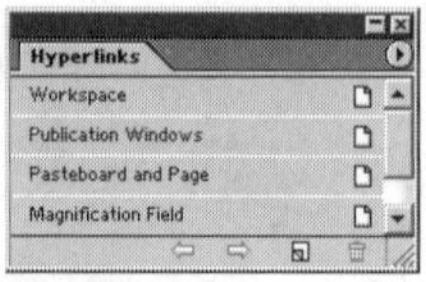

*Tags provide a link between objects and elements in the XML structure of your document. The Tags palette is where you create, manage, and apply tags.*

*Planning to export your InDesign document as HTML or PDF? If so, you might want to add navigational features. The Hyperlinks palette is where you create links and define destinations.*

*The Script palette provides a view of the files in the Scripts folder in your InDesign folder. Double-click a script in the Script palette to run it.*

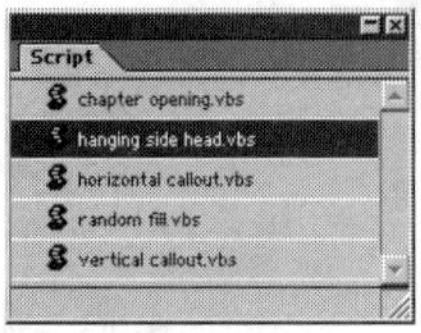

*The Script palette and the Script Label palette are not installed by default.*

*The Script Label palette shows you the label associated with the selected object.*

**All About Focus**

When a particular window, or field, or control is active, we say it has "focus"—meaning that the gadget is receiving any keystrokes you might press. If you're furiously pressing keys, and yet no text is appearing in the selected text frame, it's because something else—some other window—has focus.

Understanding and manipulating palette focus is very important—especially when you're working with text.

When you choose a menu option or click a button in a palette, InDesign applies the change and returns focus to your page layout. When you press Tab to move ahead one field (or Shift-Tab to move back one field), InDesign applies any change you made and shifts focus to the next (or previous) palette field.

InDesign offers a number of keyboard shortcuts for controlling keyboard focus:

◆ Press Enter/Return to apply a value you've entered in a palette field and return focus to your page.

◆ Press Shift-Return/Shift-Enter to apply the value you've entered in a palette field and keep that palette field in focus.

◆ If you've entered a value in a palette field and decide you don't want to apply it, press Escape/Esc. InDesign changes the field back to whatever it was before you started typing, and keeps the focus on the palette field.

◆ In any of the "list" palettes (the Swatch Library palette, for example), hold down Command-Option/Ctrl-Alt and click in the list. This transfers focus to the list—you can type the name of a list item to select that item from the list (see Figure 1-9).

FIGURE 1-9
**Palette Lists and Focus**

*Once a list has focus, you can select list items by typing—it's often quicker than scrolling.*

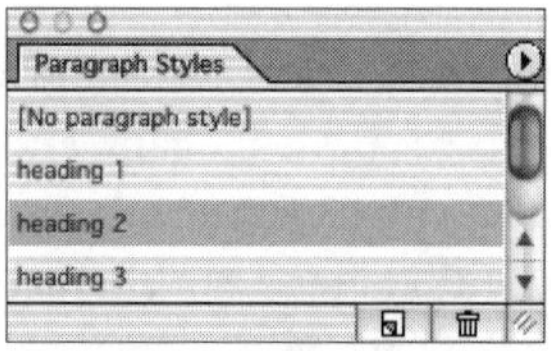

Hold down Command-
Option/Ctrl-Alt and
click to give a list focus.

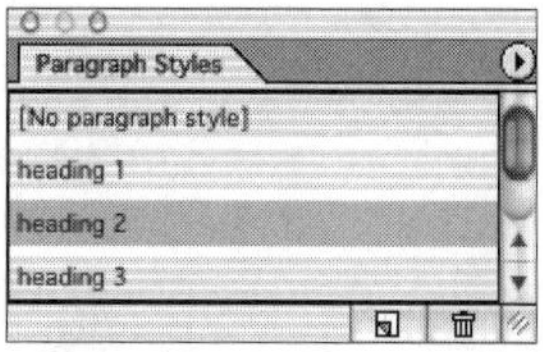

When a list has focus, InDesign
displays a dark border around it.

**Displaying and Hiding Palettes**

You can use keyboard shortcuts to show and hide palettes and save yourself lots of mouse movement (see Table 1-1). If a palette's open, but behind other palettes in the same group, pressing the keyboard shortcut brings the palette to the front of the group. To close a palette, press the shortcut again, or click the Close button on the palette's title bar.

**TABLE 1-1**
**Palette Keyboard Shortcuts**

| To display this palette: | Press: |
| --- | --- |
| Align | F8 |
| Attributes | None/Alt-W, U |
| Character | Command-T/Ctrl-T |
| Character Styles | Shift-F11 |
| Check Spelling | Command-I/Ctrl-I |
| Color | F6 |
| Edit Dictionary | None/Alt-E, Y |
| Find/Change | Command-F/Ctrl-F |
| Gradient | None/Alt-W, G |
| Index | Shift-F8 |
| Layers | F7 |
| Links | Command-Shift-D/Ctrl-Shift-D |
| Navigator | None/Alt-W, V |
| Pages | F12 |
| Paragraph | Command-M/Ctrl-M |
| Paragraph Styles | F11 |
| Story | None/Alt-T, R |
| Stroke | F10 |
| Swatches | F5 |
| Table | Shift-F9 |
| Tabs | Command-Shift-T/Ctrl-Shift-T |
| Text Wrap | Command-Option-W/Ctrl-Alt-W |
| Tools palette | None/Alt-W, O |
| Transform | F9 |
| Transparency | Shift-F10 |

**Hiding All Palettes.** Press Tab, and all of the palettes currently displayed disappear; press it again, and they reappear. This shortcut won't work when you have text selected or have an active text cursor in a text frame (it'll enter a tab character, instead). You'd think that you could use the keyboard shortcut to switch to the Selection tool (hold down Command/Ctrl) and then press Tab to hide the palettes, but you can't.

**Zipping and Unzipping Palettes.** With all these palettes, it's easy to run out of room on your screen to see anything *but* the palettes. While you can use keyboard shortcuts to display the palettes, you might like this better: Macintosh users can shrink a palette down to just its tab and title bar by clicking the zoom box; Windows users can click the Minimize button to do the same thing. You can also double-click the palette's tab.

This is called "zipping" a palette. The title bar stays on the screen (see Figure 1-10). When you want to display the entire palette, click the zoom box again if you're a Macintosh user, or click the Maximize button if you're using Windows. The palette expands to its full size. In addition, you can:

◆ Double-click the tab of the frontmost palette in a group.

◆ Click the tab of any palette in a group that is not the frontmost palette in the group.

◆ Press the keyboard shortcut for the palette.

On the Macintosh, you can shrink the palette down to its title bar by double-clicking the title bar. To expand the palette again, double-click the title bar again. In Windows, double-clicking the title bar is the same as clicking the Minimize button or double-clicking a palette's tab.

**Displaying options.** Many of InDesign's palettes can be set to display all of the available options for a particular feature, or a subset of those options. The Stroke palette, for example, can display all stroke attributes (stroke weight, stroke type, end cap type, join, and arrowheads) or the stroke weight only.

**Resizing palettes.** To resize a palette, drag the Resize box at the palette's lower-right corner (see Figure 1-11). If a palette doesn't have a Resize box, you can't resize it. In Windows, you can drag the sides of some of the palettes to resize them (this works for the Paragraph Styles, Character Styles, Pages, and Swatches palettes).

FIGURE 1-10
### Zipping and Unzipping Palettes

*When you choose Show Options from a palette menu...*

*...InDesign expands the palette to display additional options.*

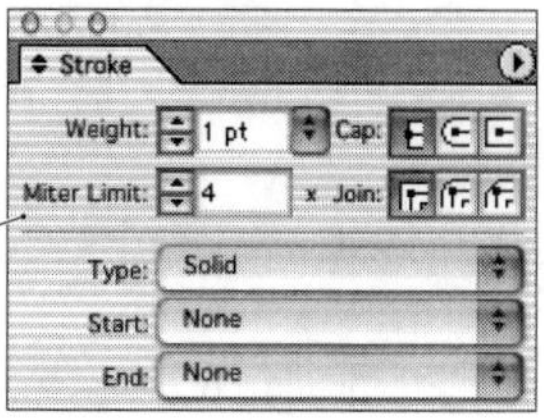

*Here's another (and possibly quicker) way to accomplish the same thing. Position the cursor over a palette tab...*

*...and click the tab. InDesign shrinks the palette to the next smaller size (if one is available).*

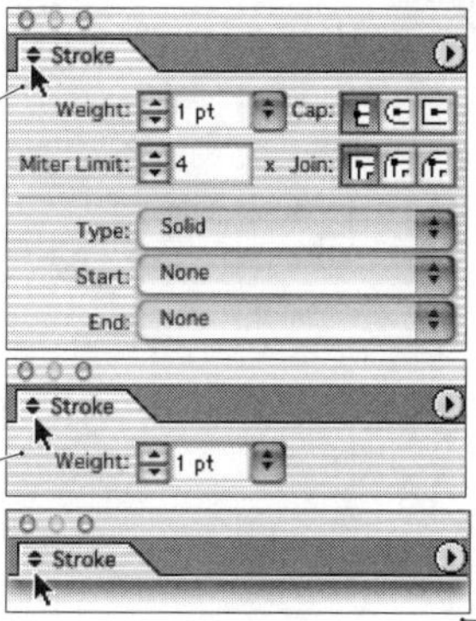

*Click again, and InDesign shrinks the palette further (if possible).*

FIGURE 1-11
### Resizing Palettes

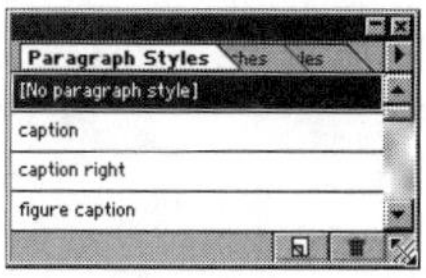

*To change the size of a palette, drag the resize box.*

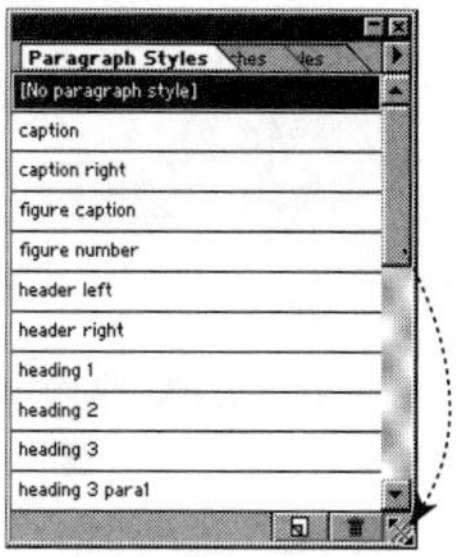

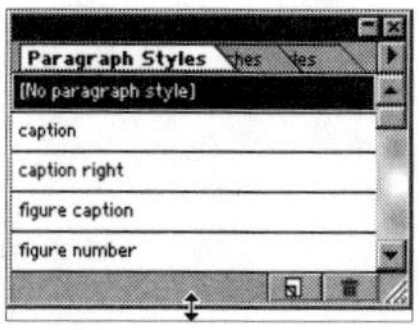

*In Windows, you can also drag the borders of the palette to resize the palette.*

**Snapping palettes into position.** When you drag a palette near to the edge of another palette, InDesign snaps the edge of the palette you're moving to the closest edge of the other palette. This makes it easy to arrange and resize palettes in relation to other palettes.

**Combining and separating palettes.** You can rearrange any of the "tabbed" palettes (see Figure 1-12). You can combine many palettes into a single palette, or you can create more palettes than you'll see when you first open InDesign (this is a mind-boggling concept, we know). Why would you want to do this? You could display the Paragraph Styles palette and the Character Styles palette at the same time (rather than having them stacked on top of each other). We all have different ways of working, and tabbed palettes give us a way of customizing InDesign to fit our particular habits and needs.

**FIGURE 1-12**

**Combining Or Separating Tabbed Palettes**

*To join two palettes:*                    *Position the cursor over a palette tab.*

*Drag the palette into another palette group.*

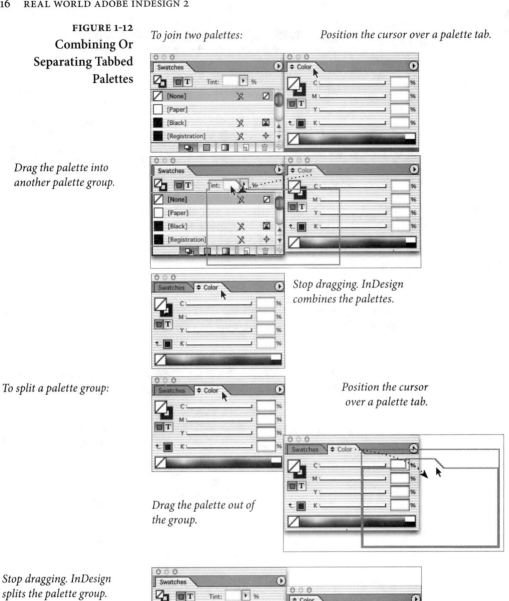

*Stop dragging. InDesign combines the palettes.*

*To split a palette group:*

*Position the cursor over a palette tab.*

*Drag the palette out of the group.*

*Stop dragging. InDesign splits the palette group.*

To combine palettes, drag the tab of one palette into the area at the top of another palette. When you combine two or more palettes, you create a "palette group." A palette group behaves as if it is a single palette—the palettes move, resize, and zip/unzip as a unit.

In any palette group, only one palette can be "on top" at a time; only the tabs of the other palettes in the group are visible. To display another palette in the group, click the palette's tab or press the keyboard shortcut for the palette.

**Docking palettes.** Another way to customize the layout of InDesign's palettes is to "dock" one palette to another. When you do this, both palettes remain visible (in contrast to combined palettes, where only the uppermost palette is visible), and move, hide, display, or resize as a single palette.

To dock one palette to another, drag the tab of a palette into the area at the bottom of another palette. As you drag, InDesign highlights the bottom of the target palette. Stop dragging and release the mouse button, and InDesign joins the palettes (see Figure 1-13).

**FIGURE 1-13**
**Docking Palettes**

*Drag the tab of one palette into the bottom of another palette. InDesign displays a highlight when the palettes are ready to dock.*

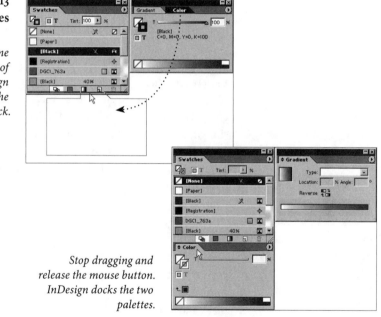

*Stop dragging and release the mouse button. InDesign docks the two palettes.*

**Palette navigation.** To move from one field in a palette to the next, press Tab. To move from one field to the previous field, press Shift-Tab. If you've made any changes in the field, InDesign applies the changes.

To "jump" back to the palette field you used most recently, press Command-` (accent grave; it's just to the left of the number 1 at the upper-left corner of your keyboard)/Ctrl-`.

When you display a palette using the corresponding menu option or keyboard shortcut, InDesign selects the first field in the palette.

**Small Palette Rows.** To reduce the height of each item in any of the "list" palettes (i.e., the Swatches, Swatch Color Library, Paragraph Styles, Character Styles, Links, and Layers palettes), choose Small Palette Rows from the palette's pop-up menu. InDesign reduces the height of the items in the list (see Figure 1-14).

FIGURE 1-14
**Small Palette Rows**

*Choose Small Palette Rows from a list palette menu…*

*…and InDesign reduces the height of each list entry.*

**Overriding Units of Measurement.** Being able to switch from one measurement system to another is great, but what do you do when you want to enter a value in a measurement system other than the one currently selected? Do you have to go to the Units & Increments Preferences dialog box and switch to another measurement system? No—all you need to do add a "measurement override" when you enter the value. Want to enter 115.3 points in a field that's currently showing decimal inches? It's easy: enter "115.3 pt," or even "0p115.3" in the field, and InDesign will take care of the conversion for you. You can use these shortcuts in any numeric field in any InDesign palette or dialog box. Table 1-2 shows you how to enter measurement overrides.

TABLE 1-15
**Measurement Overrides**

| When you want: | Enter: | Example: |
|---|---|---|
| points | pt | 136 pt |
| points | 0p | 0p136 |
| picas | p | 1p |
| picas and points | p | 1p6 |
| inches | i* | 1.56i |
| millimeters | mm | 2.45mm |
| ciceros | c | 3c |
| ciceros and didots | c | 3c4 |

*\* or "in" if you feel the need to type the extra character.*

**Doing Arithmetic in Fields.** You can add, subtract, multiply, or divide in any numeric field in any InDesign palette or dialog box. Want an object to be half its current width? Type "/2" after the value in the W (width) field in the Transform palette and press Enter. Want an object to move two picas to the right? Enter "+2p" (yes, all of the measurement unit overrides shown above work with these operations) after the value shown in the X field in the Transform palette. Enter "*" to multiply, or "-" to subtract. You get the idea.

**A Quick Tour of the Palettes**

Here's a quick description of the palettes you'll see as you work with InDesign. Most of the rest of the book is taken up by descriptions of how you use the palettes—this section is your formal introduction to the palettes and to the gadgets they contain.

**Align palette.** Use the Align palette to arrange objects relative to other objects. To display the Align palette, press F8 (see Figure 1-15). To align two or more objects, select them and then click the alignment button corresponding to the alignment you want.

Note that the Align palette's distribution options now include the ability to space objects a specific distance apart (as the alignment features in both QuarkXPress and PageMaker do). For more on working with the Align palette, see Chapter 8, "Transforming."

**FIGURE 1-16**
**Align Palette**

Align right edges
Align horizontal centers
Align left edges
Align top edges
Align vertical centers
Align bottom edges

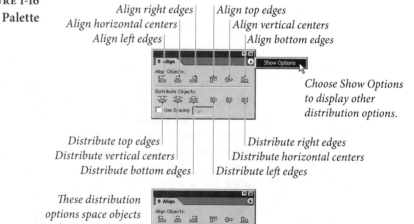

*Choose Show Options to display other distribution options.*

Distribute top edges
Distribute vertical centers
Distribute bottom edges
Distribute right edges
Distribute horizontal centers
Distribute left edges

*These distribution options space objects in the selection based on the corresponding object edge or axis...*

*...while these options create even spacing between the objects. The value you enter in the Use Spacing field sets the distance between objects.*

Vertical distribute space | Horizontal distribute space

*The tiny, but useful, Attributes palette.*

**Attributes palette.** Have you been looking for the object-level overprinting options in the Stroke palette or the Color palette? You won't find them there, because they're in the Attributes palette. We're not sure why. Choose Attributes from the Window menu to display the Attributes palette.

**Character palette.** You'll find InDesign's character formatting commands in the Character palette (see Figure 1-16). If you've grouped the Transform palette and the Character palette, InDesign will display the Character palette when you click the Text tool in a text frame. Press Command-T/Ctrl-T to display the Character palette.

FIGURE 1-17
### Character Palette

*Press Command-T/Ctrl-T
to display the Character
palette.*

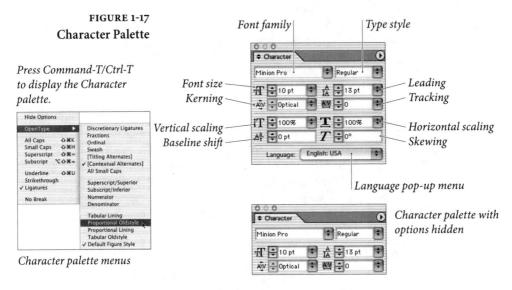

*Font family*      *Type style*

*Font size* —    — *Leading*

*Kerning* —    — *Tracking*

*Vertical scaling* —    — *Horizontal scaling*

*Baseline shift* —    — *Skewing*

*Language pop-up menu*

*Character palette with
options hidden*

*Character palette menus*

The Character palette menu contains a number of important typesetting commands, controlling features such as ligature replacement, small caps, superscript, and subscript.

In addition, the OpenType submenu of the Character palette (which only becomes active when the font you're working with is an OpenType font) offers access to a variety of OpenType features, such as Titling and Contextual alternates, true small caps, and number styles. For more on InDesign's OpenType features, see Chapter 4, "Type."

You can choose to show or hide several Character palette options: the Horizontal Scale and Vertical Scale fields, the Baseline Shift field, the Skew field, and the Language pop-up menu. To hide these controls, choose Hide Options from the Character palette's pop-up menu. To show these options again, choose Show Options.

**Character Styles palette.** You use the Character Styles palette to create, edit, and apply InDesign's character styles (see Figure 1-17).

To create a character style, select text that has the formatting attributes you want and choose New Style from the Character Styles palette menu (or click the Create New Style button at the bottom of the palette). InDesign displays the New Character Style dialog box.

**FIGURE 1-18**
**Character Styles Palette**

*Character styles*

*The Character Styles palette menu provides options for working with character styles.*

| Delete Character Style button
*New Character Style button*

At this point, you can enter a new name for the style, or otherwise tinker with the style's definition. When you close the dialog box, note that InDesign does not apply the style to the selected text.

To edit a style, hold down Command-Option-Shift/Ctrl-Alt-Shift and double-click the style name. This opens the style for editing, but does not apply it to the selected text. You can also double-click the style name to edit the style, but this applies the style to the selected text (if you have text selected) or to the document default.

To delete a character style, select the style (you might want to deselect the text before you select the style) and choose Delete Styles from the palette's pop-up menu. InDesign removes the style.

For more on character styles, see Chapter 4, "Type."

**Check Spelling palette.** As you'd expect from its name, you use this palette to check the spelling of the text in a publication (see Figure 1-18). To display this palette, press Command-I/Ctrl-I (or choose Check Spelling from the Edit menu).

For more on the Check Spelling palette, see Chapter 3, "Text."

**FIGURE 1-19**
**Check Spelling Palette**

*When InDesign finds a suspicious-looking word during a spelling check, the word appears in the Not in Dictionary field.*

*InDesign displays a list of spelling alternatives in the Suggested Corrections list.*

**Color palette.** Use the Color palette to define and apply colors (see Figure 1-19). To display the Color palette, press F6 (or choose Color from the Windows menu). You won't find colors from standard color libraries—such as Pantone or TruMatch—here. They're in swatch libraries (which you can load using the Swatches palette).

**FIGURE 1-20**
**Color Palette**

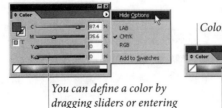

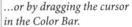

*Color palette with options hidden.*

*You can define a color by dragging sliders or entering values in the fields…*

*…or by dragging the cursor in the Color Bar.*

To define a color, choose the color model you want to work with from the Color palette's menu, then adjust the color parameters in the Color palette.

The Color palette interacts with the Swatches palette. When you select a color swatch in the Swatches palette, InDesign loads the Colors palette with the color definition of the swatch. The Swatches palette returns the favor: when you choose New Swatch from the Swatches palette menu, or click the New Swatch button at the bottom of the Swatches palette, InDesign creates a new swatch with the color definition currently in the Color palette.

For more on defining, editing, and applying colors, see Chapter 9, "Color."

**Dictionary palette.** InDesign's hyphenation and spelling features depend on dictionaries. When a word isn't in a dictionary, InDesign has no idea how to spell the word, and has to make guesses about where the word should be hyphenated. With the Dictionary palette, we can help InDesign learn new words, or change the way that it treats words it already knows (see Figure 1-20).

**FIGURE 1-21**
**Dictionary Palette**

To define a color, choose the color model you want to work with

**Find/Change palette.** As you'll see in Chapter 3, "Text," InDesign's ability to search for, find, and change text is an extremely powerful word processing and formatting tool. The key to using this feature is yet another palette: the Find/Change palette (see Figure 1-21). Press Command-F/Ctrl-F to display the Find/Change palette (or choose Find/Change from the Edit menu).

FIGURE 1-22
**Find/Change Palette**

*The pop-up menus associated with the Find what and Change to fields make searching for special characters easy.*

*Enter the text you want to search for in the Find what field...*

*...then enter the text you want to replace it with in the Change to field (if necessary).*

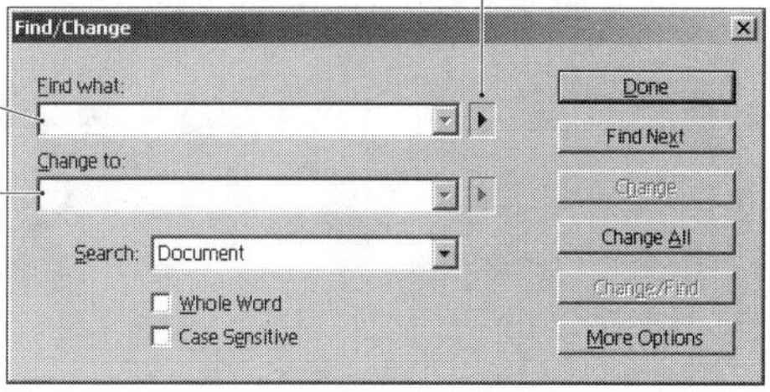

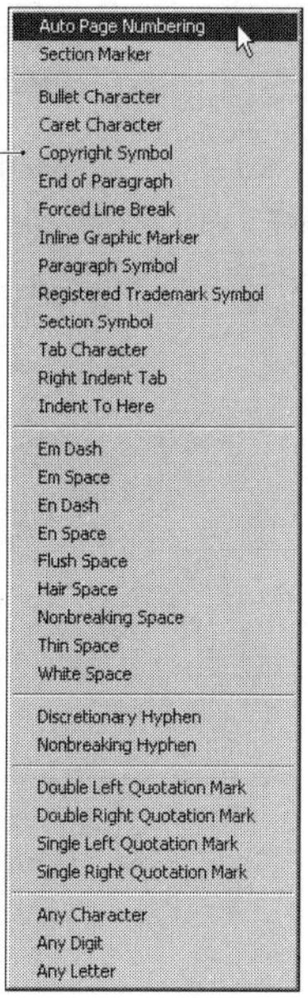

*In this example, we specified a search range (the current document), and specified formatting (click the More Options button to display the Find Style Settings and Change Style Settings options).*

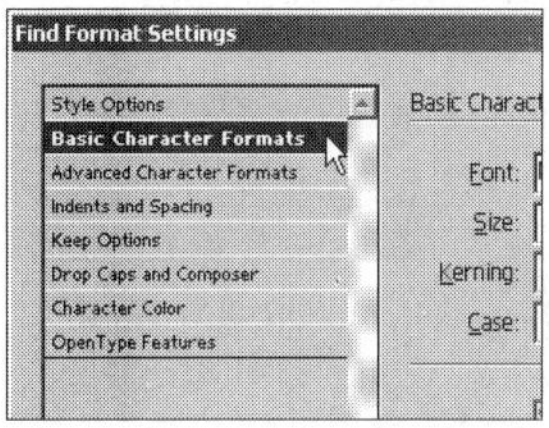

*You can find and change any formatting InDesign can apply.*

*The "alert" icons tell you that formatting attributes have been set.*

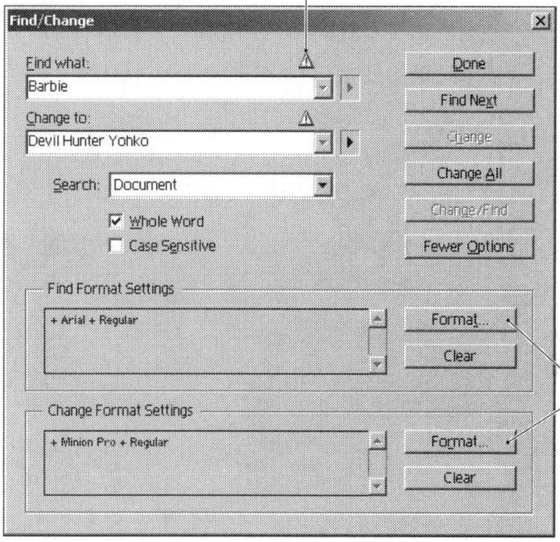

*To set formatting attributes you want to search for (or replace with), click a Format button.*

**Glyphs palette.** You know that the character you want is somewhere within a certain font...but where? In the past, we've had to resort to KeyCaps, PopChar, or the Windows Character Map utility to find special characters, but there's no need to leave InDesign. Just display the Glyphs palette (choose Insert Glyphs from the Type menu), and you can easily browse all of the characters of any font available to InDesign (see Figure 1-22).

And we do mean *every* character. Many fonts include characters which aren't normally available due to the limitations of the Mac OS or Windows character encoding. Once you've found the character you're looking for, you can double-click the character to insert it at the current text cursor location (or to replace the selected text). For more on the Glyphs palette, see Chapter 4, "Text."

**FIGURE 1-23**

**Glyphs Palette**

*The Glyphs palette menu provides various ways of sorting/filtering the character display.*

*Select a font and font style, and InDesign will display every character in the font.*

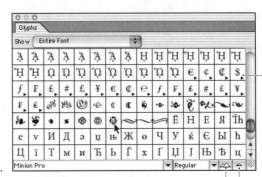

*Small arrows indicate alternate characters (in OpenType fonts).*

*Double-click a character to insert that character in text (or to replace the selected text with the character).*

*Zoom out button*
*Zoom in button*

**Gradient palette.** InDesign's ability to apply gradients to the fill and stroke of paths and text characters is one of the program's signature features, and the Gradient palette is the way you create, edit, and apply gradients (see Figure 1-23).

**FIGURE 1-24**

**Gradient Palette**

*Gradient preview*          *Gradient stop*          *Midpoint*

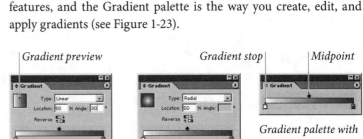

*Gradient palette with options shown (Linear gradient).*

*Gradient palette with options shown (Radial gradient).*

*Gradient palette with options hidden.*

**Hyperlinks palette.** InDesign offers the ability to attach hyperlinks to page items or to text. These hyperlinks can take you to another page, a specified chunk of text, or to a web page or email address. The hyperlinks you add to InDesign pages will function when you export your pages as PDF or HTML, but they can also be used inside InDesign itself.

You use the Hyperlinks palette (see Figure 1-24) to create hyperlinks, define hyperlink destinations, navigate using hyperlinks, and control hyperlink appearance and attributes. For more on working with hyperlinks, see Chapter 7, "Importing and Exporting."

**Index palette.** You use the Index palette (see Figure 1-25) to create, edit, delete index entries and index topics, view an index, and generate an index. We admit that indexing makes our heads spin (which is really quite something to see). For more on InDesign's indexing features, see Chapter 8, "Long Documents."

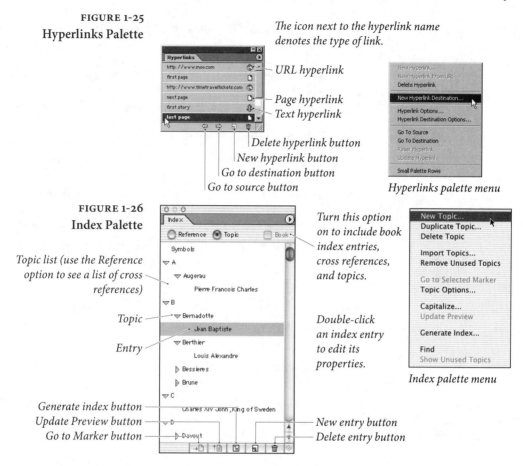

FIGURE 1-25
**Hyperlinks Palette**

*The icon next to the hyperlink name denotes the type of link.*

— URL hyperlink

— Page hyperlink
— Text hyperlink

Delete hyperlink button
New hyperlink button
Go to destination button
Go to source button

*Hyperlinks palette menu*

FIGURE 1-26
**Index Palette**

*Topic list (use the Reference option to see a list of cross references)*

*Topic*

*Entry*

*Turn this option on to include book index entries, cross references, and topics.*

*Double-click an index entry to edit its properties.*

*Index palette menu*

*Generate index button*
*Update Preview button*
*Go to Marker button*

*New entry button*
*Delete entry button*

**Layers palette.** Layers give you a way to control the stacking order of objects in your publication and also help you control the speed with which InDesign draws and redraws your publication's pages. Layers can be hidden, or locked. To work with layers, you use the Layers palette (see Figure 1-26). To display the Layers palette, press F7 (or choose Layers from the Window menu).

The following are quick descriptions of each control in the Layers palette.

◆ Show/Hide button. If you see an "eye" icon on this button, the layer is visible. Click the icon to hide the layer. To show the layer again, click the button.

◆ Lock/Unlock button. To lock a layer, click this button. When a layer is locked, a pencil with a red slash through it (as in the international "prohibited" symbol) appears on this button. To unlock the layer, click the button again.

◆ Layer color swatch. The color shown on this button determines the color of the selection handles of objects assigned to this layer.

◆ Target layer icon. This icons shows you which layer is active. Any new objects you create, objects you paste into the publication, or groups you create will appear on this layer.

◆ Layer name. The name of the layer.

◆ Selection Proxy. The Selection Proxy represents the items you've selected. If the selection contains objects from more than one layer, you'll see more than one Selection Proxy in the palette. Note that clicking on a layer does not move the selection to that layer, as it would in some other programs (notably FreeHand). Instead, you move objects from layer to layer by dragging the Selection Proxy up or down in the list of layers. This makes it harder for you to accidentally send objects to a layer.

◆ New Layer button. Click this button to create a new layer. The new layer appears at the top of the list of layers.

◆ Delete Layer button. Click this button to delete the selected layer. If, somewhere in your publication, objects are assigned to the layer, InDesign will display a dialog box that asks if you want to delete the layer. If you do, click the Yes button—InDesign will delete the layer and any objects assigned to the layer. If you don't want to delete the objects, click No.

◆ Resize handle. Drag this icon to change the width and height of the Layers palette.

Double-click a layer to display the Layer Options dialog box, where you can change the layer color, layer name, and other layer options.

For more on working with layers, see Chapter 2, "Page Layout."

**FIGURE 1-27**
**Layers Palette**

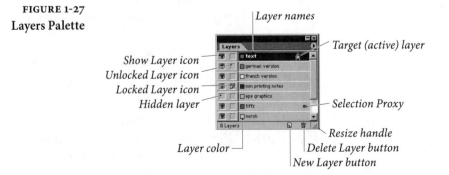

Layer names

Target (active) layer

Show Layer icon
Unlocked Layer icon
Locked Layer icon
Hidden layer

Selection Proxy

Resize handle
Delete Layer button
New Layer button

Layer color

**Library palette.** Use the Library palette (or palettes, as you can have multiple libraries open at once) to store and retrieve commonly used items (see Figure 1-27). Does your company or client have a logo they like to plaster all over every publication you lay out? Put it in a library. You open library files just as you open InDesign documents or book files—using the Open and New options on the File menu.

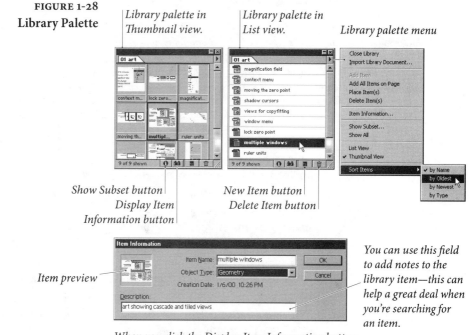

**FIGURE 1-28**
**Library Palette**

*Library palette in Thumbnail view.*

*Library palette in List view.*

*Library palette menu*

Show Subset button
Display Item
Information button

New Item button
Delete Item button

*Item preview*

*When you click the Display Item Information button, InDesign displays the Item Information dialog box.*

*You can use this field to add notes to the library item—this can help a great deal when you're searching for an item.*

*When you click the Show Subset button, InDesign displays the Subset dialog box. Specify the parameters you want and click the OK button, and InDesign displays the library items that match.*

**Navigator palette.** This palette gives you another way to get around in your publication—it's a kind of alternative to scrolling and zooming. When you display the Navigator palette, you'll see in it a thumbnail view of your page or page spread (see Figure 1-28).

Around the spread, you'll see a red rectangle (by default—you can change the color if you want). This rectangle is the View box and represents the area of the publication visible on your screen. You can

*Drag the View box
to scroll your view
of the publication.*

*To change the color used to display the View Box,
choose Palette Options from the palette menu.*

*Choose a color from the
Color pop-up menu, or...*

*The View Box represents
the area of your screen.*

*Enter a magnification
percentage in the
Magnification field, or ...*

*...click this button to zoom to the
next lower magnification preset (e.g.,
from 200% to 100%), or ...*

*...drag the Zoom slider to change the
magnification percentage (as you drag,
the View Box will change size), or ...*

*...click this button to
zoom to the next higher
magnification preset (e.g.,
from 100% to 200%).*

*...double-click to dis-
play a color picker.*

*If you don't use the Navigator
palette, turn it off—you'll get
faster screen redraw.*

drag the View box in the Navigator palette to change your view of the publication. As you drag, InDesign scrolls your view of the publication to match the area shown in the View box.

You can also zoom using the Navigator palette. Click the Zoom buttons to zoom in or out to the next "standard" magnification, or enter a new magnification in the palette's Magnification field (or choose a magnification from the pop-up menu associated with the field). Or drag the Zoom slider.

We use the Zoom tool, Hand tool, Pages palette, and keyboard shortcuts to move from place to place in our publications, rather than the Navigator palette, but you should give the palette a try—you might like it better than we do.

If you don't use the Navigator palette, turn it off to get faster screen redraw. It takes InDesign time to draw the little page preview in the palette.

**Pages palette.** The Pages palette is for creating, rearranging and deleting pages and master pages (see Figure 1-29). It's also a great way to navigate from one page to another, and it's where you apply master pages to document pages. The following are brief descriptions of the controls found in the Pages palette.

◆ Spread and page icons. These icons represent the document pages and master pages in your publication. You can drag these pages around in the Pages palette to change the page order, or apply master pages to document pages (or other master pages), or create new master pages (by dragging document pages into the master page area of the palette).

FIGURE 1-30
**Pages Palette**

*Pages display the prefix ("B" or "C," in this example) of the master page applied to them.*

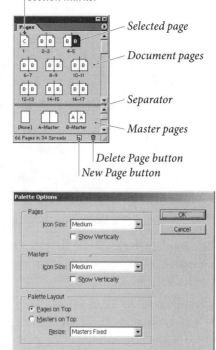

*Section marker*

*Selected page*

*Document pages*

*Separator*

*Master pages*

*Delete Page button*
*New Page button*

*Pages palette menu*

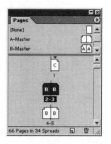

*Another way to view the Pages palette. This view means you have to scroll a lot more, but, hey, it looks like QuarkXPress.*

*Choose Palette Options from the Pages palette menu, and InDesign displays the Palette Options dialog box. Use the options in this dialog box to change the arrangement of the controls in the Pages palette.*

◆ New page button. Click this button to create a new document page.

◆ Delete page button. Click this button to delete the selected page or pages.

◆ Master/Document page separator. This bar separates the master pages in your publication (at the bottom of the palette) from the "normal" publication pages (at the top). You can drag the separator up or down to change the size of these areas.

◆ Resize box. Drag this icon to resize the Pages palette.

**Paragraph palette.** You use the controls in the Paragraph palette to specify paragraph formatting. To display the Paragraph palette, press Command-M/Ctrl-M (see Figure 1-30).

When you choose Hide Options from the Paragraph palette menu, InDesign hides the Paragraph Space Above, Paragraph Space Below, Drop Cap Characters, and Drop Cap Lines fields, and the Hyphenate checkbox and shrinks the palette to a smaller size. To display these options again, choose Show Options from the menu.

For more on working with paragraph specifications, see Chapter 4, "Type."

FIGURE 1-31
**Paragraph Palette**

*Press Command-M/Ctrl-M to display (or hide) the Paragraph palette.*

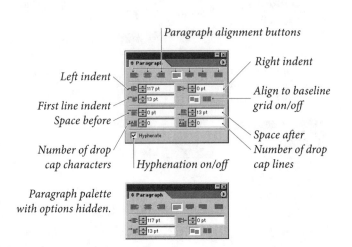

Paragraph alignment buttons

Right indent

Left indent

Align to baseline grid on/off

First line indent

Space before

Space after

Number of drop cap characters

Number of drop cap lines

Hyphenation on/off

*Paragraph palette menu*

*Paragraph palette with options hidden.*

**Paragraph Styles palette.** InDesign's paragraph styles are the most powerful text formatting feature in the program, and the Paragraph Styles palette is the way you work with them (see Figure 1-31).

◆ New Paragraph Style button. Click this button to create a new paragraph style. If you have text selected, the new paragraph style will have the formatting attributes of the first paragraph in the selection.

◆ Delete Paragraph Style button. Click this button to delete the selected paragraph style (or styles).

◆ Resize box. Drag this icon to resize the palette

FIGURE 1-32
**Paragraph Styles Palette**

*Paragraph styles*

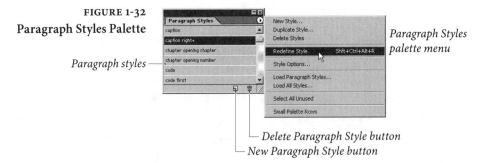

*Paragraph Styles palette menu*

*Delete Paragraph Style button*
*New Paragraph Style button*

**Story palette.** You've heard that InDesign features hanging punctuation (which, in InDesign, goes by the name "Optical Margin Alignment"), but you haven't been able to find the control for it? Relax—it's in the Story palette (see Figure 1-32). Actually, there's nothing else in the Story palette. To display the Story palette, choose Story from the Type menu.

For more on the Story palette, see Chapter 4, "Type."

FIGURE 1-33
**Story Palette**

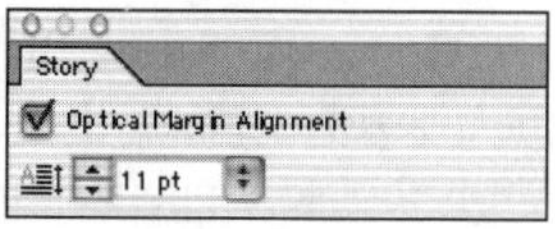

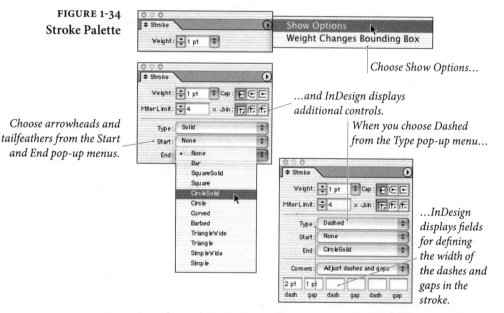

**Stroke palette.** A stroke is the outline of a path; the Stroke palette controls the formatting of that outline (see Figure 1-33).

The basic Stroke palette is minimalist: there's only the Weight option to play with. Choose Show Options, however, and InDesign expands the Stroke palette to include options controlling the line cap, miter limit, line join, stroke type, and arrowhead properties of a path. What most of these options really mean is discussed more fully in Chapter 5, "Drawing."

FIGURE 1-34
**Stroke Palette**

*Choose Show Options...*

*...and InDesign displays additional controls.*

*Choose arrowheads and tailfeathers from the Start and End pop-up menus.*

*When you choose Dashed from the Type pop-up menu...*

*...InDesign displays fields for defining the width of the dashes and gaps in the stroke.*

**Swatches palette.** Swatches can be colors, tints of colors, or gradients. They're a way of storing the values in the Color palette or the Gradient palette for future use. The Swatches palette gives you a way to organize, edit, and apply swatches in your publications (see Figure 1-34). To display the Swatches palette, press F5 (or choose Swatches from the Window menu).

While you can get by without the Swatches palette—by using the Color palette and the Gradient palette to apply fill and stroke attributes—we don't recommend it. Here's why: When you apply a fill or stroke using the Swatches palette, you create a relationship between the object's formatting and the swatch. If you later find you need to change the definition of the swatch, the appearance of any objects formatted using the swatch will change. Swatches, like paragraph and character styles, are a feature that can really save your sanity when your client/boss/whatever changes their mind about a color scheme an hour before your publication deadline.

◆ **Fill, Stroke, and Text buttons.** Click these buttons to apply a swatch to the corresponding attribute of an object (they're the same as the buttons in the Tools palette).

◆ **Tint field.** Enter a value in this field (or choose a value from the attached pop-up menu) to apply a tint of the selected color to the selection. This does not create a new tint swatch.

◆ **Show All button.** Click this button to display all of the swatches in the publication.

◆ **Show Colors button.** Click this button to display all of the color and tint swatches in the publication (and hide any gradient swatches).

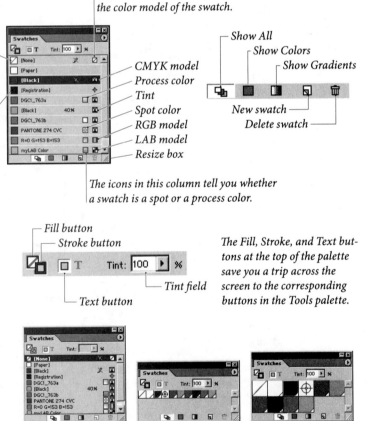

**FIGURE 1-35**
**Swatches Palette**

The icons in this column show you the color model of the swatch.

Use the default "None" swatch to remove the fill or stroke (or both).

The default "Registration" swatch prints on all separations.

Show All
Show Colors
Show Gradients

CMYK model
Process color
Tint
Spot color
RGB model
LAB model
Resize box

New swatch
Delete swatch

The icons in this column tell you whether a swatch is a spot or a process color.

Fill button
Stroke button

Text button
Tint field

The Fill, Stroke, and Text buttons at the top of the palette save you a trip across the screen to the corresponding buttons in the Tools palette.

Swatches palette menu

If you choose to use the Small Swatch or Large Swatch views, be aware that colors whose swatches are very similar in appearance can have very different color definitions.

Small Name view          Small Swatch view          Large Swatch view

◆ Show Gradients button. Click this button to display all of the gradient swatches in the publication (and hide any color or tint swatches).

◆ New Swatch button. Click this button to create a new swatch.

◆ Delete Swatch button. Click this button to delete the selected swatch or swatches.

◆ Resize box. Drag this icon to resize the Swatches palette.

For more on working with color swatches, see Chapter 9, "Color." For more on gradient swatches, see Chapter 5, "Drawing."

**Table palette.** This one is a monster (see Figure 1-35). Sure, you can set up your tables using the dialog boxes you can summon using the commands on the Table menu, but we think you'll often turn to the Table palette, which packs most of the most important table controls into a much smaller space.

FIGURE 1-36
**Table Palette**

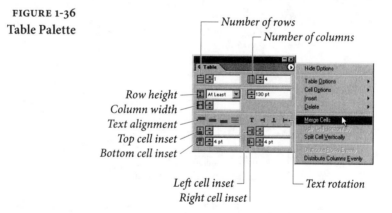

Number of rows
Number of columns
Row height
Column width
Text alignment
Top cell inset
Bottom cell inset
Left cell inset
Right cell inset
Text rotation

*The Tables palette menu provides easy access to each panel of the Table Options dialog box.*

**Tabs palette.** Use InDesign's Tabs palette to set tab stops and paragraph indents (see Figure 1-36). To display the Tabs palette, press Command-Shift-T/Ctrl-Shift-T.

◆ Tab Alignment buttons. Set the alignment of the selected tab stop (or set the default tab stop alignment).

◆ Tab stop icons. These mark the positions of the tab stops in the selected paragraph.

◆ Tab Ruler. To add a tab stop, delete a tab stop, or change the position of a tab stop, drag a tab stop icon on the Tab Ruler.

◆ Tab Position field. Enter a value in this field when you know exactly where you want to position a tab stop.

◆ Tab Leader field. Enter up to two characters in this field to apply a tab leader to the selected tab stop.

◆ Snap Palette button. Click this button to align the Tab Ruler's zero point at the left edge of the text frame.

For more on the Tabs palette, see Chapter 4, "Type."

**FIGURE 1-37**
**Tabs Palette**

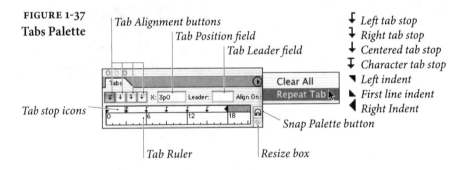

*Tab Alignment buttons*
*Tab Position field*
*Tab Leader field*

↓ *Left tab stop*
↓ *Right tab stop*
↓ *Centered tab stop*
↓ *Character tab stop*
◀ *Left indent*
◣ *First line indent*
◀ *Right Indent*

*Tab stop icons*

Clear All
Repeat Tab

*Snap Palette button*

*Tab Ruler*     *Resize box*

**Tags palette.** You use the Tags palette to control the way that objects in your page layout correspond (or "map") to elements in the XML structure of your document (see Figure 1-37). If you're confused about what we mean by this, we understand. Please see Chapter 7, "Importing and Exporting," for more on using XML in InDesign.

**FIGURE 1-38**
**Tags Palette**

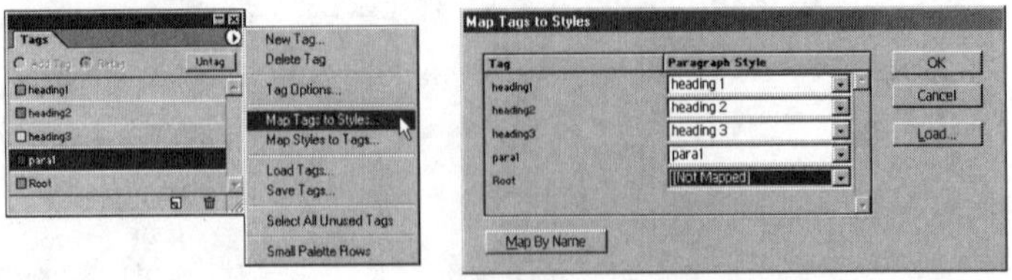

*Choose Map Tags to Styles to associate specified paragraph styles with XML tags.*

**Text Wrap palette.** When you need to tell text to avoid an object—an imported graphic, an InDesign path, or another text frame—you use the Text Wrap palette (see Figure 1-38).

FIGURE 1-39
**Text Wrap Palette**

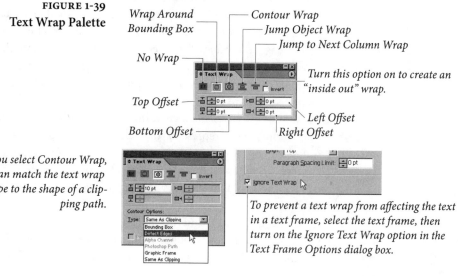

Wrap Around Bounding Box

Contour Wrap

Jump Object Wrap

Jump to Next Column Wrap

No Wrap

Turn this option on to create an "inside out" wrap.

Top Offset

Left Offset

Bottom Offset

Right Offset

*If you select Contour Wrap, you can match the text wrap shape to the shape of a clipping path.*

*To prevent a text wrap from affecting the text in a text frame, select the text frame, then turn on the Ignore Text Wrap option in the Text Frame Options dialog box.*

**Transform palette.** Look. In two-dimensional page layout and illustration programs, there's just no escape from basic geometry. So you might as well just learn to like working with numbers. Sometimes, they're the best way to get the job done. And it's not difficult—especially with InDesign's Transform palette (see Figure 1-39).

The Transform palette shows you the horizontal (X) and vertical (Y) location of the selected object (or the cursor). The coordinates that appear in the X and Y fields are shown in the current units of measurement, and are relative to the current location of the zero point. The W (for width) and H (for height) fields show you the size of the selection. The Vertical and Horizontal scaling fields show you any scaling applied to the object, the Rotation field shows you the

FIGURE 1-40
**Transform Palette**

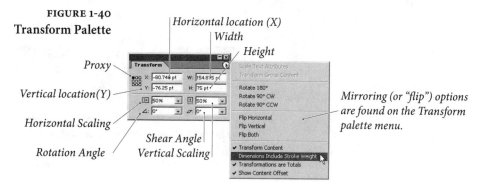

Horizontal location (X)

Width

Height

Proxy

Vertical location(Y)

Horizontal Scaling

Rotation Angle

Shear Angle

Vertical Scaling

*Mirroring (or "flip") options are found on the Transform palette menu.*

current rotation angle, and the Shear field shows you the skewing angle applied to the object. Not only do these fields give you information on the selection, they can also be used to change its location, size, rotation angle, or skewing angle.

As an object moves to the right, relative to the horizontal zero point, the object's X coordinate increases. As an object moves *down* on the page, the value of its Y coordinate increases. Note that this means that the vertical (Y) axis of InDesign's coordinate system is upside down compared to the graphs you created in junior high school (see Figure 1-40).

A "proxy" represents something else—the Proxy in InDesign's Transform palette represents the selection (see Figure 1-41). The squares at the edges and in the center of the Proxy represent the corners, sides, top, and center of the selection's bounding box, and control the way that changes in the Transform palette affect the selected object or objects.

While the X and Y fields display the current cursor position when you move the Selection tool or the Direct Selection tool, they don't change when you're using any other tool. So you can't use the X and

FIGURE 1-41
**InDesign's
Coordinate System**

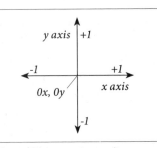

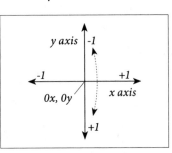

*"Classical" geometric coordinates: y values increase as you go up the vertical axis.*

*InDesign coordinates: y values increase as you go down the vertical axis.*

FIGURE 1-42
**The Proxy**

*The Transform palette's Proxy "stands in" for the selection.*

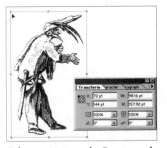

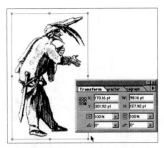

*Select a point on the Proxy, and InDesign displays the location of the point of the selection (the upper-left corner, in this example).*

*Select a different point on the Proxy, and you'll see different values in the X and Y fields (in this example, I've selected the lower-right corner).*

Y fields for positioning information as you draw a path with the Pen tool, or create a text frame with the Text tool.

Note for PageMaker users: Unlike PageMaker's Control palette, whose Proxy features both "move" and "stretch" modes, InDesign's Proxy is always in "move" mode. Entering a new X coordinate for a side handle, for example, will always move the handle to that location without resizing the selected object. You'll have to simulate the effect of "stretch" mode using the W(idth) or H(eight) fields, or the Scaling fields.

**Transparency palette.** Don't rush to the Layers palette looking for transparency options (as you would in Photoshop)—InDesign's Transparency palette (see Figure 1-42) contains the controls you're looking for.

FIGURE 1-43
**Transparency Palette**

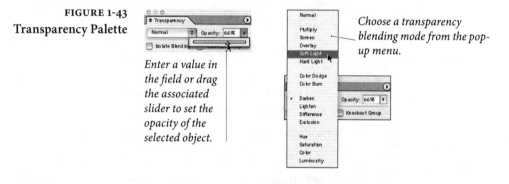

*Enter a value in the field or drag the associated slider to set the opacity of the selected object.*

*Choose a transparency blending mode from the pop-up menu.*

**Trap Styles palette.** InDesign's trap styles are collections of trapping settings you can apply to a page or range of pages in a document. Like any of the other style list palettes in InDesign (the Paragraph Styles palette or the Character Styles palette, for example), the Trap Styles palette displays a list of the styles you've defined (see Figure 1-43). For more on trapping, see Chapter 6, "Color."

FIGURE 1-44
**Trap Styles Palette**

*The Trap Styles palette is odd in that it affects pages, and not necessarily the ones that you see in your current view. Almost every other palette affects the selected page item or text.*

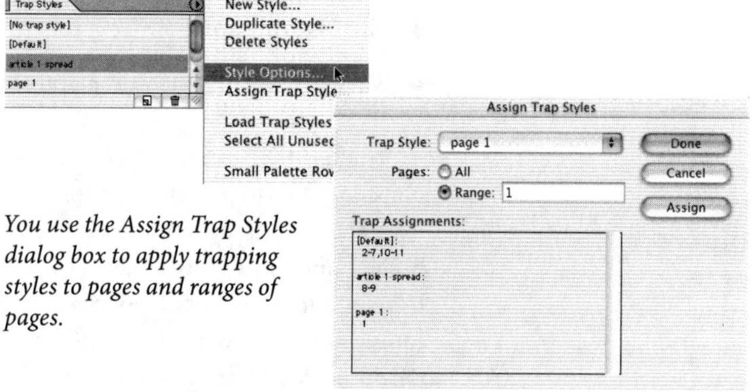

*You use the Assign Trap Styles dialog box to apply trapping styles to pages and ranges of pages.*

# Using the Tools Palette

If the publication window is the layout board where you collect the galleys of type, illustrations, and photographs you want to use in your publication, the Tools palette is where you keep your waxer, X-Acto knife, T-square, and bandages. (Note to youngsters: the foregoing are tools used by the Classical Greeks in the early days of page layout. You don't have to understand how they work to use the corresponding tools in InDesign. But it helps.)

Some of the following descriptions of the tool functions aren't going to make any sense unless you understand how InDesign's points and paths work, and that discussion falls in Chapter 5, "Drawing." You can flip ahead and read that section, or you can plow through this section, get momentarily confused, and then become enlightened when you reach the descriptions of points and paths. Or you can flip ahead for even more on points and paths. It's your choice, and either method works. This is precisely the sort of non-linear information gathering that hypertext gurus say can't be done in books.

You can break InDesign's toolbox (as shown in Figure 1-44) into six conceptual sections.

◆ Selection tools (the Selection and Direct Selection tools)

◆ Tools for drawing basic shapes (the Rectangle, Polygon, Oval, and Line tools) and their equivalent frames (Rectangular Frame, Polygonal Frame, and Oval Frame tools)

◆ Path-drawing and editing tools (the Pen, Add Point, Delete Point, Convert Point, Gradient, Pencil, Eraser, Smooth, and Scissors tools)

◆ Transformation tools (the Rotate, Reflect, Shear, Scale, and Free Transform tools)

◆ The Text tool and Path Text tool

◆ Navigation tools (the Zoom and Hand tools).

You use the Selection tool and the Direct Selection tool to select objects you want to change in some way. You can do different things with the objects depending on the selection tool you've used. The basic shape tools draw complete paths containing specific numbers of points in specific positions on the path, while the path-drawing tools draw paths point by point (or, in the case of the Scissors tool, delete points or split paths). The transformation tools change the

**FIGURE 1-45**

**The Tools Palette**

*Click the Adobe Online button to connect with Adobe's web site (and download updated plug-ins, if you want).*

*Swap fill/stroke (Shift-X)*
*Fill (X)*
*Stroke(X)*
*Default fill/stroke (D)*
*Formatting affects container*
*Apply Color (,)*
*Apply Gradient (.)*

*Formatting affects text*
*Apply None (/)*
*Preview Mode (W)*
*Normal View Mode (W)*

*Some of the "slots" in the Tools palette are occupied by more than one tool. How can you tell? When you see a tiny arrow in the corner of a tool icon, more tools lurk beneath the surface. To select a "hidden" tool…*

*…position the cursor over a tool, then hold down the mouse button.*

*InDesign displays a "flyout" menu containing the available tools.*

*Choose a tool from the menu and release the mouse button.*

*\* Hold down Command/Ctrl to switch to the Selection tool temporarily.*
*\*\* Hold down Spacebar and drag to switch to the Hand tool temporarily; hold down Option/Alt if the cursor is in a text frame.*

| | Tool name | Shortcut | | Tool name | Shortcut |
|---|---|---|---|---|---|
| | Selection | V* | | Rectangle | M |
| | Direct Selection | A | | Rectangular Frame | F |
| | Pen | P | | Polygon | |
| | Add Point | + | | Polygonal Frame | |
| | Delete Point | - | | Rotate | R |
| | Convert Point | Shift-C | | Free Transform | E |
| | Text | T | | Scale | S |
| | Path Text | Shift-T | | Shear | O |
| | Pencil | N | | Gradient | G |
| | Smooth | | | Scissors | C |
| | Eraser | | | Eyedropper | I |
| | Line | \ | | Hand | H** |
| | Ellipse | L | | Zoom | Z |
| | Elliptical Frame | | | | |

rotation angle, size, and skewing angle of objects on your pages, you use the Text tool to enter and edit text, and the navigation tools help you move around in your publication.

The tool descriptions in the following section are brief and are only intended to give you a feeling for what the different tools are and what they do. To learn more about entering text with the Text tool, see Chapter 3, "Text." For more on drawing objects with the drawing tools, see Chapter 5, "Drawing." For more on working with the Transformation tools, see Chapter 8, "Transforming."

Talking about InDesign's tools and their use can get a little confusing. When you select a tool in the Tools palette (or press the keyboard shortcut to select a tool), what does the cursor become? In this book, we will sometimes use phrases like "select a tool and drag," or "drag the tool on the page." We hope this is clear—from our point of view, the cursor *is* the tool.

**Hiding the Tools palette.** Or Not. Sometimes, you want to hide all of the palettes except the Tools palette. To do that, make sure that the cursor isn't in a text frame, and then press Shift-Tab. InDesign hides all open palettes, but leaves the Tools palette open. If you've hidden all of the palettes including the Tools palette, you can display it by choosing Tools from the Window menu.

**Tools Palette Keyboard Shortcuts.** You can choose most of the tools in the Tools palette using keyboard shortcuts. This is usually faster than going back across the screen to the palette.

**Hidden Tools/Tool Variants.** To save some of your precious screen real estate, some of the slots in the Tools palette contain more than a single tool. You can tell by looking at the tool icon—when you see a tiny triangle on a tool icon, you know that other tools are lurking beneath it. In general, tools are grouped by their function. The Rectangular Frame tool, for example, shares a slot with the Rectangle tool. One notable exception is the Scissors tool, which has nonsensically taken up residence beneath the Gradient tool. Go figure.

To use one of the "hidden" tools, position the cursor over a tool icon and hold down the mouse button (the left mouse button, for Windows users). InDesign displays a short pop-up menu, or "flyout," containing the available tools. Choose one of the tool icons, and that tool will be displayed in the Tools palette.

For each of the basic shape tools, InDesign offers a corresponding frame drawing tool. There's really very little difference between the path drawn by the Rectangle tool and a frame drawn by the Rectangular Frame tool, and paths can be converted to frames—and frames to paths—very easily. There's no penalty for drawing a path one way or another, as there is in some other programs.

**Adobe Online**     When you click the button at the top of the Tools palette, InDesign displays the Adobe Online window (see Figure 1-45). You can connect to Adobe's web site to obtain technical support or download new plug-ins. You'll also find columns, articles, and white papers on various topics related to InDesign.

**FIGURE 1-46**
**Adobe Online**

*Click the Updates button to check for the presence of new Adobe Online components.*

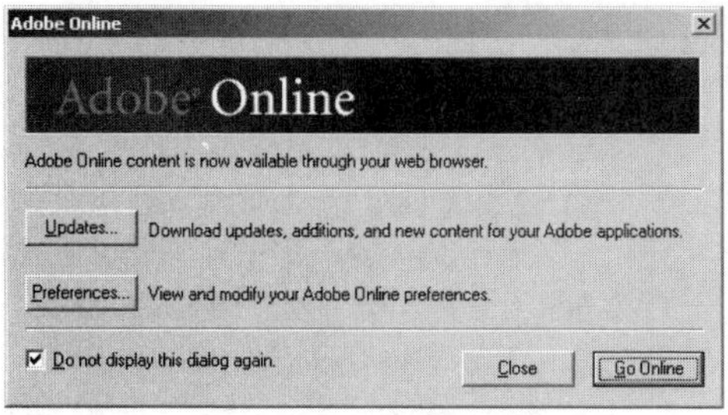

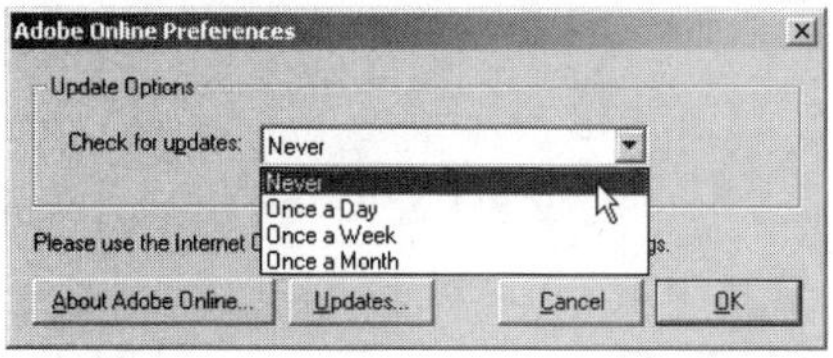

*How often would you like Adobe Online to check for updates?*

**Selection Tool**

You use the Selection tool to select and transform objects. Press V to select the Selection tool (when the cursor is not in text). To temporarily switch to the Selection tool, hold down Command/Ctrl when any other tool is selected. If you press Tab while you're holding down Command/Ctrl, you'll switch to the Direct Selection tool. To switch back to the Selection tool, press Tab again. When you release Command/Ctrl, the cursor turns back into whatever tool you were using before you summoned the Selection/Direct Selection tool.

**Direct Selection Tool**

How many selection tools does a page layout application really need? We don't know, but InDesign has two—one for everyday selection; another for selecting objects on Sundays and holidays. No, seriously, the Direct Selection tool is for selecting objects that are inside other objects, such as the following.

◆ Individual points on paths. For more on editing the shape of a path, see Chapter 5, "Drawing."

◆ Component paths of compound paths. For more on working with compound paths, see Chapter 5, "Drawing."

◆ Objects inside groups. For more on selecting objects inside groups, see Chapter 2, "Page Layout."

◆ Objects pasted inside other objects. For more on working with path contents, see Chapter 8, "Transforming."

To select the Direct Selection tool, press A. To temporarily switch to the Direct Selection tool when you have any other tool selected, hold down Command/Ctrl (to switch to the Selection tool), then press Tab.

**Pen Tool**     You use the Pen tool to draw paths containing both straight and curved line segments (that is, paths containing both curve and corner points). Illustrator users will recognize the Pen tool immediately, because it's pretty much identical to Illustrator's Pen tool (maybe there's something to all this "cross-product" talk, after all). Click the Pen tool to create a corner point; drag to create a curve point. Press P to select the Pen tool.

Under the Pen tool, you'll find the following tools:

◆ Add Point tool (press + to switch to this tool). When you click the Add Point tool on a selected path, InDesign adds a point at that location on the path.

◆ Delete Point tool (press – to switch to this tool). When you click the Delete Point tool on a point on a selected path, InDesign deletes the point.

◆ Convert Point tool. When you click the Convert Point tool on a point on a selected path, InDesign converts the point to the other kind of point—if the point you click is a corner point, InDesign converts it to a curve point; if it's a curve point, InDesign converts it to a corner point. You can also use the Convert Point tool to adjust the direction handles of a point.

For more (much more) on working with the Pen tool (and its variants) to draw and edit paths, see Chapter 5, "Drawing."

**Text Tool**     You enter and edit text using the Text tool. To create a text block, select the Text tool and drag the tool in the publication window; a text block appears with a flashing text-insertion point (or text cursor) in its first line. To edit text, select the Text tool and click in a text block. For more on entering, editing, and formatting text, see Chapter 3, "Text." To select the Text tool, press T.

**Path Text Tool**     Use the Path Text tool to enter and edit text on a path. To add text to a path, select the Path Text tool and click the tool on a path. A flashing text insertion point (or text cursor) appears on the path. At this point, text you enter will flow along the path. See Chapter 6, "Where Text Meets Graphics." To select the Path Text tool, press Shift-T.

**Pencil Tool**     If you're one of the millions of computer users who find the Pen tool—and the whole process of drawing by manipulating points, line segments, and control handles—confusing, give the Pencil tool a try. With the Pencil tool, you can sketch freeform paths. As you drag the tool, InDesign creates a path that follows the cursor, automatically placing points and adjusting curve handles as it does so.

If you don't like something about a path you've drawn using the Pencil tool, you can adjust it using any of InDesign's other drawing tools (including that scary Pen tool). You might want to start with the other tools that share the same space in the Tools palette: the Smooth tool and the Eraser tool (see below).

**Smooth Tool**

We like power tools. A good belt sander, for example, can reduce just about anything to a smooth, rounded blob in mere seconds. The Smooth tool is something like that. Select a path—any path—and drag the Smooth tool over it. It'll get smoother. Not smooth enough yet? Drag again.

As you drag the Smooth tool, InDesign adjusts the points and control handles that define the path to create a smoother transition from one line segment to another. InDesign often removes points during this process. If you continue to repeat the smoothing process, we think you'll eventually end up with a simple curve between two points.

**Eraser Tool**

The Eraser tool (press Shift-N until the Eraser tool appears) erases line segments and points. To use the Eraser tool, select a path, then drag the eraser tool over part of the path. InDesign splits the path and removes the line segments and points where you dragged the Eraser tool.

**Line Tool**

Use the Line tool to draw straight lines—paths containing two corner points. If you hold down Shift as you drag the Line tool, the lines you draw will be constrained to 0-, 45-, and 90-degree angles. Press E to select the Line tool.

**Ellipse Tool**

Use the Ellipse tool to draw ellipses and circles. Hold down Shift as you drag the Ellipse tool, and InDesign draws circles. Press L to select the Ellipse tool.

**Rectangle Tool**

Use the Rectangle tool to draw rectangles. If you hold down Shift as you drag, you draw squares. Press M to select the Rectangle tool.

If you need a rectangle with rounded corners, draw the rectangle using the Rectangle tool, then choose Corner Effects from the Object menu to display the Corner Effects dialog box (you can also get to this dialog box via the context menu, or by pressing Command-Option-R/Ctrl-Alt-R). Choose Rounded Corners from the Effect pop-up menu and enter a distance in the Size field to set the corner radius you want for the corners of the rectangle (see Figure 1-46).

If you draw a rectangle with square corners and then decide that you'd rather its corners were rounded, use the Corner Effects dialog box. The Corner Effects dialog box can provide a variety of other corner shapes, as discussed in Chapter 5, "Drawing."

**FIGURE 1-47**
**Applying Corner Effects**

*There's no special tool for drawing a rectangle with rounded corners. Instead, you use corner effects.*

Select a rectangle...

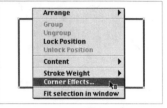

...choose Corner Effects from the Context menu (or press Command-Option-R/Ctrl-Alt-R).

*InDesign displays the Corner Effects dialog box.*

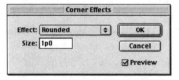

Choose a corner effect from the Effect pop-up menu. Enter a corner radius in the Size field.

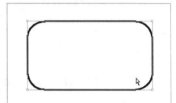

InDesign applies the corner effect.

**Polygon Tool**   The Polygon tool makes it easy to draw equilateral polygons, such as pentagons, hexagons, and dodecagons. (Polygons are closed geometric objects that have at least three sides; they're equilateral if all sides are the same length.) You can also use the Polygon tool to draw stars. Press N to select the Polygon tool. Under the Polygon tool, you'll find the Polygonal Frame tool.

To change which polygon the Polygon tool draws, double-click the tool in the Tools palette. InDesign displays the Polygon Settings dialog box (see Figure 1-47). Enter the number of sides you want in the Number of Sides field. If you want the polygon to be a star polygon, enter a percentage (from 0 to 99 percent) in the Star Inset field. If you don't want the polygon to be a star polygon, enter 100 percent in the Star Inset field.

**FIGURE 1-48**
**Polygon Settings**

**Rotate Tool**     To rotate the selection, select the Rotate tool from the toolbox and then drag the tool on your page. When you select the Rotate tool, InDesign displays the transformation center point icon on or around the selected object. The center point icon sets the center of rotation (the point you'll be rotating around), and corresponds to the selected point on the Transform palette's Proxy. Drag the transformation center point icon to a new location (or click one of the points in the Proxy) to change the center of rotation.

Hold down Shift as you drag the Rotate tool to constrain rotation to 45-degree increments (that is, as you drag the Rotate tool, InDesign snaps the selection to 0, 45, 90, 135, 180, 225, 270, and 315 degree angles).

**Scale Tool**     To scale (or resize) an object, select the object, select the Scale tool, and then drag the tool in the publication window. When you select the Scale tool, InDesign displays the transformation center point icon on or around the selected object. The location of the center point icon sets the center of the scaling transformation, and corresponds to the selected point on the Transform palette's Proxy. Drag the transformation center point icon to a new location (or click one of the points in the Proxy) to change the point you're scaling around.

Hold down Shift as you drag a corner handle to retain the object's proportions as you scale it.

**Shear Tool**     Shearing, or skewing, an object, alters the angle of the vertical or horizontal axes of the object. This makes it appear that the plane containing the object has been slanted relative to the plane of the publication window. To shear an object, drag the Shear tool in the publication window. As you drag, InDesign shears the object.

When you shear an object, InDesign distorts the stroke weights of the paths in the selection.

**Free Transform Tool**     The Free Transform (press E) tool is a combination of the Scale and Rotate tools, plus some aspects of the Selection tool, all bundled into a single tool. What the tool does depends on the position of the cursor.

◆ When the cursor is above one of an object's selection handles, the Free Transform tool acts as the Scale tool. Drag the Free Transform tool, and you scale the object around its center point.

◆ When the cursor is just outside one of the selection handles, the Free Transform tool behaves as if it were the Rotate tool. Drag the tool to rotate the object around its geometric center.

◆ When the Free Transform tool is inside the bounds of the selection, it acts as a "move" tool-drag the tool to move the object.

This last feature is of particular interest when you need to move a graphic that's inside a clipping path inside another object. As you've probably discovered, it's way too easy to move the graphic without moving the clipping path. The Free Transform tool helps keep the clipping path and the graphic together, as shown in Figure 1-48.

For more on working with the Free Transform tool, see Chapter 8, "Transforming."

**Eyedropper Tool**

The Eyedropper tool can pick up formatting attributes (from the fill and stroke of a path to the character and paragraph formatting of text) and apply them to other objects. You can also use the Eyedropper tool to sample a color in an object on an InDesign page-including imported graphics-and add it to your Swatches palette.

To "load" the Eyedropper tool, click the tool on an object (the object doesn't have to be selected). If you have an item selected when you click, InDesign applies the attributes of the item under the cursor to the selected item. Click the loaded Eyedropper tool on an object to apply the formatting (see Figure 1-49).

Double-click the Eyedropper tool to display the Eyedropper Options dialog box. Use the settings in the three panels of this dialog box to define the attributes sampled and affected by the Eyedropper tool (see Figure 1-50).

**Gradient Tool**

Use the Gradient tool to apply gradients, or to adjust gradients you've applied. When you drag the Gradient tool, you're setting the location of the beginning and ending points of an existing gradient (see Figure 1-51).

**Scissors Tool**

The Scissors tool cuts paths or points. Select a path, choose the Scissors tool (or press C), and then click the path (see Figure 1-52). InDesign splits the path at the point at which you clicked.

**Zoom Tool**

Use the Zoom tool to change the magnification in a publication window. To switch to the Zoom tool, press Z (obviously, this shortcut will work a lot better if you're not editing text). To switch to the Zoom tool temporarily, hold down Command-Spacebar/Ctrl-Spacebar (when you're done using the tool, InDesign will select the tool you were using before you switched to the Zoom tool).

Once you've switched to the Zoom tool (regardless of the method you've used), click the tool on the area you want to magnify, or drag a

**FIGURE 1-49
Selecting Objects
Inside Other Objects**

*In this example, we've pasted
a graphic with a clipping
path inside a frame.*

*When you click the Direct
Selection tool inside the
graphic, InDesign selects the
clipping path.*

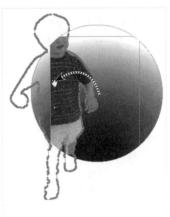

*If you drag the clipping path,
InDesign moves the clipping path
and the graphic, but leaves the
frame behind.*

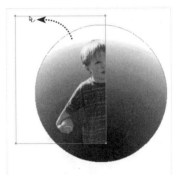

*If you select the frame of the graphic
using the Direct Selection tool and
then drag...*

*...InDesign moves the frame, but
doesn't move the graphic and the
clipping path. Argh!*

*The solution? Select the path
with the Direct Selection tool,
then press V to switch to
the Selection tool, and then
press E to switch to the Free
Transform tool.*

*Once you've selected the
Free Transform tool, you
can move, rotate, or scale
the graphic, its clipping path,
and its frame as a unit.*

*Drag the graphic with the Free
Transform tool...*

*...and InDesign moves the graphic,
the frame, and the clipping path.*

**FIGURE 1-50**
**Eyedropper Tool**

*Select an object or a series of objects and then choose the Eyedropper tool from the Tools palette.*

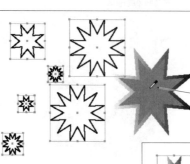

*Position the Eyedropper tool over an object that has the formatting you want to apply.*

*To format text using the Eyedropper tool, select the text using the Text tool.*

*Click the Eyedropper tool. InDesign applies the formatting of the object beneath the cursor to the selected objects.*

*Here's another method.*

*Select the Eyedropper tool from the Tools palette.*

*Position the cursor over an object and click. InDesign loads the Eyedropper tool with the formatting attributes of the object.*

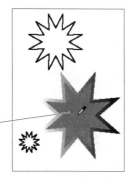

*Click another object (it doesn't have to be selected). InDesign applies the formatting attributes to the object.*

**FIGURE 1-51**
**Eyedropper Tool Options**

> Eyedropper Options
> ▷ ☑ Stroke Settings
> ▽ ☑ Fill Settings
>    ☑ Color
>    ☑ Tint
>    ☑ Overprint
> ▷ ☑ Character Settings
> ▷ ☑ Paragraph Settings
> ▷ ☑ Transparency Settings
>
> OK
> Cancel

selection rectangle around it. To zoom out, hold down Option/Alt—you'll see that the plus ("+") inside the Zoom tool changes to minus ("-")—and then click or drag to zoom out.

For more on using the Zoom tool, see "Zooming," later in this chapter.

FIGURE 1-52
**Gradient Tool**

*Once you've applied a gradient to a path, you can use the Gradient tool to change the gradient.*

*To edit a gradient, select an object and drag the Gradient tool.*

*When you stop dragging, InDesign changes the appearance of the gradient.*

 *The Gradient tool affects the formatting of either the fill or the stroke, depending on the state of the Fill or Stroke buttons.*

**Fill and Stroke**    The Fill and Stroke buttons, or "selectors," near the bottom of the Tools palette control what part (the fill or the stroke) of the selected path or text is affected when you apply a color. To make a selector active, click it. InDesign brings the active selector to the front. Here are two very useful shortcuts:

◆ To swap colors—apply the color assigned to the fill to the stroke, or vice versa—click the swap fill and stroke icon (or press Shift-X).

◆ Press X (when you're not editing text) to switch between the Fill selector and the Stroke selector.

Beneath the Fill and Stroke buttons, you'll see two very small buttons—the Formatting Affects Container button and the Formatting Affects Text button. When you have a text frame selected, you can apply a fill or stroke to either the text frame or to the characters of text inside the text frame. Click the former button to apply the formatting to the text frame; click the latter to apply it to the text.

As your eye proceeds down the Tools palette, you'll find three more buttons—they're shortcuts for applying colors or gradients, or for removing a fill or stroke from an object. Click the Apply Color button to apply the current color (in the Color palette or Swatches palette) to the fill or stroke of the selected object. The state of the Fill and Stroke selector determines which part of the object is affected. Click the Apply Gradient button to apply the current gradient (in the Swatches palette or the Gradient palette), and click the Apply None button to remove the fill or stroke from the selected object.

As you'd expect, InDesign has shortcuts for these buttons, too.

◆ To apply the most recently used color to the current fill or stroke (which attribute is affected depends on which selector is active), press , (comma—again, this won't work when text is selected).

◆ Press . (period) to apply the current gradient.

◆ Press / (slash) to remove the fill or stroke from the selected object or objects.

For more on applying colors, see Chapter 9, "Color."

## Context Menus

Context menus are menus that pop up at the location of the cursor, and change according to the location of the cursor and the object you have selected (see Figure 1-53). On the Macintosh, you summon a context menu by holding down Control as you click the mouse button. In Windows, click the right mouse button.

FIGURE 1-53
**Context Menus**

Hold down Control and click to display the Context menu on the Macintosh; in Windows, press the right mouse button.

The Context menu looks like this when you have a graphic selected.

The Context menu looks like this when you have text selected.

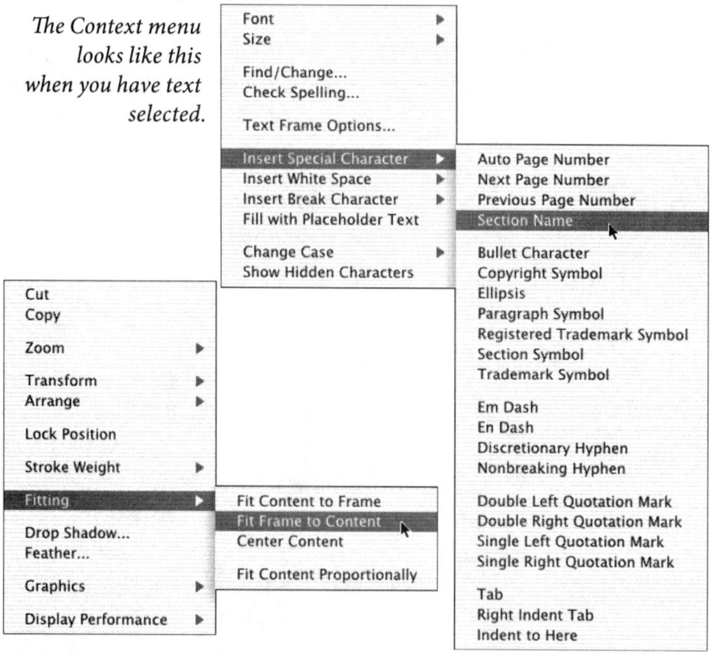

| Font ▶ |
| Size ▶ |
| Find/Change... |
| Check Spelling... |
| Text Frame Options... |
| Insert Special Character ▶ |
| Insert White Space ▶ |
| Insert Break Character ▶ |
| Fill with Placeholder Text |
| Change Case ▶ |
| Show Hidden Characters |

| Auto Page Number |
| Next Page Number |
| Previous Page Number |
| Section Name |
| Bullet Character |
| Copyright Symbol |
| Ellipsis |
| Paragraph Symbol |
| Registered Trademark Symbol |
| Section Symbol |
| Trademark Symbol |
| Em Dash |
| En Dash |
| Discretionary Hyphen |
| Nonbreaking Hyphen |
| Double Left Quotation Mark |
| Double Right Quotation Mark |
| Single Left Quotation Mark |
| Single Right Quotation Mark |
| Tab |
| Right Indent Tab |
| Indent to Here |

| Cut |
| Copy |
| Zoom ▶ |
| Transform ▶ |
| Arrange ▶ |
| Lock Position |
| Stroke Weight ▶ |
| Fitting ▶ |
| Drop Shadow... |
| Feather... |
| Graphics ▶ |
| Display Performance ▶ |

| Fit Content to Frame |
| Fit Frame to Content |
| Center Content |
| Fit Content Proportionally |

Context menus give you a great way to do a lot of things—from changing the formatting of the selected objects to changing your magnification. Let's face it—your attention is where the cursor is, and there's a limited amount of it. Dragging the cursor across the screen to reach a menu or button is distracting, time-consuming, and tiring. The only thing wrong with InDesign's context menus is that you can't add more commands to them.

In addition, some commands—such as Fit Selection In Window—appear only on the context menus.

# Keyboard Shortcuts

We hate it when software manufacturers change the keyboard short-cuts we know and love. Especially when they change an easy-to-reach, frequently used shortcut to one that's difficult to use (PageMaker users, you know exactly what we're talking about). InDesign gives us something we'd like to see in every application—editable keyboard shortcuts. This means that we can make the program's keyboard shortcuts work the way we think they ought to.

For the most part, the keyboard shortcuts you can redefine are those that correspond to menu commands—you can't redefine some of the keyboard shortcuts that modify mouse actions. If you hate having Spacebar as the shortcut for the Hand tool, you're out of luck—at least this time around.

To define or redefine a keyboard shortcut, follow these steps (see Figure 1-54 on the following page).

1. Choose Keyboard Shortcuts from the Edit menu. InDesign displays the Keyboard Shortcuts dialog box.

2. To create a new shortcut set, click the New Set button. To use an existing set, choose the set's name from the Set pop-up menu (if that's all you want to do, you can skip to Step 7). To delete a set, choose the set's name and click the Delete Set button.

3. Choose an option from the Product Area pop-up menu. InDesign fills the Commands list with the available commands for the corresponding area of the program.

4. Select a command from the list. InDesign displays the current shortcut (or shortcuts) assigned to the command.

5. To remove a selected shortcut, click the Remove button. To assign a shortcut to a command, or to replace an existing short-cut, move the cursor to the New Shortcut field and press the keys you want to use for the shortcut. If the shortcut you've entered has already been assigned to a command, InDesign displays the Replace button (even if the current command has no keyboard shortcut).

6. Click the Assign button to assign a shortcut to the command, or (if you had a shortcut selected) click the Replace button to replace the selected shortcut. Note that a single command can have multiple shortcuts assigned to it. If you want, you can save your changes without closing the dialog box by pressing the Save button.

**FIGURE 1-54**
**Editing Keyboard Shortcuts**

*When you select an option from this pop-up menu...*

*...InDesign displays a list of the available commands.*

*When you select a command, InDesign displays the shortcut in this field.*

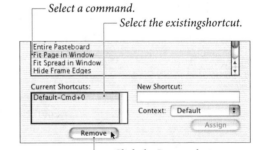

*Click the New Set button, or choose the QuarkXPress 4.0 shortcut set from the Set pop-up menu.*

*If you loaded the Quark XPress 4.0 set, and don't want to edit any shortcuts, click the Save button, then close the dialog box.*

*If you're creating a new set, InDesign displays the New Set dialog box. Enter a name for your set and click the OK button.*

*Select an option from the Product Area pop-up menu.*

— *Select a command.*

— *Select the existing shortcut.*

*Click the Remove button. InDesign deletes the shortcut.*

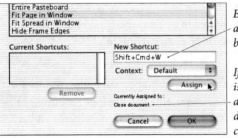

*Enter the new shortcut and click the Assign button.*

*If a keyboard shortcut is already assigned to a command, InDesign displays the name of the command here. Assigning the shortcut removes the conflicting shortcut.*

*InDesign assigns the shortcut to the command.*

7.  Once you've changed all of the shortcuts you want to change, click the OK button to close the dialog box and save the set.

Keyboard shortcut sets are saved in the Shortcut Sets folder in your InDesign folder. Want to take your keyboard shortcuts with you to another machine? Take the shortcuts file from your machine and copy it into the Shortcut Sets folder of the copy of InDesign you'll be using. Open the Keyboard Shortcuts dialog box and choose your shortcut set from the Sets pop-up menu.

To return to InDesign's default keyboard shortcuts, all you need to do is choose the Default set from the Set pop-up menu.

To view or print a complete listing of the shortcuts in a set, select the set from the Set pop-up menu, then click the Show Set button. InDesign creates a text file containing a list of the shortcuts in the set and then opens it using the default text editor on your system (SimpleText on the Macintosh, Notepad in Windows). You can print or save this file for your reference.

**A few thoughts on making up your own shortcuts.** There are two approaches to making up your own keyboard shortcuts. The first is assign shortcuts using a key that has something to do with the name of the command—like "P" for "Print." Usually, these shortcuts are easy to remember. Another, and, in our opinion, better, approach is to analyze the way you work with commands, and then take the commands you use most often and assign them shortcuts that are easy to reach with one hand (usually the left hand, given that the shortcuts for copy, cut, and paste are all located on the left side of the keyboard).

What's the most frequently used keyboard shortcut? For us, it's got to be Fit Page In Window, because we navigate by zooming in with the Zoom tool, then zooming out to the Fit Page In Window view, and then zooming in on another part of the spread. The default shortcut for the Fit Page In Window view, Command-0/Ctrl-0 doesn't work for us. It's a long reach for the left hand, and 0 (zero) is a difficult key to hit without looking at the keyboard. Consider using Command-Shift-W/Ctrl-Shift-W—it's an easy, one-handed reach.

# Setting Preferences

Why do applications have Preferences dialog boxes? We've heard more than one computer user complain about this ubiquitous feature of today's applications. It's simple: there's often more than one "right" way to do something. Rather than dictatorially decide to limit users, InDesign gives you a choice. Preferences are one way you can control the appearance and behavior of the program (defaults are the other—see "Setting Defaults," later in this chapter). They're a place where you can customize the program to better fit your work habits and personality.

To display InDesign's Preferences dialog box, choose General from the Preferences submenu of the File menu, or press Command-K/Ctrl-K. The Preferences dialog box contains a number of panels. Once you've opened the Preferences dialog box, you can move to the next panel by pressing the Next button, or display the previous panel by pressing the Previous button. Better yet, you can press Command-Down Arrow/Ctrl-Down Arrow to go to the next panel, or Command-Up Arrow/Ctrl-Up Arrow to display the previous panel.

You can also reach any panel of the Preferences dialog box directly, using the corresponding item of the Preferences submenu of the File menu.

We refer to each panel in the Preferences dialog as a separate dialog box—for example, we'll say "the General Preferences dialog box" rather than "the General panel of the Preferences dialog box."

The settings in the Preferences dialog box affect the active publication—or, if no publication is open, control the preferences settings for any new publications you create. Changes you make to the preferences of one publication do not affect other publications.

## General Preferences

The General Preferences dialog box (see Figure 1-55) is the "kitchen sink" of the dialog box universe—it contains the things that didn't fit anywhere else.

**Page Numbering.** The options on the View pop-up menu change the way InDesign displays page numbers in the Pages palette. When you choose Absolute Numbering, InDesign numbers the pages sequentially, staring with page one, and pays no attention to the page numbering options of any of the sections in the publication. Choose Section Numbering to have InDesign display page numbers based on the page numbering options you've set up in the Section Options dialog box for each section. For more on setting up sections and numbering pages, see Chapter 2, "Page Layout."

**Tool Tips.** If you're having trouble remembering the names of the tools in InDesign's palettes, choose Fast or Normal from the Tool Tips pop-up menu. When you do, InDesign displays a small window

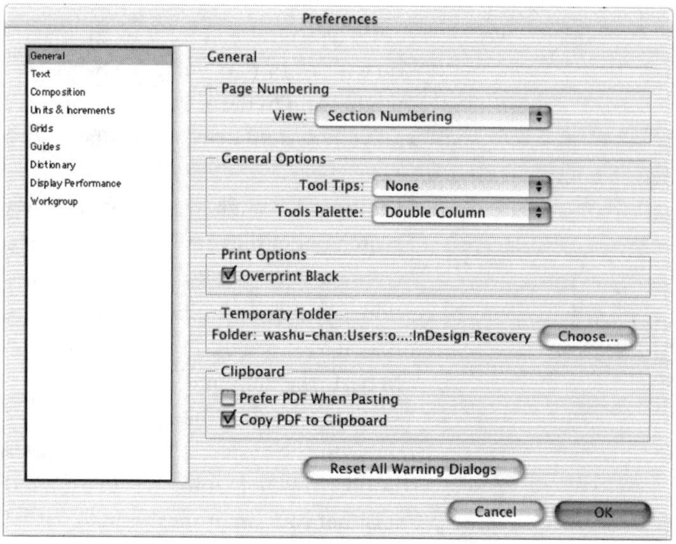

FIGURE 1-55
General Preferences
Dialog Box

containing a tool's name when your cursor passes over the tool (see Figure 1-56). Tool tips do not work for every tool or gadget in every palette. Once you're familiar with InDesign, turn this option off—showing tool tips does slow down the application.

**Tools Palette.** You can choose to display the Tools palette in one of three arrangments: Single Row, Double Column, or Single Column. Choose the option you like best.

**Overprint Black.** If you always want black ink to overprint, turn on the Overprint Black option. This setting overrides any changes you might make in the Print dialog box.

**Temporary Folder.** As you work with InDesign, the program saves information about your preference settings and keeps a record of changes you make to your document. While this makes for a lot of disk-writing activity, it also gives you InDesign's multiple undo and document recovery features.

To change the folder InDesign uses to store its temporary files, click the Choose button. InDesign displays a dialog box. Locate and select the folder you want to use and click the OK button.

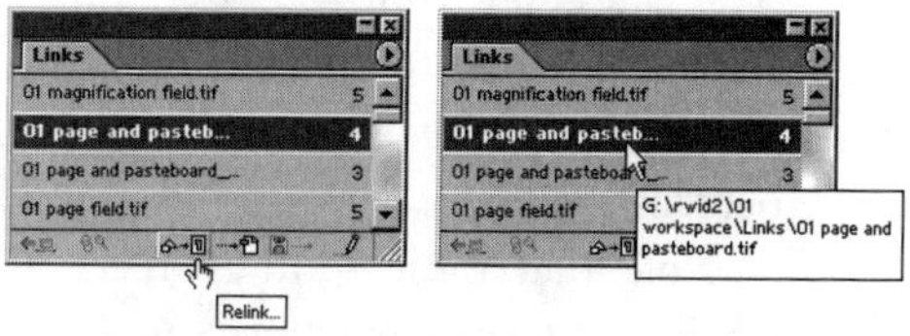

FIGURE 1-56
Tool Tips

*With Tool Tips on, InDesign displays information about the user interface item beneath the cursor.*

Why would you want to change the location? InDesign's temporary files—in particular the SavedData file, can get quite large. You might want to move them to a larger capacity drive to free disk space on your system drive, or to a faster drive to improve performance.

**Clipboard.** When you copy some data out of an application and switch out of that application, the program writes data to the system Clipboard so that it can be pasted into other applications. Applications often post multiple data formats to the Clipboard in the hope that at least one of them will be readable by the application you want to paste the data into.

Some applications (notably Illustrator) can put PDF format data on the system Clipboard. InDesign can paste this data as an imported PDF graphic. That's a good thing. The only bad thing about it is that you sometimes want to paste Illustrator paths into InDesign as editable objects (rather than as a non-editable graphic).

If you want to paste paths from Illustrator, turn off the Prefer PDF When Pasting option.

If you want InDesign to put PDF data on the Clipboard, turn on the Copy PDF to Clipboard option.

**Reset All Warning Dialogs.** Many of InDesign's warning dialog boxes include a "never ask me this again" option (if only telemarketers were so equipped!). If you have adamantly checked this option, and, for whatever reason, want to see the dialog box again, click the Reset All Warning Dialogs button.

**Text Preferences**  The Text Preferences dialog box (see Figure 1-57) contains preferences that affect the way that InDesign formats and displays text in your publications.

**Character Settings.** When you apply Superscript or Subscript to text, InDesign scales the selected characters and shifts their baseline position. How can you control the amount of scaling and baseline shift? That's where the options in this section come in. The Size fields are percentages of the size of the selected characters (you can enter from 1 to 200 percent); the Position fields are percentages of the leading (you can enter from –500 to 500 percent). When you apply Small Caps formatting to text, InDesign scales the selected characters by the percentage you enter in the Small Cap Size field (from one to 200 percent).

Note that these settings affect all superscript, subscript, and small caps formatting you've applied in the current document (like

FIGURE 1-57
Text Preferences
Dialog Box

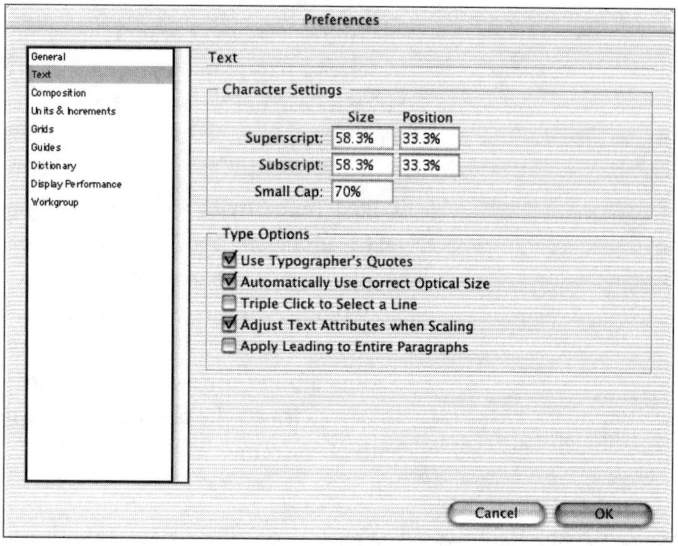

QuarkXPress, but unlike PageMaker, where superscript, subscript, and small caps formatting options are set at the character level).

For more on working with superscript, subscript, and small caps, see Chapter 4, "Type."

**Use Typographer's Quotes.** Using "typewriter" quotation marks and apostrophes (" and ') instead of their typographic (", ", ', and ') equivalents is one of the hallmarks of amateur desktop publishing design. It's sometimes difficult to remember what keys to press to get the preferred marks (press Option-Shift-]/Alt-Shift-] to produce an apostrophe for example). When you turn on the Use Typographer's Quotes option, InDesign enters the correct quotation marks for you as you type.

**Automatically Use Correct Optical Size.** This setting only comes into play when you're working with multiple master fonts—and then only with those fonts that have a defined optical size axis (not all multiple master fonts do).

If the multiple master font (or fonts) you're working with do include an optical size axis, turning this option on forces the font to use an optical size axis that matches the point size of the text, regardless of the optical size axis setting of the instance of the font. When this option is off, InDesign uses the optical size axis setting of the font instance.

**Triple Click to Select a Line.** When this option is on, triple-clicking the Text tool in text selects the line you're clicking on and quadruple-clicking selects the paragraph; when this option is off, triple-click to select a paragraph and quadruple-click to select the entire story. Since we can't agree on the "correct" setting for this option, we leave it up to you.

**Adjust Text Attributes When Scaling.** In earlier versions, scaling a text frame using the Transform palette or the Free Transform tool would change the appearance of the text, but would not affect its underlying point size. This could be confusing (see Figure 1-58).

When the Adjust Text Attributes When Scaling option is on, scaling a text frame scales the point size of the text. When it's off, InDesign leaves the point size unchanged, but applies scaling to the entire text frame.

**FIGURE 1-58**
**Scaling Text Attributes**
**(Or Not)**

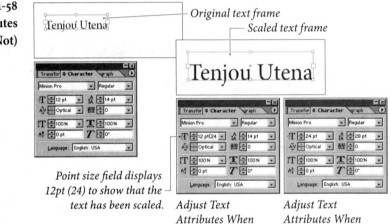

*Original text frame*

*Scaled text frame*

*Point size field displays 12pt (24) to show that the text has been scaled.*

*Adjust Text Attributes When Scaling option off*

*Adjust Text Attributes When Scaling option on*

**Apply Leading to Entire Paragraphs.** While you might, in rare instances, want to vary the leading of lines in a paragraph, you'd probably prefer to use a single leading value for all lines in a paragraph (if you're coming to InDesign from QuarkXPress, Frame-Maker, or Microsoft Word this is the behavior you expect).

In InDesign, you can apply leading at the character level, which means that you might accidentally create uneven leading between lines of a paragraph. To force InDesign to use a single leading value for an entire paragraph, turn on the Apply Leading to Entire Paragraphs option. When you do this, the largest leading value in the paragraph sets the leading of the paragraph.

**Composition**
**Preferences**

Composition is the process of making type fit in the columns and pages in your publication. The options in the Composition Preferences dialog box (see Figure 1-59) relate to various aspects of

**FIGURE 1-59**
**Composition Preferences Dialog Box**

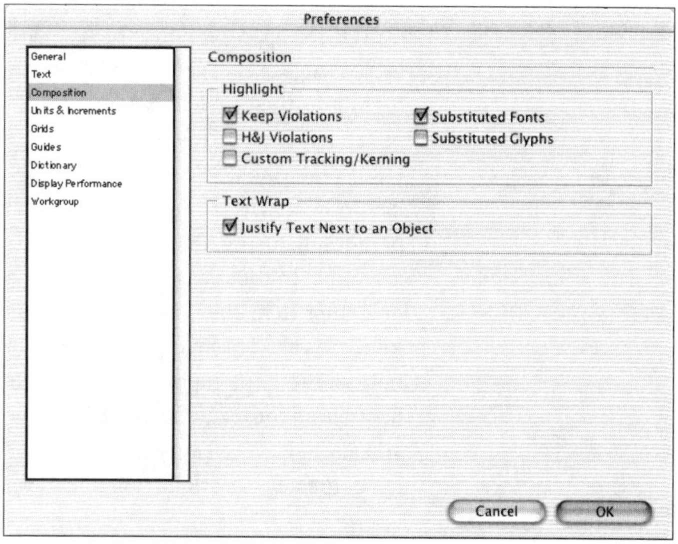
Preferences
General
Text
Composition
Units & Increments
Grids
Guides
Dictionary
Display Performance
Workgroup
Composition
Highlight
Keep Violations
Substituted Fonts
H&J Violations
Substituted Glyphs
Custom Tracking/Kerning
Text Wrap
Justify Text Next to an Object
Cancel
OK

InDesign's text composition features. To really understand how composition works, see Chapter 4, "Type."

**Highlight.** The options in the Highlight section help you spot composition problems before they become printed mistakes. All three options work the same way: when they spot a composition problem (a place where InDesign has had to break your rules to lay out a publication, or where InDesign lacks the font to properly compose a piece of text), they "highlight" the text by drawing a colored bar behind it (see Figure 1-60).

**Keeps Violations.** In the Keep Options dialog box (choose Keep Options from the Paragraph palette's menu, or press Command-Option-K/Ctrl-Alt-K), you'll see a variety of settings that determine the way the selected paragraph deals with column and page breaks. These settings, collectively, are called "keeps." InDesign will sometimes have to disobey your keeps settings in order to compose a pub-

**FIGURE 1-60**
**Highlighting Composition Problems**

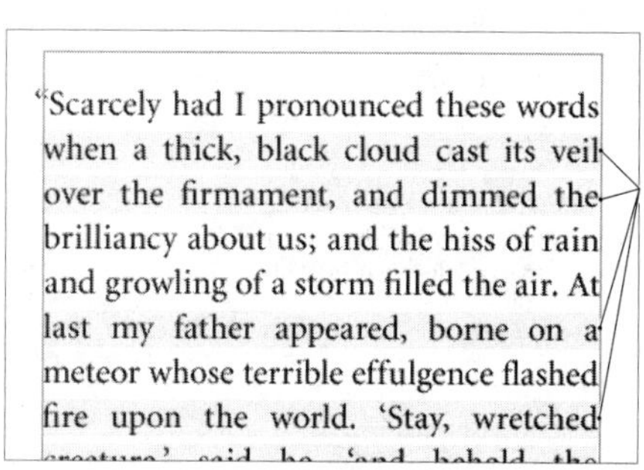
"Scarcely had I pronounced these words
when a thick, black cloud cast its veil
over the firmament, and dimmed the
brilliancy about us; and the hiss of rain
and growling of a storm filled the air. At
last my father appeared, borne on a
meteor whose terrible effulgence flashed
fire upon the world. 'Stay, wretched

*When you turn on the H&J Violations option in the Highlight section of the Text Preferences dialog box, InDesign highlights lines of text that break the spacing rules you entered in the Justification dialog box.*

lication. Keeps violations are very rare, but you can easily spot them by turning on the Keeps Violations option. When you do, InDesign highlights the problem paragraphs.

**H&J Violations.** When InDesign composes the text in your publications, it tries to follow the guidelines you've laid out for each paragraph (using the Justification dialog box), but, sometimes, it just can't. In those cases, InDesign applies word spacing that's looser or tighter than the minimum or maximum you've specified. This is known as an "H&J violation." When you turn on the H&J Violations option, InDesign highlights the problem lines by displaying a yellow bar behind the text. The intensity of the tint used to draw the bar gives you a rough indication of the severity of the "violation"—darker tints equal greater variation from your settings.

**Substituted Fonts.** When you turn on the Substituted Fonts option, InDesign highlights text formatted using fonts you do not currently have loaded. This makes it very easy to spot that space character you accidentally formatted using Hobo before you left your office. The highlight color is pink. See Figure 1-61.

**FIGURE 1-61**
**Highlighting**
**Font Substitution**

*Font (Poetica Chancery) present*

*Highlighted font substitution. The substituted text appears in the default font.*

*Font missing*

**Substituted Glyphs.** InDesign has various features that replace characters in your text with other characters (most of these options can be found on the Character palette menu). If you want to see the places where InDesign has applied these special characters, turn on the Substituted Glyphs option. The highlight color is purple. See Figure 1-62.

**FIGURE 1-62**
**Highlighting**
**Glyph Substitution**

"My father," I replied, "I am fond of action. I like to succor the afflicted, and make people happy. Command that there be built for me a tower, from whose top I can see the whole earth, and thus discover the places where my help would be of most avail."

"To do good, without ceasing, to mankind, a race at once flighty and ungrateful, is a more painful task than you imagine," said Asfendarmod. "And you, Ganigul," continued he, "what do you desire?"

"Nothing but sweet repose," replied she. "If I am placed in

*— Highlighted glyph substitution*

**Custom Tracking/Kerning.** To see the places in your text that have kerning or tracking applied to them, turn on the Custom Kerning/Tracking option. When you do this, InDesign highlights any text containing manual kerning (i.e., kerning that was not applied by one of the automatic kerning methods), or tracking values other than zero with a blue-green tint. See Figure 1-63.

**FIGURE 1-63**
**Highlighting**
**Custom Tracking**
**and Kerning**

*The paragraph style applied*
*to this paragraph specifies a*
*tracking value.*

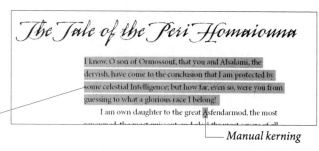

*— Manual kerning*

**Justify Text Next to an Object.** When an object bearing a text wrap appears in the *middle* of a column of text, should InDesign justify the text around the wrapped object? If so, turn on Justify Text Next to an Object. Note that this option has no effect on text wraps that do not split a line into two or more parts. The authors suggest that you never create a design that would cause you to care about this option one way or the other. See Figure 1-64.

**FIGURE 1-64**
**Justifying Text Next**
**to an Object**

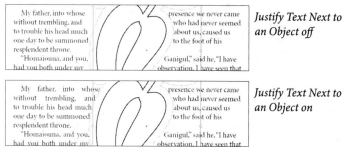

*Justify Text Next to*
*an Object off*

*Justify Text Next to*
*an Object on*

**Units & Increments**
**Preferences**

We've all got favorite units of measure—we're partial to furlongs and stone—so we should be able to choose the measurement system we use to lay out our pages. That's what the Units & Increments Preferences dialog box is for (see Figure 1-65).

**Ruler Units.** The Origin pop-up menu sets the default location of the ruler zero point. Choose Spread to have InDesign position the zero point at the upper-left corner of the spread. Choose Page, and InDesign locates the zero point at the upper-left corner of the page. Choose Spine, and the ruler zero point will appear at the top of the spine (regardless of the number of pages in the spread).

FIGURE 1-65

Units & Increments
Preferences Dialog Box

Use the Horizontal and Vertical pop-up menus to select the measurement units (inches, inches decimal, picas, points, millimeters, and ciceros) you want to use for the horizontal and vertical rulers.

In addition to the usual measurement systems, you can choose to use custom increments for either or both rulers. When you choose Custom, you can enter a distance in the field attached to the pop-up menu.

As you set up a publication's measurement units, there are two things you should keep in mind (they'll save you trips back to this dialog box):

◆ You can use the Context menu to change ruler units—Control-click (Macintosh) or right-click on the ruler, and InDesign displays a Context menu containing the same options as you see in the Units & Increments Preferences dialog box.

◆ You can always override units of measurement in any field in any palette or dialog box in InDesign. For more on entering measurement unit overrides, see "Overriding Units of Measurement," earlier in this chapter.

**Keyboard Increments.** What happens when you push an arrow key? That depends on the settings you've entered in the following fields.

**Cursor Key.** When you have an object selected using the Selection tool, you can move it by pressing the arrow keys. How far do you want it to move with each key press? Enter that value in this field.

**Size/Leading.** When you have text selected (using the Text tool), you can increase or decrease the size and/or leading of the text by pressing keyboard shortcuts (by default, you press Command-Shift->/Ctrl-Shift-> to increase the size of the text; Command-Shift-</

Ctrl-Shift-< to decrease the size; Option-Up arrow/Alt-Up arrow to increase the leading; or Option-Down arrow to decrease the leading). How much larger or smaller should the point size or leading get with each key press? Enter the amount you want in this field.

**Baseline Shift.** When you have selected text using the Text tool, you can increase baseline shift by pressing (by default) Option-Shift-Up Arrow/Alt-Shift-Up Arrow, or decrease baseline shift by pressing Option-Shift-Down Arrow/Alt-Shift-Down Arrow. How much baseline shift should each key press apply? Enter the amount you want in this field.

**Kerning.** When the text cursor is between two characters, you can apply kerning by pressing Option-Left Arrow/Alt-Left Arrow or Option-Right Arrow/Alt-Right Arrow. When a range of text is selected with the text tool, pressing this shortcut applies tracking. Enter the kerning amount you want to apply (in thousandths of an em) in this field.

**Grids Preferences**   InDesign can display two different types of grid: baseline and document. You control various aspects of their appearance using the options in this dialog box (see Figure 1-66). Both grids are very similar to the guides (ruler guides, margin guides, and column guides), and have a similar effect on items on your pages.

**Baseline Grid.** The baseline grid is an array of horizontal guides that mark off the page in units equal to a specified leading amount (note that the baseline grid isn't really a grid, as it has no vertical lines).

**Color.** Choose a color for the baseline grid using the Color pop-up menu, or double-click the color well to display a color picker.

**Start.** Enter a value in the Start field to set the distance from the top of the page at which you want the baseline grid to begin.

**Increment Every.** Enter a distance—in general, the leading value of your publication's body text—in the Increment Every field.

**View Threshold.** Set the magnification at which the grid becomes visible in the View Threshold field.

**Document Grid.** The document grid is a network of horizontal and vertical guidelines spaced a specified distance apart.

**FIGURE 1-66**
**Grids Preferences**
**Dialog Box**

*Choose one of InDesign's preset colors from the pop-up menu, or...*

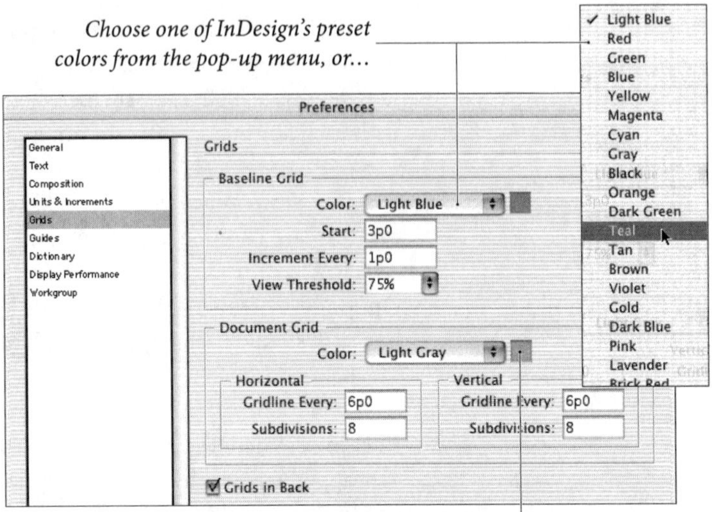

*...double-click the color swatch to display a dialog box where you can define a custom color.*

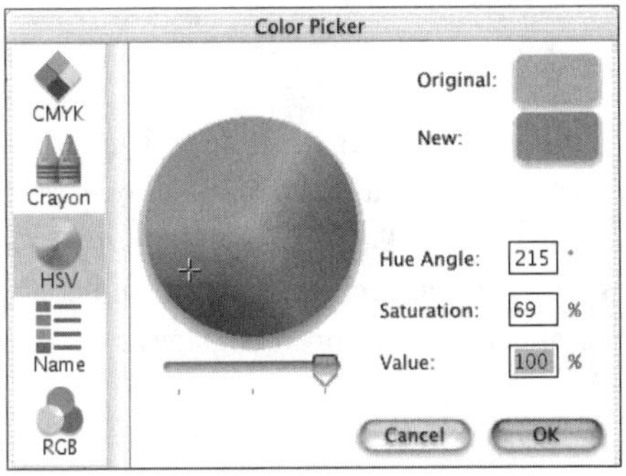

*Macintosh color picker* 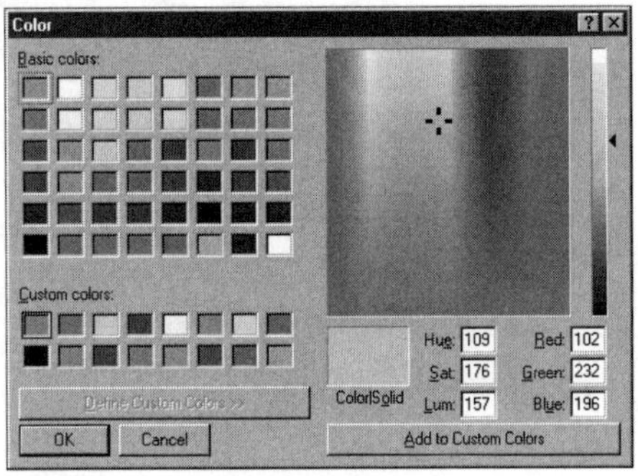          *Windows color picker*

**Color.** Choose a color for the baseline grid using the Color pop-up menu, or double-click the color well to display a color picker.

**Gridline Every.** Enter the distance you want between grid lines in this field.

**Subdivisions.** Just as the document grid divides the page, subdivisions divide the grid into smaller sections. The number you enter in this field sets the number of subdivisions between each grid line. If you don't want to subdivide the document grid, enter 1 in this field. InDesign displays the grid subdivision lines using a tint of the color you specified for the document grid.

**Grids in Back.** Turn on this option to make the grids appear at the the bottom of the stacking order.

**Guides Preferences**    Use the Guides Preferences dialog box (see Figure 1-67) to set the color you want to use to display margin and column guides. Why isn't there an option for setting the color of ruler guides? You don't have to use the same color for all of your ruler guides—you specify the color using the Ruler Guides dialog box.

**Snap to Zone.** Use this option to set the distance, in screen pixels, at which guides begin to exert their mysterious pull on objects you're drawing or dragging.

**Guides in Back.** Turn on this option to position the guides at the bottom of the stacking order of the layer they're on.

FIGURE 1-67
Guides Preferences
Dialog Box

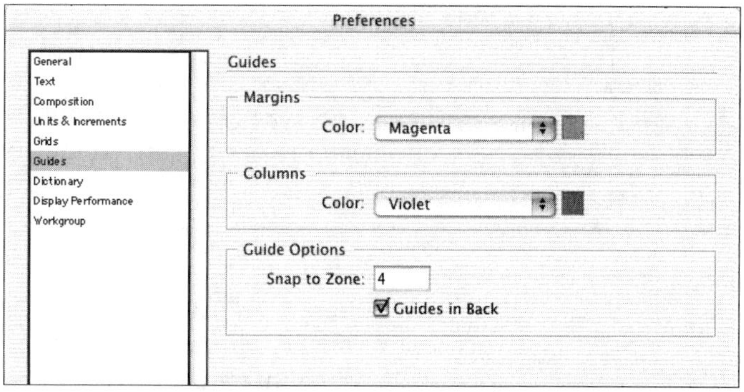

**Dictionary Preferences**    Choose a language from the dictionary pop-up menu to set the default dictionary used by the paragraphs in the publication (see Figure 1-68). Any selection you make using the Language pop-up menu in the Paragraph palette overrides this setting. Some dictionaries might offer more than one option for hyphenation vendor and spelling vendor—if you're working with one that does, you'll see more than one choice on the corresponding pop-up menus. We've only ever seen the Proximity dictionaries.

**Double Quotes.** Enter the pair of characters you want to use for double quotes, or select them from the pop-up menu.

**Single Quotes.** Enter the pair of characters you want to use for single quotes, or select them from the pop-up menu.

**Compose Using.** When you add a word to the user dictionary (including changes you make to hyphenation points), InDesign adds the word to the user dictionary's exceptions list. Choose user Dictionary to use the exceptions list in the current user dictionary;

FIGURE 1-68
Dictionary Preferences
Dialog Box

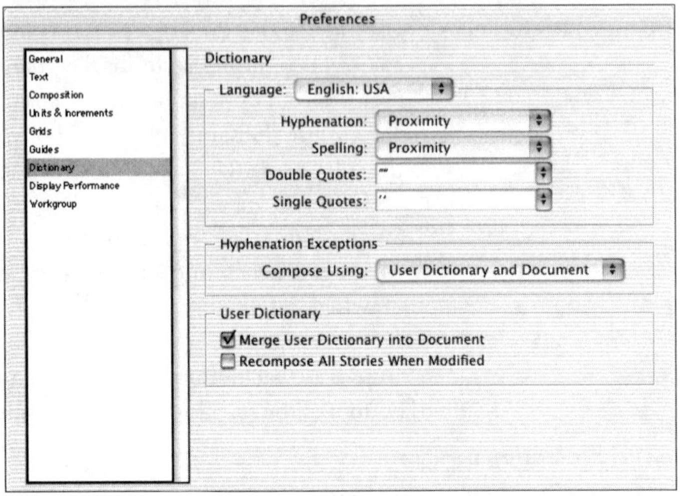

choose Document to use the hyphenation exceptions stored in the document; or choose User Dictionary and Document to use both exception lists.

**User Dictionary Options.** Choose Merge User Dictionary into Document to copy the hyphenation and spelling excptions list from the user dictionary into each document you open. Clearly, this isn't an option you want to turn on if you frequently open documents from other people.

Choose Recompose All Stories When Modified to recompose all stories in a document when the user dictionary changes (or when you change the setting of the Compose Using pop-up menu). Recomposing all stories in a document can be a time-consuming process; most of the time, we think you should leave this option turned off.

**Display Performance Preferences**  The options in this panel of the Preferences dialog box control the way that InDesign draws text and graphics on your screen. The choices you make here can dramatically speed up—or slow down— the process of drawing and redrawing the screen (see Figure 1-69).

**Default View Settings.** Choose an option on this pop-up menu to set the default view setting for the document.

**Ignore Local Settings.** Turn this option on to ignore view settings applied to individual windows and objects.

**Adjust View Settings.** You can apply one of three display settings— which are named "Optimized," "Typical," and "High Quality"—to

**FIGURE 1-69**

**Display Performance Preferences Dialog Box**

*This text changes to Gray Out or High Resolution, depending on the slider setting.*

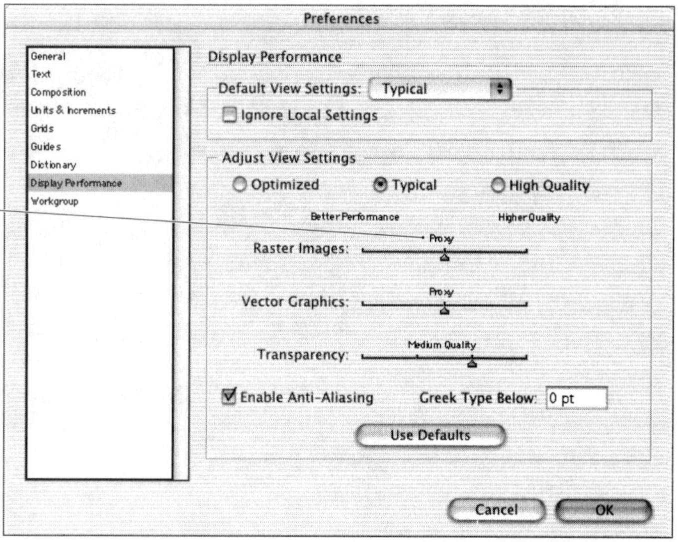

any InDesign window or object, and you can define the parameters of each setting. Note that the names of these settings do not necessarily apply to the quality of the display; "High Quality" can be redefined to produce a lower quality display than "Optimized." (We urge you not to do this, as you will only drive yourself mad.)

To edit the parameters of a view setting, choose the setting and then adjust the values of the options.

◆ **Raster Images.** Choose an option on this slider to define the method InDesign uses to draw imported bitmap images (TIFF, JPEG, GIF). Note that images saved in the EPS (including DCS) and PDF formats are considered "vector graphics," see below. See Figure 1-70.

Choose Gray Out to draw every image as a gray box.

Choose Proxy to have InDesign construct a low-resolution screen version of the imported graphic and use that image for display at all magnification levels.

When you choose High Resolution from the Raster Images slider, InDesign gets its information about how to render an image from the original file that's linked to your publication, which means that InDesign renders the best possible display of the image for the current magnification.

This setting has no effect on the way the images print.

◆ **Vector Graphics.** Choose an option from the slider to define the method InDesign uses to display vector graphics (EPS and PDF). See Figure 1-71.

**FIGURE 1-70**
**Raster Images**
**View Settings**

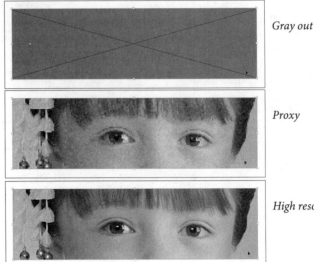

*Gray out*

*Proxy*

*High resolution*

Choose Gray Out to draw every graphic as a gray box.

Choose Proxy to have InDesign construct a low-resolution screen version of the imported graphic and use that image for display at all magnification levels.

When you choose High Resolution from the Vector Graphics slider, InDesign gets its information about how to render the graphic by reinterpreting PostScript/PDF instructions in the graphic file. InDesign then renders the best possible view of the graphic for the current screen resolution. Note, however that this process can be very time consuming.

This setting has no effect on the way the images print to a PostScript printer.

**FIGURE 1-71**
**Vector Graphics**
**View Settings**

*Proxy*

*High Resolution*

◆ **Transparency.** The Transparency slider controls the appearance of transparency on your screen—it has nothing to do with the way that transparency prints. Choose Off to omit previews for transparency altogether, or choose Low Quality, Medium Quality, or High Quality to control the accuracy of the preview (see Figure 1-72).

**FIGURE 1-72**
**Transparency View Settings**

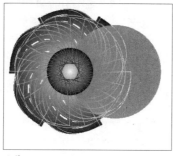

*Off*

*Low Quality*

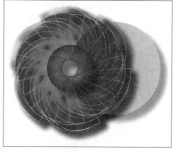

*Medium Quality*

*High Quality*

◆ **Enable Anti-Aliasing.** Anti-aliasing smoothes the edges of InDesign objects (text characters and things you've drawn using the drawing tools) by adding pixels around the edges of the object. See Figure 1-73.

**FIGURE 1-73**
**Anti-Aliasing**

*Anti-aliasing off (enlarged)*

*Anti-aliasing on (enlarged)*

◆ **Greek Type Below.** It takes time to draw text characters, and, frankly, it's not always worth doing. You might have noticed that when you zoom out to the 12.5% page view, InDesign doggedly attempts to give the best preview it can of the (now very tiny) text on your pages. To tell InDesign not to bother, and to speed up your screen redraw, use greeking.

When you enter a value in the Greek Type Below field that's greater than zero, InDesign represents text characters that are equal to or smaller than that value as a gray bar (see Figure 1-74).

The value shown in the field is in points, but it doesn't refer to the point size of the text. Instead, it refers to the size of the text as it appears on your screen at the current magnfication. The advantage of using this option is that the gray bar draws much faster than the actual characters. Greeking has no effect on text composition.

**FIGURE 1-74**
**Greeking**

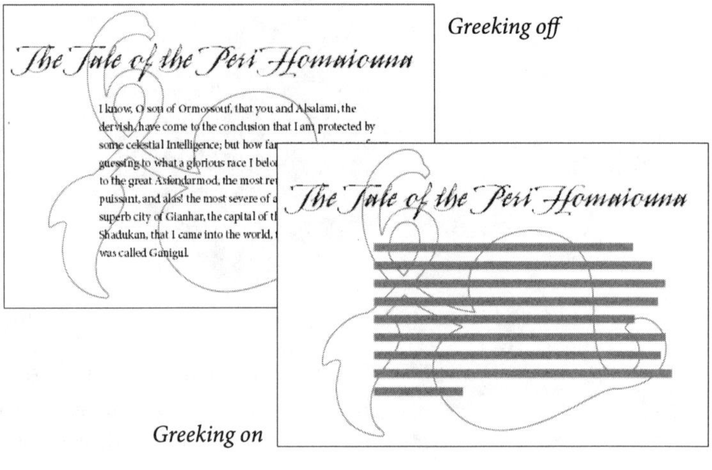

*Greeking off*

*Greeking on*

◆ **Use Defaults.** Click this button to return the options for the selected display setting to their default value.

**Workgroup Preferences**

WebDAV is a file control system for people who regularly read Dave Barry's "humor" columns. We are not making this up. No, actually, we are. WebDAV stands for Web Distributed Authoring and Versioning, and provides a web-server based set of tools for managing a collaborative workgroup environment. InDesign's Workgroup preferences dialog box gives you a way to set preferences for your WebDAV server (see Figure 1-75).

**FIGURE 1-75**
**Workgroup Preferences**

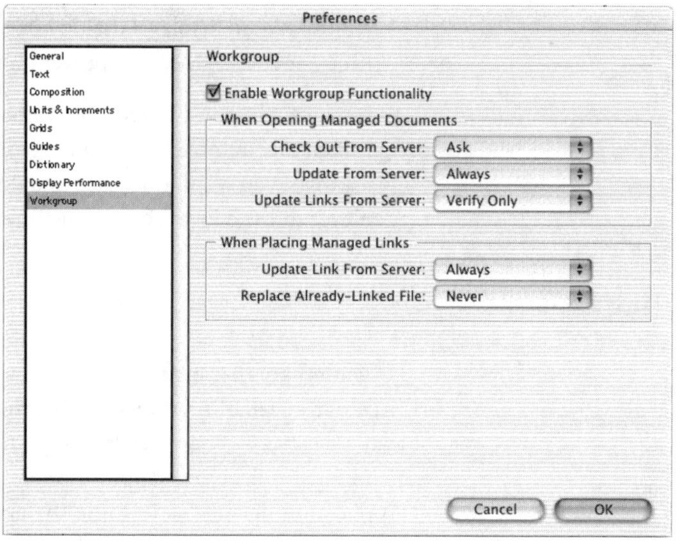

**Enable Workgroup Functionality.** To enable InDesign's workgroup features, turn this option on.

**When Opening Managed Documents.** The options in this section of the dialog box control the way that InDesign works with files you open from the server.

◆ **Check Out from Server.** Choose Always to check out and create a local copy of the file. Choose Ask to display a warning before checking out a file. Choose Never to open a local copy of the file without checking it out.

◆ **Update from Server.** Choose Always to download the latest version of the document, choose Ask to display a dialog box if the file on the server has changed, or choose Never to open a local copy of the document without checking for an updated version.

◆ **Update Links from Server.** Choose Always to update links automatically, choose Ask to have InDesign display a dialog box asking if you want to update changed links, or choose Never to prevent InDesign from updating links. Choose Verify Only to update broken links only.

**When Placing Managed Links.** The options in this section of the dialog box define the way that InDesign works with linked files stored on your workgroup server.

◆ **Update Link from Server.** Choose Always to automatically update linked graphics files when their link status changes, choose Ask to display a dialog box asking if you want to update links, or choose Never to prevent links from updating.

◆ **Replace Already-Linked File.** Choose Always to replace the linked files automatically, choose Ask to display a dialog box asking if you want to replace updated linked files, or choose Never to use a local copy of the linked file.

## Setting Defaults

"Defaults" are the settings you begin with when you start InDesign. InDesign's defaults control page size, fill type and stroke color, available styles, type specifications, and other details. InDesign has two kinds of defaults—application defaults and document defaults. Application defaults determine the appearance and behavior of all new publications; document defaults control the specifications of objects you create in a particular publication.

Neither document defaults nor application defaults change any existing objects or publications—you can change the defaults at any time without harming publications you've already laid out.

When you create a new InDesign publication, do you immediately add a set of colors to the Colors palette, change the default line weight, display the rulers, or add styles to the Style palette? If you do, you probably get tired of making those changes over and over again. Wouldn't it be great if you could tell InDesign to create new documents using those settings?

You can. To set InDesign's application defaults, close all publications (without closing InDesign), then, with no publication open (what we like to call the "no pub state," or, as our good friend Steve Broback would say, "Utah"), add or remove styles and colors, set type specifications, and otherwise make the changes you've been making in each new publication.

The next time you create a new InDesign publication, it'll appear with the settings you specified.

Some document properties cannot be set as application defaults—you cannot, for example, create a new layer or add master pages.

**Reverting to InDesign's Original Defaults**

If you want to return to InDesign's original defaults, quit InDesign and then throw away two files: InDesign Defaults and InDesign SavedData (they're in different places on different systems, so the easiest way to find them is to search for the file names). When you restart InDesign, the program will regenerate the files using its original "factory" settings.

# Publication Navigation

InDesign offers three ways to change your view of the publication: zooming, scrolling, and moving from page to page. Zooming changes the magnification of the area inside the publication window. Scrolling changes the view of the publication in the publication window without changing the magnification.

**Zooming**

Most of the time, we use zooming (that is, changing magnifications of the view of the publication) rather than scrolling (that is, changing the view of the publication without changing magnification) to move from one area of the page or pasteboard to another.

**Zooming with the View menu.** The View menu offers InDesign's "standard" magnifications, or views, and provides keyboard shortcuts for most of them (see Table 1-3).

All of these commands except Fit to Page center the object you've selected in the publication window. If you don't have an object selected, these shortcuts zoom in or out based on the center of the current view. Fit Page In Window centers the current page in a publication window. This makes Fit Page In Window the perfect "zoom-out" shortcut.

**Fit Selection In Window.** Another view command we use all of the time is Fit Selection In Window. Don't bother looking for it on the View menu—it's not there. Instead, it appears on the context menu when you have an object selected. It does just what it says—zooms (in or out) on the current selection and centers it in the publication window (see Figure 1-76). Press Command-Option-=/Ctrl-Alt-= to zoom to the Fit Selection In Window view.

**TABLE 1-3**
**View Shortcuts**

| To zoom to this view: | Press: |
| --- | --- |
| Actual size (100%) | Command-1/Ctrl-1 |
| 200% | Command-2/Ctrl-2 |
| 400% | Command-4/Ctrl-4 |
| 50% | Command-5/Ctrl-5 |
| Fit Page in Window | Command-0/Ctrl-0 |
| Fit Spread in Window | Command-Option-0/Ctrl-Alt-0 |
| Zoom in | Command-+/Ctrl-+ |
| Zoom out | Command-- (minus)/Ctrl--(minus) |

FIGURE 1-76
Fit Selection in Window

*It doesn't really matter where the selection is hiding...*

*... "Fit Selection in Window" will find it and make it more visible.*

**Zooming with the Zoom tool.** Another zooming method: choose the Zoom tool, point at an area in your publication, and click. InDesign zooms to the next larger view size (based on your current view—from 100% to 200%, for example), centering the area you clicked on in the publication window. Hold down Option/Alt and the plus ("+") in the Zoom tool changes to a minus ("-"). Click the Zoom tool to zoom out.

**Switching to the Zoom Tool.** Press Command-Spacebar/Ctrl-Spacebar to temporarily switch from any tool to the Zoom tool to zoom in; or hold down Command-Option-Spacebar/Ctrl-Alt-Spacebar to zoom out.

**The Best Way to Zoom.** To zoom in, press Command/Ctrl and hold down Spacebar to turn the current tool (whatever it is) into the Zoom tool, then drag the Zoom tool in the publication window. As you drag, a rectangle (like a selection rectangle) appears. Drag the rectangle around the area you want to zoom in on, and release the mouse button. InDesign zooms in on the area, magnifying it to the magnification that fits in the publication window (see Figure 1-77).

To zoom out, use one of the keyboard shortcuts—Command-0/Ctrl-0, for Fit Page In Window, is especially handy (it's even better if you redefine the shortcut to make it easier to reach with one hand—why take your hand off of the mouse if you don't need to?).

**Entering a magnification percentage.** To zoom to a specific magnification percentage, enter the percentage in the Magnification field and press Return/Enter. To "jump" into the Magnification field, press Command-Option-5/Ctrl-Alt-5. InDesign zooms to the percentage you specified (centering the selection, if any, as it does so).

**FIGURE 1-77**
**Drag Magnification**

*Hold down Command-*
*Spacebar/*
*Ctrl-Spacebar to switch*
*to the Zoom tool.*

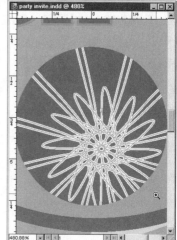

Drag the Zoom tool around the area    InDesign zooms in on the area you
you want to magnify.    defined by dragging.

**Scrolling**    As we said earlier in this chapter, we rarely use the scroll bars to
scroll. So how do we change our view of our publications? We use the
Hand tool (also known as the "Grabber Hand"), or we let InDesign
do the scrolling for us as we move objects.

**Scrolling with the Hand Tool.** So how do *you* use the Hand tool?
Sure, you can always click on the Hand tool in the Tools palette, or
press the keyboard shortcut to switch to the Hand tool, but there's a
better way. Provided you're not editing text, holding down the Spacebar turns the cursor into the Hand tool. Avoid this shortcut if you
are editing text—you'll enter spaces. Instead, hold down Option/Alt
to switch to the Hand tool. Drag the Hand tool, and InDesign scrolls
in the direction you're dragging (see Figure 1-78). When you stop
dragging, InDesign switches back to the tool you were using before
you used the Hand tool.

**Another Hand Tool Shortcut.** You think it's a bother remembering
two shortcuts for the Hand tool? Try this: hold down Command/
Ctrl (which switches to the Selection tool), then press Spacebar and
release Command/Ctrl. InDesign displays the Hand tool. Drag until
you see the part of the publication you want to see, then release the
Spacebar.

InDesign switches back to whatever tool you had selected before
you pressed Command/Ctrl. If you were editing text, InDesign
switches back to the Text tool and puts the cursor back where it was
(see Figure 1-79).

FIGURE 1-78
**Using the Hand Tool**

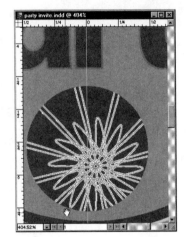

*If the cursor is in a text frame, or if text is selected, hold down Option/Alt instead of Spacebar.*

*Hold down Spacebar to switch to the Hand tool, then drag the Hand tool to scroll.*

*When the publication window looks the way you want it to, stop dragging.*

**Scrolling as you drag objects.** Don't forget that you can change your view by dragging objects off the screen. If you know an object should be moved to some point outside your current view, select the object and do one of the following things:

◆ To scroll down, drag the cursor into the scroll bar at the bottom of the publication window. Don't drag the cursor off the bottom of the screen—InDesign won't scroll if you do this (for some unknown reason).

◆ To scroll to the right, move the cursor into the vertical scroll bar, or drag the cursor off of the left edge of the screen.

◆ To scroll to a point above your current view, drag the cursor into the horizontal ruler.

◆ To scroll to the left, drag the cursor into the vertical ruler (or off the screen, if the ruler is not visible).

The window scrolls as long as the mouse button is down. Sometimes it's the best way to get something into position.

InDesign won't let you drag objects to an area in the publication window that is behind a palette. If you drag the cursor into any palette other than the Library palette, InDesign displays the "prohibited" symbol. When you drop objects you're dragging into an area covered by a palette, InDesign bounces the objects back to their original locations. You can't hide palettes while you're dragging objects, so you might want to hide the palettes before you begin dragging.

# Place Icons

When you place (that is, import) a file, InDesign changes the cursor into an icon called a "place icon," or "place gun" (see Figure 1-79). You can click the place icon to specify the position of the upper-left corner of the incoming file, or you can drag the place icon to define the width and height of the file.

◆ To "unload" a place icon without placing the file, click the place icon on any of the tools in the toolbox.

◆ If you had a frame selected, InDesign places the file in that object. This is, in general, a very useful feature, but it can sometimes mean that imported files end up in frames you didn't want to fill with the file. When this happens to you, press Command-Z/Ctrl-Z (or choose Undo from the Edit menu), and InDesign will display the loaded place icon. Now you can click or drag the place icon to place the file.

We'll talk more about place icons in the next chapter, and in Chapter 7, "Importing and Exporting."

**FIGURE 1-79**
**Place Icon**

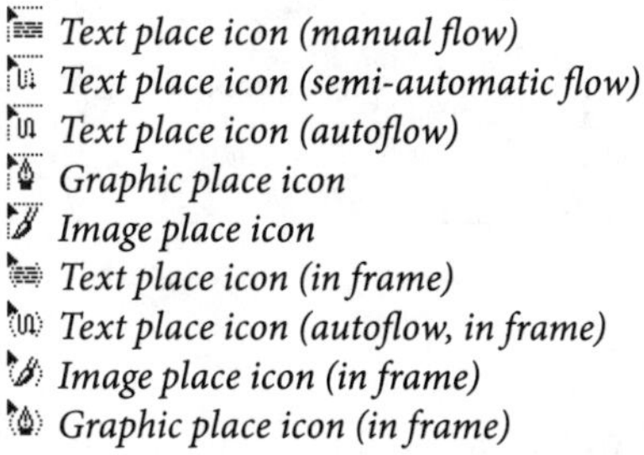

*Text place icon (manual flow)*
*Text place icon (semi-automatic flow)*
*Text place icon (autoflow)*
*Graphic place icon*
*Image place icon*
*Text place icon (in frame)*
*Text place icon (autoflow, in frame)*
*Image place icon (in frame)*
*Graphic place icon (in frame)*

# Managing InDesign's Plug-Ins

Everything you see in InDesign is provided by a plug-in. The "application" itself is little more than a plug-in manager. The functions we traditionally think of as being central to a page layout application—things like text composition, text editing, or basic drawing tools—they're all plug-ins. We're not kidding.

This means that you can turn plug-ins on and off to customize InDesign to the way that you work and the publications you work with. Specifically, you can turn off the plug-ins you don't use.

To define the set of plug-ins InDesign will load the next time you start the program, choose Configure Plug-ins from the Apple menu on the Mac OS, or from the Help menu in Windows. InDesign displays the Configure Plug-ins dialog box (see Figure 1-80).

Why would you want to turn plug-ins off? Simple—to reduce the amount of memory taken up by InDesign and to increase the speed of the application (slightly).

Some plug-ins are required by InDesign—they're the ones with the little padlock next to them. But all of the other plug-ins are fair game. Never use the Navigator palette? Turn it off!

Our favorite candidate for shutdown is Adobe Online. Yes, it's cool to be able to go to adobe.com and download new plug-ins. But *how often do you really need to do that?* Once a month? Never?

FIGURE 1-80

**Configure Plug-Ins Dialog Box**

*If you're not using a particular plug-in, click the check mark to the left of the plug-in's name to turn it off. The next time you start InDesign, the plug-in will not be loaded.*

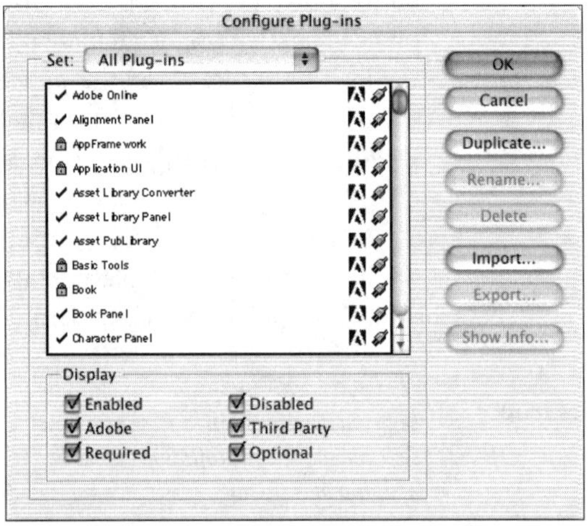

## Getting Help

If you installed InDesign's online help system, you can display information on the meaning and use of specific InDesign features. InDesign's online help consists of HTML pages you can view in your web browser. Press Help/F1 to open the help system.

## On with the Tour

At this point in the InDesign tour, we've seen most of the sights. Don't worry if you're a little confused—it's hard to take it all in at once. In the following chapters, we'll help you put the tools in context—so far, we've just talked about what the tools *are*. In the rest of the book, we'll talk about that you can *do* with them.

# Page Layout

## CHAPTER 2

Now that you know what's what, and what's where, in InDesign, it's time to create an InDesign publication and set up some pages. As you work your way through the process of defining the page size, margins, column layout, and master pages for your new publication, think ahead. How will the publication be printed? How will it be bound? Will you need to create a different version of the publication for a different paper size (such as switching from US Letter to A4 for an international edition)? Will you need to create a different version of the publication for online distribution?

We know—having to think about these things and make design decisions early in the process can be boring. And InDesign makes it relatively easy to make changes to your layout late in the production process. Easy, but not without a certain amount of trouble. How high is your threshold of pain? Will it decrease as your deadline approaches? You decide.

## Creating a New Publication

When you choose New from the File menu, InDesign displays the New Document dialog box (see Figure 2-1). You use the controls in this dialog box to set up the basic layout of the pages in your publication. Don't worry—you're not locked into anything; you can change these settings at any time, or override any of them for any page or page spread in your publication. Getting them right at this point, however, might save you a little time and trouble later on.

FIGURE 2-1

**The New Document Dialog Box**

*Note: To enter the starting page number, you use section options (in the Pages palette).*

*Enter the number of pages you want.*

*Should InDesign create a text frame on the master page? If so, turn this option on. The width and height of this "automatic" text frame are defined by the area inside the page margins; its column settings correspond to the column settings for the page.*

*Choose a page size from this pop-up menu...*

*...or enter a custom page size using these fields.*

*Enter page margin settings in the fields in this section. Note that the margin settings of individual master pages override these settings.*

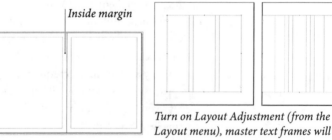

*Page Size pop-up menu*

*Enter the number of columns you want. This setting can be overridden on document pages or master pages.*

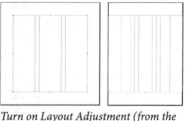

*Inside margin*

*If you turn off the Facing Pages option, the "Inside" and "Outside" fields change to read "Right" and "Left."*

*Outside margin*

*Turn on Layout Adjustment (from the Layout menu), master text frames will not resize when you change page size, margin, or column settings.*

**Setting New Document Defaults**

Do you find that you frequently have to change the settings in the New Document dialog box? If you're in the United States and work with a magazine printed on A4 paper, for example, you'll rapidly tire of the New Document dialog box—because you'll have to choose the A4 paper size from the Page Size pop-up menu for each new publication you create. But you can't change the defaults in the New Document dialog box, because doing so simply creates another new publication. The following steps tell you how to change the defaults used by the New Document dialog box.

1. Close all documents, then open the Document Setup dialog box (press Command-Option-P/Ctrl-Alt-P or choose Document Setup from the File menu). Change the options in the dialog box to match the basic page layout you most commonly use. Press OK to close the dialog box when you're done.

2. Open the Margins and Columns dialog box (choose Margins and Columns from the Layout menu) and adjust the settings in the dialog box to match your typical publication. Click the OK button to close the dialog box.

The next time you display the New Document dialog box, you'll see that it contains the settings you specified.

**Skip the dialog box.** You work on a tabloid newspaper. You never use any other page size. You've already set up your document defaults the way you want them. You're not even sure what a letter-sized page *looks like* anymore. Why in the world should you have to look at the New Document dialog box every time you create a layout?

You don't. Instead of pressing Command-N/Ctrl-N to create a new document, press Command-Shift-N/Ctrl-Shift-N. This creates a new document of your default page size without displaying the dialog box.

## Opening Publications

You know, we've often been asked why we bother writing about the process of opening documents. Doesn't everyone know the drill by now? Nevertheless, we'll cover it because some readers might be new to computing altogether, and because InDesign offers a couple of slightly unusual options.

Choose Open from the File menu, or press Command-O/Ctrl-O, and InDesign displays the Open a File dialog box (see Figure 2-2). Locate and select the InDesign document you want to open, then click the Open button and InDesign opens the selected document in a new window.

The "twist" InDesign adds to the standard process has mainly to do with publications you've saved as templates (also known as

FIGURE 2-2
The Open a File
Dialog Box

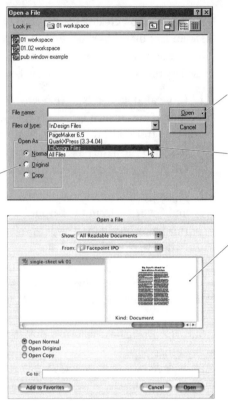

*Locate and select a file
using the file listing.*

*Click the Open button to
open the publication.*

*Choose Normal to open the
publication; choose Original
to open and edit a file you've
saved as an InDesign
template file; and choose
Copy to open a file as an
untitled publication.*

*The option you choose from
the Files of Type menu
determines which files you
see in the file list.*

*The Mac OS X version of
InDesign can display a
preview of InDesign
documents.*

"stationery" on the Macintosh), or documents you want to treat as templates (later in the chapter, we'll describe templates). To open a copy of the file, turn on the Open Copy option. InDesign opens an untitled copy of the file you selected. To open a template file for editing, turn on the Open Original option.

InDesign can also open PageMaker or QuarkXPress files. To do this on the Macintosh, choose All Documents from the Show pop-up menu in the Open dialog box; in Windows, choose the file type you want to open from the Files of Type pop-up menu, or choose All Documents. Select the file you want to convert, and then click the Open button. InDesign converts the file and opens it as a new, untitled InDesign publication.

How well does this conversion process work? That depends on the publication you're trying to open, but you should never expect the conversion process to be perfect. There are simply too many differences in the capabilities of the different products.

InDesign will usually manage to capture the basic geometry of a publication, the position of imported graphics, and the content of text frames. InDesign will also do a good job of converting text formatting, though line endings may change due to InDesign's superior composition features (the Adobe Paragraph Composer is applied by default by the conversion process). The following sections provide more detail on what you can expect to see when you convert publications from other page layout programs.

**QuarkXPress Files**    InDesign can open QuarkXPress 3.3-4.11 documents and templates. This useful ability is subject to a number of terms and conditions, which we'll outline in this section. First, InDesign cannot open:

◆ QuarkXPress 5.x files (but you can open QuarkXPress 4.x documents saved from version 5.x)

◆ Multi-language documents created using QuarkXPress Passport (unless you save in single-language format)

◆ QuarkXPress documents (any version) created using XTensions that require you have the XTension to open the document (the infamous Pasteboard XT, for example)

◆ QuarkXPress book or library documents

Provided the document you want to convert does not fall into one of the above accursed categories, InDesign will convert the document setup, pages, and page items into their InDesign equivalents. As you might expect, there are a number of details you need to be aware of. Rather than list all of the features which are converted, we'll stick to the ones that aren't converted, or are converted with certain differences.

◆ **Non-printing objects.** If you've turned on the Suppress Printout option in the Modify dialog box for any objects in the QuarkXPress document, InDesign places those objects on a separate, non-printing layer (named "Non-printing items") in the converted publication.

◆ **Guides.** Ruler guides can shift slightly on the page or pasteboard during the conversion process. In general, the amount of the shift depends on the measurement system you're using. If you're using points, or picas and points, InDesign rounds guide positions to the nearest whole point. If you're using inches, you can count on InDesign correctly positioning a guide when the guide's position uses two decimal places (e.g., .25), or when the guide's position falls on an "even" location (such as .125 or .625), but not when the position is less common (.306, for example, is usually changed to .3056).

◆ **Master Page items.** While InDesign converts QuarkXPress master pages and items on those pages to their InDesign equivalents, it also converts master page items to document page items (in essence, it copies the page items to document pages formatted using the master page). This means that reapplying the master page will result in duplicated page items. To avoid having stacks of objects on your pages, delete all of the copied master items before you reapply the master page.

◆ **Dashed strokes and "fancy" borders.** InDesign converts strokes formatted using QuarkXPress' "Solid," "Dotted," "Dotted 2," "Dash Dot," stroke types but does not convert the "All Dots" stroke type, the multi-line stroke types ("Double," for example), or any of the border styles ("Yearbook," for example). Paths formatted using the unsupported stroke types are converted to paths formatted using the Solid stroke type.

◆ **Text on a path.** InDesign and QuarkXPress have different ways of aligning text to a path. Expect the position of the text to change.

◆ **Table of contents.** InDesign imports table of contents (known as "lists" in QuarkXPress), but does not retain the option to sort the entries alphabetically (the Alphabetical option in the Edit List dialog box in QuarkXPress).

◆ **Leading.** InDesign and QuarkXPress use different methods to calculate the position of the first baseline of text in a text frame, so you can expect to see the position of the text in converted text frames move up or down on the page (depending on the settings in the First Baseline section of the Text tab of the Modify dialog box in QuarkXPress and the First Baseline section of the Text Frame Options dialog box in InDesign).

◆ **Keyboard shortcuts for styles.** QuarkXPress allows a wider range of keyboard shortcuts for paragraph and character styles than InDesign does. Any keyboard shortcuts in the QuarkXPress document outside the range of shortcuts supported by InDesign (keys on the numeric keypad plus Command/Ctrl or Option/Alt) are not assigned to the styles in the converted publication.

◆ **Special characters.** InDesign converts all em spaces in the QuarkXPress publication to standard em spaces (versions of QuarkXPress prior to 4.0 use the composed width of two zeros to set the width of an em space; version 4.0 and higher use this value as the default width of an em). QuarkXPress "flex space" characters convert to standard word spaces. Uppercase characters with accents display and print differently in InDesign than they do in QuarkXPress.

◆ **Superior type style.** InDesign does not have a "superior" formatting attribute. InDesign applies the superscript type style to text formatted using this attribute..

◆ **"Colorized" images.** InDesign can apply colors to bilevel (black-and-white) and grayscale TIFF images; QuarkXPress can apply color to other image file formats. When, during the conversion process, InDesign encounters a "colorized" image in one of the other formats, it converts the image, but does not apply the color.

◆ **Gradients.** InDesign can distinguish properly between linear and radial gradients, but the gradients applied to the resulting InDesign objects will contain only two gradient stops, regardless of the gradient's definition in the QuarkXPress document.

◆ **Graphics file formats.** QuarkXPress can import several graphic formats that InDesign does not support (PhotoCD, for example), and can import using import methods not supported by InDesign (Publish and Subscribe on the Mac OS and OLE in Windows). When you try to open a QuarkXPress document containing graphics in any unsupported format, InDesign displays a warning dialog box. In general, you'll have to create a new version of the graphic and place the new graphic in the document. Note that the image you see (if you see anything at all) will be a preview image, and probably won't be suitable for printing.

**PageMaker Files**    As you convert, or prepare to convert, publications from PageMaker to InDesign, keep the following in mind.

◆ **Pasteboard items.** Any objects on the pasteboard in a PageMaker publication are placed on the pasteboard of the first spread in the converted publication.

◆ **Master page items.** All master page items are assigned to a layer named "Master."

◆ **Ruler guides.** All ruler guides in the PageMaker publication are converted and are placed on a new layer named "Guides."

◆ **Non-printing objects.** If you've suppressed the printing of an object in PageMaker (to do this, you select the object and choose Non-Printing from the Element menu), InDesign moves those objects to a new layer named "Non-printing items," and then makes that layer a non-printing layer.

◆ **Book list.** InDesign has no corresponding feature, so the book list of the PageMaker publication is not copied to the InDesign version of the publication.

◆ **Composition.** InDesign applies the Adobe Paragraph Composer to all of the paragraphs in the converted publication. Because this composition method is very different from (and better than) the composition system found in PageMaker, many of the line endings and column depths in the publication will change. The Adobe Single Line Composer is similar to PageMaker's composition system, and you can apply it to the paragraphs in the publication if you like. If you do this, the resulting line endings might be more similar to those of the original PageMaker publication (then again, they might not, as the composition system and hyphenation settings differ).

◆ **Leading.** PageMaker has three leading methods: Top of Caps, Proportional, and Baseline. InDesign's leading method is most similar to PageMaker's Baseline leading method. When you convert a PageMaker publication, you can expect text in paragraphs using the other PageMaker leading methods to shift up or down on the page (usually down).

In addition, the position of the first baseline of text in a text frame is determined by the Offset pop-up menu in the First Baseline section of the Text Frame Options dialog box. By default, InDesign applies the Ascent option—which can make text in converted PageMaker publications shift vertically. If you've been using the Baseline leading method in your PageMaker publications (as we think you should), choose Leading from the Offset pop-up menu to restore the position of your text baselines to their original position.

◆ **Text position.** In PageMaker, you can choose to position the text in a text frame at the top, bottom, or middle of the frame (to do this, you use the options on the Vertical Alignment pop-up menu in the Frame Options dialog box). InDesign lacks these options, and positions text at the top of the frame.

◆ **Font and type style conversion.** When, during the process of converting a PageMaker publication, InDesign encounters a font change or type style change, it tries to map the PageMaker formatting into its InDesign equivalent. This isn't always possible. When you apply the font "Minion" and type style "Bold" to text in a PageMaker publication, PageMaker applies Minion Semibold—and that's what InDesign applies. When you apply the type style "Bold" to Minion Bold or Minion Black however, InDesign displays an error message (see Figure 2-3) and applies Minion Bold. The conversion is actually better than we'd expected, given the differences in specifying fonts in the two programs—but you'll have to closely check converted publications against your original PageMaker versions.

InDesign does not support the PageMaker type style Shadow, and formats any text using that type style as plain text. InDesign converts text formatted using the Outline type style to text formatted with a hairline (.25 point) stroke and a fill of the color "Paper." You'll also notice that the position and thickness of the bar in text using the Underline or Strikethrough type styles changes slightly in the InDesign version of the publication.

**FIGURE 2-3**
**Fonts Not Found**
**During Conversion**

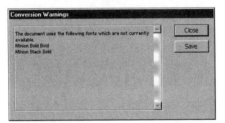

◆ **Tracking.** InDesign removes all kerning applied by PageMaker's Expert Tracking command (the tracks "Very Loose," "Loose," "Normal," "Tight," and "Very Tight"). InDesign's "tracking" is the same as PageMaker's Range Kerning feature, not PageMaker's Expert Tracking feature.

◆ **Colors.** Colors defined using the HLS and Hexachrome color models are converted to RGB colors. Tints are converted to new colors in the Swatches palette (tints based on colors defined using the HLS or RGB model will become new RGB colors; tints based on process colors will become new process colors).

◆ **Image control settings.** InDesign doesn't have a set of features corresponding to those found in PageMaker's Image Control dialog box, and any settings you've applied to images using these controls will be removed from the images in the converted version of the publication. Note that InDesign doesn't have a way to apply halftone screen settings to individual images.

◆ **Masks and masked objects.** If you've used an object to mask other objects in a PageMaker publication, those objects will be pasted into the masking object in the InDesign publication (you can select them using the Direct Selection tool).

◆ **Fill patterns.** PageMaker features a variety of goofy fill patterns (making possible what Edward Tufte dubbed "chartjunk") that date from the early Stone Age of desktop publishing. InDesign doesn't have a similar feature, so these anachronisms are converted to solid fills during the conversion process.

◆ **Imported graphics.** Even if an image is embedded in a PageMaker publication, InDesign requires an up-to-date link to the original version of the graphic. If InDesign can't find the original graphic, it uses the screen preview image in the PageMaker publication (if any such image exists).

If you've placed a PDF in the PageMaker publication you're converting, InDesign will always place the first page of that PDF in the InDesign version of the publication—regardless of the page you selected to place in PageMaker.

Finally, any graphics you've placed in a PageMaker publication using OLE (Object Linking and Embedding) methods (usually the Insert Object command in the Windows version of PageMaker) will not be converted.

## Saving Publications

To save a publication, choose Save from the File menu (or press Command-S/Ctrl-S). To save a publication under a different name, choose Save As (or press Command-Shift-S/Ctrl-Shift-S), and InDesign will display the Save File As dialog box. Use this dialog box to set a location for the new file, assign a file name, and decide whether the file should be saved as a publication file or as a template.

If you're trying to save the file in a format other than an InDesign file, the command you want is not "Save" but "Export." For more on exporting publications or parts of publications in file formats other than InDesign's native format, see Chapter 7, "Importing and Exporting."

**Saving As a Template**

Here's a process we've gone through many times, and we bet you have, too. Stop us if you've heard this one before. You need to base a new publication on the design of a publication you've already laid out. You want to open the older publication, then save it under a new name, and then change its content. You open the publication, replace a few elements and delete others, and edit and format text. Then you save the file.

And only then do you realize that you haven't renamed the publication, and that *you've just written over a publication you probably wanted to keep.* You can undo many stupid actions in InDesign—but an inadvertent "Save" isn't one of them.

Has this ever happened to you? If not, please accept our hearty congratulations. If so, you should know that the ability to save or open a file as a template is something that was developed for marginally competent people like us. When you try to open a file that was saved as a template, InDesign automatically opens a copy of the file (though it doesn't select the Copy option in the Open dialog box). If, at that point, you try to save the file, InDesign will display the Save As dialog box. Which means you can proceed with your plan to save the publication under a new name. Remember? Your plan?

To save an InDesign publication as a template in Windows, choose Save As from the File menu. InDesign displays the Save As dialog box. Enter a name for the template file and then choose InDesign Template from the Save As Type pop-up menu. Click the Save button to save the template file.

In Mac OS 9.x, choose Save As from the File menu to display the Save As dialog box. Choose Stationery Option from the Format pop-up menu. InDesign displays the Stationery Option dialog box. Turn on the Stationery option, then click OK to close the dialog box. Click the Save button in the Save As dialog box to save your publication.

You can also choose to open any publication as a template by turning on the Open Copy option in the Open a File dialog box. InDesign will open a new, untitled publication with the contents of the file you selected.

# Crash Recovery

It will happen. At some point, your computer will suddenly stop working. A wandering child, dog, or co-worker will trip over the power cord, or accidentally press the reset switch. A storm will leave your area without electrical power. Or the software we jokingly refer to as the "operating system" will fail for some unknown reason.

At this point, it's natural to assume you've lost work—and maybe that you've lost the file forever. That is, after all, the way things work in most other programs.

But it's not true for InDesign. InDesign keeps track of the changes you've made to a document—even for an untitled document you haven't yet saved. When you restart InDesign after a system failure, the program reads from a file named InDesign SavedData. This file is saved in different places on different operating systems, so the best way to find it is to use your operating system's Search utility (Sherlock on most Macintosh systems; Find Files or Folders on the Start menu in most Windows systems) to find the file. InDesign uses this file to reconstruct the publication or publications that were open when your system crashed. Because InDesign uses the SavedData file to keep a record of your actions—which is how you get the "Undo" feature—you'll be right back where you left the program.

If you don't want to recover the most recent changes you made to a publication before a crash (which you might want to do if you felt that your changes caused the crash), delete this file. You should also delete this file if InDesign is crashing on startup as it tries to read the file. In this case, the file has been damaged and cannot be opened—you'll have to rebuild the publication from a previous version (or from scratch, if you hadn't saved the file). You should also delete the files in the InDesign Recovery folder (which you'll find in the same folder as the InDesign SavedData file).

## Setting Basic Layout Options

As we stated earlier, you can always change the margins, columns, page size, and page orientation of a publication. You change the margin and column settings using the Margins and Columns dialog box, and you can apply these changes to any page, page spread, or master page in a publication.

**Changing Page Size and Orientation**

Page size and page orientation affect the entire document (you can't mix page sizes and page orientations in a file), and you use the Document Setup dialog box (press Command-Option-P/Ctrl-Alt-P to display this dialog box, or choose Document Setup from the File menu) to change these settings. To change the page size, choose a new page size for the publication from the Page Size pop-up menu (or enter values in the Width and Height fields); to change the page orientation, click the orientation button corresponding to the page orientation you want.

If you have turned on the layout adjustment (from the Layout menu), InDesign might move objects and guides on your pages when you change the page size or page orientation. See "Adjusting Layouts," later in this chapter, for more on this topic.

**Specifying Margins and Columns**

You aren't stuck with the margin and column setup you specified in the New Document dialog box—you can change margin and column settings for any page, at any time. To change margin and column settings, navigate to the page you want to change, then choose Margins and Columns from the Layout menu (see Figure 2-4). Click the OK button to close the dialog box, and InDesign applies the new margin and column settings.

To reset the fields in the dialog box to the publication's default margin and column settings, hold down Option/Alt. InDesign changes the Cancel button into the Reset button. Click the Reset button to return the fields to their default state.

To create columns of unequal width, drag the column guides on the page (see "Adjusting Column Guides," later in this chapter).

What happens to the objects on a page when you change the margin and column settings for that page? Do they reposition themselves relative to the new margins? Or do they stay put? That depends on the settings in the Layout Adjustment dialog box. See "Adjusting Layouts," later in this chapter, for more on adjusting layouts.

**FIGURE 2-4**
**Margins and Columns Dialog Box**

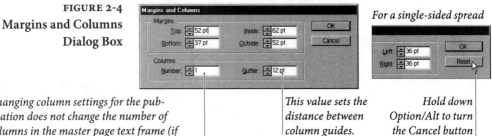

*For a single-sided spread*

*Changing column settings for the publication does not change the number of columns in the master page text frame (if any exist) unless you've turned on Layout Adjustment, and has no effect on the number of columns in other text frames.*

*This value sets the distance between column guides.*

*The value you enter here sets the number of column guides.*

*Hold down Option/Alt to turn the Cancel button into the Reset button.*

# Guides

InDesign can display three types of guide: margin guides, column guides, and ruler guides. Guides are nonprinting guidelines you can use for positioning objects on the pages and pasteboard of an InDesign publication. Margin guides appear inside the page margins for a particular page. Column guides are actually pairs of guides that move as a unit. The space between the two guides making up the column guide is the gutter, or column spacing. This built-in spacing makes these guides good for—you guessed it—setting up columns. A ruler guide is a horizontal or vertical guideline you can use as an aid to aligning or positioning page items.

You use guides to mark a position on the page or pasteboard. The most important thing about guides is not just that they give you a visual reference for aligning objects to a specific location, but that they can exert a "pull" on objects you're moving or creating. To turn on that "pull," choose Snap to Guides from the View menu. When this option is on, and you drag an object within a certain distance of a guide, InDesign snaps the object to the guide.

This is one of our favorite psychocybernetic illusions—as an object snaps to a guide, your nervous system tells you that your hand can feel the "snap" as you drag the mouse. Turning on Snap to Guides can't physically affect the movement of your mouse, of course, but the illusion is very useful.

When you want to drag an object freely, without having it snap to any guides it encounters on its path across the publication window, turn Snap to Guides off. Do not try to align an object to a guide while Snap to Guides is turned off, however—there aren't enough pixels available on your screen to allow you to do a good job of this at any but the highest magnifications (see Figure 2-5).

Objects do not snap to guides when guides are hidden. This includes guides that are on a hidden layer.

**FIGURE 2-5**
**Don't Trust Your Screen**

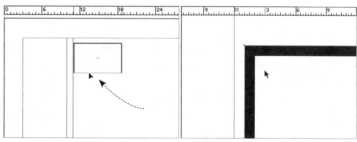

*When InDesign's Snap to Guides feature is turned off, it's easy to think that you've gotten an object into perfect alignment with a guide...*

*...but zooming in will often show you that you've missed the guide. Turning on Snap to Guides can help.*

**Hiding and Displaying Guides**

Tired of looking at all of the guides? To hide all guides, choose Hide Guides from the View menu (press Command-;/Ctrl-;). To display the guides again, choose Show Guides (press Command-;/Ctrl-; again).

To hide only the document grid, choose Hide Document Grid from the View menu, or press Command-'/Ctrl-'. Choose Show Document Grid, or press the keyboard shortcut again to show the document grid.

To hide only the baseline grid, choose Hide Baseline Grid from the View menu or press Command-Option-'/Ctrl-Alt-'. Choose Show Baseline Grid or press the keyboard shortcut again to show the baseline grid.

Note that you can also make guides disappear by changing the view threshold associated with the guides (see Figure 2-6). For the document grid, baseline grid, margin guides, and column guides, you set the view threshold using the Preferences dialog box (see Chapter 1, "Workspace."). For individual ruler guides, use the View Threshold field in the Ruler Guides dialog box (select a guide and choose Ruler Guides from the Layout menu or the context menu).

**FIGURE 2-6**
**Guide View Threshold**

*The View Threshold of these ruler guides is set to 100%...*

*...the View Threshold of these ruler guides is set to 5%.*

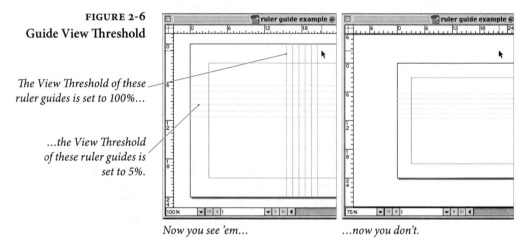

*Now you see 'em...*                    *...now you don't.*

**Adjusting Column Guides**

The method you use to adjust the position of column guides depends on what you're trying to do. If you're trying to divide the area inside the page margins into equal columns, select the page and enter a new value in the Number field in the Columns section of the Margins and Columns dialog box.

If, on the other hand, you're trying to get columns of unequal width, you can adjust the column guides by dragging them on the page (see Figure 2-7).

You can't adjust the distance between the column guides (the "gutter") by dragging—instead, you'll have to go to the Margins and Columns dialog box. To change the gutter width, enter a new value in the Gutter field (see Figure 2-8).

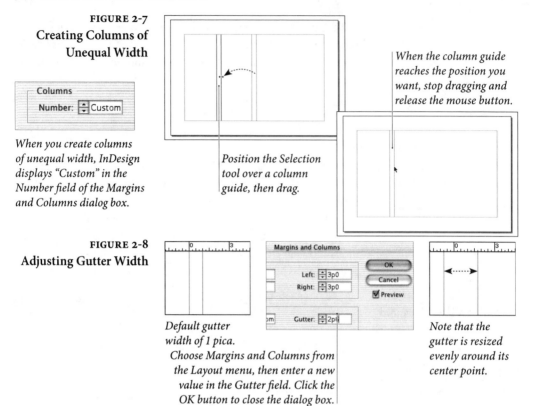

FIGURE 2-7
**Creating Columns of Unequal Width**

*When you create columns of unequal width, InDesign displays "Custom" in the Number field of the Margins and Columns dialog box.*

*When the column guide reaches the position you want, stop dragging and release the mouse button.*

*Position the Selection tool over a column guide, then drag.*

FIGURE 2-8
**Adjusting Gutter Width**

*Default gutter width of 1 pica.*

*Choose Margins and Columns from the Layout menu, then enter a new value in the Gutter field. Click the OK button to close the dialog box.*

*Note that the gutter is resized evenly around its center point.*

When you open the Margins and Columns dialog box after you've set up a custom column guide arrangement, InDesign displays "Custom" in the Number field. Do not enter a number in this field, or InDesign will move your column guides so that they evenly divide the space between the margins. If you change the gutter width without touching the Number field, InDesign leaves your column guides in their original positions, but changes the space inside each guide.

You should also bear in mind that text frames can, by themselves, contain multiple columns of equal width. For more on this topic, see Chapter 3, "Text." Sometimes it's easier to work with a single multicolumn text frame than with multiple single-column text frames.

**Creating a New Ruler Guide**

To create a new ruler guide, position the cursor over one of the rulers (for a horizontal ruler guide, move the cursor to the vertical ruler; for a vertical ruler guide, use the horizontal ruler) and then drag. As you drag, InDesign creates a new ruler guide at the position of the cursor. When you've positioned the ruler guide where you want it, stop dragging. InDesign adds a ruler guide (see Figure 2-9).

To create a horizontal ruler guide that crosses the current spread, including the pasteboard (rather than the current page), hold down

**FIGURE 2-9**

**Creating a Ruler Guide**

*To make a ruler guide snap to the tick marks on the ruler, hold down Shift as you drag the ruler guide.*

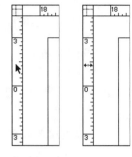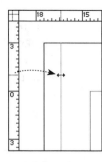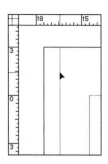

Position the cursor over a ruler, then hold down the mouse button...

...and drag. As you drag, a ruler guide follows the cursor.

When the ruler guide reaches the position you want, stop dragging.

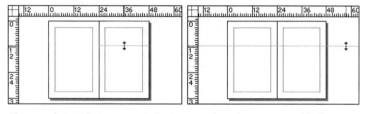

Drag a ruler guide on a page to limit the guide to that page...

...or drag the cursor outside the spread to create a guide that crosses pages in the spread.

Command/Ctrl as you drag the guide. To adjust this type of ruler guide, drag the guide on the pasteboard—if you drag it on a page, InDesign will limit the guide to that page.

When you drag a ruler guide into the pasteboard, it automatically extends to the width (for a horizontal ruler guide) or height (for a vertical guide) of the pasteboard. If you want, you can use guides on the pasteboard to align objects before dragging the objects onto a page.

You can also double-click a ruler to create a new ruler guide—InDesign creates a guide at the point at which you clicked.

If you have switched to Preview mode, your guide will appear as long as it is selected. Once you deselect it, it will disappear (just like all of the other guides). If your guides are mysteriously disappearing immediately after you draw them, you're probably in Preview mode. Click the Normal View Mode button (or press W) to view your guides.

**Adding Ruler Guides Around an Object**

InDesign doesn't have the ability to automatically position ruler guides around a selected object. Luckily, one of the scripting examples on the InDesign CD can do this for you (Olav wrote it). The script is named AddGuides, and you'll find it in the Scripting folder inside the Adobe Technical Information folder. Run the script, and InDesign adds guides around the selected object or objects. If you're using Windows, the script will display a dialog box you can use to set the positions of the ruler guides (see Figure 2-10).

This script is especially useful when you're setting up a publication for use with InDesign's layout adjustment features.

FIGURE 2-10

**Add Guides Script**

*Select an object.*      *Run the script. Choose the locations of the guides you want to add and click the Add Guides button.*      *InDesign adds guides at the locations you specified.*

**Selecting Ruler Guides**    To select a ruler guide, click on the guide using one of the selection tools, or drag a selection rectangle over the guide. This differs from PageMaker and QuarkXPress, where you cannot select a ruler guide as you would any other object. You can select multiple ruler guides at once by dragging a selection rectangle over them. If the selection rectangle touches an object, InDesign selects the object, in preference to any ruler guides touching the selection rectangle—you cannot select both ruler guides and objects in the same selection. When a ruler guide is selected, it displays in the layer color of the layer you assigned it to.

**Editing Ruler Guides**    To change the location of a ruler guide, do one of the following.

◆ Drag the guide (using the Selection or Direct Selection tool).

◆ Select the ruler guide and then enter a new position in the X field (for a vertical guide) or in the Y field (for a horizontal guide) of the Transform palette.

◆ Select the guide and press an arrow key to "nudge" the guide one direction or another.

You can also select a series of ruler guides and drag them, as a unit, to a new location (see Figure 2-11).

**FIGURE 2-11**
**Moving Multiple Guides**

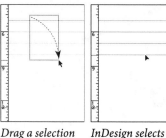

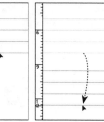

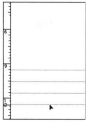

*Drag a selection rectangle over the guides you want to move.*

*InDesign selects all of the guides touched by the rectangle.*

*Drag the guides.*

*Stop dragging when the guides reach the location you want to move them to.*

**Moving a Ruler Guide to a Specific Layer**

You can assign a ruler guide to a layer as you would any other selected object—drag the Proxy that appears in the Layers palette up or down, then drop it on the layer to which you want to send the guide (see Figure 2-12).

The guide will appear on top of other objects on that layer if you turned off the Guides in Back option in the Guides Preferences dialog box, or behind them (if you turned the option on).

**FIGURE 2-12**
**Guides and Layers**

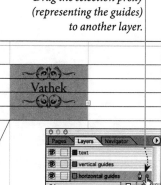

*These guides are on the "text" layer, and are selected.*

*Drag the selection proxy (representing the guides) to another layer.*

*At this point, the guides appear to be in front of the text—guides always come to the front when selected.*

*The guides are actually behind the text, as you can see when we deselect them.*

**Setting Guide Options**

When you create a ruler guide, InDesign applies the default guide color (which you specified in the Guides Preferences dialog box) and a default view threshold (usually 5%) to the guide, but you can change these options if you want (see Figure 2-13).

**FIGURE 2-13**

**Setting Guide Options**

*Enter a view threshold percentage.*

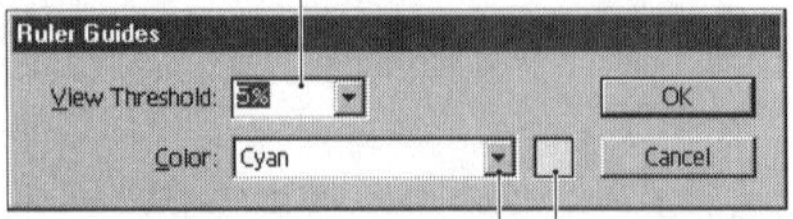

*Select a guide, then display the Context menu and choose Ruler Guides.*

*Choose a color from this pop-up menu, or...*

*...double-click this color swatch to display the Color dialog box.*

1. Select the ruler guide (or guides).

2. Choose Ruler Guides from the context menu (or choose Ruler Guides from the Layout menu). InDesign displays the Ruler Guides dialog box.

3. Choose one of InDesign's preset colors from the Color pop-up menu, or create a custom guide color by double-clicking the color well to the right of the pop-up menu. When you do this, InDesign displays the Color dialog box. Specify a color using the controls in this dialog box, then click the OK button to close the dialog box.

4. Click the OK button to close the Ruler Guides dialog box. InDesign displays the guide (or guides) in the color you chose.

5. You can also change the view threshold of the selected ruler guide by entering a new value in the View Threshold field of the Ruler Guides dialog box. The percentage you enter is the percentage magnification at and above which you want the ruler guide to appear. Enter 5% to make the guide visible at all magnifications.

Why would you want to assign different colors to guides? Guides are such useful tools that we find we use *lots* of them. Color coding guides for different tasks makes it easier for us to see what's going on. One set of guides, for example, might be used for aligning captions in one illustration; another set might be used in a different illustration. Applying colors, changing view thresholds, and assigning guides to layers helps control the way that InDesign draws the guides in the publication window.

Note that guides always take on the layer selection color of their layer when they're selected.

**Locking Ruler Guides**    To lock the position of a ruler guide, choose Lock Position from the Object menu (or press Command-L/Ctrl-L), or display the Context menu and choose Lock Position (see Figure 2-14). Once you've locked the position of a ruler guide, you can change the color of the guide, move the guide to another layer, or change its view threshold, or copy the guide, but you can't change its position.

To unlock the guide, select the guide and choose Unlock Position from the Object menu, or choose Unlock Position from the Context menu.

You can lock all ruler guides by pressing Command-Option-;/ Ctrl-Alt-; (or by choosing Lock Guides from the View menu or the context menu).

You can also lock the position of guides by locking the layer containing the guides.

Finally, you can lock all guides by choosing Lock Guides from the View menu (or the Context menu). When you do this, you're locking more than guide position—you won't be able to select a guide until you choose Unlock Guides (from the View menu or the Context menu).

**FIGURE 2-14**
**Locking Ruler Guides**

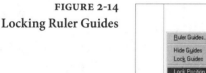

*To lock the position of a ruler guide, select the guide and choose Lock Position from the Context menu.*

*To unlock a locked ruler guide, select the guide and choose Unlock Position from the Context menu.*

**Deleting Ruler Guides**

To delete a ruler guide (or guides), select the guide (or guides) and press the Delete key. Trying to drag the guide onto a ruler or out of the publication window (the technique used in PageMaker and QuarkXPress) simply scrolls your view of the publication window, so don't bother.

**Copying Ruler Guides**

You can also copy selected ruler guides and paste them into other spreads or publications. When you paste, the guides appear in the positions they occupied in the original spread (that is, they're not pasted into the center of the publication window as page objects are), provided the page sizes are the same (see Figure 2-15). If the page sizes are not the same, InDesign gets as close to the original positions as it can.

But wait! It gets better! You can use InDesign's Step and Repeat feature to duplicate ruler guides (see Figure 2-16). For more on Step and Repeat, see Chapter 8, "Transforming."

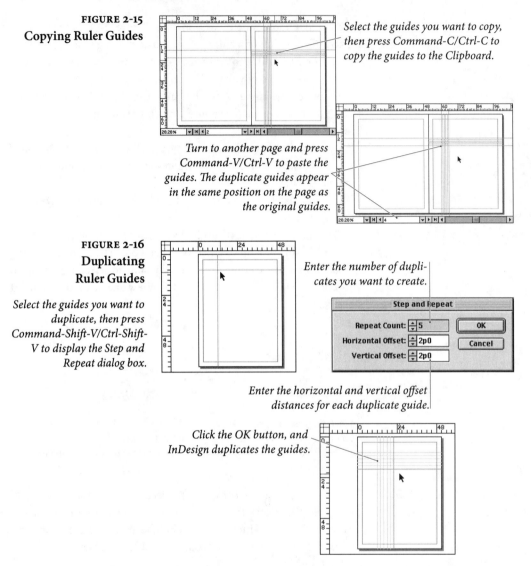

**FIGURE 2-15**

**Copying Ruler Guides**

*Select the guides you want to copy, then press Command-C/Ctrl-C to copy the guides to the Clipboard.*

*Turn to another page and press Command-V/Ctrl-V to paste the guides. The duplicate guides appear in the same position on the page as the original guides.*

**FIGURE 2-16**

**Duplicating Ruler Guides**

*Select the guides you want to duplicate, then press Command-Shift-V/Ctrl-Shift-V to display the Step and Repeat dialog box.*

*Enter the number of duplicates you want to create.*

*Enter the horizontal and vertical offset distances for each duplicate guide.*

*Click the OK button, and InDesign duplicates the guides.*

# Grids

InDesign can display two different grids: the document grid and the baseline grid. Both grids are arrangements of guidelines spaced a specified distance apart. (Note that the baseline grid is not truly a grid, as it has no vertical guidelines.)

You set up both grids using the Grids Preferences dialog box, as described in Chapter 1, "Workspace."

To display a grid, choose the corresponding option (Show Document Grid or Show Baseline Grid) from the View menu, or from the

Context menu (when nothing is selected, and when a tool other than the Text tool is active). If the magnification of the current publication window is below the view threshold of the baseline grid (again, this setting is in the Grids Preferences dialog box), you'll have to zoom in to see the grid (see Figure 2-17).

If you've turned on the Snap to Guides option (from the View menu), objects you're moving will snap to the baseline grid. If you've turned on Snap to Document Grid (on the View menu), they'll snap to the document grid. As we said earlier, the grids aren't very useful without the relevant "snap."

When you turn on the Snap to Document Grid option, objects snap to the document grid even when the grid is not visible. When you hide the baseline grid, on the other hand, objects will not snap to it even if you've turned on the Snap to Guides option.

You can also have the baselines of lines of text in a paragraph snap to the underlying baseline grid—a very useful typesetting feature. For more on working with leading grids and the baseline grid, see Chapter 4, "Type."

**FIGURE 2-17**
**Setting the View Threshold of the Baseline Grid**

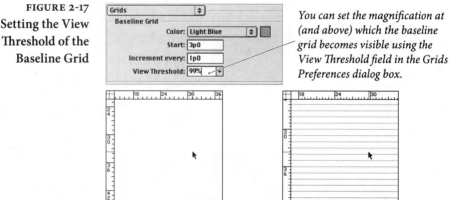

*You can set the magnification at (and above) which the baseline grid becomes visible using the View Threshold field in the Grids Preferences dialog box.*

*If you've chosen Show Baseline Grid from the View menu, and yet the baseline grid has not appeared...*

*...it's because you haven't zoomed in enough to cross the view threshold. Once you do, you'll see the grid.*

## Pages and Spreads

We considered naming this section "Pages Palette Workout," because that's what it is. You won't get far in InDesign without mastering the Pages palette, the fundamental tool for creating, arranging, deleting pages, and applying master pages (see Figure 2-18). It's also a great way to move around in your publication.

FIGURE 2-18
**Pages Palette**

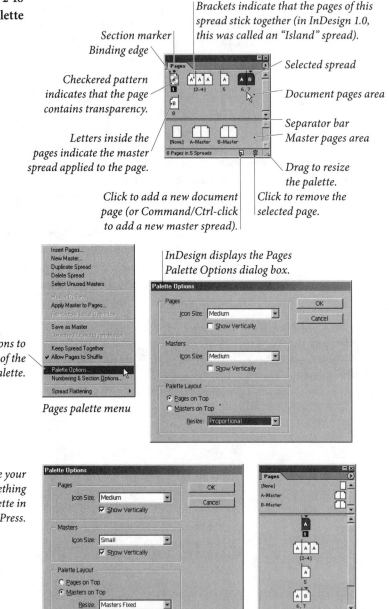

Brackets indicate that the pages of this spread stick together (in InDesign 1.0, this was called an "Island" spread).

Section marker
Binding edge

Checkered pattern indicates that the page contains transparency.

Selected spread

Document pages area

Letters inside the pages indicate the master spread applied to the page.

Separator bar
Master pages area

Drag to resize the palette.

Click to add a new document page (or Command/Ctrl-click to add a new master spread).

Click to remove the selected page.

InDesign displays the Pages Palette Options dialog box.

Choose Palette Options to change the appearance of the Pages palette.

Pages palette menu

These settings make your Pages palette look something like the Pages palette in QuarkXPress.

**Selecting Pages and Spreads**

To work with pages or spreads in the Pages palette, you've got to select them. InDesign makes different options available depending on the method you've used to select the objects (see Figure 2-19).

To select a page, click the page icon in the Pages palette. To select a spread, click the spread name—the text beneath the page icons. You can also select one page in the spread, then hold down Shift and

FIGURE 2-19
**Selecting Pages and
Spreads**

*Click a page icon
to select the page.*

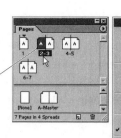

*When you select a page (rather
than a spread), InDesign
changes the options on the Pages
palette menu, making some
commands unavailable).*

*Click the label of a spread
(the name or page numbers
beneath the spread icon) to
select the spread.
InDesign activates the corresponding
options on the Pages palette menu.*

select the other page or pages, but it's slower. Note that you must
select all of the pages in a spread in order to use the Spread Options
option on the Pages palette menu—InDesign does not make it available when you select a single page of the spread.

To select more than one spread at a time, select the first spread,
then hold down Shift as you select the other spreads. Hold down
Command/Ctrl as you click pages to select non-contiguous pages
or spreads.

Double-click a page icon to scroll to that page and display it in the
publication window (see Figure 2-20). Hold down Option/Alt as you
double-click the page icon, and InDesign will change the page view
to the Fit Page in Window view.

FIGURE 2-20
**Navigating with the
Pages Palette**

*Double-click a page icon
to scroll to that page; hold
down Option/Alt as you
double-click to display the
page at Fit Page in Window
view.*

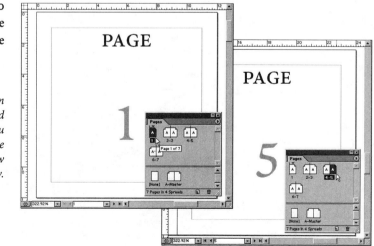

## Adding Pages

To add a page, do any of the following.

**Click the Add Page button.** InDesign adds a page to the publication and displays the new page in the publication window (see Figure 2-21). At the same time, InDesign applies the most recently applied master page to the new page. If you hold down Option/Alt as you click the Add Page button, InDesign displays the Insert Pages dialog box (see below). If you press Command/Ctrl as you click the Add Page button, InDesign adds a new master page.

**Choose Insert Pages from the Pages palette menu.** InDesign displays the Insert Pages dialog box (see Figure 2-22). Enter the number of pages you want to add in the Pages field. Use the Insert pop-up menu to select the position at which you want the inserted pages to

FIGURE 2-21
The Add Page Button

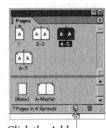 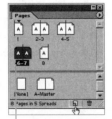 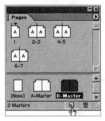

*Click the Add Page button...*

*...and InDesign adds pages after the selected page or spread.*

*Hold down Command/Ctrl as you click to add a new master spread.*

FIGURE 2-22
Using the Insert Pages
Dialog Box

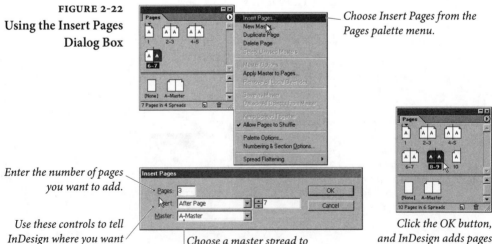

*Choose Insert Pages from the Pages palette menu.*

*Enter the number of pages you want to add.*

*Use these controls to tell InDesign where you want to add the pages.*

*Choose a master spread to apply to the new pages.*

*Click the OK button, and InDesign adds pages to your publication.*

appear. If your publication has more than one section, you can also enter the section to which you want to add the pages in the Section field (if your publication contains only a single section, this field will be unavailable). If you want to apply a master page or spread to the pages, choose that master page from the Master Page pop-up menu. Click the OK button to add the pages. If you hold down Option/Alt, InDesign turns the Cancel button into the Reset button. Click the Reset button, and the controls will be set back to the state they were in when you opened the dialog box.

**Drag a master spread icon into the document pages area of the Pages palette.** This creates a new document page or page spread and applies the master page to it (see Figure 2-23). To create a page without applying a master page to it, drag and drop the None master page.

**Hold down Option/Alt as you drag a page or page spread icon.** You can drag document pages or master pages. When you drop the page icon, InDesign will create a duplicate of the page or spread (see Figure 2-24). You can't use this technique to duplicate individual pages of a multi-page spread.

FIGURE 2-23
**Drag a Master Spread into the Document Pages Area**

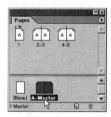

*Select a master spread icon.*

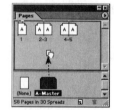

*Drag the master spread out of the masters area and into the document pages area.*

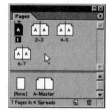

*Drop the master spread icon. InDesign adds a new spread.*

FIGURE 2-24
**Drag and Drop Duplication**

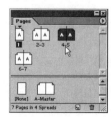

*Select a page or spread icon.*

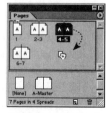

*Hold down Option/ Alt and drag.*

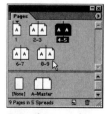

*Drop the icon where you want to add the page (or spread).*

**Choose Duplicate Spread from the Pages palette's menu.** This duplicates the selected spread (including any page objects on the spread's pages) and adds it to the current section (see Figure 2-25).

FIGURE 2-25

**Duplicating a Spread**

*Select a spread icon (not an individual page icon) and choose Duplicate Spread from the Pages palette menu.*

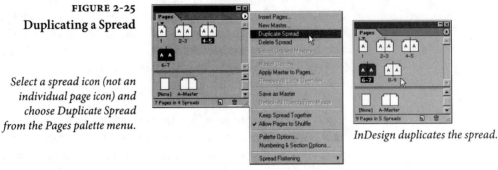

*InDesign duplicates the spread.*

## Arranging Pages

Ordinarily, the pages in your publication are arranged into spreads according to the state of the Facing Pages option in the New Document and Document Setup dialog boxes. If you've turned the Facing Pages option on, InDesign arranges the majority of pages into two-page spreads (if the first page in a section is odd, or if the last page in a section is even, InDesign will set that page as a single page spread). If the Facing Pages option is off, InDesign makes each page in the publication into a single page spread.

But you're not limited to these arrangements of pages and spreads. At any point, in any section of your publication, you can create a spread containing anything from one to ten pages. InDesign 1.0 called these custom arrangements of pages "island" spreads. We don't know what makes one of these an island, and not a peninsula or an isthmus, but we'll stick with the old terminology (because we can't think of anything better, ourselves).

An island spread pays no attention to the default arrangement of pages, but follows its own whim. It doesn't matter what you do—you can add or remove pages that precede the island spread in a section, and the island spread will remain unchanged.

To create an island spread, select a spread and then choose Keep Spread Together from the Pages palette menu. InDesign displays brackets around the name of the spread to indicate that it's an island spread (see Figure 2-26). Selecting more than a single spread before you choose Keep Spread Together converts all of the spreads to separate island spreads; it does not join them into a single island spread.

FIGURE 2-26
**Creating an Island Spread**

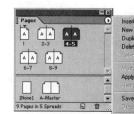

*Select a spread in the Pages palette.*

*Choose Keep Spread Together from the Pages palette menu.*

*InDesign converts the spread to an island spread (brackets around the spread's label indicate an island spread).*

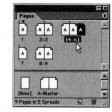

*To add a page to an island spread, select a page icon...*

*...and drag it into or adjacent to the island spread.*

*InDesign adds the page to the island spread.*

When you drag a page or spread into an island spread, InDesign adds the pages of the spread to the island spread. When you drag a page out of an island spread, InDesign does not set the page as an island spread (that is, the pages of the island spread do not inherit the spread's "island" quality).

## Defining Sections

Sections are ranges of pages that have unique page numbering properties. By using sections, you can combine front matter numbered using lowercase roman numerals starting with page one (or i) and regular pages numbered using Arabic numerals and beginning with page one. Another example would be a magazine layout containing a special advertising section that has a page numbering system that differs from that used in the rest of the magazine. With sections, setting up this sort of page numbering variation inside a single publication is easy. You can have multiple sections in an InDesign publication, and each section can have its own starting page number, page numbering system, and page numbering prefix.

To define a section, follow these steps (see Figure 2-27).

1.  Select the page icon in the Pages palette that represents the first spread in the section.

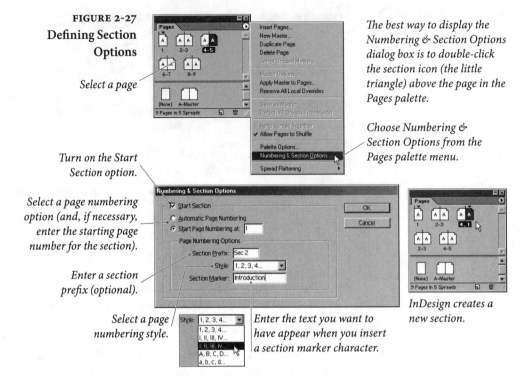

**FIGURE 2-27**

**Defining Section Options**

*Select a page*

*The best way to display the Numbering & Section Options dialog box is to double-click the section icon (the little triangle) above the page in the Pages palette.*

*Choose Numbering & Section Options from the Pages palette menu.*

*Turn on the Start Section option.*

*Select a page numbering option (and, if necessary, enter the starting page number for the section).*

*Enter a section prefix (optional).*

*InDesign creates a new section.*

*Select a page numbering style.*

*Enter the text you want to have appear when you insert a section marker character.*

2. Choose Numbering & Section Options from the palette's menu. InDesign displays the Numbering & Section Options dialog box.

3. Use the controls in the Numbering & Section Options dialog box to specify the page numbering options of your new section.

**Section Prefix.** When you turn to a page in your publication, InDesign displays the section prefix before the page number in the Page field. If you want, you can enter a label for the section in this field (you can enter up to five characters). InDesign does not display or print the section prefix on the page (if that's what you're trying to do, see "Section Marker," below).

**Style.** Choose the page numbering style you want from the Style pop-up menu.

**Page Numbering.** If you want InDesign to continue the page numbering from the previous section, choose the Automatic Page Numbering option. Otherwise, turn on the Start Page Numbering At option and enter a starting page number in the associated field.

**Section Marker.** If you want InDesign to automatically enter text on some or all of the pages of the section (such as the chapter name), enter that text in this field. Most of the time, this field will be used to enter the name of the section itself—but you can enter anything you want (up to around 100 characters).

## Numbering Pages

While you can always type the page number of a page into a text frame, there's an easier way to number a page. By entering a page number marker, you can have InDesign automatically number the page for you. If you move the page, or change the page numbering for the section containing the page, InDesign will update the page number.

To enter a page number marker, click the Text tool in a text frame and do one of the following:

◆ Display the Context menu (press Control and hold down the mouse button on the Macintosh; click the right mouse button in Windows), then choose Auto Page Number from the Insert Special Character submenu.

◆ Choose Auto Page Number from the Insert Special Character submenu of the Type menu.

◆ Press Command-Option-N/Ctrl-Alt-N.

InDesign inserts a page number marker. If you're on a master page, you'll see the master page prefix (if you're on master page "A," for example, you'll see an "A"); if you're on a document page, you'll see the page number itself (see Figure 2-28).

## Adding Section Marker Text

To have InDesign automatically enter the section marker text in a story, click the Text tool in a text frame and do one of the following:

◆ Choose Section Name from the Insert Special Characters submenu of the Context menu.

◆ Press Command-Option-Shift-N/Ctrl-Alt-Shift-N.

InDesign inserts the text you entered in the Section Marker field of the Numbering & Section Options dialog box (see Figure 2-29). If you change the contents of the Section Marker field, InDesign changes the text entered by the section marker character.

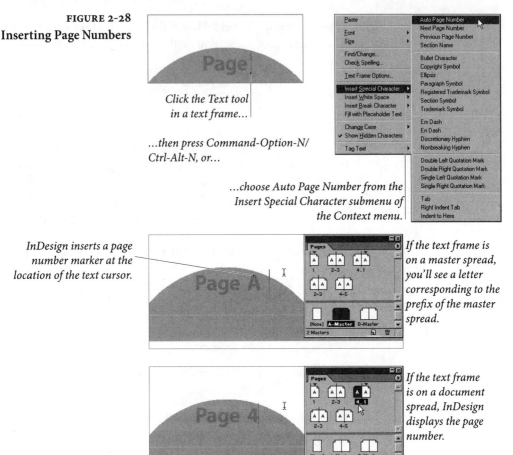

FIGURE 2-28
**Inserting Page Numbers**

*Click the Text tool
in a text frame...*

*...then press Command-Option-N/
Ctrl-Alt-N, or...*

*...choose Auto Page Number from the
Insert Special Character submenu of
the Context menu.*

*InDesign inserts a page
number marker at the
location of the text cursor.*

*If the text frame is
on a master spread,
you'll see a letter
corresponding to the
prefix of the master
spread.*

*If the text frame
is on a document
spread, InDesign
displays the page
number.*

Most of the time, you'll probably want to enter automatic page number and section marker characters in text frames on master pages—but you can also enter them on document pages.

## Working with Master Spreads

Master spreads are the background on which you lay out your publication's pages. When you assign a master spread to a document page, InDesign applies the margin and column settings of the master spread to the page. Any page items on the master spread also appear on the document page, on the layers they occupy on the master spread. Master page items cannot be edited on document pages unless you choose to override (that is, copy) the items from the master pages (see "Overriding Master Items," below).

**FIGURE 2-29**
**Inserting Section**
**Marker Text**

*Choose Section Name*
*from the Insert Special*
*Character submenu*
*of the Context menu.*

*Click the Text tool in a text*
*frame. (In this example,*
*we've added a section*
*marker to a tab at the edge of*
*the page; we then rotated the*
*text frame 90 degrees.)*

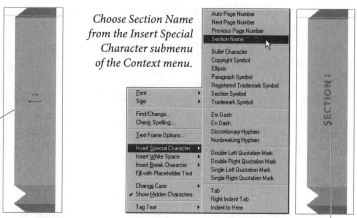

*You can also Press Command-*
*Option-Shift-N/Ctrl-Alt-Shift-N to*
*enter the section marker character.*

*If you're on a master page,*
*you'll see the word "Section"*
*where you entered the*
*section marker.*

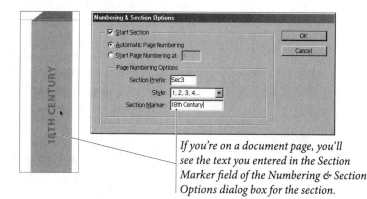

*If you're on a document page, you'll*
*see the text you entered in the Section*
*Marker field of the Numbering & Section*
*Options dialog box for the section.*

You lay out master spreads using the same techniques you use to lay out document pages. Repeating page elements, such as page numbers, headers and footers, and background images, are all great candidates for master spread page items. In addition, empty text frames can be placed on a master spread to provide a text layout template for document pages.

**Creating Master**
**Spreads**

To create a new master spread, use any of the following techniques:

◆ Hold down Command/Ctrl as you click the Add Page button at the bottom of the Pages palette. InDesign adds a new master spread to the publication (see Figure 2-30). If you've turned on the Facing Pages option in the New Document or Document Setup dialog box, the new master spread will be a two-page spread; if the option is off, InDesign creates a one-page spread.

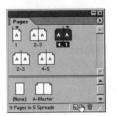

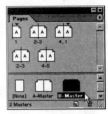

*Hold down Command/Ctrl and
click the Add Page button.*

*InDesign adds a new master spread.
This new master spread is not based
on the selected master spread.*

◆ Choose New Master from the Pages palette menu. InDesign
displays the New Master dialog box (see Figure 2-31).

◆ Drag a spread from the document pages section of the Pages
palette into the master pages section (see Figure 2-32). If you've
already laid out a document page using the layout you'd like
to use as a master page, this is the easiest way to transfer that
layout to a master page. This is called "creating a master spread
by example." When you do this, InDesign creates a new master
page with the margins, column guides, ruler guides, and content
of the document page. The new master spread is based on the
master spread applied to the example document pages. Note that
this does not remove the spread from the document pages area.

FIGURE 2-31
**Choose New Master to
Create a Master Spread**

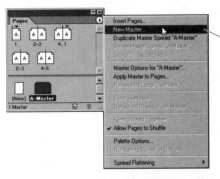

*Choose New Master from
the Pages palette menu.*

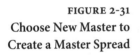

*InDesign displays the New Master dialog box.*

*Enter a name for the master
spread, if you want.*

*Enter a prefix for the master spread.*

*Choose an existing master
spread from this pop-up
menu to base the new master
spread on that spread.*

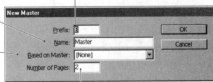

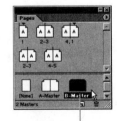

*Enter the number of pages
in the master spread.*

*Click the OK button,
and InDesign creates a
new master spread.*

◆ Hold down Option/Alt as you drag and drop an existing master spread icon in the master pages area of the Pages palette. InDesign creates a copy of the master spread (see Figure 2-33).

◆ Choose Duplicate Master Spread from the Pages palette menu. This has the same effect as the above method (see Figure 2-34).

**FIGURE 2-32**
**Basing a Master Spread on a Document Spread**

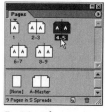  

*Position the cursor over a page spread.*

*Drag the page spread into the master spreads area of the Pages palette.*

*InDesign creates a new master spread with the same margins, guides, and page objects.*

**FIGURE 2-33**
**One Way to Duplicate a Master Spread**

*Note that you press Option/ Alt after you start dragging the master spread; pressing the key before you drag will result in an error message.*

 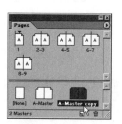

*Tap the Option/Alt key as you drag a master spread in the master spreads area of the Pages palette.*

*InDesign creates a copy of the master spread.*

**FIGURE 2-34**
**Another Way to Duplicate a Master Spread**

 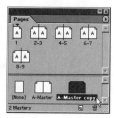

*Select a master spread and then choose Duplicate Master Spread from the Pages palette menu.*

*InDesign creates a new master spread with the margins, guides, and objects of the selected master spread.*

## Applying Master Pages and Master Spreads

To apply a master page or master spread, do one of the following.

◆ Drag and drop the master page spread icon or master page icon on a page icon or a page spread (see Figure 2-35). Or drag and drop the master spread icon on a document spread.

Note that you can apply individual pages from a master spread to individual document or master pages, or you can apply a master spread to any page spread. You can also apply a single page from a master spread to all of the pages in a spread. To do this, drag the page icon onto the document page spread name. InDesign displays a rectangle around the page spread icon. Drop the master page icon, and InDesign applies the master page to all of the pages in the spread.

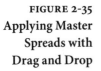

FIGURE 2-35
**Applying Master
Spreads with
Drag and Drop**

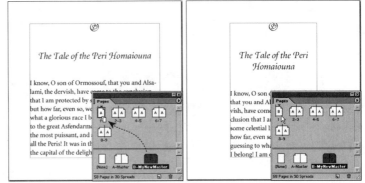

Drag a master spread icon out of the master spreads area of the Pages palette and drop it on a document page or spread.

InDesign applies the margins and columns of the master spread to the document spread.

◆ Choose Apply Master to Pages from the Pages palette menu. InDesign displays the Apply Master dialog box (as shown in Figure 2-36). InDesign sets the Apply Master field to the selected master spread. Enter the page, or pages, to which you want to apply the master spread. To enter non-contiguous pages, enter commas between the page numbers ("1, 3, 10, 12, 22"), or enter page ranges ("55-73"), or mix ranges and individual pages ("1, 3, 7-13, 44").

**Editing Master Spreads**   To edit a master spread, display the master spread (the easiest way to do this is to double-click the master spread's label in the Pages palette). Select and edit the master spread's margins and ruler guides,

FIGURE 2-36
Applying Master
Spreads Using the Apply
Master to Pages Option

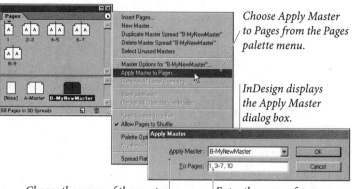

Choose Apply Master
to Pages from the Pages
palette menu.

InDesign displays
the Apply Master
dialog box.

Choose the name of the master
spread you want to apply from the
Apply Master pop-up menu.

Enter the range of pages
you want to apply the
master spread to.

and any page items on the master spread just as you would any items
and attributes of a document spread. Turn on the Enable Layout
Adjustment option in the Layout Adjustment dialog box (choose
Layout Adjustment from the Layout menu to display the Layout
Adjustment dialog box) to apply any changes you've made to the
master spread to any pages in the document to which you've applied
the master spread.

**Deleting Master
Spreads**

To remove a master spread from a publication, choose the master
spread in the Pages palette, then choose Delete Master Spread from
the Pages palette menu. InDesign removes the selected master spread
from the publication.

**Basing One Master
Spread on Another**

Imagine that you produce a catalog, and that, over the course of a
year, you produce seasonal issues of the catalog. The basic design
elements—the section, margins, columns, and page numbering—
remain the same throughout the year, but the colors used, and the
page footers change with each issue. Do you have to create a new set
of master spreads for each issue? Not when you have InDesign's ability to base a master spread on another master spread, you don't.

When you base a new master spread on an existing master spread,
the new master *inherits* the properties of the existing master spread.
This is part of the reason that we refer to the relationship between
the original style and the new style a "parent/child" relationship.
Once you've applied a master spread to another master spread, you
can work with (override) page elements on the pages of the "child"
spread, just as you can from any document page (see "Overriding
Master Items," below).

Here's how inheritance works: When the attributes between a "child" spread and its "parent" spread differ, those attributes are controlled by the definition found in the "child" spread. When you change any of the attributes defined by the "parent" spread, those changes appear in the "child" spread. Take a look at the (somewhat overwrought) example Figure 2-37, and you'll see what we mean.

## Overriding Master Items

Want to modify or delete a master page item from a document page, but leave all of the other master pages items alone? Wait! Don't cover the master page item with a white box! There's a better way. InDesign calls it "overriding" a master page item.

To override a master page item, hold down Command-Shift/Ctrl-Shift and click the master page item (or, if you're using the Text tool, click inside the master page item). InDesign copies the master page item to the document page, where you can select it, format it, or delete it as you would any other page item (see Figure 2-38).

Once you've overridden and deleted a master page item, InDesign will not display or print the original master page item (on the current page; other pages are unaffected). This isn't the same thing as deleting the overridden items, however. To remove all master page overrides, choose Remove All Local Overrides from the Page palette menu. To remove a specific local override (or a series of overrides), select the object (or objects) and choose Remove Selected Local Overrides from the Page palette menu (see Figure 2-39).

To restore the overridden master page object while retaining the copy of it that's on the document page, reapply the master page to the document page. At this point, the copy is no longer considered a local override—it's a page item. Removing local overrides from this document page will have no effect on the object.

Overridden items are not entirely free of the influence of their master page counterpart. Changes to the fill and stroke of the original path (though not to its contents, including text characters) will be reflected in the fill and stroke of the overridden version of the object, provided you haven't changed the object's fill or stroke. If you have changed the overridden object's fill and stroke, changes made to the corresponding attributes of the original master page item will not be applied to the overridden object. Other modifications to the original master page item have no effect on the overridden object.

When you reapply the master page to a document page containing overridden items, the original master page items reappear on the

**FIGURE 2-37**
**Basing One Master**
**Spread on Another**

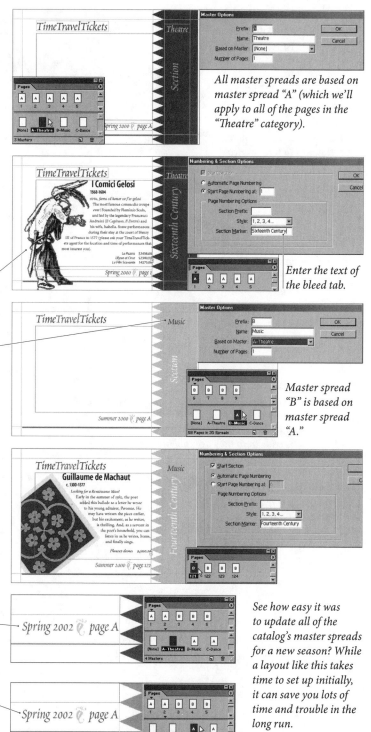

TimeTravelTickets offers time travel to agreat performances in history. Their catalog is divided into sections based on the century of the performance, each section is divided into the categories "Theatre," "Music," and "Dance." We've set up master spreads to reflect the organization of the catalog.

Master spread "A" applied to a document page.

All master spreads are based on master spread "A" (which we'll apply to all of the pages in the "Theatre" category).

Enter the text of the bleed tab.

Master spread "B" uses a different color scheme and replaces the word "Theatre" with "Music," but is otherwise identical to master spread "A."

Master spread "B" is based on master spread "A."

Here's an example of master spread "B" in another section (note the differing section text).

Ready to update the catalog? Enter a new season and year in the page footer of the "parent" master spread…

See how easy it was to update all of the catalog's master spreads for a new season? While a layout like this takes time to set up initially, it can save you lots of time and trouble in the long run.

…and that change will be reflected in all of the "child" master spreads.

FIGURE 2-38
Overriding a
Master Item

FIGURE 2-38
**Overriding a
Master Item**

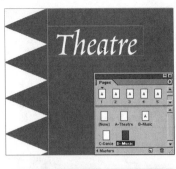

*If you click on the master spread item
you want to change, nothing happens.
This is probably a good thing, as
it prevents you from accidentally
changing master items.*

*In this example, we want to
create a new master spread
based on the "A-Theatre"
master spread. In the new
spread, we want to change
the word "Theatre" to
"Music."*

*Instead of using copy and paste to
move the master page item from the
original master page, hold down
Command-Shift/Ctrl-Shift...*

*...and click the object. InDesign copies
the object to the current page and
marks it as a "local override."*

*Now you can edit, transform, or
format, the text.*

FIGURE 2-39
**Removing
Local Overrides**

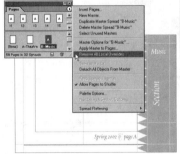

*To remove a local override,
select the object...*

*...and choose Remove Selected Local
Override from the Pages palette menu.*

*InDesign removes the object from
the current spread and displays the
original master spread object.*

*To remove all of the local
overrides on a spread, press
Command-Shift-A/Ctrl-
Shift-A to deselect any
selected objects...*

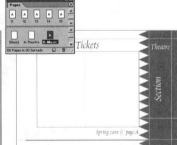

*...then choose Remove All Local
Overrides from the Pages palette
menu.*

*InDesign removes all of the local
overrides on the current spread.*

document page, but the overridden page items are not deleted. This
isn't usually a good thing—it's easy to end up with stacks of duplicated objects (which is probably not what you want).

## Layers and Master Pages

In older page layout software, objects on master pages were always displayed behind document page objects. This meant that page numbers often end up being hidden by items on your document pages, and that you have to copy the master page item to your document page to get it to display or print.

In InDesign, objects on master pages are arranged according to the layer they're on. This means that you can put page numbers on the uppermost layer in a publication without worrying about them being obscured by images or other page items on the document pages (see Figure 2-40).

**FIGURE 2-40**

**Using Layers to Control the Stacking Order of Master Spread Items**

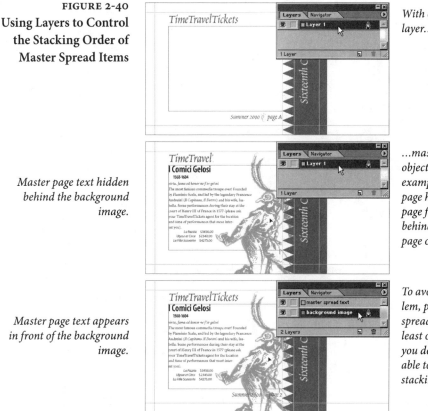

*With only a single layer...*

*...master spread objects (in this example, the tab, page header, and page footer) appear behind document page objects.*

*Master page text hidden behind the background image.*

*Master page text appears in front of the background image.*

*To avoid this problem, put your master spread items on at least one layer. If you do this, you'll be able to control their stacking order.*

## Adjusting Layouts

What happens when you change the margins of a page, or apply a different master page? Should the items on the affected pages move or resize to match the new page geometry? Or should they stay as they are? You decide. Choose Layout Adjustment from the Layout menu. InDesign displays the Layout Adjustment dialog box. What do the controls in the dialog box do? Here's a quick walk-through (see Figure 2-41).

**Enable Layout Adjustment.** Turn this option on, and InDesign adjusts the position and size of the objects on the affected pages according to the settings in this dialog box. With this option off, InDesign does not change object positions or sizes when you apply master pages, change page size, or otherwise change page geometry.

**FIGURE 2-41**
**Adjusting Layouts**

*When the Enable Layout Adjustment option is off, InDesign does not change the position or size of page objects when you change the geometry of the page...*

*...even for a change as radical as changing page orientation*

*Turn on the Enable Layout Adjustment option, and InDesign changes the position and size of page objects in response to changes in page size, orientation, column setup, or margins.*

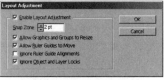

*The options in the Layout Adjustment dialog box give you a way to "fine tune" the automated adjustment process.*

*Here's the layout, as adjusted by InDesign.*

*Ruler guide positions are very important to the layout adjustment feature. In this example, changing the page size changes the shape and position of the graphics—all because of their relationship to the ruler guides that surround them.*

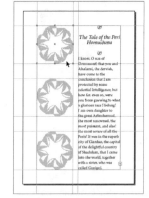

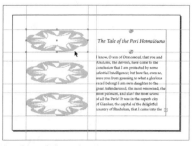

*As the ruler guides move, InDesign resizes the graphics you've "stuck" to the ruler guides.*

**Snap Zone.** How close to a guide does an object have to be to be affected by layout adjustment? That's what you're telling InDesign by the value you enter in this field. Objects within the specified distance will move or resize; objects outside that range won't.

**Allow Graphics and Groups to Resize.** When this option is off, InDesign will not resize objects while adjusting layouts. When it's on, InDesign will resize objects to match the new page layout.

**Allow Ruler Guides to Move.** Should ruler guides move when you change the layout of the page or spread? If you'd like the ruler guides to move, turn this option on; if not, turn it off.

**Ignore Ruler Guide Alignments.** When this option is off, InDesign moves and resizes objects to match the positions of ruler guides in the new page layout. When it's on, InDesign does not consider the locations of ruler guides when resizing or moving objects—only the location of margin guides and page edges. The effect of this option also depends on the state of the Allow Ruler Guides to Move option (described above).

**Ignore Object and Layer Locks.** What should InDesign do while adjusting your layout when it encounters a locked object, or an object on a locked layer? When you turn this option on, InDesign will treat the objects as if they were unlocked. To leave locked objects alone, turn this option off.

The key thing to remember is that InDesign bases all layout adjustment decisions on the positions of margin guides, ruler guides, column guides, and page edges. InDesign cannot know that you want an object to change its size or position unless you somehow associate the object with a guide or a page edge.

## Selecting and Deselecting

Before you can act on an object, you have to select it (see Figure 2-42). You select objects using the Selection tool by clicking them, dragging a selection rectangle over them, or by Shift-selecting (select one object, hold down Shift, and select another object).

When you select an object using the Selection tool, InDesign displays the object's selection handles and the object's bounding box—the smallest rectangular area capable of enclosing the selection.

**FIGURE 2-42**

**Selecting Objects**

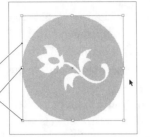

*Bounding box*

*Selection handles*

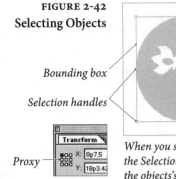

*Proxy*

*The proxy in the Transform palette represents the selection handles of the selected object.*

*When you select an object using the Selection tool, InDesign displays the objects's selection handles and bounding box.*

*When you select an object using the Direct Selection tool, InDesign displays the points on the object's path.*

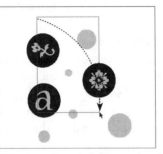
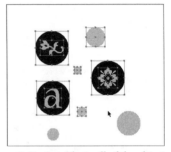

*When you drag a selection rectangle around an object or objects...*

*...InDesign selects all of the objects that the selection rectangle touched.*

The selection handles also correspond to the points on the proxy in the Transform palette.

When you select an object using the Direct Selection tool, InDesign displays the points on the object's path.

Note that you do not have to entirely surround an object with a selection rectangle to select it—if the selection rectangle touches any part of the object, InDesign will select it. Choose Select All from the Edit menu to select everything on the current spread.

To deselect all selected objects, click an uninhabited area of the page or pasteboard, or, better yet, press Command-Shift-A/Ctrl-Shift-A.

## Selecting Through Objects

Sometimes, you have to select an object that's behind another object. You might, for example, need to select and edit a background graphic behind a text frame. What can you do? Do you need to drag the text frame out of the way? Or hide the layer containing the text frame? There's a better way. Try this: click the Selection tool on the object on top of the stack, then press Command/Ctrl and click again. InDesign selects the next object in the stack. Each successive click selects the next object down in the stack (see Figure 2-43).

FIGURE 2-43
**Selecting Through
Objects**

*Want to select an object
that's behind other
objects? You don't need
to drag objects out of the
way. Instead, hold down
Command/Ctrl and click
the Selection tool above the
object you want to select.*

*Text frame selected*　　　　　　　*Background graphic selected*

*The first click selects the object on top    ...but each subsequent click selects the
of the stack of objects...                         next object in the stack.*

You can accomplish the same end using a keyboard shortcut. To
select the object behind the currently selected object in a stack of
objects, press Command-Option-[/Ctrl-Alt-[.

Once you reach the bottom of a stack of objects, InDesign stops.
Pressing the keyboard shortcut again does nothing.

To select the object above the currently selected object in a stack
of objects, press Command-Option-]/Ctrl-Alt-].

When overlapping objects are exactly or nearly the same size,
it can be difficult to see which object in a stack is selected. Don't
start dragging objects out of the way—look for clues. The color of
the selection handles, the state of the Fill and Stroke buttons in the
Toolbox, and the Stroke palette all provide information that can help
you determine which object is selected.

**Subselecting Objects**

Sometimes, you need to select an object that you've pasted inside
another object, or to select an object inside a group. The Direct Selection tool, as you might expect, is the tool you'll use to do this, and the
process is called "subselection" (and when you select an object that's
inside another object, we say the object is "subselected").

**Selecting objects inside groups.** You don't have to ungroup a group
of objects to select and edit the objects in the group—you can work
with them just as if they were outside the group. To do this, select
the Direct Selection tool and click the element that you want to edit.
InDesign selects the object. You can then change its attributes, text,
shape, or position. Deselect the subselected item, and it goes back to
being part of the group (see Figure 2-44).

**Selecting path contents.** One of the trickiest things to master in
InDesign is the process of selecting and working with objects you've
pasted inside other objects. When you click an object inside a path

FIGURE 2-44
Subselecting Objects
Inside Groups

FIGURE 2-44
**Subselecting Objects
Inside Groups**

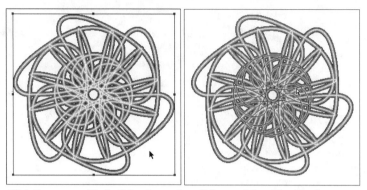

*Click the group with the Selection tool …click one of the objects in the group
to select the group, or… with the Direct Selection tool.*

using the Direct Selection tool, InDesign selects the object (see Figure
2-45). To work with the bounding box of the object, press V to switch
to the Selection tool, or E to switch to the Free Transform tool.

Imagine that you've subselected an object in a group that's pasted
inside another object. How can you move from that selection to
select the group itself? Hold down Option/Alt and click the object
again, and InDesign will move the selection to the group. Click
again, and InDesign will select the frame containing the group (see
Figure 2-46). Don't drag as you click—holding down Option/Alt will
make a copy of the selected object.

FIGURE 2-45
**Subselecting Path
Contents**

*Select the Direct Selection tool from the
Tools palette (or press A), position the
tool over the object you want to select…*

*…and click. InDesign selects
the object.*

*To work with the bounding
box of the subselected object,
press V (to switch to the
Selection tool).*

**FIGURE 2-46**
**Sub Selecting**
**Nested Groups**

*If all you want to do is select an object inside the group, it's easy—just click the Direct Selection tool on the object. But what if you want to select the entire group?*

*Click the Direct Selection tool inside the containing frame. InDesign selects the frame.*

*Hold down Option/Alt and click again. InDesign subselects the objects in the group.*

*Switch to the Selection tool (press V) to work with the group's bounding box.*

To move a group inside a frame, Option/Alt-click the object, press V to switch to the Selection tool, and then hold down Command/Ctrl as you drag the group (see Figure 2-47). Or, as we mentioned in the previous chapter, select the object with the Direct Selection tool, press E to switch to the Free Transform tool, and then drag the center point of the object.

**FIGURE 2-47**
**Moving a**
**Subselected Group**

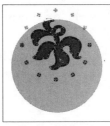
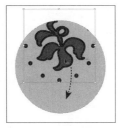

*Hold down Option/Alt and click inside the frame until all of the group objects are selected.*

*Press V, then hold down Command/Control and drag.*

*The cursor must be over one of the group objects, or you'll end up moving the containing frame.*

*Note that you can also press E to switch to the Free Transform tool and then drag the center point.*

When you've selected an object using the Direct Selection tool, switching to the Selection tool (by pressing V) will display the object's selection handles. At this point, you can scale the object by dragging one of its selection handles.

If you're trying to select an object in a group that's behind other objects, you can use the keyboard shortcut for selecting objects behind/in front of other objects that we mentioned earlier (Command-Option-[/Ctrl-Alt-[ and Command-Option-]/Ctrl-Alt-]).

See Chapter 8, "Transforming, " for more on working with path contents.

## Stacking Objects

Page items on an InDesign page can be arranged in front of or behind each other. You can imagine that every object exists on an invisible plane that it cannot share with other objects, if you like. These planes can be shuffled to place one object above another, or behind another.

Simple stacking isn't the only way to control the front-to-back order of objects on a page—layers are another, and usually better, method. Arranging objects on a single layer, however, is very similar to tasks we perform every day as we stack and sort physical objects (our lives, for example, seem to revolve around stacks of paper).

To move an object to the front, or send an object to the back of the layer it occupies, select the object and do one of the following (see Figure 2-48).

To bring an object to the front:

◆ Press Command-Shift-]/Ctrl-Shift-]

◆ Choose Bring to Front from the Arrange submenu of the Object menu.

◆ Display the Context menu and choose Bring to Front from the Arrange submenu.

To send an object to the back:

◆ Press Command-Shift-[/Ctrl-Shift-[

◆ Choose Send to Back from the Arrange submenu of the Object menu.

◆ Display the Context menu and choose Send to Back from the Arrange submenu.

**FIGURE 2-48**
**Bring to Front and**
**Send to Back**

*Note that bringing an object
to the front or sending it
to the back only changes
its position in the stacking
order of the current layer.
Objects on other layers can
still appear in front of objects
brought to the front; objects
on layers behind the current
layer will still appear behind
objects sent to the back.*

*To bring an object to the front,
select the object...*

*...and then press Command-
Shift-]/Ctrl-Shift-]. InDesign brings
the selected object to the front of the
current layer.*

*To send an object to the back of the
current layer, select the object...*

*...and then press Command-
Shift-[/Ctrl-Shift-[.*

You can also choose to bring objects closer to the front or send
them farther to the back in the stacking order of objects on a layer.
To do this, select the object and then do one of the following (see
Figure 2-49).

To bring an object closer to the front:

◆ Press Command-]/Ctrl-]

◆ Choose Bring Forward from the Arrange submenu of the Object
menu.

◆ Display the Context menu and choose Bring Forward from the
Arrange submenu.

To send an object backward:

◆ Press Command-[/Ctrl-[

◆ Choose Send Backward from the Arrange submenu of the
Object menu.

FIGURE 2-49
**Bring Forward and Send
Backward**

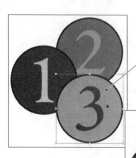

*Select an object.*

*Press Command-[/Ctrl-[ to
send the object backward.*

*You can also press
Command-]/Ctrl-]
to move the object
forward.*

*Note that the stacking
order includes all
of the objects on the
layer containing the
object you're moving.
If the next object in
the stacking order does
not intersect the object
you're moving, you
won't see any change
on your screen.*

*Press the shortcut
again to move the
object farther back
in the layer's
stacking order.*

## Layers

InDesign's layers are transparent planes on which you place page
items. You've probably heard that layers are a way to organize your
publication (that's what all the marketing materials say, after all). But
there's far more to InDesign's layers than just organization—layers
give you control over what parts of your publication display and
print, and whether they can be edited or not.

**Layers Basics**     In the old days (before personal computers and desktop publishing),
our page layouts sometimes consisted of a number of overlapping
sheets of transparent mylar and tracing paper, each sheet bearing
galleys of type, photographs, printing instructions, and scalpel-cut
windows of rubylith or amberlith (these last were sticky films you'd
use to indicate the position of an image).

The different layers of material told our commercial printers how
to create printing plates from the layout. The layers organized the
way that our pages would be photographed for printing.

InDesign's layers have a few characteristics you should understand before you start using them. First, layers affect an entire document—not individual pages or page spreads. Next, layers created in
one document do not affect layers in another document.

As far as we can tell, there's no technical limit to the number of layers you can have in a publication; it's possible to make hundreds or more of them if you have enough memory. But just because you can do that doesn't mean that you should. Too many layers can make a publication difficult to manage.

Layers are especially useful when you're working with pages containing slow-drawing graphics, when your publication features complicated stacks of objects, or when you want to add a nonprinting layer of comments or instructions to a publication. Layers are also helpful when you want to create "conditional" layers containing differing text or graphics (you could create multiple versions of the publication in different languages, for example, and store all of the versions in a single publication).

**The Layers Palette**    You use the Layers palette to create, edit, rearrange, and delete layers (see Figure 2-50). To display the Layers palette, choose Layers from the Window menu (or press F7). If you're familiar with the Layers palettes found in Illustrator and PageMaker (and, to a more limited extent, Photoshop), you'll be right at home with the InDesign Layers palette.

What do you see when you look at the Layers palette?

**Show/hide column.** When you see an "eye" icon in this column, the layer is visible. When there's no icon in this column, all of the objects

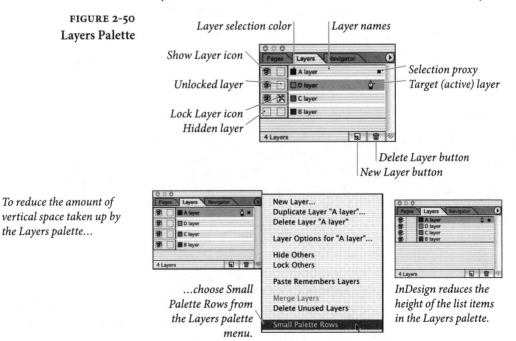

FIGURE 2-50
**Layers Palette**

*Layer selection color*    *Layer names*

*Show Layer icon*    *Selection proxy*
*Unlocked layer*    *Target (active) layer*

*Lock Layer icon*
*Hidden layer*

*Delete Layer button*
*New Layer button*

*To reduce the amount of vertical space taken up by the Layers palette...*

*...choose Small Palette Rows from the Layers palette menu.*

*InDesign reduces the height of the list items in the Layers palette.*

on the layer are hidden (invisible). Click in this column to change from one state to another. You can't select or edit objects on hidden layers, and objects on hidden layers don't print.

When you want to hide all of the layers in a publication except the selected layers, hold down Option/Alt as you click anywhere in the show/hide column (or choose Hide Others from the Layers palette menu). Clicking again in the column while holding down Option/Alt will show all layers, which is equivalent to choosing Show All Layers from the Layers palette menu (see Figure 2-51).

**FIGURE 2-51**

**Showing and Hiding Other Layers**

*To hide all but one layer, follow these steps.*

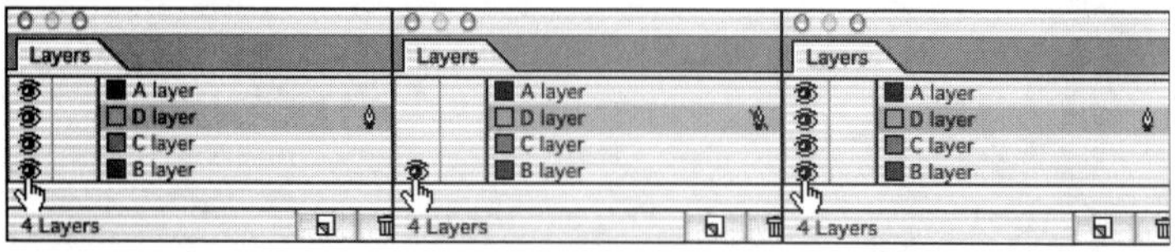

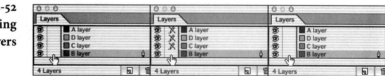

*Point at the layer's Visibility icon, hold down Option/Alt...*

*...and click. InDesign hides all of the other layers.*

*Press Option/Alt and click again to make the layers visible.*

**Lock/unlock icon.** Click in the column to the right of the show/hide column to lock a layer. InDesign displays the "lock" icon (a pencil with a red line through it) in that column. To unlock the layer (and remove the icon), click on it (see Figure 2-52).

You can't select objects on locked layers (so you can't move or format them, either), and you can't assign objects to locked layers. When you want to lock all of the layers in a publication except the currently selected layer (or layers), hold down Option/Alt and click in the lock/unlock column (or choose Lock Others from the Layers palette menu). To unlock any locked layers, hold down Option/Alt and click the lock/unlock column (this is the same as choosing Unlock All Layers from the Layers palette menu).

**FIGURE 2-52**

**Locking and Unlocking Other Layers**

*To lock all but one layer, follow these steps.*

*Point at the layer's Lock/Unlock icon, hold down Option/Alt...*

*...and click. InDesign locks all of the other layers.*

*Press Option/Alt and click again to unlock the layers.*

**Layer selection color.** Each layer has its own "selection color" that helps you see which objects are on which layers; when you select an object, its selection handles appear in the selection color of that layer. You set the selection color of a layer when you create the layer, but you can change the color at any time. To do this, either double-click a layer in the Layers palette, or select a layer and choose Layer Options from the Layers palette menu. Either method will display the Layer Options dialog box, where you can assign a new selection color.

**Layer name.** When you create a layer, you can assign a name to it—or you can let InDesign name the layer for you. You can change the layer name at any time using the Layer Options dialog box.

**Target layer icon.** This icon shows you which layer is the "target layer"—the layer on which InDesign will place any objects you create, import, or paste. You can also see this information in the lower-left corner of the Layers palette. Making a layer the target layer does not assign the current selection to that layer.

**Selection Proxy.** When you select an object, InDesign highlights the name of the layer containing the object. In addition, InDesign displays a small square to the right of the layer name. This square is the Selection Proxy, which represents the layer or layers containing the selected objects (just as the proxy in the Transform palette "stands in" for the bounding box of the selection). To move objects from one layer to another, drag the Selection Proxy to another layer.

**New Layer icon.** Click this icon to create a new layer. InDesign displays the New Layer dialog box.

**Delete Layer icon.** Click this icon to delete the selected layer or layers (to select more than one layer, hold down Shift/Ctrl as you click the layer names). If the selected layers contain objects, InDesign will ask if you want to delete the objects with the layer.

**Paste Remembers Layers.** This option takes care of a question: "If I copy objects from several layers and then paste, where should the pasted objects end up?" Should they be placed on the target layer (in a stack corresponding to their layer order)? Or should they be placed on the layers they originally came from?

We think you'll turn this option on and leave it on. If you do this, you'll be able to copy layers between publications. To do this, select objects on different layers in one publication, then copy them, and then switch to another publication and paste. When you paste, the layers will appear in the publication's Layers palette.

If layers with the same names already exist in the publication, InDesign moves the incoming objects to the corresponding layers, which is why you might want to turn the Paste Remembers Layers option off. If you don't, and if the layer stacking order is not the same as it was in the publication you copied the objects out of, the appearance of the pasted objects might change.

**Delete Unused Layers.** To get rid of layers you're not using, choose Delete Unused Layers from the Layers palette menu.

**Merge Layers.** Want to combine two or more layers into a single layer? Select the layers, then choose Merge Layers from the Layers palette menu. InDesign merges the two layers (the name of the "merged" layer will be that of the layer you selected first). InDesign arranges the objects on the layers according to the stacking order of the layers.

**Creating a New Layer**

To create a new layer, follow these steps (see Figure 2-53).

1. Choose New Layer from the Layers palette (or click the New Layer icon at the bottom of the Layers palette). InDesign adds a new layer to the top of the Layers palette. To add the layer at the bottom of the layers list, hold down Command-Option/Ctrl-Alt as you click the New Layer icon.

2. To change the layer's attributes (its name, selection color, visibility, guide behavior, and locked/unlocked status) choose Layer Options from the Layers palette menu, or double-click the layer name. InDesign displays the New Layer dialog box.

**Name.** Enter a name for the layer in this field. InDesign assigns a default name to each layer you create, but we think it's better to enter a layer name that means something in the context of your publication. It's far easier to remember that the enormous, slow drawing image of grazing Herefords is on the layer you've named "Big Slow Cows" than it is to remember that you've placed the image on the layer named "Layer 51."

**Color.** If you like, you can change the selection color of the layer. You can do this by either choosing one of InDesign's default layer colors from this pop-up menu or by double-clicking the associated color swatch. When you take the latter approach, InDesign displays a color picker where you can choose a custom selection color. We have never felt the need to change a layer's selection color in an actual project, but it's nice to know that you can.

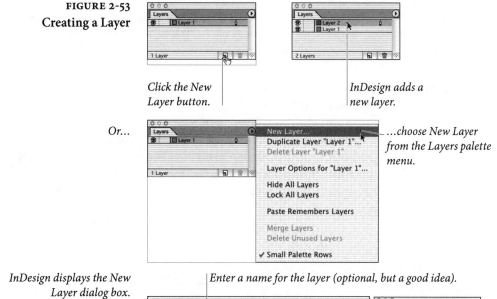

FIGURE 2-53
**Creating a Layer**

*Click the New Layer button.*

*InDesign adds a new layer.*

*Or...*

*...choose New Layer from the Layers palette menu.*

*InDesign displays the New Layer dialog box.*

*Choose a layer color from the pop-up menu, or double-click the color swatch.*

*Enter a name for the layer (optional, but a good idea).*

*Click the OK button, and InDesign adds the new layer to the Layers palette.*

*Set layer options.*

**Show Layer.** Should the layer be visible, or hidden? This option performs the same task as the show/hide column in the Layers palette.

**Lock Layer.** Should the layer be locked or unlocked? This option performs the same task as the lock/unlock icons.

**Show Guides.** Should the ruler guides on the layer be visible or hidden? Turn this option on to show the guides.

**Lock Guides.** Should the ruler guides on this layer be locked or unlocked? Turn this option on to lock the guides.

**Editing Layer Properties**

To edit the properties of a layer, double-click the layer name in the Layers palette (or choose Layer Options from the Layers palette menu). InDesign displays the Layer Options dialog box for the layer.

**Deleting Layers**

To delete a layer, select the layer and choose Delete Layer from the Layers palette menu. If there are any objects on the layer, InDesign will display a message asking if you want to remove the layer. To delete all of the unused layers (layers that have no objects assigned to them) in a publication, choose Delete Unused Layers from the Layers palette menu.

**Assigning Objects to Layers**

To move objects from one layer to another, drag the selection proxy from one layer and drop it on another layer (see Figure 2-54).

While this method of moving objects from one layer to another makes it difficult to accidentally move objects, it also makes it difficult to move objects from multiple layers to a single layer. To accomplish this, you'll have to make multiple trips up and down the Layers palette, selecting and moving the selection proxy for each layer in the selection.

To copy objects from one layer to another, hold down Option/Alt as you drag the selection proxy.

**FIGURE 2-54**
**Moving an Object to a Layer**

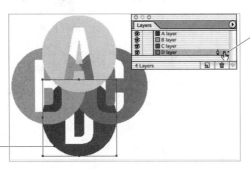

*This object is on the layer named "D layer."*

*Move the cursor over the selection proxy representing the object.*

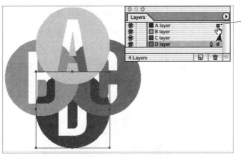

*Drag the selection proxy to another layer.*

*Object is now on the layer named "A layer."*

*Drop the selection proxy. InDesign moves the object to the layer.*

You can also move objects to a locked or hidden layer—to do this, press Command /Ctrl as you drag the selection proxy to the layer. To copy objects as you move them to a hidden or locked layer, hold down Command-Option/Ctrl-Alt as you drag.

**Changing Layer Stacking Order**

To change the stacking order of layers, drag the layer up (to bring the layer closer to the front) or down (to send the layer farther to the back) in the Layers palette. As you drag, InDesign displays a horizontal bar showing the position of the layer. When the layer reaches the point at which you want it to appear, stop dragging. InDesign moves the layer (and all the objects on it) to a new location (see Figure 2-55).

**Merging Layers**

To combine a series of layers into a single layer, select the layers and choose Merge Layers from the Layers palette menu. InDesign merges the layers into a single layer—the first layer you selected (see Figure 2-56). Note that merging layers sometimes changes the stacking order of objects on the merged layers.

**Moving Layers From One Publication to Another**

To move a layer from one publication into another publication, make sure you've turned on the Paste Remembers Layers option (on the Layers palette menu), then copy an object from that layer and paste it into the publication that lacks that layer. When you paste, InDesign adds the layer to the list of layers.

# Grouping Objects

What does it mean to "group" objects in a page layout program? When you group objects, you're telling the application to treat the objects as a single object. The objects in the group move and transform (scale, skew, and rotate) as a unit.

To group the objects in a selection, press Command-G/Ctrl-G (or choose Group from the Context menu, or choose Group from the Object menu). When you group a series of objects, the group moves to the top-most layer of the selection (see Figure 2-57). To ungroup a selected group, press Command-Shift-G/Ctrl-Shift-G (or choose Ungroup from the Context menu or the Object menu).

To select (or "subselect") an object inside a group, click the object using the Direct Selection tool.

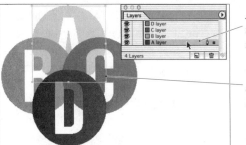

*Move the cursor over
the layer you want to
move.*

*The selected object is
on the layer named "A
layer."*

*Drag the layer to a
new position in the
Layers palette.*

*The layer named "A layer"
is now the layer closest
to the front.*

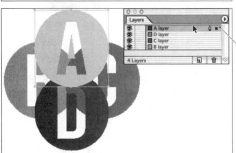

*When the layer
reaches the location
you want, stop drag-
ging. InDesign changes
the layer stacking
order.*

FIGURE 2-56
**Merging Layers**

*Select a series of layers and
choose Merge Layers from
the Layers palette menu.*

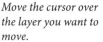

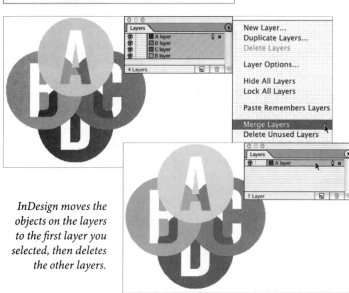

*InDesign moves the
objects on the layers
to the first layer you
selected, then deletes
the other layers.*

FIGURE 2-57
**Grouping and
Ungrouping Objects**

*Groups can come in handy
when you've created an
assemblage of objects you
want to treat as a single
object. In addition, grouping
objects speeds up screen
redraw—InDesign draws
selection handles for one
object, rather than for all of
the objects in the group.*

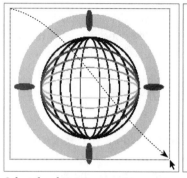

*Select the objects you want to group.*

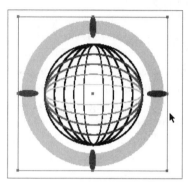

*Press Command-G/Ctrl-G.
InDesign groups the objects. You
can move, scale, shear, or rotate the
group as you do any other single
object. To select an object inside the
group, switch to the Direct Selection
tool and click the object.*

*To ungroup, select a group and press
Command-Shift-G/Ctrl-Shift-G.*

## Locking Object Positions

When you want to keep from changing the location of an object, you
can lock it. To do this, select the object and then press Command-
L/Ctrl-L (or choose Lock Position from the Context menu or the
Object menu). When an object is locked, you can select it, but you
can't change its position on the page or pasteboard. You can, however, move the object to another layer, or change its position in the
stacking order using the commands on the Arrange submenu of the
Object menu. When you try to drag a locked object, the cursor will
turn into a "padlock" icon (see Figure 2-58).

FIGURE 2-58
**Locking and
Unlocking Objects**

*Select an object and press
Command-L/Ctrl-L or
choose Lock Position from
the context menu.*

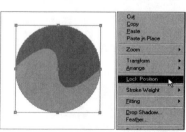
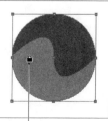

*InDesign displays the padlock icon
to show that the object is locked*

If what you're looking for is a way to keep from selecting and for-matting objects, lock the layer that contains the object (see "Layers," earlier in this chapter).

## A Good Foundation

The authors admit that they are not spectacularly organized per-sons. In general, we respond to events when something or someone catches fire, whacks one of us upside the head, or threatens some form of legal action.

We've found, however, that being methodical every now and then can save a lot of trouble later. Setting up master pages, defin-ing layers, creating layout grids, and positioning ruler guides are not the most glamorous parts of InDesign, but they're a good place to expend a little organizational energy.

Far from cramping your creative style, paying attention to basic layout options—at the very beginning of the production process, if possible—sets the stage on which you produce and direct the play of your publications.

# Text

## CHAPTER 3

Text is the stream of characters that inhabit the text frames of your publication. Text is not about what those characters look like (that's "type")—it's about the characters themselves, and the text frames that hold them.

There are areas of overlap between these definitions, of course. Changing the number of columns in a text frame, for example, definitely changes the appearance of the text, but we've put it in this chapter because it's an organizational change, not one that changes the appearance of individual characters.

The text in an InDesign publication is contained inside text frames (see Figure 3-1). Text frames are similar to the text "boxes" found in QuarkXPress, and they're also similar to the text "blocks" found in PageMaker (yes, text blocks are text frames—they just hide the frame from your view). In our opinion, InDesign's text frames present a "best of both worlds" approach—you get the flexibility and fluidity of PageMaker's text blocks combined with the precision of QuarkXPress' text boxes.

Text, in a word, is what publications are really all about. A picture might be worth a thousand words, but they're not very specific words. When you create a poster for a concert, for example, the text is what tells you where the concert will be presented, at what time, and on which day. The point of using an image, color, or a stylish layout in publication is to get people to *read the text*.

FIGURE 3-1
**Text Frame Anatomy**

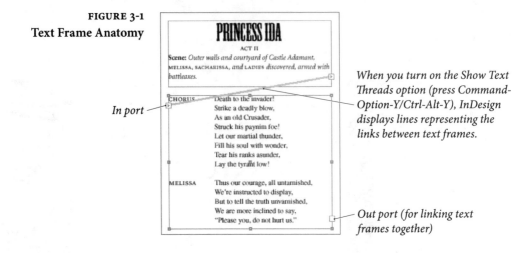

*In port*

*When you turn on the Show Text Threads option (press Command-Option-Y/Ctrl-Alt-Y), InDesign displays lines representing the links between text frames.*

*Out port (for linking text frames together)*

This chapter is all about how to get text into your InDesign publications: how to create and edit text frames, enter text, edit text, and import text files. It's also about checking the spelling of the text in your publication; and about finding and changing text. We'll even go a little bit off the deep end with a description of InDesign's tagged text import and export format.

## Creating Text Frames

Before you can add text to your InDesign publication, you've got to have something to put it in: a text frame. To create a text frame, you can use any of the following methods.

◆ Draw a frame using one of the frame drawing tools (the Rectangular Frame, Oval Frame, or Polygonal Frame tools). QuarkXPress users may think these tools only make "picture boxes" because they have an "X" in them. Not so, they're just generic frames. To convert the frame to a text frame, choose Text from the Content submenu of the Object menu, or click inside the frame using the Text tool (see Figure 3-2).

◆ Draw a frame using the Rectangle, Oval, or Polygon tools, and then convert it to a text frame by choosing Text from the Content submenu of the Object menu (or click the Text tool inside the frame; see Figure 3-3). Remember that the only difference between these tools and the frame tools is that these tools create shapes (usually with stroked borders). We recommend using the frame tools if you know you're going to be putting text or pictures in them.

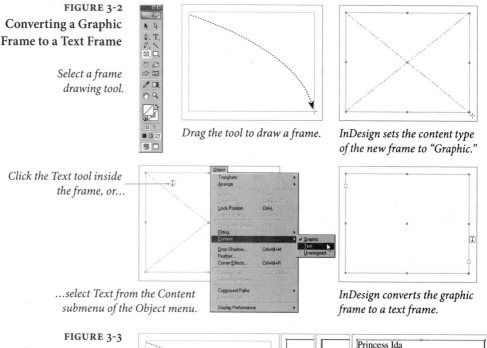

**FIGURE 3-2**
**Converting a Graphic Frame to a Text Frame**

*Select a frame drawing tool.*

*Drag the tool to draw a frame.*

*InDesign sets the content type of the new frame to "Graphic."*

*Click the Text tool inside the frame, or...*

*...select Text from the Content submenu of the Object menu.*

*InDesign converts the graphic frame to a text frame.*

**FIGURE 3-3**
**Converting a Basic Shape to a Text Frame**

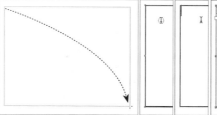

*Draw a path. InDesign creates a frame with a content type of "Unassigned."*

*Click the Text tool inside the frame...*

*...and InDesign converts the basic shape to a text frame.*

- Click the Text tool inside any empty frame. If the frame is a graphic frame, clicking it with the Text tool converts it to a text frame (see Figure 3-4).

- Drag the Text tool to create a frame whose height and width are defined by the area you specified by dragging (see Figure 3-5).

- Drag a text place icon. The text place icon appears whenever you import a text file, or when you click the in port or out port of a text frame (see Figure 3-6). For more on text place icons, and the in port and out port of a text frame, see "Importing Text" later in this chapter.

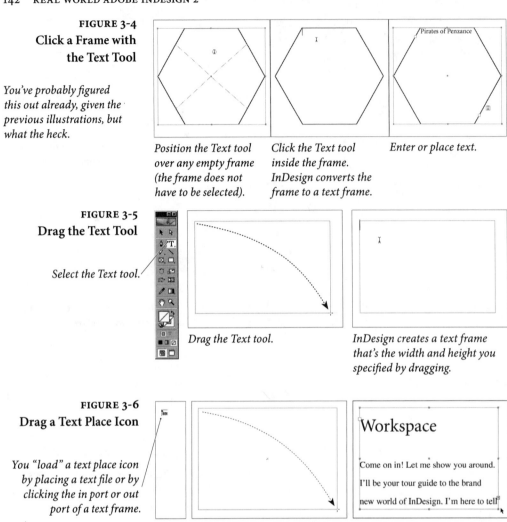

**FIGURE 3-4**
**Click a Frame with the Text Tool**

*You've probably figured this out already, given the previous illustrations, but what the heck.*

*Position the Text tool over any empty frame (the frame does not have to be selected).*

*Click the Text tool inside the frame. InDesign converts the frame to a text frame.*

*Enter or place text.*

**FIGURE 3-5**
**Drag the Text Tool**

*Select the Text tool.*

*Drag the Text tool.*

*InDesign creates a text frame that's the width and height you specified by dragging.*

**FIGURE 3-6**
**Drag a Text Place Icon**

*You "load" a text place icon by placing a text file or by clicking the in port or out port of a text frame.*

*Drag the text place icon...*

*...to create a text frame that's the width and height you specified by dragging.*

◆ Deselect all (Command-Shift-A/Ctrl-Shift-A) and then paste text into the publication (or drag it out of another application and drop it into the publication, which accomplishes the same thing). InDesign creates a text frame containing the text (see Figure 3-7).

◆ Drag a text file (or series of text files) out of your operating system's file browser (the Finder on the Macintosh, or the Windows Explorer in Windows) and drop it into an InDesign publication (see Figure 3-8).

**FIGURE 3-7**
**Paste Text**

*Copy text out of another application...*

*...and paste it into InDesign.*

**FIGURE 3-8**
**Drag and Drop Text Files**

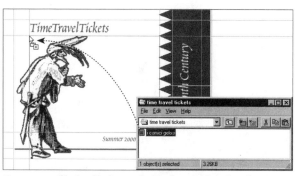

*Drag a text file (or files) out of a Finder window (on the Macintosh) or Explorer window (in Windows) into the InDesign publication window.*

*Drop the file. InDesign places the file in your publication.*

Note that InDesign does not require you to create a text frame *before* you add text, as (for example) QuarkXPress does. Most of the text frame creation methods described above dynamically create a text frame as you enter, import, or paste text.

Once you've created a text frame, you can change its size, shape, and rotation angle just as you would any other object you've created (see Chapter 5, "Drawing" and Chapter 9, "Transforming"). You can also change the shape of the text frame using InDesign's drawing and path editing tools (see Chapter 5, "Drawing").

Text can also appear *on* a path—for more on this topic, see Chapter 6, "Where Text Meets Graphics."

## Setting Text Frame Options

Text frames have attributes that are not shared with graphics frames or with frames whose content is set to "Unassigned." You can view and edit these attributes by choosing Text Frame Options from the Type menu (or by pressing Command-B/Ctrl-B). InDesign displays the Text Frame Options dialog box (see Figure 3-9). The controls in this dialog box set the number of columns, inset distances, and first baseline calculation method for the text frame.

FIGURE 3-9
Text Frame Options

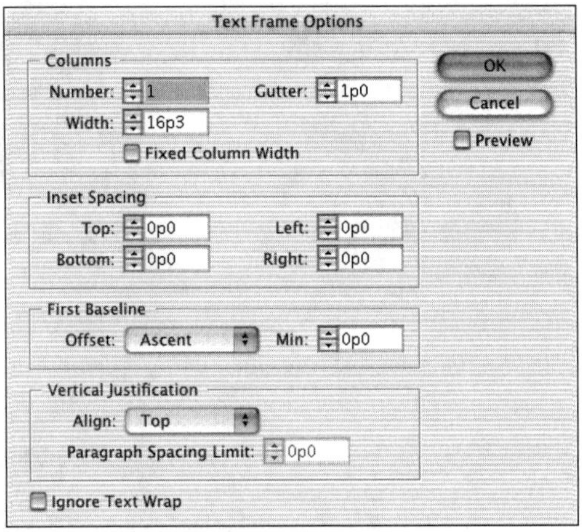

**How Many Columns?**   InDesign text frames can contain up to 40 columns—enter the number of columns you want in the Number field. To define the distance between columns, or "gutter," enter a value in the Gutter field.

**Measure for Measure**   When we think of the typesetting specifications for a block of text, we think first of the typeface, then the point size, the leading, and the measure, or column width—in that order. When we see a line of type, our thoughts go something like this: "That's Bodoni Book, eleven-on-fifteen, on a fourteen pica measure." The length of the lines of text is roughly as important as the character shapes, their size, and their leading.

QuarkXPress lets you set the number of columns in a text frame, but it doesn't let you specify the width of the columns—instead, you have to work with the width of the text box to get the column width you want. InDesign recognizes the importance of column width in typesetting by giving you the ability to determine the width of a text frame by the width of its columns. When you type the number of columns in the Text Frame Options dialog box and click OK, InDesign divides the current width of the text frame into columns for you (as

QuarkXPress does). However, if you specify a value in the Width field, then the program changes the width of your text frame so that the columns will fit.

The Fixed Column Width option tells InDesign what to do with your text frame when it gets wider or narrower. When you turn this option on, you'll notice that when you resize the text frame it snaps to widths determined by the fixed widths of the columns (and gutters) it contains (see Figure 3-10). If you leave this option turned off, the column widths change when you resize the frame.

FIGURE 3-10
**Fixed Column Width**

*When you turn on the Fixed Column Width option...*

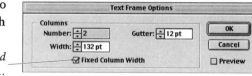

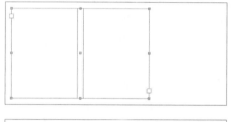

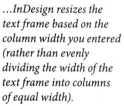

*...InDesign resizes the text frame based on the column width you entered (rather than evenly dividing the width of the text frame into columns of equal width).*

*If you resize a text frame that has a fixed column width...*

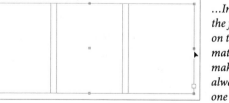

*...InDesign will "snap" the frame widths based on that column width. No matter how narrow you make the frame, it will always contain at least one column of that width.*

**Setting Text Frame Insets**

The values you enter in the Inset Spacing section of the Text Frame Options dialog box control the distances InDesign will push text from the edges of the text frame. You can enter an inset distance from 0 to 720 picas or 120 inches. (Unfortunately, you can't enter negative values to make the text hang out of the text frame.)

Inset distances work in conjunction with (and in addition to) the margins of the paragraphs in a text frame (see Figure 3-11). In

FIGURE 3-11

**Text Frame Insets**

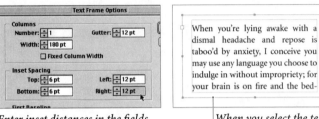

When you're lying awake with a dismal headache and repose is taboo'd by anxiety, I conceive you may use any language you choose to indulge in without impropriety; for your brain is on fire and the bedclothes conspire of usual slumber to plunder you: first your counterpane goes,

*By default, InDesign applies no inset—note that this differs from QuarkXPress, which applies a one point inset by default.*

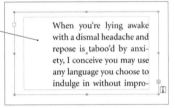

When you're lying awake with a dismal headache and repose is taboo'd by anxiety, I conceive you may use any language you choose to indulge in without impropriety; for your brain is on fire and the bed-

*Enter inset distances in the fields in the Inset Spacing section of the dialog box to push text away from the edges of the text frame.*

*When you select the text frame with the Selection tool, InDesign displays the text inset boundary.*

*Paragraph indents are applied in addition to the text frame inset distances.*

When you're lying awake with a dismal headache and repose is taboo'd by anxiety, I conceive you may use any language you choose to indulge in without impro-

general, we prefer to work with the text inset values set to zero, and use the left and right indent values of individual paragraphs to control the distance from the edges of the text to the edges of the text column. However, these inset features are sometimes helpful when you need to move all the text in a frame up or down slightly without moving the frame itself.

**Setting First Baseline Position**

The Offset pop-up menu in the First Baseline section of the Text Frame Options dialog box offers five methods for calculating the position of the first baseline of text in a text frame: Ascent, Cap Height, Leading, x Height, and Fixed (see Figure 3-12).

If you use either the Ascent or Cap Height method, the tops of characters in your text frames will touch (or come close to touching) the top of the text frame (provided, of course, that the top frame inset is zero). Choosing x Height is similar: the tops of the lowercase characters will bump up against the top of the frame (and the ascenders and uppercase letters will pop out the top of the frame). These settings come at a price, however: it's almost impossible to

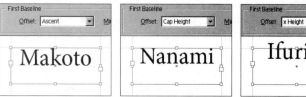

**FIGURE 3-12**

**First Baseline Position**

*Example font is Minion Pro; example leading is 24 points.*

*All baseline distances calculated using Neo-Atlantean super science, and will vary from font to font.*

*Distance from the top of the text frame to the first baseline: 17.44775390625 points.*

*Distance from the top of the text frame to the first baseline: 15.6000316143036 points.*

*Distance from the top of the text frame to the first baseline: 10.4640212059021 points.*

*If you use the Fixed or Leading options, you can know exactly where the first baseline of text will fall in relation to the top of the text frame, regardless of the font or the point size of the text.*

*Distance from the top of the text frame to the first baseline: 24 points.*

*Distance from the top of the text frame to the first baseline: 24 points.*

calculate the distance from the top of the frame to the baseline of the first line of text in the frame (without resorting to scripting).

In addition, using these methods means that InDesign will vary the leading of the first line when you enter characters from different fonts in the line, or change the size of characters, or when you embed inline graphics in the line.

Is that bad? It is, if you care about type.

It's important that you know exactly where the first baseline of text in a text frame will appear, relative to the top of the text frame. Why? Because if you know the position of the first baseline, you can snap the top of the text frame to your leading grid—and rest secure in the knowledge that the first baseline will fall neatly on the next baseline.

To control the location of the first baseline of text in a text frame, choose either Leading or Fixed from the Offset menu in the First Baseline section. When you choose Leading, the first baseline is one leading increment from the top of the text frame—regardless of the size of the characters (or the height of inline graphics) in the line. When you choose Fixed, you can specify exactly how far from the top of the frame the first baseline should fall using the Min field.

The Min field for the Offset settings other than Fixed means, "between the Min value and what the Offset would be ordinarily, use the larger value."

For more on leading, see Chapter 4, "Type."

**Ignoring Text Wrap**

In a typical magazine spread, some text wraps around graphics; some text doesn't. Imagine that you want the body text of an article to wrap around an image—but you want to place a headline on top of the same image. To keep text in a text frame from obeying a text wrap, select the frame, open the Text Frame Options dialog box, and then turn on the Ignore Text Wrap option (see Figure 3-13).

FIGURE 3-13
**Ignoring Text Wrap**

*When you try to place a text frame on top of a graphic that has a text wrap, InDesign hides the text.*

*Unless, that is, you display the Text Frame Options dialog box (select the text frame and press Command-B/Ctrl-B)and turn on the Ignore Text Wrap option.*

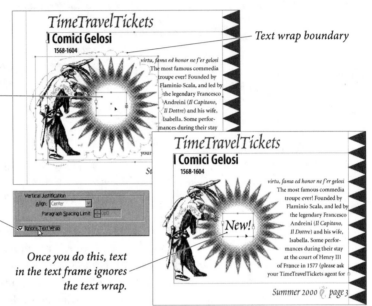

Text wrap boundary

*Once you do this, text in the text frame ignores the text wrap.*

**Vertical Justification**

Just as the alignment of a paragraph controls the horizontal position of the paragraph in a column, vertical justification controls the vertical position of the text in a text frame (see Figure 3-14). To set the vertical justification method used for a text frame, select the text frame, display the Text Frame Options dialog box, and then choose a method from the Align pop-up menu.

◆ Top. Aligns the text to the top of the text frame, positioning the first baseline of text in the frame according to the method you've selected from the Offset pop-up menu (see above).

◆ Center. Vertically centers the text in the text frame. More precisely, the program centers the text between the bottom of the text frame and the top of the first line of text (depending on the Offset and Minimum value in the First Baseline section of this dialog box. The problem is that in small text frames the text may be mathematically centered, but not actually appear centered—especially single lines of all-capitals text, or in fonts that have no ascenders or descenders. In these relatively rare cases, you

FIGURE 3-14

**Vertical Justification**

*When you choose Center from the Align pop-up menu, you might want to choose the Cap Height or Ascent option from the Offset pop-up menu (in this case, choosing Leading is not a good idea, as it pushes the text away from the visual center of the text frame).*

*When you choose Justify from the Align pop-up menu, InDesign adds space to force the text to fill the height of the frame. The method InDesign uses is based on the value you enter in the Paragraph Spacing Limit field (you can enter values from 0 to 8640 points).*

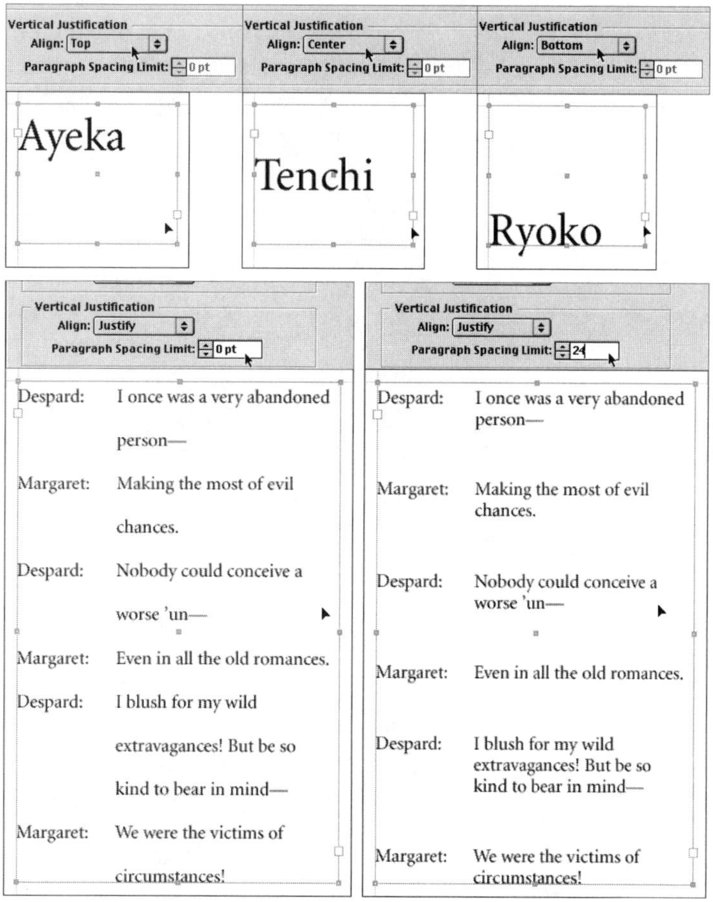

| Vertical Justification | | |
|---|---|---|
| Align: Top | Align: Center | Align: Bottom |
| Paragraph Spacing Limit: 0 pt | Paragraph Spacing Limit: 0 pt | Paragraph Spacing Limit: 0 pt |
| Ayeka | Tenchi | Ryoko |

**Vertical Justification** — Align: Justify — Paragraph Spacing Limit: 0 pt

| | |
|---|---|
| Despard: | I once was a very abandoned person— |
| Margaret: | Making the most of evil chances. |
| Despard: | Nobody could conceive a worse 'un— |
| Margaret: | Even in all the old romances. |
| Despard: | I blush for my wild extravagances! But be so kind to bear in mind— |
| Margaret: | We were the victims of circumstances! |

**Vertical Justification** — Align: Justify — Paragraph Spacing Limit: 24

| | |
|---|---|
| Despard: | I once was a very abandoned person— |
| Margaret: | Making the most of evil chances. |
| Despard: | Nobody could conceive a worse 'un— |
| Margaret: | Even in all the old romances. |
| Despard: | I blush for my wild extravagances! But be so kind to bear in mind— |
| Margaret: | We were the victims of circumstances! |

*When you enter zero, InDesign applies leading to make the text fill the height of the text frame.*

*When you enter a value, InDesign applies paragraph spacing up to that amount before changing the leading.*

may have to tweak the First Baseline or Baseline Shift settings to center the text.

◆ Bottom. Aligns the baseline of the last line of text in the text frame to the bottom of the frame. When you choose this method, the method you've chosen from the Offset pop-up menu has no effect.

◆ Justify. Adds vertical space to the text in the text frame (using paragraph spacing and/or leading to add this space) to fill the text frame with the text. Note that using the Justify method will not pull overset text into the text frame (that is, it won't lessen the leading value to make more text fit in the frame; it only adds space). The first line of the text frame will remain where it was, based on the First Baseline setting.

**Paragraph Spacing Limit.** The problem with vertically justified text is that it overrides your leading values, and we don't take kindly to anyone messing with our leading. Fortunately, when you choose Justify from the Align pop-up menu, InDesign activates the Paragraph Spacing Limit control, which sets the maximum amount of space you'll allow between paragraphs in the text frame. Once the space between paragraphs reaches this value, InDesign adjusts the leading of each line in the text frame, rather than adding space between paragraphs. To keep InDesign from changing leading at all, enter a large value (up to 8640 points) in this field. On the other hand, if you really want InDesign to change the leading instead, enter zero in this field. (This is handy if you have a long list of single-line paragraphs that you want to spread out over the height of a text frame.)

## Linking and Unlinking Text Frames

You can link one text frame to another to make the text continue—or "flow"—from frame to frame. In InDesign, the controls for linking and unlinking text frames are the "in port" and "out port" icons on the text frames themselves. This means that the process of linking text frames in InDesign is similar to working with the "window-shade handles" on PageMaker text blocks, and should feel familiar to PageMaker users. There's no need to go to the Toolbox to get a special "linking" tool, as there is in QuarkXPress.

Text frames come with their own somewhat obscure terminology. Any continuous series of text characters is a *story.* A story can be as small as a single, unlinked text frame, or as large as a series of hundreds of text frames containing tens of thousands of words and spanning hundreds of pages. When you link text frames together, you're *threading* stories through the text frames. When you place text to create a series of linked text frames, you're *flowing* text.

The text in a story has a direction—it has a beginning, a middle, and an end. When we speak, in this section, of a particular text frame appearing before or after another, we're talking about its position in the story, not relative to its position on the page.

The way that InDesign displays the in port and out port of a text frame tells you about the text frame and its position in a story (see Figure 3-15).

◆ When the in port or out port is empty, no other text frame is linked to that port. When both ports are empty, the text you see in the text frame is the entire story.

**FIGURE 3-15**
**In Ports and Out Ports**

*This text frame contains all of the text in a story. How can you tell?*

*The in port is empty, and...*    *...the out port is also empty.*

*This text frame is at the start of a story, because the in port is empty.*

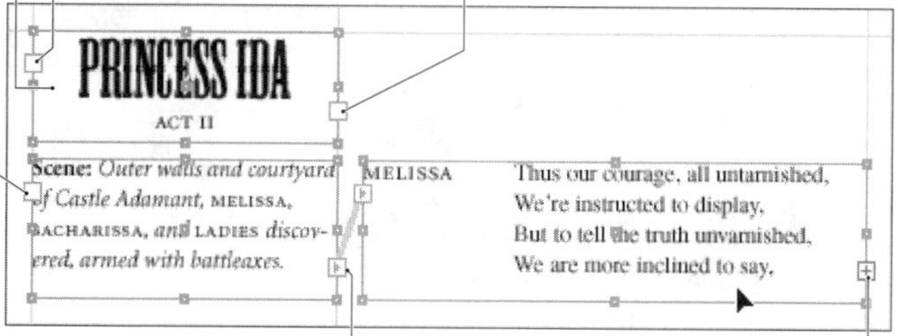

PRINCESS IDA

ACT II

**Scene:** *Outer walls and courtyard of Castle Adamant,* MELISSA, SACHARISSA, *and* LADIES *discovered, armed with battleaxes.*

MELISSA

Thus our courage, all untarnished,
We're instructed to display,
But to tell the truth unvarnished,
We are more inclined to say,

*When you see a triangle in the out port, it means that the text frame is linked to another text frame.*

*A "+" in the out port means that the text frame is the last text frame in a story, and that there's more text to place (the unplaced text is called "overset" text).*

◆ When you see a plus sign (+) in the out port, it means that not all of the text in the story has been placed. The remaining (or "overset") text is stored in the text frame, but is not displayed.

◆ When you see a triangle in the in port or the out port (or both), InDesign is telling you that the text frame is linked to another text frame.

## Linking Text Frames

To link one text frame to another, choose the Selection or Direct Selection tool, then click either the in port or the out port of a text frame. InDesign displays the text place icon. Place the cursor over another frame (when you do this, InDesign displays the text link icon, which either looks like a little chain or like some text inside big parentheses, depending on what type of frame you're hovering over) and then click. InDesign links the two frames (see Figure 3-16). That sounds pretty simple, but there are a number of details you should keep in mind:

◆ Unlike QuarkXPress, InDesign can link two text frames when both frames contain text. When you do this, the stories in the text frames are merged into a single story. If the text in the first text frame did not end with a carriage return, InDesign will run the text in the second text frame into the last paragraph of the first text frame (see Figure 3-17).

**FIGURE 3-16**
**Linking Text Frames**

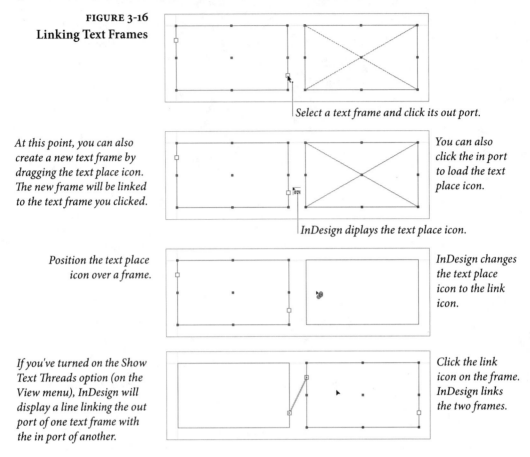

Select a text frame and click its out port.

At this point, you can also create a new text frame by dragging the text place icon. The new frame will be linked to the text frame you clicked.

You can also click the in port to load the text place icon.

InDesign diplays the text place icon.

Position the text place icon over a frame.

InDesign changes the text place icon to the link icon.

If you've turned on the Show Text Threads option (on the View menu), InDesign will display a line linking the out port of one text frame with the in port of another.

Click the link icon on the frame. InDesign links the two frames.

◆ Unlike PageMaker's text blocks, InDesign frames can be linked when they're empty. This means you can easily set up text layouts without having the copy in hand and without resorting to a "dummy text" placeholder.

◆ The port you click (the in port or the out port) sets the position of the link in the sequence of linked text frames making up the story. If you click the out port, the text frame you link to will come after the current text frame. If you click the in port and then another frame, this second frame will come earlier in the story (see Figure 3-18).

◆ When you click the out port of a text frame that contains more text than it can display (that is, an out port that displays the "+" symbol), the additional text will flow into the next text frame in the story (see Figure 3-19).

**FIGURE 3-17**
**Linking Stories**

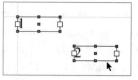

*Two unlinked text frames.*

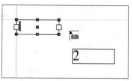

*Click the out port of one of the frames to load the text place icon.*

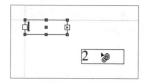

*Click the text place icon on the other frame.*

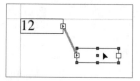

*InDesign links the two frames. If the first frame did not end with a carriage return, InDesign runs the text from the first paragraph of the second frame into the last paragraph of the first frame.*

**FIGURE 3-18**
**Controlling the Order of Text Frames in a Story**

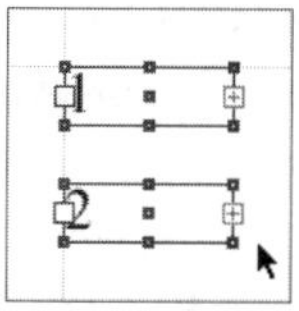

*Two unlinked text frames.* 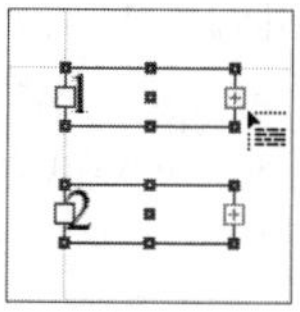    *When you load the text place icon by clicking the out port...*    *...and link to another text frame...* 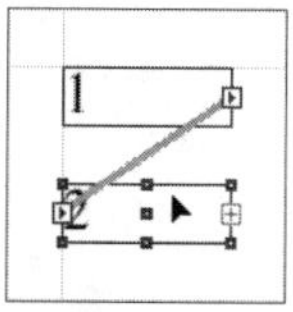    *...that frame becomes the next frame in the story.*

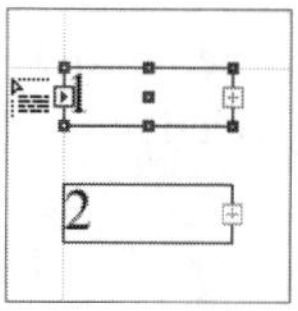

*If, on the other hand, you load the text place icon by clicking on an in port...*    *...the frame you link to becomes the previous text frame in the story.*

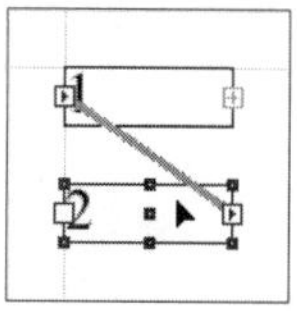

**FIGURE 3-19**
**Placing Overset Text**

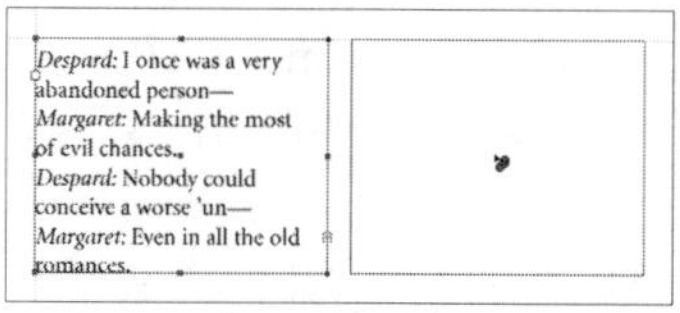

*This text frame contains overset text. When you link it to another text frame...*

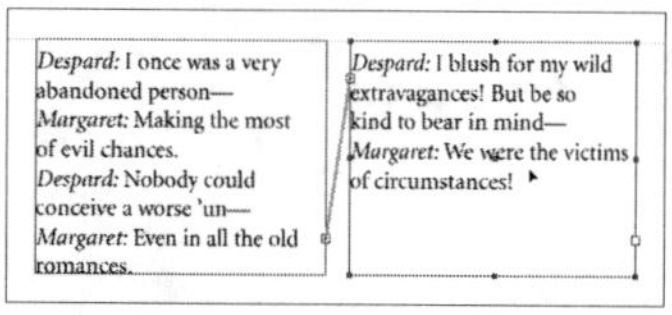

*...InDesign places the overset text in the following text frame (in this example, all of the text in the story has been placed).*

◆ You don't have to link to another text frame—you can also create a link to a graphic frame or a frame whose content type has been set to "None." In InDesign 1.0, you could link a text frame to a graphic frame that had a picture in it and InDesign would discard the picture and fill the frame with text. InDesign no longer lets you link to a frame if there's a picture in it.

◆ To create a new text frame that's linked to an existing text frame, click the in port or out port of the existing frame and then drag the text place icon.

*Link icon*    *Unlink icon*

◆ As you link and unlink text, InDesign changes the appearance of the cursor to give you a clue (or, as a more formal author would say, a "visual indication") about what you're doing or are about to do.

◆ What if you have a "loaded" text place cursor and then realize that you need to scroll, or turn to another page? Do you need to "unload" the text place cursor (see below) before issuing other commands? Probably not—you can scroll, zoom, turn pages, create or modify ruler guides, and create new pages while InDesign displays the text place cursor.

◆ To "unload" the text place cursor (disable it, like if you change your mind midstream), click on any tool in the Toolbox (or just press a key to switch tools, like "V" for the Selection tool).

◆ To view the links between text frames, choose Show Text Threads from the View menu. InDesign displays lines connecting text frames in the selection (see Figure 3-20).

## Unlinking Text Frames

To break a link between text frames, double-click the in port or out port on either side of the link (see Figure 3-21). When you break a link between text frames that have text content, the text usually becomes overset text (which is stored in the last text frame in the story).

Alternatively, you can click the out port of one frame and then click the next frame in the thread (see Figure 3-22). When you move the text place icon over the next frame, InDesign displays the Unlink Text icon (which is subtly different than the Link Text icon). When you click the Unlink Text icon on the frame, InDesign breaks the

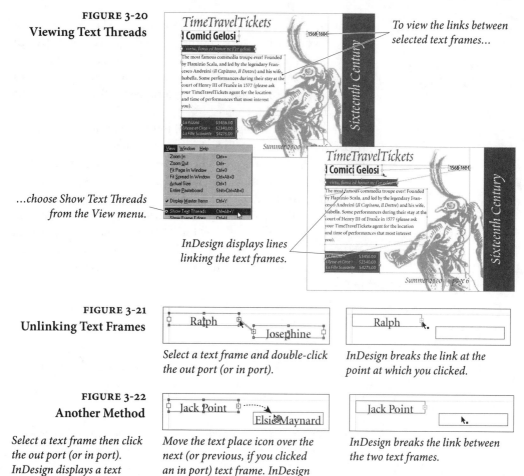

FIGURE 3-20
**Viewing Text Threads**

*To view the links between selected text frames...*

*...choose Show Text Threads from the View menu.*

*InDesign displays lines linking the text frames.*

FIGURE 3-21
**Unlinking Text Frames**

*Select a text frame and double-click the out port (or in port).*

*InDesign breaks the link at the point at which you clicked.*

FIGURE 3-22
**Another Method**

*Select a text frame then click the out port (or in port). InDesign displays a text place icon.*

*Move the text place icon over the next (or previous, if you clicked an in port) text frame. InDesign displays the unlink icon.*

*InDesign breaks the link between the two text frames.*

link. This method does the same thing, but is slower and involves more mouse movement than double-clicking—however, some people like it better.

By the way, when you break a link in the middle of multiple frames, the links before and after the break stick around. That is, if boxes A, B, C, and D are linked together, and you break the link between B and C, then C and D will stay linked together (even though there won't be any text in them).

## Cutting and Pasting Text Frames

What happens to links when you delete or cut a linked text frame or series of linked text frames? First, InDesign does not delete any text in the story—the only time it does that is when you select all of the frames in the story and delete them. Otherwise, InDesign always flows the text contained by the frames you've deleted into the remaining frames in the story. If you want to delete text, you have to select it using the Text tool first. For more on selecting text, see "Editing Text," later in this chapter.

When you cut or copy a series of linked text frames, then paste, InDesign maintains the links between the duplicated frames—but not between the duplicates and the original frames or any other frames in the publication (see Figure 3-23). The copies of the frames contain the same text as the originals.

An interesting side effect of this behavior is that you can copy text frames from a story that are not linked to each other, and, when you paste, the text frames will be linked. This can come in handy when you're trying to split a story that is in multiple frames (as you can see in Figure 3-24).

**FIGURE 3-23**
**Cutting and Pasting Linked Frames**

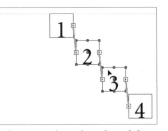
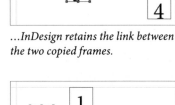

*In this example, we've selected the second and third text frames in a story. When we copy and paste...*

*...InDesign retains the link between the two copied frames.*

**FIGURE 3-24**
**More About Copying and Pasting**

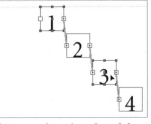

*In this example, we've selected the first and third text frames in a story. When we copy and paste...*

*...InDesign retains the link between the two copied frames—even though the original frames were not directly connected to each other.*

## Adding a New Frame to a Story

It's easy to add a text frame in the middle of a sequence of linked text frames. Just follow these steps (see Figure 3-25).

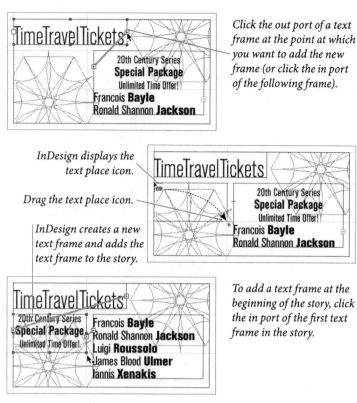

**FIGURE 3-25**
**Adding a New Frame**
**to a Story**

*Click the out port of a text frame at the point at which you want to add the new frame (or click the in port of the following frame).*

*InDesign displays the text place icon.*

*Drag the text place icon.*

*InDesign creates a new text frame and adds the text frame to the story.*

*To add a text frame at the beginning of the story, click the in port of the first text frame in the story.*

1. Use the Selection tool to click the out port at the point in the story at which you want to add the new frame.

2. Drag the text place icon to create a new text frame, or click an existing, empty, unlinked frame.

   InDesign only lets you link to empty and unlinked frames unless you're adding frames to the beginning or end of your thread.

## Flowing Text

When you select Place from the File menu (and then choose a text file), or use the Selection tool to click the in port or out port of a text frame, your cursor changes to the text place icon. You can drag this text place cursor to create a text frame, or you can click on an existing frame to flow text into it. Flowing text is all about the care, maintenance, and feeding of the text place icon (see Table 3-1 for more on text place icons).

   Once you've "loaded" the text place icon, you can use one of three text flow methods: Manual text flow, Semi-automatic text flow, or

TABLE 3-1
Text Flow Icons

| Icon: | What it means: |
|---|---|
| ▣ | Manual text flow icon. Click to flow text into a frame; click in a column to create a frame that's the width of the column, or drag to create a frame. |
| ▣ | Semi-automatic text flow icon. InDesign will "reload" the text flow icon after each click or drag. |
| ▣ | Autoflow text flow icon. Click to place all of the text in the story. |
| ▣ ▣ ▣ | The text flow icon is above a guide or grid "snap" point. |
| ▣ ▣ | The text flow icon is above a frame; clicking will place the text in the frame. |

Autoflow. These determine what happens when you click or drag the text place icon. Here's the lowdown.

◆ **Manual text flow.** By default, InDesign uses the manual text flow method. When you click the text place icon on your page, or drag the text place icon, InDesign creates a new text frame and flows the text into it (see Figure 3-26). When you click the text place icon in between column guides, the width of the text frame is determined by the width of the column you clicked in; the height of the frame is the distance from the point at which you clicked the text place icon to the bottom of the column (see Figure 3-27). In a one-column document, the text frame reaches from the page's left to right margins. InDesign then flows the text into the new text frame. When you click the text place icon on an existing text frame or series of linked text frames, InDesign flows the text into the frame or frames. In either case, once InDesign is done flowing the text, the text place icon disappears and you're back to whatever tool you had selected before you loaded the text place icon. To continue placing text, click the out port to reload the text place icon.

◆ **Semi-automatic text flow.** Semi-automatic text flow is almost exactly like manual text flow—the difference is that InDesign reloads the text place icon after you've placed some text. The advantage? You don't have to click the out port of a text frame to reload the text place icon. To turn on semi-automatic text flow, hold down Option/Alt when the text place icon is visible. InDesign displays the semi-automatic text place icon when you do this (the cursor looks like a half-solid and half-dotted curvy line; see Figure 3-28).

**FIGURE 3-26**
**Manual Text Flow**

Load the text place icon (by placing a text file or clicking the in port or out port of any text frame).

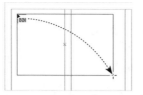

InDesign displays the manual text flow icon. Drag the icon.

InDesign flows text into the area you defined by dragging.

**FIGURE 3-27**
**Manual Text Flow and Column Guides**

Load the text place icon. InDesign displays the manual text flow icon.

Click the manual text flow icon in a column.

InDesign flows the text into the column. Click the out port to reload and place more text.

**FIGURE 3-28**
**Semi-Automatic Text Flow**

Load the text place icon. InDesign displays the manual text flow icon.

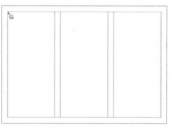

Hold down Option/Alt to switch to the semiautomatic text flow icon, then click the icon in a column.

InDesign flows the text into the column, then automatically reloads the text place icon.

Click the the semiautomatic text flow icon in the next column. InDesign creates a new text frame and links it to the previous text frame.

Repeat this process until you've placed all of the columns of text you want to place.

◆ **Autoflow.** Hold down Shift, and the text place icon turns into the autoflow icon. Click the autoflow icon, and InDesign places all of the text, creating new frames and pages as necessary (see Figure 3-29). When you click the autoflow icon in a text frame

FIGURE 3-29
**Autoflow**

*Load the text place icon.
InDesign displays the
manual text flow icon.*

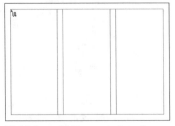

*Hold down Shift to switch to the
autoflow text flow icon, then click
the icon in a column.*

*InDesign flows the text into the
available columns or text frames,
and continues adding new text
frames and pages until there's no
more text left to place.*

or series of linked text frames, InDesign duplicates that frame
(or frames) on any new pages it creates, automatically links the
frames, and places the text in the frames. When you click the
autoflow icon in a column, InDesign creates a new text frame in
each column (adding pages until it has placed all of the text).

Note that you can also hold down Shift-Option/Shift-Alt when
you click—this is sort of a hybrid: it fills all the columns on a single
page with text frames (and links them together, of course), but won't
add additional pages.

# Entering Text

The simplest way to get text into the text frames in your InDesign
publications is to type it. To do this, create a text frame by dragging
the Text tool, or select the Text tool and click in a frame (again, it
doesn't have to be a text frame). Either method places a blinking text
cursor (or "text insertion point") inside the text frame. Type, and the
characters you type will appear in the text frame.

**Inserting Special
Characters**

We don't know about you, but we're not getting any younger, and we
have trouble remembering exactly which keys to press to produce
certain special characters. If you're like us, you'll appreciate the list
of common characters in Table 3-2. Even better, InDesign lists these
all in the Insert Special Character submenu (under the Type menu,
or in the context-sensitive menu when you Control/Right-button-
click on a text box with the Type tool; see Figure 3-30). InDesign also
offers (in the same places) the Insert White Space submenu (which
lists various white spaces such as an Em Space) and the Insert Break
Character submenu (which lists Forced Line Breaks, Column Breaks,
and other interruptions of the text flow).

TABLE 3-2
Entering Special
Characters

| Special character: | What you press: |
| --- | --- |
| Bullet (•) | Option-8/Alt-8 |
| Column break | Keypad Enter |
| Copyright symbol (©) | Option-G/Alt-G |
| Discretionary hyphen | Command-Shift--/Ctrl-Shift-- |
| Ellipsis (…) | Option-;/Alt-; |
| Em dash (—) | Option-Shift--/Alt-Shift-- |
| Em space | Command-Shift-M/Ctrl-Shift-M |
| En dash (–) | Option--/Alt-- |
| En space | undefined* |
| Even page break | undefined* |
| Figure space | Command-Shift-Option-8/ Ctrl-Shift-Alt-8 |
| Flush space | Command-Option-J/ Ctrl-Shift-Alt-J |
| Frame break | Shift-Keypad Enter |
| Hair space | Command-Shift-I/Ctrl-Shift-Alt-I |
| Indent to here | Command-\/Ctrl-\ |
| Next page number | Command-Option-Shift-] Ctrl-Alt-Shift-] |
| Non-breaking hyphen | Command-Option--/Ctrl-Alt-- |
| Non-breaking space | Command-Option-X/Ctrl-Alt-X |
| Odd page break | undefined* |
| Page break | Command-Keypad Enter Ctrl-Keypad Enter |
| Paragraph symbol (¶) | Option-7/Alt-7 |
| Previous page number | Command-Option-Shift-[ Ctrl-Alt-Shift-[ |
| Punctuation space | undefined* |
| Trademark (™) | Option-2/Alt-2 |
| Left double quote (") | Option-[/Alt-[ |
| Left single quote (') | Option-]/Alt-] |
| Right double quote (") | Option-Shift-[/Alt-Shift-[ |
| Right single quote (') | Option-Shift-]/Shift-Alt-] |
| Section name | Command-Option-Shift-N Ctrl-Alt-Shift-N |
| Section symbol (§) | Option-6/Alt-6 |
| Thin space | Command-Option-Shift-M Ctrl-Alt-Shift-M |
| Registered trademark (®) | Option-R/Alt-R |

*You can define the
undefined shortcuts (or
redefine any of the others) by
selecting Keyboard Shortcuts
from the Edit menu.

*Click the Text tool
in a text frame.*

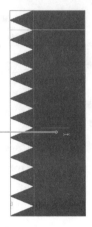

*In this example, the section
marker text (in the Section
Options dialog box) is
"Sixteenth Century."*

*Display the
context menu
and choose a
special character
from the Insert
Special Character
submenu.*

*InDesign enters
the character.*

*You can also use the
context menu to enter
space characters...*

*...and break
characters.*

**Insert Glyph**    We're sometimes stumped when it's time to type a dagger (†) or a circumflex (ˆ). And we often spend time hunting through KeyCaps (on the Macintosh) or Character Map (in Windows) looking for the right character in a symbol font (such as Zapf Dingbats).

If you also have this problem, you'll love InDesign's Glyphs palette (in version 1 it was a dialog box and was called Insert Character). You can open this palette by choosing Insert Glyphs from the Type menu or the Type submenu under the Window menu (see Figure 3-31). A "glyph," is the word for a specific shape of a character. For instance, there may be three different glyphs in a font that all look like the character "A" (one regular A, one with a swash, and one in small caps style).

The Glyphs palette is easy to use: while the text cursor is blinking in a text frame, choose the font (if different than the one you're currently using), then double-click a character from the list of characters in the font. InDesign places the character at the location of the cursor.

Now here's the cool part: If a character can be found inside a font, you can use it—even if the character is outside the range of characters supported by your system. For instance, most fonts have

**FIGURE 3-31**
**Inserting Characters**
**Using the Glyphs Palette**

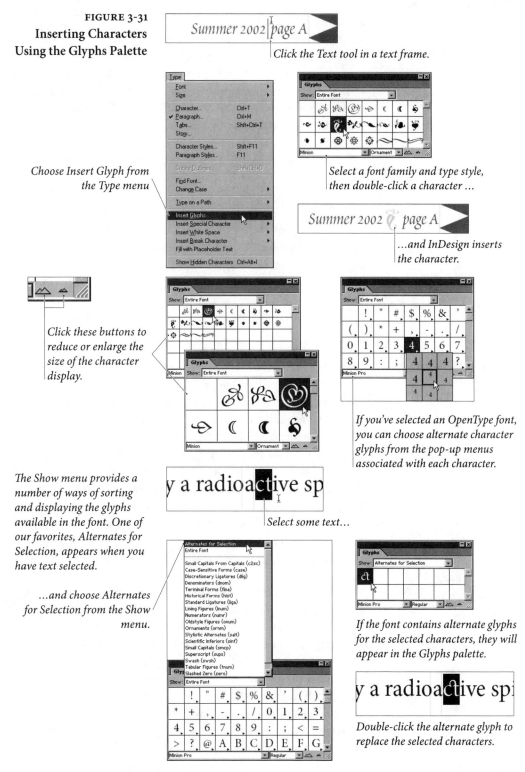

*Click the Text tool in a text frame.*

*Choose Insert Glyph from the Type menu*

*Select a font family and type style, then double-click a character ...*

*...and InDesign inserts the character.*

*Click these buttons to reduce or enlarge the size of the character display.*

*If you've selected an OpenType font, you can choose alternate character glyphs from the pop-up menus associated with each character.*

*The Show menu provides a number of ways of sorting and displaying the glyphs available in the font. One of our favorites, Alternates for Selection, appears when you have text selected.*

*Select some text...*

*...and choose Alternates for Selection from the Show menu.*

*If the font contains alternate glyphs for the selected characters, they will appear in the Glyphs palette.*

*Double-click the alternate glyph to replace the selected characters.*

a ½ character, but there's no way to type it. This seems like a silly feature—after all, why would fonts contain characters that would be inaccessible to any other program? We don't know, mate, but they do. Fonts have all kinds of foreign-language characters, weird punctuation, and even ornaments that simply can't be used in QuarkXPress or other programs. But the Glyphs palette makes it easy to get to them. Characters such as "fi" and "fl" ligatures, which aren't part of the Windows character set, suddenly become available (without switching to an "expert" font). It's well worth your time to trawl through your fonts just to see if there's anything you can use that you haven't been using.

You've got to keep in mind that just because one font has a particular glyph doesn't mean that another font will, too. When you use Insert Glyphs, InDesign remembers the Unicode value for that glyph. If you change fonts, the program tries to find the same Unicode value in the new font. If the font designer didn't include that character, or assigned it to a different Unicode value, InDesign displays the dreaded pink highlight instead of the character.

**Dummy Text**    The client wants to see the new layout. But the writer won't give you the text. You're stuck—a layout looks, so, well, incomplete without text. And the client, a singularly humorless individual, cannot be appeased by whatever snatches of text from Gilbert & Sullivan, Brecht, or Edgar Rice Burroughs come easily to mind. What you need is something that looks like text, but isn't really text at all.

Graphic artists have been prepared for this eventuality for *centuries* (rumor has it that even *Gutenburg's* writers couldn't deliver text in time for an important meeting)—we use something called "dummy text." Dummy text is a meaningless stream of fake Latin text that *looks* very much like real text (it's so realistic that it's used to fill the pages of a major national newspaper). It's just the thing you need to survive your meeting and get that approval your business depends on.

InDesign makes it easy to add dummy text to a text frame—select the text frame using the Selection tool, or click the Text tool in a text frame and choose Fill with Placeholder Text from the context menu (or from the Type menu). InDesign fills the text frame with dummy text (see Figure 3-32). By the way, InDesign's dummy text is a random compilation of words taken from the Lorum Ipsum text that so many designers have used over the years. However, if you have Caps Lock turned on when you select Fill with Placeholder Text, the Macintosh version of InDesign will, instead, fill the box with random words from an oration by Cicero.

**FIGURE 3-32**
**Filling a Frame with Dummy Text**

*Select a text frame with the Selection tool, or click the Text tool in a text frame.*

*Choose Fill with Placeholder Text from the context menu (or from the Type menu)...*

*...and InDesign fills the selected frame with dummy text.*

Even better: If you save a text file in the InDesign folder with the name "Placeholder.txt" the program will use this text instead of the fake Latin stuff. This probably isn't actually useful, but it's nice to know it's possible, ain't it?

# Importing Text

Most of the time, the text you work with in a page layout program isn't originally written using that program—it's written using a word processing program (such as Microsoft Word) or text editors (such as BBEdit on the Macintosh). To get the text into InDesign, you must import (or "place") the text files. InDesign can import text in a variety of formats, including Microsoft Word (97, 98, v.X, 2000, and 2001), Microsoft Excel (97, 98, 2000, and 2001), text-only (ASCII or Unicode), Rich Text Format (RTF), and InDesign tagged text (we discuss this last format later in the chapter).

You can view the complete list of available import filters in the Files of Type pop-up menu in the Place Document dialog box in Windows, or in the Component Information dialog box (for either platform—see Chapter 1, "Basics").

If you don't see your word processor or text editor listed as one of the available import filters, don't despair. InDesign can import text in common "interchange" formats, such as text-only and RTF, and chances are good that your word processor or text editor can save text in one of those formats.

In addition, InDesign's tagged text filter can import formatted text from any application that can write a text-only file. The tagged text format is something like RTF—it's a text-only format that uses special codes to define the typesetting of the text in the file (see "Working with InDesign Tagged Text," later in this chapter).

To place a text file, follow these steps (see Figure 3-33).

FIGURE 3-33
**Placing a Text File**

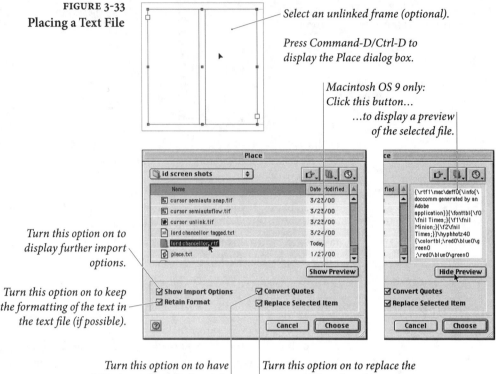

*Select an unlinked frame (optional).*

*Press Command-D/Ctrl-D to display the Place dialog box.*

*Macintosh OS 9 only:
Click this button…*

*…to display a preview of the selected file.*

*Turn this option on to display further import options.*

*Turn this option on to keep the formatting of the text in the text file (if possible).*

*Turn this option on to have InDesign replace any "straight quotes" in the text file with proper typographic quotation marks.*

*Turn this option on to replace the contents of the selected frame or text, or to insert the file at the current text cursor position.*

*Click the Choose button (in Windows, click the Open button).*

*If you turned on the Show Import Options option, InDesign displays an Import Options dialog box.*

*Click the OK button.*

*InDesign places the text file. If you had a frame selected, InDesign places the text inside the frame; otherwise, InDesign displays the text place icon.*

1. Choose Place from the File menu (or press Command-D/Ctrl-D). InDesign displays the Place dialog box.

2. Locate and select the text file you want to import. In OS 9 on the Macintosh, you can click the Show Preview button to view a preview of the file if you want—this will display the first few lines of the file in a preview window. Turning this option on can

make it take longer to browse through lists of files, as InDesign must create a preview for each file you select.

3. Set up the import options you want.

◆ **Convert Quotes.** Turn on the Convert Quotes option to convert any straight quotes (i.e., foot and inch marks) to proper typographic quotation marks and apostrophes.

◆ **Retain Format.** Turn on the Retain Format option to keep the formatting specified in the text file (if any).

What does "Retain Format" really mean? In general, InDesign imports any character or paragraph formatting attributes specified in the text file (this is mainly true for files from Microsoft Word or saved as RTF), but does not import any page layout information, such as headers and footers, or page margins. When the Retain Format option is off, InDesign strips the formatting out of the text file (including paragraph styles), and places the text using the current default formatting.

◆ **Show Import Options.** Turn on the Show Import Options checkbox to display another dialog box containing more import options for the specific type of file you're placing. This dialog box appears after you click the OK button to import the text file.

◆ **Replace Selected Item.** If you had a frame selected before you displayed the Place dialog box, InDesign makes the Replace Selected Item option available. Turn this option on to replace the contents of the frame (if any) with the text file. If you had text selected, or if you had clicked the Text tool in a text frame, turning the Replace Selected Item option on inserts the text from the file into the text frame.

**Note to PageMaker users:** If you've looked, in vain, for an option similar to the Read Tags option in PageMaker's Place Document dialog box, you can give up. InDesign cannot read paragraph style tags. Instead, you'll have to learn how to accomplish the same thing using InDesign's tagged text format (see that section, later in this chapter).

4. Click the Choose/Open Button. If you turned on the Show Import Options option, InDesign displays a dialog box containing options for the type of file you selected. Make any changes in this dialog box that you want, and then click the OK button.

5. If no frames were selected on your page, InDesign displays the Text Place cursor and waits for you to click on a frame or drag one out (for more on flowing text using the Text Place icon, see "Flowing Text," earlier in this chapter). If the incoming text file contains fonts that aren't currently loaded, InDesign warns you of their presence. If you had selected a frame before opening the Place dialog box, and you turned on the Replace Selected Item checkbox, InDesign fills the frame with the file you selected—even if it was a graphic frame with a picture in it! This can be very annoying if you had forgotten to deselect all frames first. Fortunately, you can always press Command-Z/Control-Z to undo the Place and reload the Text Place cursor.

**Show Options Shortcut:** Hold down Shift and double-click a text file in the Place dialog box. Or hold down Shift as you click the Choose/Open button. InDesign displays the Import Options dialog box for the type of file you're importing.

**Word and RTF Import**

In general, InDesign imports the text formatting in Word and RTF text files, and does not import any page layout ("page geometry") information saved in the file. This means, for example, that InDesign imports paragraph indents, but does not import page margins.

For a more complete list of the formatting imported by the Word and RTF import filters, see the Filters ReadMe file (you'll find it in your InDesign folder).

When you turn on the Show Import Options option and place a Word or RTF file, InDesign displays the corresponding Import Options dialog box (see Figure 3-34).

**FIGURE 3-34**
**Word/RTF**
**Import Options**

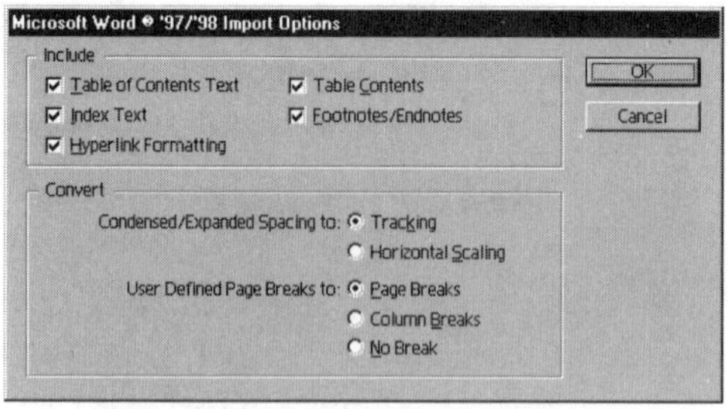

**Table of Contents Text.** Turn this option on to import the table of contents text (if any) in the Word file. However, the table of contents entries lose their special qualities. The page numbers appear as they were in the Word or RTF document the last time the file was saved, and do not change as you place the text on the pages of your InDesign publication. The table of contents also loses its navigational (i.e., hyperlink) properties. To InDesign, it's just text. InDesign's Table of Contents feature is not linked with this at all; if you're going to build a table of contents with the InDesign feature, you might as well leave this checkbox turned off.

**Index Text.** Turn this option on to import an index (or indices) you've inserted in the Word/RTF document. Note that individual index entries that you make in Word are imported whether this option is on or off; this only controls whether any built indexes get imported. We usually leave this turned off.

**Footnotes/Endnotes.** When you turn on this option, InDesign places any footnotes or endnotes at the end of the story. Leave this option off to omit any footnote or endnote text.

**User Defined Page Breaks.** What should InDesign do when it finds a page break setting? (In Word, you can set up automatic page breaks in the Line and Page Breaks tab of the Paragraph dialog box, or by pressing Shift-Enter.) We typically want InDesign to ignore these, so we choose No Break. However, if those breaks are there for a good reason, you can choose Page Breaks or Column Breaks to have InDesign automatically apply the page and column break settings (which is usually done manually using the Start Paragraph pop-up menu in the Keep Options dialog box). Manually entered section breaks (press Command-Enter/Ctrl-Enter in Word) are always ignored.

**Beware the Fast Save.** It's so seductive. It's hard to resist the natural impulse to turn on the Allow Fast Saves option in Word's Options dialog box (it's on by default; see Figure 3-35). It sounds like such a good idea. Faster saves mean you spend less time waiting for Word to save files—and saving time is good, right?

Not in this case, it isn't. The Word file format is very complicated, and using this option sometimes produces files that import filters can't read. Heck, when you turn this option on, Word sometimes writes files that *Word* can't read.

FIGURE 3-35
Word's Allow Fast
Saves Option

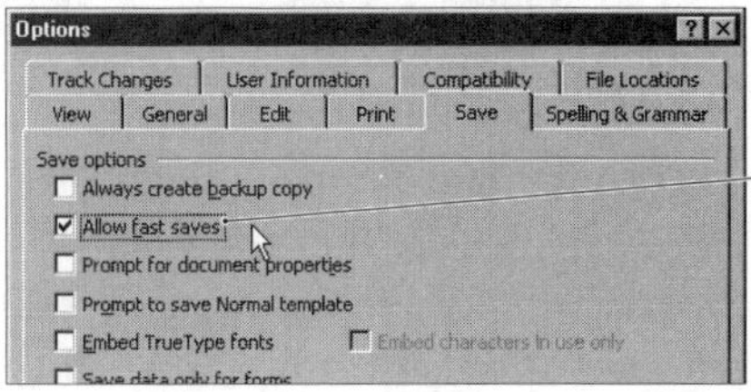

Turn it off!

And, if you're having trouble importing a Word file, open the file in Word (if you can) and save it under another file name—it's very likely the person who gave you the file had forgotten to turn off the Allow Fast Saves option.

**Text-Only Import Options**

Text-only files often arrive full of extra characters—usually spaces and carriage returns added to change the appearance of text on screen. Text prepared for online viewing, for example, often contains a carriage return at the end of each line, as well as carriage returns between paragraphs. The options in the Text Import Options dialog box give you a way to have the import filter do some of the clean-up for you (see Figure 3-36).

**FIGURE 3-36**
**Text Import Options**

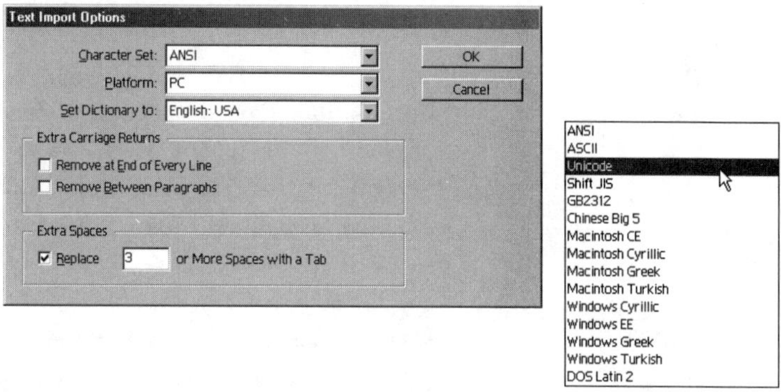

**Character Set.** If you're seeing odd characters in the text files you import, it might be that the character set of the computer used to create the files is not the same character set as the one in use by your copy of InDesign. As you import a text file, you can choose a character set that matches the character set of the text file.

**Platform.** Windows and the Macintosh use different character sets and also use different ways of ending a paragraph. If you're using Windows and know that the text file you're placing came from a Macintosh—or vice versa—choose the appropriate platform from this pop-up menu.

**Set Dictionary To.** Use this pop-up menu to apply a default spelling and hyphenation dictionary to the incoming text.

**Extra Carriage Returns.** The people who prepare the text files for you want to help. They really do. That's why they entered all of those carriage returns (to force a page break). Why they entered all of those spaces (to center the headline). They are trying to do some of the formatting so that you don't have to. The only trouble, of course, is that they usually make a mess that you're left to fix. InDesign's Text Import filter can solve many of the problems your helpful co-workers create. The options in the Extra Carriage Returns section of the Text Import Options dialog box help you clean up the extraneous carriage return characters.

**Extra Spaces.** Why do people enter extra spaces in text? Usually, they're trying to indicate to you, their trusted typesetter, that they want to enter some amount of horizontal space. In other words, a tab. InDesign can replace some number of spaces in the incoming text file with tabs—just enter a value for the number of contiguous space characters you want replaced. Note that this approach often enters multiple tab characters in the story, but that problem is easily cleaned up using Find and Change.

**Excel Import Options**    Use the options in the Excel Import Options dialog box to specify the range of cells you want to import and the formatting applied to those cells (see Figure 3-37). Note that Excel tables are automatically formatted as InDesign tables when you import them. If you want to import the data without InDesign making a table, you should save the file as Text (tab-delimited) from Excel. (See Chapter 6, "Where Text Meets Graphics," for more on Tables.)

FIGURE 3-37
**Excel Import Options**

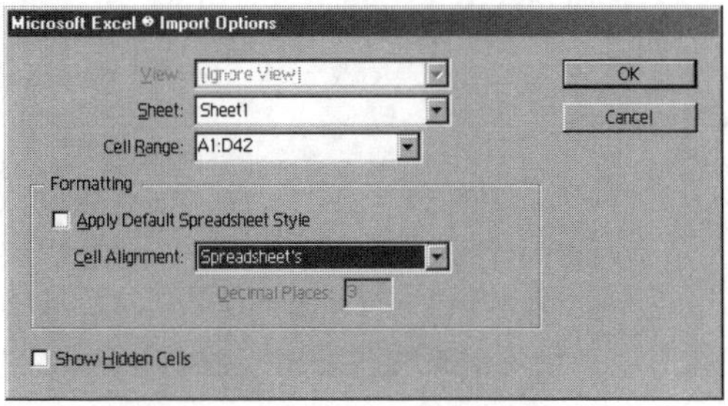

View, **Sheet**, and **Cell Range**. Use these options to define which custom view, worksheet, and range of cells you want to import. By default, the Cell Range field selects the filled cells of the worksheet you've selected.

**Apply Default Spreadsheet Style.** If you want to apply Excel's default formatting (the General settings in Excel's Format Cells dialog box) to the incoming text, turn this option on. However, if you do, you won't be able to use the Cell Alignment and Decimal Places options. We'd rather leave this turned off.

**Cell Alignment.** How do you want InDesign to align the text from the cells you're importing? The default setting is Spreadsheet's, which tells InDesign to copy the alignment from Excel. However, unless you have done a lot of formatting in your Excel spreadsheet that you want to keep, we recommend changing this to Left and then applying your alignment once the table is built in InDesign.

**Decimal Places.** If you choose the Decimal Cell Alignment, you can choose the number of decimal places you want to use in the imported spreadsheet cells. For example, a spreadsheet cell might be 3.1415926, but if you specify only three decimal places, only 3.142 shows up in the table (it rounds off to the nearest decimal digit).

**Show Hidden Cells.** Turn this option on to import any cells in the Excel file that have been formatted as hidden cells.

**Tagged Text Import Options**

InDesign's Tagged Text import filter, as we said earlier, gives you a great way to get formatted text from any application that can create a text-only file. You can use FileMaker Pro, vi on a UNIX workstation, or even the original Quark word processor for the Apple II (dongle-equipped, of course) to enter tags in a text file that specify InDesign formatting. For more on creating tagged text files, see "Working with InDesign Tagged Text," later in this chapter. When you import a tagged text file, you can set some import options (see Figure 3-38).

FIGURE 3-38
**Tagged Text Import Options**

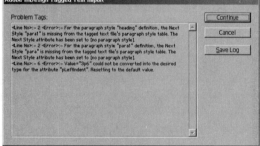

*Turn this option on...*

*...and InDesign will list any errors it finds in your tagged text file.*

**If Text Style Conflicts Use.** If the name of an incoming style (character or paragraph) matches a style that already exists in the publication, which style definition should InDesign use? Choose the

Publication Definition option to apply the formatting defined by your document (this is what we almost always use), or Tagged File Definition to import the style defined in the tagged text file. When you choose the latter method, InDesign adds the style to the publication and appends the word "copy" to the style's name. This does not affect the formatting of any text in the publication tagged with the original style.

**Show List of Problem Tags Before Place.** If you're not getting the formatting you expect from your tagged text files, turn this option on to have InDesign display a list of errors. If InDesign does find errors, you can choose to place the file, or to cancel the place operation. You can write the error list to a text file by clicking the Save Log button.

## Text Files and File Linking

When you import a text file, InDesign maintains a link to the text file itself, and adds the link to the Links palette (to display the Links palette, choose Links from the File menu, or press Command-Shift-D/ Ctrl-Shift-D). This is similar to what programs have done for many years with graphics. If you later edit the Microsoft Word document (or RTF file, or whatever), InDesign recognizes that it has changed and lets you update the file.

This sound cool, but watch out: Updating the file is the same as re-importing it, so you completely lose any edits or formatting you've applied in InDesign. Instead, we recommend embedding your text files (breaking the link to the disk file) immediately after importing them, by clicking the Update Link button in the Links palette. (For more on links, see Chapter 7, "Importing and Exporting.")

However, if you have a workflow in which you need to edit text in a word processor and have it update on your InDesign page, this text-linking feature can be a great help—as long as you never make edits or formatting changes in InDesign.

## Exporting Text

When you need to get your text back out of an InDesign publication and back into some other program—a text editor, word processor, or database—you can export the text in a variety of text formats. To export a story, follow these steps (see Figure 3-39).

**FIGURE 3-39**
**Exporting Text**

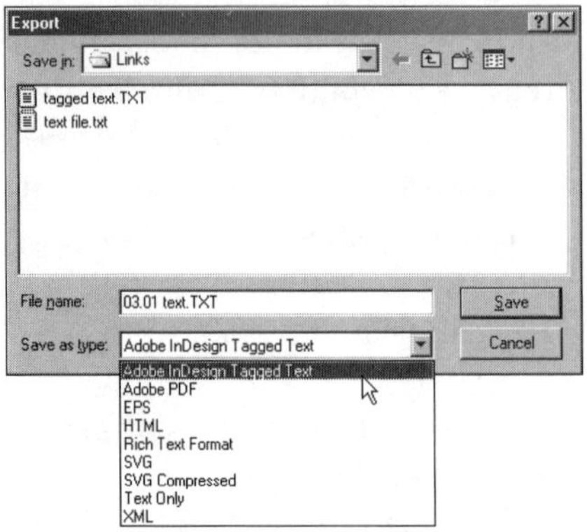

1.  Select the story you want to export (click the Text tool in the story) and choose Text from the Export submenu of the File menu (or press Command-E/Ctrl-E). InDesign displays the Export dialog box.

2.  Choose an export format for the text from the Format pop-up menu. Note that some of the items in this pop-up menu, like EPS or PDF, don't export your story; they export the whole page (or document). To export the text, choose Text Only (which will export the text without any formatting), Rich Text Format (RTF), or Adobe InDesign Tagged Text (which we'll discuss in "Working With InDesign Tagged Text," later in this chapter).

3.  Specify a name and location for the file.

4.  Click the Save button to export the story.

## Editing Text

Once you've entered or imported text, chances are good you're going to have to change it. InDesign includes most common word processing features, such as the ability to move the cursor through text using keyboard shortcuts, check the spelling of text, or find and change text and formatting. Unfortunately, InDesign doesn't yet have a Story Editor feature (which PageMaker users have come to know and love)—so all your text editing must be done right on the page itself.

**Moving the Cursor**
**Through Text**

When we're entering text, one of the last things we want to do is take our hands away from the keyboard. We don't want to have to use the mouse to move the text cursor or select text. That's why we like to use keyboard shortcuts to move the cursor and select text—they keep our hands where they belong: on the keyboard.

InDesign comes with a fairly complete set of keyboard shortcuts, as shown in Table 3-3. Note that some of the shortcuts have several keys associated with them—pick the combination that works best for you. You can always change the shortcuts by choosing Keyboard Shortcuts from the Edit menu. For example, David changed his so that they better matched those in QuarkXPress, which he has become used to.

Whatever keyboard shortcuts you use, remember that you can typically add Shift to them to select text as you move. For example, Command-End/Ctrl-End jumps to the end of a story, so adding Shift to that will select the text to the end of the story. Let's say you've got too much text in a text frame and it overflows, producing an overset mark. You could make the frame bigger or link the text to a new frame, but sometimes it's faster and more convenient to place the cursor after the last word in the text frame and press Command-Shift-End/Ctrl-Shift-End. This selects the overset text (even though you can't see it). Now you can delete it or cut it.

We like the shortcuts on the numeric keypad, even though it takes our right hand away from the "home row." To use the keypad shortcuts, turn Num Lock off.

Of course, if you do happen to have one hand on the mouse already, it's worth noting that various combinations of clicks can be used to select text. *Which* clicks, exactly depends on your preferences settings. Double-clicking always selects a word. If you've turned on

**TABLE 3-3**
**Moving the Cursor**
**Through Text**

*Hold down Shift as you press these shortcuts to select text as you move the cursor.*

| To move the cursor: | Press |
| --- | --- |
| Right one character | Right arrow, Keypad 6 |
| Left one character | Left arrow, Keypad 4 |
| Right one word | Command-Right arrow<br>Ctrl-Right arrow, Ctrl-Keypad 6 |
| Left one word | Command-Left arrow<br>Ctrl-Left arrow, Ctrl-Keypad-4 |
| Up one line | Up arrow, Keypad 8 |
| Down one line | Down arrow, Keypad 1 |
| Up one paragraph | Command-Down arrow<br>Ctrl-Down arrow, Ctrl-Keypad 8 |
| Down one paragraph | Command-Down arrow<br>Ctrl-Down arrow, Ctrl-Keypad 1 |
| End of line | End, Keypad 1 |
| Start of line | Home, Keypad 7 |
| Start of story | Command-Home/Ctrl-Home, Keypad 7 |
| End of story | Command-End/Ctrl-End, Keypad 1 |

the Triple Click to Select a Line option in the Text Preferences dialog box, triple-clicking selects a single line (not a sentence), and quadruple-clicking selects a whole paragraph; if that option is off, triple-clicking selects a paragraph and quadruple-clicking selects the entire story.

**Showing and Hiding "Invisibles"**    Sometimes, the best tools are the simple ones. When you're handed another person's file to clean up, choose Show Hidden Characters from the Type menu (or press Command-Option-I/Ctrl-Alt-I). InDesign displays the carriage returns, tabs, spaces, and other invisible characters in the text (see Figure 3-40).

FIGURE 3-40
**Showing Hidden Characters**

Space                          End of story

*TimeTravelTickets*#

I·Comici·Gelosi|                          ———— Carriage return

Em space ————   — 1568-1604 . »  Italy/France|

*virtu, fama ed honor ne f'er gelosi*|

Tab ————   The·most·famous·commedia·troupe·ever!⤶· ———— Line end

# Checking Spelling

Toward the end of a project, we fall prey to the delusion that everything, every last word, on all of our pages, is misspelled. We find ourselves staring blearily at relatively simple words. Is "dog" really spelled "D-O-G?" In our typical pre-deadline panic, we don't know. Everything looks wrong.

We don't know what we'd do without psychotherapy—and, of course, the spelling checkers in the page layout and word processing programs we use.

InDesign can check the spelling of any text in an InDesign text frame, and can also catch duplicated words ("the the") and possible capitalization errors. InDesign uses the language dictionary or dictionaries associated with your text to perform the spelling check.

To check spelling, follow these steps (see Figure 3-41).

1. Press Command-I/Ctrl-I (or choose Check Spelling from the Edit menu) to display the Check Spelling palette (note that this really is a palette, even though it looks like a dialog box—which means you can leave it open while editing text).

**FIGURE 3-41**

**Checking Spelling**

*InDesign scrolls to display any suspect words it finds while checking spelling.*

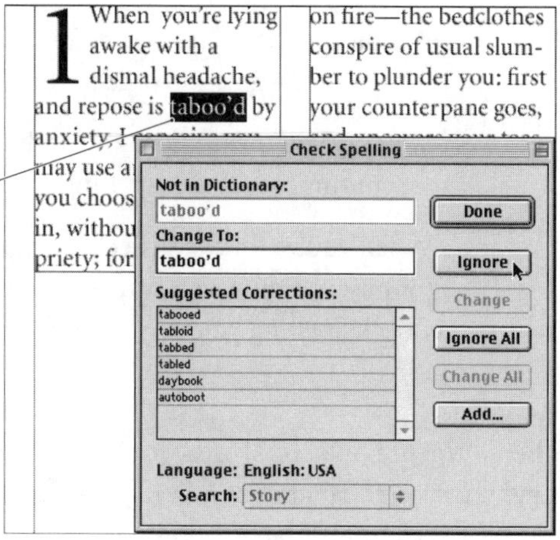

2. Define the scope of the spelling check using the Search pop-up menu at the bottom of the palette. Note that InDesign can check the spelling of all of the open publications, if you want, or you can restrict the spell check to the current story, or—if you have one or more words highlighted—even just to the selected words.

3. Click the Start button to start checking the spelling of text in the range you've chosen. When InDesign finds a potential misspelled word, the word appears in the Not in Dictionary field, and a number of possible corrections appear in the Suggested Corrections list. At this point, you can:

   ◆ Skip the word without making any change. To do this, click the Ignore button. InDesign continues with the spell check. To have InDesign ignore every occurrence of the word, click the Ignore All button.

   ◆ Replace the word with one of the suggestions. Select the suggestion, and InDesign enters the suggested word in the Change To field. Click the Change button to replace the selected word with the suggestion. Click the Change All button to replace every instance of the selected text with the text in the Change To field.

   ◆ Enter replacement text in the Change To field. Click the Change button to replace the selected word with the text you've entered, or click the Change All button to replace every instance of the selected text.

   ◆ Add the word to the user dictionary. This is a good thing to do with technical terms and names that appear frequently in your publications. For more on entering words in the dictionary, see "Adding Words to the User Dictionary," below.

After you've taken any of the above actions, InDesign continues with the spelling check.

4. When you've finished checking the spelling of the publication (or publications), you can click the Done button to close the Check Spelling palette.

**Adding Words to the User Dictionary**

We use lots of words in our publications that aren't found in InDesign's dictionary. Even quite common, household words such as "Kvern" and "Blatner" will provoke an angry query from the spelling checker. You can allay InDesign's fears by entering these words in a separate dictionary, the "user dictionary." When InDesign can't find a word in its dictionary, it consults the user dictionary before questioning the spelling of the word. If a word appears in both the standard dictionary (which can't be edited) and the user dictionary, InDesign favors the word in the user dictionary.

You can add a word to the user dictionary in two ways: from within the Check Spelling palette or from the Dictionary palette (see Figure 3-42). When you're checking your document's spelling and a "misspelled" word pops up, you can temporarily open the Dictionary palette by clicking the Add button. If you want to add or remove items from your user dictionary without first checking spelling (or without even having the word on your page), you can open the Dictionary palette by choosing Dictionary from the Edit menu.

1. Enter the word you want to add in the Word field of the Dictionary palette, if necessary (if you're in the middle of a spelling check, InDesign enters the word displayed in the Not in Dictionary field for you, though you can edit it if you want).

2. Click the Hyphenate button when you want to view the word's hyphenation points (for more on hyphenation, see Chapter 4, "Type"). InDesign displays the hyphenation points (or the proposed hyphenation points) in the word.

Hyphenation points are ranked—the best hyphenation point is indicated by a single tilde ("~"), the next best point is indicated by two tildes ("~~"), and, at the least good hyphenation points, you'll see three tildes ("~~~"). You can enter hyphenation points in words you're adding to the user dictionary, or change the hyphenation points of words already in the user dictionary.

FIGURE 3-42
**Adding a Word to the
User Dictionary**

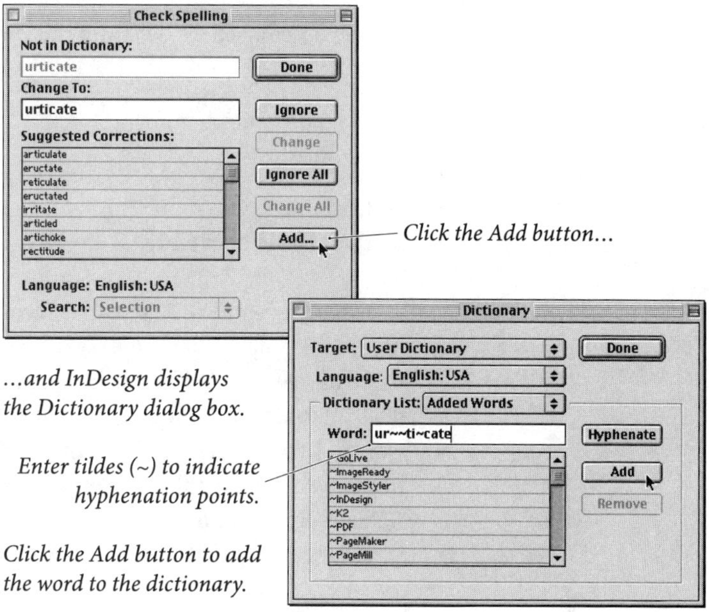

*Check Spelling*

Not in Dictionary:
urticate                                    Done

Change To:
urticate                                    Ignore

Suggested Corrections:
articulate                                  Change
eructate
reticulate                                  Ignore All
eructated
irritate                                    Change All
articled
artichoke                                   Add...
rectitude

— *Click the Add button...*

Language: English: USA
Search: Selection

*...and InDesign displays
the Dictionary dialog box.*

*Dictionary*

Target: User Dictionary                    Done
Language: English: USA
Dictionary List: Added Words

Word: ur~~ti~cate                          Hyphenate

*Enter tildes (~) to indicate
hyphenation points.*

~GoLive                                     Add
~ImageReady
~ImageStyler                                Remove
~InDesign
~K2
~PDF
~PageMaker
~PageMill

*Click the Add button to add
the word to the dictionary.*

If you do not want InDesign to hyphenate the word, enter a tilde before the first character of the word.

3.  Choose either the User Dictionary or your document's name from the Target pop-up menu. Generally, you'll want to add words to the user dictionary which can be used by all your documents. However, if you choose your current file, then the word will only appear spelled correctly in that document, and no others. This might come in handy if you're building an annual report for a medical company and you don't want to add "fluoxetine" to your general user dictionary.

4.  Click the Add button to add the word to the user dictionary.

**Removing Words From
the User Dictionary**

Obviously, once you add a word to your user dictionary you can remove it: Just choose Dictionary from the Edit menu, select the word you want to remove, and click the Remove button. But you can also tell InDesign to remove a word from the regular dictionary by adding it to the Removed Words list.

1.  Open the Dictionary palette and choose a Target. (If you choose User Dictionary, the change will affect all your documents; if you choose just the open document from the Target pop-up menu, the word is only removed from this document.)

2. Select Removed Words from the Dictionary List pop-up menu.

3. Type the word in the Word field (if you're in the middle of checking your document's spelling, it should show up here automatically).

4. Click the Add button. This *adds* the word to the list of words that should be *removed*.

Now, that word will appear as incorrect when you check its spelling. For example, sometimes when we want to type "Ctrl" we type "Control" instead. Since this is a word that we don't use a lot (what does this tell you about us?), it's easy to add it to our list of "removed" words. Then, when we check the spelling, we can quickly fix the places where we should have typed "Ctrl".

Later, if you want to take it off the "removed" list, you can open the Dictionary palette, select the word, and click Remove.

## Find and Change

Economists and productivity experts keep telling us that personal computers have not lived up to their promise of increased productivity. Workers, they say, are no more productive than they were before the microcomputer revolution.

They are, of course, wrong—or maybe they've never worked as typists or typesetters. Since the advent of word processing and desktop publishing software, we "text workers" have been enjoying a productivity increase that is nothing short of mind boggling. Although we're not sure "enjoying" is quite the right word.

One of the key innovations made possible by the text processing renaissance is the ability to find text in a document and, if necessary, to change it to something else—and all in an automated fashion. It doesn't matter what you call it—"find and change" or "search and replace," it's a kind of text-manipulation tool we didn't have in the "good ol' days."

Find and change is all about pattern recognition. Most of what we do in InDesign (or in life, for that matter) is repetitive. We work our way through text, selecting each occurrence of "f f i" and changing it to "ffi" (the ligature). Or we select each bullet character we've typed, and replace it with a character from Zapf Dingbats. In each case, we're searching for one pattern in our text and replacing it with another.

Finding and changing text is all about working with strings. A *string* is any range of text—a single character, a word, or a phrase. Strings can also contain special, nonprinting characters, such as tab characters, em spaces, or carriage returns.

There are at least four different ways to perform a search-and-replace mission.

◆ Search for a text string and replace it with a different text string.

◆ Search for formatting and replace that formatting with "other formatting.

◆ Search for a text string and apply formatting to it.

◆ Search for formatting, and replace it with a string.

**Finding Text**     If you need to find some text, follow these steps (see Figure 3-43).

1. Open the Find/Change palette (press Command-F/Ctrl-F).

2. Enter the string you want to find in the Find What field.

3. Choose one of the options on the Search pop-up menu to set the scope of the search: Story, To End of Story, Document, or All Documents. Story always begins the search from the beginning of the story, while To End of Story only searches from the current text cursor position onward. All Documents means every currently open document; this is helpful when you need to find something that may appear in multiple chapters of a book.

4. Turn on the Whole Word checkbox if you want to find only exact matches for the text you entered in the Find What field (if you've entered "dog" and want to find only that word, and not "dogged" or "underdog"). Turn on the Case Sensitive option to find only text with the same capitalization as the word you entered (this way, you'll find "dog," but not "Dog").

5. Click the Find Next button. InDesign finds an occurrence of the string you entered in the Find what field and displays it in the publication window, turning pages and scrolling to display the text, if necessary. You can continue clicking the Find Next button to find the next occurrence of the text in the specified search range until, eventually, you'll return to the first instance InDesign found.

**About metacharacters.** You can't enter invisible characters—such as tab characters, line-end characters, or carriage returns—in the

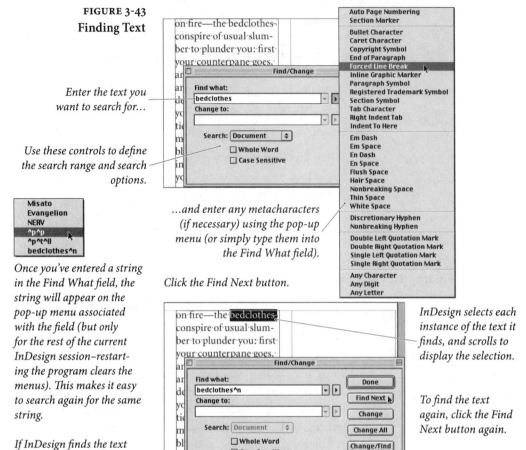

**FIGURE 3-43**
**Finding Text**

*Enter the text you want to search for...*

*Use these controls to define the search range and search options.*

*...and enter any metacharacters (if necessary) using the pop-up menu (or simply type them into the Find What field).*

*Click the Find Next button.*

*Once you've entered a string in the Find What field, the string will appear on the pop-up menu associated with the field (but only for the rest of the current InDesign session–restarting the program clears the menus). This makes it easy to search again for the same string.*

*If InDesign finds the text in overset text, the phrase "Overset Text" appears above the Find What field.*

*InDesign selects each instance of the text it finds, and scrolls to display the selection.*

*To find the text again, click the Find Next button again.*

Find What or Change To fields. To get around this, you enter codes—known as "metacharacters"—representing those characters. We've listed all those codes in Table 3-4, but if you don't have this book sitting next to your computer all the time InDesign makes the process of entering metacharacters easy—they're on the pop-up menus attached to the Find What and Change To fields.

To enter a metacharacter in the Find What or Change To fields, you can either enter it directly (if you know the code) or choose it from the pop-up menus associated with the fields.

**Wildcard Metacharacters**

Imagine that you need to find all of the part numbers in a publication. Your part numbers start with the string "IN" and are always followed by four letters, a dash, and four numbers. How can you find all of the strings?

| TABLE 3-4 | To search for this character: | Enter: |
|---|---|---|
| **Metacharacters** | Automatic page number | ^x |
| | Bullet | ^8 |
| | Caret | ^^ |
| | Copyright | ^2 |
| | Carriage return | ^p |
| | Line end | ^n |
| | Inline graphic | ^g |
| | Paragraph | ^7 |
| | Registered trademark | ^r |
| | Section | ^6 |
| | Tab | ^t |
| | Right indent tab | ^y |
| | Indent to here | ^i |
| | Em dash | ^_ |
| | Em space | ^m |
| | En dash | ^= |
| | En space | ^> |
| | Flush space | ^f |
| | Hair space | ^\| |
| | Nonbreaking space | ^s |
| | Thin space | ^< |
| | White space | ^w |
| | Discretionary hyphen | ^- |
| | Nonbreaking hyphen | ^~ |
| | Double left quotation mark | ^{ |
| | Double right quotation mark | ^} |
| | Single left quotation mark | ^[ |
| | Single right quotation mark | ^] |
| | Any character | ^? |
| | Any digit | ^9 |
| | Any letter | ^$ |

You can use InDesign's "wildcard" metacharacters—these give you a way to find patterns containing unspecified characters. To match any single, character, type "^?" in the Find What field. Enter "^9" to find any single digit, or "^$" to find any single letter.

To find all of the part numbers in the example, you'd enter "IN^$^$^$-^9^9^9^9" in the Find What field. Note that using wildcard metacharacters also helps you avoid finding the strings you don't want to find—if, in our example, we'd used the wildcard-laden string "IN^?^?^?^?^?^?^?^?^?" we'd run the risk of finding the word "INdubitable," which appears in our imaginary catalog many times, rather than the part numbers.

Be careful—entering these wildcard characters in the Change To field results in text being replaced by the metacharacter codes themselves, which is almost certainly *not* what you want. That's why the wildcards don't appear on the Change To field's pop-up menu.

**Replacing Text**    To replace one text string with another, you enter text in both the Find What and Change To fields of the Find/Change palette (see Figure 3-44). Once you've done this, you have two choices:

◆ You can choose to have InDesign replace all instances of the string in the Find What field with the string you entered in the Change To field throughout the search range by clicking the Change All button.

◆ You can find each occurrence of the string in the specified search range and decide to replace it or not. To do this, click the Find Next button, view the found text, and then click the Find Next, Change, or Change/Find button. The Find Next button moves on to the next instance of the string *without* making any changes; the Change button replaces the selected text with the contents of the Change To field, and waits to see what you'll do next. The Change/Find button replaces the string, then finds the next instance and waits.

Note that the Case Sensitive checkbox determines the case of characters it's replacing, too. However, when the Case Sensitive

FIGURE 3-44
**Replacing Text**

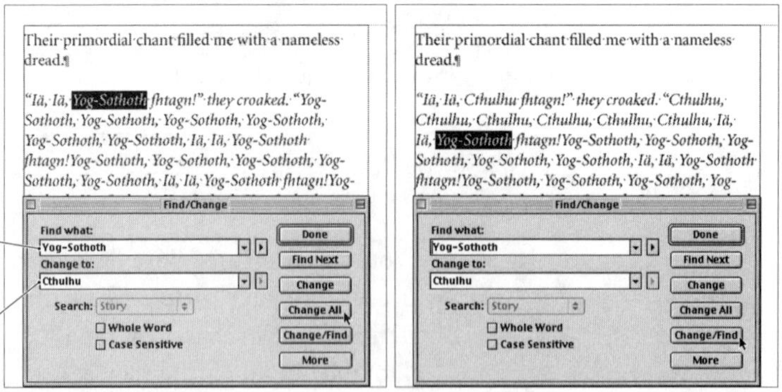

*Enter the text you want to find in the Find What field.*

*Enter the replacement text in the Change To field.*

*Click the Find Next button to find the first instance of the text.*

*Click the Change button to replace the selection with the text in the Change To field, or click the Change All button to change all occurrences of the text in the Find What field...*

*...or click the Change/Find button to make each change yourself.*

option is turned off, InDesign still pays attention to the capitalization of the word: If the word it finds is capitalized, then it will replace it with a capitalized word, even if the word you typed in the Change To field was in all lowercase.

**Finding and Changing Formatting Attributes**

What do you do when you want to find all of the occurrences of the word "Zucchini" formatted as 10-point Helvetica bold? And, for that matter, change the word's formatting to 12-point Adobe Caslon italic? It's easy—use the Find Format Settings and Change Format Settings controls at the bottom of the Find/Change dialog box (if you can't see these settings, it's because you need to expand your Find/Change dialog box—click the More Options button, and InDesign expands the dialog box to display these options).

To choose the formatting attributes you want to find, click the Format button in the Find Style Settings field. InDesign displays the Find Format Settings dialog box (see Figure 3-45). This dialog box is another of those multi-panel extravaganzas InDesign will no doubt be famous for. And, as in the other dialog boxes, the best way to get through it is to hold down Command/Ctrl as you press the up or down arrow key.

The eight panels of the Find Format Settings dialog box give you the ability to specify any formatting that can be applied to text in InDesign. Navigate through the panels until you find the formatting options you want, then use them to specify the formatting you want to find. When you're done, click the OK button to return to the Find/Change dialog box. InDesign displays a list of the options you've chosen in the field in the Find Format Settings section.

Note that when you first set up the Find Format Settings dialog box, all the pop-up menus and fields are blank. Let's say you select a format—such as 6 point text—and then change your mind; you can simply select the field and press Delete to make it blank again. This comes in handy when searching for fonts. If you select the font Palatino, the styles field automatically changes to "Roman," which means InDesign will *only* search for the roman characters and won't find italic or bold text in that font. However, if you delete "Roman" from that field, the program searches for all cases of Palatino, no matter what the style.

To set up the formatting options you want to apply to any text you find, click the Format button in the Change Format Settings field. This displays the Change Format Settings dialog box, which is identical in all but name to the Find Format Settings dialog box. Use the Change Format Settings dialog box to specify the formatting you want to apply, then return to the Find/Change dialog box. InDesign

FIGURE 3-45
**Find and Change Formatting Attributes**

*Click the More Options button (which then becomes the Fewer Options button) to display Find/Change formatting options.*

*The Find Format Settings and Change Format Settings dialog boxes contain the same set of panels and options.*

*Click the Format button to display the Find Format Settings dialog box.*

*Click the Format button to display the Change Format Settings dialog box.*

*Use the panels of the Find Format Settings dialog box to specify the formatting you want to find.*

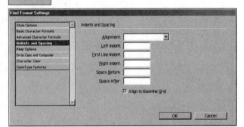

*Or use the Change Format Settings dialog box to set up the formatting you want to apply to any text you find.*

 *When you've specified formatting, InDesign displays an alert icon.*

displays the formatting you've chosen in the field in the Find Format Settings section.

When you've specified formatting in the Find Format Settings section, InDesign displays a yellow "alert" triangle above the Find What field. When you enter formatting in the Change Format Settings field, InDesign displays the yellow triangle above the Change To field.

To clear the formatting you've set in either the Find Format Settings or the Change Format Settings dialog boxes, click the Clear button in the corresponding section of the Find/Change dialog box.

Once you've specified the formatting you want to find and/or change, you can use the Find/Change dialog box in the same manner as you would when finding/changing text strings.

Note that when you have specified formatting in the Find Format Settings or Change Format Settings dialog boxes, you can:

◆ Leave the contents of the Find What and Change To fields empty. When you do this, InDesign searches for any instances of the formatting you've specified in the Find Format Settings dialog box, and replaces it with the formatting you've entered in the Change Format Settings dialog box.

◆ Enter text in both the Find What and Change To fields. In this case, InDesign searches for an instance of the string you entered in the Find What field that has the formatting specified in the Find Format Settings section, and replaces the text it finds with the string you entered in the Change To field. InDesign applies the formatting from the Change Format Settings section to the replacement text.

◆ Enter text in only the Find What field and leave the Change To field blank. When you do this, InDesign searches for the string you entered in the Find What field (and any formatting you've specified in the Find Format Settings section), and changes the formatting of the found text to the formatting specified in the Change Format Settings section (but won't change the text string itself).

◆ Enter text only in the Change To field and leave the Find What field blank. In this case, InDesign searches for the formatting you entered in the Find Format Settings area (InDesign won't start a search in which the Find What field is empty and no formatting is specified in the Find Format Settings section), and replaces any text it finds with the string you entered in the Change To field (plus any formatting you've specified in the

Change Format settings section). While you aren't very likely to use this find/change method (it's pretty obscure), it's nice to know it's available.

**Automating Run-in Headings**    If you've been in this business for a while, you've probably seen that bane of the desktop publisher's existence—a run-in heading. What's a run-in heading? It's a heading that starts a paragraph of body text. The text of the heading "runs into" the body text. You'll often see them used for paragraphs starting with "Note:" or "Warning:" or "Tip:" or the like (you'll even see them scattered through this book).

The trouble is, writers and editors usually want to keep the heading as a separate paragraph so that they can view it as a heading level in the outline mode of their word processing program (Microsoft Word, for example). It's only when the text reaches you for layout that it needs to be formatted using run-in headings.

Luckily, in InDesign, you can use the Find and Change feature to make this change. The technique we're about to show involves a two-step process—first, you find and format the text of the headings; next, you make the headings "run in" to the body text paragraphs after them. In the following example, the paragraph style applied to the run-in headings is called "heading 2," the paragraph style of the body text is "para1," and the character style we want to apply to the new run-in headings is "run-in heading" (see Figure 3-46). Of course, you can call your own paragraph styles whatever you want (see Chapter 4, "Type"). Ready?

1. Press Command-F/Ctrl-F to display the Find/Change palette.

2. Clear any formatting in the Find Format Settings or Change Format Settings sections (click the Clear button in each section), if necessary. Set the scope of the find/change operation by choosing one of the options on the Search pop-up menu.

3. Click the Format button in the Find Format Settings section. Select the Style Options panel in the Find Format Settings dialog box, if it's not already visible. Choose the name of the paragraph style containing the headings ("heading 2") from the Paragraph Style pop-up menu. Click the OK button to close the Find Format Settings dialog box.

4. Click the Format button in the Change Format settings section. Select the Style Options panel of the Change Format Settings dialog box and choose the character style you want to use for

**FIGURE 3-46**
**Formatting Run-in**
**Headings with**
**Find and Change**

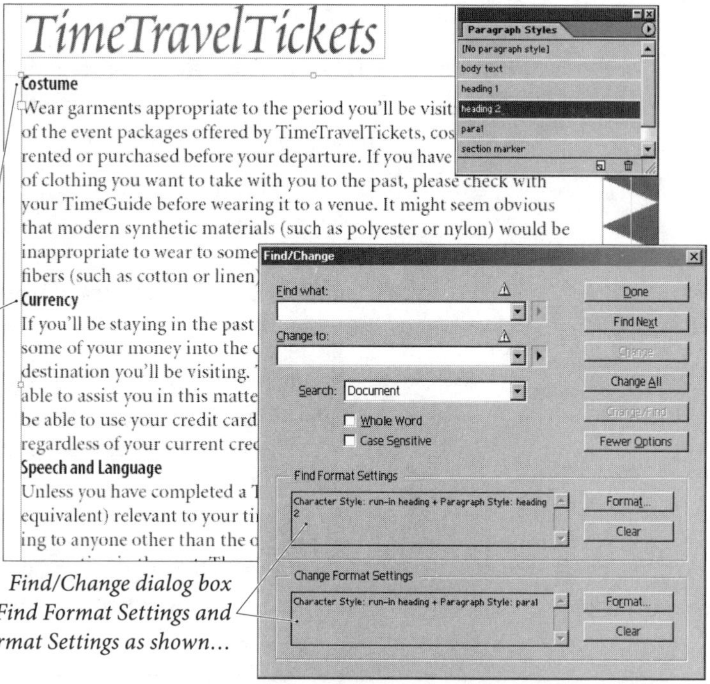

*This text contains heading paragraphs (in this example, they've been formatted using the paragraph style "heading 2"). To convert these paragraphs into run-in headings...*

# TimeTravelTickets

**Costume**
Wear garments appropriate to the period you'll be visit of the event packages offered by TimeTravelTickets, cos rented or purchased before your departure. If you have of clothing you want to take with you to the past, please check with your TimeGuide before wearing it to a venue. It might seem obvious that modern synthetic materials (such as polyester or nylon) would be inappropriate to wear to some fibers (such as cotton or linen

**Currency**
If you'll be staying in the past some of your money into the c destination you'll be visiting. able to assist you in this matte be able to use your credit card regardless of your current cre

**Speech and Language**
Unless you have completed a T equivalent) relevant to your ti ing to anyone other than the d

**Paragraph Styles**
[No paragraph style]
body text
heading 1
heading 2
para1
section marker

**Find/Change**

Find what: ⚠
Change to: ⚠
Search: Document
☐ Whole Word
☐ Case Sensitive

Find Format Settings
Character Style: run-in heading + Paragraph Style: heading 2

Change Format Settings
Character Style: run-in heading + Paragraph Style: para1

Done
Find Next
Change
Change All
Change/Find
Fewer Options

Format...
Clear

Format...
Clear

*...display the Find/Change dialog box set up the Find Format Settings and Change Format Settings as shown...*

*...and then click the Change All button. InDesign applies the character style to all of the characters in the heading paragraphs (and sets the paragraph style to that of the body text paragraph following the heading).*

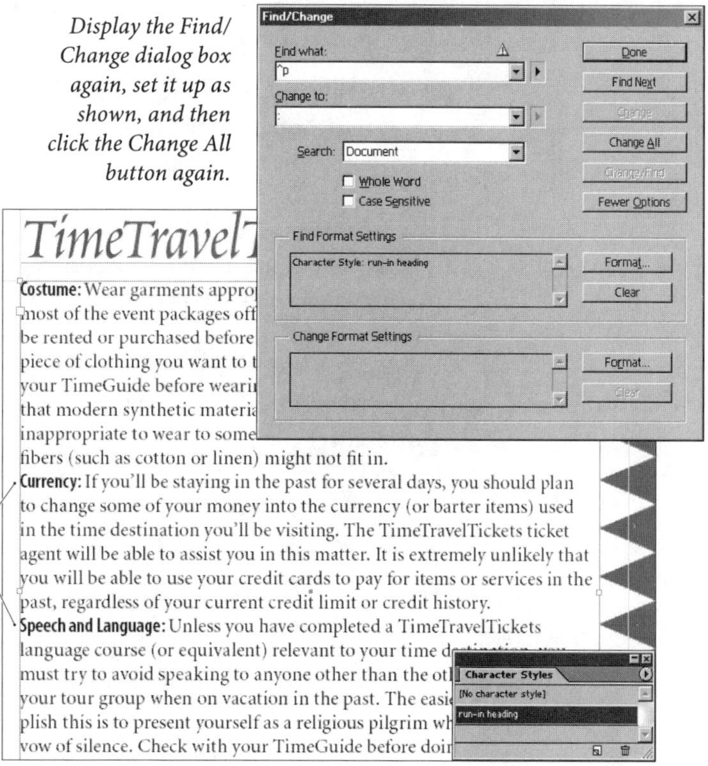

*The second search replaces all carriage returns formatted using the run-in heading character style—and replaces them with a separator character (a colon, in this example) followed by a space.*

*InDesign runs the headings into the text.*

*Display the Find/Change dialog box again, set it up as shown, and then click the Change All button again.*

**Find/Change**

Find what: ⚠
^p
Change to:
:
Search: Document
☐ Whole Word
☐ Case Sensitive

Find Format Settings
Character Style: run-in heading

Change Format Settings

Done
Find Next
Change
Change All
Change/Find
Fewer Options

Format...
Clear

Format...
Clear

# TimeTravelT

**Costume:** Wear garments appro most of the event packages off be rented or purchased before piece of clothing you want to t your TimeGuide before wearir that modern synthetic materia inappropriate to wear to some fibers (such as cotton or linen) might not fit in.
**Currency:** If you'll be staying in the past for several days, you should plan to change some of your money into the currency (or barter items) used in the time destination you'll be visiting. The TimeTravelTickets ticket agent will be able to assist you in this matter. It is extremely unlikely that you will be able to use your credit cards to pay for items or services in the past, regardless of your current credit limit or credit history.
**Speech and Language:** Unless you have completed a TimeTravelTickets language course (or equivalent) relevant to your time destination, you must try to avoid speaking to anyone other than the ot your tour group when on vacation in the past. The easie plish this is to present yourself as a religious pilgrim wh vow of silence. Check with your TimeGuide before doir

**Character Styles**
[No character style]
run-in heading

the run-in headings (in this case, "run-in heading"). Choose the paragraph style of the paragraph following the headings ("para1") from the Paragraph Style pop-up menu. Click the OK button to return to the Find/Change dialog box.

5. Because you are completely fearless (and because you know InDesign can undo this action if something goes terribly wrong), click the Change All button. InDesign applies the character style ("run-in heading") and paragraph style ("para1") to all of the headings. Don't close the Find/Change dialog box yet!

6. Now, enter a carriage return metacharacter ("^p") in the Find What field. Enter the separator (usually a period or colon, followed by a space) you want to use for the run-in heading in the Change To field.

7. Click the Clear buttons in both the Find Format Settings and Change Format Settings areas. Click the Format button in the Find Format Settings section. InDesign displays the Find Format Settings dialog box. Display the Style Options panel, if it's not already visible. Choose the character style you're using for the run-in heading ("run-in heading") from the Character style pop-up menu, then close the dialog box.

8. Click the Change All button. InDesign runs all of the headings into the paragraphs following them, creating run-in headings out of the heading paragraphs.

Does this sound like a lot of work? We can tell you from years of experience that it's much (much!) faster than doing all this by hand throughout a document. And it goes pretty fast once you've done it a few times.

**Goodbye, Paragraph!**  We frequently work with publications containing notes written to us by other people—you know, things like, "Ole, this section still needs work." We don't want to see that paragraph in the printed version of the piece (and we have, believe us!), so we tag these paragraphs with a paragraph style named "Comment."

When we're laying out the publication, we remove all of the paragraphs tagged with this style name. Do we hunt through the text, laboriously selecting each paragraph and pressing the Delete key? No way—we use an unexpected and probably unintended feature of InDesign's Find/Change dialog box. Here's the easy way to delete paragraphs tagged with a particular style (see Figure 3-47).

**Removing All
Paragraphs Tagged
with a Specific
Paragraph Style**

*This text contains
paragraphs tagged with the
style "editorial comment"—
they're left over from the
writing process. To remove
them all, display the
Find/Change dialog box...*

*...make sure that the Find
What and Change to fields
are empty...*

*...choose the style name from the Paragraph
Style pop-up menu in the Style Options panel
of the Find Format Settings dialog box...*

*...and click the Change All
button. InDesign removes all
paragraphs tagged with the
paragraph style you selected.*

1.  Press Command-F/Ctrl-F to display the Find/Change palette.

2.  Leave the Find What and Change To fields empty. Choose a
    search range from the Search pop-up menu to define the scope
    of the find/change operation.

3.  Click the Clear buttons in both the Find Format Settings and
    Change Format Settings areas, if necessary. Then, click the
    Format button in the Find Format Settings section to open the
    Find Format Settings dialog box.

4.  Select the Style Options panel, if it's not already visible. Choose
    the paragraph style you want to annihilate from the Paragraph
    Style pop-up menu, then close the Find Format Settings dialog
    box by pressing OK.

5.  Click the Change All button. InDesign deletes every paragraph tagged with the paragraph style from the search range.

There are hundreds of other cool (and often non-intuitive) uses for the Find/Change palette; let your imagination go wild!

## Working with InDesign Tagged Text

It's been pointed out to us that we live on another planet. This planet, everyone agrees, is one very much like Earth. In fact, almost everything is the same—right down to the existence of a desktop publishing program named "InDesign." At that point, however, things get different. Disturbingly, subtly different.

The most recent reason for the "Kvern and Blatner are alien weirdos" talk around our offices is that one of the features that excites us most about InDesign is rarely mentioned in the marketing materials. Or on the back of the box. It's not the typesetting features, nor it it the ability to place native Photoshop and Illustrator files. We think those are great features, but they're not it.

What is this mystery feature? It's the ability to save and read tagged text. To explain why this is so important, we've got to explain a little bit about what tags are.

**The Land That WYSIWYG Forgot**

Tags have been around for a long time. Before desktop publishing appeared, the world of typesetting was ruled by dedicated typesetting systems. As we set type on these machines, we didn't see anything that looked like the type we were setting. Instead, we saw the text of our newspapers, books, and magazines surrounded (and sometimes obscured) by cryptic symbols: typesetting tags and codes.

To see what these symbols meant, we had to print the file. Only then would we see our type with its formatting applied. (If you have ever messed around with HTML text, you have played with a kind of tagged text, where <B> means make the text bold, but you can't actually see the bold text until you open it in a Web browser.)

Then came the Macintosh, PageMaker, the LaserWriter, and WYSIWYG (What you See Is What You Get) publishing. This revolution made it easier for more people to set type—in part because it freed us from having to learn and use the obscure codes and tags of the dedicated typesetting systems. These days, modern desktop publishing programs are better typesetting systems than anything we had in the old days—and you can see what you're doing.

**Why Bother with Tags?** So why should you mess with tags in this day and age? It turns out that they can make some jobs easier, and sometimes they can make it possible to do things that wouldn't be practical to do using menus, dialog boxes, and the Character and Paragraph palettes.

The tagged text export filter takes formatted InDesign text and turns it into tags in a text file. The tagged text import filter reads tags—strings of text you've entered in the text file—and turns them into formatted ("WYSIWYG") text. There's a key point to make here: InDesign's tagged text export filter is the only text export filter that doesn't change the appearance of the text you're exporting.

Here are some of the reasons you might want to use tags:

◆ If you have employees using text editors (such as BBEdit on the Macintosh) instead of full-featured word processors, they cannot apply formatting such as bold or italic or paragraph styles. However these programs are small, fast, and can do lots of things word processors cannot. In short, we want to be able to take advantage of all of InDesign's text formatting features, but create and manage our text using a program that speaks nothing but ASCII (text only) format. You can do that with tagged text.

◆ Any application that can save files in text-only format can be used to create formatted text for use in InDesign. This means that your catalog clients can use FileMaker database to mark up their text—Visual Basic, Microsoft Excel, and Microsoft Access are other obvious choices. It might even help your old uncle who lives in a cave and uses nothing but EDLIN.

◆ You can store frequently used formatted text as tagged text files. It's far quicker to place a tagged text file than it is to open another InDesign publication and copy/paste the text you want. In addition, the tagged text file takes up far less disk space than an InDesign publication or InDesign library file.

**Getting Started with Tagged Text** To learn how tags work, the best thing you can do is to export some formatted text from InDesign (select the story, choose Export from the File menu, and change the Format pop-up menu to InDesign Tagged Text) and then use a text editor to look at the file (you can't, unfortunately, place a tagged text file in InDesign without converting the tags to formatting).

While it is possible to open these tagged text files in a word processor like Microsoft Word, those programs often assume that because there are tags in the file, it must be HTML (so you either get errors or things get really weird). That's why text editors (like

Windows Notepad or BBEdit) are better—they just deal with plain text and never try to format anything.

The "official word" on tagged text is the Tagged Text.pdf file, which you'll find inside the Adobe Technical Info folder on your InDesign installation CD. This guide includes basic instructions and a list of all of the tags you can use.

**What Tags Can Contain**

InDesign's tags can specify character formatting (such as font, point size, color, or baseline shift), paragraph formatting (such as indents, tabs, and paragraph space before and after), and styles (both paragraph styles and character styles). Everything that you can apply to text can be formatted with tags. In InDesign 2, even tables can be exported or imported as tagged text. (That means you can program your database to export fully formatted, ready-to-import InDesign tables.)

**Tag Structure**

InDesign tags are always surrounded by open (<) and close (>) angle brackets (which most of us also know as "greater than" and "less than" symbols). The first characters in a tagged text file must state the character encoding (ASCII, ANSI, UNICODE, BIG5, or SJIS), followed by the platform (MAC or WIN). So the typical Windows tagged text file begins with <ASCII-WIN>, and the Macintosh verison begins with <ASCII-MAC>. If InDesign doesn't see one of these tags at the start of the file, InDesign won't interpret the tags in the file, and all the tags show up as part of your text. Here are a few more details about tagging conventions.

◆ When you need to refer to a font, style, or color name inside a tag, you must surround the name with straight quotes—not typographic ("curly") quotation marks. For example:

```
<FONT "Zapf Dingbats">
```

◆ Any characters you enter outside a tag will appear as characters in the imported text.

◆ Enter an empty tag to return the formatting affected by the tag to its default state. For example:

```
Baseline <cBaselineShift:3>Shift<cBaselineShift:> text following
should be back to normal.
```

**Paragraph Style Tags**

If you're a long-time PageMaker user, you may have worked with PageMaker's style tags to apply paragraph formatting to text files. InDesign's tagged text format is different than PageMaker's, but you can create a "minimalist" tagged text file that's almost as easy to work with as PageMaker's paragraph style tags. Here's the header for an example tagged text file:

```
<ASCII-WIN>
<DefineParaStyle:heading><DefineParaStyle:para1><DefineParaStyle:para>
<ColorTable:=<Black:COLOR:CMYK:Process:0,0,0,1>>
```

Note that the paragraph style definitions in this tagged text file do not contain any formatting—our assumption is that you'll set up corresponding paragraph styles in your publication. Then all you need to do is paste the appropriate header at the top of a text file, and then enter the paragraph style tags for each paragraph. If, when preparing a file for import into PageMaker, you entered "<heading>" then enter "<ParaStyle:heading>" for InDesign.

Here's an example (very simple) text file marked up with Page-Maker paragraph tags:

```
<heading 1>TimeTravelTickets
<subhead>Travel through time to experience the greatest artistic per-
formances in history!
<para>We are pleased to announce our Summer, 2002 series.
```

Here's the same text, marked up with InDesign tags:

```
<ASCII-WIN>
<DefineParaStyle:heading><DefineParaStyle:subhead><DefineParaStyle:para>
<ColorTable:=<Black:COLOR:CMYK:Process:0,0,0,1>>
<ParaStyle:heading>TimeTravelTickets
<ParaStyle:subhead>Travel through time to experience the greatest
artistic performances in history!
<ParaStyle:para>We are pleased to announce our Summer, 2002 series.
```

A few things to note about converting PageMaker paragraph style tags to InDesign tagged text:

◆ For each paragraph style used in the file, you must include a (blank) paragraph style definition with exactly the same name in the InDesign tagged text file header.

◆ While PageMaker paragraph style tags don't require that you tag each paragraph, you should tag each paragraph in the InDesign version of the file.

◆ InDesign's tagged text import filter is very fragile, and will crash the program when it encounters a tag it doesn't understand. Always save your work before importing a tagged text file (yes, even a tagged text file exported from InDesign).

◆ This would be a great process to automate using a search and replace tool or a script.

**What About**
**XPresstags?**

InDesign 1.5 could import text files marked up using QuarkXPress' tagged text format, but InDesign 2 can't. While we decry this loss of capability (many publishing systems are built around XPressTags), we're happy to note that Late Night Software (already dear to our hearts for their excellent Script Debugger) has created XPressTags import and export filters for InDesign. The product is named "TagOn," and you can download a demo version from Late Night Software's web site (http://www.latenightsw.com).

# After Words

In academic circles, debate continues on whether we're born with the ability to understand language, or whether it's something we're taught. We don't know the answer, and, most of the time, we don't even know which side of the argument we're on. What we do know is that language is the most important technology humans have developed.

In this chapter, we've shown how to get words into InDesign, how to organize them in your publications, and how to get them out again. Next stop—typesetting with InDesign!

# Type

## CHAPTER 4

Ole's sordid tale: "Late night. The pale glow from the monochrome monitor of my Compugraphic phototypesetter. The smell of the office standard 'French Vanilla' coffee—warming, now, for several hours and resembling nothing so much as battery acid. The gentle snoring of one of the staff writers, who is curled up in the warmth of the unit that holds the spinning filmstrips containing the fonts I'm using to set his story.

"These are the things I think of when I hear the word 'typesetting'—they're memories from my job at Seattle's free rock and roll newspaper *The Rocket*, circa 1982. Desktop publishing didn't exist yet, and digital (as opposed to photo) typesetting systems—with their WYSIWYG displays—were rare. The code and characters I saw on my screen wouldn't look anything like type until they were printed, one character at a time, on a strip of photographic film and developed. I could set just about any kind of type using that machine, provided the characters would fit on a piece of film not more than seven inches wide, and provided I didn't need to use characters from more than six fonts."

When desktop publishing systems appeared, we found that they couldn't do everything Ole could do with his Compugraphic—but that being able to see what our type would look like *before we printed it* more than made up for any deficiencies in precision, automation, and flexibility. These days, page layout programs are far more capable than Ole's trusty EditWriter. Does that mean, however, that there's no more room for improvement? For surprising new features? Is typesetting "done?"

Not a chance—InDesign offers a number of improvements and surprises in the area of typesetting. It's an evolutionary product—not a revolutionary one, but, on its release, InDesign became the best desktop typesetting program, and raised the bar for its competition.

In this chapter, we'll walk through InDesign's typesetting features. We'll start with character formatting (font, point size, kerning, and baseline shift are examples of character formatting), move on to paragraph formatting (indents, tabs, space above and below, and composition), and then dive into formatting using character and paragraph styles. Along the way, there may be a joke or two.

## Selecting and Formatting Text

Generally, when you want to change the formatting of some text, you have to select it with the Text tool. However, there are two caveats to this. First, because paragraph formatting (which we'll discuss later) always applies to an entire paragraph, you don't have to select every character in the paragraph before applying it—you can simply place your text cursor anywhere in the paragraph.

Second (and more interesting) is that beginning in InDesign 2, you can apply text formatting to text frames you've selected using the Selection tool or the Direct Selection tool. When you do this, the InDesign applies the formatting to all of the text in the text frame, including any overset text. InDesign won't let you use this method to apply formatting to text frames that are linked to other text frames. Tired of using the Text tool to select and format every photo caption on a page? Use the Selection tool to select them all and apply your formatting—it's easier, and it's quicker (see Figure 4-1).

The ability to apply formatting with the Selection tools is very powerful, but it's also slightly dangerous. Let's say you set a single character to Zapf Dingbats somewhere in your text frame. If you select the text frame using the Selection tool and then apply a new font, every character—including that dingbat—gets changed.

The only warnings that InDesign gives you that some of the text in the selected text frame uses a different font are: the Font field in the Character palette is blank, and the Font submenu (under the Type menu) has hyphens next to each font.

**FIGURE 4-1**

**Formatting the Text in Text Frames**

*Use the Selection tool to select the text frames you want to format...*

*...and apply formatting. InDesign applies the formatting to all of the text in the text frames. That's all there is to it. In this example, we've changed character attributes (font, font style, and leading) and paragraph attributes (alignment).*

## Character Formatting

Character formatting is all about controlling the appearance of the individual letters characters in your publication. Font, type size, color, and leading are all aspects of character formatting. (Longtime QuarkXPress users won't think of leading as a character format, but we'll cover that below.)

We refer to all formatting that can be applied to a selected range of text as "character" formatting, and refer to formatting that InDesign applies at the paragraph level as "paragraph" formatting. Tab settings, indents, paragraph rules, space above, and space after are examples of paragraph formatting. There are areas of overlap in these definitions. Leading, for example, is really a property that applies to an entire *line* of text (InDesign uses only the largest leading value in a line to set the leading for that line), but we'll call it "character" formatting, nonetheless, because you can apply it to individual characters.

In addition to these distinctions, InDesign's paragraph styles can include character formatting, but apply to entire paragraphs. See "Styles," later in this chapter.

**Character Palette**    The key to character formatting in InDesign is—you guessed it—the Character palette (see Figure 4-2). To show the Character palette and shift the focus to the palette's Font field, press Command-T/Ctrl-T. If the palette is already visible when you use this keyboard shortcut, InDesign hides it; so you may need to press it twice.

FIGURE 4-2
Character Palette

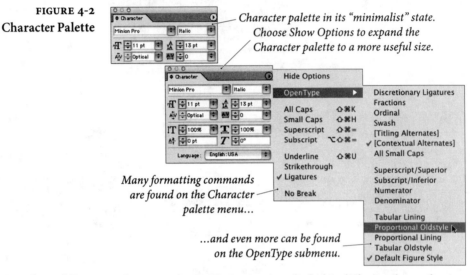

*Character palette in its "minimalist" state. Choose Show Options to expand the Character palette to a more useful size.*

*Many formatting commands are found on the Character palette menu...*

*...and even more can be found on the OpenType submenu.*

**Font Family and Font**    Selecting a font in InDesign is a little bit different than selecting a font in most other page layout programs. To InDesign, fonts are categorized as font "families," and each family is made up of one or more type styles. A font family is a set of typefaces designed to have a common "look." A "font," then, is specified by its font family and type style. In this book, we've used the font family Minion Pro, and the type style Regular for the body text—so the font of the body text is "Minion Pro Regular."

InDesign's user interface for selecting fonts mirrors this approach. When you choose a font from the Font submenu of the Type menu, you must select both the font family and a specific type style (that is, you can't simply select the font family).

Using the Character palette to select a font is a two-part process. First, you choose the name of a font family from the Font Family pop-up menu. Next, you specify a member of that family using the Type Style pop-up menu. Note that InDesign does not have "type styles" in the same way that other programs do—it makes no assumption that the selected font family has a "bold" or "italic" member, and will never *generate* a fake bold or italic version of a font. The names that appear on the Type Style pop-up menu are all taken from the fonts themselves—if you don't have a font for a particular type style, you won't see it listed in the Type Styles menu (see Figure 4-3).

## FIGURE 4-3
### Selecting a Font

*Select a font family...*

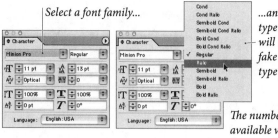

*...and then select a type style. InDesign will not generate fake bold or italic type styles.*

*Sometimes, when you change to a symbol font (such as Zapf Dingbats), you may encounter font subtitution (the dreaded pink highlight). This happens because InDesign is attempting to map the character from one font to another. To avoid this problem, hold down Shift as you apply the font.*

*The number of type styles available varies from family to family.*

To select a font family or type style in the Character palette, you can type into the appropriate field—you don't have to use the menu. As you type the name of a font family or type style, InDesign will display the available font or fonts that match the characters you typed. For instance you can type "T" and it will guess "Tekton" (if you have that font installed); if you meant "Times" then you may have to type "Ti" or even "Tim". Note that you can also press the up and down arrow keys, which is especially helpful in the Style field to move from Regular to Bold to Italic, and so on.

**Font Style Keyboard Shortcuts.** Although InDesign won't generate a bold or italic weight, you can type Command-Shift-B/Ctrl-Shift-B to make your text bold and Command-Shift-I/Ctrl-Shift-I to make it italic. If a font doesn't have a bold or italic version, InDesign will not change the text.

**Size** You can change the size of text by entering the point size you want in the Size field of the Character palette, or choose a point size from the attached pop-up menu (see Figure 4-4). If you type the size, you can specify it in .001-point increments. After you've entered the size you want, apply the change by pressing Enter or by pressing Tab to move to another field.

## FIGURE 4-4
### Point Size

*Click the "nudge" buttons, or...*

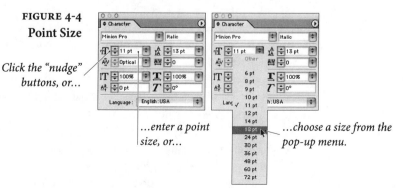

*...enter a point size, or...*

*...choose a size from the pop-up menu.*

**Size Adjustment Keyboard Shortcuts.** You can increase the size of selected type by pressing Command-Shift->/Ctrl-Shift->, or decrease the size by pressing Command-Shift-</Ctrl-Shift-<. The amount that InDesign increases or decreases the point size when you use these shortcuts depends on the value in the Size/Leading field in the Units and Increments Preferences dialog box.

To increase or decrease the size of the selected text by five times the value entered in the Size/Leading field, you can add the Option or Alt key: Command-Option-Shift->/Ctrl-Alt-Shift->, or Command-Option-Shift-</Ctrl-Alt-Shift-<.

**Leading**

Text characters—usually—sit on an imaginary line, which we call the baseline. Leading (pronounced "ledding") is the vertical distance from the baseline of one line of text to the next text baseline. When you hear "10 on 12" or see "10/12", it means "10-point text on 12-point leading." In InDesign, leading is measured from the baseline of the current line of text to the baseline of the line of text above (see Figure 4-5). When you increase the leading in a line of text, you push that line farther from the line above it, and farther down from the top of the text block.

*You set the leading of selected characters using the Leading control—enter a value, click the arrows, or choose a value from the pop-up menu. You can also choose Auto from the pop-up menu to base the leading on the point size of the text.*

In InDesign—as in PageMaker or FreeHand—leading is an attribute of individual characters, but the largest leading value in a line predominates (see Figure 4-6). This differs from QuarkXPress, where leading is a paragraph attribute (although if you use QuarkXPress's relative leading mode, the largest leading in a line predominates).

For those of us who came to desktop publishing from typesetting, the idea of leading being a character attribute seems more natural than QuarkXPress' method of setting it at the paragraph level. Fortunately, InDesign lets you have it both ways: When you turn on the Apply Leading to Entire Paragraphs option in the Text tab of the Preferences dialog box, the program automatically sets the leading of every character in a paragraph to the same value. Most QuarkXPress users will find it more comfortable to turn this on.

FIGURE 4-6
The Largest Leading
in a Line Wins

KING PARAMOUNT:
To a monarch who has been

accustomed to the free use of his
limbs, the costume of a British
Field Marshal is, at first, a little
cramping. Are you sure it's all
right? It's not a practical joke, is
it?

*This word has a larger
leading value than the other
characters in the line.*

KING PARAMOUNT:
To a monarch who has been
accustomed to the uncontrolled

use of his limbs, the costume
of a British Field Marshal is, at
first, a little cramping. Are you
sure it's all right? It's not a practical joke, is it?

*When the word moves to another
line (due, in this example, to a
change in the text), the larger
leading is applied to that line.*

However, this preference only affects paragraphs that you change *after* you set it. For instance, you could have it on most of the time, then turn it off in order to vary the leading of lines within a paragraph—something you sometimes have to do to optically balance display copy—and then turn the preference back on again.

**How to Avoid
Wacky Leading**   The disadvantage of making leading a character attribute (when "Apply Leading to Entire Paragraphs" is turned off) is that it requires a bit more vigilance on your part than the "leading-as-a-paragraph-attribute" approach taken by QuarkXPress and most word processors. Most of the time, leading values should be the same for all of the characters in the paragraph. If, as you apply leading amounts, you fail to select all of the characters in a paragraph, you'll get leading that varies from line to line—which, most of the time, is a typesetting mistake.

You can also get this effect if you leave your paragraph's leading set to the default Auto leading, which always sets the leading to some percentage (usually 120%)of the text size—or, more specifically, some percentage of the largest character on a line. This is true even when Apply to Entire Paragraph is turned on. We strongly urge you not to use Auto leading. Ever.

If you've seen paragraphs where the leading of the last line of the paragraph is clearly different from that of the lines above it, you know exactly what we're talking about (see Figure 4-7). Why does this happen?

It's simple—the carriage return, that sneaky invisible character, can have a different leading value that the other lines in the paragraph. When the person formatting the text selected the paragraph, they failed to select the carriage return. You can avoid this by triple-clicking (or quadruple, if you've turned on the Triple Click to Select a

FIGURE 4-7
**That Crazy
Carriage Return**

*In this example, the carriage
return character carries an
Auto leading value and point
size left over from previous
paragraph formatting (the
leading of the rest of the text
in the paragraph is
13 points).*

*To avoid this problem, triple-
click to select the entire
paragraph before applying
character formatting—this
selects the carriage return
character.*

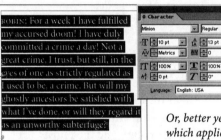

*The large leading value applied
to the carriage return distorts the
leading of the last line of text.*

*Or, better yet, apply a paragraph style,
which applies the same leading to all
characters in the paragraph.*

Line option in the Text Preferences dialog box) a paragraph to select
it, rather than dragging the text cursor through the text. Or you can
apply a paragraph style—when you apply a paragraph style, InDesign
applies the character formatting specified in the style—including
leading—to every character in the paragraph.

**Leading Shortcuts**  You can decrease the leading of selected type by pressing Option-Up
arrow/Alt-Up arrow or increase the size by pressing Option-Down
arrow/Alt-Down arrow (yes, this does seem counter-intuitive). The
amount that InDesign increases or decreases the leading depends
on the value you entered in the Size/Leading field in the Units and
Increments Preferences dialog box (see Chapter 1, "Basics").

To increase the leading of the selected text by five times the value
in the Size/Leading field, press Command-Option-Up arrow/Ctrl-
Alt-Up arrow. To decrease the leading by the same amount, press
Command-Option-Down arrow/Ctrl-Alt-Down arrow.

**Leading Techniques.** Here are a few tips and tricks for adjusting
your leading.

◆ Increase leading as you increase line length (the column width).
 Solid leading (12 point text on 12 points leading, for example)
 produces almost unreadable text for all but the narrowest of
 lines.

◆ Use extra leading for sans serif or bold type.

◆ Fonts with a small x-height (the height of the lowercase "x" in relation to the height of the capital letters) can often use a smaller leading value than those with a large x-height.

◆ Decrease leading as point size increases. Large display or headline type needs less leading than body copy. You can often get by with solid leading or less—just make certain that the descenders of one line don't bump into the ascenders of the line below.

**Kerning**

The goal of kerning—the adjustment of the space between characters—is to achieve even spacing. InDesign offers both pair kerning (the adjustment of the space between adjacent characters) and tracking (or "range kerning")—the adjustment of all of the inter-character spaces in a series of characters.

For each space between any pair of characters in a publication, InDesign applies the total of the pair kerning and tracking values (so if you set kerning to 50 and tracking to –50, you will not see any change in the composition of the text).

InDesign adjusts kerning using units equal to one-thousandth of an em. An *em* is equal in width to the size of the type—for instance, in 18 point text, an em is 18 points wide, and so each unit in the kerning or tracking fields equals 18/1000 point (about .00025 inch). You can enter values from –1000 (minus one em) to 10000 (plus 10 ems) in the Kerning and Tracking fields of the Character palette.

**Manual Kerning**

To adjust the spacing between a pair of characters, move the text insertion point between the characters and apply manual kerning (see Figure 4-8). You can apply kerning using any of the following techniques.

◆ Enter a value in the Kerning field of the Character palette. If the kerning field already contains a value entered by one of the automatic kerning methods (see below), you can replace the value by typing over it, or add to or subtract from it (by typing a "+" or "-" between the value and the amount you want to add or subtract).

◆ Click the arrow buttons attached to the Kerning field in the Character palette. Click the up arrow button to increase the kerning amount by the value you entered in the Kerning field in the Units and Increments Preferences dialog box, or click the down arrow button to decrease kerning by the same amount.

◆ Press a keyboard shortcut (see Table 4-1).

FIGURE 4-8
Kerning Text

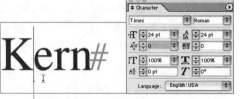

*Click the Text tool between the characters you want to kern.*

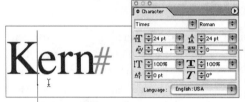

*Enter a value in the Kerning field, or choose a value from the associated pop-up menu, or click the arrows, or press a kerning keyboard shortcut.*

*InDesign adjusts the spacing between the characters.*

TABLE 4-1
Kerning Keyboard
Shortcuts

| To change kerning by: | Press: |
| --- | --- |
| +20/1000 em* | Option-Right arrow/ Alt-Right arrow |
| -20/1000 em* | Option-Left arrow/Alt-Left arrow |
| +100/1000 em** | Command-Option-Right arrow/ Ctrl-Alt-Right arrow |
| -100/1000 em** | Command-Option-Left arrow/ Ctrl-Alt-Left arrow |
| Reset Kerning | Command-Option-Q/ Ctrl-Alt-Q |

\* This is the default value in the Kerning field of the Units & Increments Preferences dialog box.

\*\* Or five times the default kerning amount.

To remove all kerning and tracking from the selected text, press Command-Shift-Q/Ctrl-Shift-Q (this sets tracking to zero and sets the kerning method to Metrics).

You can't apply pair kerning when you have a range of text selected—if you try, InDesign displays an error message. When you want to apply a kerning value to a range of text, use Tracking.

**Automatic Kerning**   InDesign offers two automatic kerning methods: pair kerning based on kerning pairs found in the font itself (choose Metrics from the Kerning pop-up menu), and kerning based on the outlines of the characters (choose Optical). What's the difference between the two methods (see Figure 4-9)?

**FIGURE 4-9**
**Automatic**
**Kerning Methods**

*Choose Optical or Metrics
from the Kerning pop-up
menu.*

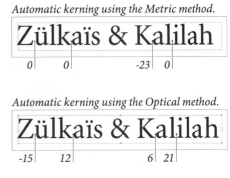

*Automatic kerning using the Metric method.*

Zülkaïs & Kalilah

0    0    -23   0

*Automatic kerning using the Optical method.*

Zülkaïs & Kalilah

-15   12    6   21

◆ **Metrics.** When you turn on the Metrics automatic kerning method, InDesign reads the kerning pairs built into the font by the font's designer (or publisher). These kerning pairs cover—or attempt to cover—the most common letter combinations (in English, anyway), and there are usually about 128 pairs defined in a typical font.

You'd think that using the kerning pairs defined in the font would be the perfect way to apply automatic kerning to your text. Who, after all, knows the spacing peculiarities of a given font better than its designer? Would that this were true! In reality, very few fonts contain well-thought-out kerning pairs (often, pair kerning tables are simply *copied* from one font to another), and the number of kerning pairs defined per font is inadequate (a really well-kerned font might contain one or two *thousand* kerning pairs, tweaked specifically for the characters in that typeface).

We really need a better method—a method that can adjust the spacing between *every* character pair, while taking into account the peculiarities of the character shapes for a particular font. We also need a kerning method that can automatically adjust the spacing between characters of different fonts. With InDesign's Optical kerning method, we get both.

◆ **Optical.** What's new and different about kerning text in InDesign is the Optical kerning method, which considers the composed shapes of the characters and applies kerning to even out spacing differences between characters.

If you've ever worked with PageMaker's Expert Kerning dialog box, you'll understand the basic technology behind Optical Kerning, but you'll be surprised by the speed with which InDesign automatically kerns your type.

In general, the kerning applied by InDesign when you use the Optical kerning method looks looser than that applied by the Metrics kerning method. That's okay—once you've accomplished even spacing, you can always track the text to tighten or loosen its overall appearance. Because tracking applies the same kerning value to all of the text in the selection, in addition to any pair kerning, the even spacing applied by the Optical kerning method is maintained.

**Viewing Automatic Kerning Amounts.** As you move your cursor through the text, you'll be able to see the kerning values applied to the text in the Kerning field of the Character palette. Kerning values specified by Optical kerning or Metrics kerning are displayed surrounded by parentheses; manual kerning values you've entered are not (see Figure 4-10).

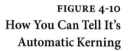 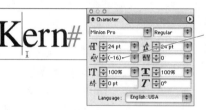

*InDesign displays automatic kerning amounts in parentheses.*

**Changing Word Spacing.** It's not entirely true that you can't apply kerning when more than one character is selected. You can select a range of text and select Metrics, Optical, or 0 (zero) from the pop-up menu next to the Kerning field in the Character palette.

If you want to increase the spacing between words but don't want to change the letterspacing of a range of text, press Command-Option-\ or Ctrl-Alt-\ (backslash) to add the base kerning increment (as defined by the value in the Kerning field in the Units & Increments Preferences dialog box) after each space character in the range. Hold down Shift as you press this shortcut, InDesign adds kerning by five times the base kerning amount. To decrease word spacing, press Command-Option-Delete/Ctrl-Alt-Backspace (add Shift to the shortcuts to multiply the effect by five).

This keystroke works simply by changing the kerning after each space character. You can always go back and change the kerning, or use Find/Change to remove it.

**Tracking**    Tracking, in InDesign, applies the same kerning value to every character in a selected range of text (see Figure 4-11). When you change the tracking of some text, InDesign applies the tracking in addition to any kerning values applied to the text (regardless of the method—

FIGURE 4-11
Tracking

Select a range of text.

Enter a new value in the Tracking field.

InDesign changes the spacing of the selected text.

manual or automatic—used to enter the pair kerning). Note that this is the same as the definition of tracking used by QuarkXPress, and is different from the definition used by PageMaker. In PageMaker, tracking also applies kerning, but the amount of kerning applied varies depending on the point size of the selected text and the tracking table in use. In PageMaker, InDesign's tracking would be called "range kerning."

Just as you cannot apply kerning using the Kerning field when you have multiple characters selected, you can't change the Tracking field when the text insertion point is between two characters—you have to have one or more characters selected. (Actually, you *can* change it, but it doesn't do anything.)

Note that the default keyboard shortcuts for tracking are exactly the same as those for kerning; which one you get depends on whether or not you have a range of text selected.

**Tracking Tips.** The following are a few of our favorite tracking tips.

◆ If you're setting text in all capitals or the small caps style, add 20 or 50 units of tracking to the text. Do not add tracking to the last character of the last word in the text, as that will affect the amount of space after the word, too.

◆ Printing white text on a black background often requires a little extra tracking, too. That's because the negative (black) space makes the white characters seem closer together.

◆ Larger type needs to be tracked more tightly (with negative tracking values). Often, the larger the tighter, though there are aesthetic limits to this rule. Advertising headline copy will often be tracked until the characters just "kiss."

♦ A condensed typeface (such as Futura Condensed) can usually do with a little tighter tracking. Sometimes we'll apply a setting as small as -10 to a text block to make it hold together better.

♦ When you're setting justified text and you get bad line breaks, or if you have an extra word by itself at the end of a paragraph, you can track the whole paragraph plus or minus one or two units without it being too apparent. Sometimes that's just enough to fix these problems.

**Horizontal and Vertical Scaling**    Enter a value in the Horizontal Scaling or Vertical Scaling fields (or both) to change the size of the selected text (see Figure 4-12). When the values you enter in these fields are not equal, you're creating fake "expanded" or "condensed" type. We say "fake" because true expanded or condensed characters must be drawn by a type designer—when you simply scale the type, the thick and thin strokes of the characters become distorted.

Note that entering values in these fields does not affect the point size of the type.

**FIGURE 4-12**
**Squashing and Stretching Type**

*Select some text.*

*Enter a scaling value in the Horizontal Scaling field (and/or Vertical Scaling field).*

*InDesign squashes and stretches the characters of the selected text.*

**Baseline Shift**    Sometimes, you need to raise the baseline of a character or characters above the baseline of the surrounding text (or lower it below the baseline). In pre-DTP typesetting, we would accomplish this by decreasing or increasing the leading applied to the character. However, that won't work in modern programs—remember, in InDesign the largest leading in the line predominates. Instead, you use the Baseline Shift field in the Character palette (see Figure 4-13).

Enter an amount in the Baseline shift field to shift the baseline of the selected text by that amount. As you'd guess, positive values

**FIGURE 4-13**
**Baseline Shift**

*Select the character or characters you want to shift...*

*...then enter a baseline shift distance in the Baseline Shift field (positive values move the baseline up; negative values move it down).*

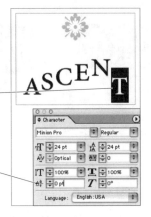

*InDesign shifts the baseline of the selected character or characters.*

move the selected text up from the baseline; negative values move the selected text down from the baseline.

While it's tempting to use Baseline Shift to adjust numbers in formulas, registered trademark symbols, and so on, it's better to use the Superscript or Subscript features for these things (see "Superscript and Subscript," later in this section).

**Baseline Shift Keyboard Shortcuts.** You can apply baseline shift using your keyboard. To do this, select some text and press Option-Shift-Up Arrow/Alt-Shift-Up Arrow to move the baseline of the text up two points—or whatever value you've entered in the Baseline Shift field of the Units and Increments Preferences dialog box, or Option-Shift-Down Arrow/Alt-Shift-Down Arrow to shift the baseline down by the same distance.

To shift the baseline of the selected text *up* by a distance equal to five times the value you entered in the Units & Increments Preferences dialog box, press Command-Option-Shift-Up Arrow/Ctrl-Alt-Shift-Up Arrow. To shift the baseline down by the same amount, press Command-Shift-Down Arrow/Ctrl-Alt-Shift-Down Arrow.

**Skewing**    When you apply skewing to a range of characters in an InDesign text frame, InDesign slants the vertical axis of the type by the angle you enter here (see Figure 4-14). You can enter from -85 degrees to 85 degrees. Positive skew values slant the type to the right; negative values slant it to the left.

This might be useful as a special text effect, but you shouldn't count on it to provide an "italic" version of a font family that lacks a true italic type style. Why? Because there's more to an italic font than simple slanting of the characters (see Figure 4-15).

FIGURE 4-14
**Skewing Text**

*Select some text.*

*Enter a value
in the Skew field.*

*InDesign skews the characters
of the selected text.*

FIGURE 4-15
**Real and Fake
Italic Characters**

*AaBbCcDdEeFf*

Real: Minion Italic

*Note the differences in
character shapes.*

*AaBbCcDdEeFf*

Fake: Minion Regular
with -10 degree skewing.

**Language**    The language you choose for a range of text determines the dictionary InDesign uses to hyphenate and check the spelling of the text (see
Figure 4-16). Because language is a character-level attribute, you can
apply a specific language to individual words—which means you can
tell InDesign to stop flagging "frisson" or "gemütlichkeit" as misspelled words, if you want. The only languages that show up in the
Language pop-up menu in the Character palette are those for which
you have a dictionary installed. If the language you're looking for
isn't in this list, then you can use the InDesign installer to install that
dictionary for you.

FIGURE 4-16
**Assigning a Language**

*Select a word or phrase, then
select a language from the
Language pop-up menu.*

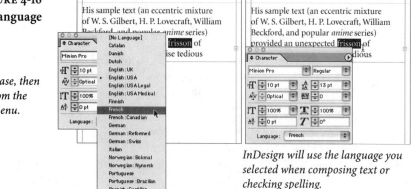

*InDesign will use the language you
selected when composing text or
checking spelling.*

**Case Options**

You can change the case of selected characters to All Caps or Small Caps by choosing All Caps or Small Caps from the Character palette menu (see Figure 4-17 and Figure 4-18). Note that InDesign does not replace the characters themselves, it simply changes they way they look and print. To InDesign's spelling checker or Find and Change features, the text is exactly as it was entered—not the way it appears on your screen.

When you choose Small Caps from the Character palette menu (or press Command-Shift-K/Ctrl-Shift-K), InDesign examines the font used to format the selected text. If the font is an OpenType font, and if the font contains a set of true small caps characters, InDesign uses true small caps. InDesign is also smart enough to do this if you have a non-OpenType font that has an "Expert" version. If the font is not an OpenType font, doesn't have an Expert font available, or doesn't contain small caps characters, InDesign scales regular uppercase characters down to 70 percent (or whatever value you entered in the Small Cap field of the Text Preferences dialog box—see Chapter 1, "Basics").

FIGURE 4-17
All Caps

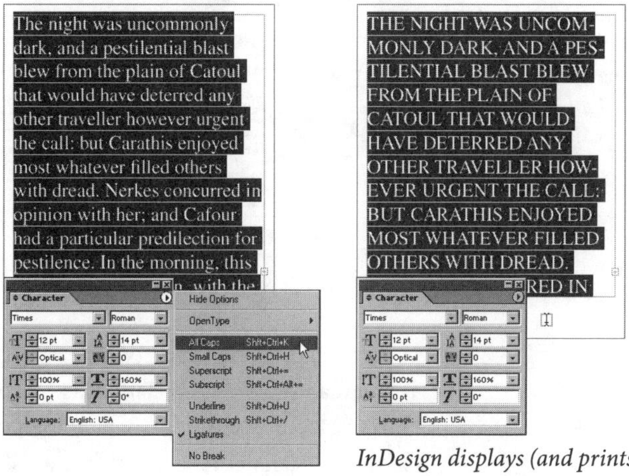

*Select the text you want to capitalize, then choose All Caps from the Character palette menu.*

*InDesign displays (and prints) the selected text in all caps.*

**Changing Case**

If Chapter 3, "Text," was all about entering text, why didn't we put the Change Case command there? Because, frankly, that chapter is already laid out and we don't want to upset our indexer.

In addition to being able to temporarily change the case of characters using the case options, you can have InDesign change the case of the characters by typing new characters for you using the Change Case submenu (which you'll find on the Type menu and on the context menu when text is selected).

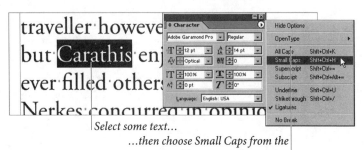

*Select some text...*

*...then choose Small Caps from the
Character palette menu*

*If you're using an OpenType
font (as in this example),
InDesign displays the small
caps version of the selected
characters (if the OpenType
font contains small caps
alternate characters).*

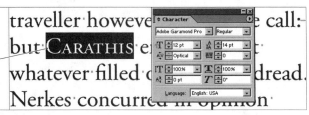

*If you're using a PostScript Type 1 or TrueType font, InDesign
displays scaled, capitalized versions of the selected characters.*

*If you're using a PostScript
Type 1 font, don't use the
Small Caps character
formatting option; instead,
change the font of the text to
an "expert set."*

*Adobe Garamond Pro (OpenType)*

THESE ARE TRUE SMALL CAPS

*Adobe Garamond (PostScript Type 1)*

THESE ARE NOT TRUE SMALL CAPS

To change the case of selected characters, choose an option: Uppercase, Lowercase, Title Case, or Sentence Case. Uppercase and Lowercase are self-explanatory. Sentence Case capitalizes the first letter of each sentence. Title Case is very simpleminded: it capitalizes the first character of each word in the selection, even if the word is "the," "and," or other preposition or article (see Figure 4-19).

**Underline**   When you choose Underline from the Character palette menu (or press Command-Shift-U/Ctrl-Shift-U), InDesign applies an underline to the selected text (see Figure 4-20). To remove the Underline text effect, select the text and choose Underline from the Character palette menu (when you select text containing the Underline effect, InDesign displays a check mark next to the Underline menu item). Unfortunately, the Underline style is pretty unsophisiticated: There's no way to change the stroke weight (it varies depending on the size

FIGURE 4-19
**Changing Case**

*Select some text.*

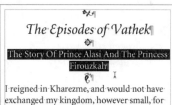

*InDesign's Title Case command capitalizes the first character of each word (you'll have to fix articles and prepositions yourself).*

*Choose a case conversion option from the Change Case submenu (on the Type menu or the context menu).*

*InDesign converts the case of the selected text. This conversion, unlike the All Caps and Small Caps formatting options, actually enters new characters in the text.*

FIGURE 4-20
**Underline**

*Underline stroke weights vary, because they're based on the size of the text.*

*Select the text you want to underline.*

*Choose Underline from the Character palette menu.*

*InDesign applies an underline to the selected text.*

of the text), the color, the style (it's always the color of the text), or the position, and there's no way to make it break across descenders (so it crosses out the bottom of "p" and "j").

InDesign's underline also includes any spaces in the selection. Some designs require that underlines break at spaces in the text. You could laboriously select each space and turn off the underline attribute, by why not use Find/Change to do the work for you? Find a space in the selection with the Underline attribute, then replace it with a space with Underline turned off.

**Strikethrough**

When you choose Strikethrough from the Character palette menu (or press Command-Shift-?/Ctrl-Shift-?), InDesign applies the strikethrough text effect to the selected text (see Figure 4-21). To remove the Strikethrough text effect, select the feature or press the keystroke again.

FIGURE 4-21
**Strikethrough**

*The stroke weight of the Strikethrough effect varies based on the size of the text.*

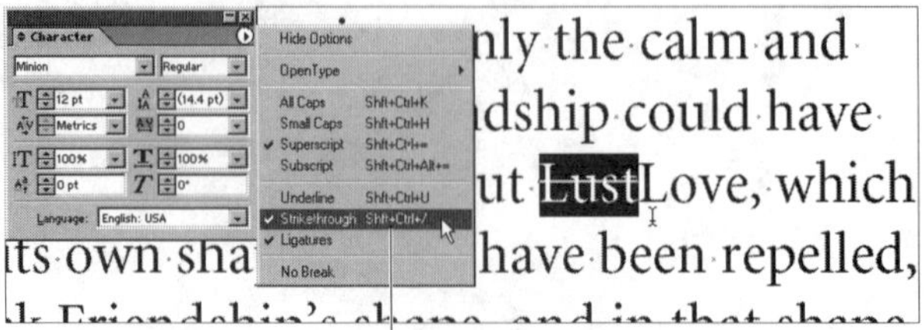

*Select some text, then choose Strikethrough from the Character palette menu.*

**Ligatures**     Some character combinations are just trouble—from a typesetting standpoint, at least. In particular, when you combine the lowercase "f" character with "f," "i," or "l," the tops of the characters run into each other. To compensate for this, type designers provide ligatures—special characters "tied" ("ligature" means "tie") together.

When you choose Ligatures from the Character palette's menu, InDesign replaces some of the character combinations in the selected range of text with the corresponding ligatures (see Figure 4-22).

If the font you've selected is not an OpenType font, InDesign replaces only the "fl" and "fi" character combinations. In Windows, InDesign uses these ligature characters if they're available in the font (and they are, for most PostScript Type 1 fonts), even though they are not part of the Windows character set—that is, there is usually no way to type them. If the font you've selected is an OpenType font, InDesign makes the ligature substitutions are suggested by the font.

OpenType fonts can also feature discretionary ligatures—for more on this topic, see "OpenType Fonts," later in this chapter.

FIGURE 4-22
**Ligatures**

*Select some text and then choose Ligatures from the Character palette menu.*

*If you're using an OpenType font, InDesign uses additional ligatures defined in the font. In this example, InDesign applies the "ffi" and "ffl" ligatures.*

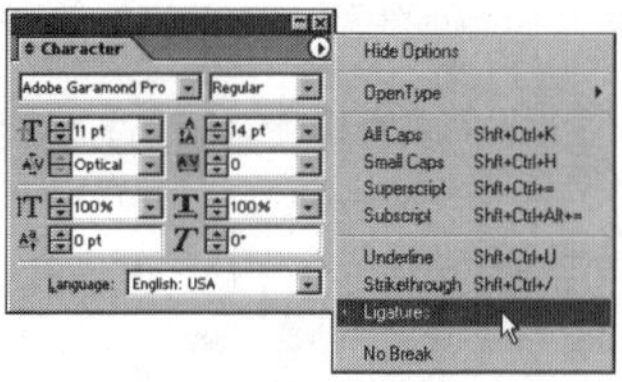

*Ligatures off*
*Adobe Garamond Pro (OpenType)*
file difficult reflect affliction

*Adobe Garamond (PostScript Type 1)*
file difficult reflect affliction

*Ligatures on*
*Adobe Garamond Pro (OpenType)*
file difficult reflect affliction

*Adobe Garamond (PostScript Type 1)*
file difficult reflect affliction

**Superscript and Subscript**     While you can always create superscript or subscript characters (for use in fractions or exponential notation) by changing the point size and baseline shift of selected characters, InDesign provides a shortcut: the Superscript and Subscript text effects (see Figure 4-23).

**FIGURE 4-23**
**Superscript and**
**Subscript**

*Select a character or series of characters...*

*...choose Superscript from the Character palette menu.*

*InDesign scales the text and shifts its baseline...*

*...according to the values you entered in the Text Preferences dialog box.*

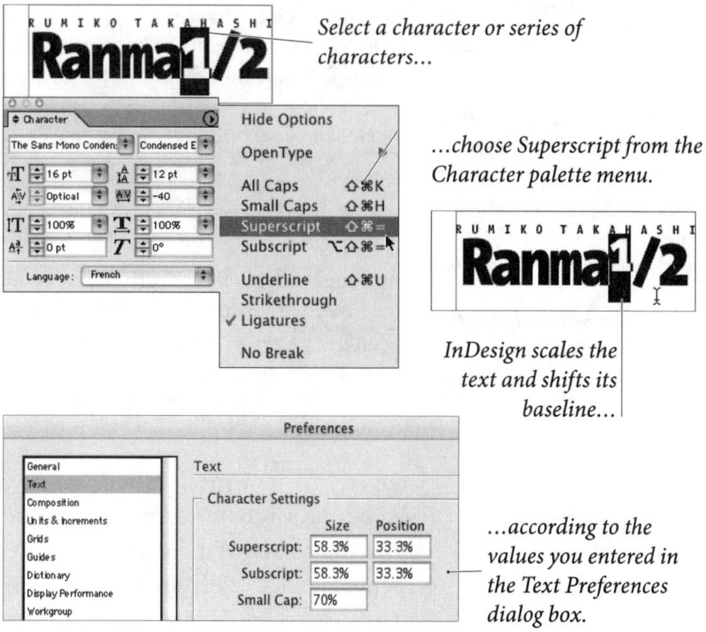

When you select Superscript or Subscript from the Character palette menu, InDesign scales the selected text and shifts its baseline. (You can also press Command-Shift-=/Ctrl-Shift-= or Command-Option-Shift-=/Ctrl-Alt-Shift-=.) InDesign calculates the scaling and baseline shift by multiplying the current text size and leading by the values you've set in the Size fields (Superscript or Subscript) in the Text Preferences dialog box (see "Text Preferences" in Chapter 1, "Basics").

Note that InDesign does not display the effective point size or baseline shift values in the corresponding fields of the Character palette when you select the text. If you are using an OpenType font that has true Superscript and Subscript characters, you'd be better off using the Superscript/Superior and Subscript/Inferior formatting in the OpenType submenu (see below).

**No Break**    This one is really easy to explain: To prevent a range of text from hyphenating across lines, select the text and turn on the No Break option in the Character palette's menu (see Figure 4-24).

## Opentype Fonts

We've mentioned OpenType fonts a few times in the chapter so far; however, we should probably take a moment to discuss them. The

**FIGURE 4-24**

**No Break**

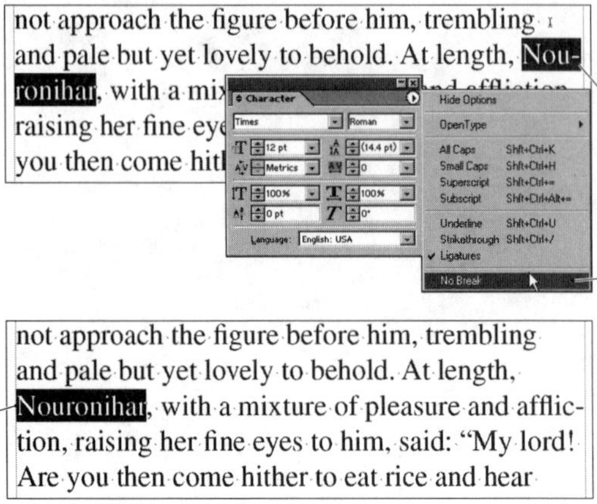

*It should be obvious that applying No Break to large amounts of text can make your text disappear (as it cannot be composed in a single column).*

*InDesign will not break the text when it falls at the end of a line.*

*Select the text you want to keep from breaking across lines (in this example, a name).*

*Choose No Break from the Character palette menu.*

OpenType font specification was created jointly by Microsoft and Adobe as a way to represent a font with only a single file on both Macintosh and Windows (so you can move the font cross-platform). Plus, the characters are encoded using the international standard Unicode, so each font can have hundreds, or even thousands of different characters—even the very large character sets in foreign languages like Japanese.

OpenType fonts act just like PostScript Type 1 or TrueType fonts in programs like Microsoft Word or QuarkXPress, but InDesign can perform special tricks with them, such as replacing characters with swashes (fancy versions of a letter), or with ligatures for character pairs such as ct and ffi. InDesign ships with several OpenType fonts, including Adobe Garamond Pro, Adobe Caslon Pro, Caflisch Pro, and Kozuka Mincho Pro (a Japanese typeface).

Most of the special OpenType typesetting features in InDesign are hidden in the OpenType submenu in the Character palette's menu (see Figure 4-25). If a font doesn't support one of these features, it appears in the menu within square brackets ("[Swash]").

**Alternative Characters**

All the OpenType features work by replacing one or more glyphs with another single glyph. The basic "fi" and "fl" ligatures that we discussed earlier are a great example of this, but they're only the beginning.

**Discretionary Ligatures.** Font designers love making ligatures, but they recognize that users won't usually want to use ones like "ct" or "st" in everyday text. If you select some text and turn on the Discretionary Ligatures feature, InDesign uses these lesser-known ligatures (if they're available in the font). We usually turn this off except

FIGURE 4-25
**OpenType Features**

*Select some text...*

*Arcana Manuscript is an interesting, if somewhat overwrought, OpenType font.*

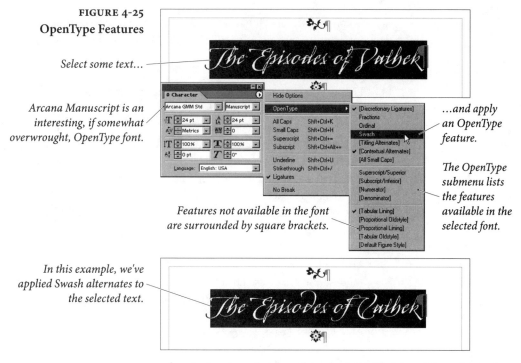

*...and apply an OpenType feature.*

*The OpenType submenu lists the features available in the selected font.*

*Features not available in the font are surrounded by square brackets.*

*In this example, we've applied Swash alternates to the selected text.*

when trying to make something look "old fashioned," or when using a script typeface like Caflisch Pro.

**Fractions.** Changing fake fractions (such as $^1/_2$) to real fractions (½) has long been a thorn in the side of anyone laying out cookbooks or construction manuals. Fortunately, you can now just turn on the Fractions feature and anything that looks like a fraction will convert to the proper character automatically. (In some OpenType typefaces, only very basic fractions such as ½, ¼, and ⅔ are converted. In others, even arbitrary fractions like 355/113 are changed (sadly, not in this font). It depends on the design of the font.) This feature has no effect on non-fractions, so we usually just turn this on and leave it on.

**Ordinal.** Ordinal numbers are like "first" and "second," and InDesign can automatically set the "st", "nd", and "rd" (or the "o" and "a" when typesetting in Spanish) to superscript when you turn Ordinal on in the OpenType submenu. For instance 3rd becomes 3ʳᵈ.

**Swash.** When you need to give a character a little more flair, select it and turn on the Swash feature. Swashes are typically used at the beginning or ending of words or sentences. You can see if a particular OpenType font has any swash characters by opening the Insert

Glyph palette and looking for Swash in the Show pop-up menu; some fonts (such as Adobe Caslon Pro) have swashes in their italic styles only.

**Titling Alternates.** Some OpenType fonts have special "titling" characters that are designed for all-uppercase type set at large sizes.

**Contextual Alternates.** A few OpenType fonts—mostly script faces—have contextual ligatures and connecting alternates, which are very similar to ligatures. Set a paragraph in Adobe Caflisch Pro, for instance, and then select it and turn on Contextual Alternates. The result is looks more like handwriting, because the alternate characters connect to each other.

**All Small Caps.** When you turn on the Small Caps feature (which we described in "Case Options," earlier), InDesign leaves uppercase characters alone. All Small Caps, however, forces uppercase characters to appear as lower case small caps. This is useful when formatting acronyms such as DOS, NASA, or IBM.

**Raised and Lowered Characters**

Typesetting a treatise on Einstein's theory of relativity? If so, you'll be mighty happy about InDesign's ability to use true superscripts and subscripts instead of the faked scaled versions that you get with the Superscript and Subscript features in the Character palette's menu. You have four choices in the OpenType submenu (each one is mutually exclusive of the others):

◆ Superscript/Superior

◆ Subscript/Inferior

◆ Numerator

◆ Denominator

However, note that most OpenType fonts only have a small set of characters designed to be superscript or subscript, so you can't set any and all characters you want in these styles. For example, if you set the word "turkey" to Superscript/Superior style, only every other character changes. Plus, in many cases you get the same result when you choose Denominator or Subscript/Inferior, and so on.

**Formatting Numerals**

We like "old style" numerals (you know, the kind with descenders: 1234567890) better than full-height "lining figures" (1234567890), and we've always gotten them by changing the font of the characters to an "expert" version of whatever font we were using (if one was available). So we were very happy to see that there are four different ways InDesign can format numerals: Proportional Oldstyle, Tabular Oldstyle, Proportional Lining, and Tabular Lining (see Figure 4-26).

The default style is Tabular Lining, which is great for financial pages in an annual report because all the numbers have equal widths, so they line up from one line to the next. If you choose Tabular Oldstyle from the OpenType submenu, the numerals line up, but InDesign uses old style characters. Proportional Lining numerals are all the same height, but vary in width. David prefers this style for everything other than tables, especially when interspersing numbers and uppercase characters. Ole would rather use Proportional Oldsyle, which uses old style figures of varying widths.

The last OpenType numeral formatting option is Default Figure Style, which applies the figure style defined as the default by the type designer (so the effect varies from font to font).

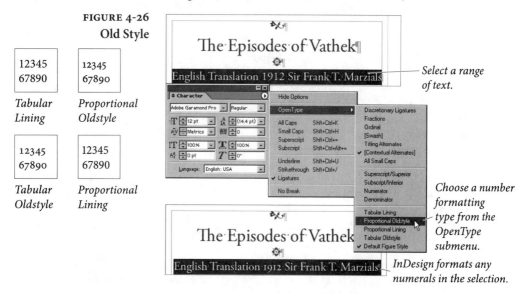

**FIGURE 4-26**
Old Style

12345
67890

*Tabular
Lining*

12345
67890

*Proportional
Oldstyle*

12345
67890

*Tabular
Oldstyle*

12345
67890

*Proportional
Lining*

*Select a range
of text.*

*Choose a number
formatting
type from the
OpenType
submenu.*

*InDesign formats any
numerals in the selection.*

## Filling and Stroking Characters

Most page layout programs—at least on the Macintosh—give you the ability to apply an "outline" type style to text. When you do this, you get a stroke around the text that varies in size depending on the point size of the text. But what if you want to apply a stroke of a particular width to the text? What if you want to apply a fill of a different color?

With InDesign, you can fill or stroke text as you would any other path. Once you've selected text (you can use the Selection tool to select unlinked text frames), you can set the fill color, or the stroke color and stroke weight (see Figure 4-27).

You can even apply gradients to the fill and stroke of the type—without converting the type to outlines. However, while gradients are easy to apply, it's not always easy to get the effect you're looking for. The reason is that gradients are based on the bounding box of the text frame (the bounding box is the smallest imaginary rectangle inside which the frame will fit). In general, while we think the gradient-in-text feature is kind of fun, in the real world we usually convert the text to outlines first (see "Converting Text to Outlines" in Chapter 6, "Where Text Meets Graphics").

**FIGURE 4-27**
**Character Fill and Stroke**

Select an unlinked text frame using the Selection tool, then click the Formatting Affects Text button.

*In addition to the method shown here, you can select characters using the Text tool, then apply a fill and/or stroke to the text using the controls you use to apply a fill and stroke to any path.*

You can also click the Formatting Affects Text button in the Swatches palette.

Format the text using any of the fill and stroke formatting tools. In this example, we used the Swatches palette to apply a tint to the fill and stroke of the text, and then used the Stroke palette to set the stroke weight.

A character without a fill quickly becomes unreadable as you increase the stroke weight.

Note that the fill retains the shape of the character as you increase stroke weight.

## Paragraph Formatting

What makes a paragraph a paragraph? InDesign's definition is simple—a paragraph is any string of characters that ends with a carriage return. When you apply paragraph formatting, the formatting applies to all of the characters in the paragraph. Paragraph alignment, indents, tabs, spacing, and hyphenation settings are all examples of paragraph formatting.

You don't have to select all of the text in a paragraph to apply paragraph formatting—all you need to do is click the Text tool in the paragraph. To select more than one paragraph, drag the cursor through the paragraphs you want format. The selection doesn't have to include all of the text in the paragraphs, it only has to *touch* each paragraph.

If what you're trying to do, however, is apply character formatting (like font, size, and so on) to all of the characters in the paragraph, you should triple (or quadruple, if you've turned on the Triple Click to Select a Line option in the Text Preferences dialog box)-click the paragraph with the Text tool—that way, you'll select all of the characters, including the invisible carriage return character. (Note that you can force a line break without creating a new paragraph—called a "soft return"—by typing Shift-Return/Shift-Enter.)

You can find all of InDesign's paragraph formatting features in the Paragraph palette: press Command-M/Ctrl-M to display the palette if it's not already visible.

**Alignment**    Click the alignment buttons at the top of the Paragraph palette to set the alignment of the selected paragraphs (see Figure 4-28).

InDesign supports the usual set of paragraph alignments—left aligned (also known as "rag right"), right aligned (also known as "rag left"), centered, and justified, but also adds a couple of variations on the justified alignment you might not be familiar with.

In addition to the standard "justified" alignment, which treats the last line of the paragraph as if it were left aligned, InDesign offers the force justified, right justified and center justified alignments. These each tell InDesign to treat the last line of the paragraph differently. When you force justify the text, the last line is spread out all the way to the right margin, even if it's only a single word. In some cases, when the Paragraph Composer is turned on (see "Multi-line Composition," later in this chapter), turning on force justify actually reflows the paragraph significantly.

Right justified and center justified treat the last line as right aligned and center aligned, respectively. In the old days of typesetting, these alignments were known as "quad right" and "quad center."

**Indents**    InDesign paragraphs can be indented from the left and right sides of the column using the Left Indent and Right Indent fields in the Paragraph palette (see Figure 4-29). You can enter values from zero

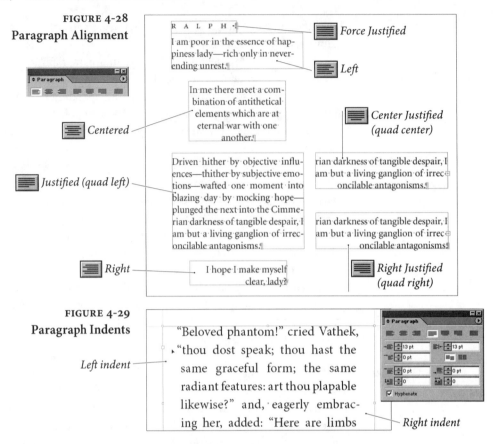

FIGURE 4-28
**Paragraph Alignment**

FIGURE 4-29
**Paragraph Indents**

Left indent

Right indent

(0) to 720 picas in these fields, but you can't enter negative numbers to make the edges of the paragraph "hang" outside the edges of the column or text frame.

Note that the left and right indents are always added to the text inset, as specified in the Text Frame Options dialog box. That is, if you have a left inset of 6 points and a left indent of 12 points, then the left edge of the paragraph will sit 18 points from the edge of the box.

There's also a special indent, called First Line, that applies to the first line of the paragraph alone. The value you enter in the First Line field sets the distance between the first line indent and the left indent. The First Line indent may be positive or negative, but cannot be a negative number greater than the left indent (see Figure 4-30). You should *never* create an indent by typing five spaces at the beginning of a paragraph to indent; instead, use First Line indent.

How large your First Line indent should be depends on your design and on the typeface you're working with. Typically, the larger the x-height of the font, the larger first-line indent you should use.

**FIGURE 4-30**
**First Line Indent**

*Don't use tab characters to apply a first line indent...*

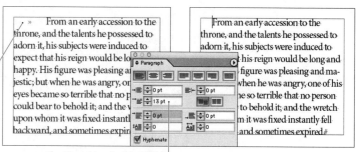

*...use the First Line Indent field.*

Book designers often use a one- or two-em indent, so in an 11-point type, the indent might be 11 or 22 points.

To change an indent value, select a paragraph and then do one of the following things:

◆ Display the Paragraph palette, then enter a value in the First Line Indent, Left Indent, and/or the Right Indent fields (see Figure 4-31).

◆ Display the Tabs palette (press Command-Shift-T/Ctrl-Shift-T), and drag one of the indent icons (see Figure 4-32).

**FIGURE 4-31**
**Setting an Indent**

*Click the Text tool in the paragraph you want to format.*

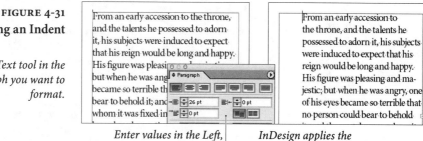

*Enter values in the Left, Right, or First fields.*

*InDesign applies the indents you've specified.*

**FIGURE 4-32**
**Indents on the Tabs Palette**

*First Line indent*

Left indent

Right indent

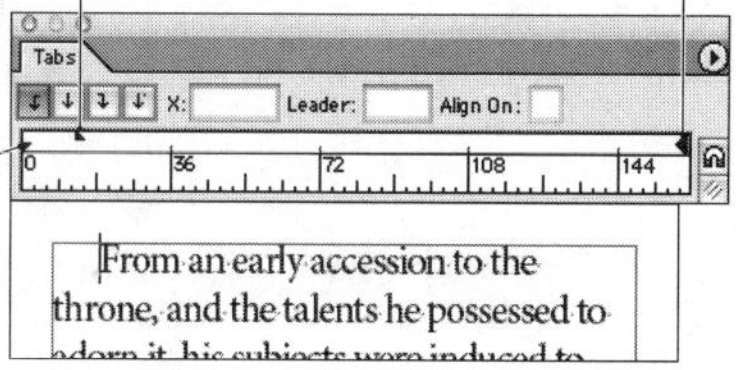

**Creating a**
**Hanging Indent**

If you learn nothing else from this chapter, we'd like you to come out of it knowing how to set a hanging indent—a paragraph format you use for numbered lists, bullet lists, or any of several other situations. Use hanging indents, rather than breaking and indenting each line using carriage returns and tabs—you'll thank yourself for it later, when you need to edit the text.

To create a hanging indent that adapts when you change the width of a text block, edit copy, or change formatting in other ways, follow these steps (see Figure 4-33).

1. If you haven't already done this, type a bullet, a number, or some other character, followed by a tab at the beginning of the paragraph.

2. While the cursor is still blinking in the paragraph, press Command-Shift-T/Ctrl-Shift-T to display the Tabs palette. Hold down Shift and drag the Left indent icon to the right—leaving the First Line indent marker in position. Press the same keystroke to make the palette go away.

You can also set your hanging indent using the Paragraph palette—to do this, enter a positive left indent and a negative first-line indent. Either way, there's no need to set a tab stop because InDesign assumes the left indent is the first tab stop.

FIGURE 4-33
**Setting a
Hanging Indent**

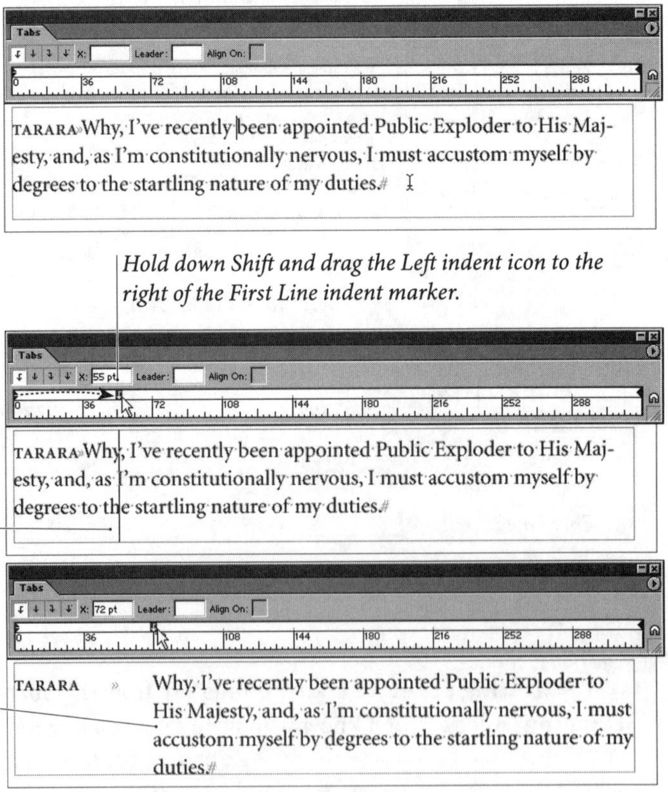

*Click the Text tool in a
paragraph, then press
Command-Shift-T/
Ctrl-Shift-T to display
the Tabs palette.*

*Hold down Shift and drag the Left indent icon to the
right of the First Line indent marker.*

*As you drag, InDesign
displays a vertical guide that
follows the location of the
Left indent icon.*

*Stop dragging, and InDesign
applies a hanging indent to
the selected paragraph.*

Here's one other way to create a hanging indent: Set the Left indent for the paragraph where you want the bullet to be, then set a tab stop (see "Tabs," below, for more on this) where you want the Left indent for the rest of the paragraph to be. Now place the text cursor immediately after the tab character and press Command-\ or Ctrl-\ (backslash). This is the keyboard shortcut for the Indent Here character (you can also get this character from the Insert Special Character submenu in the Type menu or the context sensitive menu). This invisible character causes the rest of the lines in a paragraph to indent to this place. If you want to delete it, you can place the cursor after it (since it's invisible and has no width, you might have to use the arrow keys to position it) and then press Delete.

While the Indent Here character is easy to type, we like using the negative First Line indent trick more because we can use it in a paragraph style.

**Tabs**

A classic Ole anecdote: "Whiz! Clunk. Whiz! Clunk. Ding! My father brought home a large, black typewriter—a machine so antiquated that even his school district (he was a high school math teacher) didn't want it anymore. It was a behemoth, a leviathan among type-writers. I couldn't lift it, and typing a letter took the entire strength of my seven-year-old arm.

"My brother and I were fascinated by the movement of the car-riage. For one thing, the spring that pulled it was massive—probably capable of launching a small aircraft—so pressing the Tab key was, by itself, pretty exciting. But what really caught our attention were the tabs themselves: thick slabs of metal you "set" by pushing them into the teeth of a bar set below the carriage. With each press of the Tab key, the carriage would leap to the right—then a protruding part would slam into one of the tabs. Bam! Unstoppable force meets immovable object. The rear of the typewriter would jump half an inch to the right. This was cool."

**Tabs, Mice, and History**

Tabs come to desktop typesetting from typewriters, by way of word processing (with a stopover along the way at the Linotype machine). They solve a problem that didn't exist in hand-set metal type—namely, how do you position characters at precise locations in a line of type when you can't simply slide them into place with your finger?

There are two methods of controlling the horizontal position of text in a line. First, you can use space characters—word spaces, thin spaces, en spaces, and em spaces. This method places characters at *relative* positions in the line—where they appear depends on the width of the spaces and of the other characters in the line. Tabs, by contrast, provide *absolute* position on the line—a tab stop set at 6 picas will remain at that position, regardless of the text content of the line.

Before we go any farther, we'd better make sure we're using the same terminology. *Tab stops* are formatting attributes of paragraphs. *Tab characters* are what InDesign enters in a line of text when you press the Tab key. Tab characters push text around in a line; tab stops determine the effect of the tab characters. Each tab stop has a position (relative to the left edge of the text frame), an alignment (which specifies the composition of the text following a tab character), and, potentially, a leader (a tab leader is a series of repeated characters spanning the distance from beginning of the tab character to the beginning of the following text). Put tab stops and tab characters together, and you get *tabs*, the feature.

**A Little Tab Dogma**    Look. We try to be reasonable. We try not to insist that everyone work the way that we do, or that our way of doing things is necessarily the best way (in fact, we sometimes know it's not). But tabs are different—if you don't do it our way, you'll be causing yourself needless pain. Let's review the rules:

◆ Use tabs, not spaces, to move text to a specific position in a line of text.

◆ Use a First Line indent, not a tab, when you want to indent the first line of a paragraph.

◆ Do not force lines to break by entering tab characters (or multiple tab characters) at the end of a line! If you do, you'll find tab characters creeping back into the text as editing changes force text recomposition. To break a line without entering a carriage return, use the "soft return" (press Shift-Return/Shift-Enter).

◆ Don't use multiple tab characters when you can use a single tab character and an appropriately positioned tab stop. While there are some cases where you'll have to break this rule, putting two or more tab characters in a row should be the exception.

**Types of Tab Stops**    InDesign features five types of tab stop (see Figure 4-34).

**Left, Right, and Centered Tab Stops.** InDesign's left, right, and centered tab stops are the same as the basic tab stops you'll find in any word processor.

FIGURE 4-34
**Tab Stop Alignment**

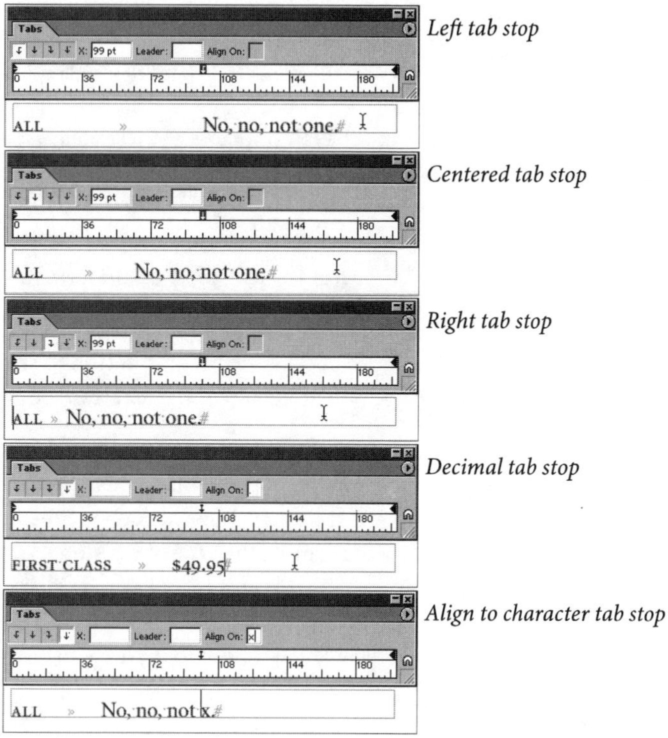

*Left tab stop*

*Centered tab stop*

*Right tab stop*

*Decimal tab stop*

*Align to character tab stop*

◆ Left tab stops push text following a tab character to a specific horizontal location in a column, and then align the text to the left of the tab stop position.

◆ Right tab stops push text to a location and then align the text to the right of the tab stop position.

◆ Centered tab stops center a line of text at the point at which you've set the tab stop.

**Decimal Tab Stops.** Decimal tab stops push text following a tab character so that any decimal point you've entered in the text aligns with the point at which you set the tab stop. Actually, the Decimal tab stop will use *any* non-numeric character. This turns out to be very useful when trying to align a column of numbers when some of them have footnotes, asterisks, or other symbols after them, because the numbers form to the left and the symbols "hang" off to the right. If there's no number followed by a character, InDesign treats the decimal tab stop as a right tab stop.

**Align to Character Tab Stops.** Align to character tab stops are just like decimal tab stops, but align to a character you specify (rather than a decimal point). If the character is not found in the text, the program treats the tab stop as a right tab stop.

**Setting Tab Stops**    To set a tab stop, follow these steps (see Figure 4-35).

1. If you haven't already entered tab characters in the text, enter them.

2. Select the text you want to format.

3. Display the Tabs palette (press Command-Shift-T/Ctrl-Shift-T), then click the Magnet button to snap the Tabs palette into position at the top of the text frame (if possible).

4. Click in the tab ruler and drag. As you drag, the X field shows you the position of the tab icon (relative to the left edge of the text frame). Then click one of the tab stop alignment buttons to determine the type of tab stop.

   If you want to add a tab leader, enter one or two leader characters in the Leader field in the Tabs palette (if you can't see this field, you'll need to increase the width of the palette).

You can also add a tab stop at a specific location on the tab ruler. To do this, enter the position you want in the X field in the Tabs palette and then press Enter. InDesign adds the tab stop. The new tab stop uses the current tab stop alignment, or you can click on a different one to change it.

FIGURE 4-35
**Setting a Tab Stop**

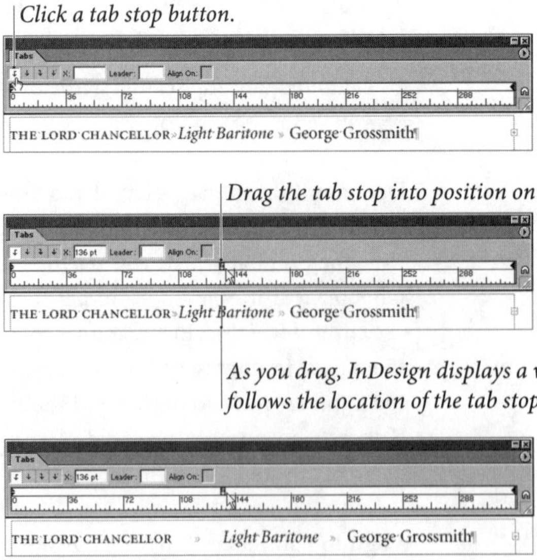

*Click a tab stop button.*

*Drag the tab stop into position on the tab ruler.*

*As you drag, InDesign displays a vertical guide that follows the location of the tab stop icon.*

*When the tab stop icon is in position, stop dragging.*

**Removing Tab Stops.** To remove a tab stop, drag the tab stop icon off the tab ruler (see Figure 4-36). Note that this doesn't remove any tab characters you've typed in your text, though it does make them behave differently (because you've taken away their tab stop).

FIGURE 4-36
**Removing a Tab Stop**

Select a tab stop icon...

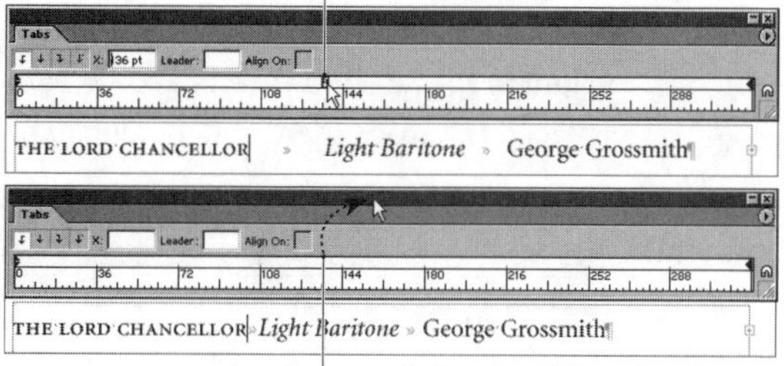

...and drag it off the tab ruler.

**Editing Tab Stops.** To change a tab stop's position, drag the tab stop on the tab ruler (see Figure 4-37). Alternatively, you can select the tab stop (click on it), then enter a new value in the x field or give it a leader. Don't forget that if you want to move the tab stop by a specific amount, you can add a + or – character after the value that appears in the x field and then type the amount you want to move it ("+14mm").

To change a tab stop's alignment (from left to decimal, for instance), select the tab stop on the tab ruler and then click the tab stop button corresponding to the alignment you want. Or you can Option/Alt-click on the tab stop to rotate through the alignment types.

**FIGURE 4-37**
**Editing a Tab Stop**

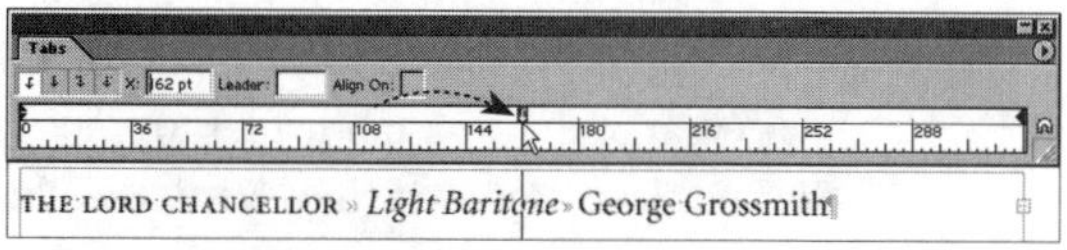

To change the position of a tab stop, drag the tab stop icon on the tab ruler.

To change the alignment of a tab stop, select the tab stop icon...

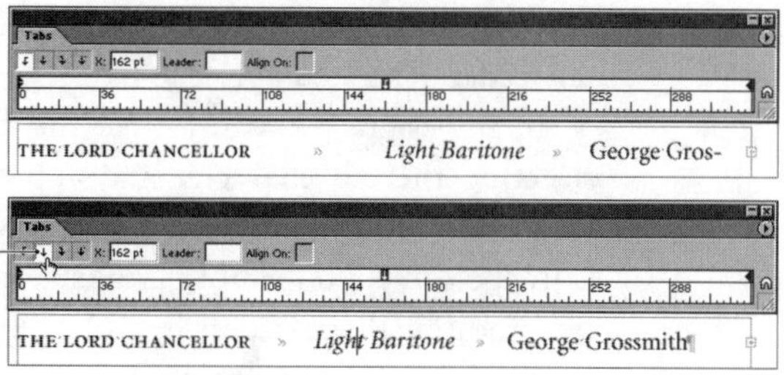

...and click one of the tab stop alignment buttons.

**Repeating Tab Stops.** To create a series of tab stops spaced an equal distance apart, select a tab stop on the tab ruler and choose Repeat Tab from the Tabs palette menu (see Figure 4-38). InDesign repeats the tab across the width of the current column. The distance between the new tab stops is equal to the distance between the tab stop you selected and the previous tab stop (or indent) in the column. InDesign 2 now also deletes all the tab stops that were already to the right of the tab stop you clicked on (which can be frustrating if you've placed tab stops there and weren't expecting them to disappear).

FIGURE 4-38
**Repeating a Tab Stop**

*Select the tab stop icon you want to repeat...*

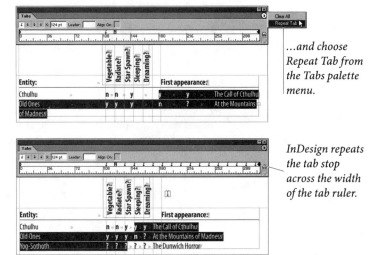

*...and choose Repeat Tab from the Tabs palette menu.*

*InDesign repeats the tab stop across the width of the tab ruler.*

**Working with Tab Leaders.** A tab leader is a series of repeated characters that fill the area taken up by the tab character (see Figure 4-39). The most common tab leader character is a period—think of all of the "dot" leaders you've seen in tables of contents.

Characters in a tab leader are not spaced in the same fashion as other characters—if they were, the characters in tab leaders on successive lines would not align with each other. That would be ugly. Instead, characters in a tab leader are monospaced—positioned as if on an invisible grid. This means you'll see different amounts of space between the last character of text preceding a tab leader and the first tab leader. It's a small price to pay.

In InDesign, you can format the characters in a tab leader by selecting the tab character and applying formatting, just as you would any other character. For instance, dotted tab leaders typically look like a bunch of periods. You can make them look more like traditional dot leaders by adding a space after the period (in the Leader field of the Tab palette), then selecting the tab character and reducing its size slightly.

FIGURE 4-39
Applying a Tab Leader

Select some text. ——

——— Select a tab stop.

*Enter the character or characters you want to use for the tab leader in the Leader field. Press Enter...*

*...and InDesign applies a tab leader to the selected tab stop.*

**Right-aligned Tabs.** Setting a tab stop precisely at the right margin can be a bother, it's an even bigger bother if your art director says, "make that column narrower." So, instead of using tab stops, try using a right-aligned tab character, which you can enter by pressing Shift-Tab (or add with the Insert Special Characters submenu in the Type menu). The text that follows the right-aligned tab character always aligns with the right margin, even when you change the right indent or the width of the text frame.

Unfortunately, at the time of this writing, there's no way to add leaders to right-aligned tab characters.

**Adding Space Before and After Paragraphs**

When you want to add extra space between paragraphs, don't use carriage returns (not even one). If you do, you're certain to end up with unwanted carriage returns at the tops of text frames when text recomposes due to editing or formatting changes. Instead of carriage returns, use the Space Before and Space After fields in the Paragraph palette. When you add space using these controls, InDesign removes the space when the paragraph falls at the top of a text frame (see Figure 4-40). If you need to add space before a paragraph at the top of a text frame, use First Baseline offset (see Chapter 3, "Text").

In addition, adding an exact amount of space is easier when you use the Paragraph palette. Want to add four picas of vertical space above the paragraph? Enter it in the Space Before field. There's no need to guess how many carriage returns it would take to make up that vertical distance.

**Align to Grid**

When you have more than one column of text on a page, it's important that the baselines of the text line up across the columns. The idea is that the leading should be consistent with an underlying "leading

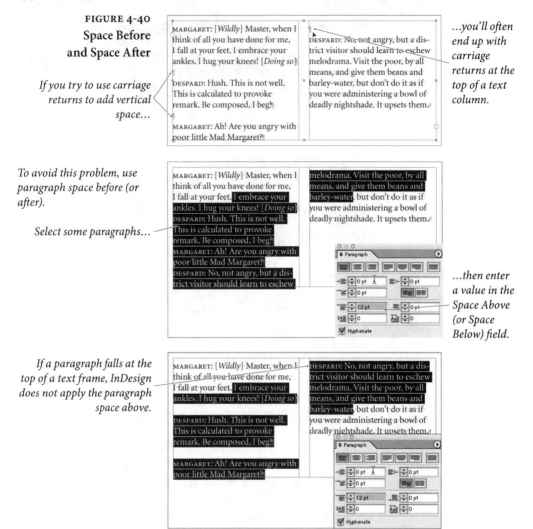

FIGURE 4-40
**Space Before
and Space After**

*If you try to use carriage
returns to add vertical
space...*

*...you'll often
end up with
carriage
returns at the
top of a text
column.*

*To avoid this problem, use
paragraph space before (or
after).*

*Select some paragraphs...*

*...then enter
a value in the
Space Above
(or Space
Below) field.*

*If a paragraph falls at the
top of a text frame, InDesign
does not apply the paragraph
space above.*

grid"—an invisible set of rules for where the baselines of text should
lay. Many designers even work with leading grids on pages with a
single column.

Unfortunately, in most page designs, you'll find elements that
have to have leading values that differ from the leading applied to
the body text. Inline graphics, paragraph rules, and headings are all
examples of the sort of elements we're talking about. When one of
these elements appears in a column of text, the leading of the lines in
that column gets thrown off.

You need a way to compensate for leading variations inside a
column of text. "Leading creep," the misalignment of baselines in
adjacent text columns, is one of the hallmarks of amateur typesetting, so you want to avoid it.

While you could adjust the space above and below such intrusions to compensate, there's an easier way: use InDesign's Align to Baseline Grid command. Select a paragraph and click the Align to Baseline Grid button in the Paragraph palette, and InDesign forces the baselines of the lines in the paragraph onto the baseline grid (see Figure 4-41). You can change the leading and position of the baseline grid in the Grids panel of the Preferences dialog box. To see this grid, select Show Baseline Grid in the View menu.

**Align to Grid**

*This is all very pretty...*

*...but it throws the leading of the following paragraph off of the leading grid.*

She spoke, sighed deeply, and then began her story in the following words.

THE TALE OF THE PERI HOMAÏOUNA

I know, O son of Ormossouf, that you and Alsalami, the dervise, have come to the conclusion that I am protected by some celestial Intelligence; but how far, even so, were you from guessing to what a glorious race I belong!

*To fix this problem, select the paragraph and click the Align to grid button.*

She spoke, sighed deeply, and then began her story in the following words.

THE TALE OF THE PERI HOMAÏOUNA

I know, O son of Ormossouf, that you and Alsalami, the dervise, have come to the conclusion that I am protected by some celestial Intelligence; but how far, even so, were you from guessing to what a glorious race I belong!

*InDesign snaps the baselines of the text in the paragraph to the baseline grid.*

**Why We Rarely Align to Baseline.** While there's no doubt that a careful study and practice of baseline grids can make your documents better looking, we rarely use the Align to Basline Grid feature. The reason: you can get the same quality by simply making sure your leading, Space Before, and Space After always adds up to a multiple of the leading value.

For example, if your body text has 15-point leading, then make sure your headings also have 15- or 30-point leading. If you use Space Before or Space After, make sure those values are set to a multiple of 15, like: 15, 30, or 45 points. If you have a list, you could place 7.5 points between each item, and as long as there are an even number of items, the leading after the list will end up on the leading grid. Finally, snap the tops of your frame to the baseline grid and set the First Baseline setting to Leading, and you can't go wrong.

**Align First Line to Grid.** Often, sidebars in magazines or newsletters are set in a different font and leading than the main body text, and they're placed in their own text frame. You can make the first baseline of that sidebar align with the leading grid by using the Only Align First Line to Grid feature. This forces the first line of a selected paragraph to snap to the baseline grid, but then leaves the rest of the paragraph alone. However, you can only turn this on with a keyboard shortcut, and you'll have to provide your own: You can assign a shorcut to this feature by finding it in the Text and Tables product area of the Keyboard Shortcuts dialog box (in the Edit menu).

**Drop Caps**

Drop caps are a paragraph-level attribute in InDesign (as they are in QuarkXPress). To apply a drop cap to a paragraph, enter a value in the Number of Lines field of the Paragraph palette (this sets both the baseline shift and the point size of the drop cap). To make InDesign apply the drop cap formatting to more than one character, enter a number in the Number of Characters field. InDesign enlarges the characters you specified and shifts their baseline down according to the value you entered in the Number of Lines field (see Figure 4-42).

You can also make an initial cap that drops down *and* raises up by selecting the drop cap character (or characters) and increasing the point size. To add or remove space between the drop cap and the characters that follow it, place the cursor after the drop cap and adjust the Kerning value (see "Kerning," earlier in this chapter). The only good way to get your text to follow the shape of a drop cap ("A" or "W," for example) is to convert the character to an outline, cut it out of the text frame, place it above or below the frame, and then apply a text wrap.

**Type in the Margin.** In InDesign, the edges of text frames are usually inviolable (apart from the adjustments applied by optical margin alignment). There's no margin release, no handy command for moving one line a bit over the edge. Or is there? Instead of a single-character drop cap, specify a two-character drop cap. Add a space to the left of the first character in the paragraph—if your paragraph is justified, this should be a space that doesn't get wider, such as an en space (Command-Shift-N/Ctrl-Shift-N). Place the cursor between the space and the drop cap and apply negative kerning until the left edge of the character moves outside of the text frame. Note, too,

FIGURE 4-42

**Drop Caps**

*Select a paragraph.*

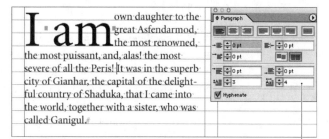

I am own daughter to the great Asfendarmod, the most renowned, the most puissant, and, alas! the most severe of all the Peris! It was in the superb city of Gianhar, the capital of the delightful country of Shaduka, that I came into the world, together with a sister, who was called Ganigul.

I am own daughter to the great Asfendarmod, the most renowned, the most puissant, and, alas! the most severe of all the Peris! It was in the superb city of Gianhar, the capital of the delightful country of Shaduka, that I came into the world, together with a sister, who was called Ganigul.

*Enter the number of lines you want to "drop" the initial character(s).*

I am own daughter to the great Asfendarmod, the most renowned, the most puissant, and, alas! the most severe of all the Peris! It was in the superb city of Gianhar, the capital of the delight-ful country of Shaduka, that I came into the world, together with a sister, who was called Ganigul.

*Enter the number of characters you want to apply the drop cap format to, if necessary.*

that using optical margin alignment might provide the effect you're looking for.

**Multi-Line Composition**

Composition—the method our desktop publishing program uses to fit text into a line—isn't glamorous. It's not going to be the focus of any glossy magazine advertisement. In fact, most people never consciously notice good or bad composition. We are convinced, however, that readers perceive the difference between well spaced and poorly spaced text. Good spacing not only improves readability, it also conveys an aura of quality to the publication or organization. In short, it's worth caring about. There are four basic ways to fit text onto a line.

◆ Controlling the spacing between the letters.

◆ Controlling the spacing between the words.

◆ Adjusting the size of the characters themselves.

◆ Breaking the words at line endings by hyphenating.

If you're serious about type, you already know that a large part of your typesetting time is spent fixing bad line breaks and lines with poor word and letter spacing. In our experience, fully one third of our typesetting and production time in QuarkXPress or other program is spent "walking the lines"—fixing spacing problems.

Other desktop publishing programs use a "single line composer" to compose lines of text. As the program arranges the characters on each line, it only considers the spacing of that line, which means that adjacent lines may have dramatically different spacing. The greater the variation of letter and word spacing among lines in a paragraph, the harder it is to read (and the less appealing it is to look at).

InDesign, however, has both a single-line composer and a multi-line composer, which can examine an entire paragraph's worth of lines at a time.

**How does it work?** The multi-line composer (called Adobe Paragraph Composer) creates a list of possible line break points in the lines it examines. It then ranks the different sets of possible break points, considering the effect of each break point on spacing and hyphenation. Finally, it chooses the best of the alternatives. You'd think that this would take a lot of time—but it doesn't. When you use the default settings, you get composition speed that's equal to that of a single-line composition system, and you get better-looking text (see Figure 4-43).

Multi-line composition takes some getting used to, however, because characters *preceding* the cursor will sometimes *move* as you enter or edit text—something you won't see in most page layout, word processing, or illustration programs. You really can't be certain of the position of the line breaks in a paragraph until you've entered

**FIGURE 4-43**
**Multi-Line Composition**

*Note the extreme variation in word and letter spacing from line to line in the text composed using the Single-line composer.*

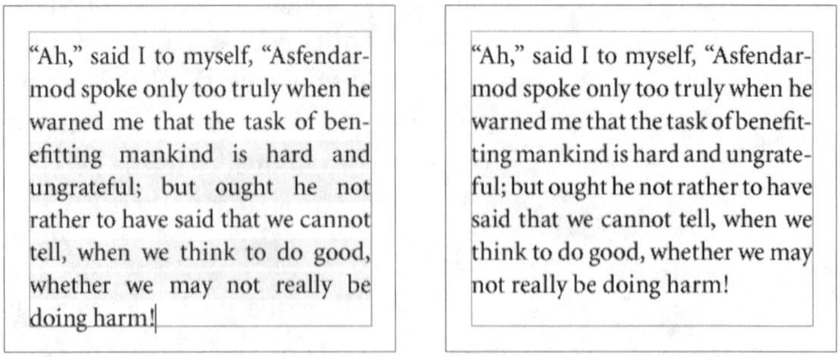

"Ah," said I to myself, "Asfendar-mod spoke only too truly when he warned me that the task of ben-efitting mankind is hard and ungrateful; but ought he not rather to have said that we cannot tell, when we think to do good, whether we may not really be doing harm!

"Ah," said I to myself, "Asfendar-mod spoke only too truly when he warned me that the task of benefit-ting mankind is hard and ungrate-ful; but ought he not rather to have said that we cannot tell, when we think to do good, whether we may not really be doing harm!

*Single-line composition.*

*Multi-line composition.*

the last word in the paragraph. Luckily, it doesn't take long to adjust to this behavior—especially when the results are so much better than what you're used to.

In some rare cases you might want or need to turn the Adobe Paragraph Composer off and exercise manual control over the line breaks in a paragraph—when lines absolutely must break a particular way. Also, single-line composition is faster than multi-line, so if quality isn't an issue, you might consider turning it off. However, ultimately, we leave it on most of the time.

Multi-line composition is on by default; to use the single-line composition method, select a paragraph and choose Adobe Single-line Composer from the Paragraph palette menu. To turn multi-line composition back on again for the paragraph, choose Adobe Paragraph Composer.

(If you used InDesign 1.5, you might be looking for the Multi-line Composer controls in the Preferences dialog box. They're not there—Adobe took them out in version 2.)

**Hyphenation Controls**

If you're tired of having your favorite page layout program hyphenate the word "image" after the "m," you'll like InDesign's hyphenation controls. To set the hyphenation options for a paragraph, choose Hyphenation from the Paragraph palette's menu or press Command-Option-H/Ctrl-Alt-H. InDesign displays the Hyphenation dialog box (see Figure 4-44). QuarkXPress users are used to having both hyphenation and justification settings in one dialog box; in InDesign they're broken into two. Also, in QuarkXPress, you have to make and save an H&J setting first, and then apply it to a paragraph. In InDesign, you simply select a paragraph (or paragraphs) and change its hyphenation and justification settings.

The first checkbox in the Hyphenation dialog box, simply labeled Hyphenate, controls whether the selected paragraph or paragraphs will be hyphenated. This is identical to turning on and off the Hyphenate checkbox in the Paragraph palette. Then there are seven other controls that determine the hyphenation rules.

**FIGURE 4-44**
**Hyphenation Dialog Box**

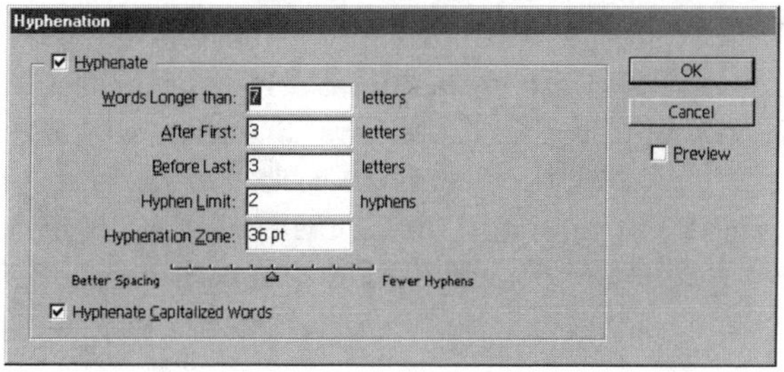

**Words Longer Than.** You can direct InDesign's hyphenation system to leave short words alone using the Words Longer Than option. If you don't want words like "many" to hyphenate, you can set this to 5 or higher.

**After First.** The value you enter here sets the minimum size, in characters, of the word fragment preceding a hyphen. Many typesetters dislike two-letter fragments, so they increase this value to three.

**Before Last.** The value you enter here sets the minimum size, in characters, of the word fragment following a hyphen. Some people don't mind if the "ly" in "truly" sits all by itself on a line. You care about type, so you set this to at least three.

**Hyphen Limit.** You can limit the number of consecutive hyphens you'll allow to appear at the left edge of a column of text using the Hyphen Limit field. Enter a value greater than one to allow consecutive hyphens.

**Hyphenation Zone.** Another way to limit the number of hyphens in a paragraph is the Hyphenation Zone setting. The idea is that there is an invisible zone along the right margin of each paragraph. If InDesign is trying to break a word at the end of a line, it looks to see where the hyphenation zone is. If the word *before* the potentially hyphenated word falls inside the zone, then InDesign just gives up and pushes the word onto the next line (without hyphenating it). If the previous word does not fall into the zone, then InDesign will hyphenate the word.

That's the concept, at least. As it turns out, InDesign's composition algorithms are complex enough that the hyphenation zone is often overridden by other factors, especially when using the Paragraph Composer. In addition, the Hyphenation Zone setting doesn't have any effect at all on justified text. In general, though, for non-justified text, larger amounts mean fewer hyphens but more variation in line lengths ("rag").

**Hyphenation Slider.** Someone, somewhere must have complained that InDesign's hyphenation controls weren't flexible enough, because those wacky engineers at Adobe have added the Hyphenation Slider to the Hyphenation dialog box. We're sure there's a lot of math behind what this slider is doing, but all you really need to know is that you can move the slider back and forth between Better Spacing and Fewer Hyphens to get a more pleasing appearance (turn on preview to see the effect of the slider).

This control is called "Nigel" because it goes all the way to eleven.

**Hyphenate Capitalized Words.** To prevent capitalized words (i.e., proper names) from hyphenating, turn off this option.

**Discretionary Hyphens.** There's another way to control hyphenation: Use a discretionary hyphen character. When you type a discretionary hyphen (Command-Shift-hyphen/Ctrl-Shift-hyphen) in a word, you're telling InDesign that you wouldn't mind if the word hyphenates here. This doesn't force the program to hyphenate the word at that point; it just gives it the option. This is much better than typing a regular hyphen because if (or when) your text reflows, you won't be stuck with hyphens littered in the middles of your paragraphs—the discretionary hyphen "disappears" when it's not needed. Another way to get a discretionary hyphen is to use the Insert Special Character submenu (in the Type menu or the context-sensitive menu).

By the way, longtime QuarkXPress users know that in that program you can place a discretionary hyphen before a word to make it not break. Not so in InDesign. Here, if you want a word (or phrase) not to hyphenate, you can select the text and turn on the No Break option in the Character palette's menu. If it's a word that you think should never be hyphenated, or should always be hyphenated differently than InDesign thinks, you can add it to your user dictionary (see "Adding Words to the User Dictionary" in Chapter 3, "Text").

**Controlling Word and Letter Spacing**

When InDesign composes the text in your publications, it does so by following the spacing rules you've laid down using the controls in the Justification dialog box (choose Justification from the Paragraph palette menu or press Command-Option-Shift-J/Ctrl-Alt-Shift-J to display the dialog box; see Figure 4-45). Contrary to popular opinion, this dialog box controls all text composition, not only that of justified text.

**FIGURE 4-45**
**Justification Dialog Box**

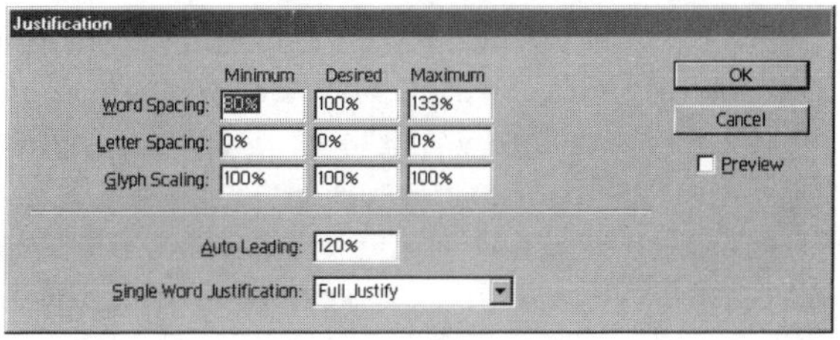

This dialog box offers five controls: Word Spacing, Letter Spacing, Glyph Scaling, Auto Leading, and Single Word Justification. The important thing to remember is that you will never find a set of spacing values that will work for all fonts, point sizes, and line lengths. In addition, the text that you are typesetting plays a role. Spacing settings that work for one writer's copy may not work for copy composed by a different author, even when the typesetting specifications are exactly the same. You just have to experiment to discover the settings that work best for you and your publications.

InDesign's default settings give you a reasonable starting point, these spacing values encourage wide word spacing over narrow word spacing, and attempt to discourage letter spacing.

**Word Spacing.** You can adjust the amount of space InDesign places between words by changing the Minimum, Desired, and Maximum percentages. In non-justified text, only the Desired value matters. In InDesign, the values in the word spacing fields are *percentages of* the standard word space in a font (the width of the space is defined by the font's designer, and is stored in the font—inside the screen font on the Macintosh, or in the .PFM file in Windows). The default settings tend to encourage slightly wide word spacing over narrow word spacing in justified text.

**Letter Spacing.** You can adjust the amount of space the program places between each character in your paragraphs by changing the Minimum, Desired, and Maximum percentages. Again, in non-justified text, only the Desired value makes a difference. These percentages represent the *amount of variation* from a standard spacing unit—the "spaceband" defined in the font. By default, the percentages are all set to zero, which discourages adjusting letter spacing at all.

**Glyph Scaling.** QuarkXPress and PageMaker both allow you to set the letterspacing and wordspacing values. The Glyph Scaling option, however, is something new, different, and, potentially, more than a little strange.

When you enter anything other than 100% in any of the Glyph Scaling fields, you give InDesign permission to horizontally scale the characters in the paragraph to make them fit. We are always opposed to distorting character shapes (our opposition doesn't extend to Multiple Master typefaces, which are designed to be squashed and stretched), but we have to admit that, used in very small doses (like 1-2% variation), this feature could come in handy. You can also enter larger values to use Glyph Scaling as a wacky design effect, but you'll have to endure the scowls of typesetting purists (see Figure 4-46).

FIGURE 4-46
**Glyph Scaling**

*Watch out—abuse of the Glyph Scaling option can result in obvious differences in the shape of characters from line to line.*

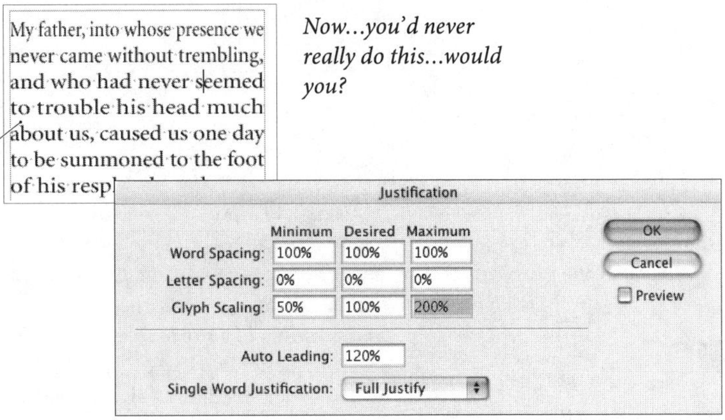

My father, into whose presence we never came without trembling, and who had never seemed to trouble his head much about us, caused us one day to be summoned to the foot of his resp

Now...you'd never really do this...would you?

| Justification | | | |
|---|---|---|---|
| | Minimum | Desired | Maximum |
| Word Spacing: | 100% | 100% | 100% |
| Letter Spacing: | 0% | 0% | 0% |
| Glyph Scaling: | 50% | 100% | 200% |
| Auto Leading: | 120% | | |
| Single Word Justification: | Full Justify | | |

OK  
Cancel  
☐ Preview

**Auto Leading.** The Auto Leading feature is easy: This controls how InDesign calculates the leading of characters that have a leading of Auto (see "Leading," earlier in this chapter, for why we never use Auto leading). This control is here, rather than in one of the Preferences dialog boxes, because the base autoleading percentage is a property of individual paragraphs (unlike QuarkXPress, where the autoleading percentage is set at the document level.).

**Single Word Justification.** What do you want InDesign to do when a word in the middle of a paragraph is so long (or a column so narrow) that only that one word fits on the line? If the line isn't justified, it's no big deal. But if the line is justified, do you want InDesign to add letterspacing to spread the word out across the line? Or make it flush left, flush right, or centered. That's what the Single Word Justification pop-up menu controls.

**Highlighting Typographic Problems**

Like PageMaker, InDesign can "flag" text composition problems—cases where the program has had to break your rules for composing text, or where substituted fonts appear in your publication. Choose Composition from the Preferences submenu of the Edit menu, then turn on the options in the Highlight section of the Composition Preferences dialog box. Lines in which InDesign has had to violate composition rules you've established (using the controls in the Justification and Keep Options dialog boxes) are highlighted in yellow; substituted fonts are highlighted in pink (see Figure 4-47). We usually work with these turned on so we can quickly identify "problem" lines.

FIGURE 4-47
**Highlighting Loose
and Tight Lines**

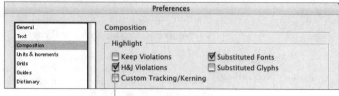

*When you turn on the H&J
Violations option...*

*...InDesign highlights lines
that break the spacing ranges
you set in the Justification
dialog box.*

"Scarcely had I pronounced these words
when a thick, black cloud cast its veil
over the firmament, and dimmed the
brilliancy about us; and the hiss of rain
and growling of a storm filled the air. At
last my father appeared, borne on a
meteor whose terrible effulgence flashed
fire upon the world. 'Stay, wretched

*InDesign uses three shades
of yellow to highlight loose
or tight lines—darker
shades indicate more
severe spacing problems.*

**Paragraph
Keep Options**

Widows and orphans are the bane of a typesetter's existence. A
widow is the last line of a paragraph that winds up all by itself at the
top of a column or page. An orphan is the first line of a paragraph
that lands all by itself at the bottom of a column or page.

Designers sometimes also refer to the single-word last line of a
paragraph as either a widow or an orphan. To avoid the confusion,
we often just use the word *runt*.

All typographic widows and orphans are bad, but certain kinds
are really bad—for example, a widow line that consists of only one
word, or even the last pat of a hyphenated word. Another related
typographic horror is the heading that stands alone with its following paragraph on the next page.

Fortunately, InDesign has a set of controls that can easily prevent
widows and orphans from sneaking into your document. These controls—along with a setting that lets you force a paragraph to begin
at a particular place—live in the Keep Options dialog box, which
you can find by selecting Keep Options from the Paragraph palette's
menu, or by pressing Command-Option-K/Ctrl-Alt-K (see Figure 4-
48). There are three parts to this dialog box: Keep with Next, Keep
Lines Together, and Start Paragraph.

**Keep with Next.** The Keep With Next Lines feature helps you ensure
that headings and the paragraphs that follow them are kept together.
If the paragraph is pushed onto a new column, a new page, or below
an obstructing object, the heading follows. It's rare that we need to
type more than 1 in the Lines field.

FIGURE 4-48
Keep Options

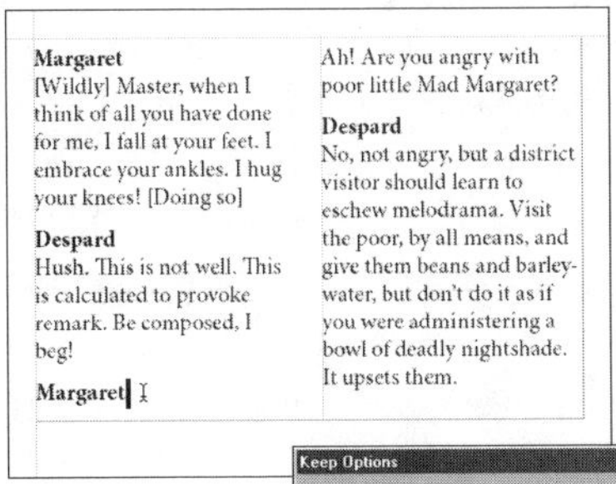

*This heading has come "unstuck" from the paragraph following it.*

*To prevent this, select the heading paragraph and display the Keep Options dialog box.*

*In addition to the Keep with Next control demonstrated in this example, the Keep Options dialog box contains other options that you can use to control the way that paragraphs break (or don't break) across columns and pages.*

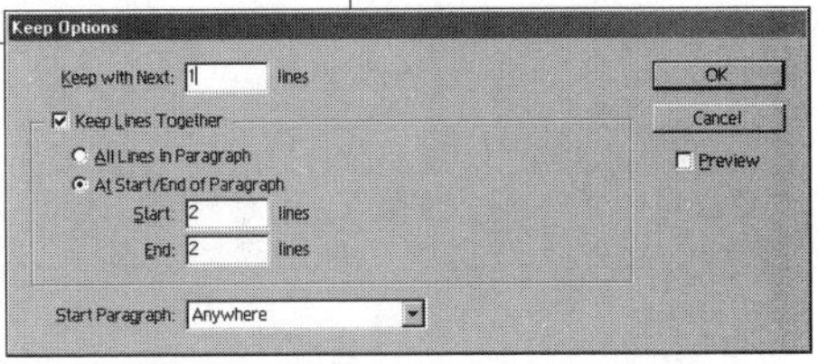

*Enter a value in the Keep with Next field. This way, when the paragraph following the heading moves to a new page or column, the heading follows along.*

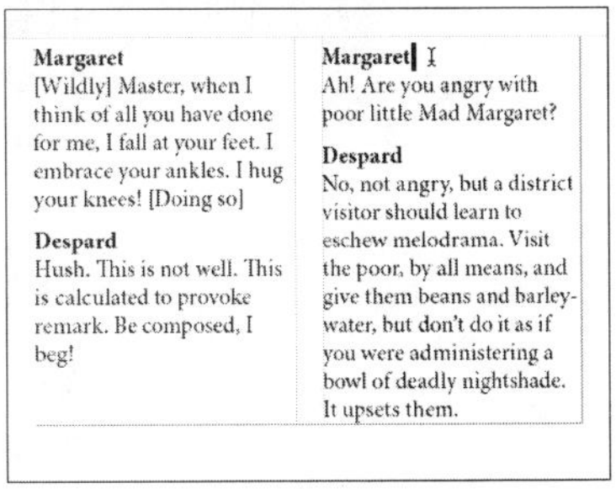

**Keep Lines Together.** The Keep Lines Together feature is the primary control over widows and orphans. When you turn on the Keep Lines Together checkbox and choose All Lines in Paragraph, InDesign not break the paragraph across column or pages. For example, if a paragraph spans across two pages, enabling All Lines In Paragraph results in that entire paragraph being pushed onto the next page to keep it together.

You can control the number of lines that should be kept together at the beginning and end of the paragraph by choosing At Start/End of Paragraph. The value you type in the Start field determines the minimum number of lines that InDesign allows at the beginning of a paragraph. For example, a Start value of 2 means that if at least two lines of that paragraph cannot be placed on the page, then the entire paragraph is pushed over to the next page. The value specified in the End field determines the minimum number of lines that InDesign lets fall alone at the top of a column or after an obstruction. Setting both Start and End to 2 means you'll never get an widow or orphan.

**Start Paragraph.** Use the options on the Start Paragraph pop-up menu to force a column or page break before your selected paragraph. For example, if you always want a particular paragraph to sit at the top of a page, select the paragraph and choose On Next Page from the Start Paragraph pop-up menu. The options are: Anywhere (this is the default value for paragraphs), In Next Column, In Next Frame, On Next Page, On Next Odd Page, and On Next Even Page.

Note that you can also get a similar effect by choosing an item from the Insert Break Character submenu in the Type menu (or the context-sensitive menu). The Start Paragraph feature is better, however, because you can use it in a definition of a paragraph style (see "Styles," next).

# Styles

When you think about the text in your publication, chances are good you're thinking of each paragraph as being a representative of a particular kind of text. You're thinking, "That's a headline, that's a subhead, and that's a photo caption." Chances are also good that you're thinking of those paragraphs as having certain formatting attributes: font, size, leading, and indents.

That's what text styles do—they bundle all those attributes together so you can apply them to text with a single click. But there's more—if you then change your mind about the formatting, you can edit the style, and all the text with that style applied to it (that is, "tagged" with the style) is reformatted automatically.

Once you've created a text style for a specific kind of text, you'll never have to claw your way through the Character palette or Paragraph palette again to format that text. Unless, of course, you want to apply a local formatting override to your styled text, which you're always free to do.

**Global versus Local Formatting.** We just mentioned "local" formatting. What are we talking about? The key to understanding text styles is understanding the difference between style-based formatting and local formatting.

Local formatting is what you get when you select text and apply formatting directly, using the Character palette or the choices on the Type menu. When you apply formatting using text styles, on the other hand, you're applying "global" formatting (that is, formatting specified by the selected style).

You can tell if there's local formatting applied to a styled paragraph by looking at the Paragraph Styles palette. Click the text tool in a styled paragraph, and you'll see a "+" before the style name if the paragraph contains local formatting (see Figure 4-49).

FIGURE 4-49
Styles and
Local Overrides

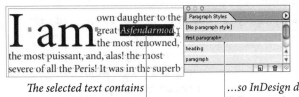

*The selected text contains
local formatting...*

*...so InDesign displays a
"+" next to the style name.*

**Plus What?** When you see that the text you've selected in a styled paragraph contains a local override, how can you tell what that local override is? It's easy—choose New Style from the Paragraph Styles palette menu (or Option/Alt click the New Style button in the palette), and InDesign displays the New Style palette. Look at the listing of attributes in the Style Settings list at the bottom of the palette—it'll say "<stylename> + next: Same Style +" (where "<stylename>" is the name of the style applied to the paragraph) and a list of formatting. The items in the list are the local formatting (see Figure 4-50). Now you can click Cancel (or press Command-period/Esc) to close this dialog box without actually creating a new style.

FIGURE 4-50
**Local Formatting?
What Local Formatting?**

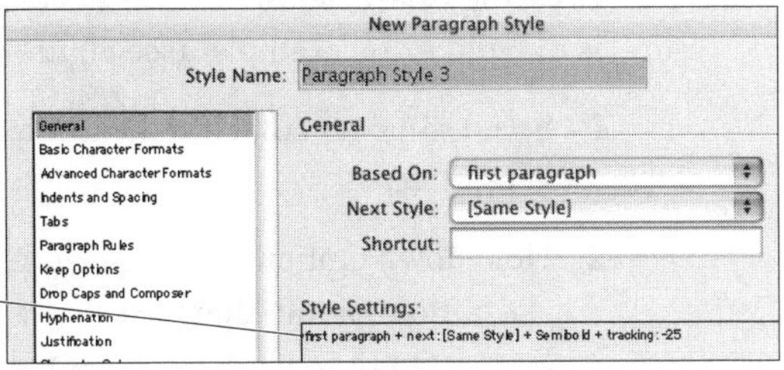

*InDesign lists the formatting
that varies from the formatting applied by the style.*

| | New Paragraph Style | |
| --- | --- | --- |
| | Style Name: Paragraph Style 3 | |
| General | General | |
| Basic Character Formats | | |
| Advanced Character Formats | Based On: first paragraph | |
| Indents and Spacing | Next Style: [Same Style] | |
| Tabs | Shortcut: | |
| Paragraph Rules | | |
| Keep Options | | |
| Drop Caps and Composer | | |
| Hyphenation | Style Settings: | |
| Justification | first paragraph + next: [Same Style] + Semibold + tracking: -25 | |

*What does the
"+" mean? To find
out, choose New
Style from the
Paragraph Styles
palette menu.*

**Styles Are More than Formatting.** When you apply a style to a paragraph (which we call "tagging" a paragraph with a style), you're doing more than just applying the formatting defined by the style. You're telling InDesign what the paragraph is—not just what it looks like, but what role it has to play in your publication. Is the paragraph important? Is it an insignificant legal notice in type that's intentionally too small to read? The style says it all.

The most important thing to remember when you're creating and applying styles is that tagging a paragraph with a style creates a link between the paragraph and all other paragraphs tagged with that style, and between the paragraph and the definition of the style. Change the style's definition, and watch the formatting and behavior of the paragraphs tagged with that style change to match.

If and when you start using XML to mark up your text (see Chapter 7, "Importing and Exporting"), you'll find that using text styles becomes really important.

**Character Styles**    By now, most of us are used to the idea of paragraph styles, which give us a way to apply multiple paragraph formatting attributes to an entire paragraph with a single action. (If you're not familiar with paragraph styles, we discuss them in the next section.) Character styles are just like paragraph styles, except that they can be applied to ranges of text smaller than an entire paragraph (and, obviously, they lack paragraph formatting features, such as alignment). Applying a character style to a text selection establishes a link between that text and the definition of the style—edit the style, and the formatting of the text changes.

Use character styles for any character formatting you use over and over again. Run-in headings, drop caps, and special ornamental characters are all good candidates for character styles. Each time you use a character style, you're saving yourself several seconds you would have spent fiddling with settings in the Character palette or the Type menu. It might not seem like much, but saving a few seconds several hundred times a day can add up.

**Creating Character Styles.** The easiest way to create a character style is to build it "by example" (see Figure 4-51).

1. Select some text that has the formatting you want in your character style.

2. Hold down Option/Alt while clicking the New Style button at the bottom of the Character Styles palette (or just select New Style from the Character Styles palette menu). InDesign displays the New Character Style dialog box.

3. At this point, if you want to create a relationship between this style and another character style, you can choose that style from the Based On pop-up menu (see "Creating Parent-Child Style Relationships," later in this chapter).

4. Now give your style a name. You can also assign a keyboard shortcut to the character style—the key used must use a modifier key (Command, Ctrl, or Shift and a number key from the numeric keypad; NumLock must be on to define the shortcut).

When you create a character style, InDesign does not automatically apply the style to the text you selected in step 1.

**QuarkXPress Users Beware:** InDesign's character styles are really different (and we think more powerful). In QuarkXPress, a character style always defines *all* the character formatting of the text—font,

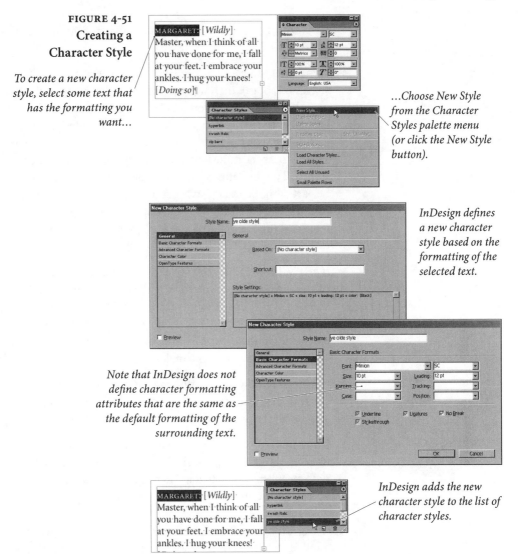

**FIGURE 4-51**

**Creating a Character Style**

*To create a new character style, select some text that has the formatting you want…*

*…Choose New Style from the Character Styles palette menu (or click the New Style button).*

*InDesign defines a new character style based on the formatting of the selected text.*

*Note that InDesign does not define character formatting attributes that are the same as the default formatting of the surrounding text.*

*InDesign adds the new character style to the list of character styles.*

color, size, and so on. InDesign's character styles, however, are defined by differences between the character formatting of the selected text and the default character formatting of the surrounding text. In InDesign you can create a character style defined as "+Size: 18, +Color: Red" which, when applied to a word, changes only its size and color, and retains all other underlying formatting.

This is actually a good thing—it means you can create character styles that affect some, but not all, of the attributes of a selection. It's different from the way that every other application defines character styles, and it takes some getting used to.

Here are a few things to keep in mind when defining character styles.

◆ If you're building a character style based on example text (as we suggested above), InDesign only picks up the formatting differences between the text you've selected and the paragraph style applied to the paragraph. For example, if the underlying paragraph style uses the font Minion Pro Italic, and the text you've selected uses the same font, the Font attribute of the character style will not be defined automatically. If you want the font to be part of the character style definition, you can add it once you have the New Character Style dialog box open (just select the font from the Font pop-up menu in the Basic Character Formats tab).

◆ If you want your character style to be defined by every attribute of your text selection, you can use the CreateCharacterStyle script (it's on your InDesign installation CD, inside the Scripting folder in the Adobe Technical Information folder). Or you can create the character style from scratch (not from example text), specifying the font, size, color, leading, and so on.

◆ Clicking the New Style button in the Character Styles palette creates a new character style based on whatever style was selected in the palette. It doesn't open a dialog box or anything.

◆ If you want to "undefine" an attribute in a character style (maybe you accidentally picked up the "Times" font when you didn't want the Font attribute to be defined at all), simply select and delete the current value (see Figure 4-52).

**Applying Character Styles.** To apply a character style, select some text and click the character style name in the Character Styles palette, or press the keyboard shortcut you assigned to the character style (see Figure 4-53).

Remember that when you apply a character style, only the attributes that are defined in the character style are changed. This can cause grave confusion and hair-pulling if you're used to the way QuarkXPress does it. For example, if you apply a character style that applies only the underline type style and color (see Figure 4-54)—it leaves all other character formatting (font, size, and so on) as is.

To remove a character style from a text selection, click No Character Style in the Character Styles palette. Note that this does not change the formatting of the selected text—it simply applies the formatting applied by the character style as local formatting. This

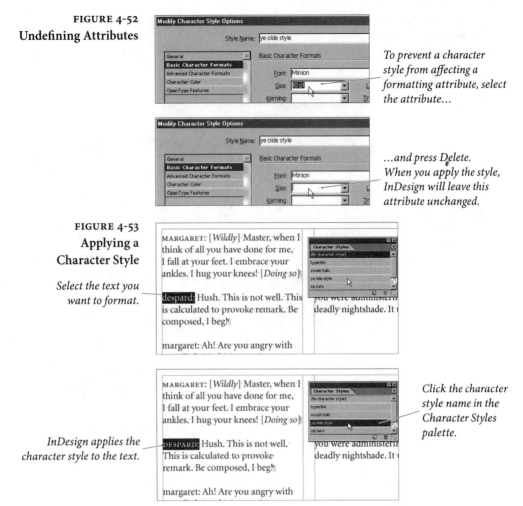

FIGURE 4-52
**Undefining Attributes**

*To prevent a character style from affecting a formatting attribute, select the attribute...*

*...and press Delete. When you apply the style, InDesign will leave this attribute unchanged.*

FIGURE 4-53
**Applying a Character Style**

*Select the text you want to format.*

*InDesign applies the character style to the text.*

*Click the character style name in the Character Styles palette.*

is sometimes useful when you want some text to be formatted like a character style, but you don't want it actually linked to that style (because you know the style definition might change). Selecting No Character Style breaks the link between text and its style definition.

If you want to remove a character style *and* reset the formatting to the publication's default formatting, hold down Option/Alt as you click No Character Style in the Character Styles palette.

**Editing Character Styles.** The great thing about styles is that that you can always change them later, and those changes ripple throughout your document. To edit a character style, hold down Command-Option-Shift/Ctrl-Shift and double-click the character style name in the Character Styles palette. InDesign will display the Modify Character Style dialog box.

FIGURE 4-54
**Character Styles Affect
Only Defined Attributes**

*The character style
"hyperlink" in this example
affects only the Underline
character format...*

*...and the fill color
of the text.*

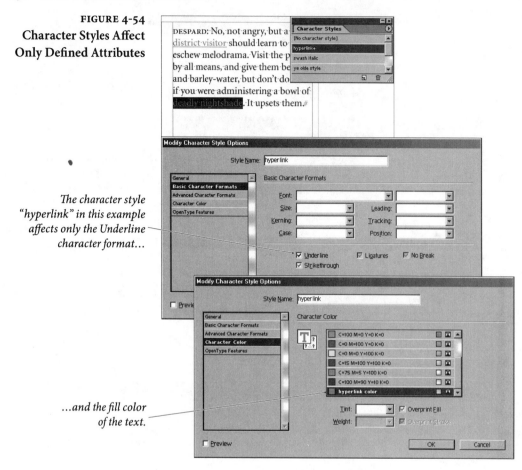

All of the other methods for editing the character style—double-clicking the character style name, or selecting the character style and choosing "Edit Style" from the Character Styles palette menu—apply the style before opening the dialog box. This means that the only time you can use these methods safely (that is, without applying the character style) is when your cursor is in text that has been formatted using the character style.

Remember—clicking a character style in the Character Styles palette when you have no text selected sets the publication default—the next time you create a text frame, the text in the text frame will be formatted using that character style.

So get used to using Command-Option-Shift/Ctrl-Shift-double-click. It's safer.

**Redefining Character Styles.** Editing a character style through the Modify Character Style Options dialog box works fine, but is kind of boring. For quick changes, try this: Find some text tagged with the character style you want to redefine and apply local formatting to it (change it to the way you want the style to be defined). A "+" will appear next to the character style name in the Character Styles palette. Next, without deselecting the text, press Command-Option-Shift-C/Ctrl-Alt-Shift-C. InDesign automatically redefines the character style based on the selected text (see Figure 4-55).

Alternatively, you can select the text and choose Redefine Style from the Character Style palette menu. But the keyboard shortcut is more fun.

FIGURE 4-55
**Redefining a
Character Style**

*Apply local formatting to
an instance of the character
style you want to redefine.
Select a character or
characters...*

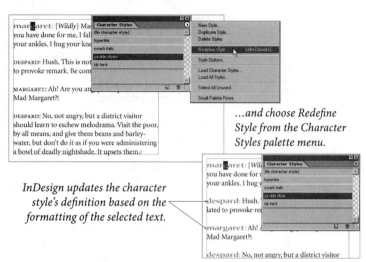

*...and choose Redefine
Style from the Character
Styles palette menu.*

*InDesign updates the character
style's definition based on the
formatting of the selected text.*

**Deleting character styles.** To remove a character style, press Command-Shift-A/Ctrl-Shift-A to deselect everything (do this so that you don't accidentally apply the character style to text), then select the character style and choose Delete Styles from the Character Styles palette menu (or click the Delete Style button in the palette).

What happens to the text you've tagged with that style? Note that InDesign does *not* give you an option to replace the style with another one (as QuarkXPress does). The formatting you applied throughout your document using the character style does not change in appearance, but becomes local formatting.

**Paragraph Styles**    Paragraph styles encapsulate all text formatting—both paragraph formatting and character formatting.

**Creating Paragraph Styles.** The easiest way (in our opinion) to create a text style is to format an example paragraph using local formatting, then create a new style based on that paragraph (see Figure 4-56).

FIGURE 4-56
Defining a
Paragraph Style

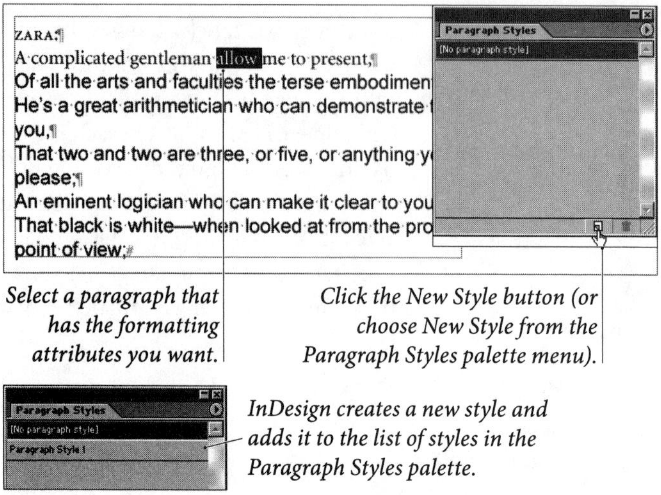

ZARA:¶
A·complicated·gentleman allow me·to·present,¶
Of·all·the·arts·and·faculties·the·terse·embodimen
He's·a·great·arithmetician·who·can·demonstrate·
you,¶
That·two·and·two·are·three,·or·five,·or·anything·y
please;¶
An·eminent·logician·who·can·make·it·clear·to·you
That·black·is·white—when·looked·at·from·the·pro
point·of·view;#

Paragraph Styles
[No paragraph style]

*Select a paragraph that
has the formatting
attributes you want.*

*Click the New Style button (or
choose New Style from the
Paragraph Styles palette menu).*

Paragraph Styles
[No paragraph style]
Paragraph Style 1

*InDesign creates a new style and
adds it to the list of styles in the
Paragraph Styles palette.*

1.  Select a formatted paragraph.

2.  Display the Paragraph Styles palette, if it's not already visible
    (press F11).

3.  Choose "New Style" from the Paragraph Styles palette menu (or
    Option/Alt-click the New Style button) to open the New Para-
    graph Style dialog box.

4.  Enter a name for the style in the Style Name field. You could
    leave the name set to the default, but we think it's better to enter
    a descriptive name—"heading 1" is quite a bit easier to remem-
    ber than "Paragraph Style 6."

    You can also assign a Next Style (see "Next Styles," later in
    this chapter) and a keyboard shortcut to the style—the shortcut
    must use a modifier key (Shift, Command/Ctrl, Option/Alt, or
    some combination of the above) and a number key from the
    numeric keypad (NumLock must be on to define the shortcut).

5.  Click the OK button.

When you're done, InDesign adds a new paragraph style. The
style definition includes all the character and paragraph formatting
applied to the first character in the selected "example" text.

That's all there is to it—you've created a paragraph style. InDesign
does not apply the style to the selected paragraph, so you'll probably
want to do that now (see "Applying Styles," below).

If you work by the hour you might prefer to create a style by using
the style definition dialog boxes, rather than basing your style on an
example.

1. Choose "New Style" from the Styles palette menu. InDesign displays the New Style dialog box.

2. Work your way through the dialog box, setting the options as you want them for your new style. When everything looks the way you want it to, press Return to close the dialog box.

Creating a style this way is a little bit more awkward than simply basing a style on an example paragraph, but some people prefer it. We've met at least one person who likes setting tabs "without all that pesky text in the way."

**Applying Paragraph Styles.** To apply a paragraph style, select a paragraph or series of paragraphs (remember, you don't have to select the entire paragraph to apply paragraph formatting—for a single paragraph, simply clicking the Text tool in the paragraph will do) and click a style name in the Paragraph Styles palette (see Figure 4-57). Alternatively, if you've defined a keyboard shortcut for the paragraph style, you can press the shortcut.

When you simply click a paragraph style to apply it, InDesign retains all the local formatting, so italic text remains italic, and so on. The one exception to this rule is when every character in the paragraph has local formatting—that stuff always gets removed.

To remove all local formatting as you apply a paragraph style, hold down Option/Alt as you click the paragraph style name. Any formatting applied using character styles is retained.

**FIGURE 4-57**

**Applying a Paragraph Style**

*Select the paragraphs you want to format (remember, you don't need to select the entire paragraph).*

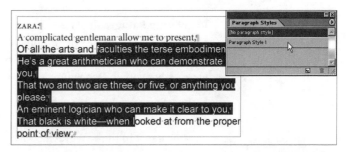

*Click a style name in the Paragraph Styles palette. InDesign applies the paragraph style to the selected paragraphs.*

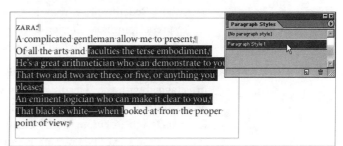

To remove all local formatting and remove formatting applied by character styles, hold down Option-Shift/Alt-Shift as you click the paragraph style name.

To remove a paragraph style from a text selection, click No Paragraph Style in the Paragraph Styles palette. Note that this does not change the formatting of the selected paragraphs—it simply applies the formatting applied by the paragraph style as local formatting. As we said in the "Character Styles" section, you can think of this as breaking the link between the paragraph and the style definition.

To remove a paragraph style and reset the formatting to the publication's default formatting, hold down Option/Alt as you click No Paragraph Style in the Paragraph Styles palette.

**Editing Paragraph Styles.** To edit a paragraph style, hold down Command-Option-Shift/Ctrl-Alt-Shift and double-click the paragraph style name in the Paragraph Styles palette. InDesign displays the Modify Paragraph Style dialog box, in which you can change the various character and paragraph attributes.

As we said earlier, all of the other methods for editing a style (you can double-click the style name, or select the style name and choose Edit Style from the Paragraph Styles palette menu) apply the style to the paragraph you're in (or, if the cursor isn't in text, this becomes the default style you'll get next time you create a text frame). So it's really worth using the Command-Option-Shift/Ctrl-Alt-Shift keyboard shortcut.

**Redefining Paragraph Styles.** The easiest way to *create* a paragraph style is to base the style's definition on the formatting of an example paragraph. The easiest way to update the style definition? The same. Here's what you do (see Figure 4-58).

1. Pick any paragraph tagged with the style you want to change, and apply local formatting to it (a "+" will appear next to the style name in the Paragraph Styles palette).

2. Choose Redefine Style from the Character Style palette menu (or press Command-Option-Shift-R/Ctrl-Alt-Shift-R). InDesign redefines the style based on the selected paragraph.

**Next Style.** If you're typing in InDesign, and the paragraph you're in is tagged with the "Heading" style, you probably don't want the next paragraph to be tagged with "Heading" too, right? You can force InDesign to automatically change the subsequent paragraph style with the Next Style pop-up menu in the New Paragraph Style

**FIGURE 4-58**
**Redefining a**
**Paragraph Style**

*Change the formatting of an example paragraph tagged with the paragraph style you want to change. A "+" appears next to the style name in the Paragraph Styles palette.*

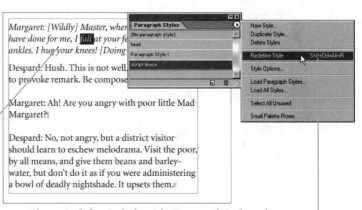

*Choose Redefine Style from the Paragraph Styles palette menu.*

*InDesign updates all instances of the style with the formatting of the selected paragraph.*

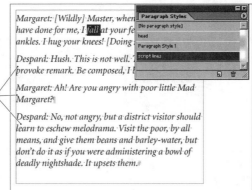

or Modify Paragraph Style Options dialog box (see Figure 4-59). For example, if you want the subsequent paragraph to be "BodyText," then choose "BodyText" from the Next Style pop-up menu.

Note that this only works if the insertion point is at the end of a paragraph when you press Return/Enter. If the insertion point is anywhere else, you'll simply break that paragraph in two, and both new paragraphs will have the same style as the original one. In other words, this feature is intended to be used while you're typing, not editing or formatting. That said, it certainly can come in handy once in a while.

**Selecting Unused Paragraph Styles.** Choose Select All Unused from the Paragraph Styles palette menu to select all paragraph styles that are not applied to any text in the publication. Typically, the only reason you'd want to do this is to delete them all.

**Deleting Paragraph Styles.** To remove a paragraph style from your document, first deselect everything (press Command-Shift-A/Ctrl-Shift-A), then select the style name in the Paragraph Styles palette

**FIGURE 4-59**
**Next Style**

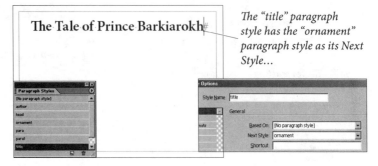

*The "title" paragraph style has the "ornament" paragraph style as its Next Style...*

*In this example, we have set the Next Style option for each paragraph style to automatically apply the paragraph style we want when we press Return/Enter.*

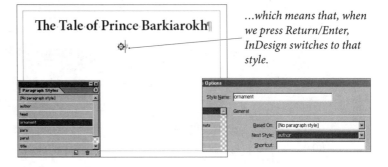

*...which means that, when we press Return/Enter, InDesign switches to that style.*

*The "ornament" style, in turn, has the paragraph style named "author" as its next style, so pressing Return/Enter as we type text switches to the "author" style.*

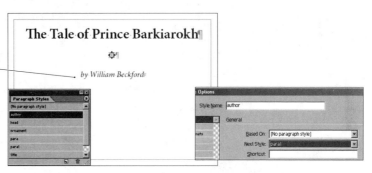

*When we enter text following the "author" paragraph style, InDesign applies the "para1" style, which includes drop cap formatting.*

*The wonderful thing about the Next Style property is that all of these paragraph style assignments take place as we type; we never have to reach for the Styles palette.*

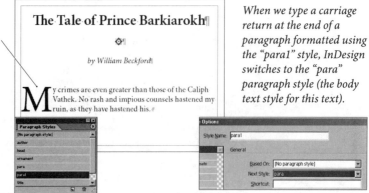

*When we type a carriage return at the end of a paragraph formatted using the "para1" style, InDesign switches to the "para" paragraph style (the body text style for this text).*

and choose Delete Styles from the palette's menu (or click the Delete Style button at the bottom of the palette). InDesign deletes the style.

Unfortunately, InDesign won't give you a choice of how to handle paragraphs already tagged with that style (as QuarkXPress does). Instead, when you delete a paragraph style, InDesign simply assigns No Paragraph Style to the paragraph, and changes the formatting of each paragraph to local formatting. In the meantime, if you want to replace one paragraph style with another throughout a document, use the Find/Change palette (see Chapter 3, "Text").

**Creating Parent-Child Style Relationships**

One powerful feature of InDesign's character and paragraph styles is the ability to base one style on another, also called parent-child relationships (see Figure 4-60). You can base a style on another one by choosing a style from the Based On pop-up menu in either the New Style or the Modify Style dialog box (this works for either character or paragraph styles).

For example, in this book, there are body text styles for paragraphs that follow headings, paragraphs that are in lists, paragraphs that have run-in heads, and so on—but they're all based on one "parent" paragraph style. If we need to make the text size a half-point smaller, we could edit the parent style and the change would ripple throughout the book.

FIGURE 4-60
**Using Based On**

heading 1

heading 2

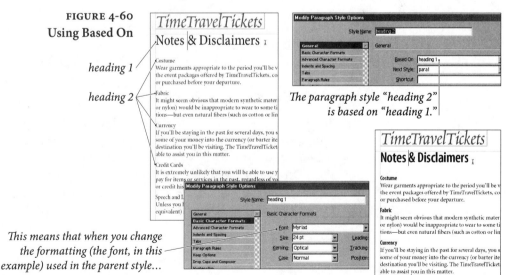

The paragraph style "heading 2" is based on "heading 1."

This means that when you change the formatting (the font, in this example) used in the parent style...

...the change affects all of the child styles.

When one style is based on another, InDesign keeps track of the differences between the base style and the new style. Let's say you have a style called "Head1" and it's 18-point Futura with a 3 pica left indent, and a style called "Head2" that's based on "Head1," except that it's 12-point Futura. The difference between the two is the point size. If you change Head1's font, color, or anything *except* its point size, the edit ripples through to Head2. Nothing happens if you just edit the point size of Head1 because the "point size link" is broken between the two styles.

Later, if you edit Head2 so that it has the same point size as Head1, then that link is re-established, and changing Head1's size *will* ripple through to Head2.

If this all is making your head spin, try making your own styles based on other styles and you'll get the hang of it in a jiffy.

By the way, if your text cursor is in a paragraph when you create a new style, that paragraph's style becomes the "based on" style. If you don't want your new style to be based on anything, make sure the Based On pop-up menu is set to No Paragraph Style.

## Copying Styles From Other Publications

One of the great things about character and paragraph styles is that you can use them to unify standard formatting across a range of publications—the chapters of this book, for example. While you can't define a "master" style sheet and have all publications get their style definitions from it (as you can in FrameMaker), you can easily copy styles from one InDesign publication to another.

◆ To copy character styles from another publication, choose Load Character Styles from the Character Styles palette menu. InDesign displays the Open a File dialog box. Locate and select the InDesign publication file containing the styles you want and click the Open button. InDesign copies the character styles from that publication into the current document.

◆ To copy paragraph styles from one publication to another choose Load Paragraph Styles from the Paragraph Styles palette menu.

◆ To import both character and paragraph styles from another publication, choose Load All Styles from the palette menu of either the Character Styles palette or the Paragraph Styles palette.

When you import styles that have the same name as styles that already exist in the publication, InDesign overrides the attributes of the existing styles with the attributes of the incoming styles.

You can also move styles by copying text tagged with the styles you want from one publication and pasting it into another document (or dragging a text frame from one document into another). If the styles do not exist in the document you've pasted the text into, InDesign adds them. If the styles already exist, InDesign overrides the style definitions in the incoming text with the style definitions of the existing styles.

You can also synchronize style sheets among all the documents in a book when you use the Book palette, which we talk about in Chapter 8, "Long Documents."

**Libraries of Styles.** One of our favorite uses for libraries (see "Library palette" in Chapter 1, "Workspace") is to save paragraph and character styles that we use in multiple documents. In a small text frame, we type a few words (usually the name of the style) and then apply one or more styles to them. Then we drag the text frame into a library (select Library from the New submenu, under the File menu, if you haven't already made one) and double-click on the library thumbnail to give it a name and description. Later, when we need that style in some other document, we can open the library file, drag that text frame into our document, and then delete the text frame—the styles remain. Of course, this works with libraries of color swatches, too.

## Optical Margin Alignment

Ever since Gutenberg set out to print his Bible, typesetters have looked for ways to "balance" the edges of columns of text—particularly lines ending or beginning with punctuation. Because the eye doesn't "see" punctuation, it can sometimes appear that the left or right edges of some columns of type (especially justified type) are misaligned. Some other programs compensate for this problem by using a "hanging punctuation" feature, which pushes certain punctuation characters outside the text column. But there's more to making the edges of a column look even than just punctuation. Some characters can create a "ragged" look all by themselves—think of a "W," at the beginning of a line, for example.

When you select an InDesign story (with either the Selection or the Type tool) and turn on the Optical Margin Alignment option in the Story palette (choose Story from the Type menu to display the Story palette), the program balances the edges of the columns based on the appearance of *all* of the characters at the beginning or end of the lines in the column. This adjustment makes the columns appear more even—even though it sometimes means that characters are extending *beyond* the edges of the column (see Figure 4-61).

The amount that InDesign "hangs" a character outside the text column depends on the setting you enter in the Base Size field of the Story palette (that's the field with the icon that looks like it would make a drop cap). In general, you should enter the point size of your body text in this field.

Unfortunately, it turns out that many designers don't like the look of Optical Margin Alignment. It's not that the feature is flawed; it's that designers (especially younger folks) have become accustomed to the lower quality of type set without this feature. Nevertheless, we encourage you to try turning it on and seeing how your readers like it—we think they'll find the text actually easier to read.

**FIGURE 4-61**
**Optical Margin Alignment**

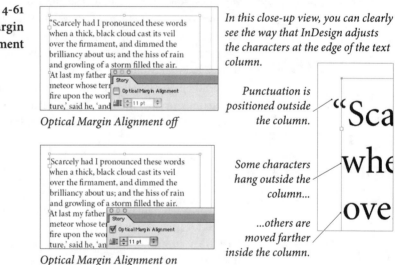

*Optical Margin Alignment off*

*Optical Margin Alignment on*

*In this close-up view, you can clearly see the way that InDesign adjusts the characters at the edge of the text column.*

*Punctuation is positioned outside the column.*

*Some characters hang outside the column...*

*...others are moved farther inside the column.*

## An Old Typesetter Never...

Late night. The sound of the espresso machine in the kitchen about to reach critical mass and melt down, destroying the office and civilization as we know it. The office is different, the equipment and the coffee are better, but we still seem to be up late at night setting type.

And, to tell you the truth, we're not sure we would have it any other way.

# Drawing

## CHAPTER 5

Fifteen of the twenty-seven tools in the InDesign toolbox are drawing tools. Using these tools, you can draw almost anything—from straight lines and boxes to incredibly complex freeform shapes.

The drawing tools can be divided into three types: the Rectangle, Polygon, Oval, and Line tools are for drawing basic shapes; the Pencil, Smooth, Eraser, Pen, Add Point, Delete Point, and Convert Point tools draw or edit more complex paths (see Figure 5-1). The Scissors tool gives you a way of cutting paths.

Some of the path drawing tools (the Rectangle, Oval, and Polygon tools) have counterparts that draw frames (the Rectangular Frame, Oval Frame, and Polygonal Frame tools). The only thing different about these tools is that the "frame" versions draw paths whose content type has been set to "Graphic" (the "regular" versions of these tools draw paths whose content type is "Undefined"). That's it.

In this book, we'll use the default variant of the tool to refer to both tools—when we say "the Rectangle tool," we're referring to both the Rectangle tool and the Rectangular Frame tool.

FIGURE 5-1
**Drawing Tools**

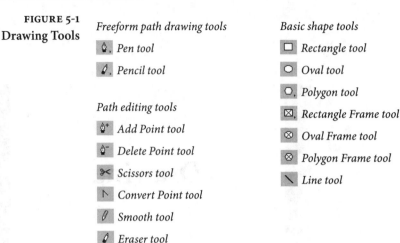

Which path drawing tools should you use? Don't worry too much about it—the basic shapes can be converted into freeform paths, and the freeform drawing tools can be used to draw basic shapes.

The paths you draw in InDesign are made up of points, and the points are joined to each other by line segments (see Figure 5-2). An InDesign path is just like a connect-the-dots puzzle. Connect all the dots together in the right order, and you've made a picture, or part of a picture. Because points along a path have an order, or winding, you can think of each point as a milepost along the path. Or as a sign saying, "Now go this way."

**A Brief Note on Path Drawing Terminology.** Adobe likes to refer to points on a path as "anchor points," and to control handles as "direction lines." We don't.

FIGURE 5-2
**Parts of a Path**

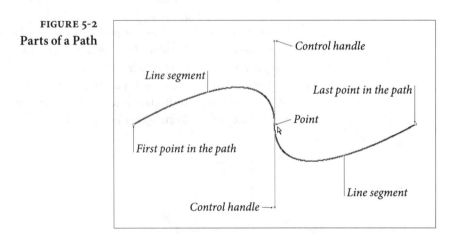

# Drawing Basic Shapes

The basic shapes tools (the Rectangle, Polygon, Oval, and Line tools, and their frame-drawing counterparts) don't draw anything you couldn't draw using the Pen tool (discussed later in this chapter) or (even) the Pencil tool; they just make drawing certain types of paths easier. They're shortcuts.

The operation of the basic shapes tools is straightforward: drag the tool and get a path of the corresponding shape. If you want to draw a frame, you can either use the frame-drawing variant of the tool, or draw the path and then convert it to a frame.

To draw a rectangle, oval, polygon, or line, follow the steps below (see Figure 5-3).

1. Select the appropriate tool from the Toolbox.

    To specify what type of polygon you'll be drawing, double-click the Polygon tool and choose the shape you want in the Polygon Settings dialog box before you start drawing.

2. Position the cursor where you want one corner of the shape, then drag. InDesign draws a path, starting where you first held down the mouse button.

    To draw squares, hold down Shift as you drag the Rectangle tool. To draw circles, hold down Shift as you drag the Oval tool. When you hold down Shift as you drag, the Polygon tool produces equilateral polygons. Holding down Shift as you drag the Line tool constrains the angle of the line to 45-degree tangents from the point at which you started dragging.

    Hold down Option to draw a basic shape from its geometric center point.

3. When the basic shape is the size and shape you want it to be, stop dragging and release the mouse button.

FIGURE 5-3
**Drawing a Basic Shape**

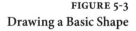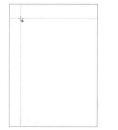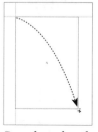

*Select a basic shape tool (in this example, the Rectangle tool).*

*Drag the tool on the page.*

*InDesign creates a basic shape.*

You can also create rectangles and ellipses by specifying their width and height (see Figure 5-4).

1. Select the Rectangle tool or the Ellipse tool from the Toolbox.

2. Position the cursor where you want to place one corner of the basic shape, or hold down Option/Alt and position the cursor where you want to place the center point of the shape.

3. Click. InDesign displays the Rectangle dialog box (if you've selected the Rectangle tool) or the Ellipse dialog box (if you've selected the Ellipse tool).

4. Enter values in the Width and Height fields, then click the OK button.

**FIGURE 5-4**
**Adding a Basic Shape**
**"by the Numbers"**

*Select a basic shape tool.*

*You can control the origin of the basic shape by selecting a point on the Transform palette's Proxy before you click.*

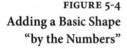

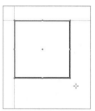

*Click the tool on the page or pasteboard.*

*InDesign displays a dialog box (Rectangle, Polygon, or Ellipse). Enter the dimensions of the basic shape and click the OK button.*

*InDesign creates a basic shape with the dimensions you entered.*

## Points and Paths

Why is it that the most important things are often the most difficult to learn? Drawing by manipulating Bezier paths—the geometric construct used to represent path shapes in most of today's vector drawing programs—is one of those difficult things. When we first approached FreeHand and Illustrator, the process of drawing by placing points, and manipulating control handles struck us as alien, as nothing like drawing at all. Then we started to catch on.

In many ways, we had been drawing lines from the point of view of everything *but* the line; in a Bezier-path-drawing program such as InDesign, we draw lines from the point of view of the line itself. This is neither better nor worse; it's just different and takes time to get used to. If you've just glanced at the Pen tool and are feeling confused, we urge you to stick with it. Start thinking like a line.

**Thinking like a Line**    Imagine that, through the action of some mysterious potion or errant cosmic ray, you've been reduced in size so that you're a little smaller than one of the dots in a connect-the-dots puzzle. For added detail and color, imagine that the puzzle appears in a *Highlights for Children* magazine in a dentist's office.

The only way out is to complete the puzzle. As you walk, a line extends behind you. As you reach each dot in the puzzle, a sign tells you where you are in the puzzle and the route you must take to get to the next dot in the path.

Get the idea? The dots in the puzzle are points. The route you walk from one point to another, as instructed by the signs at each point, is a line segment. Each series of connected dots is a path. As you walk from one dot to another, you're thinking like a line.

Each point—from the first point in the path to the last—carries with it some information about the line segments that attach it to the previous and next points along the path.

Paths and their formatting (fill and stroke) attributes are different things. Even if the fill and stroke applied to the path is "None" or the stroke weight is 0 there's still a path there.

When you select a point, the point "fills in," becoming a solid square (see Figure 5-5). Note that this is the way that Illustrator displays a selected point, but the opposite of FreeHand's method.

**FIGURE 5-5**
**Selected and**
**Unselected Points**

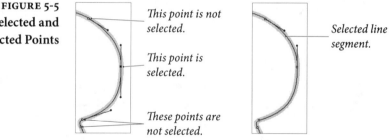

This point is not selected.

This point is selected.

These points are not selected.

Selected line segment.

**Point Types**    Points on an InDesign path are either *corner points* or *curve points*. Each type of point has its own special properties.

◆ A curve point adds a curved line segment between the current point and the preceding and following points along the path. Curve points have two control handles extended from them, and moving one control handle affects the position of the other control handle. The control handle following the point controls the curve of the line segment following the curve point on the path; the control handle preceding the point controls the curve of the line segment preceding the curve point on the path. Curve points are typically used to add smooth curves to a path (see Figure 5-6).

◆ A corner point adds a straight line segment between the current point and the preceding point on the path (see Figure 5-7). Corner points are typically used to create paths containing straight line segments.

**FIGURE 5-6**
**Curve Points**

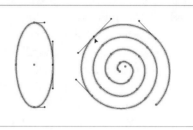

*Curve points curve the line segments attached to the point. All of the points in this example are curve points.*

**FIGURE 5-7**
**Corner Points**

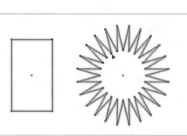

*Corner points, by default, apply no curve to the line segments attached to the point. All of the points in this example are corner points.*

What type of points should you use? Any type of point can be turned into any other type of point, and anything you can do with one kind of point can be done with the other kind of point. Given these two points (so to speak), you can use the kinds of points and drawing tools you're happiest with and achieve exactly the results you want. There is no "best way" to draw with InDesign's Pen tool, but it helps to understand how the particular method you choose works.

**Winding**    Paths have a direction, also known as "winding" (as in "winding a clock"—nothing to do with the weather) that generally corresponds to the order and direction in which you placed their points (see Figure 5-8). In our connect-the-dots puzzle, winding tells us the order in which we connect the dots.

To reverse the direction of a path, select the path and choose Reverse Path from the Object menu (in InDesign 1.0, you had to use the Direct Selection tool to select a point before InDesign would let you reverse the path). InDesign reverses the direction of the path.

**FIGURE 5-8**
**Winding**

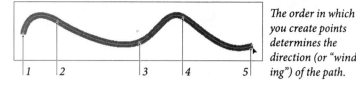

*The order in which you create points determines the direction (or "winding") of the path.*

1  2  3  4  5

**Control Handles**

You control the curvature of the line segments before and after each point using the point's control handles. Points can have up to two control handles attached to them. By default, new corner points have none and curve points have two. Note that each line segment has up to two control handles defining its curve—the "outgoing" control handle attached to the point defining the start of the line segment and the "incoming" control handle attached to the next point.

If you retract the control handle (by dragging it inside the point), the control handle has no effect on the curvature of the path. This doesn't necessarily mean that the line segment is a straight line, however—a control handle on the point at the other end of the line segment might also have an effect on the curve of the line segment.

The most significant difference between corner points and curve points is that the control handles attached to a corner point can be adjusted independently, while changing the angle of one control handle of a curve point changes the angle of the other control handle (see Figure 5-9). This difference, in our opinion, makes corner points more useful than curve points—you can do anything with a corner point you could do with a curve point or a connector point.

To convert a point from one point type to another, click the point using the Convert Point tool. If you click a curve point, this retracts both control handles. To convert a curve point to a corner point while leaving one of its control handles in place, drag the other control handle using the Convert Point tool (see Figure 5-10).

**FIGURE 5-9**
**Curve Points Vs.**
**Corner Points**

*When you adjust one control handle on a curve point, InDesign adjusts the other control handle, as well.*

*To adjust the curvature of a line segment without changing the curve of the following line segment, use a corner point.*

FIGURE 5-10
**Converting From One Point Type to Another**

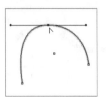
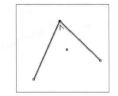

*Position the Convert Point tool over a curve point...*

*...and click. InDesign converts the curve point to a corner point.*

*To convert a corner point to a curve point, drag the Convert Point tool over the point.*

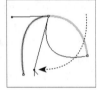

*To convert a curve point to a corner point, drag one of the control handles using the Convert Point tool.*

*InDesign converts the curve point to a corner point. As you drag the control handle...*

*...InDesign adjusts the curve of the corresponding line segment, but leaves the other line segment unchanged.*

## Drawing Paths with the Pencil Tool

The quickest way to create a freeform path on an InDesign page is to use the Pencil tool. Click the Pencil tool in the Tools palette (or press N), then drag the Pencil tool on the page. As you drag, InDesign creates a path that follows the cursor, automatically placing corner and curve points as it does so (see Figure 5-11).

FIGURE 5-11
**Drawing with the Pencil Tool**

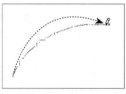

*Select the Pencil tool and position it where you want the path to start.*

*Drag the Pencil tool on the page or pasteboard.*

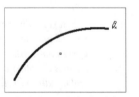

*When the path looks the way you want it to, stop dragging.*

*As you drag the Pencil tool, InDesign positions curve and corner points.*

# Drawing Paths with the Pen Tool

You use the Pen tool and its variants (the Remove Point, Add Point, and Convert Point tools)—to create and edit paths.

When you *click* the Pen tool in the publication window, InDesign places a corner point. *Drag* the Pen tool, and InDesign places a curve point where you started dragging—you determine the length of the control handles (and, therefore, the shape of the curve) by dragging as you place the curve point (see Figure 5-12).

**FIGURE 5-12**

**Placing Curve and Corner Points**

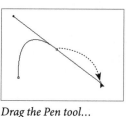

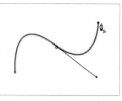

*Drag the Pen tool...*                    *...and InDesign creates a curve point.*

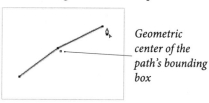

Geometric center of the path's bounding box

*Click the Pen tool...*                    *...and InDesign creates a corner point.*

To curve the line segment following a *corner* point, place the corner point, position the Pen tool above the point (this switches to the Convert Point tool), and then drag. As you drag, InDesign extends a control handle from the point (see Figure 5-13).

The trickiest thing about using the Pen tool this way is that you don't see the effect of the curve manipulation until you've placed the next point. This makes sense in that you don't need a control handle for a line segment that doesn't yet exist, but it can be quite a brain-twister.

**FIGURE 5-13**

**Dragging a Control Handle Out of a Corner Point**

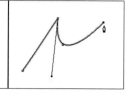

*Position the Pen tool above a point (it will change into the Convert Point tool).*

*Drag a control handle out of the point.*

*Click the Pen tool to add a point. InDesign curves the line segment connecting the points.*

To convert a curve point you've just placed to a corner point, position the Pen tool above the point (to switch to the Convert Point tool) and then click the point. InDesign converts the point to a corner point and retracts the point's control handles.

You can change the position of points, as you'd expect, by selecting the point with the Direct Selection tool and then dragging the point to a new location.

## Drawing Techniques

Now that you know all about the elements that make up paths, let's talk about how you actually use them.

**Path Drawing Tips**   When you're drawing paths, don't forget that you can change the path after you've drawn it. We've often seen people delete entire paths and start over because they misplaced the last point on the path. Go ahead and place points in the wrong places; you can always change the position of any point on the path. Also, keep these facts in mind:

◆ You can always split the path using the Scissors tool.

◆ You can always add points to or subtract points from the path.

◆ You can always change tools while drawing a path.

It's also best to create paths using as few points as you can—but it's not required. We've noticed that people who have just started working with Bezier drawing tools use more points than are needed to create their paths. Over time, they learn one of the basic rules of vector drawing: Any curve can be described by two points and their associated control handles. No more, no less.

**Manipulating Control Handles**   The aspect of drawing in InDesign that's toughest to understand and master is the care, feeding, and manipulation of control handles. These handles are fundamental to drawing curved lines, so you'd better learn how to work with them.

To adjust the curve of a line segment, use the Direct Selection tool to select a point attached to the line segment. The control handles attached to that point—and to the points that come before and after the selected point on the path—appear. If you don't see control handles attached to the point you selected, the curve of the line segment is controlled by the points at the other end of the line segments. Position the cursor over one of the control handles and drag. The curve of the line segment associated with that handle changes as you drag. When the curve looks the way you want it to, stop dragging (see Figure 5-14).

To retract (delete) a control handle, drag the handle inside the point it's attached to.

You can also adjust the curve of a curved line segment by dragging the line segment itself. To do this, select the line segment (click the line segment with the Direct Selection tool, or use the tool to drag a selection rectangle over part of the line segment) and then drag. As you drag, InDesign adjusts the curve of the line segment (see Figure 5-15).

**Adding Points to a Path**

To add a point to an existing line segment, select the path, switch to the Pen tool, and then click the Pen tool on the line segment. InDesign adds a point to the path (see Figure 5-16).

You don't need to select the Add Point tool—InDesign will switch to it when you move the Pen tool above a line segment.

**FIGURE 5-14**
**Adjusting Curve Points**

 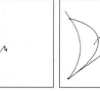 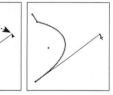

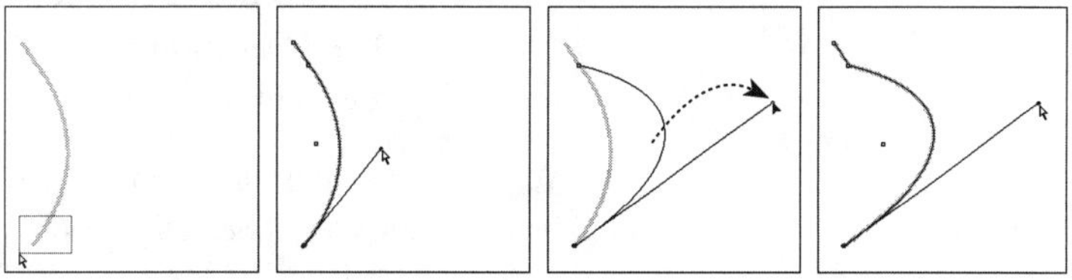

*Select a point using the Direct Selection tool.*   *Drag the control handle attached to the point to a new location.*   *InDesign curves the line segment.*

**FIGURE 5-15**
**Another Way to Adjust the Curve of a Line Segment**

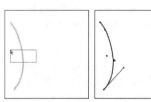 

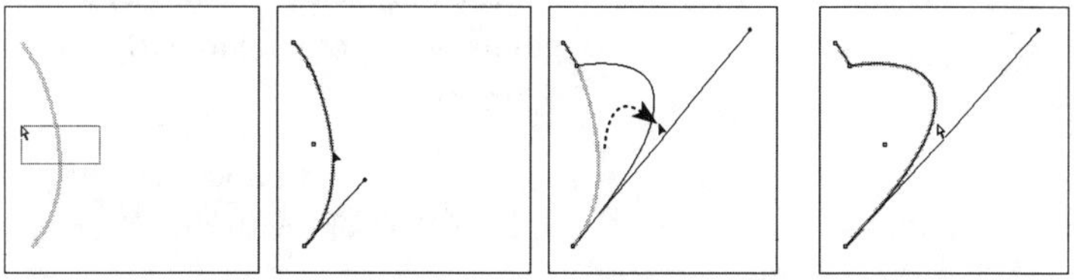

*Select a line segment using the Direct Selection tool (drag a selection rectangle over the line segment).*   *Drag the line segment. As you drag, InDesign adjusts the curve of the line segment.*

**FIGURE 5-16**
**Adding a Point to a Path**

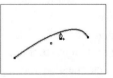 

*Position the Pen tool above a line segment. InDesign switches to the Add Point tool.*   *Click on the path, and InDesign adds a point to the path.*

**Removing Points From a Path**

To remove a point from a path, select the path, switch to the Pen tool, and then click the Pen tool on the point. InDesign removes the point from the path (see Figure 5-17).

**FIGURE 5-17**
**Removing a Point From a Path**

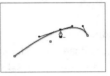

*Position the Pen tool above an existing point on a path. InDesign switches to the Delete Point tool.*

*Click the point, and InDesign removes the point from the path.*

**Selecting and Moving Points**

If you've gotten this far, you probably know how to select points, but here are a few rules to keep in mind.

◆ To select a point, click it with the Direct Selection tool, or drag a selection rectangle over it (using the same tool).

◆ You can select more than one point at a time. To do this, hold down Shift as you click the Direct Selection tool on each point, or use the Direct Selection tool to drag a selection rectangle over the points you want to select.

◆ You can select points on paths inside groups or compound paths by using the Direct Selection tool.

◆ When you move a point, the control handles associated with that point also move, maintaining their positions relative to the point. Note that this means that the curves of the line segments attached to the point change, unless you're also moving the points on the other end of the incoming and outgoing line segments.

◆ To move a straight line segment and its associated points, select the line segment with the Direct Selection tool and drag.

**Opening and Closing Paths**

Paths can be open or closed (see Figure 5-18). An open path has no line segment between the beginning and ending points on the path. You don't have to close a path to add contents (text or a graphic) or apply a fill to the path.

To close an open path, select the path, select the Pen tool, and then click the Pen tool on the first or last point on the path (it doesn't matter which). Click the Pen tool again on the other end point. InDesign closes the path (see Figure 5-19).

To open a closed path, select the Direct Selection tool and click the line segment between two points on the path (you can also drag a selection rectangle over the line segment. Press Delete, and InDesign removes the line segment, opening the path between the points on either side of the line segment (see Figure 5-20).

To open a path *without* removing a line segment, select the Scissors tool and click the path. Click on a point to split the path at that point, or click a line segment to split the path at that location (see Figure 5-21).

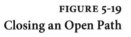

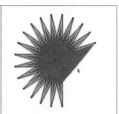

*Closed path.*       *Open path.*       *A path does not have to be closed to have a fill.*

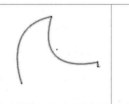

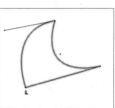

*Move the Pen tool over an endpoint of an open path.*    *Click the Pen tool, then move it over the other endpoint on the path.*    *Click on the endpoint. InDesign closes the path.*

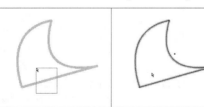

*Select the Direct Selection tool, then drag a selection rectangle over a line segment.*    *Press the Delete key to delete the line segment.*

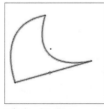
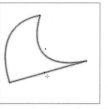

*Click a line segment or point with the Scissors tool.*    *InDesign opens the path.*    *You can drag the path's endpoints apart, if necessary.*

The point closest to the start of the path (following the path's winding) becomes the point farther to the back, and the point farthest from the start of the path is on top of it.

**Joining Open Paths**    You can join two open paths to create a single path, or you can join two closed paths to create a compound path. In this section, we'll talk about joining open paths. For more on joining closed paths to create compound paths, see the section "Compound Paths," below.

To join two open paths, follow these steps (see Figure 5-22).

1.  Select the Pen tool.

2.  Position the Pen tool above the start or end point of one of the open paths (you don't need to select either path). InDesign changes the cursor to indicate that it's ready to add a point to the path.

3.  Click the Pen tool, then position the cursor over the start or end point of the second path. InDesign changes the cursor to show that it's ready to connect the current path to the point.

4.  Click the Pen tool. InDesign joins the two paths.

5.  Repeat this process for the other two end points to close the path, if necessary.

FIGURE 5-22
**Joining Open Paths**

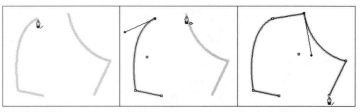

*Position the Pen tool over an endpoint of an open path.*

*Click the Pen tool to continue the path, then move the cursor over the endpoint of another open path.*

*Click the Pen tool on one of the remaining endpoints.*

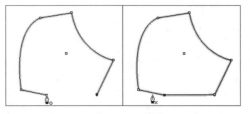

*Click on the other endpoint to close the path.*

# Compound Paths

In the old days, not only did Ole have to walk miles to school in freezing cold weather, but he also had to work his way through an impossibly difficult series of steps just to create holes inside closed paths. While the process was kind of fascinating, it did nothing improve his already gloomy outlook on life.

These days, creating holes in paths is easier—just make them into compound paths. Compound paths are made of two or more paths (which must be unlocked, ungrouped, and closed) that have been joined using the Make option on the Compound Paths submenu of the Object menu. Areas between the two paths, or areas where the paths overlap, are transparent. The following steps show you how to make a torus, or "doughnut" shape (see Figure 5-23).

1. Select the Oval tool from the toolbox.

2. Draw two ovals, one on top of the other.

3. Fill the ovals with a basic fill.

4. Select both ovals.

5. Press Command-8/Ctrl-8 to join the two ovals.

**FIGURE 5-23**
**Creating a**
**Compound Path**

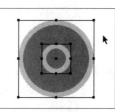

*Choose Make from the Composite Paths submenu of the Object menu.*

*Select the paths you want to turn into a compound path.*

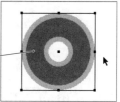

*InDesign creates a compound path from the selected objects.*

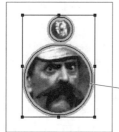

*Compound paths don't have to have holes in them—this example shows a compound path that we've used as a container for an image.*

If you decide you don't want the paths to be compound paths, you can change them back into individual paths by selecting the compound path and then choosing Release from the Compound Paths submenu of the Object menu.

When you join paths with different lines and fills, the compound path takes on the stroke and fill attributes of the path that's the farthest to the back.

Compound paths can be transformed just as you'd transform any other path.

When you convert characters to paths, InDesign automatically converts the characters into compound paths.

**Editing Compound Paths**

You can subselect the individual points that make up a compound path in the same way that you subselect objects inside a group—select the Direct Selection tool and click on the point. Once a point is selected, you can alter its position (see Figure 5-24).

**FIGURE 5-24**
**Editing a Compound Path**

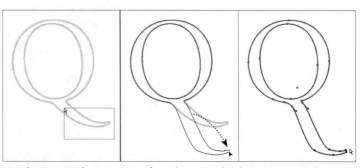

Use the Direct Selection tool to select some points.

Transform (move, scale, shear, or rotate) the points. In this example, we've dragged the points to a new location.

**Splitting Compound Paths**

To convert a compound path back into two or more normal paths, select the compound path and choose Release from the Compound Paths submenu of the Object menu (or press Command-Option-8/Ctrl-Alt-8). InDesign converts the compound path into its component paths. Note that the paths do not return to their original formatting when you do this.

## Smoothing Paths

You like using the Pencil tool. But your mouse hand isn't perfectly steady. Or the jerk you share office space with can't resist the urge to bump your arm while you're drawing. Either way, you need a way to smooth the path you've drawn in InDesign. Are you doomed to an after-hours workout with the Pen tool? Not with the Smooth tool on your side. This handy gadget can help you smooth out the rough patches in your InDesign paths.

To use the Smooth tool, select the tool from the Tools palette (it's usually hiding under the Pencil tool). Or select the Pencil tool and hold down Option/Alt to change the Pencil tool to the Smooth tool. Drag the tool along the path you want to smooth (see Figure 5-25). As you drag, InDesign adjusts the control handles and point positions on the path (sometimes deleting points as you drag).

**FIGURE 5-25**
**Smoothing a Path**

*Select the Smooth tool from the Tools palette.*

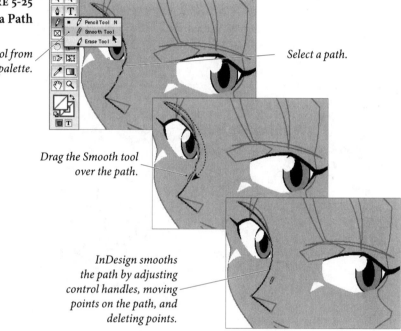

*Select a path.*

*Drag the Smooth tool over the path.*

*InDesign smooths the path by adjusting control handles, moving points on the path, and deleting points.*

To control the operation of the Smooth tool, double-click the Smooth tool in the Tools palette. InDesign displays the Smooth Tool Preferences dialog box (see Figure 5-26). The Fidelity slider controls the distance, in screen pixels, that the "smoothed" path can vary from the path of the Smooth tool (higher values equal more adjustment and greater variation from the existing path). The Smoothness slider controls the amount of change applied to the path (higher values equal greater smoothing).

**FIGURE 5-26**
**Smooth Tool Preferences**

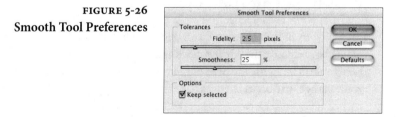

# Erasing Paths

Imagine that you want to remove an arbitrary section of a path, and that the beginning and end of the section do not correspond to existing points on the path. In InDesign 1.0, deleting this section of the path would have involved splitting the path using the Scissors tool (at either end of the section you wanted to delete) and then deleting the path segment between the two points.

These days, it's much easier. Select the Erase tool from the Tools palette, then drag the tool over the area of the path you want to delete (see Figure 5-27).

**FIGURE 5-27**
**Erasing Part of a Path**

*Select the Erase tool from the Tools palette (or press Shift-N until InDesign selects it for you).*

*Select a path.*

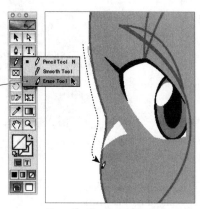

*Drag the Erase tool over the parts of the path you want to erase.*

*When you drag the Erase tool over a line segment on a closed path, InDesign opens the path. When you drag the Erase tool over an open path, InDesign splits the path into two paths.*

# Corner Effects

InDesign can apply a number of distortions to the corners of the paths in your publication. These distortions are known as "Corner Effects," and are controlled by the settings you enter in the Corner Effects dialog box. The most common use of this feature is to add rounded corners to rectangles and squares.

To apply a corner effect, select a path and then choose Corner Effects from the Object menu. InDesign displays the Corner Effects dialog box. Choose the effect you want from the Effect pop-up menu, then enter a value in the Size field and then press Return to apply your change. InDesign changes the corners of the path based on the corner effect you selected (see Figure 5-28).

**FIGURE 5-28**
**Corner Effects**

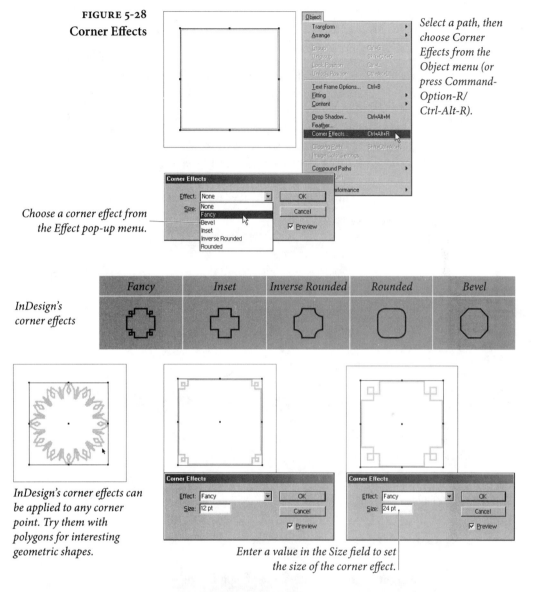

*Select a path, then choose Corner Effects from the Object menu (or press Command-Option-R/ Ctrl-Alt-R).*

*Choose a corner effect from the Effect pop-up menu.*

*InDesign's corner effects*

| Fancy | Inset | Inverse Rounded | Rounded | Bevel |
|-------|-------|-----------------|---------|-------|

*InDesign's corner effects can be applied to any corner point. Try them with polygons for interesting geometric shapes.*

*Enter a value in the Size field to set the size of the corner effect.*

*Shapes created by overlapping corner effects*

# Strokes

Once you've created a path, you'll probably want to give the path some specific line weight, color, or other property. The process of applying formatting to a path is often called "stroking a path," and we refer to a path's appearance as its "stroke." Strokes specify what the outside of the path *looks like*.

To define a stroke for a path, select the path, then display the Stroke palette by pressing F10 (see Figure 5-29). Use the Type pop-up menu to choose the type of stroke you want to use—solid, dashed, or any of the "scotch" (i.e., multi-stroke) types.

**FIGURE 5-29**
**Stroke Palette**

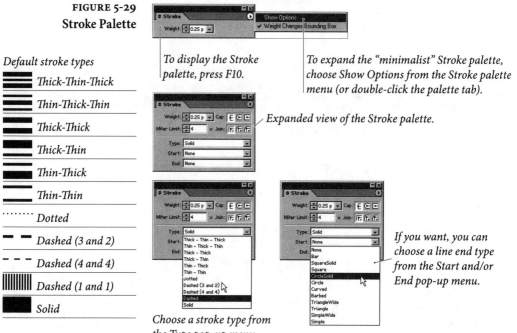

*Default stroke types*

Thick-Thin-Thick

Thin-Thick-Thin

Thick-Thick

Thick-Thin

Thin-Thick

Thin-Thin

Dotted

Dashed (3 and 2)

Dashed (4 and 4)

Dashed (1 and 1)

Solid

*To display the Stroke palette, press F10.*

*To expand the "minimalist" Stroke palette, choose Show Options from the Stroke palette menu (or double-click the palette tab).*

*Expanded view of the Stroke palette.*

*If you want, you can choose a line end type from the Start and/or End pop-up menu.*

*Choose a stroke type from the Type pop-up menu.*

**Weight**    You can enter a line weight for the stroke of the selected path using the Weight field, or you can choose a predefined line weight from the pop-up menu associated with the field. To remove a stroke from a path, enter zero in the Weight field.

**Historical Note:** In the old days of desktop publishing, some programs created hairlines using the PostScript command "0 setlinewidth," which generates a one-pixel wide stroke on a PostScript printer. Provided you were printing to a 300-dpi laser printer, this worked pretty well—you'd get a stroke that was approximately the width of a hairline (between .2 and .25 points). When imagesetters appeared, however, this approach led to strokes that were $^1/_{1200}$th of an inch wide or even smaller—stroke weights too fine to be printed on most presses. So, we grizzled graybeards advised all of our younger cohorts to avoid entering zero for the weight of a stroke. In InDesign, at least, it doesn't matter—entering zero won't result in a "0 setline-width" stroke.

**Weight Changes Bounding Box**

By default, changing the weight of a stroke changes the position of the points on the path. This means that increasing the stroke weight of, say, the border of an ad in your magazine layout keeps the stroke inside the area the advertiser is actually paying for (see Figure 5-30). That's how QuarkXPress works, so that must be the correct way to do it. Right? (At least one of us violently disagrees.)

FIGURE 5-30
**Weight Changes Bounding Box**

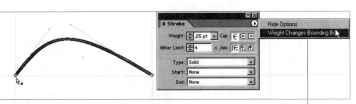

*The starting and ending points of this path fall exactly on ruler guide intersections. What happens when you change the width of the stroke?*

*That depends on the state of the Weight Changes Bounding Box option.*

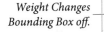

*Weight Changes Bounding Box off.*

*You should be able to see that the points in the path to the left have moved, and that the path shape has (therefore) changed.*

*Weight Changes Bounding Box on.*

*This path is the same shape as the original—the location of the path points has not changed.*

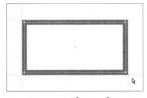

*Here's a rectangle with a stroke width of zero points. If you increase the stroke width...*

*...InDesign makes the stroke width increase equally around the path when you have the Weight Changes Bounding Box option turned on...*

*...or increases the stroke weight inside the path when you have Weight Changes Bounding Box turned off.*

It also enrages and upsets geometric purists (like the authors), who believe that the positions of the points on a path are sacred and should not be altered just to keep a path inside its bounding box. Not by some smartypants page layout program, anyway—we'll change the shape of the path ourselves if we, the omnipotent users, feel we should. Luckily, someone at Adobe agrees with us, and added the Stroke Weight Changes Bounding Box option to the Stroke palette.

When you turn on the Weight Changes Bounding Box option, InDesign leaves the position of the path alone when you increase or decrease stroke weight. Choosing this option has no effect on existing paths.

**Cap**   Select one of the Cap options to determine the shape of the end of the stroke (see Figure 5-31). The Cap option you choose has no visible effect on a closed path.

**FIGURE 5-31**
**Cap Options**

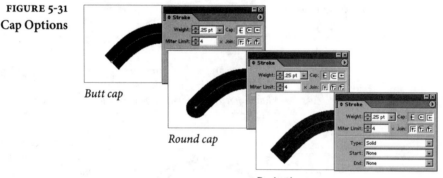

*Butt cap*

*Round cap*

*Projecting cap*

**Join**   The Join option determines the way InDesign renders corners—the place where two line segments in a path meet in a corner point (see Figure 5-32).

**FIGURE 5-32**
**Join Options**

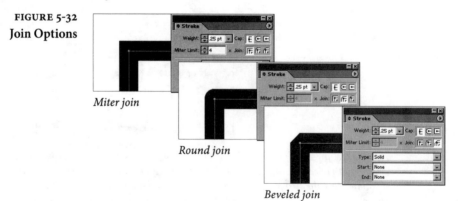

*Miter join*

*Round join*

*Beveled join*

**Miter Limit**    When paths go around corners, some weird things can happen. Asked to corner too sharply, the stroke skids out of control, creating spiky elbows that increase the effective stroke weight of a path's corners. The value you enter in the Miter Limit field sets the distance, as a multiple of the stroke weight, that you'll allow the corner to extend before InDesign applies a beveled join to the corner (see Figure 5-33). If, for example, you enter "2" in the Miter Limit field, InDesign will flatten corners when the stroke weight of the corner is equal to or greater than two times the weight of the stroke.

The Miter Limit field is only available when you're using the Miter Join option, and applies only to corner points.

**FIGURE 5-33**
**Miter Limit**

*When angles get small, corners go out of control. In this example, a Miter Join creates a projecting "elbow."*

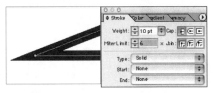

*Increase the value in the Miter Limit field to cause corners with tight angles to be rendered using a Beveled miter join.*

**Dash**    If you want a dashed line, choose Dashed from the Type pop-up menu, and use the Dash and Gap fields that appear at the bottom of the Stroke palette to specify the appearance of the dashed stroke (see Figure 5-34).

**FIGURE 5-34**
**Applying a**
**Dashed Stroke**

*To apply a dashed stroke, choose Dashed from the Type pop-up menu.*

*InDesign applies the default dashed stroke pattern.*

*Edit the dashed stroke pattern, if necessary, by entering new values in the Dash and Gap fields (these fields use standard measurement units).*

**Creating Layered Strokes**

We've heard a number of people complain that InDesign doesn't include their favorite "fancy" rules—if you can't find what you're looking for on the Type menu in the Stroke palette, you can make your own. To create a simple multi-stroke effect, follow these steps (see Figure 5-35).

1. Select a path.

2. Clone the path. To do this, press Command-C/Ctrl-C to copy the path, then press Command-Option-Shift-V/Ctrl-Alt-Shift-V. InDesign creates a copy of the selected path exactly on top of the original path.

3. Turn on the Stroke Weight Changes Bounding Box option on the Stroke palette menu (if it's not already on).

4. Change the stroke weight, stroke type, or color of the copy of the path.

5. Select the original path and the clone and group them (note that you can't make them a compound path, as that would apply one of the two strokes to both paths and would undo your multi-stroke effect).

**FIGURE 5-35**
**Creating a Complex Stroke by Stacking Paths**

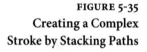

*This complicated-looking stroke is made up of three separate strokes applied to three paths.*

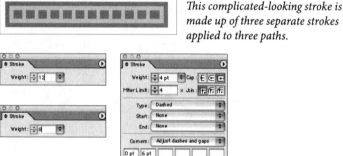

**Arrowheads**

You can add arrowheads or tailfeathers to any open path you want by choosing an arrowhead from the Start and End pop-up menus at the bottom of the Stroke palette. The Start pop-up menu applies to the first point in the path (according to the direction of the path); the End pop-up menu applies to the last point in the path. You don't have to make choices from both of the pop-up menus (see Figure 5-36).

To swap the arrowheads on the beginning and end of a path, select the path using the Direct Selection tool and choose Reverse Path from the Object menu (see Figure 5-37).

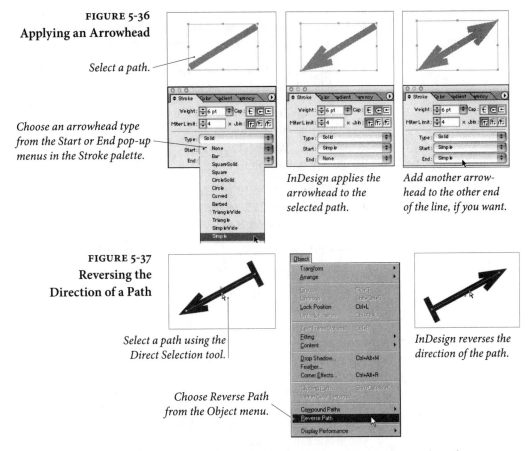

**FIGURE 5-36**
**Applying an Arrowhead**

*Select a path.*

*Choose an arrowhead type from the Start or End pop-up menus in the Stroke palette.*

*InDesign applies the arrowhead to the selected path.*

*Add another arrowhead to the other end of the line, if you want.*

**FIGURE 5-37**
**Reversing the Direction of a Path**

*Select a path using the Direct Selection tool.*

*Choose Reverse Path from the Object menu.*

*InDesign reverses the direction of the path.*

**Overprint**  You won't find this basic stroke option in the Stroke palette, so stop looking. Instead, it's in the Attributes palette (choose Attributes from the Window menu). Checking the Overprint Stroke option makes the stroke overprint (rather than knock out of) whatever's behind it. This might not seem like much, but if you're creating color publications, you'll find it's one of the most important features in InDesign (see Chapter 8, "Color").

**Editing Strokes**  Once you've applied a stroke to a particular path, you can change the stroke using any of the following methods. Again, there's no "right" way to edit a stroke—which method is best and quickest depends on how you work and which palettes you have open at the time you want to change the stroke.

◆ Display the Stroke palette, then make changes in the palette.

◆ Click the Stroke selector in the Color palette, then click a color in the palette (see Chapter 8, "Color," for more on applying colors using the Color palette).

♦ Use the Stroke button at the bottom of the Toolbox to apply or remove colors and gradients from the path.

♦ Select the path, then choose a new stroke weight from the Stroke Weight submenu of the Context menu.

♦ Use the Eyedropper tool to pick up the stroke of a path and apply that formatting to another path.

**Removing Strokes**    To quickly remove a stroke from a path, use one of the following techniques.

♦ Select the path, click the Stroke selector (at the bottom of the Toolbox), then click None.

♦ Select the path, display the Swatches palette, click the Stroke selector at the top of the palette, and then click the None swatch.

♦ Enter 0 in the Weight field of the Stroke palette.

# Fills

Just as strokes determine what the *outside* of a path looks like, fills specify the appearance of the *inside* of a path. Fills can make the inside of a path a solid color, or a linear or radial gradient. Any path you create can be filled, including open paths.

To apply a fill, select a path and do one of the following.

♦ Click the Fill selector at the top of the Swatches palette, then click a color swatch (see Figure 5-38).

♦ Click the Fill selector at the bottom of the Tools palette, then click the Apply Color button (or press comma). This applies the most recently selected color or swatch (see Figure 5-39).

♦ Drag a swatch out of the Swatches palette or Color palette and drop it on a path (see Figure 5-40). The path doesn't have to be selected.

♦ Click the Fill selector in the Color palette, then define a color in the palette (see Figure 5-41).

♦ Select the Eyedropper too. Click an object formatted with the fill you want, then click on another object to apply the fill (see Figure 5-42).

**FIGURE 5-38**
**Applying a Fill**
**(Swatches Palette**
**Method)**

*Select an object.*

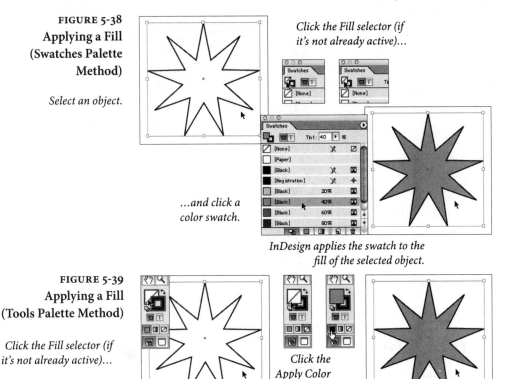

*Click the Fill selector (if it's not already active)...*

*...and click a color swatch.*

*InDesign applies the swatch to the fill of the selected object.*

**FIGURE 5-39**
**Applying a Fill**
**(Tools Palette Method)**

*Click the Fill selector (if it's not already active)...*

*Click the Apply Color button.*

*InDesign applies the most recently selected swatch to the fill of the selected object.*

**FIGURE 5-40**
**Applying a Fill**
**(Drag and Drop**
**Method)**

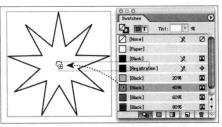

*Drag a color swatch out of the Swatches palette...*

*Note that you don't need to select the object when applying a fill using drag and drop.*

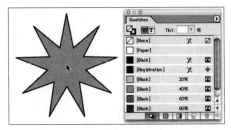

*...and drop it in the interior of a path.*

FIGURE 5-41<br>**Applying a Fill**<br>**(Color Palette Method)**

*Select an object.*

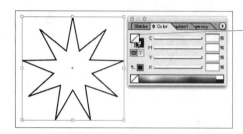

*Click the Fill selector in the Color palette.*

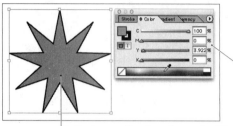

*Define a color. You can change color models, drag the sliders, enter values in the fields, or click anywhere in the color (as we have in this example).*

*InDesign applies the color to the fill of the object.*

**FIGURE 5-42**
**Applying a Fill**
**(Eyedropper Method)**

*Use the Eyedropper tool to pick up the color you want from another path...*

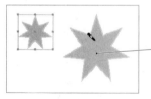

*...and then click the Eyedropper tool on the path you want to format.*

**Removing Fills**   To quickly remove a fill from a path, do one of the following:

◆ Click the Fill selector in the Tools palette, then click the None button (or, better yet, press X and then press /).

◆ Click the Fill button in the Color palette and then click the None swatch (if you can't see the None swatch, it's because you've hidden the Color palette's option—choose Show Options from the Color palette menu to expand the palette and display the options).

◆ Click the Fill button at the bottom of the Toolbox, then click the None swatch in the Swatches palette.

# Gradients

A "gradient" is a type of fill or stroke that creates a graduation from one color to another—an effect also known as a "fountain," "blend," or "vignette." InDesign offers two types of gradients: "Linear" and "Radial." For either type of gradient fill, you can set the colors used in the gradient, the rate at which one color blends into another, and the colors used in the gradient (gradients can contain two or more colors). For Linear gradients, you can set the angle that the graduation is to follow.

Linear gradients create a smooth color transition (or series of transitions) from one end of a path to another; Radial gradients create a graduation from the center of a path to its edges. Gradients applied to paths are calculated relative to the geometric bounds of the path; gradients applied to text characters use the geometric bounding box of the text frame containing the text (not the individual characters themselves).

**Applying Gradients**

To apply a gradient to a path, follow these steps (see Figure 5-43).

1. Select the path using the Selection tool or the Direct Selection tool, or select text using the Text tool or Path Text tool.

2. Do one of the following.

   ◆ Click the Fill or Stroke selector in the Tools palette (to specify which part of the path you want to apply the gradient to). Click the Apply Gradient button at the bottom of the Tools palette.

   ◆ Display the Gradient palette (choose Gradient from the Window menu), and then click the gradient ramp.

   ◆ Click an existing gradient swatch in the Swatches palette (press F5 to display the Swatches palette). You can also drag the gradient swatch out of the Swatches palette and drop it on a path (the path doesn't have to be selected).

   ◆ Select the Eyedropper tool and click an object formatted with a gradient, then click the tool again on the selected path.

   ◆ Select the Gradient tool and drag the tool inside the path.

**Gradient Controls**

When you create or edit a gradient, you work with InDesign's gradient controls: the gradient ramp, gradient stop icons, and centerpoint icons. What the heck are we talking about? See Figure 5-44.

**Applying a Gradient**

*Click the Fill or*
*Stroke selector...*

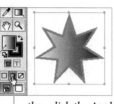
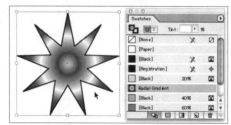

*...then click the Apply*
*Gradient button.*

*Select an object, then click a gradient*
*swatch in the Swatches palette.*

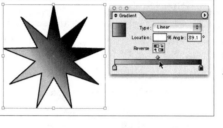

*...or display the Gradi-*
*ent palette, then click the*
*gradient ramp.*

*...or drag a gradient swatch*
*out of the Swatches palette*
*and drop it on a path*
*(the path does not have*
*to be selected).*

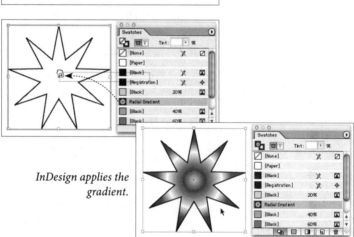

*InDesign applies the*
*gradient.*

**Creating a**
**Gradient Swatch**

In our opinion, the best way to apply gradients is to use the Swatches palette. Just as applying a color from the Swatches palette establishes a link between the color swatch and the object you've applied it to, so applying a gradient swatch links the swatch and the objects you've formatted with it. This means that you can edit the definition of the gradient swatch and update the formatting of all of the objects you've applied the swatch to.

To create a gradient swatch, follow these steps (see Figure 5-45).

1.  Select an object formatted using a gradient that has the attributes you want (this step is optional).

FIGURE 5-44
**Gradient Controls**

FIGURE 5-44
**Gradient Controls**

Gradient ramp                    Centerpoint

Gradient stop                    Gradient stop

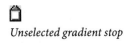

Unselected gradient stop

Selected gradient stop

To change the position of a centerpoint, select it...

...and then drag it to a new location on the gradient ramp.

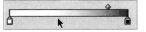

To change the position of a gradient stop, select it...

...and then drag it to a new location on the gradient ramp.

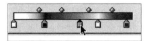

To add a new gradient stop, position the cursor below the gradient ramp...

...and click.

To remove a gradient stop, select it...

...and then drag it away from the gradient ramp.

FIGURE 5-45
**Creating a Gradient Swatch**

Choose New Gradient Swatch from the Swatches palette menu.

InDesign displays the New Gradient Swatch dialog box.

Enter a name for the gradient (optional, but a good idea).

Set up the gradient. If you selected an object formatted using a gradient, that gradient's properties will appear here.

Click the OK button, and InDesign adds the gradient to the list of available swatches.

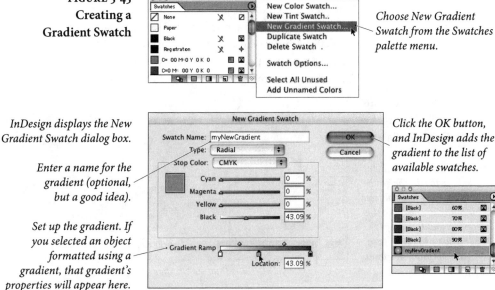

2. Display the Swatches palette, if it's not already visible, then choose New Gradient Swatch from the Swatches palette menu. InDesign displays the New Gradient Swatch dialog box. If you selected an object in Step 1, InDesign picks up the attributes of the gradient applied to the object and displays them in this dialog box. If you did not select an object, the controls in the dialog box reflect the document's default gradient formatting.

3. If you're creating a gradient based on the gradient applied to a selected object, enter a name for the gradient swatch (this step is optional) and click the OK button to save the gradient swatch. If you're creating a new gradient swatch "from scratch," specify the colors and gradient stop positions for the gradient. Once the gradient looks the way you want it to, click the OK button to save the gradient swatch. InDesign adds the gradient swatch to the list of swatches in the Swatches palette.

**Using the Gradient Palette**

You can also apply and edit gradients using the Gradients palette (see Figure 5-46). Like the New Gradient Swatch and Gradient Options dialog boxes, the Gradient palette contains a gradient ramp, with centerpoints above the ramp and gradient stops below.

To apply a gradient, select a path, then display the Gradient palette, then click the gradient ramp. InDesign applies the gradient to the selected object.

To edit a gradient you've applied to a path, select the path, then display the Gradient palette (if it's not already visible). InDesign loads the gradient applied to the selected path into the Gradient palette. Adjust the gradient stop positions, or add gradient stops, or change the  position of centerpoints or colors, and InDesign applies the changes to the selected path.

**FIGURE 5-46**
**Using the Gradient Palette**

*You can use the Gradient palette to edit the gradient applied to an object. You could, as shown in this example, change the position of a centerpoint on the gradient ramp.*

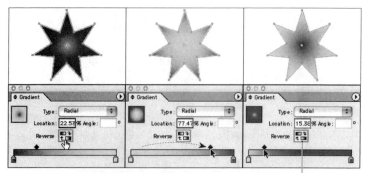

*One thing that the Gradient palette has that you won't find elsewhere—the Reverse button, which reverses the direction of the gradient.*

**Editing Gradients**

To edit the color, gradient type, or angle of a gradient you've applied to an object, select the object and then display the Gradient palette. You can use any of the following techniques to change the gradient.

◆ Drag a gradient stop to a new position on the gradient ramp.

◆ Select the stop and enter a new value in the Location field.

◆ Add a new gradient stop by clicking below the gradient ramp.

◆ Change the position of the centerpoint by dragging it above the gradient ramp. Or you can select the centerpoint and enter a new value in the Location field.

◆ Remove a stop by dragging it away from the gradient ramp.

◆ Reverse the gradient ramp by clicking the Reverse button.

◆ Change the angle of a linear gradient by entering a new value in the Angle field.

◆ Change the color of a gradient stop using a color from the Swatches palette. To do this, select the stop, then hold down Option/Alt and click a color swatch in the Swatches palette (see Figure 5-47).

◆ Change the color of a gradient stop to an unnamed color. To do this, select the gradient stop, then display the Color palette. Specify a color. As you change color values in the Color palette, InDesign changes the color applied to the gradient stop.

◆ Change the gradient type using the Type pop-up menu.

**FIGURE 5-47**
**Getting a Swatch Color into a Gradient Stop**

*It's something every InDesign user has done at least once—you select a gradient stop, then click a color swatch in the Swatches palette, expecting to apply the color to the gradient stop. Instead, InDesign fills (or strokes) the path with the color. How the heck do you get a swatch color into a gradient stop?*

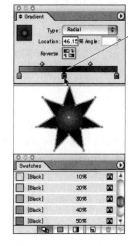

*Select a gradient stop.*

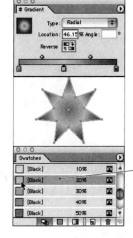

*Hold down Option/ Alt and click the color swatch in the Swatches palette. InDesign assigns the color to the gradient stop.*

**Applying a Gradient
to Multiple Paths**

To apply a gradient to more than one path, select the paths (which need not already have gradients applied to their fills or strokes), then drag the Gradient tool. The point at which you start dragging defines the starting point of the gradient (see Figure 5-48).

**FIGURE 5-48**

**Applying a Gradient to
Multiple Objects**

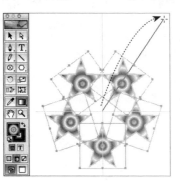

*Select a series of paths. In this example, each path has been formatted using a radial gradient fill. Position the Gradient tool over the point at which you want to place the center point (for a radial gradient) or start (for a linear gradient), and then drag the tool.*

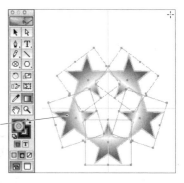

*InDesign applies a single gradient to the selected paths.*

# Transparency

If this were an introductory logic class, rather than a somewhat illogical computer book, we could present the following syllogism: PostScript's basic drawing model does not allow for transparency; InDesign is a PostScript-oriented page layout program. Therefore, it follows that you cannot have transparent objects in InDesign. Right?

Well…not quite.

While PostScript itself does not handle transparency, InDesign's drawing model—the part of the software that draws elements on the screen—can. So how does InDesign print transparent objects to a PostScript printer? Simple: it cheats. When the time comes to print, InDesign does what Illustrator and FreeHand (and possibly Corel-DRAW, we have no idea) users have done for years—it uses clipping paths to create the illusion of transparency and/or rasterizes the transparent objects and sends the printer separated image data. All of this takes place in the background—InDesign does not change the objects in your document. Instead, it changes the way that the objects are sent to the printer.

The way that InDesign sends the transparent objects to the printer is defined by the Transparency Flattener settings for the spread containing the objects. Flattener settings are described in Chapter 11, "Printing." As a rule of thumb, however, transparent objects make documents somewhat harder to print, and putting one transparent object on top of another transparent object can make a document much harder to print.

This brings us to our patented "With Power Comes Responsibility" speech. It's very easy to come up with combinations of transparent objects and flattener settings that create a document that is impossible to print on any PostScript printer. It's also easy to create documents that can slow a printer to a crawl, or to produce files that take up enormous amounts of space on your hard drive.

This doesn't mean that you should avoid using transparency. That would be silly, given that there's sometimes no other way to create a specific creative effect. It's just that you must bear in mind that using the feature comes at a cost, and that you need to weigh the potential risks (slow printing, no printing) against the benefit (a cool layout). In other words, it's fine to use scissors, just don't run with them.

If you're familiar with Photoshop's approach to transparency, you'll find InDesign's a bit different: In Photoshop, transparency is an attribute of layers; in InDesign, transparency is an attribute of individual page items. Transparency applies equally to the fill and stroke of an item; you cannot apply one level of transparency to the fill and another to the stroke.

**Applying Transparency**

To apply transparency to a page item, work your way through the following steps (see Figure 5-49).

1. Select a page item.

2. Display the Transparency palette, if it's not already visible (choose Transparency from the Window menu).

4. Choose an option from the Blending Mode pop-up menu, if necessary.

3. Drag the transparency slider or enter a value in the Opacity field.

**Blending Modes**

The transparency blending modes define the way that the colors in the transparent objects interact with objects that fall behind them (see Figure 5-50).

When you apply transparency, InDesign calculates the resulting color based on each color component of the foreground and back-

FIGURE 5-49
**Applying Transparency
to an Object**

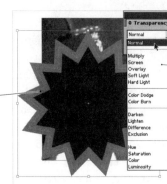

*Enter an opacity
percentage.*

*Choose a blending mode.*

*Select an object.*

*Display the Transparency
palette, if it's not already
visible (press Shift-F10)*

*InDesign makes
the selected object
transparent. Is that
cool, or what?*

ground colors. For two overlapping process colors, for example, the effect of the blending mode will almost certainly differ for each of the four inks. When we say that a blending mode behaves in a particular way for a specific gray percentage value, we mean the percentage of a color component.

The effect of a blending mode is dependent on the current color management settings. The ink values of the colors in a stack of transparent objects, for example, will never exceed the maximum ink coverage for the current color management profile. (For the sake of your press operator's sanity, don't try to prove us wrong.)

The following notes provide a quick description of the most useful of the blending modes. For a color illustration of the effect of each option (which is the only way to make sense of the color, Hue, Luminosity, and Saturation blending options), see Color Figure 10 on color page 8. In these descriptions, the term "foreground color" refers to the color applied to the front-most object; "background color" refers to the color of the background object, and "resulting color" is the color you see where the two object intersect.

**Normal.** The Normal blending mode adds the foreground color to the background color. If the foreground color is black, and the opacity percentage is 10%, then 10% black is added to the background color to produce the resulting color. The Normal blending mode at 100% opacity turns transparency off.

**Multiply.** The Multiply blending mode always results in a darker color. The one exception is when the foreground color is white or Paper color, in which case this blending mode has no effect at all.

**FIGURE 5-50**
## Transparency Blending Options

*Here are all of InDesign's transparency blending options. Luckily, we were able to use a page from Ole's high school yearbook as an example.*

*For a color illustration of the effect of the blending options, see Color Figure 10. Hue, Luminosity, Color, and Saturation make a lot more sense in color.*

Multiply is very similar to overprinting one object over another (see Chapter 10, "Color," for more on overprinting), or overlapping lines when drawing with felt pens. We think the Multiply blend mode is the best choice for drop shadows (see below).

**Screen.** This blending mode almost always produces a resulting color that is lighter than the background color (unless the foreground color is black, which has no effect in this mode). The best real-world definition of this blending mode comes from Adobe's Russell Brown: Screen is like projecting two slides on the same screen. The result is always lighter than either of the two sources. If the background color is black or white, the background color remains unchanged.

**Overlay.** The Overlay blending mode compares the foreground and background colors, accentuating highlights and shadows in each by lightening light colors and darkening dark colors. If either the foreground or background color is 50-percent gray, then this mode has no effect. Overlay increases color contrast and can get out of hand quickly; we usually reduce the Opacity slider to temper the effect.

**Soft Light.** While most people describe the Soft Light blending mode as shining a soft spotlight on the background color, we like to think of this mode in terms of playing with semi-translucent colored acetate. Soft Light has no effect if the background color is black or white, but it subtly enhances any other color, making darker colors (in either the foreground or background) a little darker and lighter colors a little lighter.

**Hard Light.** The Hard Light mode is something like two blending modes in one: If the foreground color is lighter than 50-percent gray, the Hard Light mode lightens the background color similar to the Screen mode; if the foregrond color is darker than 50-percent gray, it darkens it using a method similar to the Multiply mode. Hard Light tends to wash out colors, and we rarely use it.

**Darken.** The resulting color is equal to the darker of the foreground and background colors.

**Lighten.** The resulting color is equal to the lighter of the foreground and background colors.

**Hue.** The Hue blending mode creates a new color by blending the color of the foreground object with the luminance (brightness) and saturation of the background. Putting a black object set to Hue over a colored object simply desaturates the background colors.

**Saturation.** The Saturation mode creates a new color by blending the foreground color's saturation and the hue (color) with luminance values of the background color.

**Color.** The Color mode is slightly different from the Hue mode; it combines the color and the saturation of the foreground color with with the luminance of the background color. Placing a solid color set to Color over an image colorizes the image, like a fake duotone.

**Luminosity.** Luminosity creates a new color by blending the brightness of the foreground color with the hue and saturation of the background color.

**Transparency Options**

So what about those options at the bottom of the Transparency palette? The meaning of the terms "Isolate Blending" and "Knockout Group" is hardly self evident. Both options apply only to groups (which makes us think they should be inactive when you have objects other than a group selected, but never mind).

**Isolate Blending.** When you turn on the Isolate Blending option, and objects in the group you've selected use blending modes other than the Normal blending mode, InDesign changes the way that the object in the group interact with objects behind the group. Regardless of the blending mode you've assigned to the group objects, InDesign treats them as if the Normal blending mode were assigned. *Inside* the group, however, blending modes behave as you specified (see Figure 5-51).

**FIGURE 5-51**
**Isolate Blending**

*The selected group contains three circles. Each circle is filled with Black, set to 50% transparency, and uses the Multiply blending mode.*

*The half circle is outside and behind the group.*

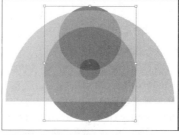

*With Isolate Blending turned off, the foreground colors blend with the background colors according to their blending modes.*

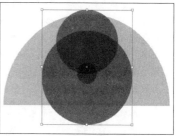

*Turn Isolate Blending on, and InDesign changes the way that the foreground colors interact with the background colors.*

**Knockout Group.** When you select a group containing transparent objects and turn on the Knockout Group option, InDesign makes the objects in the group opaque to each other (see Figure 5-52). In other words, the option should really be named "Knockout Objects Inside the Group," but there's not room in the palette. Objects *outside* the group are treated according to the state of the Isolate Blending option (see above). And yes, it is possible to have both Isolate Blending and Knockout Group turned on (see Figure 5-53).

**FIGURE 5-52**
**Knockout Group**

*The selected group contains three circles. Each circle is filled with Black, set to 50% transparency, and uses the Multiply blending mode.*

*The half circle is outside and behind the group.*

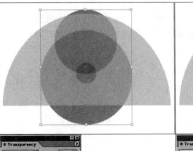

*With Knockout Group turned off, the objects inside the group affect each other.*

*Turn on Knockout Group, and the objects in the group become opaque to each other, but are still transparent to any background objects.*

**FIGURE 5-53**
**Isolate Blending Plus Knockout Group**

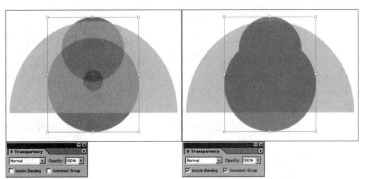

*Both options off.*

*Objects inside the group knock each other out, and the group behaves as if the Normal blending option is applied to all members of the group.*

**Groups and Transparency**

There's a difference between applying transparency to a group and applying transparency to the objects inside a group (see Figure 5-54). When you apply transparency to a group, InDesign will override the transparency settings for any objects in the group that have no transparency applied to them, but will leave any transparent objects unchanged.

**FIGURE 5-54**
Applying Transparency
to a Group

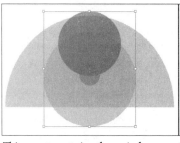 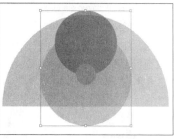

*This group contains three circles. Each circle is filled with a tint of Black, and each uses the Multiply blending mode.*

*This is the same group of objects, but the 50% transparency has been applied to the group rather than to each individual object.*

# Drop Shadows

What is it about drop shadows? Does everyone want their page items to appear as if they are the highly mobile space battleship *Nadesico*, floating defiantly above the page? We're not sure, but we do know that these ubiquitous two-dimensional impersonations of three-dimensional space are something no graphic designer will leave home without—at least until clients stop asking for them.

Any object on an InDesign page can have a drop shadow, you can control the offset distance, color, transparency, and sharpness/blur of the shadow. Drop shadows come with many of the same cautions and warnings as transparency; used to excess, they can make a page difficult to print. Rather than repeat a rant here, we'll simply direct you back to the section on Transparency, above, on the benefits and dangers of using transparent objects in your page layouts. In short: It's OK, but use caution.

To apply a drop shadow follow these steps (see Figure 5-55).

1. Select an object.

2. Choose Drop Shadow from the Context menu or Object menu. InDesign displays the Drop Shadow dialog box.

3. Turn on the Drop Shadow option (that's why you're here, after all), and then use the controls in the dialog box to specify the appearance of the drop shadow. It helps to turn on the Preview option—this way, you can see what you're doing without having to close the dialog box.

4. When you're through adjusting the drop shadow settings, click the OK button to close the dialog box and apply the drop shadow.

FIGURE 5-55
**Applying a Drop Shadow**

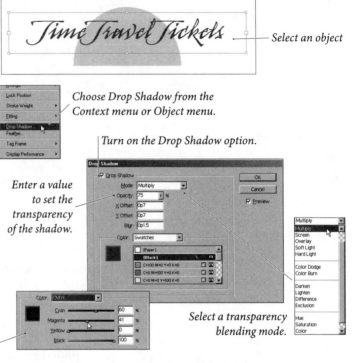

Select an object

*Typical Display*

*High Quality Display*

*Display performance settings have a big effect on the way that InDesign displays drop shadows.*

*You can change the color mode to CMYK, RGB, or LAB, or swatches.*

*Choose Drop Shadow from the Context menu or Object menu.*

*Turn on the Drop Shadow option.*

*Enter a value to set the transparency of the shadow.*

*Select a transparency blending mode.*

*Click the OK button, and InDesign applies the drop shadow.*

**Drop Shadow Controls**  The Opacity field and its associated pop-up menu control the opacity or transparency of the drop shadow (see Figure 5-56).

The Mode pop-up menu sets the transparency blending mode for the drop shadow. We've described all of the useful blending modes in the section on Transparency, above. The Multiply blending mode works well with drop shadows. For a color illustration of the blending modes, see Color Figure 10.

The X Offset and Y Offset fields define the distance (in horizontal and vertical measurement units, respectively) by which the drop shadow is offset from the selected object (see Figure 5-57).

A hard-edged shadow is probably not what you were looking for—what you need is a way to soften  the edges of the shadow so that it looks more realistic. That's exactly what the Blur field does (see Figure 5-58).

You can define the color of the drop shadow using swatches, or by creating a color using the RGB, CMYK, or LAB color models (switch among these color models using the Color pop-up menu).

FIGURE 5-56
Shadow Transparency

FIGURE 5-56
Shadow Transparency

The blending mode and
the Opacity field set the
transparency of the
drop shadow.

In this example, the drop
shadow isn't transparent at all.

The blur around the edges
of a drop shadow is always
partly transparent.

In this example, adding
transparency allows the
background object to show
through the drop shadow.

You can use any of InDesign's blending modes to
change the transparency of a drop shadow.

FIGURE 5-57
Drop Shadow Offset

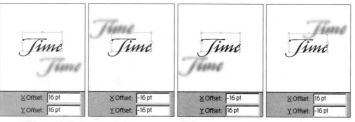

Use the X Offset (horizontal)
and Y Offset (vertical) fields to
position the shadow relative to
the object.

Entering negative values in the
X Offset field moves the shadow to
the left; in the Y Offset field, negative
values move the shadow up.

FIGURE 5-58
Blur

Enter a value in the Blur field to
control the diffusion of the drop
shadow. Entering zero produces a
hard-edged shadow.

Entering a large blur value would
make the shadow disappear altogether for this 24-point example text.

# Feathering

The usual definition of feathering goes something like this: "feathering softens the edges of page items." This isn't really quite true. Feathering softens the *interior*—the fill or contents—of a page item around the edges of the page item. If you're hoping to simulate a pencil stroke on an InDesign path...well, you'll just have to do that in Illustrator. Our disappointment aside, feathering is a useful addition to InDesign's path formatting features.

To apply the feathering effect to an object, follow these steps (see Figure 5-59).

1. Select an object.

2. Choose Feather from the Context menu or Object menu.

3. Turn on the Feather option.

4. Enter a value for feather width. This sets the distance from the edges of the object at which the feathering will take effect. Choose an option from the Corner pop-up menu (these options are described below). Turn on the Preview option if you want to see the effect before you close the dialog box.

5. Click the OK button to apply the effect.

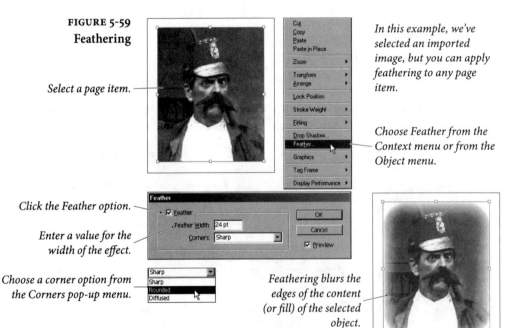

**FIGURE 5-59**
**Feathering**

*Select a page item.*

*In this example, we've selected an imported image, but you can apply feathering to any page item.*

*Choose Feather from the Context menu or from the Object menu.*

*Click the Feather option.*

*Enter a value for the width of the effect.*

*Choose a corner option from the Corners pop-up menu.*

*Feathering blurs the edges of the content (or fill) of the selected object.*

**Feather Corner Options**

The options on the Corner pop-up menu control the appearance of the feathering effect as it approaches sharp corners at the edges of the object (see Figure 5-60).

**Sharp.** When you choose the Sharp option, the feathering effect follows the outline of the path as closely as possible.

**Rounded.** When you choose Rounded, InDesign rounds the edges of the feather effect as it nears sharp corners.

**Diffused.** This effect provides a general fade from opaque to transparent, based on the geometric center of the object, rather than on the shape of the path (as is the case for the Sharp and Rounded options). This is similar to the feathering effect in Illustrator.

**FIGURE 5-60**
**Feathering**

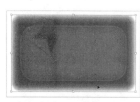

*While the Rounded corner option probably isn't a good match with the example star polygon, it's great for creating beveled buttons.*

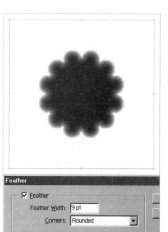

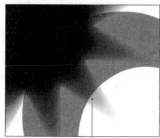

*The edges of the Diffused corner effect fade from opaque to transparent.*

## Drawing Conclusions

Earlier in this chapter, we noted that we found the process of drawing paths using Bezier curves confusing when we first encountered it. As we worked with the tools, however, we found that the parts of our brains that were used to using rapidographs (an obsolete type of pen favored by the ancient Greeks), triangles, curves, and rulers quickly adapted to the new drawing environment. Eventually, we realized that this was the easier way to draw.

Then, after reading a related article in a tabloid at the supermarket, it dawned on us that the archaic methods we'd learned were nothing less than an extraterrestrial plot, forced on us in classical antiquity by evil space gods, to some cosmic purpose which we cannot—as yet—reveal.

Just keep at it.

# Where Text Meets Graphics

Usually, we think of text and graphics as occupying two different, but parallel, universes. But there's an area—a Twilight Zone, a Bermuda Triangle of page layout—where the boundary between text and graphics blurs, frays, or becomes thin.

In this strange dimension, text characters can be bound to paths, or become paths, graphics can be embedded in text and behave as if they were text characters, and nothing, nothing is what it seems.

In spite of the repeated warnings of our scientific colleagues, we must, for the sake of humanity, tell what we have discovered in this alien landscape.

# Paragraph Rules

Ole laments, "I haven't looked at the PageMaker 3.0 documentation recently. I don't have to—I remember it too well.

"A feature of that manual's design was a rule drawn below a particular, and very common, heading. I know this, because I was one of the four people who put those rules there. For every one of those headings, one of us had to zoom in, measure from the baseline of the text in the heading, position a ruler guide, and then draw a rule. When the position of the heading changed, as it often did, we had to zoom in again, measure again, and move or redraw the rules.

"I still dream about it."

Which is part of the reason we like the paragraph rules feature found in PageMaker, QuarkXPress, and InDesign these days. Rules (or "lines") can be part of your paragraph's formatting (or, better yet, part of a paragraph style definition), and the rules you specify follow your paragraph wherever it happens to go.

**Applying Paragraph Rules**

To apply a paragraph rule to a paragraph, follow these steps (see Figure 6-1):

1.  Select the paragraph (remember, you don't need to highlight the entire paragraph—all you need to do is click the Text tool somewhere inside the paragraph).

2.  Choose Paragraph Rules from the Paragraph palette menu (or press Command-Option-J/Ctrl-Alt-J). InDesign displays the Paragraph Rules dialog box.

3.  Choose the type of paragraph rule (Rule Above or Rule Below) from the Rule Type pop-up menu, then turn on the Rule On option.

4.  Set the rule options you want using the controls in the panel. If you turn on the Preview option, you can watch InDesign apply the paragraph rule to the paragraph as you adjust the settings.

5.  Click OK to apply the paragraph rule settings to the selected paragraph, or click Cancel to close the dialog box without applying the rule.

**Ground Rules for Paragraph Rules**

Paragraphs can have up to two rules attached to them. One rule can be positioned on or above the baseline of the first line of text in a paragraph (InDesign calls this the "Rule Above"), the other line can

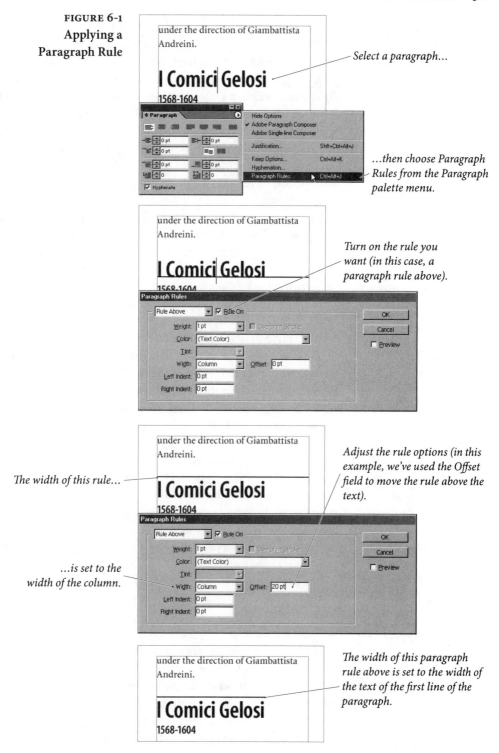

**FIGURE 6-1**

**Applying a Paragraph Rule**

*Select a paragraph...*

*...then choose Paragraph Rules from the Paragraph palette menu.*

*Turn on the rule you want (in this case, a paragraph rule above).*

*The width of this rule...*

*Adjust the rule options (in this example, we've used the Offset field to move the rule above the text).*

*...is set to the width of the column.*

*The width of this paragraph rule above is set to the width of the text of the first line of the paragraph.*

be positioned at or below the baseline of the last line of the paragraph (the "Rule Below"). You can't have two rules above a single paragraph, or two rules below, without trickery (see below). Note that these rule positions specify only the starting point of the rule—by manipulating the rule width, it's easy to create a rule below that extends far above the baseline, or a rule above that extends far below the baseline of the last line.

Paragraph rules, like any other paths you can draw in InDesign, can be up to 1000 points wide, and the stroke width can be specified in .001-point increments. Unlike other paths, however, you can't use a dotted, dashed, or multi-line stroke.

You set the position at which InDesign starts drawing a paragraph rule using the controls in the Paragraph Rules dialog box (choose Paragraph Rules from the Paragraph palette menu).

Paragraph rules above grow *up* (that is, toward the top of the text frame) from the position you specify in the Offset field in the Paragraph Rules dialog box; rules below grow *down* (toward the bottom of the text frame) as you increase their stroke weight. InDesign draws paragraph rules *behind* the text in the text frame.

You can base the width of a paragraph rule on the width of the text column or on the width of the text in the first (for paragraph rules above) or last (for rules below) line of the paragraph. Paragraph rules can also be indented from either the width of the column or the width of the text—the value you enter in the Left Indent and Right Indent fields of the Paragraph Rules dialog box determines the indent distance. You can even make paragraph rules extend beyond the width of the text or column by entering negative numbers in the Left Indent and Right Indent fields.

Paragraph rule positions have no effect on the vertical spacing of text. If you want to make room above a paragraph for a paragraph rule above, or below a paragraph for a rule below, you can use paragraph space before and after.

You can't select or manipulate paragraph rules using the Selection tool or the Direct Selection tool. Everyone tries this at least once.

**Tinting Paragraphs**    When you want to put a tint behind a paragraph (which you might want to do for a sidebar, a line in a table, or for a note or warning paragraph in your text), paragraph rules are the way to go. Provided, of course, that your paragraph isn't taller than 1000 points or so (the maximum paragraph rule width), and provided the paragraph fits inside a single text frame or text column.

To use a paragraph rules to add a tint behind a paragraph, follow these steps (see Figure 6-2).

FIGURE 6-2
**Placing a Tint Behind
a Paragraph**

*Select a paragraph.*

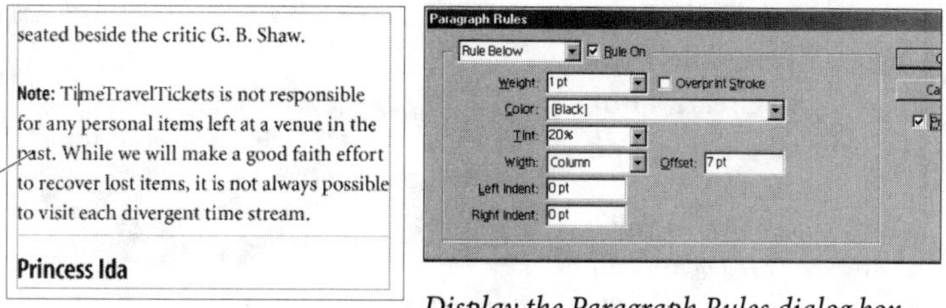

*Display the Paragraph Rules dialog box
and add a rule below.*

*Make the stroke weight of the rule at least equal to
the sum of the leading of the lines in the paragraph.*

*Move the rule up or down by
entering values in the Offset
field (we usually start with
the stroke weight, then add
or subtract smaller values to
"fine tune" the rule position).*

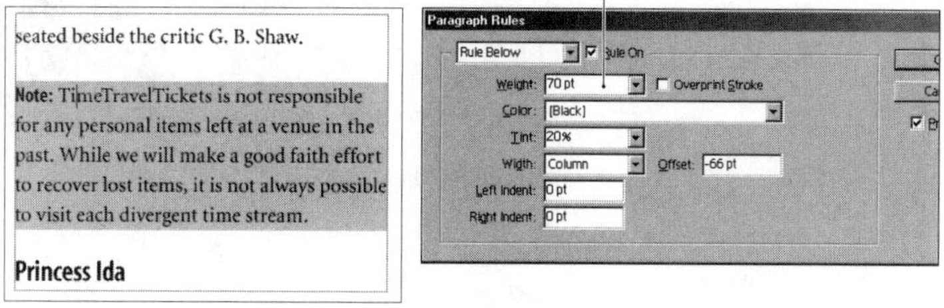

1. Calculate the height of the paragraph by adding up the leading of the lines in the paragraph.

2. Select the paragraph, then use the Paragraph Rules dialog box to apply a paragraph rule below. Use the Weight field to set the stroke width of the rule to at least the height of the paragraph.

3. Use the Color pop-up menu to set the color of the paragraph rule.

4. Enter a value in the Offset field to move the paragraph rule up or down behind the paragraph (remember, a negative value in the Offset field moves a paragraph rule below toward the top of the paragraph).

5. When the paragraph rule looks the way you want it to, click the OK button to apply it to the selected paragraph.

**Putting a Box
Around a Paragraph
Using Paragraph Rules**

Are you thinking what we're thinking? If the paragraph rule below overprints the paragraph rule above, and both rules fall behind the text in the paragraph, then you ought to be able to create a "box" around a paragraph by cleverly manipulating the width, height, and offset of the paragraph rules above and below. You can do just that, as shown in Figure 6-3.

Note that you can also use a table containing a single cell to accomplish this effect (see "Tables," later in this chapter).

FIGURE 6-3
**Using Paragraph Rules
to Create a Box
Around a Paragraph**

*Set the rule above so that it
covers the area behind the
paragraph.*

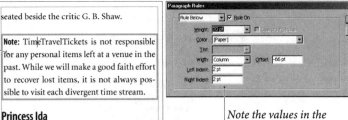

*Set the rule below so it covers
an area slightly smaller (in
this example, two points
smaller on all sides). Set the
rule color to "Paper."*

*Note the values in the
Left Indent, Right Indent,
Weight, and Offset fields.*

**Hanging Your
Head in a Bar**

Here's an effect you see often—a heading, set in a hanging indent, and knocked out of a paragraph rule. There's no trick to it—you use the same approach described in the previous section ("Tinting Paragraphs"), but you use a paragraph rule above and set the width of the rule so that it falls behind any text in the hanging indent (but not behind the text in the body of the paragraph).

To do this, set the right indent for the rule to at least the width of the body of the paragraph. Set the weight of the stroke to at least the height of the heading. Apply the paragraph rule, and you've got the effect you're looking for (see Figure 6-4).

**Instant "Bullets"**

Earlier, we mentioned that you can "hang" paragraph rules outside the text block containing the paragraphs containing the rules. Of what conceivable use is this?

Wouldn't it be great if you could make a bullet part of a paragraph style? There's a sleazy way to accomplish this using paragraph rules—provided all you want is a square bullet.

Here's what you do: apply a thick Rule Above to the paragraph, setting its right indent to a value equal to the width of the text column minus the width of the left indent. InDesign positions the paragraph rule to the left of the paragraph. Work with the offset, stroke width, and right indent until the square bullet looks the way you want it to (see Figure 6-5).

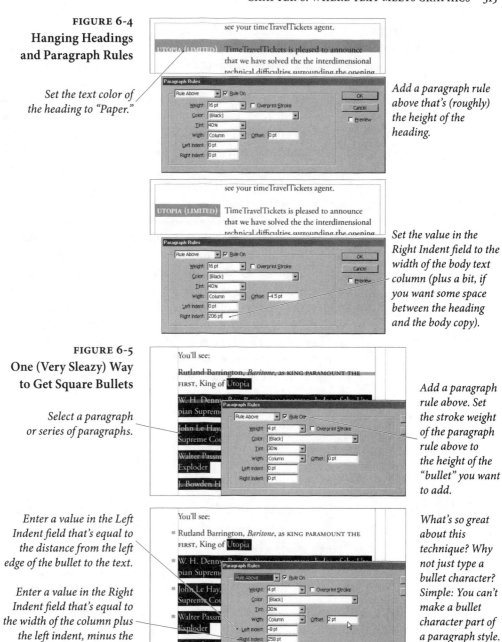

FIGURE 6-4
**Hanging Headings
and Paragraph Rules**

Set the text color of
the heading to "Paper."

Add a paragraph rule
above that's (roughly)
the height of the
heading.

Set the value in the
Right Indent field to the
width of the body text
column (plus a bit, if
you want some space
between the heading
and the body copy).

**FIGURE 6-5**
**One (Very Sleazy) Way
to Get Square Bullets**

Select a paragraph
or series of paragraphs.

Add a paragraph
rule above. Set
the stroke weight
of the paragraph
rule above to
the height of the
"bullet" you want
to add.

Enter a value in the Left
Indent field that's equal to
the distance from the left
edge of the bullet to the text.

Enter a value in the Right
Indent field that's equal to
the width of the column plus
the left indent, minus the
width of the paragraph rule.

What's so great
about this
technique? Why
not just type a
bullet character?
Simple: You can't
make a bullet
character part of
a paragraph style.

When you work with a paragraph rule (or anything else) that
extends beyond the edges of a text frame, InDesign sometimes for-
gets to redraw the rules when you edit text in the text frame. Don't
worry—the rules are still there. To see them again, force InDesign to
redraw the screen by pressing Shift-F5.

**Vertical Paragraph Rules**

What if your design calls for a vertical rule next to a specific type of paragraph? It's easy to automate this with paragraph rules—using a trick that borrows from other tricks we've discussed above. Set a paragraph rule below that's equal to the height of the paragraph (or thereabouts)—just as you would if you were placing a tint behind the paragraph. Next, make the rule's right indent (or left, if you want the rule to fall to the right of the paragraph) equal to the width of the paragraph minus the width of the vertical rule you want. If, for example, you want a 1-point rule at the left of the text frame, and the text column is 18 picas wide, enter "17p11" in the Right Indent field (see Figure 6-6).

This technique works especially well when you position the rules outside the text frame. To do this, enter a negative value in the Left Indent field (this sets the position of the left edge of the rule). Enter a value in the Right Indent field that's equal to the width of the text column plus the value you entered in the Left Indent field minus the width of the "vertical" ruler you want to create. If you want a 1 point rule 3 points to the left of an 18-picas-wide text column, enter "-0p3" in the Left Indent field and enter "18p2" in the Right Indent field.

Want to position rules on both sides of the text column? Add a paragraph Rule Below that's the same weight as the Rule Above. You should be able to get the two rules to align by adjusting the values of the Offset fields for both rules (see Figure 6-7).

**FIGURE 6-6**
**Vertical Paragraph Rules**

*This looks like a vertical rule, but it's really a horizontal paragraph rule with a very large stroke width.*

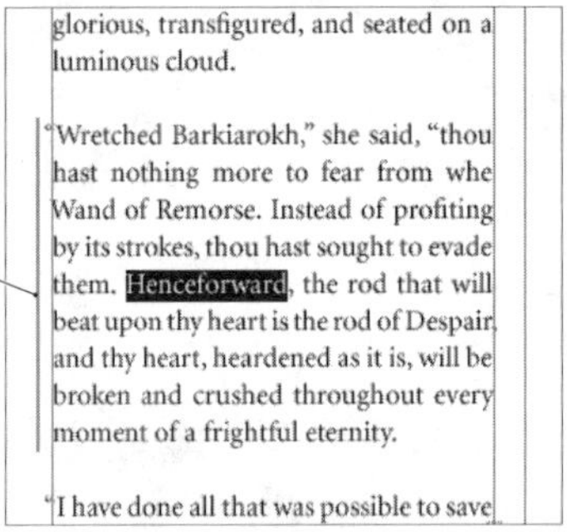

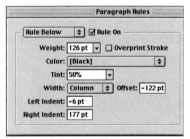

*The indents set the length of the paragraph rule to a single point.*

**FIGURE 6-7**
**Adding Vertical Rules Around a Paragraph**

*Use the paragraph rule above to add another "vertical" rule.*

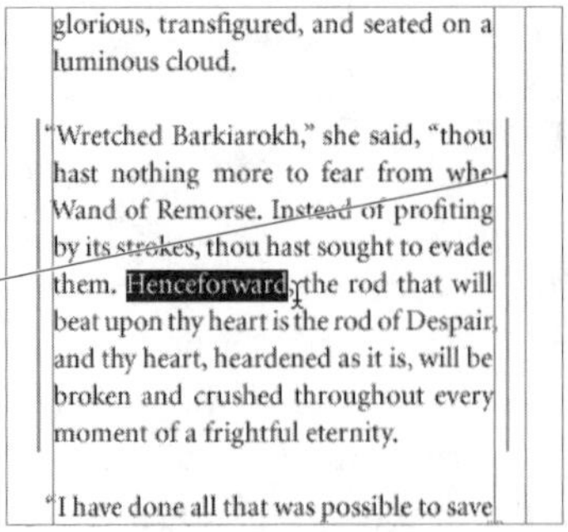

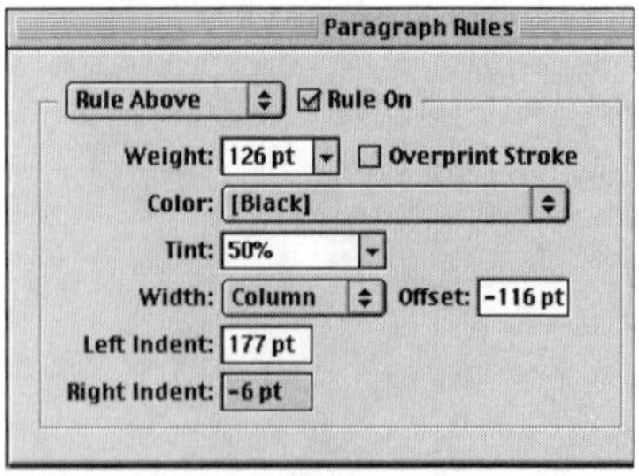

*These indent settings create a rule to the right of the paragraph.*

**Two Rules Above**    What can you do when one rule above isn't enough—when your design calls for two rules above your paragraph? A common design specification calls for two rules above a heading: a thin rule the width of the column and a thick rule the width of the text in the heading. How can you accomplish this using InDesign's paragraph rules? It's easy, as shown in the following steps (see Figure 6-8).

1.  Select a paragraph.

2.  For the paragraph rule below, choose Column from the Width pop-up menu, then enter a negative value in the Offset field that positions the rule above the tops of the characters in the first line of the paragraph (this will be something like the sum of the leading values in the paragraph). Set the line weight to a hairline (.25 points) or so.

FIGURE 6-8
Thick/Thin Rule Above

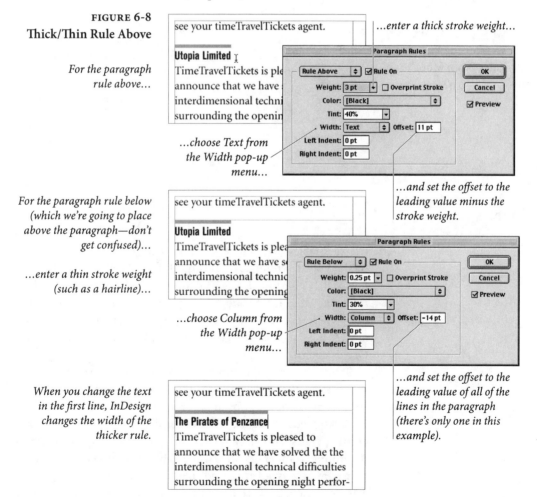

*For the paragraph rule above...*

*...choose Text from the Width pop-up menu...*

*For the paragraph rule below (which we're going to place above the paragraph—don't get confused)...*

*...enter a thin stroke weight (such as a hairline)...*

*...choose Column from the Width pop-up menu...*

*When you change the text in the first line, InDesign changes the width of the thicker rule.*

*...enter a thick stroke weight...*

*...and set the offset to the leading value minus the stroke weight.*

*...and set the offset to the leading value of all of the lines in the paragraph (there's only one in this example).*

3. For the paragraph rule above, choose Text from the Width pop-up menu, then set the stroke weight of the paragraph rule to something thicker than the stroke weight of the rule below—4 points, for example. Set the value in the Offset field so that the top edge of the rule above touches the bottom of the rule below.

**More Than Two Rules**

When you need to attach more than two rules above or below a paragraph, enter extra carriage returns before or after the paragraph, then apply paragraph rules to the resulting "blank" paragraphs. You can even set the leading of the empty paragraphs to zero, which keeps the empty paragraphs from disturbing the leading of the other text in the text column (see Figure 6-9). You can then use the Keep with Next settings of the empty paragraphs to make them "stick" to the original paragraph.

FIGURE 6-9
**Combining Paragraph Rules From More Than One Paragraph**

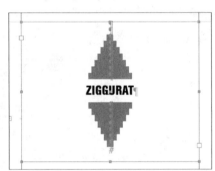

*The range of possible design effects is limited only by your imagination. (Our imaginations are running a little thin, right at the moment.)*

# Tables

Ole sees tables everywhere. He thinks they're the most common method of presenting text. This quirk is probably due to the time he spent typesetting a magazine devoted to horse racing (and its infamous "stud listing"), but he can be forgiven—tables really *are* everywhere. Looked at the business or sports section of a newspaper lately? Or a data sheet for that nifty new computer you want to buy? Or a calendar?

Tables are everywhere because they're a great way to present information that falls naturally into a set sequence of categories. If tables are so useful, why are they universally hated and despised by desktop publishing users? Since the dawn of the page layout era, creating tables has been a bother—programs that supported tables (Microsoft Word, FrameMaker, and Ventura Publisher, for example) didn't have the typesetting and color management features graphic arts professionals expect; popular page layout programs (such as

PageMaker and QuarkXPress) lacked tools for tabular composition. Plug-ins and standalone table-editing programs attempted to provide the feature, but, frankly, never worked very well.

The desktop publishing field has been waiting for someone to "do tables right" in a page layout program.

InDesign can create and edit tables, or import tables from Word, Excel, or HTML/XML. How good is this feature? It's not perfect, but it's more than good enough to alleviate most of the pain of working with tables in a layout.

**Table Anatomy**

Tables are a matrix; a grid made up of *rows* (horizontal subdivisions) and *columns* (vertical subdivisions). The area defined by the intersection of a given row and column is called a *cell*. InDesign has a complete vocabulary of terms for the various parts of rows, columns, and cells, which we've attempted to explain in Figure 6-10.

**FIGURE 6-10**
**What's That Called?**

*The basics*

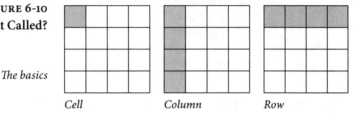

Cell    Column    Row

*Heading row made up of merged cells*

*A somewhat more complex example:*

*Table border*

*These cells have been filled with a tint.*

*Rotated merged cells make up these side headings.*

| I Gelosi (1600-1604) | |
|---|---|
| CHARACTER | ACTOR |
| Pantalone *or* Magnifico | Giulio Pasquati |
| Zanobio da Piombino | Girolamo Salimboni |
| Dottore Gratiano Forbisoni | Ludovico *of Bologna* |
| Capitano Spavento della Valle Inferna | Francesco Andreini |
| Prima Donna | Isabella Andreini |
| Burattino | Unknown |
| Arlecchino | Simone *of Bologne* |
| Franchechina | Silvia Roncagli |
| Lesbino | Silvia Roncagli |
| Ricciolina | Maria Antonazzoni |
| Olivetta | Unknown |

(PRINCIPAL ROLES / SERVANTS — rotated side headings)

**Understanding InDesign Tables**

Now that we've got the terminology out of the way, but before we dive into the details of working with tables in InDesign, there are a few conceptual points we'd like to make, as follows.

◆ Tables exist inside text frames. There is no "Table tool"—you create a text frame and then add a table to it, or convert text in the text frame to a table.

◆ From the point of view of the text frame (or story), a table acts like a single character (albeit a potentially *very large* one). Another way to look at a table is to think of it as a special type of inline frame. Like a character, a table changes position as you add or delete text preceding it in its parent story; like an inline frame, you can't apply character formatting (point size, font, or leading) to the character containing the table.

◆ Like text, tables can flow from column to column, text frame to text frame, and from page to page. Table header rows, however, do not automatically repeat when the table breaks across multiple text objects. Table rows cannot be broken from one text frame to another or from one column to another.

◆ Table cells are something akin to text frames: they can contain text, which can contain inline graphics, text frames, or tables. Any and all of InDesign's typesetting features can be used on the text in a table cell, including character and paragraph styles, indents, tab stops, and character formatting.

◆ Table cells can automatically expand (vertically) to display their content.

◆ Tables are not only for formatting tabular data—they're useful for a number of other things. Want to put a box around a paragraph? Convert the paragraph to a single-cell table. Want to compose paragraphs "side by side?" Use a two-column table (note that this can be one way to create hanging side heads). The number of possible uses are, as the cliché goes, "limited only by your imagination" and/or good sense/taste. But we're getting ahead of ourselves, as usual.

## Creating a Table

There are (at least) four ways to create a table.

◆ **"From scratch."** Click the Text tool inside an existing text frame, then choose Insert Table from the Table menu. InDesign displays the Insert Table dialog box. Enter the number of rows and columns you want in the corresponding fields and click the OK button. InDesign creates the table (see Figure 6-11).

Once you've created a table using this approach, you can add text or graphics to the table the same way you would add text to

**FIGURE 6-11**
**Creating a Table "From Scratch"**

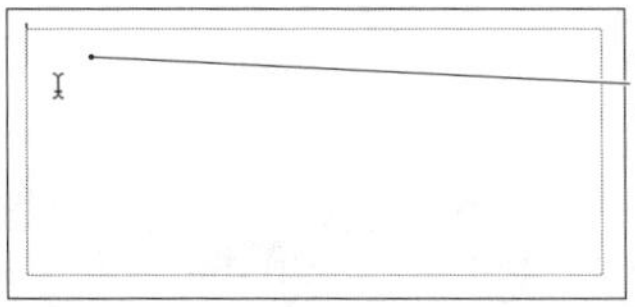

*Click the Text tool in a text frame.*

*Choose Insert Table from the Table menu (or press Command-Option-T/ Ctrl-Alt-T)*

Insert Table
Table Dimensions
Rows: 4
Columns: 4
OK
Cancel

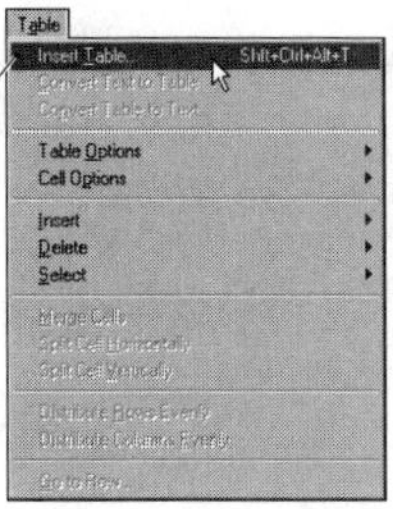

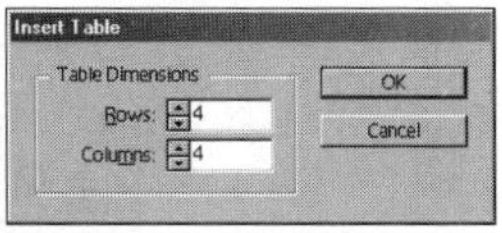

*InDesign displays the Insert Table dialog box. Enter the number of rows and columns you want and click OK.*

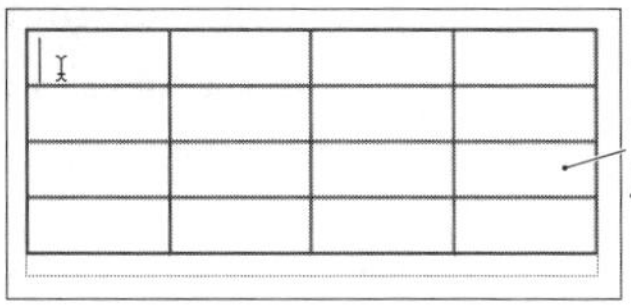

*InDesign inserts the table into the text frame.*

any text frame—click the Text tool inside a cell, then enter text, or paste text or graphics, or place text or graphics into the cell.

- **Converting Text to a Table.** To turn a range of text into a table, select the text and choose Convert text to Table from the Table Menu. InDesign converts the selected text to a table, using tab characters to split the text into table columns and return characters to split the text into table rows (see Figure 6-12). If the paragraphs of the selected text contain differing numbers of tab characters, InDesign bases the number of columns in the table on the tab characters found in the first paragraph of the selection. To convert a table to text, click the Text tool anywhere inside the table, then choose Convert Table To Text from the Table menu.

**FIGURE 6-12**
**Converting Text to a Table**

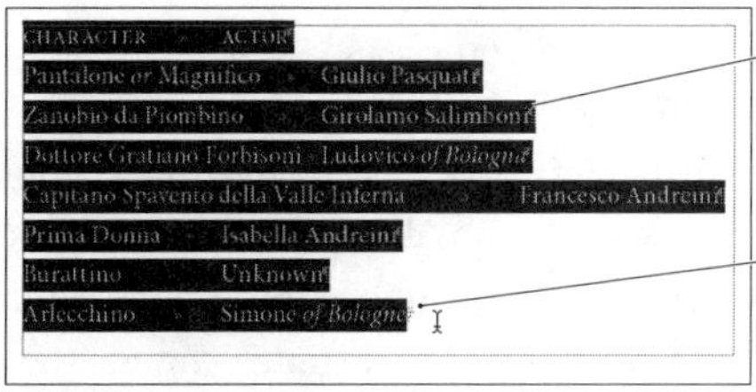

*Select some text.*

*Do not select the final carriage return character unless you want the table to end with an empty row.*

*Choose Convert Text to Table from the Table menu.*

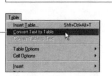

*InDesign converts the text to a table.*

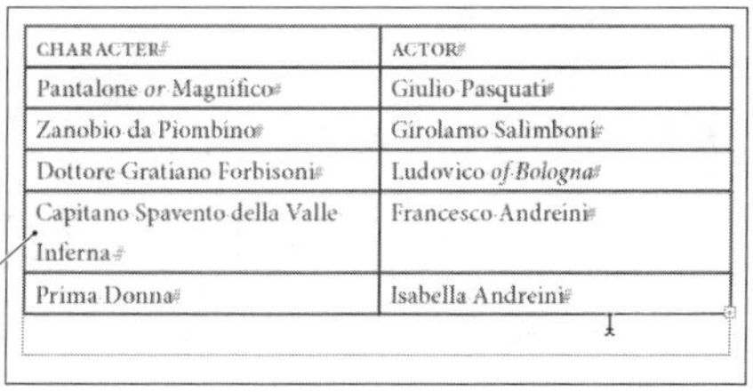

CHARACTER
ACTOR
Pantalone or Magnifico
Giulio Pasquati
Zanobio da Piombino
Girolamo Salimboni
Dottore Gratiano Forbisoni
Ludovico of Bologna
Capitano Spavento della Valle Inferna
Francesco Andreini
Prima Donna
Isabella Andreini

◆ **Importing a Table.** Another way to create a table is to import a table you've laid out in Word, Excel, or in an HTML document. There's no trick to this—simply select a file containing a table in the Place Document dialog box and place it, just as you'd place any other type of tile. If there is a table in the document, InDesign will convert it to an InDesign table as you flow the text onto a page. To import a table, place the file containing the table as you would place any other file.

◆ **Pasting a table.** You can also copy and paste tables from Word, Excel, and from HTML pages displayed in your web browser. Again, there's no trick—select the table, then copy, return to InDesign and paste. (Not all HTML tables seem to convert, nor are the results identical from browser to browser, but it does work, most of the time. David cannot get this to work at all.)

Sometimes, when you create or otherwise edit a table, you'll see a red dot in one or more of the cells in the table (see Figure 6-13). This means that the content of the cell (the text or graphic inside the cell) has become overset—it's exactly the same as having overset text in a text frame. What can you do? Either resize the cell or set the cell to automatically expand (as described in "Resizing Table Cells," later in this chapter).

**FIGURE 6-13**
**Overset Cell**

*The dot (you have to imagine it in red) indicates that the cell content is overset.*

When you create a table, InDesign sets the width of the table to the width of the text frame. But you're not limited to that width—InDesign tables can be narrower or wider than their containing text frame. As you'd expect, tables take on the alignment of the paragraph containing them. To change the position of the table in (or relative to) the text frame, change the paragraph alignment.

## Editing Tables

Once you've created a table, you can't just sit and *admire* it (as tempting as that might be for long-time page layout users), you've got to *do something* with it.

Before we talk about that, though, we'd better lay down a few ground rules about cells, rows, and columns.

◆ A column is always the width of the widest cell in the column. When you change the width of a cell, you're really changing the width of the column containing the cell.

◆ A row is always the height of the tallest cell in the row. Just as changing the width of a cell changes the width of a column, so changing the height of a cell changes the height of a row.

◆ In spite of the above restrictions, you can create tables containing cells that are wider than their parent columns or taller than their parent rows. You do this by merging cells, which we'll discuss later, in "Merging Cells."

**Selecting and Editing Table Items**

To select elements in a table, or to edit a table's content (text, rows, or columns) of a table, click the Text tool in one of the cells of the table. This activates InDesign's table tools. Once you've done this, you can enter and edit text in the cell, paste or place text or graphics in the cell, or even create another table inside the cell.

It's easy to tell when you're in this mode, because the cursor changes shape as you position it above cell, row, column, and table boundaries. What do these different cursors mean? What can you do with these tools? To find out, take a look at Table 6-1.

In addition, the Context menu changes to display options related to working with tables (see Figure 6-14).

**TABLE 6-1**
**Table Editing Cursors**

| When you see: | Your cursor is: | And you can: |
|---|---|---|
| ↘ | Above the top left corner of the table | Click to select the table. |
| → | Above the left edge of a row | Click to select the row. |
| ↓ | Above the top of a column | Click to select the column. |
| ↔ | Above the right or left edge of a cell | Drag to resize the column containing the cell. |
| ↕ | Above the top or bottom of a cell | Drag to resize the row containing the cell. |

FIGURE 6-14
**Context Menu Options
for Working with Tables**

*When you click the Text tool
in a table cell, or select text
in a table cell, InDesign adds
options to the Context menu.*

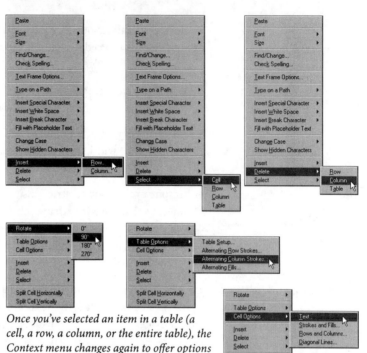

*Once you've selected an item in a table (a
cell, a row, a column, or the entire table), the
Context menu changes again to offer options
for working with the selected item.*

To select a range of cells, drag the text cursor through them. You
cannot select non-contiguous cells. Note that dragging the cursor
through multiple cells selects *all* of the text in the cells, regardless of
the starting or ending position of the cursor.

To select a row, position the cursor above the left edge of the first
cell in the row, then click; for a column, move the cursor above the
top of the first cell in the column, then click (see Figure 6-15).

You select text inside a table cell using the same methods you use
to select text in a text frame.

FIGURE 6-15
**Selecting Rows
and Columns**

*Position the cursor above the
top of a column...*

...*then click to select the column.*

*Position the cursor above the
left edge of a row...*

...*then click to select the row.*

| CHARACTER | ACTOR |
| --- | --- |
| Pantalone *or* Magnifico | Giulio |
| Zanobio da Piombino | Girola |
| Dottore Gratiano Forbisoni | Ludov |
| Capitano Spavento della Valle Inferna | France |
| Prima Donna | Isabell |
| Burattino | Unkno |
| Arlecchino | Simon |

| CHARACTER | ACTOR |
| --- | --- |
| Pantalone *or* Magnifico | Giulio Pasquati |
| Zanobio da Piombino | Girolamo Salimboni |
| Dottore Gratiano Forbisoni | Ludovico *of Bologna* |
| Capitano Spavento della Valle Inferna | Francesco Andreini |
| Prima Donna | Isabella Andreini |
| Burattino | Unknown |
| Arlecchino | Simone *of Bologne* |

| CHARACTER | ACTOR |
| --- | --- |
| Pantalone *or* Magnifico | Giulio Pasquati |
| Zanobio da Piombino | Girola |
| Dottore Gratiano Forbisoni | Ludov |

| CHARACTER | ACTOR |
| --- | --- |
| Pantalone *or* Magnifico | Giulio Pasquati |
| Zanobio da Piombino | Girolamo Salimboni |
| Dottore Gratiano Forbisoni | Ludovico *of Bologna* |

**Entering tab characters.** How the heck can you enter a tab character in a table cell? When you press Tab, InDesign moves the cursor to the next cell in the table (see "Table Shortcuts," later in this chapter). If the cursor is in the last cell of the table, pressing Tab creates a new table row. Either way, you don't get the character you're looking for. To enter a tab character, press Option-Tab/Alt-Tab (or choose Tab from the Insert Special Character submenu of the Context menu).

**Placing a Graphic in a Table Cell**

You place a graphic in a table cell in exactly the same fashion as you insert a graphic in text: click the Text tool in a cell, or select some text inside a cell, then place a file or paste a graphic you copied to the Clipboard earlier (see Figure 6-16). Note that you must select text or have an active text insertion point; selecting the cell itself will not get the graphic into the cell.

**FIGURE 6-16**
**Placing a Graphic in a Cell**

*Click the Text tool inside a table cell.*

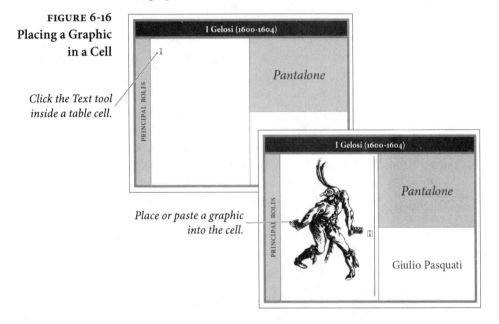

*Place or paste a graphic into the cell.*

**Changing the Size of a Table**

To resize a table by dragging, follow these steps (see Figure 6-17).

1. Click the Text tool inside the table.

2. Move the cursor over the left or right edge of the table (to change the table's width), or over the top or bottom of the table (to change its height). Position the cursor above the lower-right corner of the table to resize the width and height of the table.

3. Drag the cursor to resize the table. Hold down shift as you drag to resize the table proportionally.

FIGURE 6-17
**Resizing a Table**

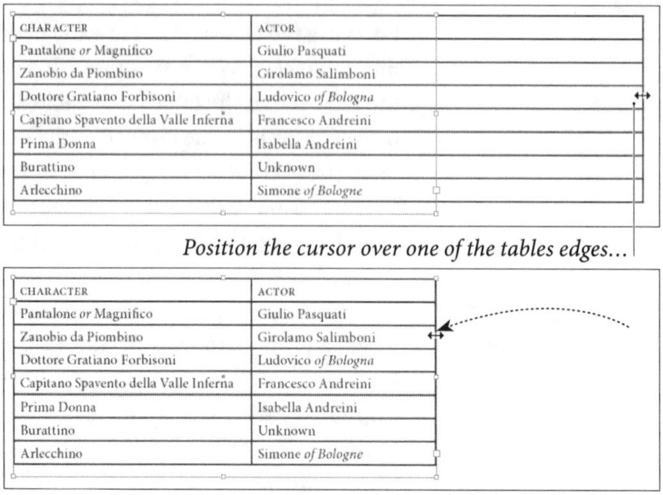

*Position the cursor over one of the tables edges...*

*...and drag. InDesign resizes the table. To resize the table proportionally, hold down shift as you drag*

When you resize the table by dragging the lower right corner of the table, or when you hold down Shift as you drag, InDesign applies the changes in size equally to all of the cells in the table. If you drag the sides of the table without holding down Shift, InDesign only changes the row or column nearest the edge you're dragging. Resizing the table using this technique does not scale the text in the table.

What? You've resized the table and now want all of the columns to be the same width? Don't start dragging columns around. Instead, select the table and choose Distribute Columns Evenly from the Table palette menu or Table menu (see Figure 6-18). If you're changed the height of the table and want to make all of the rows in the table the same height, select the table and choose Distribute Rows Evenly (again, from the Table menu or from the Table palette menu).

FIGURE 6-18
**Distributing
Columns Evenly**

*Select the columns you want to make equal in width. In this example, we've selected the entire table.*

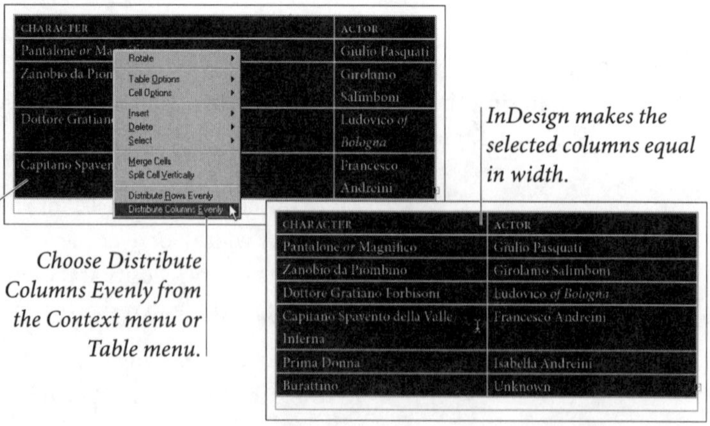

*Choose Distribute Columns Evenly from the Context menu or Table menu.*

*InDesign makes the selected columns equal in width.*

**Changing the Size of Rows and Columns**

To change the height of a row, or the width of a column by dragging, follow these steps (see Figure 6-19).

1. Click the Text tool inside a cell.

2. Move the cursor over the top or bottom of the cell to change the height of the row containing the cell, or over the left or right of the cell to change the column width.

3. Drag the cursor up or down to resize a row, or right or left to resize a column.

**FIGURE 6-19**
**Changing Row Height by Dragging**

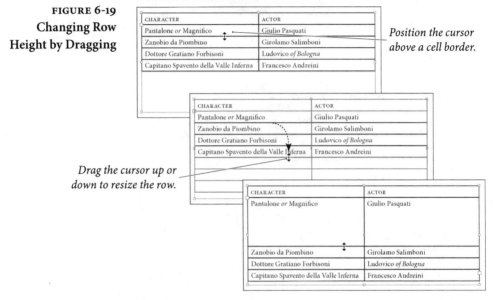

*Position the cursor above a cell border.*

*Drag the cursor up or down to resize the row.*

To change the height of a row or the width of a column using the Tables palette, follow these steps (see Figure 6-20).

1. Click the Text tool inside a cell.

2. Adjust the values in the Row Height and Column Width fields (you can type values in the fields, or use the arrow buttons associated with the fields to "nudge" the height or width up or down).

To change the height of a row or the width of a column using the Cell Options dialog box (see Figure 6-21).

1. Select a cell, a row, a column, or the entire table.

2. Choose Rows and Columns from the Cell Options submenu of the Context menu (or from the Table menu). InDesign displays the Cell Options dialog box.

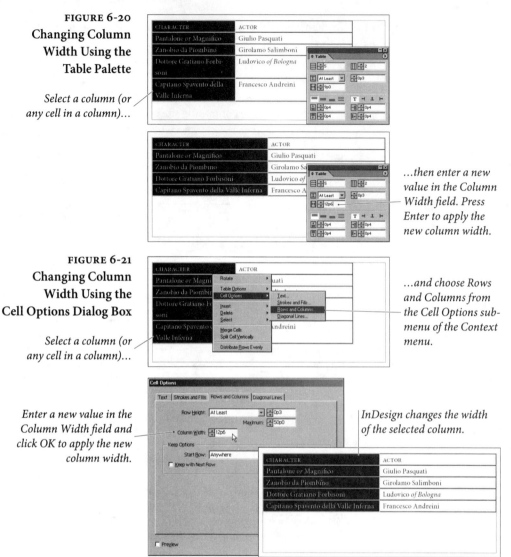

**FIGURE 6-20**

**Changing Column Width Using the Table Palette**

*Select a column (or any cell in a column)...*

*...then enter a new value in the Column Width field. Press Enter to apply the new column width.*

**FIGURE 6-21**

**Changing Column Width Using the Cell Options Dialog Box**

*Select a column (or any cell in a column)...*

*...and choose Rows and Columns from the Cell Options submenu of the Context menu.*

*Enter a new value in the Column Width field and click OK to apply the new column width.*

*InDesign changes the width of the selected column.*

3. Enter a new value in the Row Height field to change the height of the row, or in the Column Width field to change the width of a column. If you want to

**Adding Rows Or Columns**

To add a row or a series of rows to a table, follow these steps (see Figure 6-22).

1. Click the Text tool in a cell in a row that is above or below the point at which you want to add the new rows.

2. Choose Row from the Insert submenu of the Context menu. InDesign displays the Insert Row(s) dialog box.

**FIGURE 6-22**
**Adding Rows**

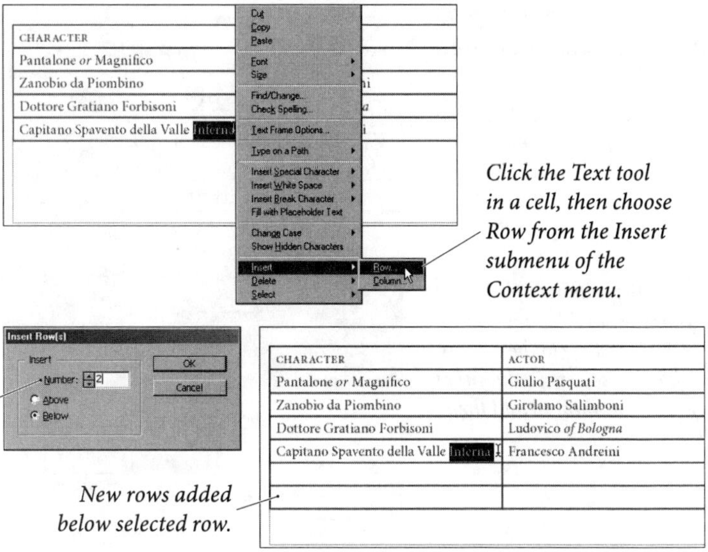

*Click the Text tool in a cell, then choose Row from the Insert submenu of the Context menu.*

*Enter the number of rows you want to add to the table, and specify whether you want them added above or below the selected row. Click the OK button to add the row or rows.*

*New rows added below selected row.*

3. Enter the number of Rows you want to add in the Number field, and choose the Above or Below option to tell InDesign where to put the rows (relative to the selected row).

4. Click the OK button. InDesign adds the empty rows.

To add a column or a series of columns to a table, follow these steps (see Figure 6-23).

1. Click the Text tool in a cell in a column that is adjacent to the point at which you want to add the new columns.

2. Choose Column from the Insert submenu of the Context menu. InDesign displays the Insert Column(s) dialog box.

3. Enter the number of Columns you want to add in the Number field, then choose the Left or Right option to tell InDesign where to put the rows (relative to the selected row).

4. Click the OK button. InDesign adds the empty columns to the table.

To add a row or column by dragging, follow these steps (see Figure 6-24).

1. Click the Text tool in a cell.

2. Position the cursor over one of the edges of the cell. To add a column, position the cursor over the left or right side of the cell; to add a row, position the cursor above the top or bottom of the cell.

FIGURE 6-23
**Adding a Column**

*Click the text tool in a cell (or select text in a cell).*

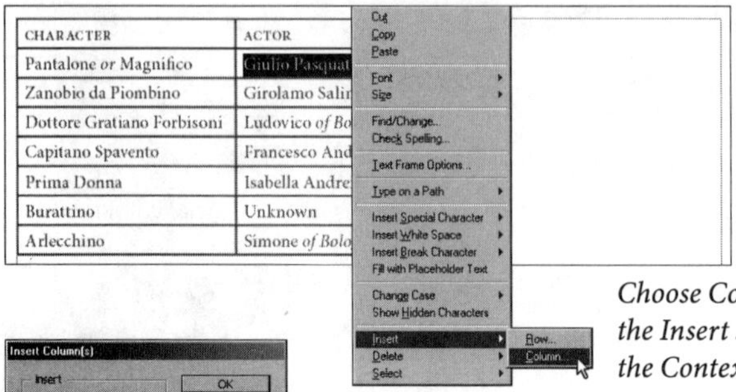

*Choose Column from the Insert submenu of the Context menu.*

*Enter the number of columns you want to add, and specify the location (to the right or left of the selected column) at which you want to add them.*

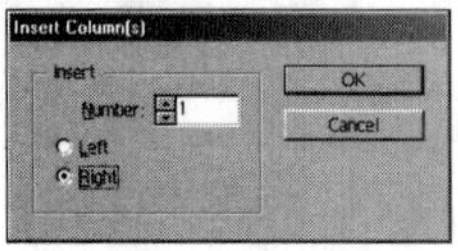

*Click the OK button to add the columns.*

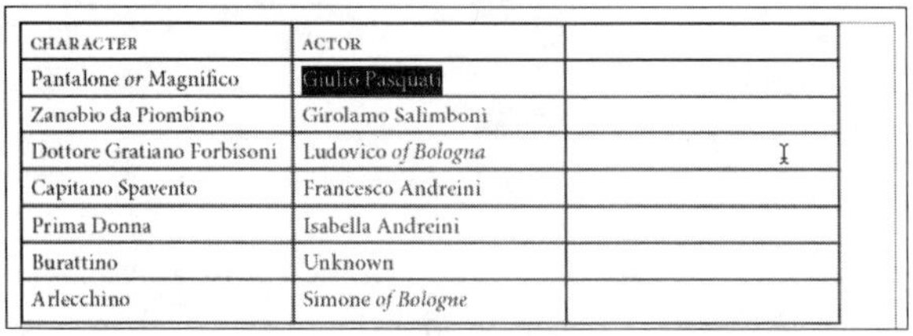

*InDesign adds the columns to the table.*

FIGURE 6-24
**Adding a Column by Dragging**

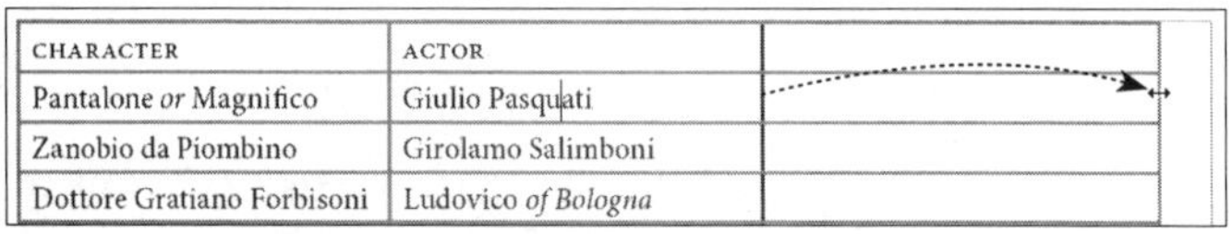

*Postion the cursor over a column edge. Hold down the mouse button, then press Option/Alt and drag.*

*Stop dragging, and InDesign adds a column to the table.*

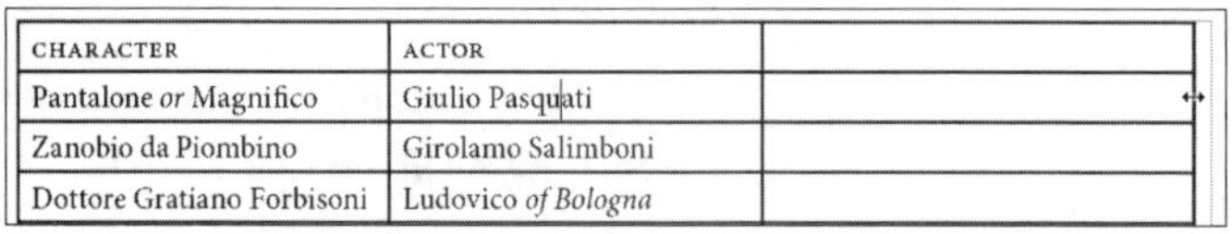

3. Hold down the mouse button, then press Option/Alt and drag. InDesign adds a row or column to the table.

To add a row to a table using the Table palette, follow these steps (see Figure 6-25).

1. Click the Text tool in a cell.

2. Display the Table palette (press Shift-F9) if it isn't already visible, then change the value displayed in the Rows field or the Columns field.

When you add a row using this technique, the new row appears below the row you selected; when you add a column, the new column appears to the right of the selected column.

**FIGURE 6-25**
**Adding a Row Using**
**the Table Palette**

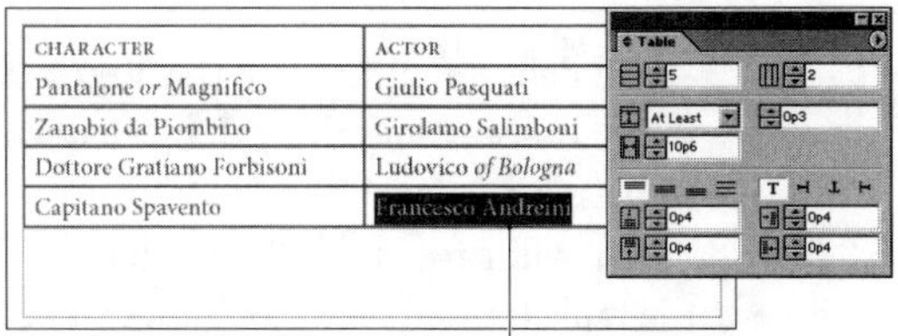

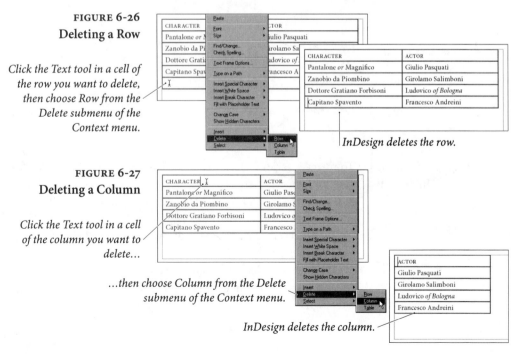

Click the text tool in a cell (or select text in a cell).

Enter a new
number of rows in
the Rows field of
the Table palette.

**Deleting Rows,**
**Columns, and Tables**

To delete a single row, click the Text tool in a cell in the row, then choose Row from the Delete submenu of the Context menu (see Figure 6-26). There's no need to select the row or cell. To delete more than one row, select at least one cell in each row you want to delete, then choose Row from the Delete submenu of the Context menu.

To delete a single column, click the Text tool in a cell in the column, then choose Column from the Delete submenu of the Context menu (see Figure 6-27). To delete more than one column, select a cell in each column you want to delete, then choose Column from the Delete submenu of the Context menu.

**FIGURE 6-26**
**Deleting a Row**

Click the Text tool in a cell of
the row you want to delete,
then choose Row from the
Delete submenu of the
Context menu.

InDesign deletes the row.

**FIGURE 6-27**
**Deleting a Column**

Click the Text tool in a cell
of the column you want to
delete...

...then choose Column from the Delete
submenu of the Context menu.

InDesign deletes the column.

To delete a table, click the Text tool in any cell in the table, and then choose Table from the Delete submenu of the Context menu. InDesign deletes the entire table containing the cell.

Or you can use the Text tool to select the character containing the table (remember: though it can be a very *large* character, it's still a single character) and press Delete.

To delete rows or columns using the Table palette, follow these steps (see Figure 6-28).

1. Click the Text tool in a cell.

2. Display the Table palette (press Shift F9) if it isn't already visible, then reduce the value in either the Rows field or the Columns field. InDesign asks if you're certain you want to remove the row(s). You are certain, so click the OK button.

FIGURE 6-28
**Deleting a Column Using the Tables Palette**

*Click the Text tool in a cell (or select text in a cell, or select a cell, row, or table).*

*Decrease the value in the Columns field by one or more.*

*InDesign asks if you want to delete the column. You do, so click the OK button.*

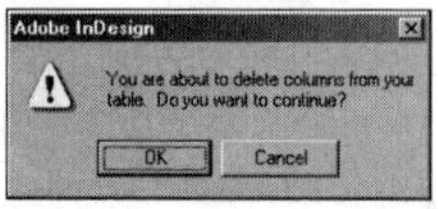

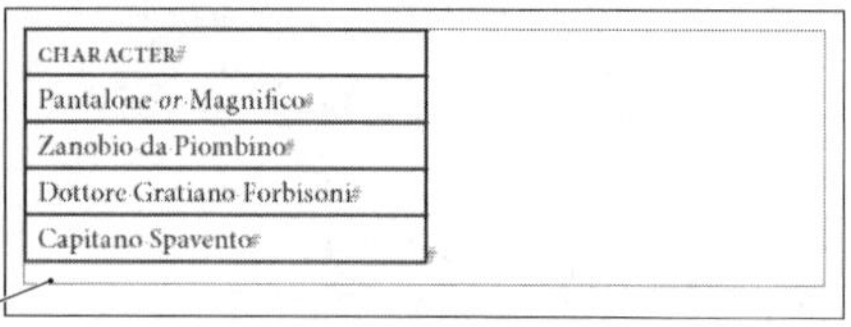

*InDesign removes columns from the table.*

**Merging and Splitting Table Cells**

To merge a series of selected table cells into a single cell, select the cells and choose Merge Cells from the Context menu (see Figure 6-29). All of the contents of all of the selected cells is placed in the new merged cell.

To split a cell, select the cell and choose Split Cell Horizontally or Split Cell Vertically from the Context menu (see Figure 6-30).

If you have selected an entire column of cells, you won't see the Split Cell Horizontally option; if you've selected a row of cells, InDesign turns off the Split Cell Vertically option.

**FIGURE 6-29**
**Merging Cells**

*Select a range of cells.*

*Choose Merge Cells
from the Context menu
(or Table menu).*

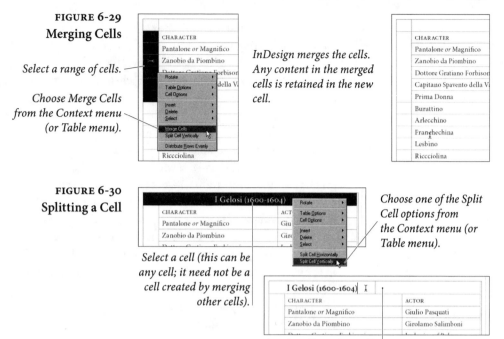

*InDesign merges the cells.
Any content in the merged
cells is retained in the new
cell.*

**FIGURE 6-30**
**Splitting a Cell**

*Choose one of the Split
Cell options from
the Context menu (or
Table menu).*

*Select a cell (this can be
any cell; it need not be a
cell created by merging
other cells).*

*InDesign splits the cell into two cells.*

**Rotating Table Cells**

Cells in an InDesign table can be rotated in 90-degree increments (see Figure 6-31). To rotate a cell and its contents, select the cell and then choose one of the options (0, 90, 180, 270) on the Rotate submenu of the Context menu (or click the corresponding button in the Table palette).

**FIGURE 6-31**
**Rotating a Cell**

*Select a cell.*

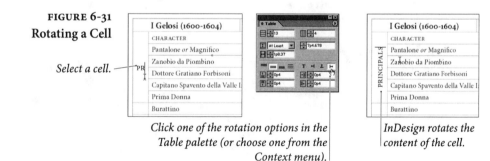

*Click one of the rotation options in the
Table palette (or choose one from the
Context menu).*

*InDesign rotates the
content of the cell.*

# Two Table Tricks

Earlier, we mentioned two of our favorite uses for tables—hanging side headings and boxed paragraphs. This section is our "best guess" attempt to find a place for these tricks in this chapter's organizaitonal structure.

**Using a Table to Create a Box Around a Paragraph**

Sometimes, you need to place a box around a paragraph—you often see this formatting used to set off notes and warnings in technical manuals. While you could always draw a box behind the paragraph, you would then have to move the box when the paragraph changes its position on the page due to text editing or layout changes. What you really need is a way to "stick" the box to the paragraph, so that it will follow the paragraph wherever it goes.

In the interest of completeness, we've shown two other methods for accomplishing this end elsewhere in this chapter (involving paragraph rules and inline frames)—but the best way to put a box around a paragraph is to convert the paragraph to a single-cell table. We do not know if single-cell tables can reproduce by fission, as other single-cell animals can, but they're certainly useful nonetheless.

To convert a paragraph to a single-cell table, select all of the text in the paragraph up to, but not including, the return at the end of the paragraph. Then choose Convert Text to Table from the Table menu (see Figure 6-32). Apply whatever formatting you want to the fill and stroke of the table's single cell.

**FIGURE 6-32**
**Placing a Box Around a Paragraph (Table Method)**

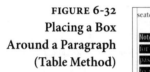

*Choose Convert Text to Table from the Table menu.*

*Select the text of the paragraph, leaving the return character unselected.*

*InDesign creates a table containing a single cell.*

*Apply formatting to the table.*

**Using a Table to Create a Hanging Side Head**

To create a hanging side head (like the one attached to this paragraph) using a table, follow these steps (see Figure 6-33).

1. Enter and format the heading and the body text as separate paragraphs.

2. Replace the return between the two paragraphs with a tab character.

3.  Select the text in the paragraph. Do not include the return in the selection.

4. Choose Convert Text to Table from the Table menu.

5.  Format the table.

FIGURE 6-33
**Creating a
Hanging Side Head
(Table Method)**

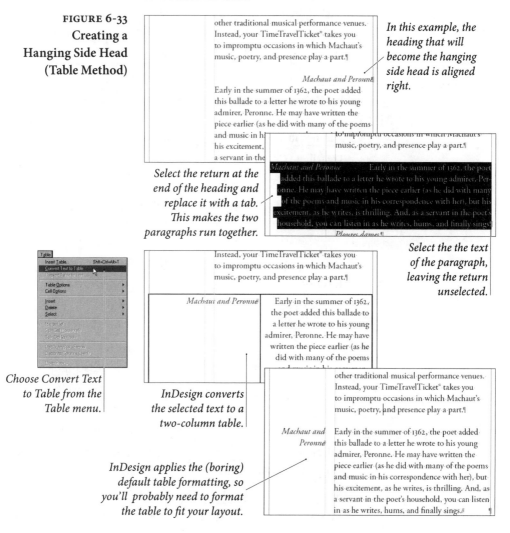

In this example, the heading that will become the hanging side head is aligned right.

Select the return at the end of the heading and replace it with a tab. This makes the two paragraphs run together.

Select the the text of the paragraph, leaving the return unselected.

Choose Convert Text to Table from the Table menu.

InDesign converts the selected text to a two-column table.

InDesign applies the (boring) default table formatting, so you'll probably need to format the table to fit your layout.

## Table Shortcuts

As you might expect, InDesign has a number of keyboard shortcuts related to working with tables (see Table 6-2 on the following page). Note that there are some very cool shortcuts that, by default, have no key assigned to them. Go to Row, in particular, is worth sacrificing an existing default shortcut for.

**TABLE 6-2**
**Table Shortcuts**

| Function | Shortcut |
|---|---|
| Diagonal Lines Options | not defined |
| Rows and Columns Options | not defined |
| Strokes and Fills Options | not defined |
| Text Options | Command-Option-B/Ctrl-Alt-B* |
| Convert Table to Text | not defined |
| Convert Text to Table | not defined |
| Delete Column | Shift-Backspace* |
| Delete Row | Command-Backspace/ Ctrl-Backspace* |
| Delete Table | not defined |
| Distribute Columns Evenly | not defined |
| Distribute Rows Evenly | not defined |
| Go to Row | not defined |
| Insert Table | Command-Shift-Option-T/ Ctrl-Alt-Shift-T |
| Insert Column | Command-Option-9/Ctrl-Alt-9* |
| Insert Row | Command-9/Ctrl-9* |
| Merge Cells | not defined |
| Next Cell | Tab |
| Previous Cell | Shift-Tab |
| Select Cell | Command-/(slash)/ Ctrl-/ (slash) or Esc* |
| Select Column | Command-Option-3/Ctrl-Alt-3* |
| Select Row | Command-3/Ctrl-3* |
| Select Table | Command-Option-A/Ctrl-Alt-A |
| Split Cell Horizontally | not defined |
| Split Cell Vertically | not defined |
| Alternating Column Strokes | not defined |
| Alternating Fills | not defined |
| Alternating Row Strokes | not defined |
| Table Setup | Command-Option-T/Ctrl-Alt-T* |

* This command is only active when you have an active text
insertion point in a text frame or table cell.

# Formatting Tables

Earlier, we mentioned that table cells are similar to InDesign text frames—and we now want to point out that that similarity extends to the realm of formatting, as well. Table cells can be filled using any fill you could apply to a frame, and can use most—but not all—of the strokes in InDesign's Stroke palette.

To format table cells, however, you don't (usually) use the same controls you use to format text frames, rectangles, ellipses, or other page items. Instead, you use a special set of table formatting controls, most of which you'll find in the Table Options (see Figure 6-34) and Cell Options dialog boxes (see Figure 6-35).

**FIGURE 6-34**
**Table Options**

*To open the Table Options dialog box, select a cell and choose one of the items on the Table Options submenu of the Context menu (or Table menu).*

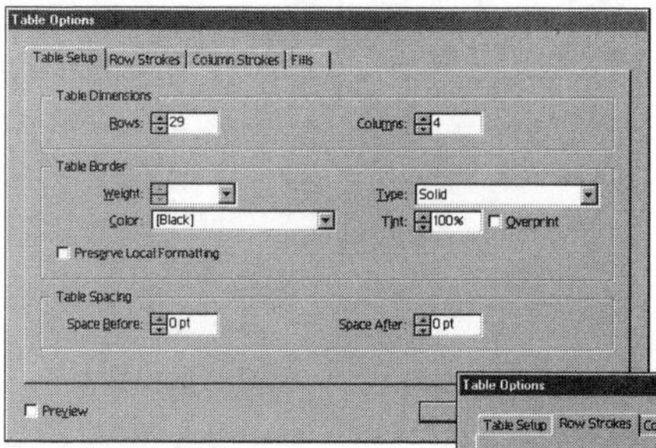

*The Row Strokes, Column Strokes, and Fills panels all feature an Alternating Pattern pop-up menu, which gives you a way to make the corresponding formatting vary in a predetermined fashion.*

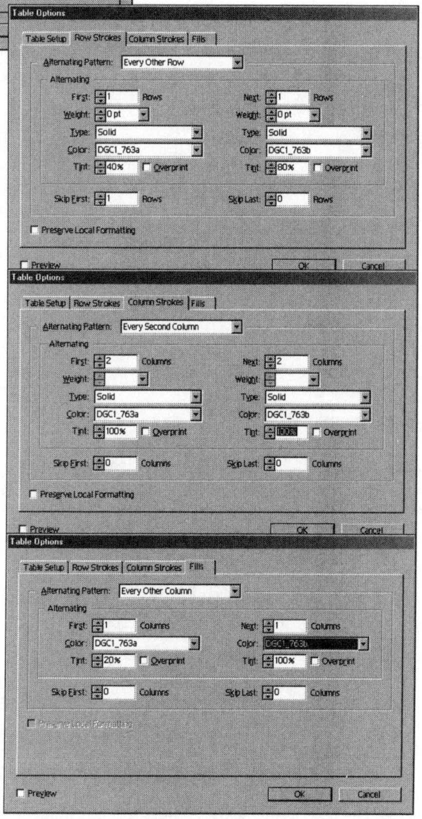

*When you choose one of the Alternating Pattern options, you can use the First and Next fields to define the pattern of alternation.*

*The Skip First and Skip Last fields give you a way to exclude certain table features (header and footer cells, for example) from the alternating pattern of formatting.*

FIGURE 6-35
**Cell Options**

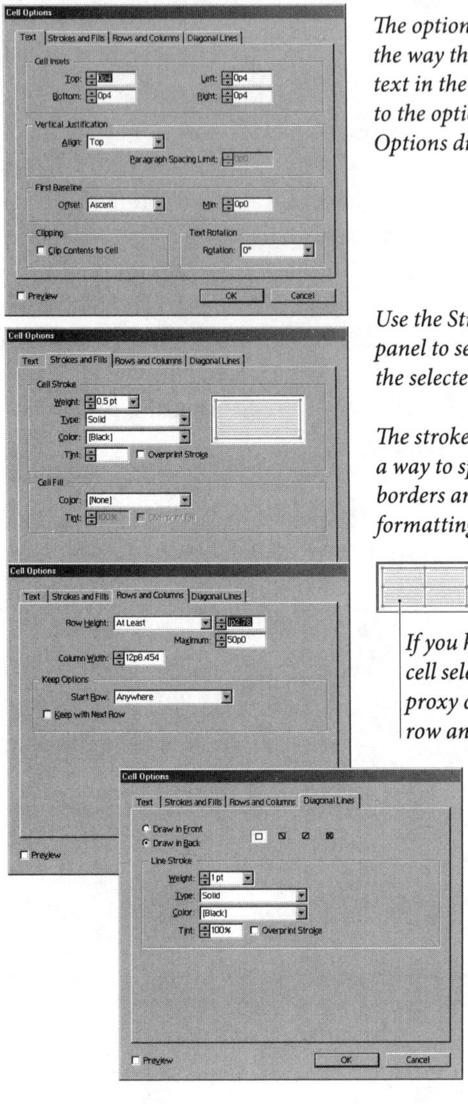

The options in the Text panel control the way that InDesign composes text in the cell—they're very similar to the options in the Text Frame Options dialog box.

To open the Cell Options dialog box, select a cell and choose one of the items on the Cell Options submenu of the Context menu (or Table menu).

Use the Strokes and Fills panel to set the formatting of the selected cells.

The stroke proxy gives you a way to specify which cell borders are affected by the formatting.

The controls in the Rows and Columns panel set the number of rows and columns in the table and their height/ width. As most of these controls are duplicated in the Table palette, the main reason you'll need to come here is the Keep Options section, which you can use to force a row to the next page or text frame.

If you have more than one cell selected, the stroke proxy changes to include row and column strokes.

Diagonal lines are often used to fill in empty cells in some table designs—the Diagonal Lines panel, as you'd expect, provides for-matting options for this feature.

**Table Cell Strokes and Fills**

Before we start talking about table formatting, it's important that you understand that applying a stroke to a column is exactly the same as applying a stroke to the left and right edges of all of the cells in that column. There are not separate stroke properties for rows and columns. If you change the stroke property of a column, the strokes on the corresponding cell borders in the column also change. The same thing is true for table border strokes—these properties apply to the outside edges of the cells at the top, right, bottom, and left edges of the table.

**Applying Strokes to Cells.** InDesign offers a number of different ways to set the fill or stroke of a cell. You can set the stroke weight using the Stroke palette or the Strokes and Fills panel of the Cell Options dialog box. You can set the fill of a cell using the Swatches palette, the Color palette, the Strokes and Fills panel of the Cell Options dialog box. The is not a complete listing of the different methods you can use to format cells, but we think you get the idea.

When you want to apply a stroke to all of the borders of a cell or cells, follow these steps (see Figure 6-36).

1. Select the cell or range of cells you want to format.

2. Display the Stroke palette or display the Strokes and Fills panel of the Cell options dialog box (choose Strokes and Fills from the Cell Options submenu of the Context menu).

3. Enter a stroke weight in the Weight field and press Enter (or otherwise apply the new value).

4. Apply a stroke color. If you're applying the stroke using the Stroke palette, you can use the Swatches palette, the Color palette, the Gradient palette, or any of the other color controls. If you're using the Strokes and Fills panel of the Cell Options dialog box, you can use the Color pop-up menu.

**FIGURE 6-36**
**Applying a Stroke to All Cell Borders**

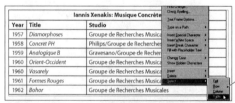

*Select a range of cells. In this example, we've selected the entire table.*

*Choose Strokes and Fills from the Cell Options submenu of the Context menu.*

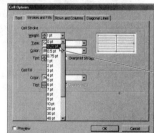

*Specify the stroke weight and color of the stroke and click the OK button to apply your changes.*

*InDesign applies the stroke to the selected range of cells.*

Each border of a cell in an InDesign table can have a different stroke. Note, however, that cells share borders with adjacent cells. Applying a stroke to the right border of a cell affects the left border of the next cell in the row.

The Cell Proxy (in the Strokes panel of the Cell Options dialog box, or in the Stroke palette) is the way that you tell InDesign which border you want to work with (see Figure 6-37). Just as the Proxy in the Transform palette "stands in" for the current selection, the Cell Proxy represents the selected cell or cell range.

When the borders in the Cell Proxy are highlighted (in light blue), changes you make to the stroke color or stroke weight will affect the corresponding cell borders. To prevent formatting from affecting a cell border, click the corresponding active border in the Cell Proxy. To make an inactive border active again, click it again.

FIGURE 6-37
**Cell Proxy**

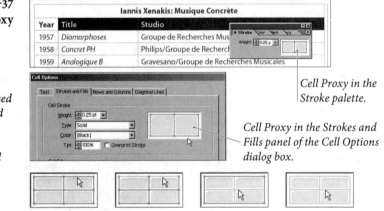

*Actually, we don't know what this control is supposed to be called—we could find no reference to it in any "official" documentation. So we're calling it the "Cell Proxy." You got a problem with that?*

*Cell Proxy in the Stroke palette.*

*Cell Proxy in the Strokes and Fills panel of the Cell Options dialog box.*

*Click a cell border in the Cell Proxy to exclude the corresponding cell edges from formatting. Click again to activate the cell border.*

*Double click to deactivate a group of cell borders, or triple-click to deactivate all cell borders.*

If you want to apply a stroke to some, but not all, of the borders of a cell, follow these steps (see Figure 6-38).

1. Select the cell or range of cells you want to format.

2. Display the Stroke palette or display the Strokes and Fills panel of the Cell options dialog box (choose Strokes and Fills from the Cell Options submenu of the Context menu).

3. Use the Cell Proxy to select the cell borders you want to format.

4. Apply stroke formatting using the Strokes and Fills panel of the Cell Options dialog box, or the Stroke and Swatches palettes.

FIGURE 6-38
**Applying a Stroke to
Selected Cell Borders**

*In this example, we want to
remove the strokes around
the outside edges (top, left,
and right) of the first row in
the table, but we don't want
to remove the stroke at the
bottom of the row. To do this,
we use the Cell Proxy in the
Stroke palette.*

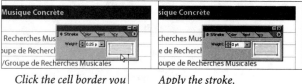

Select the cell you want
to format.

InDesign displays the Cell
Proxy in the Stroke palette.

Click the cell border you
want to protect from
formatting.

Apply the stroke.

*The top, left, and right
borders of the first row have
been set to zero point strokes,
but the bottom border of
the row retains its original
stroke weight.*

**Applying Fills to Cells.** To apply a fill to a cell, follow these steps (see Figure 6-39).

1.  Select a cell or a range of cells.

2.  Display the Strokes and Fills panel of the Cell Options dialog box (to display this panel, choose Strokes and Fills from the Cell Options submenu of the Context menu).

3.  Choose a color swatch from the Color pop-up menu, and enter a tint value in the Tint field, if necessary. Note that you can also set the fill to overprint using the Overprint option.

4.  Click the OK button to close the dialog box and apply the fill to the selected cells.

Alternatively, you can apply a fill to a cell using the Swatches palette or Color palette (see Figure 6-40).

1.  Select a cell or range of cells.

2.  Click the Fill selector at the top of the Swatches palette or Color palette to make it active (if it's not already active).

FIGURE 6-39
Applying a Fill to a Cell
(Dialog Box Method)

Select a cell or series of cells.

Choose Strokes and Fills from
the Cell Options submenu of
the Context menu.

Specify fill options in the
Strokes and Fills panel of
the Cell Options dialog
box. Click the OK button to
apply your changes.

InDesign applies the fill to the selected cells.

FIGURE 6-40
Applying a Fill to a Cell
(Palette Method)

Select a cell or a range of cells.

Click the Fill selector at
the top of the Swatches
palette (if it's not
already active).

Click a swatch.

InDesign applies the fill to the selected cells.

3. Click the swatch (if you're using the Swatches palette) or define a color (if you're using the Color palette) to apply it to the background of the cell.

**Applying Gradients to Table Cells.** You can apply a gradient to the fill and stroke of a cell, but the results might not be what you'd expect (see Figure 6-41).

1. Select the cells.

2. Display the Gradient palette, if it's not already visible.

3. Click in the Gradient Ramp to apply a gradient to the selected cells. Adjust the gradient settings to define the type, color, and angle of the gradient (as discussed in Chapter 5, "Drawing").

Note that the gradient is based on the width and height of the table, rather than on the selected cell or cells. This may or may not give you the effect you're looking for.

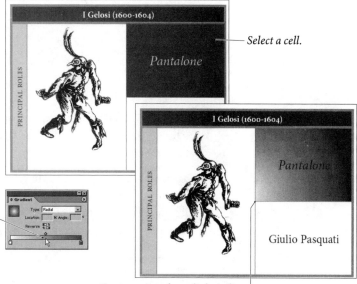

**FIGURE 6-41**
**Applying a**
**Gradient to a Cell**

*Note that InDesign calculates the position of the start and end of the gradient (in this example, the center point of a radial gradient) based on the width and height of the entire table— not the width of the cell itself.*

*Display the Gradient palette and click the Gradient Ramp to apply a gradient fill.*

*Select a cell.*

*Center point of a radial gradient applied to the cell.*

**Applying Diagonal Lines.** To apply diagonal lines to a cell, use the options in the Diagonal Lines panel of the Cell Options dialog box (see Figure 6-42).

1. Select a cell, row, column, or table (table border strokes apply to the entire table, so you need only select part of the table).

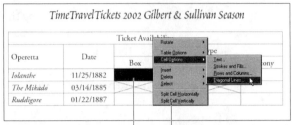

FIGURE 6-42

**Applying Diagonal
Lines to a Cell**

*In this example table,
a diagonal line in a cell
indicates that the seats in
that section are no longer
available. TimeTravelTickets
has run out of seats for
the November 11th, 1882
premiere of "Iolanthe," so we
have to apply diagonal lines
to the corresponding cell.*

*Select a cell.*   *Choose Diagonal Lines from the Cell
Options submenu of the Context menu.*

*Turn on one of the diagonal
lines options and specify the
formatting of the lines.*

*InDesign applies the diagonal
lines to the cell.*

2.  Display the Diagonal Lines panel of the Cell Options dialog box
    (choose Diagonal Lines from the Cell Options submenu of the
    Context menu).

3.  Turn on one of the diagonal lines options. Choose a stroke
    weight, stroke type, color, and tint. If you want the diagonal
    lines to overprint, turn on the Overprint option. If you want the
    diagonal lines to appear in front of the table, turn on the Draw
    in Front option.

4.  Click the OK button to apply the diagonal lines.

**Formatting Table Borders.** To apply a stroke to the edges of a table,
use the options in the Table Border section of the Table Setup panel
of the Table Options dialog box (see Figure 6-43)

1.  Select a cell, row, column, or table (table border strokes apply to
    the entire table, so you need only select part of the table).

2.  Display the Table Setup panel of the Table Options dialog box
    (press Command-Option-T/Ctrl-Alt-T).

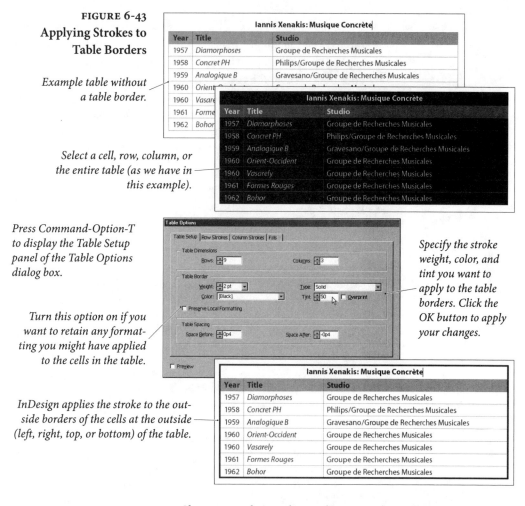

FIGURE 6-43
**Applying Strokes to
Table Borders**

*Example table without
a table border.*

*Select a cell, row, column, or
the entire table (as we have in
this example).*

*Press Command-Option-T
to display the Table Setup
panel of the Table Options
dialog box.*

*Turn this option on if you
want to retain any formatting you might have applied
to the cells in the table.*

*InDesign applies the stroke to the out-
side borders of the cells at the outside
(left, right, top, or bottom) of the table.*

*Specify the stroke
weight, color, and
tint you want to
apply to the table
borders. Click the
OK button to apply
your changes.*

3. Choose a stroke weight, stroke type, color, and tint. If you want
   the stroke to overprint, turn on the Overprint option.

4. If you want to prevent the table border formatting from overriding formatting you've applied to the cells in the table (i.e., any
   formatting other than the default table formatting), turn on the
   Preserve Local Formatting option.

**Applying Alternating Fills and Strokes.** The options in the Row
Strokes, Column Strokes, and Fills panels of the Table Options
dialog box provide a way for you to vary the formatting of rows and
columns in a table according to a predefined pattern. Shading table
rows or columns is often a more visually pleasing way to format a
table than using strokes (this depends on the design of the piece in
which the table appears).

All of these panels work the same way—you select a pattern from the Alternating Pattern menu, and then you specify the formatting applied by that pattern. If the pattern you've chosen is None, InDesign does not alternate the corresponding fill or stroke properties in the table. Otherwise, InDesign applies one of two formats to the rows and columns in the table. Formatting you apply using alternating fills or strokes overrides any cell formatting you've already applied to the cells in the table (this has no effect on text formatting).

To apply an alternating fill or stroke pattern to a table, follow these steps (see Figure 6-44).

1. Select a cell, row, column, or table (this formatting applies to the entire table, regardless of the selection, so do whatever is easiest for you).

**FIGURE 6-44**
**Applying**
**Alternating Fills**

*Select a cell.*

*Choose Alternating Fills from the Table Options submenu of the Context menu.*

*Note that we've directed our alternating pattern to skip the first two rows in the table (to avoid the table header row and title).*

*Select a pattern from the Alternating Pattern pop-up menu, then specify the formatting you want to apply.*

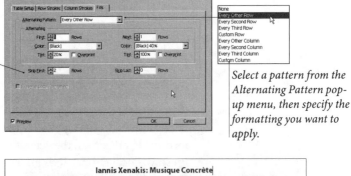

*InDesign applies the alternating fill pattern to the rows in the table.*

2. Display the panel of the Table Options dialog box that cor-responds to the attribute you want to work with (i.e., Row Strokes, Column Strokes, or Fills). You might want to turn on the Preview option—it can help you understand the effect of the formatting options.

3. Choose an option from the Alternating Pattern pop-up menu.

4. Choose a color for the alternating pattern (until you do this, you probably won't see any changes to the table, even if you have turned on the Preview option).

5. If you want the alternating pattern to ignore rows at the begin-ning or end of the table (for alternating row strokes) or at the left or right edges of the column (if you're working with alternating column strokes), enter the number of cells in the Skip First and Skip Last fields.

It should be clear that quite complex alternating formatting can be applied using these options. We don't mean to avoid the topic, but the only real way to learn how the different alternating formatting features work is to experiment with the settings. So create an exam-ple table, open the Table Options dialog box, turn on the Preview option, and play!

# Text Wrap

Any independent object in an InDesign publication can have a text wrap—a boundary that repels text—applied to it. Wrapping text around an object is something like the opposite of flowing text inside a path. When you flow text inside a path, you want text to stay inside a path; when you apply a text wrap, you want to keep it out. To set the text wrap for an object, follow these steps (see Figure 6-45).

1. Select an object—any frame or group—on an InDesign page.

2. Display the Text Wrap palette, if it's not already visible (press Command-Option-W/Ctrl-Alt-W).

3. Click one of the Text Wrap buttons in the Text Wrap palette. InDesign displays the text wrap boundary around the selected object, and pushes any text falling inside the text wrap boundary to the outside of the boundary. If you applied the text wrap to a text frame, the text in that frame is unaffected by the text wrap boundary.

FIGURE 6-45
**Text Wrap**

*To wrap text around an object, select the object and then click one of the text wrap options in the Text Wrap palette (we've listed the "official" name of the text wrap type below each example).*

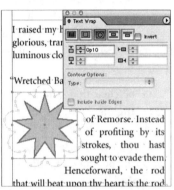

*No Text Wrap*

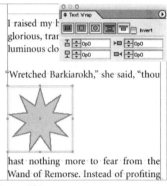

*Wrap Around Bounding Box*

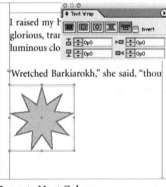

*Wrap Around Object Shape*

*Jump Object*

*When you choose one of the rectangular text wrap options (Wrap Around Bounding Box, Jump Object, or Jump to Next Column), you can adjust the offset values for the top, right, left, and bottom independently. If you choose Wrap Around Object Shape, you can only enter a single offset value that applies to all sides of the text wrap.*

*Jump to Next Column*

*The Jump Object text wrap option causes text in any column touching the text wrap boundary to jump over the text wrap—it's as if the wrap extends to the width of the column. The Jump To Next Column text wrap option pushes any text in the column below the top of the text wrap boundary to the top of the next column.*

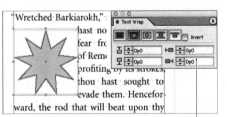

*Enter a value in one of the offset fields...*

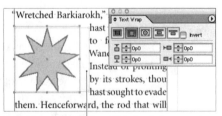

*InDesign changes the offset for the corresponding side.*

4.  Set the text wrap offset distances using the Top, Left, Bottom, and Right fields in the Text Wrap palette. If you've selected anything other than a rectangular frame, you'll only be able to adjust a single field (the Left field) to set the offset distance.

You can make individual text frames immune to text wrap—select the frame and turn on the Ignore Text Wrap option in the Text Frame Options dialog box.

InDesign can apply an *inverted* text wrap to an object, which causes text to wrap to the inside of the text wrap (see Figure 6-46).

The text wrap boundary is a path, and can be edited and adjusted just as you'd change the shape of any path in InDesign (see Figure 6-47). You can draw new line segments using the Pen tool, or change the location of path points using the Direct Selection tool.

**FIGURE 6-46**
**Inverted Text Wrap**

*Regular text wrap*          *Inverted text wrap*

**FIGURE 6-47**
**Editing a Text Wrap**

*The text wrap boundary appears in a tint (we think it's 50 percent) of the selection color of the layer containing the object—this can make it difficult to see.*

*You can also use the Pen tool to add points, delete points, or change the control handles of points of a text wrap boundary.*

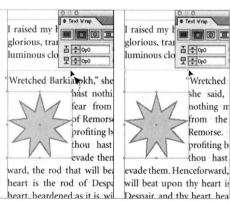

*Select points on the text wrap boundary just as you would select points on any path.*

*Drag the points to a new location.*

*InDesign wraps the text around the edited text wrap boundary.*

# Converting Text to Outlines

When you work in graphic design, you frequently need to alter character shapes for logos or packaging designs. For years, we dreamed about the ability to turn type into paths (or "outlines") we could edit. Finally, applications such as FreeHand and Illustrator added the feature. And, as you'd expect in a modern page layout program, InDesign has it.

You can convert characters from just about any font (TrueType, PostScript Type 1 and OpenType fonts) for which you have the printer (outline) font.

Once you've converted the characters into outlines, you lose all text editing capabilities, but you gain the ability to paste things inside the character outline, to use the path as a frame, and to change the shapes of the characters themselves.

To convert characters of text into paths, follow these steps (see Figure 6-48).

1. Select the text you want to convert. You can select text using either the Text tool, or select the text frame using the Selection tool or the Direct Selection tool.

2. Choose Convert to Outlines from the Type menu (or press Command-Shift-O/Ctrl-Shift-O). InDesign converts the characters into paths. If you selected the characters using the Text tool, InDesign positions the paths on the current line as an inline graphic; if you selected the text frame using the Selection tool or the Direct Selection tool, InDesign joins the resulting outlines into a compound path.

When you convert individual characters containing interior space (such as "P," or "O") into paths, InDesign turns them into composite paths (see "Compound Paths" in Chapter 5, "Drawing"). This is handy. Not only are multiple-part characters (such as i, é, and ü) treated as single paths, but characters with interior paths (such as O, P, A, and D) are transparent where they should be, and fill properly.

You can always make the characters into normal (not composite) paths. To do this, select the character and choose Release from the Compound Paths submenu of the Object menu (see Figure 6-49).

**If Your Characters Won't Convert**   If you weren't able to convert the text into paths, make sure that you have the outline (printer) fonts and that they're somewhere InDesign can find them. If you don't have the outline fonts, InDesign won't be able to convert your text into paths.

**FIGURE 6-48**
**Converting Text**
**to Outlines**

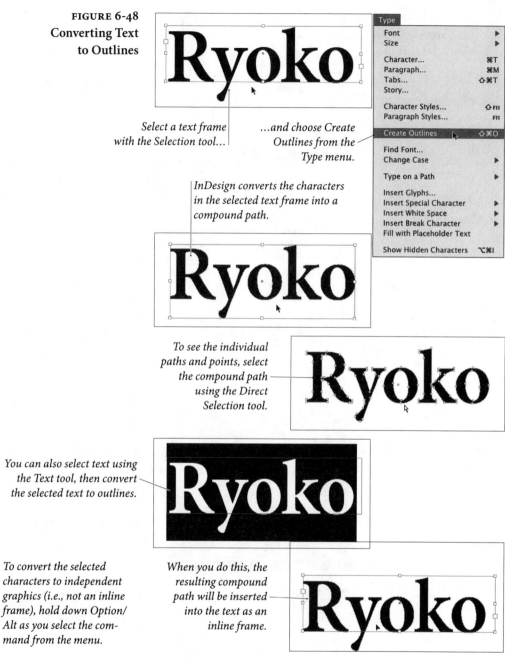

*Select a text frame*
*with the Selection tool...*

*...and choose Create*
*Outlines from the*
*Type menu.*

*InDesign converts the characters*
*in the selected text frame into a*
*compound path.*

*To see the individual*
*paths and points, select*
*the compound path*
*using the Direct*
*Selection tool.*

*You can also select text using*
*the Text tool, then convert*
*the selected text to outlines.*

*To convert the selected*
*characters to independent*
*graphics (i.e., not an inline*
*frame), hold down Option/*
*Alt as you select the com-*
*mand from the menu.*

*When you do this, the*
*resulting compound*
*path will be inserted*
*into the text as an*
*inline frame.*

**Making Type Glow**   When you want to add a glowing outline to your type, follow these steps (see Figure 6-50).

1. Convert the text to outlines. In this case, select the text using the Selection tool.

FIGURE 6-49
**Working with
Character Outlines**

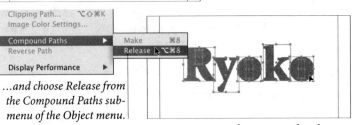

*Select the compound
path containing the
character outlines...*

*...and choose Release from
the Compound Paths sub-
menu of the Object menu.*

*InDesign converts the compound path
into normal paths.*

*The same formatting (fill
and stroke) is applied to all
of the resulting paths—even
the paths that create
the hollow areas inside
characters.*

*To put the characters back
together again, use the Direct
Selection tool to select the
path representing the hollow
area or areas of a character...*

*...and choose Reverse Path
from the Object menu.*

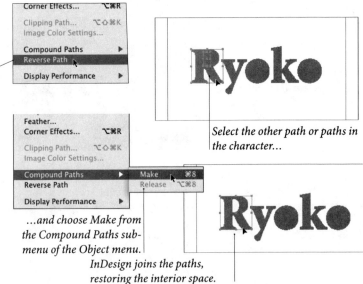

*Select the other path or paths in
the character...*

*...and choose Make from
the Compound Paths sub-
menu of the Object menu.*

*InDesign joins the paths,
restoring the interior space.*

2. Select the compound path containing the paths.

3. Increase the stroke weight to something fairly heavy—say,
   6 points or more.

FIGURE 6-50
### Glowing Type

*Turn on the Width Changes Bounding Box option.*

*Select a text frame with the Selection tool and convert the text to outlines.*

*Apply a thick stroke to the converted characters.*

*Run the "Neon" script.*

*If you're using Windows, you'll see a dialog box—you won't if you're using the AppleScript version of the script.*

*InDesign creates a group containing the objects making up the "glow."*

4. Display the Stroke palette and choose Width Changes Bounding Box from the Stroke palette menu.

5. Run the "Neon Glow" script (it's on your InDesign CD, inside the Scripting folder in the Adobe Technical Info folder).

InDesign creates a series of copies of the selected paths, changing the stroke weight and stroke color of each copy as it does so. When it's done adding paths, InDesign groups the "neon glow" effect.

## Inline Frames

It was the Dark Age of page layout. The flame of classical desktop publishing knowledge flickered but dimly, kept barely alive by devoted acolytes in isolated monasteries. Pestilence and famine stalked the narrow aisles between our unheated cubicles. And, almost worst of all, page layout programs could not paste graphics into text. Producing publications featuring graphics "anchored" to a specific piece of text was a nightmare. It went something like this. Scroll. Zoom in. Measure. Pull a guide down from a ruler. Select a graphic. Drag the graphic until it snaps to the guide. Sigh heavily. Repeat.

These days, we embed graphics in lines of text whenever the graphics have some defined relationship to the text. You know what we mean—illustrations that should appear immediately after a paragraph (think of the screen shots in a typical manual), or icons "hanging" to the left of a column of text, or graphic symbols in a line of text. If you embed the graphics in the text, they'll follow the text as it flows through the text blocks or text frames containing the story. In QuarkXPress, these are called "anchored boxes," but In InDesign they're "inline frames."

With InDesign, you can paste any kind of frame into a text frame. You're not limited to graphic frames—you can use text frames and groups as well, opening up new ways to solve old problems and adding capabilities that are entirely new. You can create inline frames using frames that contain other frames or other inline frames.

Using inline frames does more than just "stick" a frame to a particular location in a story—it also makes it easier for you to control the space between the graphic and the text. Complicated spacing arrangements that would be difficult (and involve lots of measuring and moving) without inline frames become easy to implement using leading, tabs, indents, and paragraph space above and below.

**Creating an Inline Frame**

You can use any of the following methods to create an inline frame (see Figure 6-51).

◆ Paste a frame into a text frame.

◆ Use the Text tool to select a character or a range of characters and choose Convert to Outlines from the Type menu. InDesign creates a path for each character in the selection and embeds the paths, as a group, in the text.

◆ Place a graphic when you have an active text insertion point.

InDesign treats each inline frame as a single character of text. You can select an inline frame using the Text tool, and adjust its leading and baseline shift using the Character palette. You can adjust the horizontal distance between the inline frame and the other characters on the line using kerning or tracking—you can even kern text following the inline frame back into the frame (you can't, however, kern the frame back into characters preceding it on a line).

You can select an inline frame using the Selection or Direct Selection tools, and you can edit the shape of the inline frame using the path drawing tools (the Pen, Add Point, Delete Point, and Convert Point tools). You can also drag an inline frame up or down in the text frame using either of the selection tools. This produces the same effect as applying a baseline shift amount using the Character palette (see Figure 6-52).

**FIGURE 6-51**

**Creating an**
**Inline Frame**

*Select the object (graphic*
*frame, text frame, or group)*
*you want to embed in the*
*text and cut or copy it to the*
*Clipboard.*

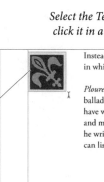

*Select the Text tool and*
*click it in a text frame.*

*Paste the object into the text.*
*At this point, you can select*
*the object using the Selection*
*tool (or select object contents*
*using the Direct Selection*
*tool) and adjust the object's*
*vertical position relative to*
*the line of text.*

*You can also select the object*
*as if it were a single character*
*of text by using the Text tool.*

**Inline Frames**
**and Leading**

When you insert an inline frame into a text frame, InDesign gives it the leading value of the surrounding text. If you're using "auto" leading, and if the inline frame is taller than the height of the text, InDesign pushes the line down to prevent the inline frame from overlapping the text on the lines above it. If, on the other hand, you're using a fixed leading value, you'll see the inline frame overlap the text. By default, InDesign positions the bottom of the inline frame at the baseline of text.

This works perfectly for us—when the inline frame shares a line with other text, we usually want the leading of the line to stay the same as the other lines in the paragraph—and we can get this effect using fixed leading values. When we place an inline frame in a paragraph by itself, however, we usually want the height of the paragraph to equal the height of the inline frame—and we can get that effect by using "auto" leading for the paragraph.

The rules are a little different when an inline frame falls on the first line of text in a text frame. The position of the baseline of the

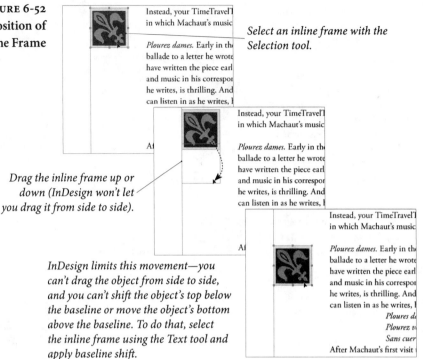

*Select an inline frame with the
Selection tool.*

*Drag the inline frame up or
down (InDesign won't let
you drag it from side to side).*

*InDesign limits this movement—you
can't drag the object from side to side,
and you can't shift the object's top below
the baseline or move the object's bottom
above the baseline. To do that, select
the inline frame using the Text tool and
apply baseline shift.*

first line of text is controlled by the First Baseline option in the Text Frame Options dialog box.

If the height of the inline frame is greater than the height of the characters in the line (and it usually is), choosing "Ascent" positions the top of the inline frame at the top of the text frame. This pushes the first line down to accommodate the height of the inline frame. If you adjust the vertical position of the inline frame, the position of the first line of text moves up or down. The same thing happens when you choose "Cap Height" (note that these two settings produce different results for text, but are the same for inline frames).

When you choose "Baseline," however, InDesign positions the baseline of the first line of text according to the largest leading value in the line. If you're using a fixed leading value, and you've set the leading of the inline frame to the leading of the surrounding text, the position of the baseline of the first line of text won't change, regardless of what you do with the inline frame.

We always use the "Baseline" option for my first baseline position, and we always set the leading of a graphic that shares a line with text characters to the leading of those characters. This way, we always know where the first baseline of text will fall, and we don't have to worry that changes to the shape, size, or baseline position of the inline frame will mess up the leading.

The only time we use "auto" leading is when we're working with a paragraph that contains only an inline frame. The only trouble is that we want the vertical distance taken up by the paragraph to be exactly equal to the height of the inline frame—no more, no less. By default, InDesign's "auto" leading value is equal to 120% of the point size of the type (or, in this case, the height of the inline frame). How can we get the base "auto" leading percentage down to 100%?

The percentage used to calculate "Auto" leading, as it turns out, is a paragraph-level attribute. To view or adjust this percentage, choose Justification from the Paragraph palette's menu. InDesign displays the Justification dialog box. Enter 100 in the Auto Leading field and click OK to close the dialog box (see Figure 6-53). Once you've done this, the leading of the paragraph will equal the height of the inline frame. If you want, you can add this to a paragraph style definition.

**FIGURE 6-53**
**Inline Frames and "Auto" Leading**

*Height of inline graphic: 56 points (4 \* 14).*

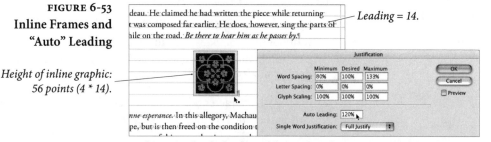

*In this example, the leading of the paragraph containing the inline frame is set to "Auto," and the Auto Leading value is set to 120 percent, which means that the lines following the graphic do not align to the 14-point baseline grid.*

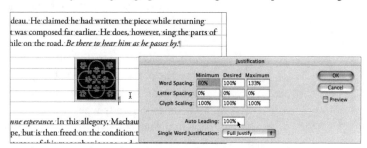

*Set the Auto Leading value to 100 percent, and InDesign makes the vertical space occupied by the inline frame equal to the height of the frame.*

**What Can't You Do with Inline Frames?**

In spite of their tremendous flexibility, there are a few things you can't do with inline frames.

◆ You can't link (or "thread") a text frame you've pasted inline to another text frame.

◆ You can't apply a text wrap to an inline frame.

◆ When you select an inline frame using one of the selection tools, the InDesign selects the center point of the Proxy in the Transform palette—you can't choose any other point.

◆ You can't adjust the horizontal position of a frame away from the frame's position in text. Instead, you have to move the graphic as if it were a text character.

**Creating Hanging Side Heads**

If there's one thing that inline frames make easier, it's hanging side heads. You know—the headings that appear to the left of a column of text (like the one to the left of this paragraph). In InDesign, you can create a hanging side head that follows a paragraph of text as it flows through a publication—no more dragging the headings to a new position when text reflows. You use a hanging indent and an inline frame, as shown in the following steps (see Figure 6-54).

1. Create a hanging indent. To do this, set a left indent that's the width of the "companion column" you want to the left of the paragraph, then set a negative first line indent equal to the width of the left indent. Place a tab stop at the left indent.

2. Enter a tab character before the first character of the paragraph. This pushes the text to the left indent.

3. Paste a text frame before the tab character you just entered. Adjust the position of the inline text frame, if necessary.

4. Enter the heading's text in the inline text frame.

5. Format the heading.

That's all there is to it—you now have a hanging side head that will follow the paragraph anywhere it goes.

This same technique can also be used to position graphics frames, and comes in handy when you need to "hang" an icon or a vertical rule to the left of a particular paragraph.

**Putting a Box Around Text**

How can you put a box around a paragraph that will follow the paragraph as it flows from column to column or page to page? As shown earlier in this chapter, you can use paragraph rules or a single-cell table (probably the best method), or you can use an inline rectangle, as shown below (see Figure 6-55).

1. Create a paragraph above the paragraph you want to put the box around.

**FIGURE 6-54**
**Creating a Hanging Side Head**

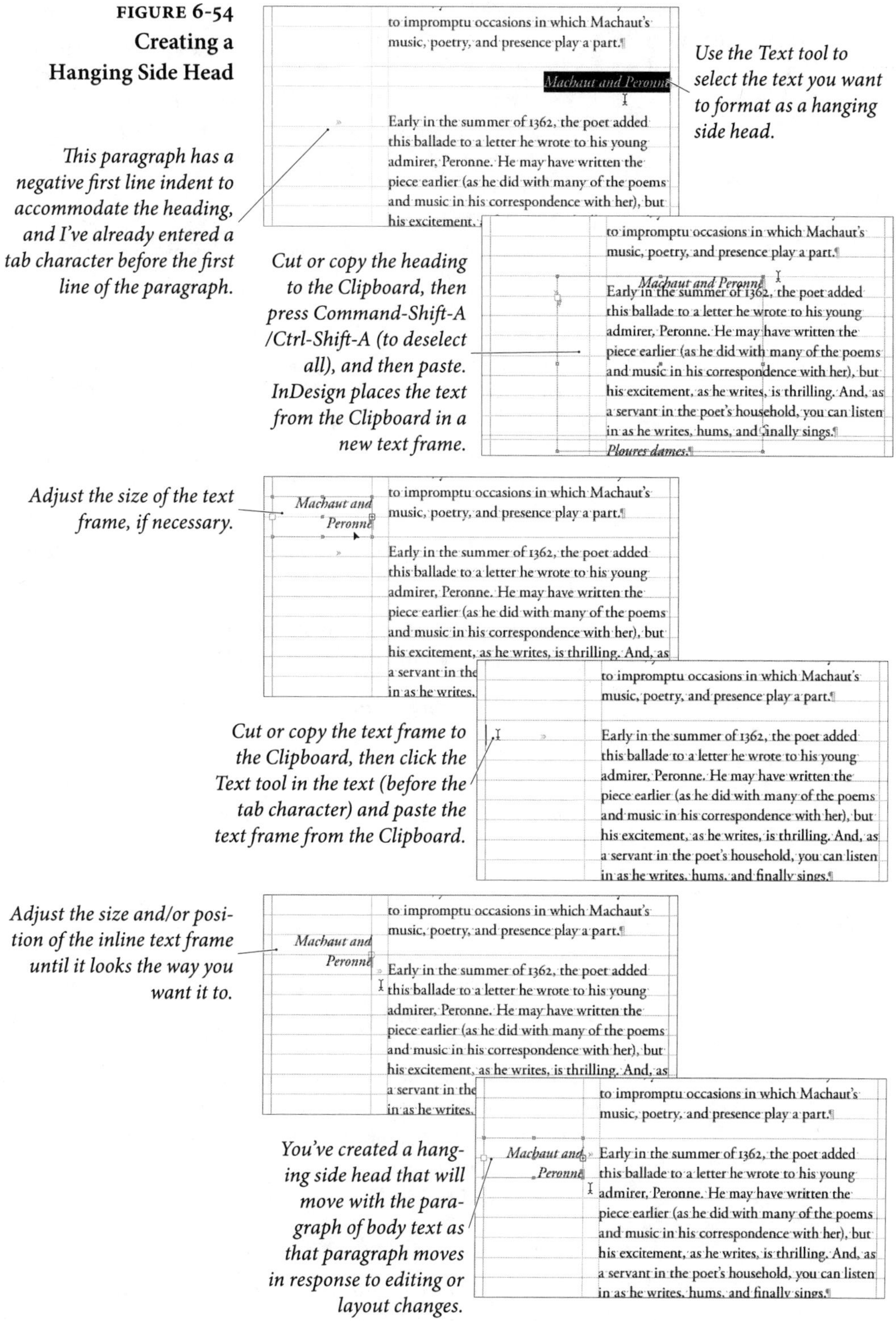
*Use the Text tool to select the text you want to format as a hanging side head.*
*This paragraph has a negative first line indent to accommodate the heading, and I've already entered a tab character before the first line of the paragraph.*
*Cut or copy the heading to the Clipboard, then press Command-Shift-A /Ctrl-Shift-A (to deselect all), and then paste. InDesign places the text from the Clipboard in a new text frame.*
*Adjust the size of the text frame, if necessary.*
*Cut or copy the text frame to the Clipboard, then click the Text tool in the text (before the tab character) and paste the text frame from the Clipboard.*
*Adjust the size and/or position of the inline text frame until it looks the way you want it to.*
*You've created a hanging side head that will move with the paragraph of body text as that paragraph moves in response to editing or layout changes.*
Machaut and Peronne
to impromptu occasions in which Machaut's music, poetry, and presence play a part.
Early in the summer of 1362, the poet added this ballade to a letter he wrote to his young admirer, Peronne. He may have written the piece earlier (as he did with many of the poems and music in his correspondence with her), but his excitement, as he writes, is thrilling. And, as a servant in the poet's household, you can listen in as he writes, hums, and finally sings.
Ploures dames.

FIGURE 6-55
Yet Another Way
to Put a Box Around
a Paragraph

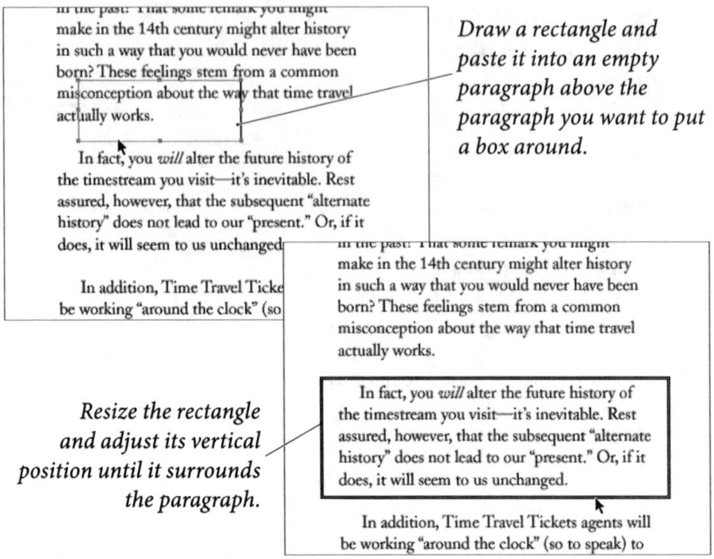

in the past? That some remark you might
make in the 14th century might alter history
in such a way that you would never have been
born? These feelings stem from a common
misconception about the way that time travel
actually works.

In fact, you *will* alter the future history of
the timestream you visit—it's inevitable. Rest
assured, however, that the subsequent "alternate
history" does not lead to our "present." Or, if it
does, it will seem to us unchanged

In addition, Time Travel Ticke
be working "around the clock" (so

*Draw a rectangle and
paste it into an empty
paragraph above the
paragraph you want to put
a box around.*

in the past? That some remark you might
make in the 14th century might alter history
in such a way that you would never have been
born? These feelings stem from a common
misconception about the way that time travel
actually works.

In fact, you *will* alter the future history of
the timestream you visit—it's inevitable. Rest
assured, however, that the subsequent "alternate
history" does not lead to our "present." Or, if it
does, it will seem to us unchanged.

In addition, Time Travel Tickets agents will
be working "around the clock" (so to speak) to

*Resize the rectangle
and adjust its vertical
position until it surrounds
the paragraph.*

2. Draw a rectangle, then paste the rectangle into the empty paragraph you just created.

3. Set the leading of the paragraph and the inline frame to some fixed value (anything other than "auto").

4. Adjust the size and baseline position of the inline frame so that it falls around the following paragraph.

5. Use the Keep With Next option to "stick" the paragraph containing the inline frame to the following paragraph.

## Placing Text on a Path

InDesign can place text *on* a path, as well as placing text *inside* a path (which is what a text frame is, after all). Once you've joined text to a path, you can select the text just as you would select any other text—select the Text tool and drag it through the characters you want to select, or click the Text tool in the text and use keyboard shortcuts. To select the path, click on the path using the Selection tool or the Direct Selection tool.

To attach text to a path, follow these steps (see Figure 6-56).

1. Select the Path Type tool.

2. Move the tool over a path. The cursor changes to indicate that InDesign is ready to place text on the path.

**FIGURE 6-56**
**Adding Text to a Path**

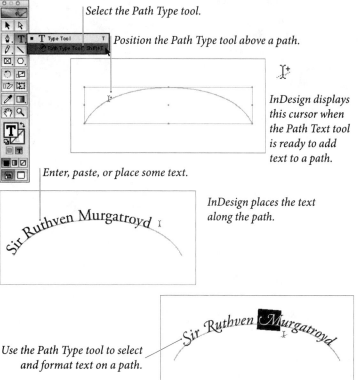

Select the Path Type tool.

Position the Path Type tool above a path.

InDesign displays
this cursor when
the Path Text tool
is ready to add
text to a path.

Enter, paste, or place some text.

InDesign places the text
along the path.

Use the Path Type tool to select
and format text on a path.

3.  Click the tool on the path. InDesign places the cursor on the path. The position of the cursor depends on the document's default paragraph alignment (if the default alignment is left, for example, the cursor will appear at the start of the path).

    Instead of clicking, you can drag the tool along the path to define the area of the path you want to fill with text.

    If InDesign cannot fit all of the text onto the path, the extra text is stored as overset text.

4.  Add text to the path just as you would add text to a text frame—by typing, pasting text from the Clipboard, or importing text from a text file. This creates a new kind of object—not a text frame, not a path, but a blending of the two I'll refer to as a "path text object" from here on out.

    Once you've attached text to a path, you can change its position on the path by dragging the Start Indicator or the End Indicator (see Figure 6-57), or change its orientation relative to the path using the Center/Flip Direction Indicator (see Figure 6-58).

FIGURE 6-57
**Changing the Position of Text on a Path**

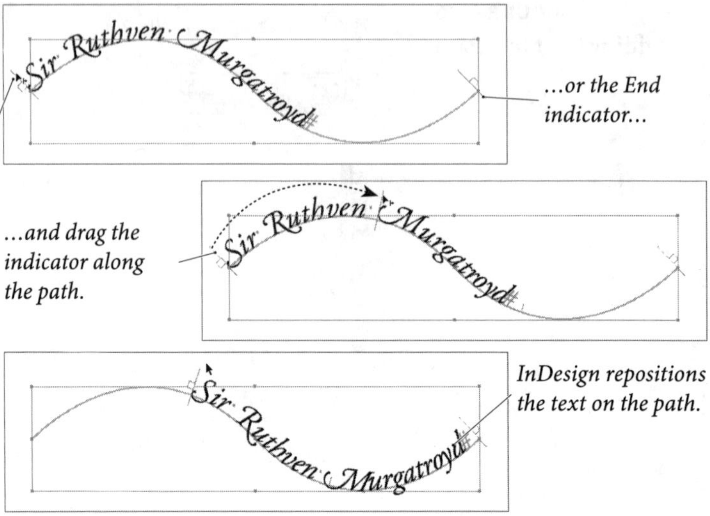

*Select the Selection tool and position the cursor above the Start indicator...*

*...or the End indicator...*

*...and drag the indicator along the path.*

*InDesign repositions the text on the path.*

FIGURE 6-58
**Flipping Text on a Path**

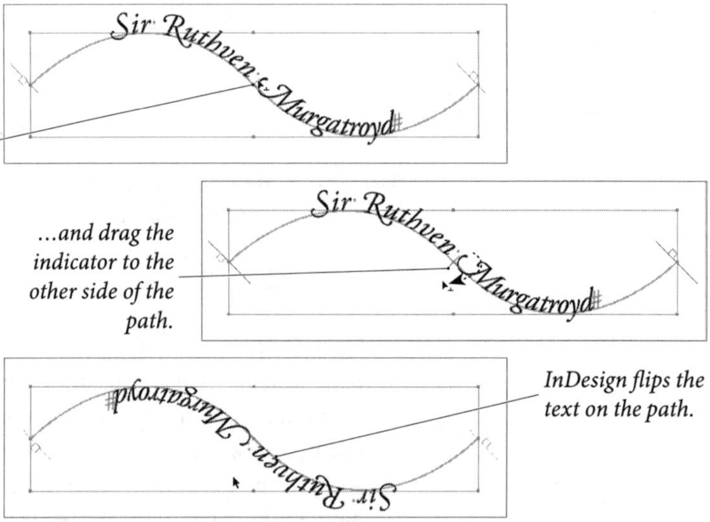

*Select the Selection tool and position the cursor above Flip indicator...*

*...and drag the indicator to the other side of the path.*

*InDesign flips the text on the path.*

Like text frames, path text objects feature an in port and an out port you can use to link the text to other text containers (text frames or other text path objects). You can even link text from a path text object to the interior of the path text object.

Note: InDesign does not apply paragraph rules to text in path text objects.

**Path Text Options**    You can control both the baseline position of text on a path and the relationship of the text to the shape of the path. To do this, select a path text object (or some of the text on a path) and then choose Options from the Path Type submenu of the Object menu. InDesign displays the Path Type Options dialog box (see Figure 6-59).

**FIGURE 6-59**
**Path Type Options**

*To set options for a path text object, select the object using the Selection tool...*

*...then display the Context menu and choose Options from the Type on a Path submenu.*

*InDesign displays the Path Type Options dialog box.*

*Drag the dialog box out of the way (if necessary) and turn on the Preview option so that you can see the effect of the changes you make in the dialog box.*

**Effect.** Do the character shapes distort in some way, or do they remain unchanged? That's the question you're answering when you make a choice from the Effect pop-up menu. What, exactly, do these oddly-named options do?

◆ Rainbow rotates the center point of each baseline to match the angle of the path at the location of the character.

◆ Skew skews the horizontal axis of the character to match the angle of the path at the location of the character, but leaves the vertical axis of the character unchanged.

◆ 3D Ribbon skews the vertical axis of each character to match the angle of the path at the location of the character, but leaves the character's horizontal axis unchanged.

◆ Stair Step aligns the center point of each character's baseline to match the angle of the path at the location of the character, but does not rotate the character.

◆ Gravity rotates the center of the baseline of each character to match the angle of the path at the character, skews the horizontal axis of the character to match that angle, and skews the vertical axis of each character around the geometric center point of the path.

These options are a bit difficult to describe with words, so take a look at Figure 6-60.

**FIGURE 6-60**
**Effect Option**

Rainbow rotates the characters around the path.

Skew skews the horizontal axis of
each character to match the angle of the
path, but leaves the vertical axis of the
character unchanged.

3D Ribbon skews the vertical
axis of each character to
match the angle of the path,
but leaves the character's
horizontal axis unchanged.

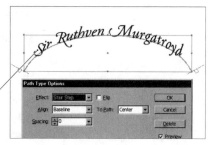

Stair Step moves the characters along the
path, but does not skew or rotate the
characters to match the path.

Gravity is like a combination
of Rainbow and Skew—it
rotates the characters around
the path and skews the horizontal axis of each character.

**Flip.** You've probably noticed that path text follows the direction of the path—the first character of the text typically appears at (or, if you've dragged the Path Text tool, nearest) the first point in the path. Given this, you'd think that you could select the path and choose Reverse Path from the Options menu to make the text read from the opposite end of the path. But you can't (not without first removing the text from the path, anyway). To do what you're trying to do, turn on the Flip option (see Figure 6-61).

FIGURE 6-61
**Another Way to Flip Text on a Path**

*Display the Path Type Options dialog box.*

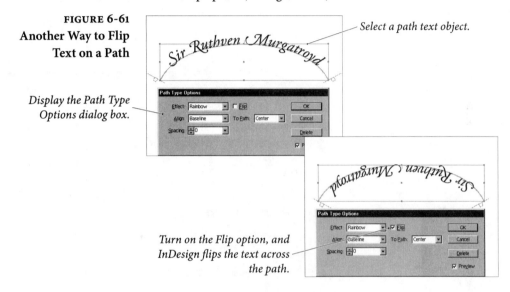

*Select a path text object.*

*Turn on the Flip option, and InDesign flips the text across the path.*

**Align.** These options control the way the text aligns to the path itself. Choose Ascender to align the top of the capital letters in the text (more or less) to the path, or choose Descender to position the bottoms of the characters on the path. Choose Center to align the text to the path at a point that's half of the height of the capital characters in the font, or choose Baseline to align the baseline of the characters to the path (see Figure 6-62).

**To Path.** The options on the To Path pop-up menu control the way that the text aligns to the *stroke* of the path. Choose Top to place the alignment point (whatever it was you chose from the Align pop-up menu) of the text at the top of the stroke; or Bottom to place the it at the bottom of the stroke; or Center to align the alignment point of the text with the center of the path (see Figure 6-63). For more precise control of the text position, use baseline shift.

**Spacing.** The Spacing field (and attached pop-up menu) control the spacing of text around curves in the path. Enter a value (in points) in

**FIGURE 6-62**
**Align Options**

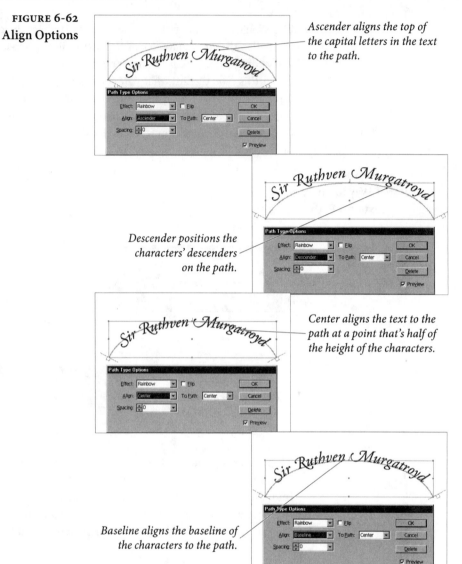

Ascender aligns the top of
the capital letters in the text
to the path.

Descender positions the
characters' descenders
on the path.

Center aligns the text to the
path at a point that's half of
the height of the characters.

Baseline aligns the baseline of
the characters to the path.

this field to tighten or loosen character spacing around curves (see Figure 6-64). Note that this setting has no effect on the kerning or tracking of text on straight line segments.

**Removing Type From a Path**    To remove the text from a path type object and convert the object back into a "normal" path, you need to do more than simply delete the text characters. If you do this, the object remains a path type object. Instead, select the path (or some of the text on the path) and choose Delete from the Path Type submenu (of the Object menu or the context menu). See Figure 6-65.

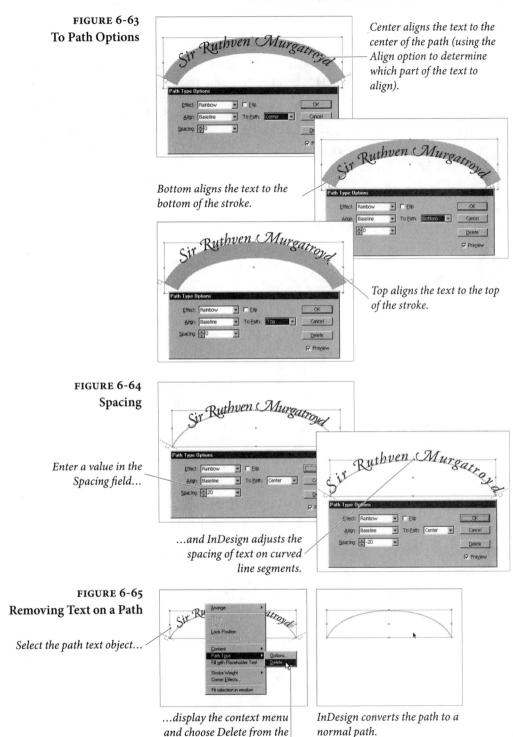

**FIGURE 6-63**
**To Path Options**

*Center aligns the text to the center of the path (using the Align option to determine which part of the text to align).*

*Bottom aligns the text to the bottom of the stroke.*

*Top aligns the text to the top of the stroke.*

**FIGURE 6-64**
**Spacing**

*Enter a value in the Spacing field...*

*...and InDesign adjusts the spacing of text on curved line segments.*

**FIGURE 6-65**
**Removing Text on a Path**

*Select the path text object...*

*...display the context menu and choose Delete from the Path Type submenu.*

*InDesign converts the path to a normal path.*

# Alternate Reality

What wonders—or horrors—exist in this weird place, where the boundary between text and graphics breaks down? Where magic works, and previously immutable laws of physics no longer apply? We have been there, reader, and, as it turns out, we have discovered new and useful techniques that can be put to immediate use in the "normal" world.

# Importing and Exporting

Someday, you'll need to do something that's beyond the drawing and typesetting capabilities of InDesign. You'll need to edit large amounts of text, adjust TIFF images, render 3-D objects, or create Web pages. Other applications do these things better than InDesign does. But you can add the files you create in other applications to your InDesign publication. And you can export InDesign pages for use in other page-layout and drawing programs.

That's what this chapter is all about: importing files from disk, and exporting your document (or pieces of it) to disk. For the most part, our discussion of importing focuses on graphics because we cover importing text in Chapter 3, "Text." However, you'll also find an exploration of InDesign's XML features at the end of this chapter (both importing and exporting XML).

# Importing

InDesign offers three ways to bring files from other applications into your publications. Here are your options:

◆ **Place the file.** The Place feature (in the File menu) is the most common method for getting files onto your pages. When you place a file, InDesign creates a link to the file on disk. In the case of graphics, InDesign stores only a low-resolution, "proxy" (or "preview") image in the publication. When you print, InDesign uses the high-resolution version of the graphic from the file on your disk. By default, placed text files are linked (this is very different than QuarkXPress), but they're also embedded, so you don't need the original file on disk to print properly. We discuss managing these links later in this chapter.

◆ **Copy and paste.** The most obvious, simplest, and least reliable method of getting information from another application is to copy it out of the application and paste it into InDesign. While this technique works well for small amounts of text, it can spell disaster for graphics and images created in other programs. We don't mean to imply that you should *never* use copy and paste, just that you should approach it with caution.

   Another thing about copy and paste is that InDesign is very picky about what it'll let you paste into a publication. Overly picky, in our opinion. You can't, for example, copy an image out of Photoshop and paste it into InDesign. Even though this is the wrong thing to do, and is likely to result in printing problems, we still believe that InDesign should let you to do it (you might have a perfectly good reason for doing so).

   A good reason to use copy and paste however, appears when you're working with Illustrator or FreeHand: When you copy paths out of these programs and paste them into InDesign, you get editable InDesign paths.

◆ **Drag and drop.** As we mentioned in Chapter 2, "Page Layout," you can drag objects out of one InDesign publication and drop them into another. You can drag files from your desktop (the Macintosh Finder or the Windows Explorer) and drop them into your InDesign publication window. This is essentially the same as importing the files using the Place command (except that you won't be able to set import options for the files, as you can if you place them). Even better, dragging from the desktop is a great way to import more than one file at a time (you can even drag a whole folder full of images if you want). You can also drag objects from some other programs (Illustrator comes to mind) and drop them into InDesign. This, in general, is the same as copying and pasting, and comes with the same cautions.

Note that you can also open QuarkXPress and PageMaker files—that's covered in Chapter 2, "Page Layout."

## Placing Anything

To get a graphic file into an InDesign publication, follow these steps (see Figure 7-1 and Figure 7-2).

1. Before you leap to the Place command on the File menu, take a second to think about where you want the graphic to appear.

   ◆ Do you want the graphic to fill an existing frame? If so, select the frame.

   ◆ Do you want the graphic to appear as an inline frame in a text frame? If so, select the Text tool and click it inside the text frame.

   ◆ Do you want to place the graphic in a new frame? If so, press Command-Shift-A/Ctrl-Shift-A to deselect everything before placing the graphic.

2. Press Command-D/Ctrl-D (or choose Place from the File menu). The Place dialog box appears.

3. Locate and select a file. You can control certain import options for some file formats. To view the available import options, turn on the Show Import Options checkbox.

4. If you have a frame selected, and want to place the file inside the frame, make sure you turn on the Replace Selected Item checkbox. If you don't want to replace the selection (perhaps you forgot to deselect all before selecting Place), turn this option off. When importing graphics, you can ignore the Retain Format and Convert Quotes checkboxes; those are only applicable to text files (we wish InDesign would just gray them out when you choose a graphic).

5. Click the Open button (or press Enter). If you turned on the Show Import Options checkbox, InDesign displays the Import Options dialog box, which looks slightly different depending

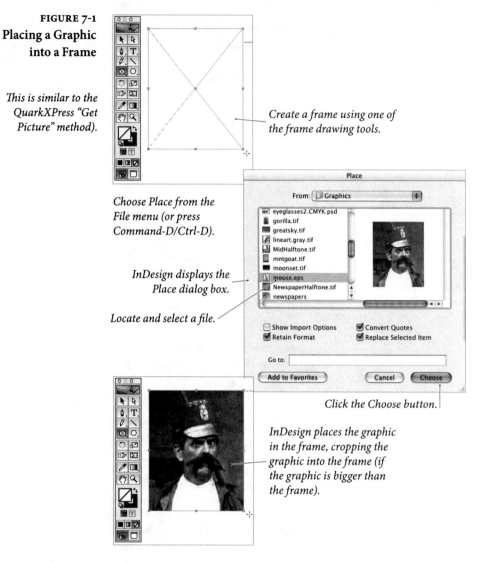

**FIGURE 7-1**

**Placing a Graphic into a Frame**

*This is similar to the QuarkXPress "Get Picture" method).*

*Create a frame using one of the frame drawing tools.*

*Choose Place from the File menu (or press Command-D/Ctrl-D).*

*InDesign displays the Place dialog box.*

*Locate and select a file.*

*Click the Choose button.*

*InDesign places the graphic in the frame, cropping the graphic into the frame (if the graphic is bigger than the frame).*

on the file type you've selected. In many cases, the options are grayed out because they aren't relevant (for example, the clipping path option is grayed out when there is no clipping path embedded in the file). Make any changes you want (or can) in this dialog box and then click the OK button (we discuss the import options for each file type in "Working with Images," later in this chapter).

What happens after you click OK depends on the choice you made in Step 1. If you had a frame selected, and turned on the Replace Selected Item option, the graphic appears inside that frame.

FIGURE 7-2
**Placing a Graphic
Without First
Making a Frame**

*Choose Place from the File
menu (or press Command-
D/Ctrl-D). InDesign displays
the Place dialog box. Locate
and select a file, then click
the Open or Choose button.*

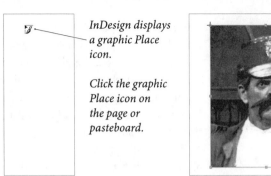

*InDesign displays
a graphic Place
icon.*

*Click the graphic
Place icon on
the page or
pasteboard.*

*InDesign places the graphic on the page, creating
a frame that is exactly the size of the graphic.*

*When you position the Place
icon near a ruler guide or
grid line, InDesign changes
the appearance of the place
icon to show that clicking or
dragging the icon will "snap"
the incoming graphic to the
guide or grid.*

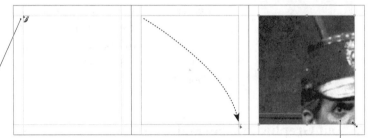

*If you drag the Place icon as you place a graphic...
...InDesign places the graphic inside a frame that's the width and
height you define by dragging. This does not scale the graphic itself.*

*When you position the
Place icon over an existing
frame, InDesign changes
the appearance of the icon
to indicate that clicking the
icon will place the file inside
the frame.*

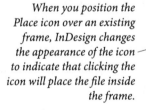

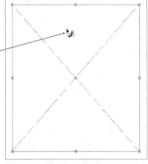

*You can also click the place
icon on an existing frame...*

*...to place the graphic
inside the frame.*

If you had an active text insertion point in a text frame, and if you
turned on the Replace Selected Item option, InDesign places the
graphic into the text frame (at the current location of the cursor) as
an inline graphic.

**The Place Icon**
On the other hand, if you deselected everything before placing, or if
you turned off the Replace Selected Item option, InDesign displays
the Place icon (some folks call this the "place gun"). Click the place

icon on a page or on the pasteboard, and InDesign imports the file you selected and positions the upper-left corner of the file at the point at which you clicked the place icon. InDesign places the graphic on the page or pasteboard at its original size.

Instead of clicking, you can *drag* the place icon. This produces a frame that's the width and height you define by dragging. Note that this does not scale the graphic itself.

To place the graphic inside an existing, empty frame, click the place icon in the frame. This frame doesn't have to be a graphic frame, and it doesn't have to be selected.

If you accidentally placed the graphic inside a frame, don't panic. Remember that Command-Z/Ctrl-Z will "undo" the action and display the place icon again, ready to place the graphic somewhere else. At this point, you can cancel the Place operation by pressing Command-Z/Ctrl-Z again, or by clicking the place icon on any tool in the Tools palette.

## About Graphic File Formats

InDesign can import a range of graphic file formats, including Adobe Illustrator and Adobe Photoshop formats, TIFF images, JPEG images, GIF images, EPS files, and PICT or WMF-type graphics. From InDesign's point of view, there are certain limitations and advantages to each of these file formats.

Just to refresh everyone's memory, here are a few quick definitions, rules, and exceptions regarding graphic file formats. There are three fundamental graphics file format types:

◆ Bitmap files store pictures as matrices (rows and columns) of squares known as pixels, with each pixel having a particular gray or color value (also known as a gray depth, color depth, or bit depth). Bitmap files are typically created by image editing programs such as Adobe Photoshop, or by the software you use to run your scanner. TIFF, JPEG, BMP, and GIF are all bitmap graphic file formats. Bitmaps are also called "raster data."

◆ Vector files contain sets of instructions for drawing graphic objects—typically geometric shapes, such as lines, ellipses, polygons, rectangles, and arcs. The drawing instructions say, "Start this line at this point and draw to that point"; or, "This is a polygon made up of these line segments." PostScript paths, such those as you'd find in an EPS, are another example of a vector format, but they're usually contained in a metafile (see below).

◆ Metafiles can contain both vector and bitmap graphics. Macintosh PICT, Adobe Illustrator, EPS, and WMF (Windows metafile) formats are all examples of metafiles. (Adobe Photoshop files can also contain a combination of vector and raster graphics, but InDesign rasterizes any visible Photoshop vector data, and uses invisible Photoshop paths only for clipping paths and text wrap.) Metafiles don't have to contain *both* vector and bitmap objects. Sometimes you'll find metafiles that contain only an image, or metafiles that contain only vector artwork.

There are a lot of different ways to talk about the files saved in these three format types. We usually refer to bitmap files as "images" and vector files as "drawings."

Note that these formats are all "interchange" formats—they're for moving information from one application to another. All programs support their own "native" file format, but many can read or write files in other formats. Some programs can open or import files saved in the native formats of other programs. InDesign can also place native Illustrator and Photoshop files—which might mean that you don't have to use an interchange format at all.

Some programs are real "Swiss Army knives," and can open and save files in lots of different formats. Photoshop, for example, can open and save files in a dozen different bitmap formats. Photoshop is a great program to have around even if you use it for nothing more than file conversions.

**A Philosophical Note**     Whether you're an explaining parent or a computer book author, there's always a temptation to simply say, "Because we say so." We feel that you deserve better. At the same time, a basic explanation of the problems inherent in, say, the Macintosh PICT vector format would consume all of the pages of this chapter. And then there's WMF, PICT's Windows counterpart, to think about. There's just not room to talk about the advantages and disadvantages of each graphic file format, so we'll try to be brief.

The biggest problem is that many graphics file formats, in spite of their being designed as "interchange" formats, make too many assumptions about the system they'll be viewed on or printed from. Most metafile and vector formats—except EPS and PDF—assume that the font list of the system they're created on will remain the same, and refer to fonts by their *number* (as they appear in the list of fonts at the time the file was created) rather than by their *name*. This can cause problems when you move to another system, or even when you install a new font. For this reason among others, we eschew WMF and PICT in favor of EPS and PDF.

It all comes down to using the formats for what they were intended for. BMP files were intended to be viewed onscreen, in Windows—not printed. PICT and WMF files were intended for printing on (different types of) non-PostScript printers. EPS and TIFF were designed to work well on high-resolution PostScript printers; GIF and JPEG were designed to carry a great deal of image information in the smallest possible package—which makes them ideal for online publishing. In addition, PDF, EPS, TIFF, JPEG, and GIF were designed for interchange between different computing environments and platforms—something you can't say of the others.

WMF is a file format for saving commands written in the Windows Graphic Device Interface (or GDI)—the language Windows uses to draw objects onscreen (or print to non-PostScript printers). PICT is based on QuickDraw, the native drawing language of the Macintosh. When you send files in these formats to a PostScript printer, they have to be translated into PostScript commands. This process isn't perfect, which means that what you see on your screen may not be what you get from your printer.

**EPS and PDF Files**    How did PDF and EPS get to be the industry-standard graphic file formats for vector graphics and type? It's because they're both based on the PostScript language—which, as you'll recall, is the language of high-resolution imagesetters. When you have to convert drawing instructions from another vector format—WMF, for example—into PostScript, you're asking for trouble. And trouble is expensive when you're printing on film at 3600 dots per inch.

Graphics saved in the PDF or EPS formats are *resolution independent,* and so paths print as smoothly as possible on whatever printer you happen to be printing to. Both formats can include color definitions (including spot colors), and store the positions of graphics and type with a very high degree of precision. All of the above make these formats ideal for prepress use.

There are two important differences between the two formats. First, PDF files can easily be viewed by the free Acrobat Reader and edited using tools such as Enfocus Software's Pitstop Professional utility. Second, EPS graphics can contain "active" PostScript code—routines that generate paths when the graphic reaches a PostScript interpreter.

For instance, a graduated fill from FreeHand or a gradient from Illustrator, is really a piece of PostScript code that tells a PostScript interpreter to fill a path with a series of paths filled with varying colors. This means that the PostScript interpreter has to work a bit—calculating the positions of the points on the generated paths, setting their color, and so on. By contrast, a gradient in a PDF is literally a series of paths—all the PostScript interpreter has to do is draw them into the image of the page it's creating in the printer's memory.

## Creating Your Own EPS Graphics

InDesign can interpret almost any PostScript file you throw at it, as long as its in the form of an EPS (Encapsulated PostScript) file. For instance, you could take a PostScript output file from a Unix machine and place it in your InDesign document. Because InDesign can interpret the PostScript, it can give you an accurate preview of what the page will look like when you print.

Similarly, some folks write their own PostScript code. We happen to be two of them, and if you think PostScript programming is fun, that makes three of us. You can create EPS graphics using a word processor or text editor, but you've got to remember two things.

◆ Try printing the file before you import it. If it doesn't print when you download it to your printer, it won't print after you've imported it into InDesign. Always test every change you make in your word processor by downloading the text file to the printer and seeing what you get before you bring the file into an InDesign publication, or at least before you take the file to a service bureau.

◆ InDesign can create a preview for any EPS graphic.

Why would you want to create your own EPS graphics? There are lots of things you can do with PostScript that InDesign doesn't do (yet). And it's fun.

Because an EPS file is a text-only file, InDesign (and other programs) need some way to distinguish it from other text-only files. They get their clues from the first few lines of the EPS (also known as the file "header"). These lines should look something like this:

```
%!PS-Adobe-2.0 EPSF-1.2
%%BoundingBox x1 y1 x2 y2
```

The values following the "BoundingBox" comment are the measurements of the EPS graphic in the following order: left, bottom, right, and top. Points are the measurement system used in an EPS graphic (unless you make other arrangements), so the bounding box of an example US letter-sized EPS graphic would be:

```
%%BoundingBox 0 0 617 792
```

Figure 7-3 shows an example of a hand-coded EPS graphic, and what it looks like when you place it in InDesign.

**Operators to Avoid.** The PostScript code you use inside an EPS should not include any of the following PostScript operators.

| | | | |
|---|---|---|---|
| banddevice | copypage | erasepage | exitserver |
| framedevice | grestoreall | initclip | initgraphics |
| initmatrix | legal | letter | note |
| nulldevice | quit | renderbands | setpageparams |
| setsccbbatch | stop | | |

## Graphic Display Properties

Once you import a graphic into InDesign, the quality of its on-screen appearance depends almost entirely on the Display Performance setting in the View menu. You can choose among three settings: Optimized Display, Typical Display, and High Quality Display. By default, these reflect low, medium, and high quality displays. However, if you hate these terms you can change each setting's meaning so that Optimized is higher quality than Typical, or whatever (see "Display Performance Preferences," in Chapter 1, "Workspace").

The basic, default settings follow these basic rules:

◆ When you choose Optimized Display, InDesign grays out both vector and bitmapped images and turns off all transparency effects. The display of these gray boxes is very fast, but somewhat lacking in detail.

◆ When you choose Typical Display, InDesign uses a proxy image—either one embedded in the image or one InDesign generated when you placed the file. (InDesign always creates a proxy preview when it imports TIFF and JPEG; it's an import option for EPS files.) InDesign uses this proxy to display the graphic at all magnification levels—which means that images are going to get pretty ugly as you zoom in on them. The advantage? The screen display of proxy images is much faster than generating new previews for every magnification change. In this setting, transparency effects are visible, but only at a reasonable quality

**FIGURE 7-3**

**Writing Your Own EPS Graphics**

*In case you ever need such a thing, this PostScript code will fill any shape with a wave pattern*

```
%!PS-Adobe 2.0 EPSF-1.2
%%BoundingBox: 0 0 200 200
%%Creator: D.Blatner
%%EndComments
%-- This Is The Main Waves Subroutine --
/waves {        %on stack: length of wave, width (height),
                %space between lines, linewidth
        setlinewidth
        /vert exch def  /height exch def  /width exch def
        /Y1 height 1.8 mul def  /Y2 Y1 neg def  /Y3 0 def
        gsave getpathbox grestore
        clip newpath
        llx lly height 4 div sub
        translate 0 0 moveto
        ury lly sub vert div 4 add cvi{   %repeat # of lines
                urx llx sub width div 2 add cvi{  %repeat # of curves
                /X0 oldX3 def
                /X3 width X0 add def
                /X1 width 2 div X0 add def
                /X2 X1 def
                /oldX3 X3 def
                X1 Y1 X2 Y2 X3 Y3 curveto
                }bind repeat
        stroke
        0 vert translate 0 0 moveto /oldX3 0 def
        }bind repeat
}bind def

%-- This Are Some Support Routines --
/oldX3 0 def
/getpathbox {{flattenpath} exec pathbbox /ury exch def /urx exch def
/lly exch def /llx exch def /middlex urx llx add 2 div def /middley
ury lly add 2 div def /pathradius urx middlex sub dup mul ury mid-
dley sub dup mul add sqrt def}bind def
```

*This is the code which actually draws the box*

```
%-- Draw The Box --
0 0 moveto 0 200 lineto 200 200 lineto closepath

%-- Then Call The Fill Routine --
24   % length of the wave pattern
6    % height of the wave pattern
4    % distance between lines
.5   % thickness of lines
waves
```

*Here's what the above PostScript code looks like when you place it in InDesign or print it.*

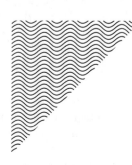

(drop shadows and feathering are displayed at low resolution, for instance).

◆ When you choose High Quality display, InDesign gets image data from the original file on your hard drive to render the best possible preview for the current screen magnification. For an EPS, it means that InDesign reinterprets the file to create a new preview (this is where those beautiful EPS previews come from). As you'd expect, either process takes more time than simply slamming a fixed resolution preview onto the screen (which is what the Proxy option does). The anti-aliasing of vector images (so they look smooth on screen) and high-quality transparency effects is also calculation-intensive.

Remember, all of these settings affect only the way that graphics appear on screen, not in print.

**Local Display Overrides**

You can also vary the display quality for individual graphics. This can come in handy when you need to see more detail in one graphic than in others, or when you want to speed up the redraw of a specific slow-drawing graphic. To control the display properties of a graphic, select the graphic, and then display the context menu (hold down Control before you press the mouse button on the Macintosh; press the right mouse button in Windows). Choose one of the display options from the Display Performance submenu (see Figure 7-4). You can also choose from the Display Performance submenu in the Object menu if you have a bizarre aversion to context menus.

## Image Import Options

When you place an image, you can turn on the Import Options checkbox and use the subsequent Image Import Options dialog box to specify a number of important things about the image (see Figure 7-5). The settings in this dialog box change depending on the file format of the graphic. Note that if you later drag and drop a graphic from the desktop into InDesign, the program remembers the import options from the last file you placed.

**Bitmapped Images**

If you are importing a bitmapped image, such as a TIFF, JPEG, GIF, or native Photoshop documents, you have two options in the Image Import Options dialog box: import clipping path, and enable color management.

FIGURE 7-4
Setting the Display
Resolution for a Graphic

| Cut |
| Copy |
| Paste |
| Paste Into |
| Paste in Place |
| Zoom ▶ |
| Transform ▶ |
| Lock Position |
| Stroke Weight ▶ |
| Fitting ▶ |
| Drop Shadow... |
| Feather... |
| Graphics ▶ |
| Tag Frame ▶ |
| Display Performance ▶ |

Optimized Display
Typical Display
High Quality Display
✓ Use View Setting

*Select a graphic, then choose a display resolution from the Context menu.*

*Choose Use View Setting to display the graphic using the display resolution you chose from the View menu.*

*Optimized Display*    *Typical Resolution*    *High Quality Display*

**Apply Photoshop Clipping Path.** If the image you're placing contains a clipping path, InDesign makes available the Apply Photoshop Clipping Path checkbox. When you turn this option on as you place the image, InDesign activates the clipping path. If you mess up, you can always turn it on or off later (see "Clipping Paths," later in this chapter).

If the image does not contain a clipping path, this option won't be available. You can always create a clipping path for the image in InDesign, or choose another path saved with the image as the clipping path (again, we cover this later in this chapter).

**Enable Color Management.** When you're importing a color bitmapped image, InDesign activates the Enable Color Management option in the Color Settings panel of the Image Import Options dialog box. Turn this option on to apply color management to the

FIGURE 7-5
**Import Options for
Bitmapped Images**

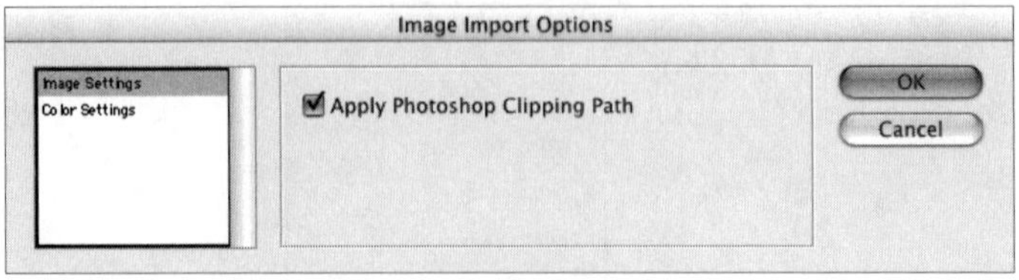

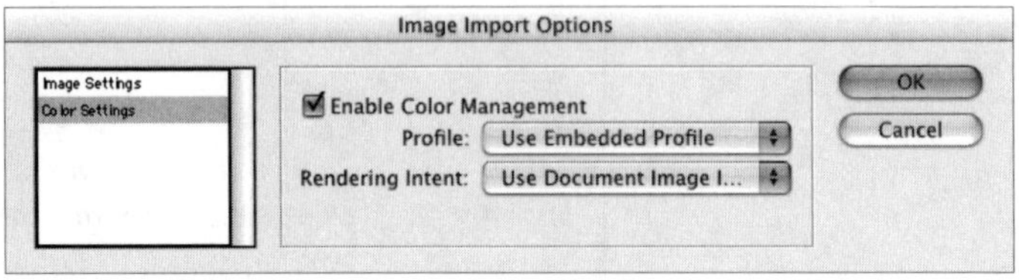

incoming image; turn it off if color consistency is not important (to you or to the graphic). Of course, even if you turn this checkbox on, InDesign won't color manage the image unless you enable color management in the Color Settings dialog box. Color management is a very complicated topic, and the following control descriptions do not attempt to discuss the finer points of each topic. For more on color management, see Chapter 10, "Color."

◆ **Profile.** If the image file you've selected contains a color management profile, InDesign selects Use Embedded Profile from the Profile pop-up menu. If you know that the embedded profile is not the one you want, choose another profile from the pop-up menu (this would be very rare).

◆ **Rendering Intent.** Choose the gamut scaling method you want to use to render the colors in the image. For most photographic images, you'll probably want to choose Perceptual (Images).

**EPS Files**    When you import an EPS graphic with Import Options turned on in the Place dialog box, InDesign displays the EPS Import Options dialog box (see Figure 7-6).

FIGURE 7-6
**Import Options
for EPS Files**

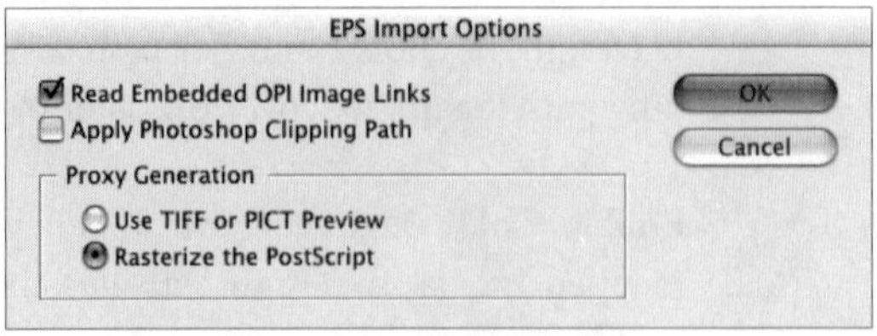

**Read Embedded OPI Image Links.** Open Prepress Interface (OPI) is a standard for maintaining image links between desktop page layout and illustration software using dedicated color prepress systems, such as those manufactured by Kodak and Creo. When you work with an OPI system, you typically work with low-resolution proxy images as you lay out a page, and then link to higher-resolution images saved on the prepress system when you print (or otherwise hand the job off to the prepress system). OPI concerns imported images only, and has nothing to do with vector graphics or type.

Turn this option off if the prepress system will take care of replacing any OPI images in the EPS; turn it on if you want InDesign to replace the images as you print. (In this case, InDesign itself is sort of acting like an OPI server.) InDesign will store the OPI image information regardless of the setting of this option.

**Apply Photoshop Clipping Path.** Turn on this option when you want to place the contents of the graphic inside the clipping path defined in the EPS graphic. This only affects Photoshop EPS images.

**Proxy Generation.** EPS graphics usually contain an embedded, low-resolution preview image. However, because InDesign can interpret almost any PostScript file, you can ask it to create a new preview image for you by selecting Rasterize the PostScript in the EPS Import Options dialog box. If you want to use the file's built-in preview, select Use TIFF or PICT Preview. We think these should have been labeled, "Use Cruddy Preview" and "Make It Look Good." We almost always make it look good by selecting Rasterize the PostScript (even though it takes a little longer to import the file). On the other hand, if you need to import 250 EPS files and on-screen quality doesn't matter, then save yourself some time and use the embedded previews.

**PDF Files**     When you import a PDF graphic, and have turned on the Import Options checkbox in the Place dialog box, InDesign displays the Place PDF dialog box (see Figure 7-7).

**Page.** PDF files can contain multiple pages (unlike EPS, which is, by definition, a single-page-per-file format), so you need some way to select the page you want to place. Scroll through the pages until you find the one you want. When you place a PDF without displaying the Place PDF dialog box, InDesign places the first page in the PDF.

FIGURE 7-7
Place PDF Dialog Box

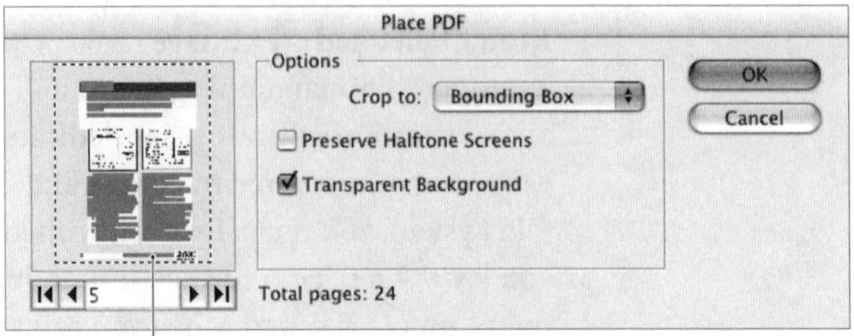

The Place PDF dialog box displays a preview of the pages of the PDF you've selected.

**Crop To.** Do you have to import the whole page? No—you can use this pop-up menu to define the area of the page you want to place. Choose one of the following options (depending on the PDF, some options may be unavailable).

◆ Choose Bounding Box to crop the incoming PDF graphic to an area defined by the objects on the PDF page.

◆ Choose Art to place the area defined by an art box in the PDF graphic (if no art box has been defined, this option will not be available). For a PDF exported from InDesign, the art box is the same as the Trim area (see below).

◆ Choose Crop to crop the area of the incoming PDF graphic to the crop area defined in Acrobat (using the Crop Pages dialog box). If the PDF has not had a crop area defined, this area will be the same as the Media setting (see below).

◆ Choose Trim to import the area defined by any trim marks in the PDF.

◆ Choose Bleed to import the area defined by any bleed marks in the PDF.

◆ Choose Media to import the area defined by the original paper size of the PDF.

**Preserve Halftone Screens.** When you turn this option on, InDesign uses the halftone screens defined in the PDF. Turn this option on to override the halftone screens defined in the PDF with the halftone screens you specify in the Colors panel of the Print dialog box.

**Transparent Background.** Turn this option on when you want to be able to see objects behind the imported PDF, or turn it off to apply an opaque white background to the PDF graphic. In general, we think you should leave this option turned on—if you want an opaque background, you can always apply a fill (of any color) to the frame containing the PDF graphic. If you turn this option off, on the other hand, the white background applied by InDesign cannot be changed by setting the fill of the frame.

**Placed PDFs and Color Management.** InDesign can't apply color management profiles to PDF graphics, but profiles embedded in the PDF will be used when you color separate the publication. If your PDFs require precise color matching, apply and embed the appropriate color profiles before saving the PDF for import into InDesign.

# Linking and Embedding

In InDesign, you can choose to embed (that is, store) imported graphics in your publication, or you can choose to store them externally and link to them.

When you link to a graphic InDesign, doesn't include the graphic file in your publication, but establishes a link between the publication and the imported file. InDesign creates a low-resolution screen preview of the graphic, and uses that preview to draw the image on your page. Linking means you don't have to store two copies of the original file—one on disk, and one in your InDesign publication—thereby saving disk space.

When you print, InDesign includes data from linked graphics in the stream of PostScript it's sending to your printer or to disk. This means that you need to take any externally stored graphics with you when you want to print your publication at an imagesetting service bureau.

Which method should you use? It's up to you. When you embed graphics, your publication size increases, but you don't have to keep track of the original files. When you link to externally stored graphics, your publications will take up less space on disk, but you'll have to keep track of more than one file. We generally recommend linking, partly because that is what the industry has come to expect (that's the way QuarkXPress works), and partly because we don't like our InDesign files becoming tens (or hundreds) of megabytes large.

If you import a bitmapped image smaller than 48K, InDesign embeds a copy of the graphic in your publication. This "automatic" embedding differs from "manual" embedding—you can maintain links to automatically embedded files, but not to manually embedded graphics.

**The Links Palette**  When you move a linked file, or change its name, you break the link between the file and any InDesign publication you've placed it in. You can also break the link when you move the publication file to another volume.

When you open a publication, InDesign looks in the folder containing the document for the linked file, and in a folder inside that folder named "Links." If InDesign can't find the linked file there, it displays an alert stating that the publication contains missing or modified linked graphics. Click the Fix Links button to locate and link to the file or files (see Figure 7-8).

The key to InDesign's linking and embedding features is the Links palette (see Figure 7-9). To display the Links palette, press Command-Shift-D/Ctrl-Shift-D, or choose Links from the Window menu. The Links palette displays the names of the linked files in the publication, and sometimes displays the following icons.

◆ If a graphic has been modified since its last update, you'll see a Caution icon (a yellow triangle with an exclamation mark).

◆ If a graphic is missing, you'll see the Missing link icon—it's a red circle with a question mark in it. This means that InDesign can't find the file—it's been moved or deleted (or maybe you've lost your connection to the server that holds the file).

◆ If you have embedded a graphic (see "Embedding a Graphic," later in this section),  a square with two shapes in it (another square and a triangle) appears.

You can change the order of the links in the Links palette—to do this, choose Sort by Status, Sort by Name, or Sort by Page from the Links palette menu.

**Getting Link Information**  Where the heck is that graphic file stored, anyway? Do we need it to print the publication? What color profile is attached to it, if any? The answers to these and other questions can be found in the Link Information dialog box. To display the Link Information dialog box, do one of the following.

◆ Select the graphic and choose Link Information from the Graphics submenu of the Context menu (to display the Context menu on the Macintosh, hold down Control and click; in Windows, press the right mouse button).

◆ Select the graphic's file name in the Links palette, then choose Link Information from the Links palette menu (or just double-click the file name in the palette).

FIGURE 7-8
**Fixing Missing Links
As You Open a File**

*When InDesign can't
find a linked file in a
publication as it opens
the publication, you'll
see the Fix Links dialog
box.*

> This publication contains missing or modified links.
> Click Fix Links to repair the links now, or click OK to
> repair them with the Links palette.
>
> 4 – Missing Links
> 1 – Modified Link
>
> [ Fix Links... ]  [ OK ]

*Click the Fix Links
button to display the
Relink dialog box.*

**Relink**

Location: `Grace:Documents:Graphics:moo:greatsky.tif`  [ Browse... ]

URL: [ Browse... ]

[ Skip ]  [ Cancel ]  [ OK ]

*Click the Browse button to display a standard file
dialog box, then locate and select the appropriate file.*

FIGURE 7-9
**Links Palette**

*Press Command-Shift-D
or Ctrl-Shift-D to display
the Links palette.*

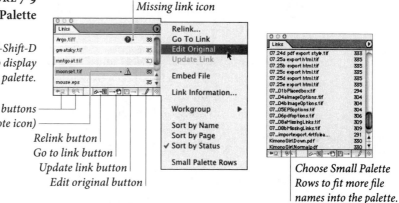

*Missing link icon*

Relink...
Go To Link
Edit Original
Update Link

Embed File

Link Information...

Workgroup ▶

Sort by Name
Sort by Page
✓ Sort by Status

Small Palette Rows

*WebDAV server buttons
Out-of-date link (note icon)*

*Relink button
Go to link button
Update link button
Edit original button*

*Choose Small Palette
Rows to fit more file
names into the palette.*

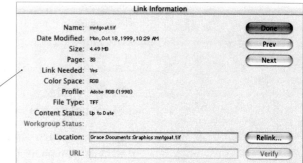

*Choose Link Information
(or double-click on a link)
to display the Link
Information dialog box.*

**Link Information**

Name: mntgoat.tif  [ Done ]
Date Modified: Mon, Oct 18, 1999, 10:29 AM  [ Prev ]
Size: 4.49 MB  [ Next ]
Page: 38
Link Needed: Yes
Color Space: RGB
Profile: Adobe RGB (1998)
File Type: TIFF
Content Status: Up to Date
Workgroup Status:
Location: `Grace:Documents:Graphics:mntgoat.tif`  [ Relink... ]
URL: [ Verify ]

The meaning of most of the items in the Link Information dialog
box is fairly straightforward—the Size field shows the amount of disk
space taken up by the graphic, for example—but a couple of the fields
deserve further explanation.

**Link Needed.** Is the linked file needed to print the publication? If the graphic has been embedded by InDesign, you won't need the original file to print the publication, so InDesign displays N/A. Very small bitmapped images (smaller than 48K) are automatically linked *and* embedded; because you don't need the original file in order to print the document properly, the Link Needed field says "No."

**Location.** Note that the Location field is the only editable field in the Link Information dialog box. While we say it's an "editable" field, we don't mean that you can change the path name in the field—you can't. But you can select the text and copy it out of the Links Information dialog box.

**URL.** The URL field at the bottom of the Link Information dialog box will be blank and grayed out unless the image has been placed from a WebDAV server using the Workgroup features (under the File menu).

**Next/Previous.** The Next and Previous buttons display link information on the next or previous file shown in the Links palette. Note that the order of the links shown in this list does not necessarily have anything to do with the location of the graphics—the "next" link could be separated from the current link by many pages (unless you've chosen Sort By Pages from the Links palette menu).

**Updating a Link**

InDesign checks the status of your graphics when you open a document or when you switch from another application back into InDesign. As soon as it notices a linked file is modified or missing, it displays an icon in the Links palette. To update the link of an imported graphic that has been modified since you last updated it or placed it, follow these steps (see Figure 7-10).

1. Display the Links palette, if it's not already visible.

2. Select the graphic you want to update, or select the corresponding link in the Links palette.

3. Choose Update Link from the Links palette menu (or click the Update Link button at the bottom of the Links palette). InDesign updates the link to the graphic file.

To update all of the modified links in a publication, deselect all of the file names in the Links dialog box (by clicking in the blank space at the bottom of the list, or clicking a linked file and then Command/Ctrl-clicking it). Then choose Update Link from the Links palette

**FIGURE 7-10**
**Updating a Link**

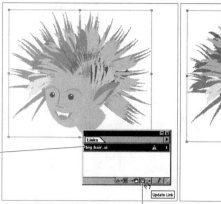

*When the link to a graphic is out of date, InDesign displays an icon next to the filename in the Links palette.*

*To update the link, select the filename and click the Update Link button.*

*InDesign updates the link to the graphic.*

menu (or click the palette's Update Link button). InDesign updates all of the links.

To replace missing links, use the Relink command, as shown below.

**Linking to Another File**

Modified files are easy to update; *missing* files are quite another matter. To link to another file, or relink to the original file in a new location, follow these steps (see Figure 7-11).

1. Display the Links palette, if it's not already visible.

2. Select the graphic you want to update, or select the corresponding link in the Links palette.

3. Click the Relink button (or choose Relink from the Links palette menu). InDesign displays the Relink dialog box.

4. Locate and select a file.

5. Click the OK button.

As we noted above, relinking to a new image retains the same transformations (scaling, rotating, and so on), which is often—but not always—what you'd want. Note that you should not use the Relink button to change the link to an image that was set up as an OPI link in an imported EPS file.

**Embedding a Graphic**

To store a graphic inside the publication, select the name of the graphic in the Links palette and choose Embed from the Links palette menu. When you embed a graphic, InDesign displays an embedded graphic icon next to the graphic's filename. Embedding a graphic has the following effects.

FIGURE 7-11
## Linking to Another File

*Select an imported graphic and then choose Relink from the Links palette menu (or click the Relink button at the bottom of the palette)...*

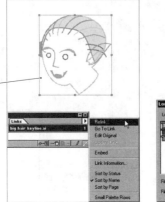

*...and select a file in the Locate file dialog box.*

*InDesign replaces the original graphic with the graphic you selected.*

*If the original graphic and the replacement graphic have different dimensions, use the Fitting options (on the Object menu, or the context menu) to fit the graphic to the frame...*

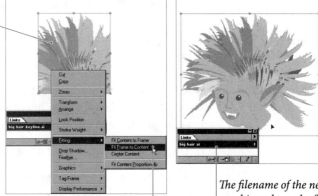

*...or, as in this example, to fit the frame to the graphic.*

*The filename of the new graphic replaces the filename of the original graphic in the Links palette.*

◆ It breaks the link to the external file, which means you won't be able to update the embedded graphic when you make changes to the original file (except by replacing the embedded graphic using the Relink command).

◆ The size of your publication file increases by the size of the graphic file. If you copy the embedded graphic and paste it elsewhere in your document, the publication grows again by the same amount. It's not true that an embedded graphic on a master page increases a publication's file size by the size of the embedded file for each use of that master page (we've seen other authors state this myth). However, file size does increase by the size of the graphic if you apply a manual override to the master page item (this is as you'd expect, as an override *copies* the master page item to the document page).

◆ You can't use the Edit Original command to open and edit the graphic file.

Ultimately, you shouldn't embed a graphic just because you want to take your publication to another system or to an imagesetting service bureau; instead, you should try using InDesign's Package and Preflight features (see Chapter 11, "Printing"). Embedding confuses service bureaus, who are used to working with QuarkXPress (which cannot embed graphics).

**Unembedding a Graphic**    Embedding a picture into PageMaker documents was almost always a dead-end street, but InDesign is smarter: You can unembed graphics, too, by selecting the graphic in the Links palette and choosing Unembed File from the palette menu. The program gives you a choice of linking to the original file on disk (if it's still there) or saving the embedded file to disk and linking to it.

**Navigating with the Links Palette**    One very nice feature of the Links palette is the Go to Link button. To display any file that appears in the Links palette, select the file and click the Go to Link button. InDesign selects and displays the graphic, centered in the publication window (jumping to another spread, if necessary, to do so).

# Working with Images

We don't think too much about the process of taking a photograph, scanning it, incorporating it into a page layout, printing color separations of the publication, and then printing it on a commercial offset printing press. But it's an amazing process.

First you record the visible light that's bouncing off of physical objects. To do this, you use a lens to project the light onto a piece of film that's coated with a chemical compound that changes on contact with light. After you expose the film to some other chemicals, an image appears. Next, you turn the photographic image into pixels using a scanner. Or you skip the film altogether and take the picture with a digital camera.

When you print from your page layout program, you turn the pixels into color halftone screens—overlapping patterns of dots, which, when printed using certain inks, produce something that resembles what you saw in the first place.

Given all of the above, is it any surprise that there's a lot to think about when it comes to images?

## Images and Halftoning

Most commercial printing equipment can only print one color per printing plate at one time. (There are some short-run printing processes based other processes, but they're still pretty rare.) We can get additional "tints" of that color by filling areas with small dots; at a distance (anything over a foot or so), these dots look like another color. The pattern of dots is called a halftone (for more on digital halftoning and commercial printing, see Chapter 10, "Color").

We use halftoning to print the different shades inside images, or the different colors in vector artwork. The eye, silly and arbitrary thing that it is, tells our brain that the printed photograph is made up of shades of gray (or color)—not different patterns of large and small dots.

## About Gray Levels

When we refer to "gray levels," we're not necessarily talking about the *color* gray—we're talking about halftone screen values less than 100 percent and greater than 0 percent that appear on a printing plate. You still need gray levels when you're printing color separations, because almost all of the colors you'll find in a typical printed color image are made up of overlapping tints of two or more inks.

## Halftone Screen Frequency and Resolution

Let us introduce you to the image resolution balancing act (in case you haven't already met). It's natural to assume that scanning at the highest resolution available from your scanner will provide the sharpest images. Unfortunately, it's just not true. When it comes to grayscale and color images, your image resolution should be no higher than twice the halftone screen frequency you intend to use. All higher scanning resolutions give you are larger file sizes, longer processing time on the computer, longer printing times, and bigger headaches.

In fact, you can almost always get away with resolutions only 1.5 times your screen frequency. For instance, at 133 lpi your images need not be any greater than 200 dpi; at 150 lpi you probably don't need more than 225 dpi images. The difference between a 300 dpi image and a 225 dpi image is more significant than you might think: A four-by-five-inch CMYK image is 6.9 Mb at 300 dpi and only 3.8 Mb at 225 dpi—about half the size. That means less time to transfer across the network (to a server or to a printer), less time to manipulate, less hassle to send it to an output provider, and so on.

Even if you don't care about transmitting or storing large files, remember that the image will always get downsampled somewhere along the line anyway, because PostScript printers always downsample to 2.5 times screen frequency, and your device won't do as good a job as Photoshop would.

We like to scan at the optical resolution of our scanner (usually 600 dpi or so), resize and downsample the image in Adobe Photoshop, and then sharpen it using Photoshop's Unsharp Masking filter (all scanned images need some sharpening). David wrote about this process in greater detail in his books *Real World Photoshop* (co-authored with Bruce Fraser) and *Real World Scanning and Halftones* (co-authored with Glenn Fleishman and Steve Roth).

**Line Art**  Line art images (which have only black and white pixels, saved in Photoshop's Bitmap mode) are different beasts than grayscale or color images. These monochrome (or bi-level) bitmapped images do not have halftone screens applied to them by the printer, and, therefore, require higher resolutions to avoid jaggy (pixelated) edges. If your final artwork is on a desktop laser printer, you don't need more than 600 dpi. Imagesetter output rarely requires more than 1200 dpi (though for a sheetfed art book, we might bump this up to 1500 dpi). Printing on uncoated stock requires less resolution because of halftone spots spreading; you can easily get away with 800 dpi for newsprint.

**Scaling in InDesign**  Ideally, you should import your bitmapped images at the same size as you intend to print them. Resolution changes when you change the size of the image in InDesign. For instance, doubling the size of a 300 dpi picture on your page cuts the effective resolution in half, to 150 dpi (because each pixel in the image has to be twice as wide and twice as tall as before, so fewer of them fit "per inch"). Conversely, making this graphic 25-percent smaller increases to 400 dpi. (If you really care why the resolution increases by a third instead of by 25-percent, e-mail us and we'll explain the unpleasant math.)

We don't mind scaling images five or ten percent up or down in InDesign. However, if the design requires any more scaling than that and we really care about the image quality, we'd rather resample in Photoshop and then apply a little more sharpening, to offset the blurriness that scaling or resampling introduces.

# Working with Graphic Frames

Getting used to the way that InDesign works with graphics and graphics frames can take some time—especially for users of

FreeHand and PageMaker (where graphics are not obviously stored inside frames). So, while this doesn't strictly have anything to do with importing or exporting images, we hope that the following sections help.

## Selecting Frames and Graphics

You can modify the size, shape, and formatting of a graphic frame, or you can modify the frame's contents, or you can change both at once. The key to making these adjustments lies in the selection method you use (see Figure 7-12).

◆ When you click the frame or frame contents using the Selection tool, or when a selection rectangle created by dragging the Selection tool touches the frame, you're selecting both the frame and its contents. At this point, any changes you make (using the Transform palette or transformation tools) affect both the frame and its contents (see Chapter 9, "Transforming").

◆ When you click the edge of the frame with the Direct Selection tool, you're selecting the frame only—not its contents. Select the frame when you want to edit the shape of the frame using the drawing tools, or transform (scale, rotate, skew, or move) the frame using the transformation tools or the Transform palette without transforming its contents.

◆ When you click *inside* the frame with the Direct Selection tool, you're selecting only the frame contents—not the frame itself. Select the graphic when you want to transform (rotate, scale, move, or skew) the graphic alone, or when you want to apply color to the graphic. If you then Option/Alt-click inside the frame again with the Direct Selection tool, InDesign selects the "parent" frame of the graphic instead.

## Resizing Imported Graphics

When you select a graphic frame with the Selection tool and drag the corner handle, InDesign resizes the frame *but does not scale the graphic*. To scale the graphic inside the frame as you scale the frame, hold down Command/Ctrl as you drag the corner handle (see Figure 7-13). Hold down Command-Shift/Ctrl-Shift as you drag to proportionally resize the frame and graphic.

You can also resize both the frame and the graphic using the Scaling tool or the Scale Horizontal and Scale Vertical fields in the Transform palette, provided you've selected the frame using the Selection tool. Or use the Free Transform tool or the Scale dialog box (see Chapter 9, "Transforming").

**FIGURE 7-12**
**Selecting a Graphic**

Click the Selection tool on the frame or graphic to select the frame and the graphic (note solid selection handles).

Click the Direct Selection tool on the frame to select the frame (note hollow selection handles).

Click the Direct Selection tool inside the frame to select the graphic. When the frame and the graphic are exactly the same size, it can be difficult to tell which is selected (in this example, it's easy, because the selected graphic is larger than the little frame). After you select the image, you can direct-select the frame by Option/Alt-clicking the image.

**FIGURE 7-13**
**Scaling a Graphic with the Selection Tool**

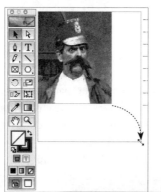

When you simply drag one of the selection handles of a frame containing a graphic, InDesign scales the frame, but does not scale the graphic.

Hold down Command/Ctrl as you drag a selection handle, and InDesign will scale the graphic as it scales the frame.

**Panning a Graphic**

When you "pan" a graphic, you move the graphic without moving the graphic's frame. To do this, select the graphic with the Direct Selection tool, then drag. As you drag, InDesign repositions the graphic inside the frame (see Figure 7-14). If you drag the contents too far, the graphic won't even be visible in the frame, which makes it virtually impossible to select again later. Select the frame and choose Center Content from the Fitting submenu (in the Object menu, or the context menu) to recover the picture.

Note that it's possible to move the graphic entirely outside the frame, off the page, and beyond the edge of the pasteboard. Don't.

**FIGURE 7-14**
**Panning a Graphic**

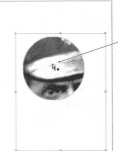

*Use the Direct Selection tool to select an image inside a frame...*

*...then drag the image. If you wait a second before you start dragging, you'll be able to see the image as you drag.*

# Working with Clipping Paths

Earlier in this chapter, we talked about InDesign's ability to use a clipping path stored in a graphic as you place the graphic—but what about creating a clipping path for a graphic that doesn't have one? First, there's nothing magical about clipping paths. In fact, you could say that every graphic you place in InDesign is inside a clipping path—its graphic frame.

A clipping path is a PostScript path, much like other Bézier lines in InDesign, Illustrator, or QuarkXPress. However, a clipping path acts like a pair of scissors, cutting out an image in any shape you want. Clipping an image is actually the same as cropping it, but because InDesign makes a distinction, we will, too: The shape of a graphic frame crops the picture, but the clipping path (if there is one) clips it.

**Why Use Clipping Paths?**

Remember that InDesign can read transparency in imported images. Even if you don't want to use any of the transparency effects, you still may want to take advantage of this feature because it means you might avoid using clipping paths altogether. Save yourself a bundle of time and just make the background of the image transparent in Photoshop.

Nevertheless, some people will still want to use clipping paths. For example, clipping paths are always drawn at the resolution of the output device, so you can get very sharp edges. If you like this sharp-edged effect, use a clipping path. Also, those folks who want to avoid the transparency flattener might still want to use clipping paths. As for us, we haven't bothered with a clipping path for months.

**Selecting an Existing Clipping Path**

If the selected graphic contains a clipping path—or, in the case of a Photoshop image, *any* path saved in Photoshop's Paths palette—you can select the clipping path you want to apply. To do this, select the graphic or its frame, then display the Clipping Path dialog box (choose Clipping Path from the Object menu or press Command-Option-Shift-K/Ctrl-Alt-Shift-K). Select Photoshop Path from the Type pop-up menu. If there are multiple paths, choose one from the Path pop-up menu (see Figure 7-15).

**Creating a Clipping Path**

You can ask InDesign to create an "automatic" clipping path using the following steps (see Figure 7-16). However, to be honest about it, we tend to shy away from this option unless we're building a quick comp for a client or we're planning on spending some time editing the resulting path. In general, you'll just get better results making clipping paths by hand in Photoshop.

1. Select a graphic. You'll have the best luck with a graphic against a white background. In addition, it's a good idea to select the graphic using the Direct Selection tool (as opposed to selecting the frame). We know this seems odd, but bear with us. We'll tell you why later.

2. Choose Clipping Path from the Object menu (or press Command-Option-Shift-K/Ctrl-Alt-Shift-K). InDesign displays the Clipping Path dialog box.

3. Choose Detect Edges from the Type pop-up menu. Turn on the Preview option, if it's not already on, and drag the Clipping Path dialog box out of the way (if necessary) so that you can see the selected image. Look at the clipping path that InDesign has built around the image. What? You can't see the clipping path? That's because you didn't select the image using the Direct Selection tool, like we told you to in Step 1. If you had, you'd be able to see the clipping path as you adjust the settings in the Clipping Path dialog box.

FIGURE 7-15
**Using an Existing
Clipping Path**

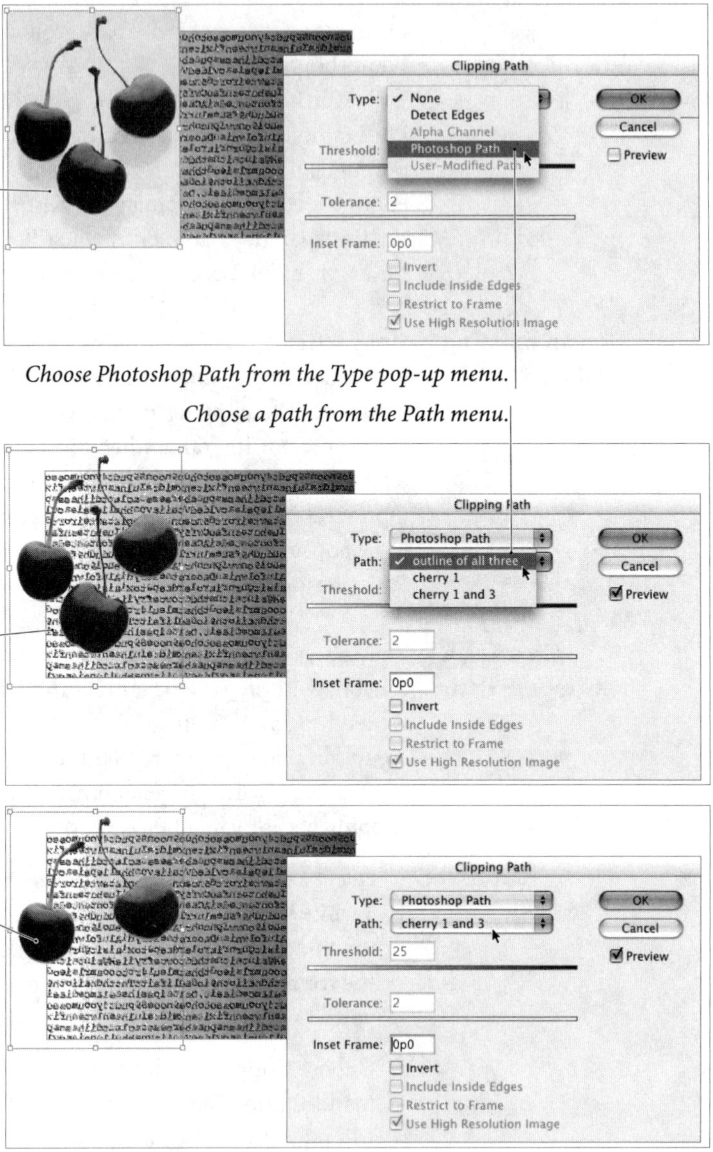

*Place a graphic contain-
ing a clipping path (in
this example, we've used
a Photoshop file).*

*Select the graphic, then press
Command-Option-Shift-K/
Ctrl-Alt-Shift-K (or choose
Clipping Path from the
Object menu) to display the
Clipping Path dialog box.*

*Choose Photoshop Path from the Type pop-up menu.*

*Choose a path from the Path menu.*

*InDesign applies
the first clipping
path defined in
the graphic.*

*If that's not the path
you wanted, choose a
different one. Here, we've
chosen "cherry 1 and 3."*

4.  Work with the controls in the dialog box.

    ◆ Adjust the values in the Threshold and Tolerance fields
      (either enter values in the fields or drag the associated sliders)
      until the clipping path looks the way you want it to.

    ◆ Turn on the Include Inside Edges option to create "holes"
      inside the clipping path for any blank (as defined by the value
      you entered in the Threshold field) areas inside the graphic.

**FIGURE 7-16**
## Creating a Clipping Path

*Select a graphic, then press Command-Option-Shift-K/ Ctrl-Alt-Shift-K (or choose Clipping Path from the Object menu) to display the Clipping Path dialog box.*

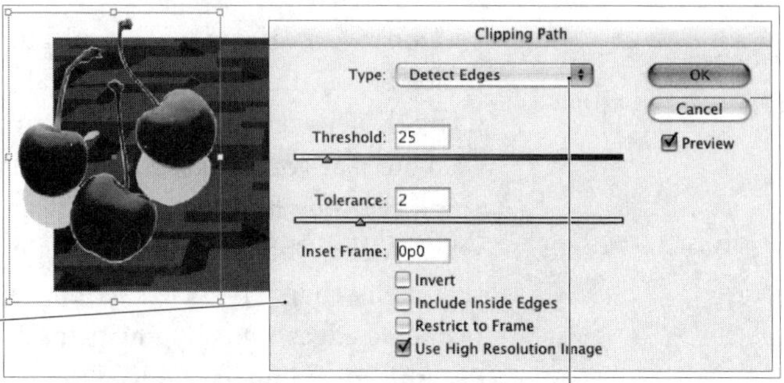

*Choose Detect Edges from the Type pop-up menu.*

*InDesign attempts to find the edges in the graphic. Of course, InDesign does a better job of this when the graphic has a simple outline and a simple background.*

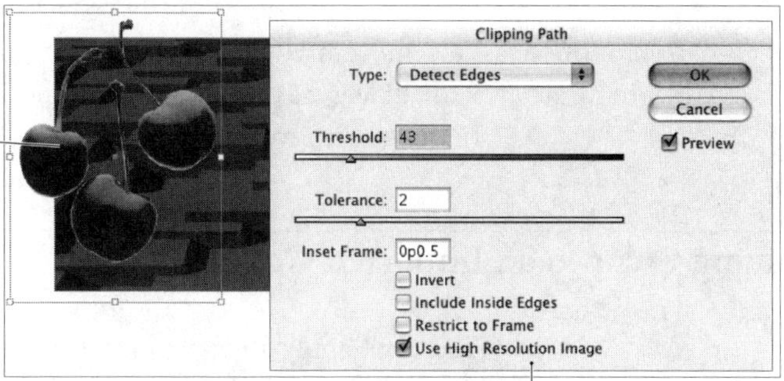

*You can fine tune the clipping path using the controls in the Clipping Path dialog box. Here, we've adjusted the Threshold and Inset Frame values to remove some off-white areas.*

◆ Turn on Invert to turn the clipping path "inside out."

◆ Turn on Restrict to Box to limit the clipping path to the boundaries of the graphic frame. (Since the image can't extend past the edges of the graphic frame anyway, this is reasonable. However, if you change your frame cropping, you'll have to rebuild your clipping path, so we leave this turned off.)

◆ Most of the time, you'll probably want to turn on the Use High Resolution Image option—it uses data from the image file on disk (rather than simply using the screen preview image) to create a more accurate clipping path.

◆ If necessary (and it usually will be), enter a value in the Inset Frame field to shrink (enter positive values) or expand (enter negative values) the clipping path. We often use a small inset value, like .5 points.

5. Once the clipping path looks the way you want it to, click the OK button.

Don't worry if you made a mistake; you can always open up this dialog box again and change the values, or change the clipping path using the Direct Select tool or the various Pen tools.

Note that you can also create a clipping path based on an alpha channel if one has been saved in an imported image. To do this, select Alpha Channel from the Type pop-up menu. The problem is that alpha channels (saved selections) can have soft anti-aliased or feathered edges, and clipping paths cannot. So, InDesign has to convert soft edges into hard-edged Bézier paths using the features above. It's hardly worth the trouble in our opinion.

**Removing a Clipping Path**    To remove a clipping path, select the image, display the Clipping Path dialog box, and choose None from the Type pop-up menu. InDesign removes the clipping path.

## Applying Color to an Imported Graphic

You can't apply a color to just any imported graphic—but you can apply colors to bi-level (*i.e.*, black-and-white) and grayscale TIFF images. To apply a color to an image, select the image using the Direct Selection tool, then apply a color as you normally would—probably by clicking a swatch in the Swatches palette (see Chapter 10, "Color," for more on applying colors).

If you want the image to overprint any objects behind it, select the image using the Direct Selection tool, display the Attributes palette (if it's not already visible), and then turn on the Overprint Fill option. You can use this technique to create duotones from grayscale images you've placed in a publication, as shown in Color Figure 7.

## Exporting Documents

Sometimes, you've got to get your pages out of your InDesign publications and into some other application or format. You can export InDesign pages as EPS, PDF, HTML, SVG, or XML (in addition to the text export options described in Chapter 3, "Text"). We explore each of these in depth in the following sections. In each case, the first step is always to select Export from the File menu (or press Command-E/Ctrl-E).

# Exporting EPS

To export an InDesign page (or series of pages) as an EPS graphic (or series of graphics, as EPS is, by definition, a single-page-at-a-time format), in the Export dialog box choose EPS from the Formats pop-up menu (Macintosh) or the Save as Type field (Windows), pick a location for the file, and then click the Save button. InDesign displays the Export EPS dialog box. This dialog box has two panels: General and Advanced. Here's a quick description of the options in each panel.

**General.** The controls in the General panel define the way that InDesign exports objects to the EPS file (see Figure 7-17).

◆ **Pages.** Which pages do you want to export? Bear in mind, as you work with the controls in this panel, that each page in the page range you specify will be exported as a separate EPS file. To export pages one, two, three, seven, and twelve, for example, enter "1-3,7,12" into the Ranges field. See "Page Ranges" in Chapter 11, "Printing," for more information. When you turn on the Spreads checkbox, InDesign exports the pages in readers spreads, just as they appear in your document window. For instance, pages 2 and 3 are combined into one wide EPS file.

◆ **PostScript.** Choose the PostScript version of the printer you expect to use to print the EPS. If you're sure you're printing on a PostScript 3 printer, choose Level 3. Choose Level 2 if your printer could be PostScript Level 2 or PostScript 3. InDesign no longer supports PostScript Level 1 printers; a Level 2 EPS file may or may not print on one of these old beasts.

◆ **Color.** Do you want to convert RGB images in your publication to CMYK as you create the EPS? If so, choose CMYK from the Color pop-up menu. The method InDesign uses for this conversion depends on the setting of the Enable Color Management option in the Color Settings dialog box (see Chapter 10, "Color," for more on color management). If the option is on, and you've assigned a color profile to an image, InDesign uses that profile to create separations of the image. If the option is turned off, or if you have not turned on color management for the image, InDesign uses its internal RGB to CMYK conversion method.

While it's pretty rare that you'd need to choose Gray or RGB, these options will convert all colors to their grayscale or RGB equivalents.

FIGURE 7-17
EPS Export Options,
General Panel

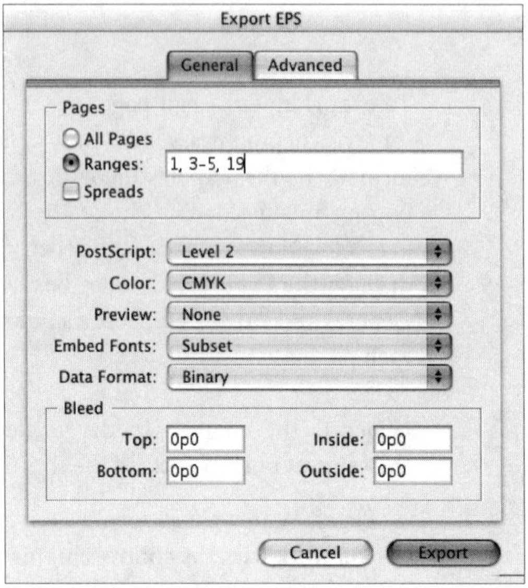

Choose Device Independent (which won't be available unless you've turned on color management) to allow output devices to apply their own color management profiles to the exported EPS. When you do this, InDesign leaves RGB and CMYK images alone during the export process.

◆ **Preview.** EPS files usually have low-resolution, built-in previews which applications use to display the EPS on screen; Macintosh EPS files typically have PICT previews, Windows EPS files must use TIFF previews. If you're re-importing the EPS file back into an InDesign document, you can leave the Preview pop-up menu set to None, because InDesign actually creates a preview on the fly when you import the file. Similarly, if you're going to open the EPS file in Photoshop (rasterizing it into a bitmapped image), Illustrator (converting it into paths), or process the EPS file with some software which doesn't require a preview image, you can leave Preview set to None. If the EPS will be used in any other program (like QuarkXPress), select PICT or TIFF (the latter is more flexible because most Macintosh programs can read both PICT and TIFF).

◆ **Embed Fonts.** To make sure that the EPS contains all of the fonts you've used, choose Complete from the Embed Fonts pop-up menu. Why not do this every time? Because your EPS files can become huge, bloated, and swollen with included fonts. To reduce the size of the EPS, choose Subset to include only the characters needed to print the text in the EPS. Choose None when you don't want or need to include any fonts in the EPS.

Some fonts cannot be embedded—the font manufacturer has included information in the font that prevents embedding. When InDesign reads this information, it will not include the fonts in the EPS, regardless of the choice you make from the Embed Fonts pop-up menu. If you find you're missing a font in an EPS, return to the InDesign publication and convert all of the characters that use the missing font to outlines and then export the EPS again.

◆ **Data Format.** Choose ASCII if you expect to print the EPS on a system connected to a printer via a serial cable, or if you plan to edit the EPS using a text editor or word processor—otherwise, choose Binary to create a compressed version of the file. Binary files are smaller and therefore transmit to the printer faster, but they sometimes choke really old networks.

◆ **Bleed.** If you do not enter values in the four Bleed fields (Top, Bottom, Inside, and Outside—or Left and Right, in a non-facing-pages document), InDesign sets the edge of the EPS bounding box to the edge of the page you're exporting. Enter value in the Bleed fields to expand the area of the page. See Chapter 11, "Printing," for more on bleeding off the edge of the page.

**Advanced.** Just because it's called the Advanced tab of the Export EPS dialog box doesn't necessarily mean that these options are any more advanced or tricky. These features let you control how images and transparency are handled in EPS files (see Figure 7-18).

◆ **Send Data.** In most cases, you want the full resolution of your bitmapped images to be included in your EPS files (so they can later be printed properly). On occasion, however, you may want only a low-resolution version of your images in the EPS file. For example, let's say you were going to rasterize the EPS in Photoshop in order to save it as a GIF or JPEG and place it on the Web; there's no need for the full-resolution images, so you could choose Proxy from the Send Data pop-up menu. Similarly, if you're planning to print the EPS through an OPI system, and plan to replace the images, or if you're creating the EPS for on-screen viewing only, choose Proxy.

◆ **OPI Image Replacement.** Turn this option on to have InDesign perform OPI image replacement as you export the EPS. If you're exporting a page containing EPS graphics containing OPI image

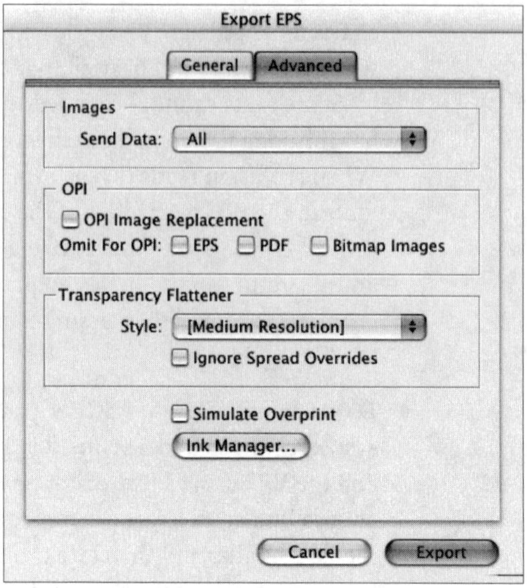

FIGURE 7-18
EPS Export Options,
Advanced Panel

links, you'll probably need to turn this option on (unless your EPS will later be processed by an OPI server).

◆ **Omit For OPI.** To keep InDesign from including a certain type of imported graphic file in the EPS, turn on the corresponding option in the Omit section (to omit placed TIFF images, for example, turn on the TIFF option). We discuss OPI in more detail in Chapter 11, "Printing."

◆ **Transparency Flattener.** In order for transparency effects to print on most devices, InDesign must "flatten" them. We discuss flattening and transparency flattening styles in great detail in Chapter 11, "Printing." Suffice it to say that you can choose a flattener style here, as well as tell InDesign to ignore any flattener style spread overrides you (or someone else) may have made in the document (by turning on the Ignore Spread Overrides checkbox).

◆ **Simulate Overprint.** If you've set various objects in your document to overprint (using the Attributes palette), but you're not going to print this EPS file on a device that can handle overprinted colors, then you may want to turn on the Simulate Overprint checkbox. However, this radically changes your EPS file, so while it may be useful for proofing, you probably shouldn't use it for final output.

◆ **Ink Manager.** The Ink Manager manages how colors trap with each other and how spot colors interact (for instance, you can use the Ink Manager to alias one spot color to another). We cover the Ink Manager in Chapter 10, "Color."

**An EPS-Related Rant**    It's inevitable—some of you are going to be asked by your imagesetting service provider to give them EPS files of your InDesign pages. This is because they want to import the EPSs into QuarkXPress 3.32. Why would they want to do this? Because they were probably raised by hyenas and this is the only way they know how to print *anything*. For what it's worth, they probably do the same thing with XPress 5 publications. In spite of the output disasters that this approach can cause, it's what they're familiar with, and is the only way they'll print your job. You're laughing now, but, believe us, these guys are out there.

So, while you're searching for a new imagesetting service bureau, you might as well give them what they want.

# Exporting PDF

InDesign can export Adobe Acrobat Portable Document Format files (what normal people call "PDF"), which can be used for remote printing, electronic distribution, or as a graphic you can place in InDesign or other programs. InDesign doesn't need to use the Acrobat Distiller (or the Distiller Assistant) to create PDF files.

Note, however, that Distiller usually makes more compact PDF files than exporting directly from InDesign, which may be important if your PDF files are destined for the Web. If you want to use Distiller to make PDF files instead of creating them directly using the Export feature, you must use the Print dialog box to write PostScript to disk first (we discuss how to do that in Chapter 11, "Printing").

While PDF is great for putting publications on the World Wide Web, or for creating other sorts of on-line publications, most of us ink-on-paper types care more about making PDF files suitable for print. Fortunately, InDesign can export PDFs for just about any purpose, on-screen or on-press. It all depends on how you set up the export options.

When you export a PDF (by selecting Export from the File menu and choosing PDF from the Type pop-up menu), InDesign displays the Export PDF dialog box. This dialog box contains six panels for setting PDF export options: General, Compression, Marks & Bleeds,

Advanced, Security, and Summary (see Figure 7-19). Remember that in all paneled dialog boxes like this one, you can jump to the second panel by pressing Command-2/Ctrl-2, the third panel with Command-3/Ctrl-3, and so on.

Above all these panels sits the Style pop-up menu, which lets you select a PDF export style (each of which is a collection of various export options). You may be familiar with these styles, as they're basically identical to those found in Illustrator and Distiller. We discuss creating your own in "Defining a PDF Export Style," later in this chapter.

**General**    The General panel of the Export PDF dialog box is a hodge-podge of options, controlling everything from what pages get exported to whether InDesign should launch Acrobat after saving the file.

**Page Ranges.** Which pages do you want to export? Just as in the General panel of the Print dialog box, you can export all document pages (click the All option) or specify individual page ranges (135-182) or non-contiguous pages (3, 7, 22) in the Range field. Note that unless you have Absolute Numbering selected in the General panel of the Preferences dialog box, you'll need to type page ranges with their actual names. For instance, if you want to export the first four pages and you're using roman numerals, you'll have to type "i-iv". If you've specified a page number prefix, like "A", you'll have to include that in the Range field, too.

**Reader's Spreads.** When you turn on the Spreads option, InDesign exports each spread in the page range you've specified (see above) as a single page of the exported PDF. This is called "reader's spreads" because the spread appears as it would to a reader flipping through a book or magazine. This does not create "printer spreads," which you need to print a saddle-stiched booklet. You need a separate plug-in to do that.

**Compatibility.** Who is your audience for this PDF file? Most people have Acrobat 5 now (or at least the free Acrobat 5 Reader), but if there's any chance your recipient only has Acrobat 4, you'll need to choose Acrobat 4 from the Compatibility pop-up menu. But there's another reason you want to pay attention here: If you have used any transparency effects in your document, the Compatibility pop-up menu controls who does the flattening. Choosing Acrobat 4 means you want InDesign to flatten the file (see "Transparency Flattner" below, and "Printing Transparency" in Chapter 11, "Printing").

FIGURE 7-19

Export PDF Options,
General Panel

FIGURE 7-19

Export PDF Options,
General Panel

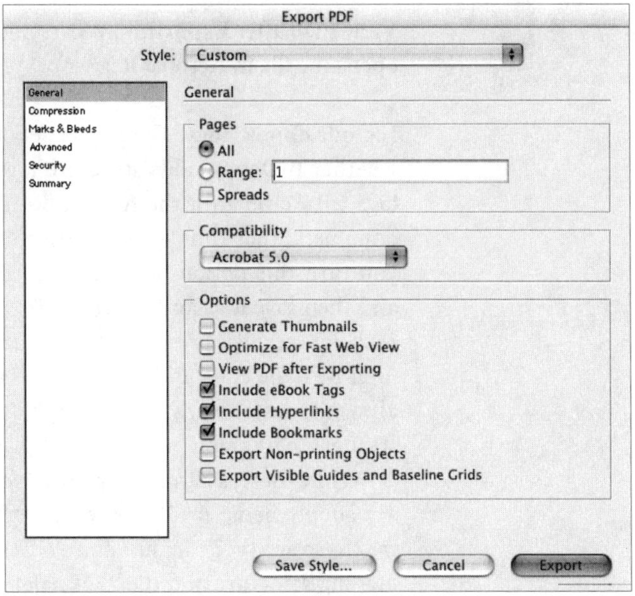

Acrobat 5 can read the unflattened transparency effects. If we're sending files to our printer or an imaging bureau that we trust knows about flattening, then we'd much rather send them Acrobat 5 PDF files.

**Generate Thumbnails.** Creates a preview image, or "thumbnail" of each page or spread (if you're exporting reader's spreads) you export. You can display thumbnails when you view the PDF using Acrobat or Acrobat Reader. They don't do much for us, and they increase the size of the file.

**Optimize for Fast Web View.** The key word here is "Web." The only time you'd want to turn this on is when you're creating a document that will only be viewed on the Web. When this option is off, InDesign includes repeated objects (such as objects from master pages) as individual objects on each page of the PDF. When you choose Optimize PDF, InDesign exports a single instance of each repeated item for the entire PDF. When the item appears on a page in the PDF, InDesign includes a reference to the "master" item. This reduces the file size of the PDF without changing the appearance of the exported pages. When on, InDesign also overrides the settings in the Compression panel with its own Web-appropriate settings, and restructures the file so that it can be downloaded one page at a time from a Web server rather than having to download the whole megillah.

**View PDF after Exporting.** When you turn this option on, InDesign opens the file in Acrobat Reader or Acrobat after exporting the PDF.

**Include eBook Tags.** The Include eBook Tags checkbox determines whether InDesign adds structure tags inside your PDF files. These tags tell Acrobat (or the Acrobat Reader) about the structure of the document, including what constitutes a paragraph. For instance, if you turn this option on, open the resulting PDF file in Acrobat 5, and then save it as an RTF (Rich Text Format) file, you can see that each paragraph is preserved. If you turn off Include eBook Tags, your final RTF file ends up with each line as a separate paragraph. After all, without structuring tags, Acrobat can't possibly know what constitutes a paragraph.

While there is hardly ever a need for these tags in documents that are simply being printed, they don't affect file size or export time much, so we typically just leave this option turned on. We discuss tagging structure and the Tags palette further in "Form and Function: XML," later in this chapter.

**Include Hyperlinks.** You can use the Hyperlinks palette to add as many hyperlinks to your document as you want, but unless you turn on this checkbox they won't appear in your PDF file. When you turn this option on, InDesign also creates hyperlinks in your table of contents and indexes (see Chapter 8, "Long Documents," for more on these features). Of course, it's not really appropriate to include hyperlinks when sending off a PDF for high-resolution printing.

**Include Bookmarks.** If you've used the table of contents feature (which we discuss in Chapter 8, "Long Documents"), you can tell InDesign to automatically build bookmarks for your PDF file based on the table of contents. Just turn on the Include Bookmarks checkbox. Again, this is a feature suitable for PDFs destined for on-screen viewing, not prepress.

**Export Non-printing Objects.** Ordinarily, non-printing objects (items on your page for which you've turned on the Non-printing checkbox in the Attributes palette) won't appear in exported PDF files. However, you can force them to export (overriding the Attributes palette) by turning on the Export Non-printing Objects checkbox in the Export PDF dialog box.

**Export Visible Guides and Baseline Grids.** If you turn on this export option, InDesign exports all visible guides (margins, ruler guides, baseline guides, and so on), which may be helpful for designers who are collaborating on a project. The only guide type that doesn't export is the document grid (even if it's visible).

**Compression**   The options in the Compression panel define the compression and/or sampling changes applied to the images in your publication as it's exported as a PDF (see Figure 7-20). Compression is almost always a good thing, but you need to choose your compression options carefully, depending on where your PDF is headed. PDFs for on-screen viewing can handle more compression, and those destined for the Web typically *need* a lot of compression to keep file sizes down. A PDF file that you're sending to a printer for high-resolution output requires very little compression, if any (unless you have to e-mail the file or it won't otherwise fit on a disk for transport).

Bitmapped images are almost always the largest part of a document, so PDF's compression techniques focus on them. InDesign has two methods of making your files smaller: lowering the resolution of the images and encoding the image data in clever ways.

**Resampling.** If you place a 300 dpi CMYK image into your document and scale it down 50 percent, the effective resolution is 600 dpi (because twice as many pixels fit in the same amount of space). When you export your PDF, you can ask InDesign to resample the image to a more reasonable resolution. If your final output is to a

**FIGURE 7-20**
**Export PDF Options, Compression Panel**

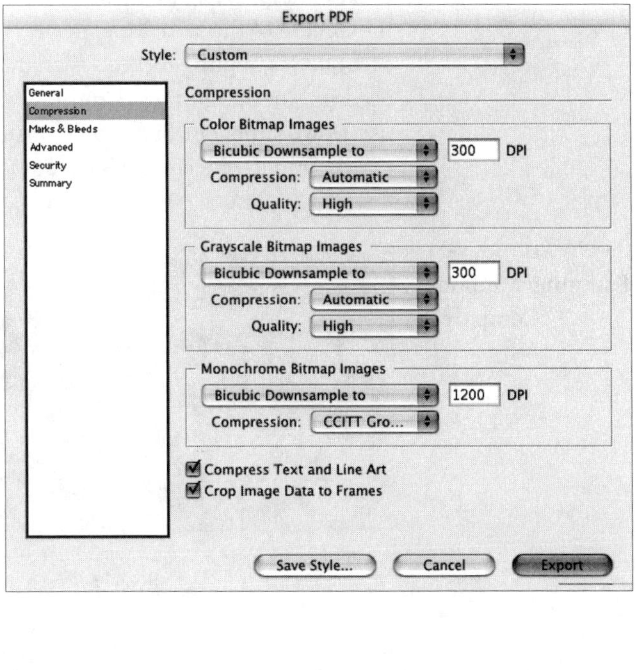

desktop inkjet printer, you rarely need more than 300 or 400 dpi. Printing on a laser printer or imagesetter (or any device that uses halftone screens) requires no more than 1.5 to 2.0 times the halftone screen frequency—a 150 lpi halftone rarely needs more than 225 dpi of data to print beautifully. Web PDFs can get away with 72 or 96 dpi, unless you want the viewer to be able to zoom in on the image and not see pixelation.

Monochrome (or bi-level) bitmapped images do not have halftone screens applied to them by the printer, and, therefore, are not subject to the same rules that govern grayscale and color images. In a monochrome image, you never need more resolution than the resolution of the printer. If your final output is your 600 dpi laser printer, you certainly never need more than 600 dpi monochrome images. Imagesetter output rarely requires more than 1200 dpi (though for a sheetfed art book, we might bump this up to 1500 dpi). Printing on uncoated stock requires less resolution because of halftone spots spreading; you can easily get away with 800 dpi for newsprint.

InDesign only downsamples when exporting PDF files. That is, it throws away data to lower image resolution (it won't add resolution). Downsampling works by turning an area of pixels into a single, larger pixel, so the method you use to get that larger pixel is crucial. When you *downsample* an image, InDesign takes the average color or gray value of all of the pixels in the area to set the color or gray value of the larger pixel. When you *subsample* an image, on the other hand, InDesign uses the color or gray value of a single pixel in the middle of the area. This means that subsampling is a much less accurate resampling method than downsampling, and shouldn't be used for anything other than proofing (see Figure 7-21). We rarely use Downsample or Subsample; instead, the best option is Bicubic Downsample, which provides the smoothest sampling algorithm.

FIGURE 7-21
**Sampling Methods
Compared**

*Normal*          *Downsampled to 300*          *Subsampled to 300*
                  *pixels per inch*             *pixels per inch*

Ultimately, however, we much prefer to just get the resolution right in Photoshop before placing the image, rather than relying on InDesign to downsample it. That way, we can see the result of resampling on the screen, and undo the change if necessary. Otherwise, we won't see the result until we view the PDF.

**Encoding.** The PDF specification supports both ZIP and JPEG encoding for grayscale and color bitmapped images; and CCITT Group 3, CCITT Group 4, ZIP, and Run Length encodings for monochrome bitmapped images. It's enough to make your head spin! Which method should you use? Again, it depends on where the PDF is going and what kind of images you've got.

Scanned images generally compress better with JPEG and synthetic images (such as screen captures that have a lot of solid colors and sharp edges) compress better with ZIP. However, JPEG compression, even at its highest quality setting, removes data from an image file (it's "lossy"). Most designers find that some JPEG compression for scanned photographs is an acceptable compromise, as it results in dramatically smaller file sizes. But when we don't need to worry about file size, we prefer to use ZIP for everything because ZIP compression does not discard image data (it's "lossless"). You never know when you might need that image data!

When making on-screen PDFs (either for the Web or for proofing), we almost always leave the color and grayscale Compression pop-up menus set to Automatic, so that InDesign decides between ZIP and JPEG for us on a per-image basis. We then make a choice from the Quality pop-up menu: You get the best compression with Minimum quality, but who wants to look at the results? Unfortunately, the only good way to choose from among the Quality options is to save two or three to disk, look at them in Acrobat, and compare their file sizes.

Exporting PDF files for print is easier: We usually just choose ZIP for both color and grayscale images, and then specify 8-bit from the Quality pop-up menu (4-bit describes fewer colors, so it's half the size but lousy quality). However, if you need to save some disk space (again, like if you're e-mailing the file to your output provider), it's usually reasonable to use Automatic compression with the Quality pop-up menu set to Maximum quality—the resulting JPEG images are usually indistinguishable from uncompressed images.

As for monochrome image encoding, it's rare to see much of a difference among the choices (they're all lossless and provide reasonable compression). We usually use Run Length or ZIP encoding, but only because we don't like the sound of CCITT.

**Compress Text and Line Art.** The Compress Text and Line Art option applies to text and paths you've drawn in InDesign—we cannot think of any reason you should turn this option off.

**Crop Image Data to Frames.** When you turn this option on, InDesign sends only the visible parts of the images in the publication. This sounds reasonable, and can result in a much smaller file for publications that contain cropped images. But it also means you won't have access to the image data if you edit the image in the PDF. Most of the time, this isn't a problem, but you might want to turn this option off if your PDF includes images that bleed (so that you or your service provider can later increase the bleed area, if necessary).

**Marks & Bleeds**   In a desperate attempt at reducing the redundancy in our overly complex lives, we're going to skip a detailed analysis of the Marks & Bleeds panel of the Export PDF dialog box and instead point out that these features are exactly the same as the features in the Print dialog box (see "Marks & Bleeds" in Chapter 11, "Printing").

**Advanced**   There's nothing particularly "advanced" about any of the options in this panel, and while you probably won't spend much time messing with these settings, it is important to understand what they do and why you'd want to change them (see Figure 7-22).

**FIGURE 7-22**
**Export PDF Options,**
**Advanced Panel**

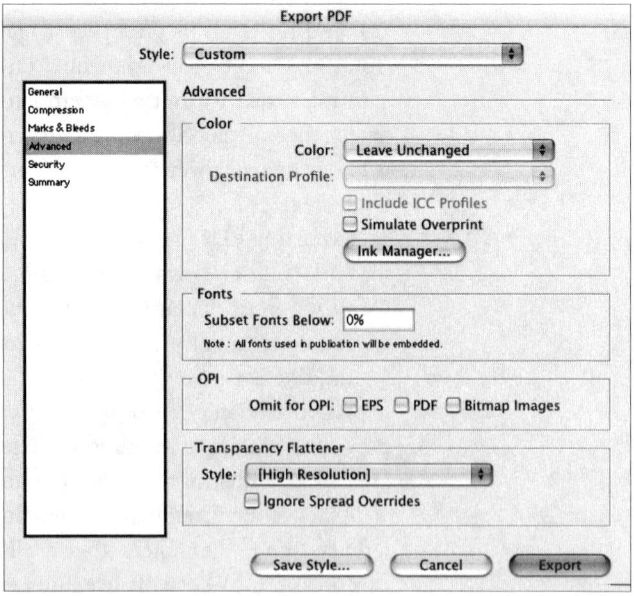

**Color.** Choose CMYK from the Color pop-up menu to convert any RGB images or RGB colors to CMYK in the exported PDF. If you've assigned a color profile to an image, InDesign uses that profile to create separations of the image. If you have not turned on color management for the image, InDesign uses its internal RGB to CMYK conversion method (the default CMYK space is based on SWOP inks; the default RGB space is AdobeRGB). When color management is enabled in the Color Settings dialog box, you can choose a destination profile for the conversion in the (surprise!) Destination Profile pop-up menu (see Chapter 10, "Color," for more on color management).

If your final output is based on RGB (like either on-screen or an inkjet printer) you can also choose RGB to convert the images and colors in the publication to the RGB color model. Choose Leave Unchanged to export the images using their current color model. The options on the Color pop-up menu have no effect on spot colors you've defined in your publication or in images.

**Include ICC Profiles.** When you've enabled color management in the Color Settings dialog box, you can tell InDesign to embed ICC profiles into its PDF files by turning on this option. In a color managed workflow, it is important that you do include profiles, or else other programs (or InDesign, if you're re-importing the PDF into another InDesign document) cannot color manage the file. Turn this option off when exporting PDF files for the Web, since the Web isn't color managed and ICC Profiles increase file size.

**Simulate Overprint.** Acrobat 4 has no way to preview overprinting instructions, so if you need to use Acrobat 4 and you need to proof overprinting, you can turn on the Simulate Overprint option. Because everyone we know is using Acrobat 5, we never have to worry about this feature. Note that Simulate Overprint should not be used for final artwork, as it radically changes your document (spot colors are changed to process colors, for instance). It's just a proofing tool.

**Ink Manager.** Have a spot color that should be a process color? Or two different spot colors that really should be one? The Ink Manager handles these kinds of troubles (for more information, see "Ink Manager" in Chapter 10, "Color").

**Subset Fonts Below.** InDesign always embeds font outline information in exported PDF files, so it doesn't matter whether the person you give the file to has the font. The exception to this is when the font manufacturer has specified that their font should not be embeddable. Many Asian fonts are not embeddable, for instance. This is a political and legal hot-potato that we're not going to touch, other than to say that if your fonts aren't embeddable, complain to your font developer, not Adobe (or us). Or, better yet, if there isn't a lot of text in that font, convert the text to outlines before printing or exporting.

Anyway, usually the question isn't whether to embed your fonts, but rather how much of the font you want to embed. The value you enter in the Subset Fonts Below field sets the threshold at which InDesign includes complete fonts in the PDF you're exporting. When you "subset" a font, you include only those characters that are used on the pages you're exporting, which keeps file size down. Enter 100 to force InDesign to always save a subset of the font's characters, or enter 0 to force InDesign to include the entire font (or fonts) in the PDF. You can also enter some other percentage value to strike a balance between the two extremes, but we generally find that either we want subsets or we don't.

One reason you might not want to subset your fonts is to maximize the potential for editing the PDF later. Let's say you subset your fonts, and later need your output provider to edit the PDF (perhaps to change a typo). If they need to change "karma" to "dharma" and you haven't used the letter "d" elsewhere in the document, they can't do it (unless they have the font installed on their system).

Another reason not to use font subsetting is if you expect users on a platform other than your own to view and print your exported PDFs. We know, it's supposed to work. In our experience, it doesn't. Platform-specific character encoding and printer driver issues always seem to cause problems when we subset fonts in a PDF. At least one of the authors (Ole!) feels strongly that font subsetting should always be avoided for this reason. The small amount of (cheap!) disk space you use to embed the entire font is a small price to pay, compared to (expensive!) last-minute print production problems.

Unfortunately, when you export PDF files from InDesign, the program embeds its fonts in a format called "CID" (which is usually reserved for Asian fonts). This wouldn't be so bad except that some laser printers (notably PostScript "emulators") cannot deal with CID fonts and so you can't print the PDF file from Acrobat. Fortunately, there's a workaround if you find yourself in this sort of situation: Turn off the Optimize for Speed option in Acrobat's Print dialog box. This allows PDFs with CID fonts to print to these sorts of PostScript devices. You can also just write PostScript to disk and use Acrobat Distiller to create the PDF for you.

**Omit for OPI.** In an OPI workflow, the high-resolution image data is kept separate from your document until it's merged in at the last minute before printing. If you have an OPI server capable of processing PDF files with OPI comments, you can keep InDesign from including a certain type of imported graphic file in the PDF file by turning on the corresponding option in the Omit section (to omit placed EPS images, for example, turn on the EPS option). We discuss OPI in more detail in Chapter 11, "Printing."

**Transparency Flattener.** While Acrobat 5 can handle InDesign's transparency effects, Acrobat 4 is clueless. So if you're exporting an Acrobat 4 file, InDesign must "flatten" all transparency effects. We discuss flattening and the Transparency Flattener Style pop-up menu in great detail in Chapter 11, "Printing." Suffice it to say that you can choose a flattener style here, as well as tell InDesign to ignore any flattener style spread overrides you may have made in the document (by turning on the Ignore Spread Overrides checkbox).

Security

Digital Rights Management (DRM) is all the rage these days. The basic issue is who gets to do what with your content? When it comes to PDF files, you have several DRM options set out in the Security panel of the Export PDF dialog box (see Figure 7-23).

In our view, most of the PDF security features are for PDFs you're exporting for online distribution (that is, the PDF is the final product of your production process), and not for prepress use. We might have our paranoid moments, but our practicality gets the better of them most of the time—and it's just not practical to lock up a PDF that's headed for printing and prepress work. Think about it—do you want your imagesetting service bureau calling you at four in the morning to ask for the password you used to lock up a PDF?

On the other hand, if you're exporting a PDF to send to a client or a printer who you don't have a close relationship with, you might want to activate some of these settings.

**Passwords.** You can give your PDF file two different passwords: one to limit who can open the document (User Password), and one to limit who can change the security settings in the document (Master Password). The two passwords must be different. If you're going to turn on *any* security settings in the PDF—even if you don't require a User Password—then we strongly encourage you to provide a Master Password (just in case you need to make changes to the PDF later).

Note that InDesign only uses the older 40-bit RC4 encryption, which isn't nearly as powerful as the new Acrobat 5 128-bit encryption. InDesign's security is good enough for most of us, but if you work for a government and really need hard-core security, you'll need to (at least) resave your PDF file out of Adobe Acrobat with 128-bit encryption.

**Permissions.** The four checkboxes in the Permissions settings are self-explanatory: No Printing; No Changing the Document; No Content Copying or Extraction, Disable Accessibility; and No Adding or Changing Comments and Form Fields. If you're sending a file to a client and you don't want them to do anything but add comments, then turn on the first three checkboxes. If you're sending a file to be printed, and you want to make sure the output provider doesn't "accidentally" change anything, then just turn on the second option.

**Summary.** The last panel of the Export PDF dialog box, Summary, simply lists all the various settings in all the tabs in one long text list (see Figure 7-24). Do we ever sit and read through this? Nope; it's more time-consuming to read through this unformatted list of settings than it is to skip through each of the panels. However, it's nice that you can click the Save Summary button to save this list to disk as a text file. If you're exporting a PDF file to disk to send to someone else, consider including this summary along with it, so they know how you set up the dialog box (and can check to see if you did any-

FIGURE 7-24
Export PDF Options,
Summary Panel

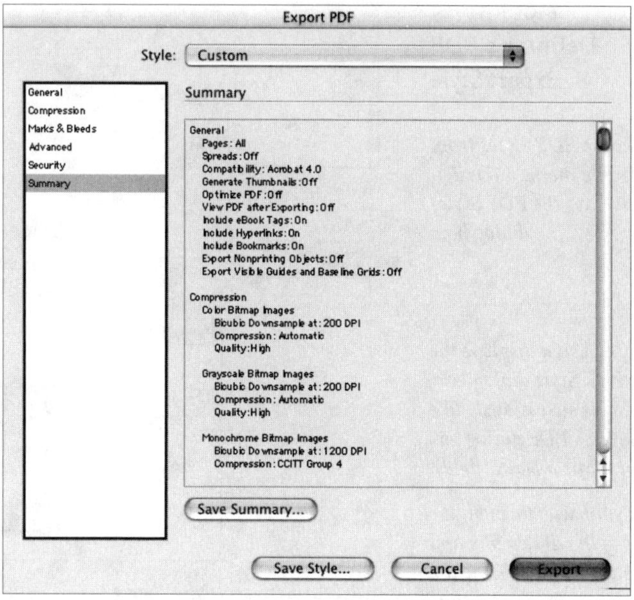

thing inappropriate). You can also use this saved summary as a log of what you did to later refer to if something prints in an unexpected fashion.

**Defining a PDF Export Style**

PDF export styles are like paragraph styles—they're bundles of attributes that can be applied in a single action. Almost all of the attributes in the PDF Export dialog box are included in a PDF export style (the Ink Manager and the Security settings aren't). It's easy to create a printer style; just set up the Export PDF dialog box with the options the way you want them, click the Save Style button at the bottom of the dialog box, and then give the style a name. You can then go ahead and export, or just cancel out of the Export PDF dialog box (if you just wanted to set up the style without exporting).

InDesign also has a second method for making PDF export styles, though we find it slightly more cumbersome (see Figure 7-25).

1. Choose PDF Styles from the File menu. InDesign displays the PDF Styles dialog box with a list of the current PDF export styles.

2. Click the New button. InDesign displays the PDF Export dialog box, but with a few differences: there's a Name field at the top, there's no Security panel, and Ink Manager and page ranges are grayed out. Note that if you select an export style before clicking New, this dialog box will be based on the style you selected.

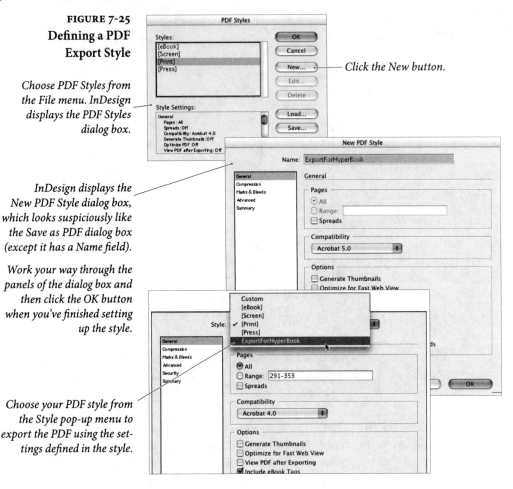

FIGURE 7-25
**FIGURE 7-25**
**Defining a PDF
Export Style**

*Choose PDF Styles from
the File menu. InDesign
displays the PDF Styles
dialog box.*

Click the New button.

*InDesign displays the
New PDF Style dialog box,
which looks suspiciously like
the Save as PDF dialog box
(except it has a Name field).*

*Work your way through the
panels of the dialog box and
then click the OK button
when you've finished setting
up the style.*

*Choose your PDF style from
the Style pop-up menu to
export the PDF using the settings defined in the style.*

3. Enter a name for the PDF export style in the Name field, then
   set up the PDF export options using the panels of the dialog box.
   Click the OK button when you're done. InDesign returns you to
   the PDF Styles dialog box and adds the new style to the list of
   available styles.

   To export a PDF using the settings in a PDF export style, choose
   the style name from the Style pop-up menu in the Export PDF dialog
   box. InDesign applies the settings of the PDF export style to the controls in the Export PDF dialog box. You'll still need to enter a page
   range in the General panel—the export style does not include that
   information.

**Managing PDF
Export Styles**

You can use the PDF Styles dialog box to add, delete, rename, edit,
and import or export PDF export styles.

◆ To delete a PDF export style, select the style name and click the Delete button. (You can't delete the four preset styles: eBook, Screen, Print, and Press.)

◆ To export PDF export styles, select the style names and click the Save button. InDesign displays the Save PDF Styles dialog box. Specify a file name and location and click the OK button.

◆ To import a PDF export style or set of styles, open the PDF Styles dialog box and click the Load button. InDesign displays the Load PDF Styles dialog box. Locate and select a document (or an InDesign publication containing PDF export styles), then click the OK button. If the PDF export styles you're importing already exist in the publication, InDesign will create copies (InDesign appends a number—usually "1"—to the duplicate styles).

◆ To edit or rename a PDF export style, select the style name in the PDF Styles dialog box, then click the Edit button.

## Exporting HTML

You can export your InDesign publication as HTML (hypertext markup language), which creates a page or pages that can be viewed using a Web browser, such as Netscape Navigator or Microsoft Internet Explorer.

When you export as HTML, keep in mind that the resulting document might bear little resemblance to your laid out publication—if maintaining control over the appearance of your material is important, you should use PDF or SVG, rather than HTML. In addition, InDesign lacks the ability to add more than rudimentary (next page/previous page) navigational features.

To export pages from an InDesign publication as HTML, follow these steps (see Figure 7-26).

1. Choose Export from the File menu. InDesign displays the Export dialog box.

2. Enter a filename and navigate to the folder in which you want to save the file, then choose HTML from the Format (Macintosh) or Save As Type (Windows) pop-up menu.

3. Click the Save button. InDesign displays the Export HTML dialog box.

**FIGURE 7-26**
**Exporting As HTML**

*The Documents panel of the Export HTML dialog box changes depending on the Export As option you choose.*

*When you choose the Multiple HTML Documents option, you can specify the filename and title for each exported page.*

*The options in the Formatting panel control the appearance of text and the background of the page (or pages).*

*When you choose Appearance, InDesign will convert some text to graphics files during the export process.*

*The options in the Layout panel control the conversion of your InDesign page layout to HTML.*

*The options in the Graphics panel control the conversion of graphics on your InDesign pages.*

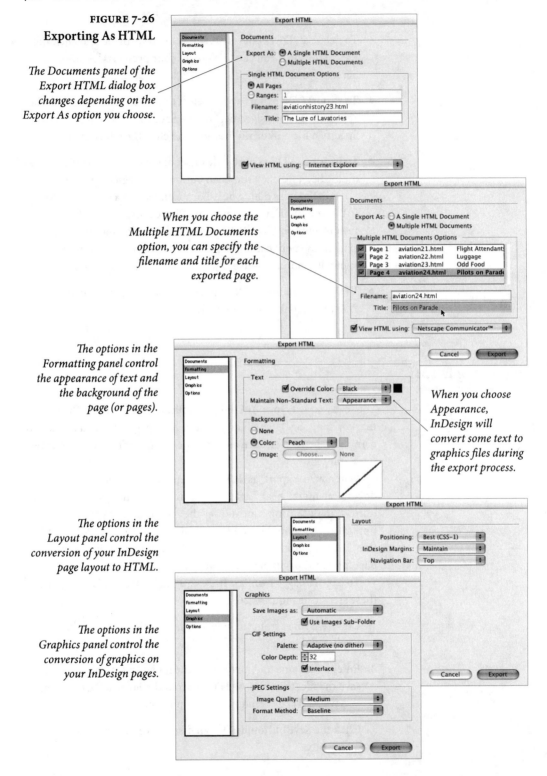

4. Set options in the five panels of the dialog box (which we describe in detail below). As in other InDesign multi-panel dialog boxes, you can move to the next panel by pressing Command-Down Arrow/Ctrl-Down Arrow or to the previous panel by pressing Command-Up Arrow/Ctrl-Up Arrow. Or, you can hold down Command/Ctrl and then press a number from one to five (for the first through fifth panels).

5. Click the Export button to export the publication as HTML.

**A Short Rant About InDesign and HTML**

InDesign is *not* a good tool for building Web pages. It's not even a good tool for starting Web pages that will later be edited in an HTML editor like Dreamweaver or GoLive. No page layout program is. Sure, InDesign can convert TIFF files to JPEGs and GIFs, but you'll get much more control and quality if you perform these conversions in Photoshop.

The best that can be said is that InDesign's HTML export feature can be a somewhat helpful first step toward repurposing your content for the Web. However, if you really need to repurpose a lot of content (like for a magazine or newspaper), then XML is a much better—though somewhat more complex—solution (see "Form and Function: XML," later in this chapter).

**Documents**

The options in this panel control the structure of the exported HTML document. The basic choice here is whether you want your document pages (assuming there are more than one) saved as a single HTML file or in multiple files.

**Single HTML Document.** To export all of the pages in the publication into a single (long, scrolling column) HTML file, choose A Single HTML Document from the Export As pop-up menu. If you choose this option, InDesign makes more controls available.

◆ Choose the All Pages option when you want to include the entire document in the HTML file.

◆ You can enter a page range in the Ranges field to export specific pages. When you enter a page range, you can use commas to indicate noncontiguous pages and dashes to indicate ranges, for example: "1, 3, 5-12, 14."

◆ InDesign automatically fills in the File Name field with the file name you typed in the Export dialog box, but you can change it if you want. (Hey, it's not often you get a second chance.)

◆ Enter a title for the HTML page (or pages) in the Title field—this determines the text your browser displays in the title bar of the window containing the file.

**Multiple HTML Documents.** To export each page as a separate HTML file, choose Multiple HTML Documents. When you do this, InDesign displays the Multiple HTML Options section—a list of the pages in the publication.

◆ To export a page, turn on the checkbox to the left of the page name. If you have a lot of pages and you only want to specify certain pages, you might find it faster to switch to A Single HTML Document, type in your pages in the Range field, then switch back to Multiple HTML Documents (the checkboxes reflect the ranges you typed).

◆ To set an export file name (and file path, in Windows) for the HTML file, select the page from the list and type the file name in the Filename field.

◆ To set a title for the HTML file, enter the title in the Title field. When you open the page, your Web browser displays the title in its title bar.

**View HTML Using.** If you want InDesign to open the HTML file (or the first HTML file in the list, in the case of multiple files) in a Web browser after exporting, then turn on the View HTML Using option and select a browser from the pop-up menu. If you're going to import your HTML into an HTML editor like GoLive or Dreamweaver, select Other from this pop-up menu, and then choose the editor here. Or just leave this option turned off to export without any subsequent action.

**Formatting**   The controls in the Formatting panel give you some (a little—we're not promising much) control over the appearance of text and graphics in the exported HTML file.

**Text Override Color.** The color you choose here changes the color of the text in the HTML file to the color you specify. The pop-up menu displays a list of colors matching some of the colors in the standard color lookup table in today's browsers (see the discussion of "Web-safe colors" in Chapter 10, "Color"), or you can define a color by double-clicking the color swatch to the left of the pop-up menu. This is especially helpful when your document includes colored text (like white on black) that you don't want on the Web page.

**Maintain Non-Standard Text.** HTML—through cascading style sheets—*does* support a lot of text formatting: typeface, text size, color, underlining, strikethrough, leading, paragraph alignment, indents, and space before and after. However, InDesign supports all sorts of text formatting that HTML does not: ligatures, small caps, drop caps, kerning, tracking, baseline shift, and so on. You can also do stuff to text that HTML can't handle, like rotate it, convert it to outlines, or apply a gradient. The Maintain Non-Standard Text pop-up menu controls what happens to that non-standard text.

When you choose Appearance from the Maintain Non-Standard Text pop-up menu, InDesign looks for deviant text formatting (it ignores some "minor deviant behavior," such as kerning, tracking, and baseline shift), and if it finds any, it converts *the entire text frame* to a GIF image. (Yes, you heard that right, a GIF.) And, to add insult to injury, it does a *really* poor job of the conversion. The result (at least at the time of this writing) is so bad as to be entirely useless.

To remove the "non-standard" formatting (in the HTML file, not in the InDesign file), choose Editability from this pop-up menu instead. This, clearly, is the sensible choice most of the time.

**Background.** Use the controls in the Background section of the Formatting panel to define the background of the HTML file or files you're creating. You can choose to set the background to a color, or to an image. To apply a background color, choose the color from the Color pop-up menu (the pop-up menu displays a limited list of Web-safe colors) or double-click the color swatch to the right of the pop-up menu to display a system color picker. Turn on the Image option and click the Choose button to locate and select an image file. The image you select will be tiled vertically and horizontally in the background of the HTML pages you export.

**Layout**  What do you want InDesign to do with your document's page geometry (where text and graphics actually sit on the page)? The Layout panel controls whether the HTML file looks like your original page or ignores the page geometry entirely.

**Positioning.** If you choose Best (CSS-1) from the Positioning pop-up menu, InDesign includes absolute positioning controls (using cascading style sheets) in the exported HTML file. That means a block of text in the upper right corner of your InDesign page will appear in the upper right corner of the Web browser window (as long as the HTML is opened in a browser that supports CSS commands, and most do these days). If you do this, there's a better chance of your

HTML pages resembling the InDesign pages they're based on. If you choose None, InDesign leaves out the positioning controls, so your content is laid out linearly (in a long column).

**InDesign Margins.** Choose Maintain if you want to write the margins of your InDesign publication into the HTML file(s) you're exporting, or choose None to use the browser's default margins.

**Navigation Bar.** Choose the Top, Bottom, or Both option to place a simple navigational link at the specified position on the page. To omit the navigational links, choose None. Of course, this only works when you're exporting multiple pages as individual files.

**Graphics**   You've probably used TIFF and EPS (or perhaps native Photoshop and Illustrator) files in your InDesign document, but graphics on the Web should be GIF or JPEG. InDesign can convert your images to GIF or JPEG files on the fly when it exports the HTML. Unfortunately, you have very little control over this conversion; as we said earlier, we'd much rather use Photoshop's Save for Web feature. Nevertheless, if you do want InDesign to convert your images, pay attention to the options in the Graphics panel of the HTML Export dialog box.

**Save Images As.** Choose the image file format you want to use to export the images.

◆ Choose Automatic to have InDesign export RGB, CMYK, and grayscale bitmap images (such as TIFF) as JPEG and export vector artwork, indexed color images, and any images using transparency or clipping paths as GIF.

◆ Choose JPEG or GIF to force InDesign to export your graphics using one format or another.

◆ Images already in a format supported by Web browsers (JPEG, GIF, PNG) and having a resolution of 72 pixels per inch are not converted during export (unless they're embedded—see below).

◆ JPEG, GIF, and PNG whose resolutions are anything other than 72 pixels per inch will be exported in the corresponding format at that resolution—which can mean that JPEG images get compressed again. This is a bad thing, so either make sure the resolution of your JPEG graphics is 72 pixels per inch or choose GIF from the Save Images As pop-up menu (if your publication contains JPEG images at higher or lower resolutions).

◆ Embedded images (i.e., images stored inside the publication) are always converted, regardless of their resolution or format.

**Use Images Sub-Folder.** Turn this option on when you want to create a folder named "images" inside the folder to which you're exporting. InDesign will export any images on the page range you've selected to this folder. When this option is off, InDesign stores the images in the same folder as the HTML file.

**GIF Settings.** The options in this section control the way InDesign exports GIF images.

◆ **Palette.** GIF images can have no more than 256 colors. The collection of these colors is called the image's *palette*. You can choose a color palette from the Palette pop-up menu.

   ◆ **Adaptive (No Dither).** Choose the Adaptive palette to create a color palette based on a sampling of the colors in the image. Because of the limited number of colors that can be used in a GIF palette, programs that export GIF typically use dithering to simulate a larger number of colors. When you choose the Adaptive palette, InDesign does not use dithering, which means the appearance of the exported images can differ significantly from the original images (typically, the images get more pixelated, especially around the edges). Use the Adaptive palette when you're exporting line art (monochrome bitmap images) or images containing fewer than 256 colors.

   ◆ **Web.** Choose the Web palette to export images using the "Web safe" color palette (see "Swatch Libraries," in Chapter 10, "Color"). As you might expect, this can create considerable changes in the appearance of the images in your publication (though the extent of the change depends on the content of the images).

   ◆ **Exact.** When you export an image in the GIF format using the Exact color palette, InDesign attempts to create a palette containing all of the color values used in the image. If the image contains more than 256 colors (or the value you entered in the Color Depth field—see below), InDesign displays a warning message.

   ◆ **System.** Choose System to use the system's default color palette to export the GIF image. Use this option only if you created the graphics using the system color palette, and if you do not plan to distribute the HTML file widely (i.e., to other platforms or other video systems).

◆ **Color Depth.** Sets the maximum number of colors used in the color palettes (see above) of the exported GIF images. Usually, the fewer the colors, the smaller the file size. You can almost always get away with 64 colors or fewer.

◆ **Interlace.** When you turn on the Interlace option, a browser opening the HTML file will first display a low resolution version of the GIF and will add more detail to the image as additional image information is downloaded. When you turn this option off, the browser waits to display the GIF image until all of the image data has been downloaded.

**JPEG Settings.** The options in this section control the way InDesign exports JPEG images.

◆ **Image Quality.** The options on the Image Quality pop-up menu control the amount of compression applied to exported JPEG images. Low applies the most compression and produces the smallest image file (and the lowest quality); Maximum retains image quality but produces larger files.

◆ **Format Method.** Choose Progressive to make the JPEG images display in increasing detail as image data are downloaded by the browser; choose Baseline to make the browser wait until all of the image data has been downloaded before displaying the JPEG.

**Options**

The Options panel of the Export HTML dialog box contains only one setting: the Encoding pop-up menu. The Encoding setting determines how InDesign writes special characters (like fractions, foreign language characters, and so on) in the HTML. You've got five options here: Unicode (UTF-8), Western (ISO-8859-1), Japanese (Shift-JIS), Japanese (ISO-2022-JP), Japanese (EUC-JP). Unless you're using Japanese or have some important reason to change it, you can probably leave Encoding set to Unicode (UTF-8).

# Exporting SVG

Here's a file format you may not have heard about before, but we wager you'll hear more about it as time goes on: SVG (Scalable Vector Graphics). It's a vector-based file format that combines much of the power of the PostScript page-description language with the brevity of PDF (Portable Document Format), and is written using the standards of XML (eXtensible Markup Lanugage), and CSS (Cascading Style Sheets).

SVG is probably best known as an up-and-coming alternative to the Flash (.swf) format for Web graphics. True, SVG will likely be most used on the Web, but because it's built in XML, the format is useful for all sorts of things. XML can be manipulated much more flexibly than Flash, PostScript, or PDF. For example, you can open SVG files in a text editor to edit them, easily mix them with HTML codes, or search for text within them using standard search engines—none of these are easy to do with other formats.

In order to view SVG files, you have to have a program capable of reading SVG, or an SVG plug-in that works with a Web browser. An SVG plug-in comes free from Adobe (one was probably installed on your system with InDesign or any other Adobe product) or other sources. Note that SVG is *not* an Adobe file format; it's an international standard written by a number of different companies, including Quark, Microsoft, and others.

To export SVG files from InDesign (you can only export them; InDesign can't import SVG yet), select SVG from the Formats pop-up menu in the Export dialog box (or the Save as Type pop-up menu in Windows), give the file a name, click Save, and then choose from among the various SVG options. You can also choose SVG (Compressed) from the Formats pop-up menu; this creates a non-text version (also called an SVGZ file), encoded in such a way as to be much smaller (useful for Web viewing) but less editable.

**Basic SVG Export Options**    The Export SVG dialog box has a cool little feature, which we hope to see someday in other InDesign dialog boxes: a Description field at the bottom that changes depending on what your mouse is hovering over (see Figure 7-27). The descriptions are brief but really help when you've forgotten what one of these export options does.

**Pages.** An SVG file can only describe a single page, but you can export multiple pages from your InDesign document as individual SVG files. Select All, or choose one or more pages in the Range field. For instance, "3, 5-7" exports pages three and five through seven.

**Export Selection.** If you turn on the Export Selection checkbox, InDesign only exports those items on your page that are selected (you have to have first selected one or more objects, of course). This, too, is a feature that we wish other export dialog boxes would have.

FIGURE 7-27
SVG Export Options

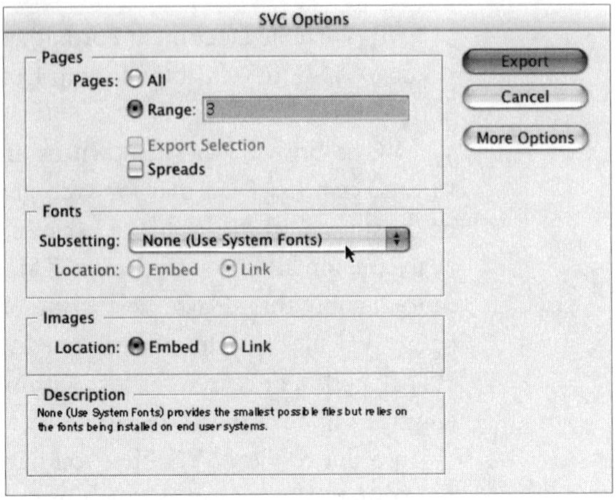

**Spreads.** The Spreads option tells InDesign to export the entire spread (like page two and three in a facing pages document) as a single SVG page. It's pretty rare that you'd want this, but it's nice that they give you the option.

**Fonts.** SVG files, like PDF files, offer the option to embed fonts, or subsets of fonts, in case your audience doesn't have the same fonts you've used. You have five choices for font embedding in the Export SVG dialog box.

◆ None (Use System Fonts). If you're sure your audience has the proper fonts, or it's okay for the fonts to change, then choose None to turn off font embedding.

◆ Only Glyphs Used. To ensure that anyone looking at this SVG file sees the fonts you specified, choose Only Glyphs Used. This embeds a subset of each font with only the characters you used, so the file size stays relatively small. However, if you later edit the SVG file and include some previously unused character, you'll be in trouble.

◆ Common English. Choosing Common English tells InDesign to embed a subset of the font with all the normal characters in english (numerals, lower case and upper case characters, common symbols). Generally, if you're going to do this, it's better to choose Common English & Glyphs Used, just in case you type something that isn't in the normal Common English subset.

◆ Common Roman. Common Roman includes a few more characters than Common English—characters that Americans would consider "foreign," such as the ç (cedilla), characters with accents, and so on. Again, Common Roman & Glyphs Used is a better choice, so other characters (like symbols) still show up properly.

◆ All Glyphs. For maximum editability of the SVG file down the road, choose All Glyphs. However, note that this makes your SVG files much larger. We certainly don't recommend this with double-byte fonts (like Japanese), each of which are several megabytes large.

The SVG specification allows for both embedding fonts and linking to external fonts. Linking to external fonts is useful when you have a bunch of SVG files that use those fonts (so you don't have to embed them in each file). If you choose the Link radio button, InDesign exports the fonts in the properly encoded XML format along with your SVG file (.cef files).

**Images.** The only thing that bulks up SVG files more than a font is a bitmapped image. If you use the same bitmapped image in multiple SVG pages, it's much more efficient to link to it (rather than embed it in the SVG file itself). You can tell InDesign whether you want to embed bitmapped images or link to them externally in the Images section of the Export SVG dialog box. If you choose Link, InDesign saves your images to disk separately, converting them to JPEG files on the fly and giving them names that relate to the SVG file. Vector artwork does not get linked separately; it's always embedded.

**More Options**    Adobe appears to be worried that you'll be scared off SVG if they show you all the options at once. We have no such concern. You can see all the controls by clicking the More Options button. True, you rarely need to actually change anything here, but it's good to know about these features, just in case (see Figure 7-28).

**Transparency Flattener.** Although the SVG specification can handle basic transparency, InDesign chooses to flatten all tranparency effects when you export an SVG file. We discuss flattening and transparency flattener styles in Chapter 11, "Printing."

**CSS Properties.** XML is a very flexible method for describing things. You can tell InDesign to write its SVG files in one of four methods—each of which is very slightly different—in the CSS Properties pop-up menu. Ultimately, the default method, Presentation Attributes, is the one you're most likely to use. If you're planning on transforming your SVG files using an XSLT (Extensible Stylesheet Language

FIGURE 7-28

**Even More SVG
Export Options**

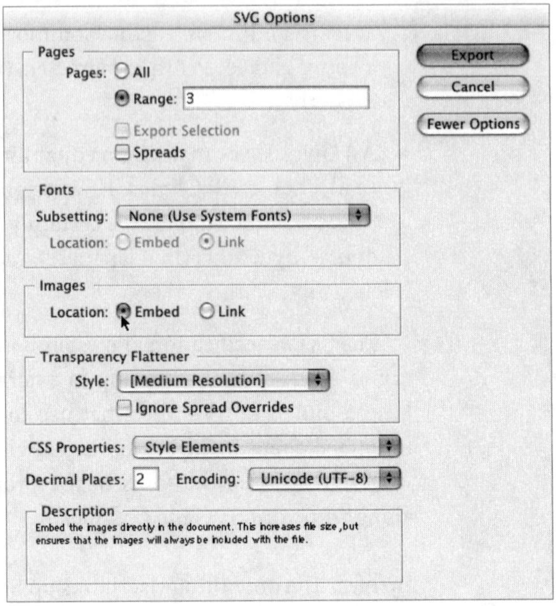

Transformation), you should choose Style Attributes, even though the file is a teensy bit larger. (We discuss XSLT later in this chapter, though the specifics of using it with SVG files is outside the purview of this book.)

If you're just trying to get the smallest, fastest SVG file you can (for Web viewing, typically), then choose Style Attributes (Entity References). The last method, Style Elements, breaks down each element into CSS elements, which can be used by multiple HTML and SVG files (if you're into hand-coding and editing files).

**Decimal Places.** How precise do you want InDesign to be in describing your objects? We think the default Decimal Places value of 3 (thousands of a point) is plenty precise enough for us. In a very complex page, you can shave a tiny bit of file size off by decreasing this to 1 or 2 decimal places.

**Encoding.** Because SVG is a regular text file, you need to tell it how to describe special characters (those outside the normal ASCII range). You've got three choices: ISO 8859-1 (ASCII), Unicode (UTF-8), and Unicode (UTF-16). The default, UTF-8, is the best choice, unless you have any double-byte characters (like Japanese or Chinese) in your file. In that case, you'd want the 16-bit version of Unicode.

# Form and Function: XML

XML stands for "Extensible Markup Language." What the heck does that mean? It's easy to be scared off—XML is usually mentioned in the same breath as SOAP, DTDs, XSL, metadata, structured content, and schema. With all of the buzzwords and jargon surrounding the topic, it's easy to lose track of something very basic: XML is simple.

XML is just a way to mark up (or tag) information in a text file. Any application that can read and write text files can be used to write XML. Like HTML, XML uses tags, such as "<h1>" to mark a piece of text. Unlike HTML, XML doesn't have a limited set of predefined tags. That's what the "extensible" part of the acronym means—that you can make up your own tags. You're not limited to <h1>, <h2>, <p>, and so on, as you are in HTML.

Given this, it would be easy to fall into the trap of thinking that XML is something like an expanded version of HTML. This isn't really the case—the two markup schemes are different in kind. HTML is all about what things *look like*; XML is about what elements *are*. The formatting of XML data—if, in fact, that data ever appears in a document—is up to you.

While we said that XML is simple (as opposed to *complex*), we never said that it couldn't be *complicated*. Indeed, the biggest problem of implementing an XML publishing workflow is figuring out the design of the XML data structures you want to work with. Users thinking about XML often end up paralyzed by the sheer number of possibilities—there are a limitless number of different ways to accomplish a given end.

In short, XML is as simple or complicated as you care to make it. Keep it simple, at least at first.

# XML Vocabulary

When we talk about XML, we'll be using a standard set of terms, for which we offer the following non-standard set of definitions.

**Tag.** A tag is a label for a piece of XML data. Tags are marked with angle brackets (also known as greater than and less than symbols), like "<title>". Tags cannot contain space characters. XML must be "well formed," which means that any "start" tag must be matched by an "end" tag. Something like this:

```
<title>Revolutionary Girl Utena</title>
```

**XML Element.** XML elements are the fundamental building blocks of an XML file. The title just shown is an example of an XML element (containing the data "Revolutionary Girl Utena"). XML elements may contain other elements, as shown in the following example.

```
<author>
    <name>Olav Martin Kvern</name>
    <address>4016 Francis Avenue North</address>
    <city>Seattle</city>
    <state>Washington</state>
    <zip>98103</zip>
</author>
```

Here, the "author" XML element contains the other elements. Each element, in turn, can contain other elements. We could easily change the structure to change the way that the name information is stored, for example.

```
<author>
    <name>
        <first>Olav</first>
        <middle>Martin</middle>
        <last>Kvern</last>
    </name>
    <address>4016 Francis Avenue North</address>
    <city>Seattle</city>
    <state>Washington</state>
    <zip>98103</zip>
</author>
```

XML elements are sometimes referred to as "nodes." Every InDesign document includes at least one XML element—by default, that's the "Root" element.

**Using Tabs.** Both of the examples above use tabs to show the nesting of elements in the file. This is not the best way to write XML for import into InDesign, as every character in the XML file is imported (unless you really do want tab characters in those locations).

**XML Attribute.** One way to attach data to an XML element is to add an element inside the element—an XML attribute is another way of doing the same thing. In general, you use attributes to add information about the element (or "metadata"). In our example, we might want to store the last time that the XML element was updated. We can do that by adding an XML attribute to the "author" tag.

```
<author last_update="11/19/02">
```

**XML Structure.** The structure of an XML document is nothing more than the way that the elements fit together. Don't let anyone tell you otherwise.

**DTD or Schema.** These are both simply descriptions of what elements can appear, and in which order, in a defined XML structure. They're not really something you need to know about, however, as InDesign doesn't use them. This annoyed David, as it meant we could not re-use his extensive research on the topic that went into one of his other titles for another page layout program (one which requires that you construct a DTD in order to use XML).

## Where Should You Work with XML?

Given that InDesign's Structure view (see below) gives you a way to add, delete, and rearrange XML elements in the XML structure of a document, you might think that you could take care of all XML creation and editing tasks without ever leaving the friendly confines of the program.

We urge you, however, not to do this. While InDesign's XML editing tools can be used in this fashion, they're really intended more for quick-and-dirty touch-up work than for industrial strength XML editing.

Instead, if you must create XML files from scratch, find yourself a good text editor (such as BBEdit or Style on the Macintosh, or Notepad in Windows). Ole prefers Marrowsoft Xselerator, which is more of an XSL (see below) debugging tool than an XML editor, or XMLSpy for XML editing. Remember, too, that if you can't find an XML editor you like, you can always use InDesign to enter and then export the text of an XML file (as we said, there's nothing magical about it—it's just a simple text file). At the moment, the system platforms (Windows and the Mac OS) are adding to their XML support. There are far more system tools for working with XML (such as the MSXML3.DLL XML parser for Windows from Microsoft) outside InDesign than there are inside InDesign.

But we expect that, most of the time, you probably won't be writing the XML yourself. Instead, you'll be getting your XML documents from some automated process, such as an Excel VBA macro, an export from FileMaker or Access, or from an InDesign document you've exported as XML.

## About XML Workflow

Before we dive into the details of working with the XML structure, we'd better explain how we think XML fits into a page layout process. As usual, we risk getting ahead of ourselves by presenting a conceptual overview before we talk about the details of the feature, but there's just no other way to do it. The following is an outline of the main approach we see for working with XML in an InDesign document.

1.  Create an InDesign document. You can use empty placeholder frames, dummy text, fixed text (that is, text you don't expect to have in the XML data file), or you can mark up an existing document.

2.  Load XML tags from an XML file. This doesn't have to be the file containing your data, and it doesn't even have to be an XML file with the same structure as you'll be using. All it needs to include are the names of the elements you expect to have in the XML data you plan to import.

    Alternatively, you can create XML tags from scratch. You'll have to remember, however, to make sure that the XML tag names match the element names for the XML files you'll be importing.

3.  Apply XML tags to frames in your template document.

4.  Map styles to XML tags using the Map Tags to Styles dialog box.

5.  Import XML into the document. When you do this, the data in your XML file (including any graphics specified in the XML structure) will appear in your layout.

When you import a new XML file and choose to replace the existing structure, InDesign will apply the formatting you've already applied. This makes this workflow particularly useful for setting up a document with a repeating publication schedule (newsletters, product data sheets, and so on). To make certain that new XML files match the layout, you might want to export the XML from the document to use as a template (see "Exporting XML Tags," later in this chapter) for the next iteration of the publication, or for use in a Web site or database.

## Inside the Structure View

It's all about structure. No matter how crazy and free-form your layout, your brain—and the brains of your audience—impose a structure on the content of your document. This is true, whether you're conscious of it or not. So don't be afraid of the word "structure" or try to deny that your documents have it. It's there. You can choose to work with it or not. Once you're out of your "denial" phase, you'll find InDesign's Structure view a powerful ally.

Using the options in the Structure view, you can create XML elements and attributes, associate elements with InDesign page items or text, rearrange XML elements, and delete XML elements (see Figure 7-29). Even if you don't work with XML you've probably already found the Structure view—it's all too easy to expand it by accident when you're trying to add a ruler guide or reposition the zero point.

**FIGURE 7-29**
**Structure View**

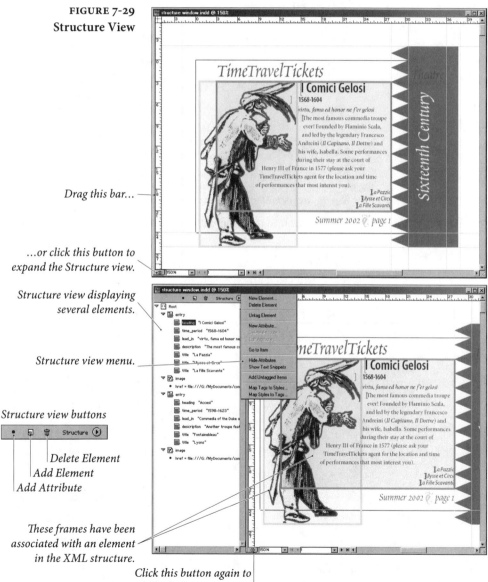

*Drag this bar...*

*...or click this button to expand the Structure view.*

*Structure view displaying several elements.*

*Structure view menu.*

*Structure view buttons*

*Delete Element*
*Add Element*
*Add Attribute*

*These frames have been associated with an element in the XML structure.*

*Click this button again to hide the Structure view.*

If you don't see the Structure view, it's because you have not installed or have turned off the relevant plug-ins. Install the plug-ins and restart InDesign. This also probably means that you're still using InDesign 2.0—go to the Adobe Web site and download version 2.0.1 or the most current update. Not only will certain bugs disappear, but you'll get the newest version of the XML-related plug-ins.

The Structure view uses icons to give you various clues about the nature of the elements in the document's XML structure, as shown in Table 7-1.

**TABLE 7-1**
**Structure View Icons**

| Icon | Representing | What it means |
|------|-------------|---------------|
| ⟨·⟩ | The Root XML element | The Root element is the base, or top-level, XML element in your XML structure. All XML elements are contained by the Root element. |
| 📄 | Story element | An InDesign story. |
| 📄 | Text element | A range of text. |
| 🖼 | Graphic element | A graphic. |
| 📄 | Unplaced text element | A text element that has not yet been associated with a page item. |
| 🖼 | Unplaced graphic element | A graphic element that has not yet been associated with a frame. |
| ⊠ | Empty element | An element associated with an empty frame. |
| • | Attribute | An attribute of an element. Attributes are always optional, and are only visible in the Structure window. |
| ▼ | Collapse/Expand | Click this icon to collapse or expand an element. If you hold down Command/Ctrl as you click this icon, InDesign will expand all elements contained within the element. |

**Showing/Hiding Text Snippets.** To see a short passage of the text associated with the XML elements, choose Show Text Snippets from the Structure view menu (see Figure 7-30). To hide text snippets, choose Hide Text Snippets.

**FIGURE 7-30**
**Showing Text Snippets**

*Without being able to see a bit of the text in each text element, it can be difficult to tell which element is which.*

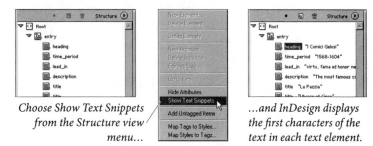

*Choose Show Text Snippets from the Structure view menu...*

*...and InDesign displays the first characters of the text in each text element.*

**Tagged Frames and Tag Markers.** Want to see which frames are associated with XML elements? Turn on the Show Tagged Frames option on the View menu (see Figure 7-31). To see text that's been associated with an XML element, choose Show Tag Markers from the View menu (see Figure 7-32).

**FIGURE 7-31**
**Viewing Frame Tags**

*Some of these frames must be tagged, right? How can you tell?*

*Choose Show Tagged Frames from the View menu...*

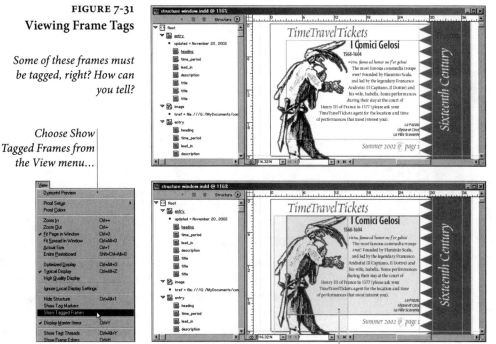

*...and InDesign highlights tagged frames with the tag color.*

**FIGURE 7-32**
**Viewing Tag Markers**

*Some of this text must
be tagged, right?
How can you tell?*

*Choose Show Tag
Markers from the
View menu...*

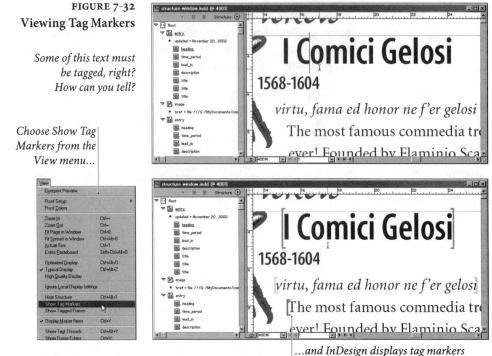

*...and InDesign displays tag markers
(brackets in the tag color) around text
associated with an XML element.*

**Adding XML Elements**    To add an element to the XML structure, select the element you want to contain the new element, then choose New Element from the Context menu (or click the New Element button). Select a tag in the Select Tag for Element dialog box, and InDesign adds a new element inside the element you selected (see Figure 7-33).

**Changing XML
Element Data**    When you add an XML element using the Structure view, it's natural to assume that you can somehow enter the data for the element in that window. You can't. We know this, because we've clicked on the element in every imaginable way trying to do it. Remember: the data for an XML element in InDesign is stored in the page item or text object that the element is associated with. The only case in which you can have element data that's not associated with a frame on your page is when you've imported XML and have not yet assigned an element to a page item, or when you've deleted the object the element was originally associated with.

To change the data in an XML structure, simply edit the text or the frame that the element is associated with.

**FIGURE 7-33**
**Adding an**
**XML Element**

*Click the New Element
button. If you want to add
the element to an element
other than the Root element,
select an element first.*

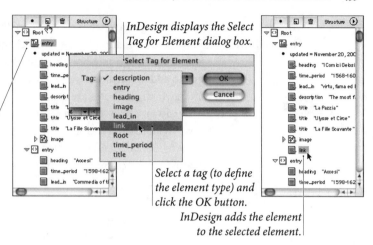

*InDesign displays the Select
Tag for Element dialog box.*

*Select a tag (to define
the element type) and
click the OK button.*

*InDesign adds the element
to the selected element.*

**Duplicating**
**XML Elements**

To duplicate an XML element (and any elements it contains), select the element in the Structure view and copy the element. Select another XML element (such as the Root element) and paste. InDesign pastes the copied element into the selected element.

**Moving XML Elements**

To move an element in the XML structure (including all of the elements it contains), simply drag the element up or down in the Structure view (see Figure 7-34). To move the element inside another element (and thereby change the hierarchy of elements), drag the element inside another element.

**FIGURE 7-34**
**Moving an**
**XML Element**

*You can move elements in
the XML structure without
changing their parent
element, or you can change
the parent element by
dragging an element into
another element. We'll do
the latter in this example.*

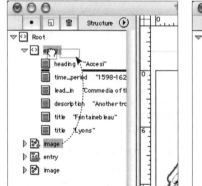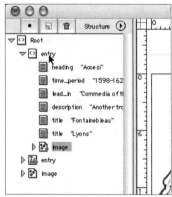

*Select the element and drag it up or
down in the Structure view. In this
example, we'll drag the element into
another element.*

*Stop dragging, and InDesign moves
the element in the XML structure.*

**Deleting**
**XML Elements**

To delete an element in the XML structure, select the element and choose Delete Element from the Context menu (or click the Delete Element button).

**Working with
XML Attributes**

XML attributes are what's called "metadata"—they're information about the information in the XML element they're associated with. You can't really do much with attributes in InDesign, but you might want to add an attribute if the XML is destined to appear in a situation in which attributes are necessary.

To add an attribute to an element, select the element and choose New Attribute from the Structure view menu. InDesign displays the New Attribute dialog box. Enter a name (like XML element names, attribute names cannot contain spaces) and value for the attributes, then click OK to save the attribute (see Figure 7-35).

To change an attribute, double-click the attribute. InDesign displays the Edit Attribute dialog box. Change the name or text of the attribute and click the OK button.

To delete an attribute, select the attribute and choose Delete Attribute from the Structure view menu.

**FIGURE 7-35
Adding an Attribute to
an XML Element**

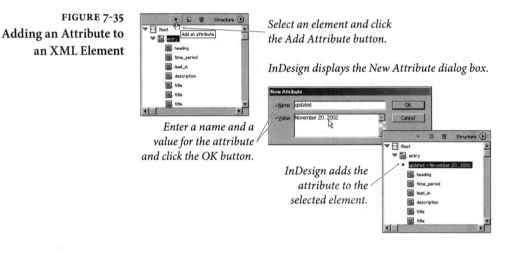

Select an element and click the Add Attribute button.

InDesign displays the New Attribute dialog box.

Enter a name and a value for the attribute and click the OK button.

InDesign adds the attribute to the selected element.

## XML Tags and the Tags Palette

XML tags provide the connection between the general name of an XML element and a specific instance of that element in the XML structure. It's important to understand that the XML tag and the XML element are different things. Associating a tag with a frame or a text object adds an instance of the element type to the structure, but the tag itself has nothing to do with the structure.

The Tags palette is the key to applying and managing XML tags in InDesign (see Figure 7-36).

FIGURE 7-36
**Tags Palette**

*When you select a tagged item, InDesign activates the Retag button.*

*Click the Untag button to remove a tag from a tagged object.*

*When you select an untagged item, InDesign activates the Add Tag button.*

*Tag colors give you a way of telling which tags are associated with which objects.*

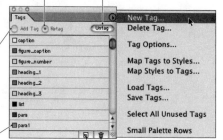

*Double-click any tag to edit its name or tag color.*

*Click the Delete Tag button to delete the selected tag or tags.*

*Click the New Tag button to add a tag.*

**Creating an XML Tag**

To create an XML tag, follow these steps (see Figure 7-37).

1. Display the Tags palette, if it's not already visible (choose Tags from the Window menu).

2. Click the New Tag button at the bottom of the palette (or choose New Tag from the Tags palette menu). InDesign creates a new tag.

3. Enter a name for the tag. You can do this by typing into the name field in the Tags palette. To change the color assigned to the tag, double-click the tag. InDesign opens the Tag Options dialog box. Choose a new color from the Color pop-up menu. Choose Other to display a color picker to define the color.

4. If you did not go to the Tag Options dialog box to change the color, press Enter. If you did, click the OK button to close the dialog box. InDesign adds the tag to the list of tags in the Tags palette.

To Delete an XML tag, select the tag and choose Delete Tag from the Tags palette menu. When you delete a tag, InDesign displays the Delete Tag dialog box, which asks you which other tag you'd like to apply to the element.

**Loading XML Tags**

To load tags from an XML file, follow these steps.

1. Choose Load Tags from the Tags palette menu. InDesign displays the Open dialog box.

FIGURE 7-37
**Adding a New Tag**

Click the New
Tag button.

InDesign creates
a new tag.

Enter a name
for the tag.

Alternatively, you can
select the tag and choose
Tag Options to edit the
name and/or color in the
Tag Options dialog box.

2.  Select an XML file and click the OK button. InDesign loads the
    element names from the XML file and creates a tag correspond-
    ing to each name.

**Exporting XML Tags**    To save tags to an XML file, follow these steps.

1.  Choose Save Tags from the Tags palette menu. InDesign displays
    the Save Tags as XML dialog box.

2.  Enter a name for the file and click the Save button. InDesign
    writes the tags to an XML file.

# Tagging Objects

You use the Tags palette to manage XML tags, and to apply tags to
frames and text. To apply a tag, select something—a frame or a range
of text—and click a tag in the Tags palette (see Figure 7-38). If the
object you're tagging is not contained by an object associated with
an XML element, InDesign will ask you which element you want to
associate with the selection. When you apply a tag, InDesign creates
an element in the XML structure. Alternatively, you can choose Tag
Text or Tag Page Item from the Context menu to apply a tag to the
selection (see Figure 7-39). You can also tag objects by simply dragging them into the Structure view (see Figure  7-40).

**FIGURE 7-38
Tagging Frames
and Text**

Select a frame.

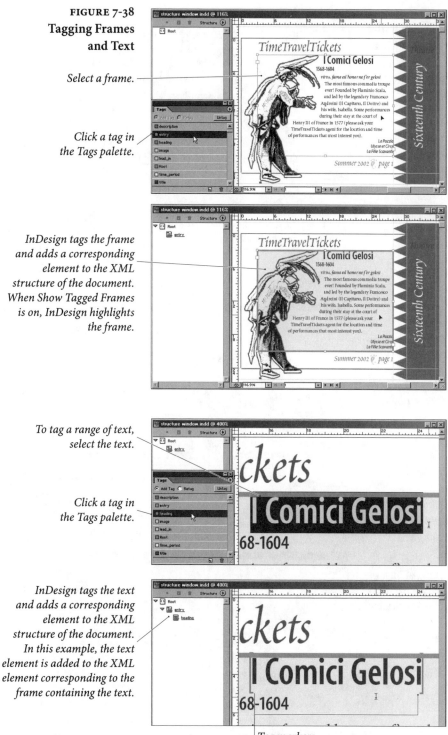

Click a tag in
the Tags palette.

InDesign tags the frame
and adds a corresponding
element to the XML
structure of the document.
When Show Tagged Frames
is on, InDesign highlights
the frame.

To tag a range of text,
select the text.

Click a tag in
the Tags palette.

InDesign tags the text
and adds a corresponding
element to the XML
structure of the document.
In this example, the text
element is added to the XML
element corresponding to the
frame containing the text.

Tag markers

**FIGURE 7-39**
**Tagging a Frame Using the Context Menu**

*You can use the Context menu to apply tags to frames and text (when you have text selected, the Context menu option will read "Tag Text").*

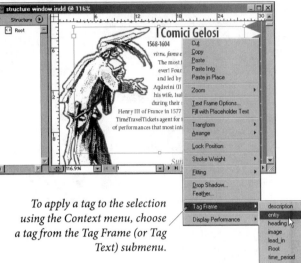

*To apply a tag to the selection using the Context menu, choose a tag from the Tag Frame (or Tag Text) submenu.*

**FIGURE 7-40**
**Tagging a Frame Using Drag and Drop**

*Drag objects out of your layout and drop them in the Structure view.*

*InDesign asks which tag you want to apply to the new XML element. Select a tag...*

*...and InDesign tags the objects and creates a new XML element.*

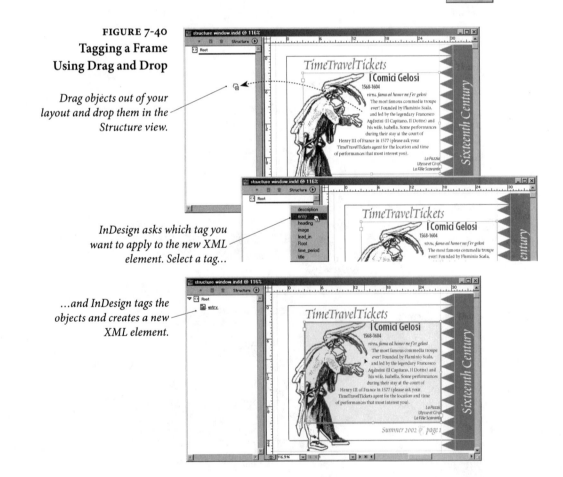

You've probably noticed the Add Tag and Retag options at the top of the Tags palette—what do they do? They answer a question: What should InDesign do when you've selected text that's already tagged and you click a tag in the Tags palette? When the Add Tag option is on, clicking a tag assigns the tag to the selected text. When Retag is active, InDesign switches the tag from the current tag to the tag you clicked.

To remove a tag from an object, select the corresponding element in the Structure view and then click the Untag button in the Tags palette.

**Mapping XML Tags to Paragraph Styles**

You've got an XML structure and a set of XML tags, and a document full of text. The task of tagging each paragraph with a specific XML tag is daunting—or is it? Not if you've used paragraph styles. If you've used paragraph styles, you can "map" those styles to XML tags, and automate the whole process.

To map XML tags to paragraph styles, follow these steps (see Figure 7-41).

1. Choose Map Tags to Styles from the Tags palette menu. The program displays the Map Tags to Styles dialog box.

2. For each XML tag, you can select a corresponding paragraph style. You don't have to map each style to a tab, and you can map multiple paragraph styles to a single XML tag. To automatically map tags to paragraph styles of the same name, click the Map By Name button. This mapping is case sensitive—the paragraph style names "Body_Text" and "body_text" will be mapped to the different XML tags. Note, also, that tag names cannot contain spaces or punctuation (so you might want to avoid using those characters in your style names).

3. When you've created as many tag-to-style correspondences as you want, click the OK button. InDesign applies the specified paragraph style to all paragraphs tagged with the corresponding XML tag.

**Mapping Paragraph Styles to XML Tags**

You've formatted all of the text in your InDesign document using paragraph styles, and you've imported or created a set of XML tags. Since you've already told InDesign what all of the paragraphs are (by way of the paragraph styles), shouldn't you be able to do so with the document's XML structure? You can, by following the steps below (see Figure 7-42).

**FIGURE 7-41**

**Mapping XML Tags to Paragraph Styles**

*You've imported XML, and you've tagged frames and text objects. So why does your text look so...unformatted? It's because you haven't created a "mapping" between the XML tags and the paragraph styles in the document.*

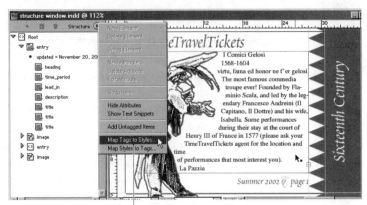

*To do that, choose Map Tags to Styles from the Structure view menu.*

*InDesign displays the Map Tags to Styles dialog box.*

*For each tag you want to associate with a style, choose a style name from the pop-up menus in the Paragraph Style list.*

*If the tags and paragraph styles have the same names, you can click the Map By Name button to have InDesign do most of the work for you.*

*Once you've set up the mapping, click the OK button to apply the styles to the tagged paragraphs.*

1. Select the Map Styles to Tags option from the Tags palette menu. InDesign displays the Map Styles to Tags dialog box.

2. Select an XML element for each paragraph style for which you want to establish a mapping. If some or all of your XML tag names are the same as the names of your paragraph styles, you can click the Map By Name button to automatically match tags and styles with the same names (this matching is case sensitive).

**FIGURE 7-42**

**Mapping Paragraph Styles to XML Tags**

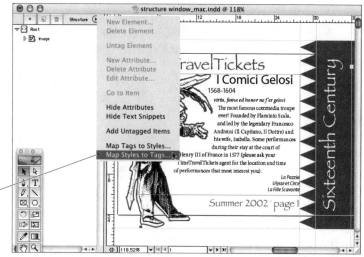

*All of the paragraphs in your document have been tagged with paragraph styles. Isn't there some easy way to add all of the text to the XML structure?*

*Select Map Styles to Tags from the Structure view menu.*

*InDesign displays the Map Styles to Tags dialog box.*

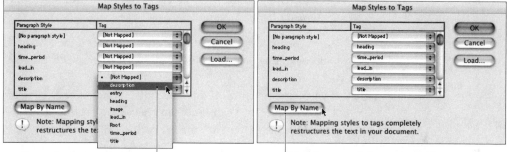

*For each paragraph style you want to add, select a tag from the pop-up menus in the Tag list.*

*If you've named the tags using the same names as the paragraph styles, you can click the Map By Name button and save a lot of time. (Hint: This is very much worth doing.)*

*Once you've finished creating a mapping, click the OK button. InDesign adds elements to the XML structure of the document based on the mapping.*

3. When you've created as many style-to-tag correspondences as you want, click the OK button. InDesign creates an XML element for all paragraphs tagged with the styles you've specified.

# Importing XML

To import XML into the structure of an InDesign document, follow these steps (see Figure 7-43).

1. Choose Import XML from the File menu. InDesign displays the Import XML dialog box.

2. Locate and select an XML file to import.

3. Click the Open button. InDesign adds the XML structure to the document

When you import XML for the first time, the incoming XML data will appear in any page items that have been tagged with the Root XML element.

If you're importing XML into a document that already contains an XML structure, you can choose to replace the existing structure, or append the incoming XML to the existing structure.

**Replacing XML**
To replace an XML structure with elements from another XML file, follow these steps (see Figure 7-44).

1. If you want to replace any element other than the Root element, select an element in the Structure view.

2. Choose Import XML from the File menu. InDesign displays the Import XML dialog box.

3. Turn on the Replace Content option. If you want to replace the selected element, turn on the Import Into Selected Element option.

4. Click the Open button, and InDesign replaces the XML elements with the elements in the XML file.

**Exporting XML**
Once you've created an XML structure in an InDesign document, you can export structure to an XML file. This is a good thing, because you can then use the exported XML file as a template for future files.

**FIGURE 7-43**
**Importing XML**

*Here's a document containing untagged frames and static text. To import XML, choose Import XML from the File menu.*

*InDesign displays the Import XML dialog box. Locate and select an XML file, then click the Open button to import the file.*

*Turn on the Replace Content option to replace existing XML elements.*

*Choose Append Content to append the elements in the XML file to the structure.*

*Turn on Import Into Selected Element to import the elements into the selected element.*

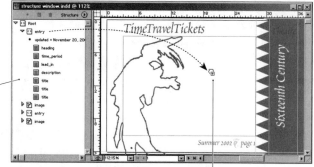

*InDesign adds the elements from the XML file to the document structure.*

*To apply an element to a frame, drag the element over the frame and release the mouse button.*

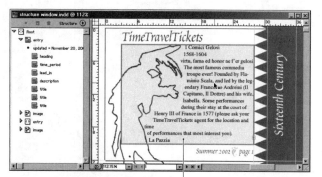

*InDesign adds the XML element content to the frame.*

FIGURE 7-44
**Replacing XML**

*Select an element.*

*Choose Import XML from the
File menu. InDesign displays
the Import XML dialog box.*

*Locate and select an XML file.*

*Turn on the Replace
Content option.*

*Turn on the Import Into
Selected Element option.*

*Click the Choose (Open in
Windows) button, and
InDesign replaces the
existing elements with the
corresponding elements from
the imported XML file.*

To export XML, follow these steps (see Figure 7-45).

1. If you want to export a selected element (and all of the elements it contains), select the XML element you want to export in the Structure view.

2. Choose Export from the File menu. InDesign displays the Export dialog box.

**FIGURE 7-45**
**Exporting XML**

To export XML, choose
Export from the File menu.

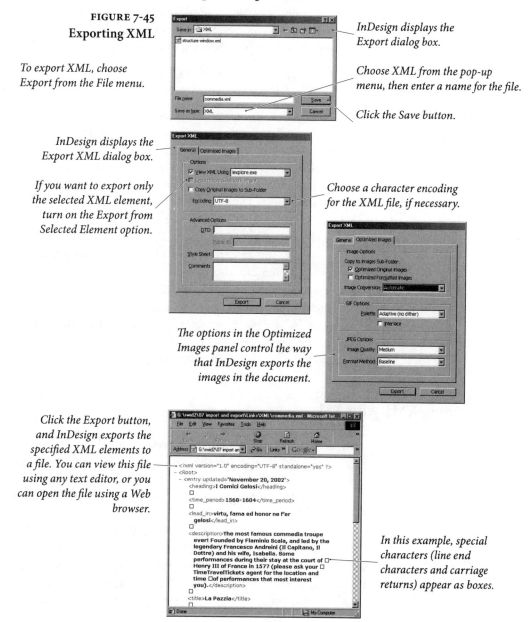

InDesign displays the
Export dialog box.

Choose XML from the pop-up
menu, then enter a name for the file.

Click the Save button.

InDesign displays the
Export XML dialog box.

If you want to export only
the selected XML element,
turn on the Export from
Selected Element option.

Choose a character encoding
for the XML file, if necessary.

The options in the Optimized
Images panel control the way
that InDesign exports the
images in the document.

Click the Export button,
and InDesign exports the
specified XML elements to
a file. You can view this file
using any text editor, or you
can open the file using a Web
browser.

In this example, special
characters (line end
characters and carriage
returns) appear as boxes.

3. Choose XML from the Format pop-up menu and enter a name for the XML file.

4. Click the Save button. InDesign displays the Export XML dialog box.

5. Select an encoding for your exported XML document from the Encoding pop-up menu. If you want, you can choose to view the XML after exporting (and the browser you want to use for that purpose). If you want to export the selected element (if any), turn on the Export from Selected Element option.

6. Click the Export button to export the XML file.

**Exporting Structure Tags to PDF**

Acrobat 5 PDF documents (PDF version 1.4 and above) can include eBook structure data. In essence, these are a defined set of XML tags that have a specific meaning to Acrobat.

The easiest way to tag the elements in your document with these tags is to choose the Add Untagged Items option from the Structure view menu. When you do this, InDesign automatically applies a tag named "Story" to untagged text frames and applies the tag "Figure" to untagged imported graphics.

If you prefer, you can create tags with these names and apply them manually. You can also use the tag name "Artifact" to mark page items you want to omit when the PDF is viewed on small-screen devices (telephones, handheld organizers, and so on).

After you've applied these tags, turn on the Include eBook Tags option as you export PDF. The PDF will then be set up to reflow when displayed by the Acrobat Reader software.

# Transforming XML with XSL

Putting all of your data into XML presents a problem—how the heck do you get it into a form that people can look at it? InDesign is certainly one answer, but there's another, and that's XSL. XSL, or Extensible Stylesheet Language, exists to transform XML into other formats.

Once upon a time, there was only one Web browser (Mosaic), which ran on a single type of device (a computer). HTML did a reasonably good job of displaying data (Web pages) in that browser on that device. But the Web grew. These days, we have multiple browsers (Netscape Navigator, Internet Explorer, Opera) running on multiple platforms (telephones, Palm OS devices, Windows, the Mac OS, television sets). An HTML format that works well for one of these viewing environments probably won't work for the others. So Web site developers faced a problem: how could they avoid writing and maintaining multiple versions of their HTML pages?

The answer lies in the combination of XML and XSL. When you use XSL, you can store the data that makes up your Web pages as XML and transform it into HTML appropriate for viewing on whatever device and browser happens to be connecting to your Web site. If you do this, you need to write and maintain the XSL templates, but the templates change far less frequently than your Web site's content.

XSL is made up of two main parts: XSL Transformations (or XSLT), which comprise the transformation language itself and XML Path Language (or XPath), a system for locating data in an XML structure.

At this point, you're probably scratching your head and wondering just exactly what a language for transforming XML into HTML has to do with InDesign. It's this: XSL can transform XML into *any* text format, including plain text, PDF, PostScript, HTML, other forms of XML, and, our favorite, InDesign tagged text.

The only trouble is that there's just no way we can cover XSL in this book. Ole's favorite reference work on the topic is more than twice the length of this title (in spite of using much smaller type). Why, then, have we brought up the topic? Mainly to get you thinking about it. People usually think of XSL as a tool for creating HTML for Web pages, and wouldn't tend to think it applicable to page layout.

Why use XSL to transform XML before placing it in an InDesign document? Well, that depends on your workflow. If you need to import lots of tabular data from your XML files, converting to tagged text first can speed things up, because tables imported from XML appear in InDesign's default table formatting. This usually means that you'll have to select and reformat each table—a task that can be time-consuming, to say the least. If you transform the same XML file to tagged text using XSL, you can specify every attribute of the tables in the file.

To further encourage you to "think outside the box," we'll have to give you an example. Rather than simply dump the XML, XSL and output (InDesign tagged text and HTML) on these pages, we will post them on the Peachpit Web page devoted to this book. We hope you'll make the trip to download the examples and check them out, because the combination of InDesign, XML, and XSL is a very powerful and useful way to work with publications.

# The Best of All Possible Worlds

Can you get there from here? When you're working with InDesign, you can almost always export or save files in a form you can use in another program, and you can usually produce files in other programs you can import or open using InDesign. There are definitely bumps in the road—sometimes, you've got to go through an intermediate program to convert files from one format to another (particularly if the files came from another type of computer).

Someday, we'll have a more complete, universal, and sophisticated file format for exchanging publications. PDF is getting very close to being that format, and it's certainly making steps in the right direction. When the great day arrives, we'll be able to take page layouts from InDesign to FreeHand to QuarkXPress to Photoshop, using each program for what it's best at without losing any formatting along the way.

And the streets will be paved with gold, mounted beggars will spend the day ducking winged pigs, and the Seattle Mariners will win the World Series.

# Long Documents

## CHAPTER 8

What constitutes a long document? Some die-hard technical writers insist that if it isn't over a thousand pages, it's not a long document. Others maintain that any document longer than five or ten pages qualifies. We think that anyone building a book, a magazine, a newspaper, a journal, or a catalog—no matter how many pages—is dealing with long documents.

There are three features in InDesign that relate directly to publishing long documents.

◆ **Books.** You can tie multiple documents together into a book, which appears in the form of a palette in InDesign. From here, you can control page numbering, printing, and such document attributes as styles and colors.

◆ **Table of Contents.** If you use paragraph styles regularly, you're going to love the Table of Contents feature, which can build a table of contents (or a list of figures, or a table of advertisers, or any number of other things) quickly and easily.

◆ **Indexes.** Building an index is a hardship we wouldn't wish on anyone (we've done enough of them ourselves), but InDesign's indexing features go a long way in helping make it bearable. We'll also discuss how indexing can be used in catalogs and other documents.

Again, even if you don't currently create what you'd consider to be "long documents," take a gander at these features; they're flexible enough to be used in documents as small as even a few pages.

# Books

Even though you can make a document thousands of pages long, you should keep your InDesign documents small. Working with smaller documents is generally faster and more efficient, especially when more than one person is working on the project at the same time. The question is: if you break up your larger project into small documents, how can you ensure style consistency and proper page numbering among them? The answer is InDesign's Book feature.

Most people think of a book as a collection of chapters bound together to act like a single document. InDesign takes this concept one step farther. In InDesign, a book is a collection of any InDesign documents on your disk or network that are loosely connected with each other via the Book palette. In other words, just because it's called a "book" doesn't mean it's not relevant for magazines, catalogs, or any other set of documents.

There are four benefits to using the Book palette.

◆ It's a good way to organize your documents, and it's faster to open them from within InDesign than using the Open dialog box.

◆ If you use automatic page numbering in your document (see "Numbering Pages" in Chapter 2, "Page Layout"), InDesign manages the page numbering throughout the entire book, so if the first document ends on page 20, the second document starts on page 21, and so on (assuming that the numbering and section options settings in that document agree, of course).

◆ You can print one or more documents from the Book palette using the same Print dialog box settings without even having the documents open. Similarly, you can export the whole book as a single PDF file.

◆ The Book palette's Synchronize feature helps you ensure that styles, colors, and other settings are consistent among the documents.

The more documents in your project, and the more pages, styles, colors, and whatnot in each document, the more useful the Book feature will be to you. Even if you're juggling two or three documents, it may be worth the minor inconvenience it takes to build a book.

**Building a Book**

To build a new book, select Book from the New submenu of the File menu. At this point, you need to tell the program where to save your new book file (you can put it anywhere you want on your hard drive or network, but you should be able to find it easily because you'll be using it a lot).

Book files appear in InDesign as palettes. As soon as you've saved your new book, InDesign displays a new, empty Book palette (see Figure 8-1).

FIGURE 8-1
**Creating a New Book**

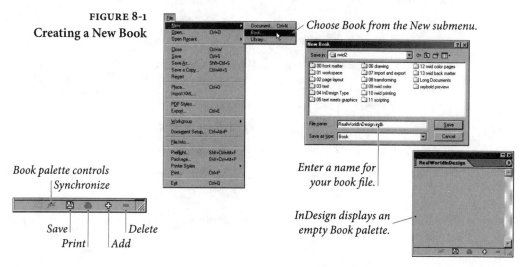

*Choose Book from the New submenu.*

*Enter a name for your book file.*

*InDesign displays an empty Book palette.*

Book palette controls
Synchronize

Save
Print   Add
Delete

**Adding and Removing Book Documents**

To add a document to your Book palette, click the Add Document button in the palette and choose a document from your disk or network (see Figure 8-2). If no documents on the palette are selected when you add a new document, the new document is added at the end of the list. If you select a document first, the new document is added after the selected document. You can also drag files directly from Windows Explorer or the Macintosh Finder windows into a book palette; this is often the fastest way to get a folder-full of files into a book.

If you accidentally insert a document in the wrong place in a Book palette, don't worry—you can move a document up and down on the list. To do this, select the book document and drag it to a new location in the list (see Figure 8-3).

Although Adobe's documentation points out that you can copy a document from one book palette to another by Option-dragging/ Alt-dragging, we don't recommend this. Having the same document in more than one book can cause pagination problems and general confusion.

To remove a document from a Book palette, select the document and click the Remove Document button. If you want to remove more than one document, select the documents (use Shift for contiguous selections, or Command/Ctrl for discontinuous selections on the list) and then click the Remove Document button (see Figure 8-4). Note that deleting a document from the Book palette does *not* delete the file from disk; it simply removes it from the list.

**FIGURE 8-2**
**Adding a**
**Book Document**

*Click the Add Document button.*

*Select the file you want to add.*

*InDesign adds the document to the book.*

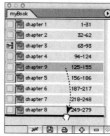

**FIGURE 8-3**
**Moving a**
**Book Document**

*To change the position of a book document in the book list, select the document...*

*...and drag it up or down in the list.*

*Drop the document, and InDesign moves the document to a new position in the list.*

**FIGURE 8-4**
**Deleting a**
**Book Document**

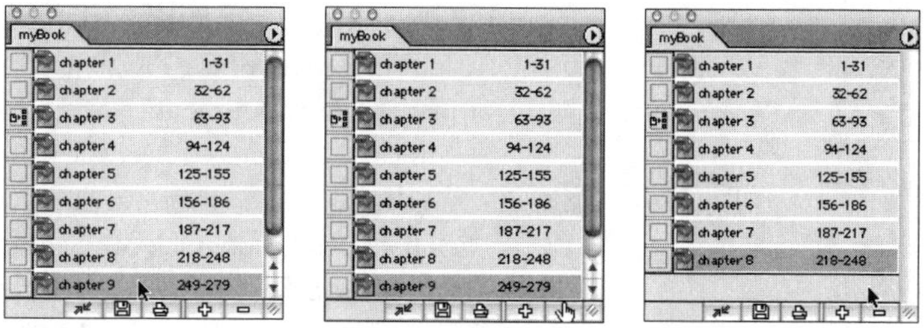

*To remove a book document, select the document...*

*...and click the Remove Document button.*

*InDesign removes the document from the book.*

**Using a Book As a Navigational Tool**

Because there is only a very loose connection among the various documents in the Book palette, you could use this feature as an informal database of documents. For instance, let's say you've built 15 different product data sheets and three small brochures for a client, and the client is forever updating them. Even though the documents may each use very different colors, styles, and so on, you could put them all on one Book palette and save this collection under the client's name. Next time the client calls for a quick fix, you don't have to go searching for a document; just open the Book palette and double-click the document name to open it.

**Editing Your Book**

Once you've added documents to your Book palette, you can go about your regular routine of editing and preparing the documents. There are, as usual, a few things you should keep in mind.

♦ Whenever possible, you should open your book's documents while the Book palette is open. (The fastest way to open a document is to double-click the document name in the Book palette.) When you open and modify a document while the palette is not open, the palette isn't smart enough to update itself (see "File

Status," below). If InDesign can't find your document (perhaps it's on a server that is not mounted), it'll ask you where it is.

◆ If you want to print more than one document in a book at a time, you should use the Print button on the Book palette (see "Printing and Exporting Books," later in this section).

◆ You should use caution when using the Numbering and Section Options feature to renumber any of the documents in the book (see "Page Numbering and Sections," later in this section). In general, if you're going to use automatic page numbering, you should let the Book palette handle your page numbering for you.

◆ We use the Save As feature to track revisions of our documents. Each time we use Save As, we change the name slightly ("mydocument1," "mydocument2," and so on), so we can always go back to an earlier version if necessary. If you do this, however, note that the Book palette doesn't catch on to what you're doing; it just lists and keeps track of the original document. So every time you use Save As, you have to select the original file and select Replace Document from the Book palette's menu.

Note that you cannot Undo or use Revert to Saved for changes in the Book palettes, so be careful what you do in these beasts. Also, the changes you make to your Book palette, including adding, removing, and reordering documents, aren't saved until you close the palette, quit InDesign, or select Save Book from the palette's menu.

**File Status**  As you work with book documents, the Book palette monitors and displays the status of each document in the book. There are five possible icons in the Status column of the palette: Available, Open, Modified, Missing, or In Use (see Figure 8-5).

◆ **Available.** The normal status of a document is Available (no icon). This means that no one has the document open for editing and that the document has not changed since the last time it was open on the computer you're using.

◆ **Open.** When you have a document open on your Macintosh or Windows system, the status of that file is listed as Open (an open book icon).

◆ **Modified.** When you or anyone else who has access to the file opens and changes a document while the Book palette is not open, the status will be listed as Modified in the Book palette (triangle icon). It's easy to change the status from Modified back

FIGURE 8-5
**Book Palette
Status Icons**

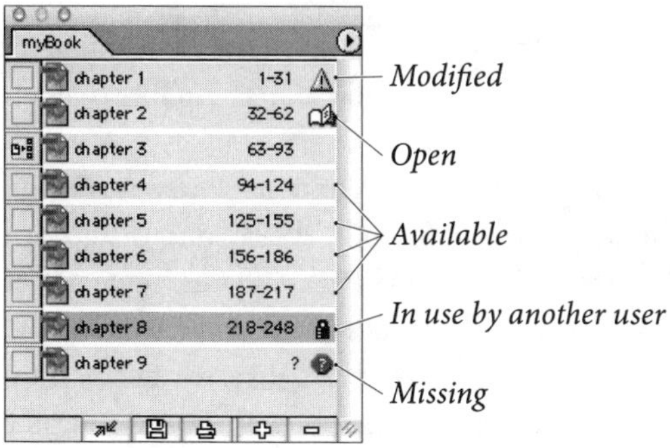

to Available: open the file while the Book palette is open, then close the document again. Or, even easier: select Repaginate from the palette's menu.

◆ **Missing.** If you move a document after adding it to the Book palette, InDesign won't be able to find it, and the status is listed as Missing (red stop sign icon). To "find" a file again, double-click the chapter name in the Book palette; InDesign displays the Replace Document dialog box in which you can tell it where the document now resides.

◆ **In Use.** If someone else on your network opens one of the documents in your book via the Book palette, the Status field of the Book palette lists that chapter as in use (padlock icon).

It's important to pay attention to the Status column readings, because documents must be either Available or Open in order to synchronize, print, or renumber properly.

**Books and Networks**   People are increasingly working on projects in groups rather than individually. Adobe anticipated this, and if you put your book file and documents on a server, more than one person can open the palette at the same time. (Only one person can open an InDesign document at a time, however.) While this isn't nearly as powerful as a full-blown document management system, it's certainly useful if a group of people have to work on different documents in the book at the same time.

The thing is, we don't like working on documents when they're on a server. It just makes us nervous. Plus, it's really slow. Instead, we prefer to copy the file to our local hard drive, edit it at our leisure, and then return the file to the server when we're done with it.

There are two problems with this. First, the Book palette doesn't update properly. Second, other people on your network might not realize that you've got the "live" file, so make it clear to them: hide the document on the server, or put it in another folder called "work in progress" or something like that.

## Synchronizing Your Book Documents

The more documents you're working with, the more likely it is that one or more of them contain settings inconsistent with the others in the book. Perhaps you decided to change a style definition in one document out of 20, and then forgot to change it in the other 19. Or perhaps your art director decided to change a Pantone color in a document and you now need to update the color in all of the other documents in the book.

Fortunately, the Synchronize Book button on the Book palette lets you ensure that all styles and color settings are consistent throughout the documents in a book. Here's how it works.

## The Master Document

One document on the Book palette is always marked as the *master document* (by default, it's the first document you add to the palette; InDesign's documentation refers to this document as the *style source document*). The master document—which has a cryptic little icon to the left of it—is the document to which all the other documents will be synchronized. That means that if you add a new color to the master document and click the Synchronize Book button, the color will be added to all of the other documents in the book. If you add a new color to a document that is not the master document, the color won't be added when you synchronize the documents.

You can always change which document is the master document. To do that, click in the left column of the Book palette next to the document you want to set as the master document.

## Synchronize

In order to synchronize your book documents, you must first select which files you want to synchronize in the Book palette; remember that you can Shift-click to select contiguous documents or Command-click/Ctrl-click to select discontinuous documents. Or, if you want to synchronize all the files, make sure that no documents (or all documents) are selected in the palette.

- ◆ A style or color swatch that is defined in the master document but not in another document gets added to that other document.

- ◆ If a setting is named the same in both the master document and another document, the definition for that setting in the master document overrides the one in the non-master document.

- ◆ If a setting is not defined in the master document but exists in some other document, it's left alone. (This means you can have "local" settings that exist in one document that don't have to be copied into all the others.)

♦ By selecting Synchronize Options in the Book palette's menu, you can choose which settings will be synchronized among the documents (see Figure 8-6). However, if the master document contains table of contents styles (which we talk about later in this chapter) and you turn on the TOC Styles checkbox in the Synchronize Options dialog box, all the character and paragraph styles are synchronized, even if you've turned off the Character Styles and Paragraph Styles checkboxes.

Note that synchronizing a document can be a time-consuming process—the more documents and the more settings there are, the longer it takes.

**FIGURE 8-6**
**Synchronization Options**

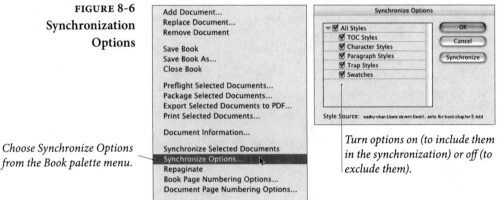

*Choose Synchronize Options from the Book palette menu.*

*Turn options on (to include them in the synchronization) or off (to exclude them).*

**Page Numbering and Sections**

Perhaps the most helpful aspect of the Book feature is that it keeps track of your page numbering for you and updates the page numbers when you add pages to or delete them from a document, or if you add a new document between two other documents in a book. Of course, this only works if you've placed automatic page numbers on your document pages (see "Numbering Pages" in Chapter 2, "Page Layout").

Let's say you've got one 16-page document in your Book palette already. When you add another document, InDesign automatically sets its first page number of the new document to 17 (provided you had not already specified the first page as a section start in the Numbering and Section Options dialog box). If you later open the first document and add two pages, InDesign automatically renumbers the second document—the next time you open it, you'll see that it starts on page 19.

If, on the other hand, you use the Numbering and Section Options dialog box (you can jump to this feature quickly by double-clicking on the page numbers in the Book palette) to create a section start, the Book palette respects that. Any subsequent documents in the Book palette continue the page numbering from where the previous document's page numbering left off.

If you don't use automatic page numbers, or you have manually specified page numbers for each document in your book, you will probably tire of watching InDesign repaginate your book. Fortunately, you can turn this feature off by selecting Book Page Numbering Options from the Book palette's menu, and unchecking Automatic Pagination (see Figure 8-7).

FIGURE 8-7
**Book Page
Numbering
Options**

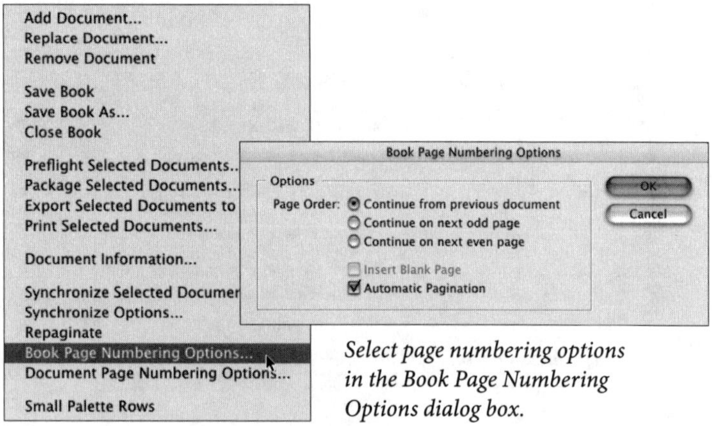

*Choose Book Page
Numbering Options from
the Book palette menu.*

*Select page numbering options
in the Book Page Numbering
Options dialog box.*

**Odd Versus Even
Page Numbers**

When chapter 2 ends on page 45, what page number does InDesign assign to the first page of chapter 3? If you're in the book business, you probably want chapter 3 to start on page 47, because it's a right-hand page (though at least one of the authors would edit and/or adjust the layout to avoid a blank left-hand page). Catalog and magazine publishers would want the third file to begin on page 46, even though it's a left-hand page. You can specify what you want InDesign to do by choosing Book Page Numbering Options from the Book palette's menu. You've got three choices: Continue from Previous Document, Continue on Next Odd Page, and Continue on Next Even Page.

When you turn on the Insert blank page option, InDesign adds a page to fill any gaps between chapters. For example, if chapter 2 ends on page 45 and you turn on the Continue on Next Odd Page, then InDesign adds a blank page at the end of chapter 2. This page is truly blank—it's not based on any master page. If you want a running head on that page, you'll have to apply the master page yourself. (By the way, David once almost drove himself mad trying to figure out why he couldn't delete the last page from a document. The answer, of course, was that he had forgotten this feature was on.)

**Printing and Exporting Books**

Even though we cover printing documents in Chapter 11, "Printing," we should take this opportunity to mention a few things that are specific to printing books.

First, each chapter in a book must be listed as Open, Available, or Modified on the Book palette in order for the document to print. This is because InDesign invisibly opens each document at print time (you don't see the document open on screen, but it does).

Second, if you only want certain documents in a book to print, select them in the Book palette. Remember that you can select contiguous documents on the list by holding down the Shift key, and discontinuous documents with Command/Ctrl. If no documents are selected, then they'll all print. When you're ready to print, click the Print Book button in the Book palette or select Print Book (or Print Selected Documents) from the palette's menu. The settings you choose in the Print dialog box apply to every document in the book.

Similarly, you can export your book as an Acrobat PDF file by choosing Export Book to PDF (or Export Selected Documents to PDF) from the palette's menu.

# Table of Contents

Don't get fooled into thinking the Table of Contents feature (under the Layout menu) is only for making book tables of contents. This feature lets you build collections of paragraphs that have been tagged with specific styles. For instance, if you use even two styles when you're formatting a book—one for the chapter name and another for your first-level headings—you can build a basic table of contents by collecting all the paragraphs tagged with these two styles. But if you use paragraph styles to tag your product names, you could just as easily build an index of products for a catalog. Anything you can tag with a paragraph style, you can build into a "table of contents." (While QuarkXPress 5 can also make these kinds of lists based on character styles, InDesign currently only works with paragraph styles.)

This all depends entirely on your using styles. You should be using styles anyway—if you're not, you're working way too hard. If you don't currently use styles, refer to Chapter 4, "Type," to see why you should.

**Making a Table of Contents**

Making a table of contents (or a list of figures, or whatever) is easy, but it requires a methodical approach to the Table of Contents dialog box (see Figure 8-8).

1. If you only have one list (table of contents, list of figures, etc.) in your document, you can leave the Style pop-up menu set to [Default]. We'll cover table of contents styles later in this section.

2. Fill in a name for your list in the Title field. InDesign places this title at the beginning of the list, so you might want to type "Table of Contents" or "Advertisers" or something like that. To be honest, we usually leave this field blank and later make our own titles on the document page. If you do include a title, choose a paragraph style for it from the Style pop-up menu to the right of the Title field. (InDesign automatically adds a paragraph style called "TOC title" to your document when you open this dialog box, but you don't have to use that style if you don't want to.)

3. Choose the paragraph styles that you want included from the list on the right. You can press the Add button to add them to the list, but double-clicking the style names is faster. You can also select more than one style (by Command/Ctrl-clicking each one) and then click Add to add them all at once (in which case they're added alphabetically—if you want to rearrange the order, just click and drag the style names after adding them).

4. One by one, click each style in the Include Paragraph Styles list and choose a paragraph style for it from the Entry Style pop-up menu. This is helpful because you'd rarely want a heading from your document to appear in your table of contents in the actual Heading style; instead, you'd probably create a new style called "TOC-head" or something like that. If you want certain paragraphs to be indented on your final list, you should apply styles here that include indentation. Note that InDesign adds a paragraph style called "TOC body text" to your document when you open this dialog box, but you don't have to use it—we typically just roll our own.

5. If your document is included in a Book palette, you can choose to include the entire book in your list by turning on the Include Book Documents checkbox. We'll talk about the Replace Existing Table of Contents checkbox below.

6. Finally, when you click OK, InDesign builds the table of contents (which might take a little while, especially if you have many documents in a book). When it's done, InDesign displays the

**FIGURE 8-8**
**Creating a Table of Contents**

*Select a paragraph style from the Other Styles list and click the Add button.*

*InDesign adds the style to the Include Paragraph Styles list (the list of styles included in the table of contents).*

*Choose a paragraph style to use to format the selected table of contents style.*

*Add other paragraph styles to the list as necessary.*

*When you're ready to build your table of contents, click the OK button.*

*Unless you've chosen to replace an existing table of contents, InDesign displays a place icon. Click the place icon to place the table of contents story.*

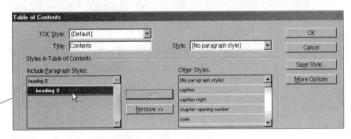

text place icon, just as if you had imported a text file (see Chapter 4, "Text," if you need to know more about placing text).

That's it! Note that InDesign captures only the first 255 characters of each paragraph when it builds a table of contents, something you should keep in mind as you think of uses for this feature (255 characters make about 40 words—more than enough for most headlines, bylines, and such).

**More Table of Contents Options**

The default Table of Contents dialog box gives you the basic controls you need for a simple table of contents, but for most lists we make we click the More Options button, which gives us more options for fine-tuning the table of contents (see Figure 8-9).

◆ **Page Number.** You may not want every entry in your table of contents to be followed by a page number. For instance, you might want page numbers after the headings, but not after the chapter titles in a book. You can control how page numbers will appear on your printed page with the Page Number pop-up menu. You've got three options for numbering: After Entry, Before Entry, and None. The first two tell InDesign to include the page number (either before or after the entry), separated from the text of the paragraph by a tab character. We typically create a character style for the page numbers and select it from the Style pop-up menu to the right of the Page Number menu. This way, all the page numbers appear the same rather than appearing in the Entry Style.

◆ **Between Entry and Number.** By default, InDesign places a tab character between the entry and the page number (whether the page number is before or after the entry). However, you can change this to some other character or characters. For instance, we usually replace the ^t character (which is code for a tab) with ^y (a right-indent tab, which always sits flush on the right margin, even if you haven't placed a tab stop). If you're planning on including dot leaders between the entries and the page numbers (which you would set up in the Tabs palette), you may want to pick a character style from the Style pop-up menu. A regular dot leader looks too much like periods in a row (which is exactly what it is), so we often make a character style of 7-point text with 500 units of tracking, then apply this style to the leader.

◆ **Sort Entries in Alphabetical Order.** If you turn on the Sort Entries in Alphabetical Order option in the Table of Contents dialog box, InDesign sorts the list in alphabetical order when you build it. Whether or not you want your final list alphabetized is up to you; you probably wouldn't want it when you build the table of contents for a book, but you might if you're creating a list of items in a catalog.

◆ **Level.** Each paragraph style you include appears with a different indent in the Include Paragraph Styles list. You can control how much indent with the Level feature. This only adjusts the display in this dialog box; it has no effect on the final list unless your list is alphabetized—in which case, the entries are alphabetized by level.

◆ **Run-in.** Some tables of contents, such as those found in academic journals, are "run-in"—that is, the headings are all in one paragraph, separated by semicolons. If you want this sort of list, turn on this option (see Figure 8-10).

◆ **Include Text on Hidden Layers.** This option is pretty self-explanatory. If you have multiple layers in your document, you can choose whether to include the text on those layers even when the layers are hidden. While it's rare that you'd turn this on, you might do so if you have made a layer that contains keywords or explanatory text that you want in the table of contents but don't want in print (see the next section).

**FIGURE 8-9**
**More Table of**
**Contents Options**

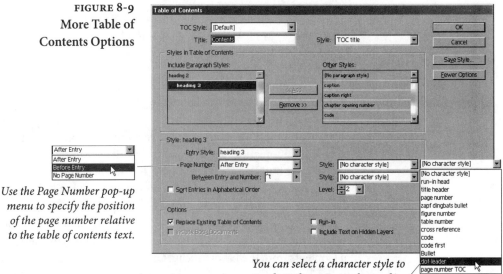

*Use the Page Number pop-up menu to specify the position of the page number relative to the table of contents text.*

*You can select a character style to apply to the page number and/or to the separator character.*

FIGURE 8-10
**The Run-in Option**

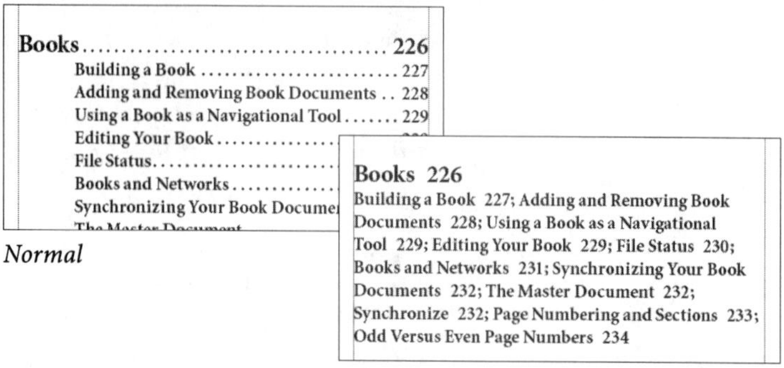

*Normal*

*Run-in*

**Using Dummy Text for Lists**

One of our favorite aspects of tables of contents is that they're document-wide rather than simply story-wide. That means that any text in any text frame can be included in a table of contents—even text in a non-printing text frame. With this in mind, you can add "tags" to items on your page that don't appear in print, but do appear in your table of contents.

One of the best examples of this is an advertiser index. You can place a text frame with an advertiser's name on top of that company's ad in your document. Set the text frame's color to None and turn on Nonprinting Object in the Attributes palette (or put the frame on a hidden layer), and it's almost as though this were a "non-object"—the text won't print, and it won't affect the ad underneath. But if that advertiser's name is tagged with a style, you can include it on a list of advertisers.

The same trick applies to building a list of pictures in a catalog, or for any other instance where what you want on the list doesn't actually appear on the page.

**Building and Rebuilding Tables of Contents**

There is nothing magic about the text or page numbers in your table of contents—they're just regular text and numbers. That means if you update the document on which the list is based (like adding pages or changing the text), the entries and page numbers in the table of contents don't automatically update, and you will have to rebuild it. We find that we build and rebuild a table of contents several times for each document or book. It isn't that we're having so much fun with the feature—it's that we make mistakes.

To update a table of contents, use the Selection tool or Text tool to select the text frame containing the list, then choose Update Table of Contents from the Layout menu. Or, if you want to make a change to the Table of Contents dialog box settings, you can choose Table of Contents from the Layout menu, make the changes, turn on the Replace Existing Table of Contents checkbox, and click OK.

**Table of Contents Styles**

Everything we've said about table of contents so far is based on the idea that you have only one of these in your document. However, you can define lots of different table of contents styles in a single document—one for headings, one for figures, one for bylines, and so on. The easiest way to do this is to build various table of contents styles, which are simply saved collections of settings. Once you set up the Table of Contents dialog box just the way you want it, you can click the Save Style button to save this setup as a style (see Figure 8-11). Later, you can reload those settings by choosing your style from the TOC Style pop-up menu at the top of the dialog box.

A second way to build a "style" is to select Table of Contents Styles from the Layout menu and click New. You get a nearly identical dialog box, but when you click OK your settings are saved for use later. You can also use the Table of Contents Styles feature to delete and edit styles, or load them from other InDesign documents.

Note that if you save your table of contents style after building a table of contents in your document, InDesign isn't smart enough to match your built list to the style name. That means you can't use the Replace Existing Table of Contents feature. Instead, you'll have to delete the already-built list and replace it with a new one.

**FIGURE 8-11**
**Creating a Table of Contents Style**

*To save the current settings of the Table of Contents dialog box as a table of contents style, click the Save Style button.*

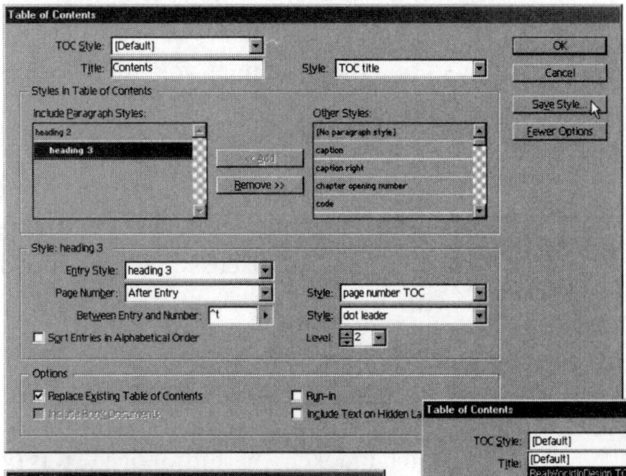

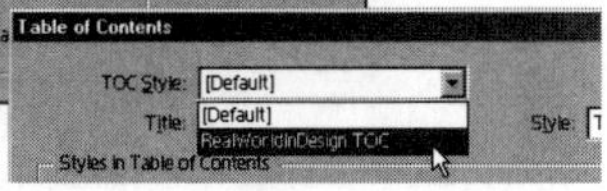

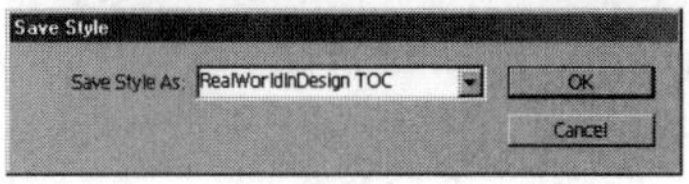

*Enter a name for the style in the Save Style dialog box and click the OK button.*

*InDesign adds the style to the list of available styles.*

# Indexes (Or Indices)

Sitting down and indexing a book is—in our experience—the most painful, horrible, mind-numbing activity you could ever wish on your worst enemy. And yet, where this is the kind of task that a computer should be great at, it's actually impossible for a computer to do a good job of indexing a book by itself. A good index requires careful thought, an understanding of the subject matter, and an ability to keep the whole project in your head at all times. In short, it requires *comprehension*—a quality computer software, at this early stage of its evolution, lacks. Plus, until recently, it required a large stack of note cards, highlighter pens, and Post-It notes.

Fortunately, InDesign has a built-in indexing feature, which, while it won't make the index for you, does remove the note card and highlighter requirements.

Some people ask us, "Why can't a computer build an index? InDesign should just give me a list of all the words in my document and what page they're on." Unfortunately, this is not an index; it's a concordance. A concordance records the location of *words*, an index records the location of *ideas*. There are times when a concordance can be useful, especially in catalogs. In those cases, you might want to use a plug-in like Sonar Bookends, which can build concordances automatically and very quickly. But in general, if you're looking for an index, you're going to have to do it manually with InDesign's indexing features.

You can index a document at any time in the production cycle, but it's almost always best to wait until the text has become fixed— until no text in the document will be deleted, copied, cut, pasted, and so on. The reason: as you edit the text, you may accidentally delete index markers.

The Index palette (choose Index from the Window menu) lets you add either single words or whole phrases to the index, and it displays a list of currently indexed words and phrases (see Figure 8-12). First we're going to discuss how to add, edit, and remove index entries with the Index palette. Then we'll explore how to collect all the tagged entries and build a finished index on your document pages.

**A Note to the Author Contemplating Self-Indexing.** Hire a professional indexer. The author of a text is *the worst person* for the job. You simply know the material too well (or, if you don't, why in the world did you write the book?) to create a useful index. A professional indexer will read and understand your text, and will create an index that opens it up to a wider range of possible readers than you ever could. It's what they do.

**Adding a New First-Level Index Entry**

There's very little that is automatic about building an index. Again, it's not difficult, but you have to be methodical about it. Here are the steps you should go through for each new index entry. (Note that we always differentiate between a new index entry or topic and a new reference

**FIGURE 8-12**

**The Index Palette**

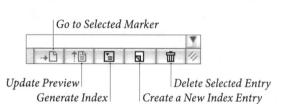

*Index palette in Reference mode.*        *Index palette in Topic mode.*

Go to Selected Marker

Update Preview          Delete Selected Entry
    Generate Index        Create a New Index Entry

to an index entry. For example, "Pigs" might be a new entry for page 34, but when it appears again on page 59, it would simply be a new reference to your already added index entry—see "Adding a New Reference to an Entry," later in this section.)

To add an index entry, follow these steps (see Figure 8-13).

1. If the word or phrase you want indexed appears on the page, select it and click the New Entry button at the bottom of the Index palette, or select New Page Reference from the palette's menu (there's no keystroke for this, but you can assign one with the Keyboard Shortcuts feature). If the index entry isn't found on the page, just place the text cursor anywhere in the text related to the topic and press the New Entry button. For example, you may be discussing cows on your document page, but you want to index the word under the phrase "Farm animals." In this case, you would simply insert the cursor in the text and click New Entry.

2. In the New Page Reference dialog box, edit the entry under the Topic Levels heading, if needed. Whatever you type here will be what shows up in the index. Since we're focusing on first-level entries right now, you can just skip over the other two Topic Levels fields. (We'll discuss the finer points of second-level entries in "Adding a New Second-level Index Entry," later.)

FIGURE 8-13
**Adding an Index Entry**

*In this example, we've gotten lucky: the text we want to add to the index is present on the page.*

> I knew only too well. I raised my head and saw Hamaïouna, glorious, transfigured, and seated on a luminous cloud.
>
> "Wretched Barkiarokh," she said, "thou hast nothing more to fear from the Wand of Remorse. Instead of profiting by its strokes, thou hast sought to evade them. Henceforward, the rod that will beat upon thy heart is the Rod of Despair, and thy heart, hardened as it is, will be broken and crushed throughout every moment of a frightful eternity."

*Select the text...*

*...and click the New Entry button.*

*If necessary, edit the text in the Topic Levels field (or fields). For this example, we don't need to edit the text.*

*Choose an indexing range from the Type pop-up menu.*

*Turn on the Number Style Override option if you want to apply a specific character style to the page number in the index (we don't, so we left the option unchecked).*

*If our index contained more than this single index entry, we'd see a list of other topics in this field.*

*InDesign adds the page reference to the index.*

3.  Index entries always appear in alphabetical order. However, occasionally you may not want your index entry to appear where it would normally be alphabetized. For instance, the famous "17-Mile Drive" would ordinarily be placed at the beginning of the index, before the "A"s. You can place it along with other words that begin with "S" by typing "Seventeen" in the first Sort As field of the New Page Reference dialog box. You'll probably leave this field blank most of the time.

4.  The Number Style Override feature is yet one more control that you will ignore most of the time. Let's say you want the page numbers that refer to an illustration (rather than to just text on the page) to appear bold in the final index. You can build a character style to define how you want the page numbers to appear and—when you're indexing that illustration—you can turn on the Number Style Override checkbox and choose that character style from the pop-up menu.

5.  If your treatise on pigs and goats spans six pages of your document, you don't want to have to make a separate index entry for each and every page. Instead, you can specify one index entry and choose a range of pages in the Type pop-up menu. There are nine page-range choices in the Type pop-up menu, plus six more cross-reference choices. We cover those last six in "Cross References," later in the chapter.

    ◆   Current page, the default page range, indexes the page that includes the index marker.

    ◆   To Next Style Change tells InDesign to index from the paragraph containing the index marker to the next paragraph style change.

    ◆   To Next Use of Style is the option we use most often. This indexes from the paragraph containing the index marker to the next use of a specific style, which you can choose in a pop-up menu next to the Type pop-up menu. For instance, let's say you've got a book about farm animals where each animal's heading is tagged with a paragraph style called "Heading-A." You could select the heading "Rabbit" and set the Type to "To Next Use of Style." Then you could choose Heading-A from the pop-up menu of styles. If the "Horse" section starts three pages after the Rabbit section, the page range in the index will span three pages; if it starts 14 pages after, the page range will span 14 pages, and so on.

        Unfortunately, there is currently a bug in InDesign so that if you put the index entry in the Rabbit heading, the program only indexes from Rabbit to Rabbit (in other words, that one page). The workaround is to put the index entry marker in the paragraph following the heading.

    ◆   To End of Story tells InDesign to index from the paragraph containing the index marker to the end of the current story. Note that InDesign assumes that the story falls on every page. If your story starts on page 1, then skips to page 9, and ends on page 12, the index will display page 1–12, ignoring the skipped pages.

◆ To End of Document is the same as To End of Story, but it spans from the paragraph containing the index marker to the end of the file. In the example of the farm animals chapter, you could index the entire chapter by placing the cursor anywhere on the first page of the chapter, specifying an index entry labeled "Farm animals," and choosing To End Of Document.

◆ To End of Section is the same as the previous two options, but the page range extends from the index marker to the end of the current section (see Chapter 2, "Page Layout").

◆ For Next # of Paragraphs works when you know exactly how many paragraphs you want indexed. Unfortunately, currently InDesign only spans to the beginning of the final paragraph, rather than the end of the paragraph—a problem if that paragraph spans two pages.

◆ For Next # of Pages indexes from the index entry marker for the number of pages you specify.

◆ Suppress Page Range. Some first-level index entries don't include page numbers at all. For instance, in the book we've been discussing, "Animals" is too broad a topic to include page numbers (every page in the book would be indexed). So you might specify Suppress Page Range for this one entry, and then follow it with 15 second-level entries, each with appropriate page numbers listed. (Again, we discuss second-level entries later.)

6. After you've chosen the scope from the Type menu, click OK and InDesign adds the index entry to the Index palette, along with the page range. If the indexed text sits on a master page or on the pasteboard, the master page label or "PB" shows up in the Index palette, but these items will not actually appear in the final index.

If you're happy with the default settings of the New Page Reference dialog box, you can streamline this process significantly by selecting a word or phrase on your page and typing Ctrl-Alt-U/Command-Option-U, which adds the selection to the index, skipping the dialog box. Or, if the selection is a proper name, press Ctrl-Shift-F8/Command-Shift-F8, which indexes the selection based on the last word (so James Joyce would show up as Joyce, James). You can control how words in a proper name show up by placing nonbreaking spaces between them; for example, if you put a non-breaking space between "King" and "Jr.," then this keyboard shortcut will index the name under King instead of Jr.

**Add and Add All**    You may already have spotted the Add and Add All buttons in the New Page Reference dialog box. Clicking the Add button adds the index entry but leaves the dialog box open so that you can add more entries. This is very helpful—you frequently need to index the same text using more than one entry.

Add All searches throughout your document for every instance of the index entry and adds it automatically to the index. If you select the word "Bee" on your page and then click Add All, InDesign places another identical index entry at each instance of the word "Bee" in your file. (If you have turned on the Book option in the Index palette, InDesign also adds all instances of the index entry in other documents, too—as long as those documents are open.)

When you press Add All, InDesign uses the same scope (Type) settings for every instance of the entry text. Whether this is a great feature or a potential problem depends on the formatting of your index. If each instance of an indexed topic needs special attention (this one only showing up on this page, the next one using a To Next Use of Style scope, and so on), you should avoid this feature.

You also need to be careful with Add All because it only finds exact matches. That is, if you type "Cow" in the New Page Reference dialog box and click Add All, InDesign won't find "Cows" or even "cows".

**Cross-References**    As you build an index, think of all the ways that your reader might
**(X-Refs)**    look for a topic and include those words in your index. For instance, because you're familiar with your own book, you might include an index entry called "Llamas." However, another reader might look for "Cute wool-producing animals that spit." Fortunately, InDesign lets you add cross-references in your index like "Spitting animals. *See* Llamas" and "Wool 34–46. *See also* Llamas."

To add a cross-reference to your index, you go through the same steps as you would to add a normal index entry. The one difference is that you set the Type pop-up menu to one of the six cross-reference settings: See [also], See, See also, See herein, See also herein, and Custom Cross-Reference. When you select any of these, InDesign provides a text field in which you can enter the cross-referenced word or phrase. If you want your index entry to be "Koi. *See* Carp" you would type "Koi" in the first Topic Levels field, and type "Carp" in the Referenced field (see Figure 8-14).

FIGURE 8-14
**Adding a
Cross-Reference**

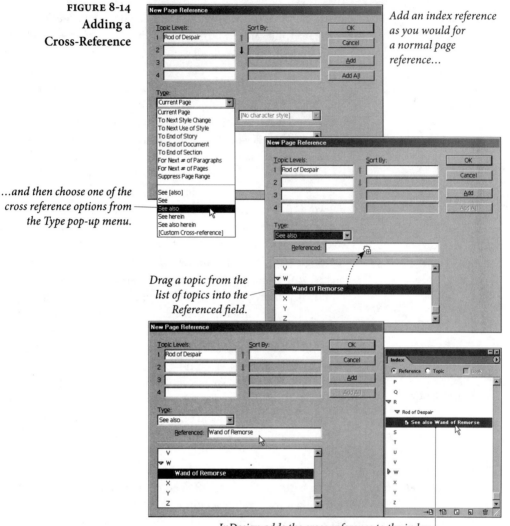

*Add an index reference
as you would for
a normal page
reference...*

*...and then choose one of the
cross reference options from
the Type pop-up menu.*

*Drag a topic from the
list of topics into the
Referenced field.*

InDesign adds the cross-reference to the index.

◆ *See* is generally used when an index entry has no page number
references, such as "Supermarket. *See* Grocery."

◆ *See also* is used when an index entry does have page references,
but you also want to refer the reader to other topics, such as
"Grocery 34–51. *See also* Farmer's Market."

◆ We like the *See [also]* option best, because it uses either See or
See also, depending on whether you've specified page references.

◆ *See herein* is a special case in which you are cross-referencing to
a second-level entry within the same entry as the cross-reference
itself, and it's used more in legal indexes than anywhere else.

◆ If you choose Custom Cross-Reference, you can type any kind of cross-reference you like, such as "Hey dude, go look at page".

Note that if you're cross-referencing to an index entry that you've already added to your index, you can find that entry in the list of entries at the bottom of the dialog box and drag it to the Referenced field. That's certainly faster (and probably more accurate) than typing the words again.

Because no page number is involved in a cross-reference, it doesn't matter where in your document you specify it (though it must be in a text frame).

Some people like putting cross-references at the end of a list of second-level index entries rather than directly after the first-level entry. InDesign won't do this for you automatically, but you can fake it by creating a dummy second-level entry (see "Adding a New Second-Level Index Entry," below) and setting its Type to a cross-reference. The dummy second-level entry should just be named with "zzz" so that it automatically falls at the end of the alphabetized list of second-level entries. Later, once you build the index onto your document pages, you will have to perform a Find/Change to remove these symbols.

**Adding a New Reference to an Entry**

Once you've got an entry on your Index palette, you can easily add more page references to it. Let's say you added the name "Farmer Jones" to your index back on page 13 of your document. Now, "Farmer Jones" appears again on page 51.

1. Place the cursor in the appropriate place in the text story. In this case, you'd probably put the cursor next to the word "Farmer" on page 51.

2. Click the entry in the Index palette. Here, you'd select "Farmer Jones."

3. Alt/Option-click the New Entry button. Make sure that the Type pop-up menu is set up according to how you want your new reference to appear, and then press OK. If you want to use the default New Page Reference dialog box settings, you can just drag the index entry on top of the New Entry button instead.

Note that while you don't necessarily have to click the entry in the Index palette in step 2 (you could just retype the entry in the New Page Reference dialog box or select it on the page), we recommend clicking because it ensures consistency. For example, if you relied on your typing ability, you might create the index entry "Chickens" and then later—meaning to type the same thing—create a new entry, "Chicken," causing two different entries to be made when you only meant to make one.

**Adding a New Second-Level Index Entry**

Now that you've specified first-level index entries, you can—if you wish—add second-level entries. As we mentioned earlier, second-level entries are subcategories of the first-level entries. For example, under the first-level index entry "Grape Varieties," you might find the second-level entries "Merlot," "Chardonnay," and "Syrah." You can make a second-level index entry just as you would make the first-level index entry, but with two added steps.

After you open the New Page Reference dialog box, click the down arrow button to move your index entry to the second Topic Level field. Then, double-click the first-level entry in the list at the bottom of the dialog box (which enters it in the first Topic Level field).

Once you've created a second-level entry, you can place a third-level entry under it. Similarly, you can put fourth-level entries under third-level entries.

**Importing Topics**

Many people prefer to index their text in Microsoft Word before placing the text in InDesign. Fortunately, InDesign can import Word's index markers, adding the index entries to the Index palette automatically. In fact, if you delete the Word file after importing it, the index topics remain in the Index palette. This is one good way to import a list of topics into the palette without having to type them manually in InDesign. Another way to import index topics is to choose Import Topics from the Index palette's menu, which lets you select any other already-indexed InDesign document.

Index entries in your palette that don't have corresponding index markers in the text won't show up in your final index. If you don't want to see these topics in your Index palette, select Hide Unused Topics in the palette's menu to them. To view the topics you've hidden, choose Show from the palette menu.

**Deleting Entries**

There are several ways to delete an entry from your index.

◆ To delete an entire entry, including all its page references, select it in the Index palette and click the Delete button. Note that this also deletes all the subcategories under it and their page references, too.

◆ To delete a single page reference, you can select it in the Index palette (click the gray triangle next to the index entry to display its page references) and click the Delete button.

◆ To remove a particular page reference in your index, delete the index marker. The marker is a zero-width character, but it is a character nevertheless. To view the character, choose Show Hidden Characters form the Type menu. To delete it, put the text cursor immediately after it (you may have to use the arrow keys to accomplish this) and press Backspace/Delete.

**Editing Entries**    We make mistakes, so it's a good thing that InDesign gives us a way to edit our flubbed index entries. When you're editing an index entry, you have to decide whether you want to edit the entry itself or a particular page reference of the entry.

Let's say that halfway through indexing your document, you realize that the index entry "Martha Washington" should have been indexed as "Washington, Martha." You can select the entry in the Index palette and choose Topic Options from the palette's menu—or even faster, you can just double-click the entry. In this case, you'd change the first Topic Level field to "Washington, Martha," and then click OK.

One of the most common entry edits is capitalizing an entry, so the folks at Adobe snuck a Capitalize feature into the Index palette's menu (see Figure 8-15). While this is nice, we wish there were a further option to change an entry to lowercase (useful for level 2 entries, which are usually set in lowercase). Maybe next version.

**Editing References**    You can also change the scope (type) or style of a particular page reference. For instance, let's say the reference to Martha Washington on page 47 should have spanned nine paragraphs, but you accidentally set it to Current Page instead. To fix this, click the gray triangle next to the index entry; this displays the page references for the entry. Double-click the page reference that corresponds to the one you want to change (in this case, you'd double-click the number 47). Go ahead and change the index entry options, and when done, press Enter.

If you actually wanted the above reference to begin on page 48 instead of page 47), you have to select the entry, cut it to the clipboard, and then paste it in the new location. Selecting entries can be difficult, so make use of the arrow keys and the Shift key.

**FIGURE 8-15**
**Capitalizing**
**Index Topics**

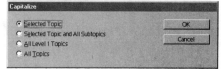

*Choose Capitalize from the Index palette menu to display the Capitalize dialog box.*

**Finding Entries**    Know you indexed "bugs" as a second-level entry, but can't remember which first-level entry it was under? Just select "Find" from the Index palette's menu to display the palette's Find field. After typing "bugs" into the field, you can click the down arrow to see the next instance of this entry in your palette. (Or click the up arrow to see the previous instance.)

**Building the Index**    You've reached the finish line—and it's finally time to place your index on a document page so you can see it in all its glory. This is the fun part, because you can just sit back, choose Generate Index from the Index menu's palette, and let InDesign do the work of collecting the index entries and page numbers for you. There is still one more dialog box you need to pay attention to: the Generate Index dialog box (see Figure 8-16).

The Generate Index dialog box presents a (somewhat bewildering) array of choices you need to make in order to get the index of your dreams. InDesign shows you a few controls by default; you can see the others by clicking More Options. Fortunately, once you make your choices in this dialog box, InDesign will remember them the next time you build an index for this document.

**FIGURE 8-16**
**Generate Index**
**Dialog Box**

*Generate Index dialog box with options hidden. Click More Options...*

*...and InDesign displays this monster. Daunting though they may be, these options give you a tremendous amount of control over the appearance of your index.*

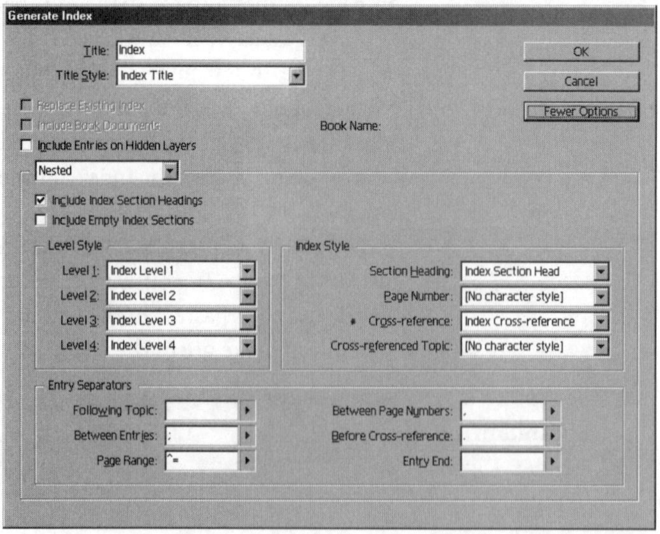

**Title.** Fill in a name for your index in the Title field. InDesign places this title at the beginning of the list, so you might want to type "Index" or "My Indexio Grandioso" or something like that. We tend to leave this field blank and later make our own titles on the document page. If you do include a title, choose a paragraph style for it from the Style pop-up menu to the right of the Title field. (InDesign automatically adds a paragraph style called "Index Title" to your document when you open this dialog box, but you don't have to use that style if you don't want to.)

**Replace Existing Index.** InDesign knows when you've already built an index in a document, and it automatically replaces that index with a new one unless you turn off the Replace Existing Index option. Probably the only time you'd turn this off would be if you wanted to compare two indexes to find differences between them.

By the way, note that when InDesign replaces one index with another, it doesn't just replace the text. It actually deletes all the index pages and then rebuilds them from scratch. So if you've spent two hours adding extra formatting to the index, or adding boxes or lines to the pages, all those additions are removed when you build the new index.

**Include Book Documents.** If your document is part of a book (see "Books," earlier in this chapter), you can choose to build an index for the book by turning on the Include Book Documents option. Note that InDesign can generate the index from all the documents even if they're not currently open, as long as they're available in the Book palette (not missing or opened by someone else on the network).

**Include Entries on Hidden Layers.** If you have multiple layers in your document, you can choose whether to include the text on those layers even when the layers are hidden. While it's rare that you'd turn this on, you might do so if you have made a layer that contains keywords or explanatory text that you want in the index but don't want in print (see "Using Dummy Text for Lists," above).

**Nested versus Run-In.** There are two primary types of index formats in the world: nested and run-in (see Figure 8-17). In a nested index, each entry occupies its own paragraph; in a run-in index, the second-level entries merge with their first-level entry to form one big paragraph. Which you choose is entirely up to you, though it should depend in part on the content of the index. Run-in indexes make no sense when you have third- or fourth-level entries. On the

FIGURE 8-17
Nested and Run-in
Index Formatting

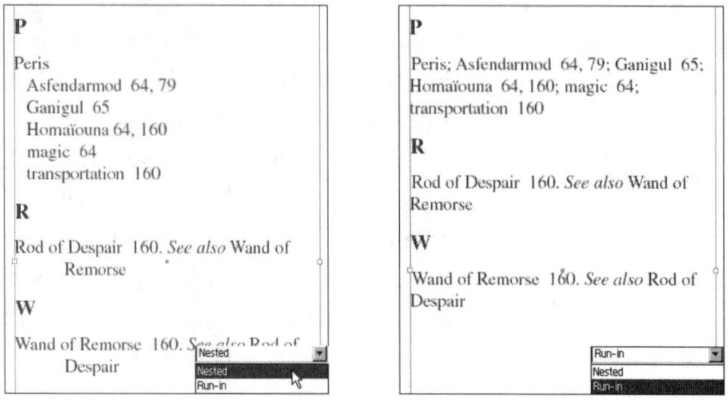

other hand, run-in indexes typically conserve space, especially when they're set in wide columns (because more than one entry fits on a single line).

**Include Index Section Headings.** In this context, "section" doesn't have anything to do with page numbering sections (which we discuss in Chapter 2, "Page Layout"). Rather, the section heads refer to index sections: "A", "B", "C", and so on. Even when you turn on Include Index Section Headings, InDesign only includes the headings for which you have made index entries. So, if you have no entries that begin with "b", the index won't include a "B" section heading. If you really want the empty sections, you can turn on the Include Empty Index Sections checkbox. We're not sure why you'd want to do that, but it's nice to know you can.

**Level Style.** The Level Styles section of the Generate Index dialog box lets you apply a paragraph style to each entry in the index. In a run-in index, there's only one kind of paragraph: the first-level entry (all the second-level entries are merged into the same paragraph). In a nested index, however, each entry level is tagged with its own paragraph style. If you want all your second-level index entries to be slightly indented from the first-level entries (you probably do), make a new style that includes indentation, and choose it from the Second Level pop-up menu (see Figure 8-18).

Once again, designing a readable index is as much an art as a science. Take some time to peruse other people's indexes, checking for details like indentation (what does a first-level entry do when it's longer than one line, for example?) and punctuation.

Note that InDesign builds styles for you called "Index Level 1", "Index Level 2", and so on. If you haven't already created your own styles, then use these and adjust their definitions in the Paragraph Styles palette later.

FIGURE 8-18
Selecting Level Styles

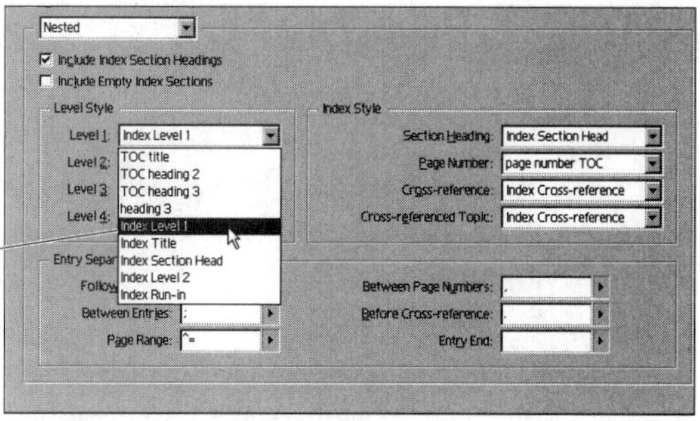

*You can use the Level Style
pop-up menus to assign
any style you've defined to a
specific index level.*

**Index Style.** One of our favorite aspects of making indexes in InDesign is the ability to apply paragraph or character styles to every index element, down to the page numbers and the cross-reference words (like "See" or "See also"). By assigning styles, you can later make global changes to the look and feel of the index by changing the style definitions. While we often apply styles in the Section Heading and Cross-reference pop-up menus, we usually leave the Page Number and Cross-referenced Topic settings alone. It all depends on the index.

**Entry Separators.** Index formatting is as varied as art directors' whims—or the whims of the indexers, which tend to be even more obscure. One of the main differences revolves around the incredibly picayune art of choosing punctuation. Do you want an en dash between numbers in a page range or a hyphen? An en dash is more appropriate, but the ends of the dash bump up against some numbers. Fortunately, you can type thin spaces on each side of the en dash in the Page Range field in the Generate Index dialog box. (Actually, we never type these characters themselves; we just select them from the menu to the right of the field.)

You can change the punctuation for Following Topic, Between Entries (which only applies in run-in indexes or where there are multiple cross-references per line), Page Range, Between Page Numbers, Before Cross-reference, and Entry End (see Figure 8-19).

FIGURE 8-19
Specifying
Entry Separators

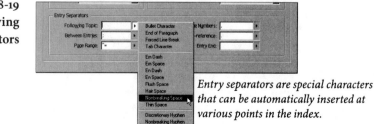

*Entry separators are special characters
that can be automatically inserted at
various points in the index.*

## Putting It Together

The Book, Table of Contents, and Indexing features in InDesign go a long way toward making the process of creating long documents more bearable. Whether you're building a magazine, a book, a journal, a catalog, or even a newsletter, we're sure you'll be able to find good use for these features. Remember that a little work up front—building styles, putting documents in a Book palette, and so on—can go a long way to saving lots of time in the long run.

## CHAPTER 9

# Transforming

In the previous chapters, we've covered the process of getting text and graphics into your InDesign publication. This chapter is all about what you can do with those elements once you've wrestled them onto your pages. The process of moving, rotating, scaling, reflecting, or shearing an object is called *transformation*.

Many of the topics in this chapter have been touched on in the preceding chapters—mainly because everything you can do in InDesign is interconnected. In the old days, software was entirely linear or modal: one had to proceed from this screen to that screen following a particular sequence of steps. These days, software is extremely nonlinear and nonmodal (that is, you can do things many different ways in many different orders), and, therefore, much harder to write about. It's enough to drive one mad! Your purchase of this book will make our time at Looney Farm that much more pleasant. Thank you.

# Transformation Basics

There are many ways to transform an object on an InDesign page or pasteboard. Select the object using the Selection tool, then:

◆ Drag one of the object's selection handles to scale the object (but not necessarily the contents of that object).

◆ Select a transformation tool from the Tools palette, set the center of transformation (if necessary), and drag the tool.

◆ Display the Transform palette and enter values in the palette field corresponding to the transformation you want to apply—or choose a preset value from the pop-up menu associated with that field.

◆ Choose one of the "preset" rotation or reflection options from the Transform palette menu.

◆ Double-click one of the transformation tools in the Toolbox to display the corresponding transform dialog box (double-click the Rotate tool, for example, to display the Rotation dialog box).

◆ Select the Free Transform tool, then apply a transformation by dragging inside the object, outside the object, or on the object's selection handles. See "Using the Free Transform Tool," later in this chapter.

◆ Scale an object by pressing keyboard shortcuts. See "Scaling an Object with the Keyboard," later in this chapter.

There's no "right" or "best" way to do transformations—you can experiment with the different methods and see which you like best. We change methods depending on the situation (and our mood).

**Setting the Center of Transformation**

When you select an object and then choose one of the transformation tools from the Tools palette, InDesign displays the center of transformation icon (it looks something like a small registration mark) on or around the object (see Figure 9-1). The initial position of the icon is determined by the point selected in the Transform palette's Proxy (by default, it's in the center).

When you scale, rotate, or shear an object, InDesign transforms the object around the Center of Transformation. To reposition the center of transformation icon, either drag it to a new position (with whatever transformation tool you have selected) or click a point on the Proxy in the Transform palette.

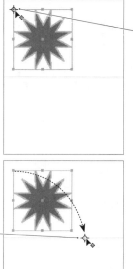

**FIGURE 9-1**
**Center of**
**Transformation**

*When you select an object and choose a transformation tool, InDesign displays the center of transformation icon.*

*When you move the cursor over the icon, InDesign changes the cursor to show that dragging will move the icon.*

*Drag the center of transformation icon to a new location, if necessary.*

*Drag the tool to transform the object. As you drag, InDesign transforms (in this example, rotates) the object around the center of transformation.*

**Transforming Line Segments and Points**

To transform a point or line segment on a path, select the path or point using the Direct Selection tool, then transform it as you would any other object (drag it, or enter values in the X and Y fields of the Transform palette, or press the Arrow keys, or display the Move dialog box, or use any of the other transformation techniques). This can produce some very interesting effects (see Figure 9-2).

You can also select the points and/or line segments of a path and then copy as you transform the object by holding down the Option/ Alt key after you start dragging or clicking the Copy button in the any of the transformation tool's dialog boxes. In this case, InDesign splits the path at the unselected points on the path. This takes a little getting used to, but might come in handy. If you want to transform line segments or points of a copy of a path, copy the path first, then apply the transformation.

**Transforming Path Contents**

When you transform a path that contains other objects (an image frame with a picture in it, for example), you can control whether the content is transformed, too. By default, dragging the handles of a frame to scale it does not scale the content, but using any of the transformation tools in the Tool palette or using the Transformation palette to alter a frame *does* scale the content.

**FIGURE 9-2**
**Transforming**
**Points, Not Paths**

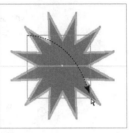

*Select some points using the Direct Selection tool.*

*In this example, the points on the inside of the star polygon are selected; the outside ones aren't.*

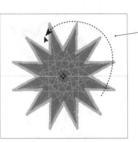

*Apply a transformation. In this example, I've rotated the selected points.*

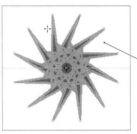

*InDesign applies the transformation to the selected points; not to the entire path.*

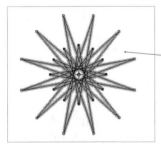

*Note: If you're transforming selected points using one of the transformation dialog boxes and click the Copy button...*

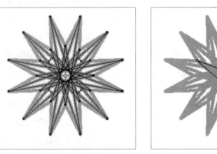

Rotate

Angle: 180°        OK

                   Cancel

Options            Copy

☑ Rotate Content   ☑ Preview

*Copy button*

*...and InDesign splits the path at the location of the unselected points.*

To transform a frame without its contents when you're scaling (or rotating or skewing) an object using the Transform palette, turn off the Transform Content option on the Transform palette menu (see Figure 9-3). You can transform a frame without its contents using the tools by first Option/Alt-clicking on the edge of the frame with the Direct Select tool—this way the frame is selected but the content is not. Or you can turn off the Transform Content checkbox in the transform tool's dialog box (double-click on the tool in the Tool palette).

FIGURE 9-3
Transforming
Path Contents

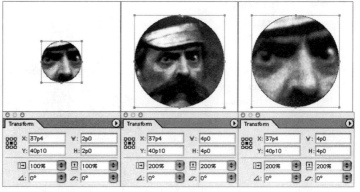

*Untransformed object*    *Object scaled with the*    *Object scaled with the*
                          *Transform Content*          *Transform Content*
                          *option turned off.*          *option turned on.*

## The Transform Palette Is Your Friend

If numbers scare you, you're going to be scared by the Transform palette. Don't give in to math anxiety—the palette is too useful to avoid. The first step in taming the Transform palette is to understand what it is these controls are called, and what they can do for you (see Figure 9-4). To display the Transform palette, press F9.

**The Proxy**    A "proxy" is something that stands in for something (or someone) else. The Proxy in the Transform palette stands in for the object or objects you've selected (see Figure 9-5). The points on the Proxy icon correspond to the selection handles InDesign displays around an object when you select it with the Selection tool (not the Direct Selection tool).

**FIGURE 9-4
Indesign's
Transform Palette**

*\*Coordinates of the point
corresponding to the point
selected on the Proxy, and
are measured relative to the
current zero point on the
ruler.*

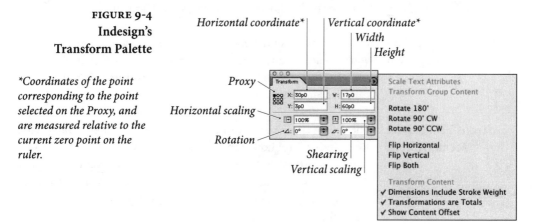

*Horizontal coordinate\**|   |*Vertical coordinate\**
                              |*Width*
                              |*Height*

*Proxy*
*Horizontal scaling*
*Rotation*

*Shearing*|
*Vertical scaling*|

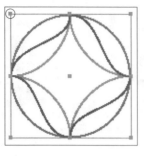

*The points you see on the Proxy correspond to the selection handles you see when you select an object.*

*The point you select on the Proxy also sets the center of transformation.*

*The point you select in the Proxy determines the content of the X and Y fields in the Transform palette—select the upper-left corner (as in this example), and you'll see the coordinates of that corner of the selection.*

When you select a point on the Proxy, you're telling InDesign that whatever changes you make in the Transform palette affect that point (the X and Y fields), or are centered around that point (the Width, Height, Horizontal Scaling, Vertical Scaling, Rotation Angle, and Shear Angle fields).

**Understanding Page Coordinates**

An InDesign page—or any other flat object—is a two-dimensional surface; a plane. You can define the position of any point on a plane using a pair of coordinates: the horizontal location (traditionally referred to as "X") and the vertical location ("Y"). The numbers you see in the X and Y fields of InDesign's Transform palette represent the horizontal and vertical distance of the selected point on the Proxy from the zero point.

As you move farther to the right of the horizontal zero point, the value in the X field increases; move the object to the left, and the value in the X field decreases. Horizontal locations to the left of the zero point are represented by negative numbers. As you move farther down on the page, the value in the Y field increases. Vertical locations above the zero point are represented by negative numbers. Note that this means that InDesign's vertical coordinate system is *upside down* relative to the two-dimensional coordinate system you learned in junior high school geometry class (see Figure 9-6).

**Duplicating As You Transform**

Hold down Option/Alt as you press Return/Enter to apply a change you've made to any of the Transform palette fields, and InDesign copies the object and then applies the transformation to the duplicate (see Figure 9-7).

**Transform Palette Menu Options**

The options in the Transform palette menu apply preset transformations and control how transformations affect objects and their contents. While these features give you unprecedented control over your objects, they can be overwhelming at first. Fortunately, the default settings are good enough most of the time. But the more you understand these, the more power you'll have.

**FIGURE 9-6**
**Page Coordinates**

*InDesign's two dimensional coordinate system. All coordinates are measured from the zero point. x represents the horizontal location of a point; y represents the vertical location.*

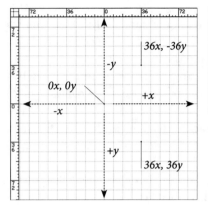

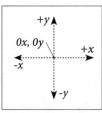

*Traditional two dimensional coordinate system (note that values on the y axis increase as you go up—the opposite of InDesign's approach).*

**FIGURE 9-7**
**Duplicating As You Transform**

*Enter a value in the Horizontal Scaling, Vertical Scaling, Width, or Height fields...*

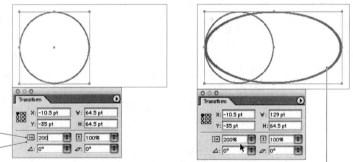

*...and press Option-Return (Macintosh) or Alt-Enter (Windows). InDesign applies the transformation to a copy of the selected object.*

**Scale Text Attributes.** Transforming text frames in InDesign 1.x was incredibly frustrating because the program would scale the frame (and the text in it), but the Character and Paragraph palettes would still display the original measurements. For example, if you used the Scale tool or the Transform palette to double the size of a text frame containing 12-point text with a two-pica indent, the Point Size field in the Character palette would still show "12 pt", the Left Indent field in the Paragraph palette would show "2p", and the Transform palette would show "200%".

Fortunately, Adobe changed this behavior. Now, when you select a text frame with the Selection tool and scale it, InDesign immediately applies the transformation to the text, and the Transform palette reverts back to 100%. In the example above, the text size would show "24 pt" and the indent would appear as "4p". However, you can go back to the old ways by turning off the Adjust Text Attributes When Scaling option in the Text panel of the Preferences dialog box (press Command/Ctrl-K, then Command/Ctrl-2). You might want to do this if there's a good chance you'll need to set the frame back to 100% later.

Now back to the feature at hand: If you have set the preferences so that InDesign works the old way, you can force the program to apply the scaling to the text (effectively resetting the transform palette back to 100%) by selecting the text frame with the Selection tool and choosing Scale Text Attributes from the Transform palette menu.

**Transform Group Content.** Select several objects on the page, group them together (Command/Ctrl-G) and then apply a transformation (scale, rotate, etc.). InDesign transforms the group as a whole around the *group's* point of transformation and displays the change in the Transform palette. For instance, if you rotate the group 30 degrees, the Transform palette shows "30°". You can reset the Transformation to zero degrees by selecting Transform Group Content in the Transform palette menu. Each item in the group stays transformed, but the group as a whole is no longer considered transformed.

**Rotate and Flip.** Some transformations are so common that Adobe just added presets in the Transform palette: Rotate 180 degrees, Rotate 90 degrees clockwise, Rotate 90 degrees counter-clockwise, Flip Vertical, Flip Horizontal, Flip Both (see "Rotating Objects," and "Reflecting Objects," later in this chapter).

**Transform Content.** As we noted earlier, the Transform Content option (in the Transform palette menu) determines whether InDesign scales, rotates, or skews the *content* of frames (either nested pictures or other nested objects) as you make changes to the frame. This setting only affects transformations you apply using the Transform palette, and it has no effect on text frames.

**Dimensions Include Stroke Weight.** What defines the dimensions of a path? Is it the geometric representation of the path itself? Or is it the area taken up by the path, including the stroke weight applied to the path? We prefer to work with the geometric bounds of a path, so we turn off the Dimensions Include Stroke Weight option. You might prefer to work with the visible bounds of objects—if you do, turn this option on (it's on by default).

**Transformations Are Totals.** When you select an object that's contained by a frame, should the Transform palette fields reflect the state of the selected object relative to the pasteboard, or relative to the frame containing the object? That's the question you answer by turning the Transformations are Totals option on the Transform palette menu on or off (it's on by default). When you turn this option on, InDesign displays the rotation, scaling percentages, and shear angle of the selection relative to the pasteboard. Turn this option off to display the information relative to the frame (see Figure 9-8).

**Show Content Offset.** If you nest one object inside another (like a picture in a graphic frame), and then select that nested item with the Direct Select tool, what should appear in the X and Y fields of the Transform palette? By default, the Show Content Offset option is turned on in the Transform palette menu, so the X and Y fields display the offset of the nested object from the "parent" frame. For example, if you simply place an image on the page and then select it with the Direct Select tool, the fields will both show 0 (zero) because the image has not moved relative to the frame. If you turn off this option, the X and Y fields display exactly where the image sits on the page, relative to the ruler's zero point.

**FIGURE 9-8**
**Transformations**
**Are Totals**

*The frame containing this image has been rotated 20 degrees, as you can see by looking at the Rotation field in the Transform palette. If you use the Direct Selection tool to select the image...*

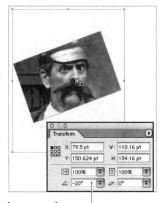

*...InDesign displays its rotation relative to the parent frame...*

*...unless you turn on the Transformations Are Totals option on the Transform palette menu.*

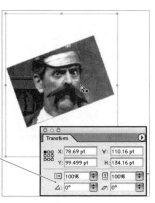

*When you do that, InDesign displays the angle relative to the pasteboard or the scaling percentages relative to the original size of the image.*

# Moving Objects

There are (at least) four ways to move objects in InDesign—select the object and then try any of the methods shown below. (To move the content of a frame without moving the frame itself, select the Direct Selection tool and click inside the frame.)

◆ Drag the objects with the Selection or the Direct Selection tool.

◆ Enter values in the X and Y fields in the Transform palette.

◆ Drag the object using the Free Transform tool.

◆ Press the arrow, or "nudge" keys.

**Moving Objects by Dragging**

InDesign is just like any other program: If you want to move an object, select the object with the Selection tool or the Direct Selection tool and drag. Hold down Option/Alt as you drag to duplicate the object.

If you select an object and then immediately start dragging, you'll see only a box representing the object. If, on the other hand, you hold down the mouse button for a second before dragging, you'll see the object as you drag it. Dragging quickly is great for snapping objects into position by their outlines; waiting a second before dragging is best when you want to see the objects in a selection as you position them on the page.

**Moving Objects with the Transform Palette**

When we need precision, we always move objects by entering numbers in the X and Y fields of the Transform palette (see Figure 9-9). And it's not just because we're closet rocket scientists; it's because we don't trust the screen display, even at 4000 percent magnification. You shouldn't either, when it comes to making fine adjustments in your InDesign publication.

1. Select the object you want to move.

2. Display the Transform palette, if it's not already visible (press F9 to display or hide the palette).

3. Enter values in the X field (to move the object horizontally) and the Y field (to move the object vertically). If you want to move the object to an *absolute* position (relative to the current position of the zero point), enter a new value in the field; to move the object some distance *relative* to its current location, add or subtract that distance from the value in the palette field.

4. Press Return/Enter. InDesign moves the selected object.

FIGURE 9-9
**Moving Objects with
the Transform Palette**

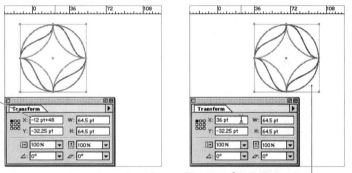

*To move an object to a
specific location on the page
or pasteboard...*

*...enter the position
in the X or Y field.*

*Press Return/Enter, and InDesign moves
the object to the location you entered.*

*To move an object by
a certain amount add (to
move to the right or down)
or subtract (to move to the
left or up) the amount to the
value in the the X or Y field.*

*Press Return/Enter, and InDesign moves
the object relative to is current position.*

**Moving Objects with
the Move Dialog Box**

To move objects using the controls in the Move dialog box, follow
these steps (see Figure 9-10).

1. Select an object.

2. Double-click the Selection tool (or choose Move from the Transform submenu of the Object menu). InDesign displays the Move
dialog box.

3. Set movement options using the controls in the dialog box.
Values here are always relative to the current position. If you
want to move a frame but not its contents, turn off the Move
Content option. To see the effect of the current settings, turn on
the Preview option.

4. Press Return/Enter to move the object, or click the Copy button
to move a copy of the object.

**Using the Free
Transform Tool**

You can use the Free Transform tool to move objects—position the
tool over any part of the object other than the selection handles, and
the Free Transform tool will work just like the Selection tool. Drag

**FIGURE 9-10**

**Moving Objects with the Move Dialog Box**

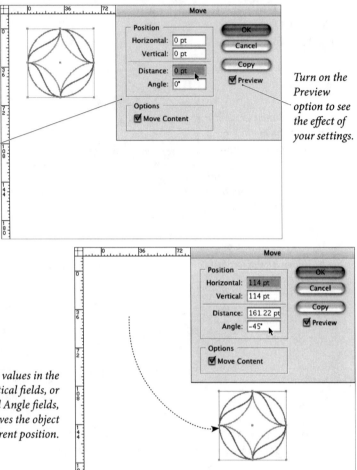

*Choose Move from the Transform submenu of the Object menu to display the Move palette (or double-click the Selection tool in the Tools palette), and InDesign will display the Move dialog box.*

*Turn on the Preview option to see the effect of your settings.*

*Whether you enter values in the Horizontal or Vertical fields, or use the Distance and Angle fields, InDesign moves the object relative to its current position.*

an object by its center point, and InDesign snaps the center point to any active grids or guides. Hold down Option/Alt as you drag to duplicate the object as you move it.

**Moving Objects by Pressing Arrow Keys**

As if dragging by eye and specifying coordinates weren't enough (in terms of movement options), InDesign also sports "nudge" keys. Select an object and press one of the arrow keys, and the element moves in that direction, using the increments you set in the Cursor Key field in the Units and Increments Preferences dialog box.

To move the selected object by ten times the distance you entered in the Cursor Key field, hold down Shift as you press the arrow key. To duplicate the selection as you move it, hold down Option/Alt as you press the arrow key.

# Scaling

To change the size of an object, select the object and then use any of the following techniques.

◆ Drag the Scale tool.

◆ Drag a selection handle with the Selection tool or the Free Transform tool.

◆ Enter values in the fields of the Transform palette.

◆ Enter values in the Scale dialog box.

◆ Press a keyboard shortcut.

You can also change the width of text frames by changing the width of the columns in the text frame (see Chapter 3, "Text").

**Scaling with the Scale Tool**

When you want to scale an object until it "looks right," use the Scale tool (see Figure 9-11).

1. Select the object you want to scale.

2. Select the Scale tool from the Tools palette (or press S).

3. Change the location of the center of transformation icon, if necessary. To do this, either drag the icon to a new location or click one of the points in the Proxy in the Transform palette.

4. Drag the Scale tool horizontally to scale the object's width, or drag vertically to scale the object's height. Dragging diagonally sizes the object's width and height. Hold down Shift as you drag to scale the object proportionally. Hold down Option/Alt as you drag to duplicate the object and scale the duplicate.

**FIGURE 9-11**
**Scaling an Object with the Scale Tool**

*Select an object, move the center of tranformation icon (if necessary), and then drag the Scale tool on the page or pasteboard.*

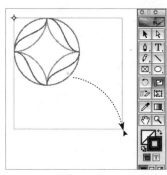

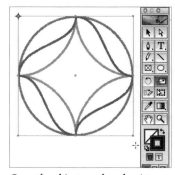

*Hold down Shift to scale the object proportionally, or Option/Alt to scale a duplicate.*

*Once the object reaches the size you want, stop dragging.*

**Scaling with the Selection Tool**

As in almost any other drawing or page-layout application, you can change the size of objects by dragging their corner handles with the Pointer tool (see Figure 9-12). As you drag, the object you're dragging gets larger or smaller. Hold down Shift as you drag to resize the object proportionally.

When you scale a frame, InDesign, by default, does not scale the frame's contents. To do this, hold down Command/Ctrl as you drag one of the selection handles.

**Scaling with the Free Transform Tool**

To scale an object using the Free Transform tool, follow these steps.

1. Select an object.

2. Select the Free Transform tool from the Tools palette.

3. Position the tool above one of the object's selection handles, then drag. Hold down Option/Alt to scale the object proportionally around its center point, or hold down Shift as you drag a corner handle to scale the object proportionally.

**Scaling with the Transform Palette**

When you know you want to make an object larger or smaller by an exact percentage, or to scale the object to a specific width or height, use the Transform palette (see Figure 9-13).

1. Select the object you want to scale.

2. Display the Transform palette if it's not already visible.

**FIGURE 9-12**
**Scaling an Object Using the Selection Tool**

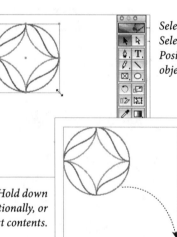

*Select an object, then select the Direct Selection tool from the Tools palette. Position the cursor over one of the object's selection handles.*

*Drag the selection handle. Hold down Shift to scale the object proportionally, or Command/Ctrl to scale object contents.*

*Once the object reaches the size you want, stop dragging.*

**FIGURE 9-13**
**Scaling an Object Using the Transform Palette**

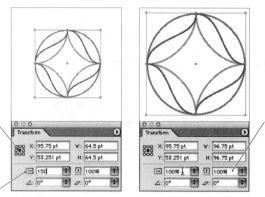

*Why do the scaling fields display 100% after we've applied the scaling? Because we have multiple objects selected. Select a single object, and you'll see the correct scaling percentage.*

*Set the center of transformation by selecting a point on the Proxy, if necessary.*

*Enter a scaling percentage in the Horizontal Scale or Vertical Scale field, or enter a new value in the Width or Height field.*

*Press Return/Enter to apply the scaling change. Hold down Command/Ctrl as you apply the change (as we have here), and InDesign scales the object proportionally.*

3. Enter a new value in the Width or Height fields (or in both fields), or enter a scaling percentage in the Horizontal Scaling field or the Vertical Scaling field.

4. Press Return/Enter to scale the object. To apply proportional scaling, hold down Command/Ctrl as you press Return/Enter.

**Scaling with the Scale Dialog Box**

To scale using the Scale dialog box, select one or more objects and follow these steps (see Figure 9-14).

1. Double-click the Scale tool (or choose Scale from the Transform submenu of the Object menu). InDesign displays the Scale dialog box.

2. Set scaling options using the controls in the dialog box. To scale the object proportionally, turn on the Uniform option and enter a scaling percentage in the Scale field. To scale an object non-proportionally, turn on the Non-Uniform option, then enter scaling percentages in the Horizontal and Vertical fields. To scale the contents of a path, turn on the Scale Content option. To see the effect of the current settings, turn on the Preview option.

3. Press Return/Enter to scale the object, or click the Copy button to scale a copy of the object.

**Scaling with Keyboard Shortcuts**

You can also scale the selected object by pressing keyboard shortcuts. Note, however, that these changes don't appear in the scaling percentages of the Transform palette (except for when you select an image with the Direct Selection tool).

- ◆ Press Command-. (period)/Ctrl-. to increase the size of the object by one percent.

- ◆ Press Command-, (comma)/Ctrl-, to decrease the size by one percent.

- ◆ Press Command-Shift-. (period)/Ctrl-Shift-. to increase the size by five percent.

- ◆ Press Command-Shift-, (comma)/Ctrl-Shift-, to decrease the size by five percent.

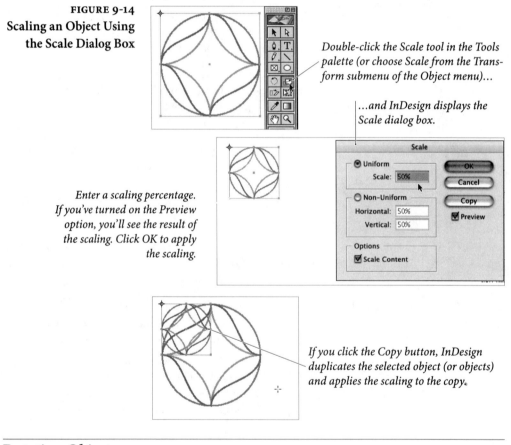

**FIGURE 9-14**
**Scaling an Object Using the Scale Dialog Box**

*Double-click the Scale tool in the Tools palette (or choose Scale from the Transform submenu of the Object menu)...*

*...and InDesign displays the Scale dialog box.*

*Enter a scaling percentage. If you've turned on the Preview option, you'll see the result of the scaling. Click OK to apply the scaling.*

*If you click the Copy button, InDesign duplicates the selected object (or objects) and applies the scaling to the copy.*

## Rotating Objects

InDesign can rotate any object on a page, in .001-degree increments. The rotation angle is always shown relative to the pasteboard (where 0 degrees is horizontal) or to the frame containing the rotated object (unless you've turned on the Transformations are Totals option). For example, if you rotate an object by thirty degrees, entering that rotation value again in the Rotation Angle field will not change the rotation of the object. To do that, you'd need to enter "+30" following the value shown in the Rotation Angle field—or use the Rotate dialog box.

**Rotating with the Rotate Tool**

To rotate an object "by eye," select the object or objects and follow these steps (see Figure 9-15).

1. Select the Rotate tool from the Tools palette (or press R).

2. Drag the Center of Transformation to the point you want to rotate around, or click a point in the Transform palette's Proxy. To rotate around the geometric center of an object, click the center point in the Proxy.

3. Drag the Rotate tool.

4. When the object looks the way you want it to, stop dragging.

**Rotating with the Free Transform Tool**

To rotate an object using the Free Transform tool, follow these steps (see Figure 9-16).

1. Select an object and then choose the Free Transform tool from the Tools palette (press E).

2. Position the tool anywhere outside of the object's selection handles, then drag. InDesign rotates the object around its center point, or hold down Shift as you drag to constrain rotation to 45-degree increments.

**Rotating with the Transform Palette**

To rotate an object using the Transform palette, follow these steps (see Figure 9-17).

1. Select the object or objects you want to rotate.

2. Click a point on the Proxy to set the point you want to rotate around, if necessary.

3. Enter a new value in the Rotation Angle field of the Transform palette. To rotate the object to a specific angle, enter that angle in the field. To rotate the object relative to its current rotation angle, add to or subtract from the value in the Rotation angle field.

   You can enter positive numbers (such as "45") or negative numbers (such as "-270") between -360 and 360 degrees. Positive rotation angles rotate the selected object counterclockwise; negative values rotate the object clockwise. You enter rotation angles in .001 degree increments.

4. Press Return/Enter to rotate the object, or Option-Return/Alt-Enter to rotate a copy of the object.

**Rotating with the Rotate Dialog Box**

To rotate an object using the Rotate dialog box, follow these steps (see Figure 9-18).

1. Select an object.

2. Double-click the Rotate tool (or choose Rotate from the Transform submenu of the Object menu). InDesign displays the Rotate dialog box.

3. Set rotation options using the controls in the dialog box.

   ◆ Enter a rotation angle in the Angle field.

   ◆ To rotate the contents of a frame or path, turn on the Rotate Content option.

   ◆ To see the effect of the current settings, turn on the Preview option.

4. Press Return/Enter to rotate the object, or click the Copy button to rotate a copy of the object.

**FIGURE 9-15**
**Rotating an Object Using the Rotate Tool**

*Select the Rotate tool from the Tools palette.*

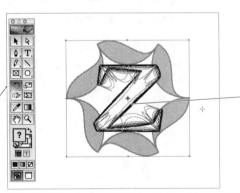

*Move the center of transformation icon, if necessary, to set the point you want to rotate around.*

*Drag the Rotate tool. If you pause for a second before you drag, InDesign displays a preview of the rotated object instead of the simple gray box (as we have in this example).*

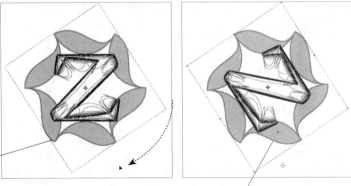

*When the object looks the way you want it to, stop dragging.*

**FIGURE 9-16**
**Rotating an Object with the Free Transform Tool**

Select the Free Transform tool from the Tools palette.

Position the cursor outside one of the object's selection handles.

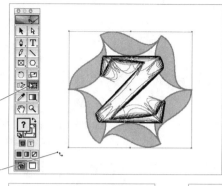

Drag the Free Transform tool. If you pause for a second before you drag, InDesign displays a preview of the rotated object rather than a simple bounding box preview.

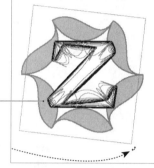

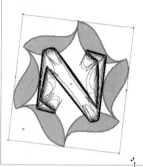

When the object looks the way you want it to, stop dragging.

**FIGURE 9-17**
**Rotating an Object Using the Transform Palette**

Set the center of transformation by clicking a point on the Proxy.

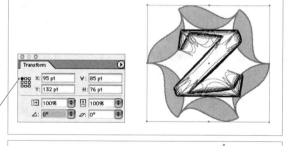

InDesign rotates the selected object.

Enter an angle in the Rotation field and press Return/Enter.

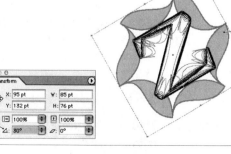

FIGURE 9-18
**Rotating an Object
Using the Rotate
Dialog Box**

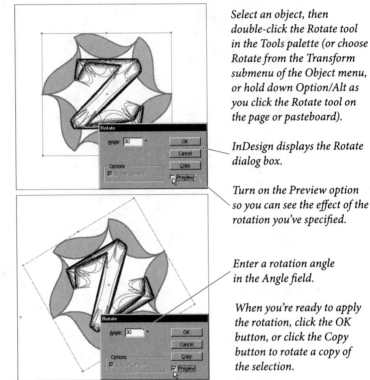

*Select an object, then
double-click the Rotate tool
in the Tools palette (or choose
Rotate from the Transform
submenu of the Object menu,
or hold down Option/Alt as
you click the Rotate tool on
the page or pasteboard).*

*InDesign displays the Rotate
dialog box.*

*Turn on the Preview option
so you can see the effect of the
rotation you've specified.*

*Enter a rotation angle
in the Angle field.*

*When you're ready to apply
the rotation, click the OK
button, or click the Copy
button to rotate a copy of
the selection.*

**Rotating Multiple
Selected Objects**    When you rotate more than one object (in this sense, I'm counting
groups as single objects), the objects rotate around a single point.
This point can be their joint geometric center, or around any other
point you've specified. They don't all rotate around their individual
center points.

## Reflecting Objects

Reflecting—or mirroring—objects in InDesign is very simple, and
you can reflect, or "flip" an object over its vertical axis, its horizontal
axis, or both its vertical and horizontal axes at once. That's it. There's
no reflection tool, no need to enter a reflection angle anywhere
(reflecting an object across an angle is the same as reflecting the
object across its horizontal or vertical axis and then rotating).

To reflect an object, follow these steps (see Figure 9-19).

1.  Select the object you want to reflect.

2.  Choose Flip Vertical, Flip Horizontal, or Flip Both from the
    Transform palette menu. InDesign reflects the selected object.

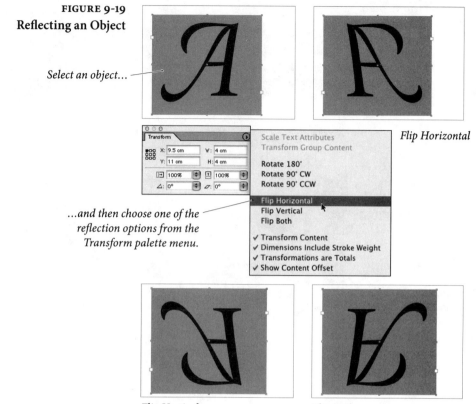

**FIGURE 9-19**
**Reflecting an Object**

Select an object...

Flip Horizontal

...and then choose one of the
reflection options from the
Transform palette menu.

Flip Vertical

Flip Both

## Shearing Objects

Shearing (or skewing) an object makes it appear that the plane the object's resting on has been rotated away from the plane of the page. It's good for creating perspective effects—but it's not a replacement for a serious 3D rotation program (see Figure 9-20).

**Shearing with the Shear Tool**

To shear an object using the Shear tool, follow the steps below (see Figure 9-21).

1. Select an object.

2. Choose the Shear tool from the Tools palette (or press O).

3. Change the location of the center of transformation icon, if necessary (you can either drag the icon to a new location, or click one of the points in the Transform palette Proxy).

4. Drag the Shear tool. As you drag the cursor, the skewing angles display in the Shearing Angle field of the Transform palette. The

FIGURE 9-20
**Shearing an Object**

*No shearing*        *Horizontal shearing*        *Vertical shearing*

FIGURE 9-21
**Shearing an Object
with the Shear Tool**

*Select an object, then
drag the Shear tool.
As you drag, InDesign
shears the selection.*

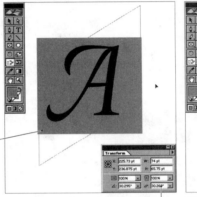

*As you drag, the Transform
palette displays the shear angle.*

*When the object looks the way you
want it to, stop dragging.*

palette shows that vertical shearing is actually done by horizontal shearing (skewing) *and* rotating the object.

5. When the object looks the way you want it to, stop dragging.

**Shearing with the
Transform Palette**

To shear an object using the Transform palette, follow these steps (see Figure 9-22).

1. Select the object you want to shear.

2. Display the Transform palette, if it's not already visible.

3. Click one of the points on the Transform palette Proxy. This sets the center of transformation.

4. Enter an angle in the Shear Angle field, or add or subtract a value from the current content of the field.

5. Press Return/Enter to shear the selected object.

Typing a value in the Shear Angle field only lets you skew (horizontal shear) the object. To create a vertical shear, type the same angle into the Rotation angle field.

FIGURE 9-22
Shearing an Object
Using the Transform
Palette

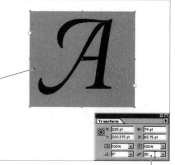 

*Select an object...*

*...enter a shear angle in the Shear field of the Transform palette.*

*Press Return/Enter to shear the selection. Press Option-Return/ Alt-Enter to apply the shear to a copy of the selection.*

**Shearing with the Shear Dialog Box**

To shear an object using the Shear dialog box, follow these steps (see Figure 9-23).

1. Select an object.

2. Double-click the Shear tool (or choose Shear from the Transform submenu of the Object menu). InDesign displays the Shear dialog box.

3. Set the shearing options using the controls in the dialog box. Enter an angle in the Shear Angle field, and pick an axis (the

**FIGURE 9-23
Shearing an Object
Using the Shear
Dialog Box**

*Select an object, then double-click the Shear tool in the Tools palette (or choose Shear from the Transform submenu of the Object menu, or hold down Option/Alt as you click the Shear tool on the page or pasteboard).*

*InDesign displays the Shear dialog box.*

*Turn on the Preview option so you can see the effect of the shearing you've specified.*

*Enter a shear angle in the Shear Angle field. Specify the shear axis you want to use.*

*Click the OK button, or click the Copy button to shear a copy of the selection.*

options are horizontal, vertical, or a specified angle). To rotate the contents of a path, turn on the Shear Content option.

4. Press Return/Enter to shear the object, or click the Copy button to shear a copy of the object.

## Locking Object Positions

In InDesign, you can lock an object's position—which means that you can't transform it. You can, however, select the object, copy the object, or change its appearance.

To lock an object, select it and press Command-L/Ctrl-L (or choose Lock Position from the Object menu). To unlock an object, press Command-Option-L/Ctrl-Alt-L (or choose Unlock Position from the Object menu).

Of course, another good way to lock an object is to place it on a layer and then lock the layer. An object on a locked layer is totally locked; you can't even select it.

## Aligning and Distributing Objects

For many of us, MacDraw ushered in the era of object alignment. You could align the left, right, top, bottom, or center of selected objects. It was the greatest. We spent whole afternoons just aligning things. You couldn't do that in MacPaint.

We consider alignment and distribution to be transformations (in case you're wondering what the topics are doing in this chapter), by the way, because they amount to automated methods of moving objects.

InDesign features both object alignment and object distribution. InDesign aligns objects based on the object's bounding box—more or less what you see when you select the object with the Free Transform tool.

When you distribute objects you're telling InDesign to evenly arrange the selected objects. Objects can be distributed inside the area occupied by the objects, or by a specific distance.

**Aligning Objects**    When you've selected the objects you want to align, press F8 to display the Align palette. Click one of the the alignment buttons to align the selected objects (see Figure 9-24).

**COLOR FIGURE 1**
## Overprint and Knockout

Objects colored with spot color 1 set to knock out (Overprint Fill option off)

*Spot color 1 plate*    *Spot color 2 plate*

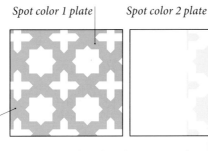
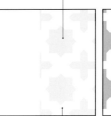

*Spot color 1 knocks out spot color 2*

Objects colored with spot color 1 set to overprint (Overprint Fill option on)

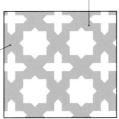

*Spot color 1 plate*    *Spot color 2 plate*

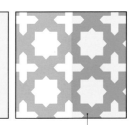

*Spot color 1 overprints spot color 2*

**COLOR FIGURE 2**
## Trapping an Open Path

*This cyan path needs to be trapped. Unless we've been very lucky, you'll see paper showing through around the stroke of the path.*

*Make sure you turn on the Weight Changes Bounding Box option on the Stroke palette menu—without it, your paths will change shape as you change their stroke weights (making manual trapping impossible).*

To create a spread (as shown here), clone the path (by copying the path and then choosing Paste In Place from the Edit menu). Increase the stroke weight of the cloned path, then turn on the Overprint Stroke option.

To create a choke, clone the path and then decrease the stroke width of the cloned path. Set the stroke of the original path to overprint.

*The thicker stroke (exaggerated in this example) overprints objects behind it.*

*The original path knocks out objects behind it.*

*Trapped path (without exaggeration)*

## Trapping Closed Paths and Text

*Again, unless we've been lucky, you'll see the paper showing through around the cyan circle in this example. To prevent the paper from showing, you need to trap the object.*

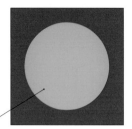

*Select the path you want to trap and press F10 to display the Stroke palette. Add a stroke to the object that's twice the width of the spread you want, and turn on the Overprint option.*

*If you could separate the fill and the stroke, you would see something like this.*

 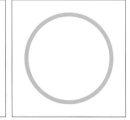 

*To create a choke, apply an overprinting stroke the color of the background rectangle to the ellipse.*

*The fill is set to knock out...*

*...the stroke is set to overprint.*

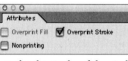

*When you print, the the stroke of the circle overprints the background square, while the fill knocks out. This creates a spread.*

*This example has not been trapped, so you'll probably see paper showing through around the text characters.*

*The cyan stroke overprints the background objects, creating a spread. In general, you want to spread the lighter color (cyan, in this example) into the darker color (magenta).*

*Trapped using a spread.*

*Because InDesign prints the fill of text over the stroke, we had to create a duplicate text frame containing characters with a magenta stroke and a fill of "None"*

*Trapped using a choke.*

*When you choke lighter characters, the apparent shape of the characters changes (not a good thing).*

COLOR FIGURE 4
## Overprinting and Process Colors

*Overprint on*
*Overprint off*

*Where the overprinting object's percentage of a process color is zero, the background color will show through.*

*Background rectangle is 80C 20M 80Y 10K*

 *0C 80M 0Y 40K*

*20C 80M 20Y 40K*

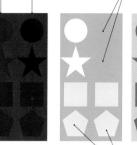

*We've always wondered what it really means to say that you're overprinting process colors, so we created this figure to explain it to ourselves. We hope it works for you, too.*

*These objects contain percentages of each process color, so overprinting and non-overprinting objects print identically on each plate.*

COLOR FIGURE 5
## InDesign Trapping

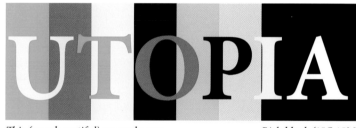

*This (very beautiful) example was trapped using InDesign's default trapping settings (shown below).*

*Rich black (15C 15M 15Y 100K)*

**Modify Trap Style Options**

Name: [Default]    OK    Cancel

**Trap Width**
Default: 0p0.25
Black: 0p0.5

**Trap Appearance**
Join Style: Miter
End Style: Miter

**Images**
Trap Placement: Center
☑ Trap Objects to Images
☑ Trap Images to Images
☐ Trap Images Internally
☑ Trap 1-bit Images

**Trap Thresholds**
Step: 10%
Black Color: 100%
Black Density: 1.6
Sliding Trap: 70%
Trap Color Reduction: 100%

**COLOR FIGURE 6**
## Rosettes

*We can't load our print-ing presses with millions of inks, so we fool the eye by printing patterns of dots of (at least) four inks when we want to print scanned natural images. The pattern made by these dots is called a "rosette."*

*In this example, we've enlarged part of the image (of Ole's son, Max). Look at the enlarged sample from a distance, and you'll see how the dots blend together to create the appearance of more than four colors.*

*We've also pulled the sample apart to show the halftone screen angle used by each ink, at right.*

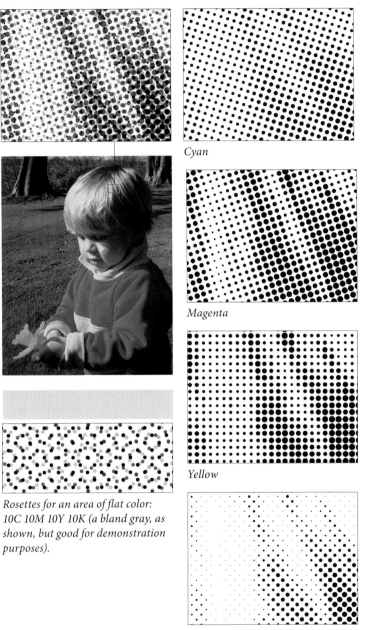

Cyan

Magenta

Yellow

*Rosettes for an area of flat color: 10C 10M 10Y 10K (a bland gray, as shown, but good for demonstration purposes).*

Black

**COLOR FIGURE 7**
## Duotones

*Photoshop duotone.*

*Two fake duotones: images in black ink over a background tint of cyan.*

*100% cyan background*

*50% cyan background*

*InDesign fake duotone: Two overlapping grayscale TIFF images colored with different inks(cyan and black).*

*Fake duotone made using transparency.*

*To apply a color to an image (black and white or grayscale only), select the image with the Direct Selection tool...*

*...and then click a color swatch in the Swatches palette.*

COLOR FIGURE 8
**Creating a
"Neon Glow" Effect**

*When you need to create a
"glow" effect, you typically
use a blend in Illustrator or
FreeHand. But, with a little
help from InDesign scripting, you can create blends in
InDesign. Here's one of
Ole's example scripts.*

*Select a path in InDesign.*

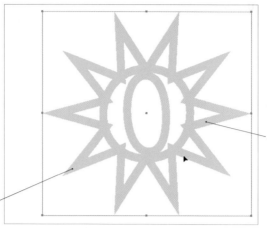

*The path should
have a fairly thick
stroke (3 points
or more), and
you should turn
on the Weight
Changes Bound-
ing Box option (on
the Stroke palette
menu).*

*Run the script. The example
Mac OS script on your
InDesign CD doesn't have a
user interface, but it does
the same thing as the
Windows version.*

*Enter the number of steps you
want for the blend, then click
the OK button. InDesign and
the script work together to
create the blend.*

*The "neon" effect looks better
on a dark background.*

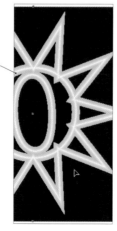

*We don't usually think of scripting as a creative
tool, but this example script gives you a way to
apply an effect that would be difficult to accomplish
without leaving InDesign for a drawing program.*

**COLOR FIGURE 9**
**Separating Color Images**

*CMYK images  as separated by Photoshop.*

*Example RGB TIFFs separated by InDesign. In this example, I used the default Adobe InDesign Default RGB profile and the Perceptual (Images) rendering intent.*

**COLOR FIGURE 10**
# Blending Modes

*For each blending mode, we've shown the effect of four overlapping rect-angles colored with 100% cyan, magenta, yellow, and black. We've applied the blending mode to each rectangle with an opacity of 50%.*

*Normal*

*Multiply*

*Screen*

*Overlay*

*Soft Light*

*Hard Light*

*Color Dodge*

*Color Burn*

*Darken*

*Lighten*

*Hue*

*Saturation*

*Color*

*Luminosity*

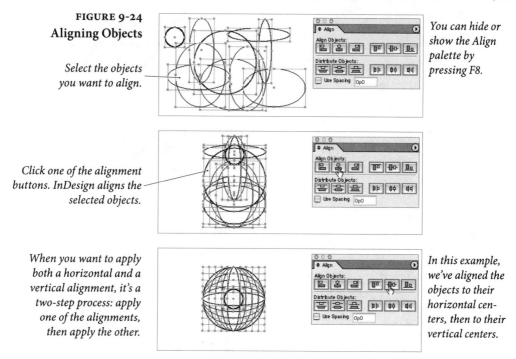

**FIGURE 9-24**
**Aligning Objects**

*Select the objects you want to align.*

*You can hide or show the Align palette by pressing F8.*

*Click one of the alignment buttons. InDesign aligns the selected objects.*

*When you want to apply both a horizontal and a vertical alignment, it's a two-step process: apply one of the alignments, then apply the other.*

*In this example, we've aligned the objects to their horizontal centers, then to their vertical centers.*

If you've locked the position of an object in the selection, InDesign does not move that object when you apply an alignment. If an object doesn't seem to be following the herd, chances are good that it's locked—choose Unlock Position from the Object menu to apply alignment to it.

**Distributing Objects**

Have you ever wanted to space a bunch of objects at even distances from each other (from each other's centers, at any rate) across a particular horizontal measurement? If you have, InDesign's Distribute feature should make your day. To distribute the selected objects inside the rectangle defined by the objects, click one of the distribute buttons in the Align palette. InDesign distributes the objects as you've specified (see Figure 9-25).

To distribute (or space) the objects by a specified distance, use the Use Spacing option in either the Distribute Objects section of the Align palette or the Distribute Spacing section.

When you click one of the buttons in the Distribute objects section, the value you enter in the Use Spacing field sets the distance between the object sides (top, bottom, right, and left) or object centers (vertical or horizontal). If you enter 12 points, for example, and then click the Horizontal Distribute Lefts button, InDesign spaces the left edges of the objects in the selection 12 points apart.

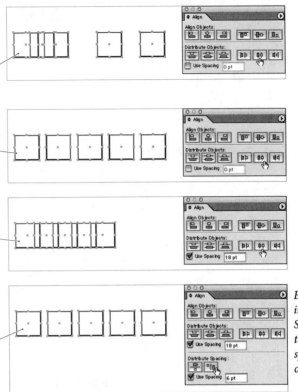

**FIGURE 9-25**
**Distributing Objects**

*Select the objects you want to distribute.*

*Click one of the distribution buttons. InDesign distributes the selected objects by spacing them evenly across the bounds of the selection.*

*...or use the Use Spacing field to space the corresponding object faces (top, bottom, side, or center) by a specific distance apart.*

*To apply even spacing between objects, expand the Align palette to show the Distribute Spacing options. Enter a value in the Use Spacing field, then click one of the associated buttons.*

*Enter zero in the Use Spacing field to remove the space between objects.*

When you use the Use Spacing option in the Distribute Spacing section, InDesign spaces the objects apart by the distance you enter in the Use Spacing field. Click the Vertical Distribute Space button to distribute the objects vertically, or click the Horizontal Distribute Space button to distribute the objects horizontally.

## Transform Your Life!

Fuzzy caterpillars turn into moths. Clark Kent jumps into a phone booth and emerges as Superman. Werewolves stalk the moors under the full moon. Bewildered authors turn into parents. These transformations are all everyday, natural phenomena.

Make InDesign's transformation tools an integral part of how you work with the program, and you'll have their powerful, almost magical forces on your side. And that means you'll have more time for other things. Like howling at the moon.

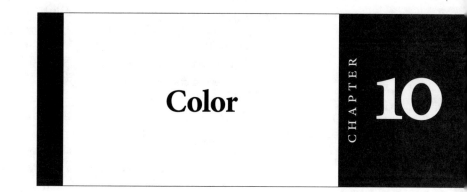

# Color

## CHAPTER 10

Color communicates, telling us things about the object bearing the color. Without color cues, we'd have a hard time guessing the ripeness of a fruit or distinguishing a poisonous mushroom from an edible one. And many animals would have a hard time figuring out when to mate, or with whom.

We associate colors with human emotions: we are green with envy; we've got the blues; we see red. Colors affect our emotions as well. Various studies suggest that we think best in a room of one color, and relax best in a room of another color.

What does all this mean? Color's important. A rule of thumb in advertising is that a color advertisement gets several times the response of a black-and-white ad. Designers of mail-order catalogs tell me that color is often cited as the reason for buying a product—and it's usually the reason a product is returned.

InDesign features a formidable array of features dedicated to creating, editing, applying, and printing colors. In addition, InDesign's color management can make what you see on your screen much closer to what you'll get when you print. Before we go any farther, however, we have to talk about color printing.

# Seeing Color, Printing Color

It's impossible to discuss the process of creating and using colors in InDesign without first talking a little about printing and visual perception. If you already know about those topics, feel free to skip ahead, though you'll miss all the jokes if you do. Everyone else should note that this is a very simple explanation of a pair of very bizarre and complex processes.

**The Color Spectrum and Color Gamuts**

The colors we see when we look at the world around us are the light reflected from objects in our field of view. In our eyes, the cornea, iris, and pupil conspire to cast this light on a rejoicing multitude of photoreceptive cells—the rods and cones at the back of the retina.

These cells, in turn, use chemical and electrical signals to pass information about the light striking them on to our visual cortex. And, after a series of profoundly *weird* things happen in the visual cortex (a friend of ours is an academic studying human visual perception—we don't understand a word she says), we see a picture.

The *visible spectrum* is the range of light wavelengths visible to the human eye (not your eye, or our eyes, but an idealized, "normal" human eye) ranging from the top of the ultraviolet (wavelengths around $7 * 10^{-5}$ centimeters, or 700 nanometers) to the bottom of the infrared (wavelengths around $4 * 10^{-5}$ centimeters, or 400 nanometers). It's the job of our scanners, monitors, printers, and printing presses to reproduce the colors we see in the visible spectrum.

Alas, they all fail miserably.

The range of color a device, color model, or printing method is capable of reproducing is referred to as its *color gamut*. There's no device, apart from your eye, that's capable of reproducing the range of light that your eye is capable of seeing. And even your eye isn't consistent from day to day.

We've settled, therefore, on a reasonably well-known and well-understood set of compromises.

**The Printing Process**

After you've printed your InDesign publication on film and delivered it to your commercial printer (we like to walk in through the loading dock), the printer takes the film and uses it to expose (or "burn") a photosensitive printing plate. (These days, you might skip all of these steps and print directly to a printing plate.) The surface of the plate has been chemically treated to repel ink. When you expose the printing plate to light, the image areas from your film become able to accept ink. Once the plate's been exposed, the printer attaches the printing plate to the cylinder of a printing press.

As the cylinder holding the plate turns, the parts of it bearing the image become coated with ink, which is transferred (via another, rubber-covered cylinder—the offset cylinder) to the paper. This transfer is where we get the term "offset," as in "offset printing," because the printing plate itself does not touch your paper.

Printing presses put ink on paper one ink at a time. Some presses have more than one printing cylinder (also called a printing "head" or "tower") and can print several colors of ink on a sheet of paper in one pass through the press, but each printing cylinder carries only one color of ink. We can make it look like we've gotten more than one color of ink on a printing plate by using screens—patterns of dots that, from a distance, fool the eye into thinking it sees a separate color.

**Spot and Process Inks**

Spot-color printing is simple: your commercial printer uses inks that exactly match the color you want (or mixes inks to get the same result), then loads the press with that ink. In spot-color printing, we sometimes use "tint builds"—screens of inks printed on top of each other—to create a new color without using another ink. In process-color printing, tint builds are where it's at; we use overlapping screens of four inks (cyan, magenta, yellow, and black) to simulate part of the spectrum of visible color. If everything's gone well, the dots of the different colored inks are placed near each other in a pattern called a rosette (see Color Figure 6 on the color pages for an example of a rosette).

Process-color printing can't simulate all the colors our eyes can see (notably very saturated colors, or metallic and fluorescent colors), but it can print color photographic images. Spot colors can print any color you can make with pigments, but aren't generally used to reproduce color photographic images (that's what process color printing was designed to be good at).

## Color in InDesign

Now that you know all about color perception and color printing, it's time to get down to the process of specifying and applying colors in your InDesign publication.

**Named and Unnamed Colors**

InDesign has two basic methods for working with color: unnamed colors and color swatches. What's the difference? Both unnamed colors and color swatches can change the appearance of an object's fill or stroke, but swatches establish a relationship between the object and the named color swatch. Change the definition of the color swatch, and the color of all of the objects you've applied that swatch to will change, as well.

Here's another way to look at it: unnamed colors are to color swatches as local character formatting is to a character style. You get the *appearance* you're looking for, but you don't get the link between the style (in this case, the color swatch) and the object.

Why do you need that link? Because people change their minds. Your publication might have started its life intended for a two-color press, but, because of a recent change in management, it's now a six-color job (lucky you!). The client's corporate color may have been Pantone 327 when you started the job, but it's now Pantone 199. You get the idea—something like this has probably happened to you.

If you've used unnamed colors, there's nothing to do but claw your way through the objects in your publication, selecting and changing each affected object. If you've used named color swatches, on the other hand, making a change of this sort is a simple task: change the definition of the swatch, and you've changed the color applied to all of the fills and strokes formatted using the swatch.

## Colors and Inks

Spot colors in your publication correspond directly to the inks you'll use to print the publication; process colors are made up of some or all of the four process inks (cyan, magenta, yellow, and black). When you create, edit, or import a color in InDesign, you're working with a single ink, or a tint of that ink, or (for a process color) a set of inks that, when printed, optically blend together to produce the color you want to see.

When it comes time to print, the ink list (in the Output panel of the Print dialog box) displays the inks needed to print the colors you have defined in your publication. You'll always see the process inks (cyan, magenta, yellow, and black) in the ink list, whether you've defined process colors or not. If you've defined spot colors, you'll see the spot inks associated with those colors in the ink list. If you want, you can print simulations of spot colors using process inks by clicking the All to Process button in the Ink Manager (we cover the Ink Manager later in this chapter). This converts the colors as you print—the color definitions are not changed in your publication.

## Spot Color Or Process Color Or Both?

Whether you use spot colors, process colors, or both depends on the needs of your specific publication—which has to do with your printing budget, your communications goals, and, most importantly, your mood. If you plan to use color photographs in your publication, you're going to have to use at least the four process inks. If you're printing on a tight budget, you'll probably want to forgo the color images and use only one or two inks.

When you're defining a color, you're offered a variety of choices: is the color a spot color, a process color, or a tint? Which color model should you use? Should you choose a color from a swatch library, or make up your own color definition? The following sections attempt to answer these questions.

**Color Models**   InDesign lets you define colors using any of three color models— CMYK, RGB, and LAB. Which color model should you use? That depends on how you plan to produce your publication.

**Spot colors.** If you're working with spot colors, you can use RGB, LAB, or a swatch book like a Pantone color, and it really doesn't matter what the color looks like on the screen, as long as you let your commercial printer know what color of ink they need to use to print your publication. How do you know what ink to use? If you use Pantone colors (the most likely scenario), you can tell them the PMS color number. If you don't, it's trickier, but your printer can help you match the color you want to an ink they can mix.

If you plan to use Pantone spot colors, save yourself some trouble: choose swatches from the Pantone swatch libraries, rather than trying to mix the color yourself. Note that, in any case, you can't use the Color palette to create a spot color from scratch—to do that, you'll have to use the controls in the New Color Swatch dialog box or the Swatch Options dialog box (both of which we talk about later in this chapter).

**Process colors.** If you're working with process colors, *specify your color using the CMYK color model or a CMYK color-matching system,* or be ready for some surprises when your publication gets printed. It's always best to look at a printed sample of the process color (like those in the Trumatch or Pantone Process swatch books) and enter the values given in the sample book for the color. In other words, trust what you see on paper, not what you see on your screen.

**On-screen colors.** If you're creating a publication for online distri-bution (on a CD-ROM or on the Web), use the RGB color model. If you're creating a publication for distribution on the Web, you may also want to stick with "browser safe" colors—colors that appear without dithering on old 8-bit color screens. For more on picking browser-safe colors, see "Swatch Libraries," later in this chapter.

**Tints.** If you're trying to create a tint of an existing color (process or spot), use the Swatches palette—don't try to approximate the right shade by mixing colors. You can base your tint on a spot color or a process color, but you can't base tints on another tint.

**Color Conversion Errors.** When you convert a color from one color model to another—from RGB to CMYK, for example—a certain amount of error is introduced by the process of conversion. This is because the color models don't cover the same color gamut, and because the color models have differing approaches to defining colors. Each time you convert the color, the rounding error is compounded: if you convert 100C 10M 50Y 0K to RGB, you'll get 0R 230G 128B—converting that RGB color back to CMYK will yield a color defined as 90C 0M 40Y 10K. There's no "round trip" in color model conversion.

**Swatch Libraries**

InDesign's swatch libraries support the most frequently used color-matching systems in the graphic arts industry, like Pantone and Trumatch. There's nothing magical about these color libraries—they're just sets of agreed-upon industry standards. Colors from swatch libraries are always named colors, and appear in your publication as swatches. InDesign changed the way it handles swatch libraries between version 1.5 and 2.0; we'll cover those differences when we discuss defining colors later in this chapter.

**DICColor.** A spot-color specifying system corresponding to inks manufactured by Dainippon Ink and Chemicals, Inc. It's something like a Japanese version of Pantone—and not seen frequently in North America or Europe—except in printing subsidiaries of Japanese printers. Still, it's a nice set of colors, which you might want to use if you can get a printer to match them.

**Focoltone.** A process-color specification system (mostly used in Europe). Colors in the Focoltone library are organized in sets of colors with common percentages of at least one process color. The idea is to create a library of colors that, when applied to objects, are easy to trap, or don't need trapping at all.

**HKS_E, HKS_N, HKS_D, HKS_K.** Where do these colors come from, and what do they want? No one knows (except perhaps some secret U.S. government agency, and they're not telling). There's no mention of them in the documentation, and the only information we've been able to glean from our usually reliable European sources says they're used almost exclusively by architects and industrial designers in Germany. Snooping around in the library itself, we see that they're spot colors defined using the CMYK model.

**Pantone Coated, Pantone Matte, Pantone Uncoated.** Sets of spot-color inks manufactured by Pantone, Inc. These inks are the industry standard for spot color in the North American printing business (as always, ask your commercial printer). The on-screen preview of the colors changes slightly in each set, attempting to simulate how this color would appear on each type of paper stock.

**Pantone Process.** A set of Pantone process-color tint builds. These colors have no relation to the Pantone spot colors.

**System (Macintosh), System (Windows).** These two swatch libraries contain the 8-bit RGB color palettes for their respective systems. We can't find any good reason to use these.

**TOYO Color Finder.** A spot-color library for matching inks from the Toyo Ink Manufacturing Company, Ltd., and corresponding to their Toyo 88 Color Guide ink sample book. Like DIC, Toyo is primarily used in Asian countries, and isn't seen much in Europe or North America.

**Trumatch.** A process-color specifying system featuring small percentage changes from one process color to another. The Trumatch swatch book gives you a good set of printed examples for specifying process color (this is David's favorite process-color swatch book because it's laid out in a very intuitive manner).

**Web.** In the bad old days, most computers could only display 8-bit color—only 256 different colors at any one time, and some of those colors were reserved by the operating system. Any color outside of these 256 would get dithered (like an airbrush spatter of two different colors to simulate a third). If you're choosing colors for an on-screen purpose (like the Web), you can avoid dithering on those old systems by using a color from the Web palette. However, we rarely build Web pages in InDesign, and almost no one in the industrialized nations has an 8-bit video system anymore anyway, so we usually just ignore these.

# InDesign's Color Controls

InDesign's controls for working with color are found in several palettes and menus. The most important palettes are the Toolbox, because it contains the Fill selector and the Stroke selector, and the Swatches palette, because it contains tools for defining, editing, and applying swatches (which can be colors, gradients, or tints) to objects.

You can also use the Color palette and the Gradient palette to create and apply unnamed colors and gradients—but, as we've noted earlier, you'll be better off if you use named color swatches. If you apply a color to an object using the Color palette, there is no swatch associated with it—it's an *unnamed color.* Unnamed colors are a nightmare for service bureaus and printers because it's hard for them to figure out what colors you used if they need to troubleshoot your file. They can also be a nightmare for you if you ever need to go back to change a color. Given that everything you can do using the Color palette can be accomplished using the Swatches palette, we recommend just leaving the Color palette closed.

**Fill and Stroke Selectors**

*Stroke selector active*

*Fill selector active*

*Fill text selector active*

At the bottom of the Tool palette and in the upper-left corner of the Swatches palette and the Color palette, you'll see the Fill selector and the Stroke selector. These aren't labeled in any way (unless you count the tool help we always turn off), but the Fill selector is the filled square on the left (here's proof that InDesign's user interface, while easy to use, is hard to write about). When you want to work with an object's fill, click the Fill selector; to work with an object's stroke, press the Stroke selector (the outlined square). InDesign shows you which selector is active by bringing it to the front.

Honestly, we almost never actually click on those squares; rather, we use these favorite shortcuts for working with the Fill and Stroke selectors.

◆ Press X (this is another of those keyboard shortcuts that doesn't work when you're editing text) to toggle between the Fill selector and the Stroke selector.

◆ Press Shift-X to swap fill and stroke colors (this shortcut is the same as clicking the double-headed arrow Swap Fill and Stroke icon).

◆ Press D to apply the default fill and stroke colors to the selected object (black stroke and a "None" fill).

◆ To apply the currently selected swatch to an object's stroke or fill, click the corresponding selector, then click the Apply Color button (or click the swatch itself, or press comma). To remove a fill or stroke from the selected object, click the appropriate selector and then click the Apply None button (or click the None swatch in the Swatches palette, or press /). To apply the last-used gradient, click the Apply Gradient button at the bottom of the Tool palette (or press period).

**Swatches Palette**

The Swatches palette is InDesign's "color control center"—it's where you create, edit, and apply colors, tints, and gradients. The Swatches palette often displays a bewildering array of icons and symbols. What does it all mean? To find out, take a look at Figure 10-1.

Press Command-Option/Ctrl-Alt and click inside the Swatches palette to activate the list. Once you've done this, you can select a color by typing its name, or move up and down in the list of swatches using the arrow keys. (But note that this will change the color of any

FIGURE 10-1
**Swatches Palette**

*To display the Swatches palette, press F5.*

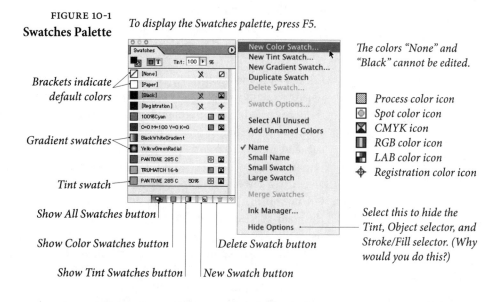

Brackets indicate default colors

Gradient swatches

Tint swatch

Show All Swatches button

Show Color Swatches button

Show Tint Swatches button

Delete Swatch button

New Swatch button

*The colors "None" and "Black" cannot be edited.*

▨ *Process color icon*
◉ *Spot color icon*
☒ *CMYK icon*
▮ *RGB color icon*
▦ *LAB color icon*
✥ *Registration color icon*

*Select this to hide the Tint, Object selector, and Stroke/Fill selector. (Why would you do this?)*

*Alternative views of the Swatches palette*

*Small name*

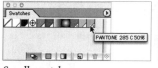

*Small swatches (hover cursor over color to see title)*

*Large swatches*

selected objects on any page. We prefer to press Command-Shift-A/
Ctrl-Shift-A to deselect all objects before messing with swatches.)

**Creating a color swatch.** To create a color swatch, follow these steps
(see Figure 10-2).

1. Choose New Color Swatch from the Swatches palette menu.
   InDesign displays the New Color Swatch dialog box, set to duplicate whatever the currently selected color is. As long as None
   or Paper are not selected in the Swatches palette, you can also
   open this dialog box by Option/Alt-clicking on the New Swatch
   button at the bottom of the palette.

2. Enter a name for the new color swatch (it's optional—InDesign
   will have filled in the Name field with a default name for the
   color).

3. Define the color using the controls in the New Color Swatch
   dialog box.

4. Click the OK button or press Enter to close the dialog box.
   InDesign adds the new color swatch to the list of swatches
   shown in the Swatches palette.

**Adding Unnamed Colors.** As we said earlier, if you've used the Color
palette to apply a color to an object, that color will not appear in the
Swatches palette; it's an unnamed color. Fortunately, there are two
ways to add unnamed colors to your Swatches palette. First, you
can add unnamed colors by selecting the object colored with the
unnamed color, then clicking the New Swatch button (or choose
New Color Swatch from the Swatches palette menu, then click the
OK button in the New Color Swatch dialog box). InDesign adds
the color applied to the object to the list of colors in the Swatches
palette.

If you've created more than one unnamed color, or you're working with a document in which someone else applied unnamed colors,
you can add all these colors to the Swatches palette at once by selecting Add Unnamed Colors from the palette's menu.

**Adding Colors from a Swatch Library.** Most of the time, we think
you should add colors from swatch libraries. Why? Because your
commercial printer wants you to (when they talk in their sleep, they
call out Pantone numbers and common process tint builds), and
because it's the quickest way to add a named color. To choose a color

FIGURE 10-2

**Creating a
Color Swatch**

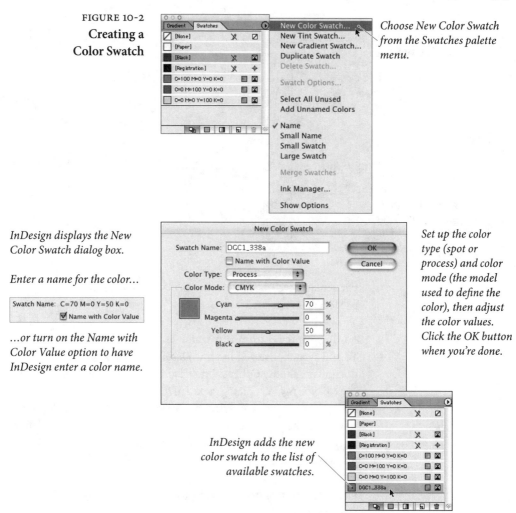

*Choose New Color Swatch
from the Swatches palette
menu.*

*InDesign displays the New
Color Swatch dialog box.*

*Enter a name for the color...*

*...or turn on the Name with
Color Value option to have
InDesign enter a color name.*

*Set up the color
type (spot or
process) and color
mode (the model
used to define the
color), then adjust
the color values.
Click the OK button
when you're done.*

*InDesign adds the new
color swatch to the list of
available swatches.*

from a color library, follow the steps for adding a color, above, but choose a swatch library from the Color Mode menu in the New Color Swatch dialog box (see Figure 10-3). Note that this is significantly different than in earlier versions of InDesign, which forced you to open special swatch library palettes (as in Adobe Illustrator).

In some cases, you can also change the Color Mode after selecting a color swatch. For example, if you need to simulate a Pantone spot color using process colors, first specify the Pantone color, then change the Color Mode pop-up menu to CMYK and the Color Type pop-up menu to Process. (This is based on the Pantone Spot to Process library rather than the ProSim library that you might be familiar with.) Of course, some Pantone colors don't convert to process colors

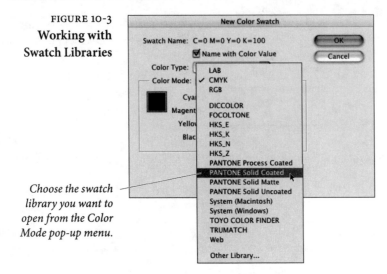

*Choose the swatch
library you want to
open from the Color
Mode pop-up menu.*

particularly well because you can't make any given hue just using
process colors.

**Adding Swatches from Illustrator or Other InDesign Publications.**
To add swatches stored in an InDesign publication or an Illustrator
document, choose Other Library from the Color Mode menu in the
New Color Swatch dialog box. InDesign displays the Open a File
dialog box. Locate and select an InDesign or Illustrator document,
then click the Open button. InDesign displays the swatches defined
in that document, and you can add them to the current publication
just as you'd add swatches from any swatch library.

**Creating a tint swatch.** To create a new tint swatch, follow these steps
(see Figure 10-4).

1.  Select a color swatch in the Swatches palette. If you select a tint
    swatch, the new tint will be based on the same color as the exist-
    ing tint swatch—you can't create a tint based on a tint.

2.  Choose New Tint Swatch from the Swatches palette menu.
    InDesign displays the New Tint Swatch dialog box.

3.  Enter a new value in the Tint field or drag the slider.

4.  Click the OK button or press Enter to close the dialog box and
    add the tint to the list of swatches in the Swatches palette.

    If you remove a color (see "Deleting a Swatch," later in this chap-
    ter), all tint swatches based on that color will change to tints of the
    color you choose in the Delete Color dialog box. If, as you remove a

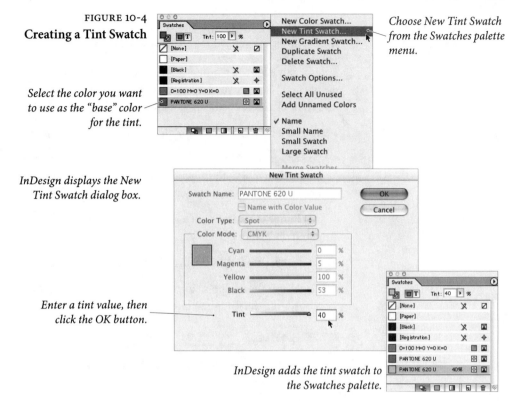

FIGURE 10-4
**Creating a Tint Swatch**

*Choose New Tint Swatch from the Swatches palette menu.*

*Select the color you want to use as the "base" color for the tint.*

*InDesign displays the New Tint Swatch dialog box.*

*Enter a tint value, then click the OK button.*

*InDesign adds the tint swatch to the Swatches palette.*

color, you choose to convert the color to the default colors "None" or "Paper," InDesign removes all of the tints based on that color from the Swatches palette. This is also what happens when you remove a color swatch and choose the Unnamed Swatch option in the Delete Color option.

*Out of gamut warning*

**Out of Gamut Warning.** InDesign constantly monitors the values of the colors you create, and when a color swatch definition falls outside the gamut defined by the default CMYK document profile, InDesign displays an alert icon next to the color sliders in the New Color Swatch or Swatch Options dialog box. To adjust the color definition so that it falls in the gamut of the separations profile, click the alert icon. We discuss document profiles in detail when we explore color management later in this chapter. Note that as long as you are choosing colors from swatch libraries or using the CMYK mode, you won't see this alert.

**Creating a gradient swatch.** To create a gradient swatch, follow these steps (see Figure 10-5).

1. Choose New Gradient Swatch from the Swatches palette menu. InDesign displays the New Gradient Swatch dialog box.

2. Enter a name for the gradient (the default name of "New Gradient Swatch" isn't particularly useful). Edit the gradient's ramp and color attributes using any or all of the following techniques.

   ◆ To add a new gradient stop, click below the gradient ramp.

   ◆ To change the color of a gradient stop, select the stop, then adjust the color definition using the controls above the gradient ramp.

   ◆ To change the position of a gradient stop, drag it along the ramp.

   ◆ To delete a gradient stop, drag it away from the ramp.

   ◆ To change the midpoint location between any two gradient stops, drag the midpoint icon along the top of the ramp.

FIGURE 10-5
**Creating a
Gradient Swatch**

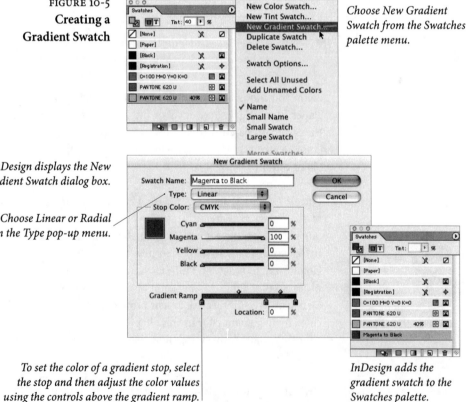

Choose New Gradient Swatch from the Swatches palette menu.

InDesign displays the New Gradient Swatch dialog box.

Choose Linear or Radial from the Type pop-up menu.

To set the color of a gradient stop, select the stop and then adjust the color values using the controls above the gradient ramp.

InDesign adds the gradient swatch to the Swatches palette.

3.  Once the gradient looks the way you want it to, click the OK button to add the gradient swatch to the Swatches palette. You can then apply this gradient to any object (or even text) as easily as applying a color swatch.

Once you've created a gradient swatch and applied it to an object on your page, you can fine-tune that object's gradient using the Gradient palette—reversing the order of the blend, dragging the gradient stops, and so on.

**Changing the order of the swatches in the Swatches palette.** To change the order in which colors appear in the Swatches palette, point at a color name and then drag the color name up or down in the Swatches palette. Once you've got the color where you want, drop it. This can be handy when you've got a long list of colors and want to position frequently used colors near the top of the palette. (Unfortunately, there's no way to drag swatches without applying them to selected objects on the page, so be careful to deselect all objects before playing in this palette.)

**Editing a Swatch.** To edit a swatch, do one of the following:

◆   Double-click the swatch in the Swatches palette. (We don't use this shortcut because the first click applies the swatch to the fill or stroke of any object we've selected, or applies the swatch to the default fill or stroke if no object is selected.)

◆   Select a swatch in the Swatches palette, then choose Swatch Options from the Swatches palette menu. Again, this method applies the swatch to the selection or to the document defaults, so we tend to avoid it.

◆   Press Command-Option-Shift/Ctrl-Alt-Shift and double-click a swatch to open the swatch for editing. We always use this method, as it does not apply the swatch to the selection or to the document default fill or stroke.

After any of the above actions, InDesign displays the dialog box appropriate to the type of swatch you clicked (the Edit Color Swatch, Edit Tint Swatch, or Edit Gradient Swatch dialog box). Make changes to the swatch definition, then click the OK button to close the dialog box. InDesign updates the appearance of all the objects formatted using the swatch.

Note that if you're looking for a different shade of the same basic CMYK color, you can hold down the Shift key while dragging one of the sliders. This moves the other sliders at the same time to achieve a lighter version of the same hue.

**Deleting a Swatch.** To delete a swatch from a publication, follow these steps (see Figure 10-6).

1.  Select the swatch in the Swatches palette (you may want to deselect all objects on the page first). To select a range of swatches, hold down Shift as you click the swatch names. To select non-contiguous swatches, hold down Command/Ctrl as you click the swatch names. If you want to select all the swatches that appear in the palette but aren't used anywhere in your document, choose Select All Unused from the palette menu.

2.  Click the Delete Swatch button in the Swatches palette (or choose Delete Color Swatch from the palette's menu). InDesign displays the Delete Swatch dialog box.

3.  If you want to replace the color you're deleting with an existing swatch, turn on the Defined Swatch option and choose the name of the swatch from the attached pop-up menu. To replace the swatch with an unnamed color (why would you want to do this?), turn on the Unnamed Swatch option.

4.  Click the OK button. InDesign deletes the swatch and applies the replacement swatch (if you selected the Defined Swatch option) or an unnamed color (if you selected the Unnamed Swatch option) to all of the objects formatted using the swatch you're deleting.

As we noted earlier, when you remove a swatch that you've used as a basis for tint swatches, InDesign bases the tint swatches on the color you specified (if you selected the Defined Swatch option), or just deletes the tint swatch if you choose Unnamed Swatch, Paper, or None.

Note that at the time we go to press, InDesign has a bug in which spot color swatches added by imported EPS graphics cannot easily be deleted, even if you delete the EPS file. The workaround is to choose Select All Unused from the Swatches palette menu, deselect all the swatches you want to keep (using Shift-clicking or Command/Ctrl-clicking), and then choosing Delete Swatch from the palette menu.

**Merging Swatches.** The folks at Adobe threw a rather confusing little feature into InDesign called Merge Swatches. The idea is simple: Take two or more swatches in the Swatches palette, merge them

FIGURE 10-6
**Deleting a Swatch**

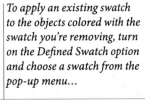

Select the swatch
(or swatches) you
want to delete.

Choose Delete Swatch from the
Swatches palette menu or click
the Delete Swatch button.

*To apply an existing swatch
to the objects colored with the
swatch you're removing, turn
on the Defined Swatch option
and choose a swatch from the
pop-up menu...*

*...or choose Unnamed Swatch
to have InDesign apply an
unnamed swatch of the same
color to the objects.*

together into a single swatch, and delete the others). The problem is few people ever figure out how it works. The key is that the first swatch you select will be the one that survives, the one that the other swatches will get merged into. After clicking on one swatch (make sure nothing is selected first, or else this click will apply the color to the selected object), then Command/Ctrl-click on one or more other swatches in the palette. Finally, select Merge Swatches from the Swatches palette menu. We find this only helpful when you've got a lot of swatches you want to merge together; for one or two, we usually just use Delete Swatch.

**Duplicating Swatches.** If you want to base a swatch on an existing swatch, select the swatch in the Swatches palette and then choose Duplicate Swatch from the palette's menu. (You can also click the New Swatch button in the Swatches palette, but that also applies the duplicate to any selected objects.) InDesign creates a copy of the swatch and assigns it a name (the default name is the name of the original swatch plus the word "copy"). At this point, you can edit the swatch by Command-Option-Shift/Ctrl-Alt-Shift double-clicking on it.

# The Color Palette

Given that we've already stated that you should use the Swatches palette instead of the Color palette, you might wonder why we're bothering to write the next section. Over the years, we've come to realize that our methods are not necessarily for everyone, and that some people have very different working habits from our own. For some of you, working with the Color palette and unnamed colors might be better than the process of creating named swatches—and there's nothing wrong with that.

The Color palette is always *on*—whenever you adjust the controls in the palette, you're applying them to something (either the selected object or the document's default fill and stroke formatting). For a look at the Color palette, see Figure 10-7.

The Color palette does have one thing that the Swatches palette's methods for defining colors lack: the Color Bar. To apply a color, drag the cursor in the Color Bar.

**Color Palette Shortcuts**

The Color palette has shortcuts, too.

◆ To display (or hide) the Color palette, press F6.

◆ To change the color mode of the palette, select RGB, Lab, or CMYK from the palette menu. Even faster, just Shift-click on the color bar to rotate through these options. If you're using a named swatch, Shift-clicking will also offer you a tint bar of the current color.

◆ When you enter a value (or a mathematical expression) in one of the color value fields, you can hold down Command/Ctrl as you press Return/Enter to apply the same percentage change to all of the color value fields. This works best when using CMYK colors in the Color palette.

FIGURE 10-7
**The Color Palette**

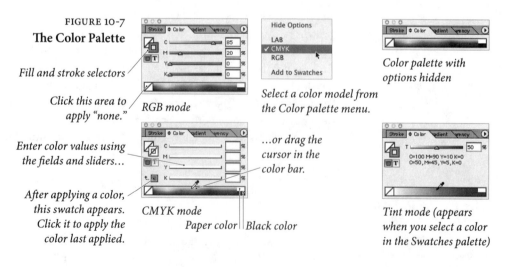

Fill and stroke selectors

Click this area to apply "none."

*RGB mode*

Enter color values using the fields and sliders...

After applying a color, this swatch appears. Click it to apply the color last applied.

*CMYK mode*

Paper color | Black color

Select a color model from the Color palette menu.

...or drag the cursor in the color bar.

*Color palette with options hidden*

*Tint mode (appears when you select a color in the Swatches palette)*

◆ To select a color that is similar in hue, but different in shade, hold down Shift as you drag a color value slider. This moves the other sliders in tandem (unless you're dragging the Black slider, or one of the other sliders is set to zero).

**Out-of-Gamut Warning.** The out-of-gamut warning that we discussed in the New Color Swatch dialog box appears in the Color palette, too, when a color swatch definition falls outside the gamut defined by the default CMYK document profile (see Figure 10-8). To adjust the color definition so that it falls in the gamut of the separations profile, click the alert icon. We discuss document profiles in detail when we explore color management later in this chapter. Note that as long as you are choosing colors in the CMYK mode, you won't see this alert (because they're all in gamut, by default). Also, note that you won't see this icon when you've chosen Hide Options from the palette menu.

FIGURE 10-8
**Fixing Out of Gamut Colors**

*When the current color cannot be printed by the separations printer you've selected, InDesign displays the out-of-gamut warning.*

*Click the icon to redefine the color so that it falls within the gamut of the output device.*

## Applying Colors and Gradients

Once you've selected an object, you can use any (or all) of the following techniques to apply a color, tint, or gradient to the object (see Figure 10-9).

◆ Click one of the selectors (Fill or Stroke) at the bottom of the Toolbox or in the Swatches palette, then click a color in the Swatches palette. InDesign applies the color to the object's fill or stroke.

◆ Click the Fill selector or the Stroke selector, then click the Apply Color button, Apply Gradient button, Apply None button, swap fill and stroke icon, or the default fill and stroke icon. Or press any of the keyboard shortcuts corresponding to the buttons (comma, period, slash, Shift-X, or D, respectively).

◆ Select an object, then adjust any of the controls in the Color palette (our least favorite method, as we've mentioned earlier).

◆ Drag a color swatch out of the Swatches palette and drop it on the fill or stroke of an object. You don't have to select the object on the page first.

◆ Use the Eyedropper tool to pick a color from an existing object, then click on another object to apply that color to it.

FIGURE 10-9
**Applying a Color**

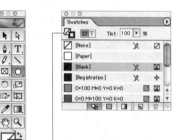

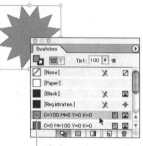

*Press X to switch between the Fill selector and the Stroke selector.*

*These three buttons apply last-used color swatch, gradient swatch, or None.*

*Select the Fill or Stroke selector in the Tools palette or the Swatches palette.*

*Click a color swatch.*

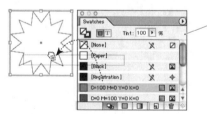

*Press F5 to display the Swatches palette.*

*Drag a color swatch out of the Swatches palette (note that you do not need to select an object to apply a color via this method) on to an object's fill or stroke.*

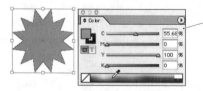

*Press F6 to display the Color palette.*

*Click the cursor in the color bar, or adjust one of the color controls in the Color palette, and InDesign applies the color to the selected object.*

**Applying Colors to Text**

You can apply a fill or stroke to the characters of text in your publication. Characters of text act just like individual objects on your page, so to apply a color to text, select it with the Text tool and apply a color using any of the techniques described above. Note that this means you can apply any color swatch, including gradients or None, to text. (The only reason we can think of to apply a fill of None to text is if you have also applied a colored stroke.) Of course, if you select the text block with the Selection tool and apply a color, InDesign applies the color to the fill or stroke of the text frame, not the text.

**Applying Colors to Imported Graphics**

You can apply colors to bi-level (black and white only) TIFFs, and grayscale TIFFs (or native Photoshop .PSD files). To apply a color to an imported image, select the image using the Direct Selection tool, click the Fill selector in the Toolbox, and then click a color swatch. When you print, InDesign prints the image on the appropriate separation (for a spot color) or series of plates (for a process color).

## Creating Spot-Color Tint Builds

When you're working with spot-color publications, you often want to create tint builds (also known as stacked screens) of the colors you're working with to broaden the range of colors in your publication. Since you can't create a color containing percentages of two or more spot colors (20-percent black and 60-percent PMS 327, for example), as you can in QuarkXPress, it'd seem, at first glance, that you're stuck. You're not, though, as the following exercise demonstrates.

1.  Open a new publication and add a spot color (create your own, or use one from the Pantone spot-color library).

2.  Draw a rectangle.

3.  Without deselecting the rectangle, fill it with the spot color you created in step 1; change the tint in the Swatches palette if you want. Set the rectangle's stroke to None.

4.  Clone the rectangle by selecting Step and Repeat from the Edit menu (or press Command-Shift-V/Ctrl-Shift-V). Enter 1 in the Repeat Count field and zero in the Horizontal Offset and Vertical Offset fields, then click the OK button to close the dialog box.

5.  Fill the clone with black, and set it to a tint (like 20 percent) in the Swatches palette.

6. Display the Attributes palette, if it's not already visible (choose Attributes from the Window menu). Turn on the Overprint Fill option to make the black rectangle overprint the underlying spot color shape.

That's all there is to it. When you print, the gray rectangle overprints the spot-color rectangle, creating a combination of the two spot colors. To see the effect, you can turn on Overprint Preview in the View menu.

**Using Transparency**  You can also build spot color tint builds by using InDesign's transparency features. In the example above, after cloning the rectangle and changing the duplicate's color and tint, you could set that object to Multiply mode in the Transparency palette. In this case, the result is exactly the same as overprinting the rectangle. However, while using this method is convenient (you don't have to turn on Overprint Preview to see the effect), it may cause other problems, depending on whether you have problems when printing transparency (see Chapter 11, "Printing," for more on printing transparency).

# Ink Manager

One of the most common complaints among prepress service providers is that too many publishers don't understand the difference between spot and process color inks, and they're forever creating spot color inks that need to be converted to process color at print time. If you're one of those service providers, you're going to love the Ink Manager. (If you're a designer, it's still important to understand the Ink Manager, but you probably won't use it much.) The Ink Manager does three things.

♦ You can tell the Ink Manager to convert spot colors to process colors at the time of output (but it won't change the actual color swatch definitions in your document).

♦ You can alias one spot color to another, so two (or more) different spot colors will output onto the same plate.

♦ You can tell InDesign how your inks act so that the program can trap them properly.

We'll discuss converting and aliasing spot colors here, and hold off on the trapping features until later in this chapter.

The Ink Manager appears in four different places: the Output panel of the Print dialog box, the Swatches palette menu, the Advanced panel of the Export PDF dialog box, and the Advanced panel of the Export EPS dialog box. A change made in any one of these places affects the Ink Manager in all its locations.

**Converting Spot Colors**

The Ink Manager dialog box lists the four process colors, plus every spot color in your document, whether or not they're actually used (see Figure 10-10). When you click in the column to the left of a spot color, the color changes to a process color (the little four-color icon appears). Click again, and it's a spot color again. As we said earlier, this does not change the color's definition; the color only changes at print or export time.

If you want to output all the spot colors in the document as process colors, turn on the All Spots to Process checkbox at the bottom of the Ink Manager dialog box.

FIGURE 10-10

**Ink Manager**

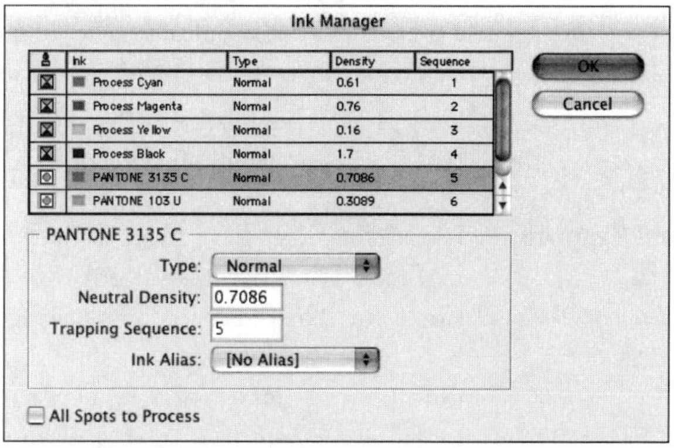

**Aliasing Spot Colors**

Let's say you create a document with two spot colors, but later find that you can only afford to print black and one spot color. You could replace one spot color with the other throughout your document by deleting one of them (see "Deleting a Swatch," earlier in this chapter). However, it's easier and more flexible to merge the two spot colors together at print time by *aliasing* one to the other.

To make an alias, select a spot color in the Ink Manager dialog box and choose a different color from the Ink Alias pop-up menu. Notice that the icon changes to the left of the color's icon (the icon, almost impossible to see without a loupe, is of an arrow pointing to a little ink well). You can still convert this color to a process color later if you want, using the techniques described above.

One of the coolest aspects of aliasing colors is that it works not only for spot colors applied to InDesign objects, but even to spot colors embedded in EPS graphics. Note that you can preview the spot color aliasing in your document by turning on both Overprint Preview and High Quality Display in the View menu.

# Trapping

A "trap" is a method of overlapping abutting colored objects to compensate for the imperfect registration of printing presses. Because registration, even on good presses with good operators, can be off by a quarter point or more, abutting elements in your publication may not end up abutting perfectly when the publication is printed by your commercial printer. What happens then? The paper shows through where you don't want it to (see Color Figures 2 and 3).

Do we need to tell you what happens when you take your work to a press that's badly out of register or run by turkeys? Disaster. Before this happens to you, talk with your commercial printer regarding the tolerances of their presses and/or operators. Don't ask them if they're turkeys—it's considered rude.

**Manual Trapping**    If you can't (or don't want to) use InDesign's automatic trapping methods (In-RIP or built-in), you can still trap your publication—you'll just have to do it yourself. We describe this process first because we believe that you should know how to add and subtract, multiply and divide before you ever use a calculator.

However, before we start describing manual trapping techniques, we need to state that InDesign's automatic trapping methods can almost always trap your publications better than you can (assuming that you have both deadlines and a finite amount of patience), and if you use them, you usually won't even have to *think* about trapping. Also, many prepress houses prefer to use post-process trapping software; in this case, they'll want you to leave trapping turned off (it's off by default). As always, check with your service provider before doing anything rash.

**Object-Level Overprinting.** The key to trapping, in InDesign and any other software, is in controlling which objects—or which parts of objects—print on top of other objects as the printing press prints your publication. The only way to make manual trapping work is to control the overprinting characteristics of individual objects (see Color Figures 1 and 4).

Luckily, you can. Any InDesign path can be specified as an overprinting object (that is, it won't knock a hole in any objects behind it when you print), regardless of the object's color. The controls for object-level overprinting are the Overprint Fill and Overprint Stroke options found in the Attributes palette (see Figure 10-11). These controls, used in combination with InDesign's Paste Into command, can be used to create virtually any trap.

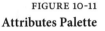

FIGURE 10-11

**Attributes Palette**

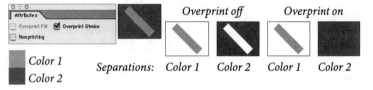

We have to stress the importance of the Weight Changes Bounding Box option on the Stroke palette menu. You cannot create traps when this option is turned off, so you'll have to make sure it's turned on as you follow any of the procedures in this section. (We don't usually have this turned on, which is one reason we prefer to use auto trapping rather than manual trapping.)

When you're working with trapping, you'll be creating *spreads* (outlines of objects, in the same color as the object, that are slightly larger than the object itself) and *chokes* (outlines of the object that are the same color as the underlying object's color). Spreads make the object larger so that the edges of the object print over the underlying object; chokes make the area knocked out of the underlying object smaller than the outline of the foreground object.

Use chokes when the foreground object is a darker color than the background object; use spreads when the foreground object is lighter. In other words, trap from light colors into darker colors. Sound subjective? It is. We use chokes when we're trapping type—text characters often look distorted when you use spreads (the eye is very critical when it comes to text). Some folks ask why you don't just always overprint every color on top of every other color. The answer is that inks are almost never fully opaque, so if you print solid cyan on top of solid magenta, you'll get purple—probably not the effect you were looking for. With trapping, you'll still get purple, but only in a tiny stripe along the edge between the cyan and magenta objects.

**Overprint Preview.** InDesign has a powerful feature called Overprint Preview (in the View menu), which gives you an on-screen preview of the strokes and fills that you set to overprint. You may not want to work with Overprint Preview turned on all the time because there is a slight performance hit, but it's certainly worth leaving it on when trapping, or when zooming in to 2000% or more to see if something is trapping correctly.

**Overprinting Black.** By default, all objects on an InDesign page knock out of all objects behind them—unless they're black. InDesign, by default, overprints black ink. Most of the time, this is a good thing. To turn off black overprinting, display the General panel of the Preferences dialog box and turn off the Overprint Black option.

Remember, however, that black ink isn't really fully opaque, even if it looks like it is on screen. Overprinting solid areas of black on an image or other page objects can look mottled, and unfortunately even Overprint Preview won't display this problem unless you have color management enabled (which we discuss later in this chapter). If you need larger areas of solid black in a full-color document, consider making a *rich black*, a CMYK black that is made of 100 percent black plus perhaps 25 percent each of cyan, magenta, and yellow.

**Solid Color Trapping.** It's more important to trap abutting color fields in publications when you're printing using spot colors or areas of single process colors (like where 100 percent cyan text sits on top of 50-percent magenta background) than it is in most process color publications. Usually when you're working with process colors, you'll almost always see some ink between abutting objects, so you're less likely to see paper-colored gaps showing a poor trap.

The easiest way to demonstrate how spot-color trapping works is to show you some examples. As you work through these examples, you'll trap an ellipse into a rectangle by manipulating the color, width, and overprinting specifications of the path that surrounds the ellipse. First, draw the colored objects.

1. Create a rectangle. Fill the rectangle with a spot color ("Color 1"). Set the rectangle's stroke color to None.

2. Draw an ellipse on top of the rectangle. Make sure that the ellipse is entirely inside the rectangle. Fill the ellipse with a different color from that of the rectangle ("Color 2"). Set the stroke of the ellipse to None.

3. Save the file.

The ellipse needs to be trapped, or you'll run the risk of having paper-colored lines appear up around the ellipse when you print the publication. You can either spread or choke the ellipse, or both.

To spread the ellipse, follow these steps (see Color Figure 3).

1. Select the ellipse.

2. Press F10 to display the Stroke palette.

3. Turn on the Weight Changes Bounding Box option from the Stroke palette menu, then enter a new line width in the Weight field. The line width you enter in the Weight field should be equal to twice the trap amount—if you enter "2", you'll get a stroke of one point on either side of the path. If your commercial printer has asked for a trap of .5 points, enter "1" in the Weight field.

4. While the object is still selected, turn on Overprint Stroke in the Attributes palette.

When you print, the fill of the ellipse knocks out the background, but the stroke overprints. That means the ellipse is larger than the hole that's been knocked out of the background rectangle. You've just created a spread.

To choke the ellipse, change the stroke color of the ellipse to the same as the background color (see Color Figure 3). Now when you print, the hole that's knocked out of the background rectangle is slightly smaller than the original ellipse.

Choose Revert from the File menu to get the file ready for the next procedure.

**Trapping Across Color Boundaries.** The techniques described above work well as long as objects don't cross color boundaries. If the objects do cross color boundaries (especially going from a color background to a white background), it's too obvious that you've changed the shapes of the objects. What do you do?

1. Drag the ellipse so that it's partially outside of the rectangle, and then press Command-Shift-[/Ctrl-Shift-[ to send it to the back (behind the rectangle).

2. Press Command-C/Ctrl-C to copy the ellipse.

3. Now select the rectangle and select Paste Into from the Edit menu (or press Command-Option-V/Ctrl-Alt-V). This duplicate should appear in exactly the same place as the original, but nested inside the rectangle. If for some reason it doesn't show up in the same place, then select the original ellipse, and note the values in the X and Y fields of the Transform palette. Then use the Direct Selection tool to select the nested ellipse, turn off

Show Content Offset in the Transform palette menu, and enter the X and Y values into the Transform palette fields. InDesign moves the copy of the ellipse into the same position as the original ellipse.

4. Without deselecting the duplicate ellipse, enter a stroke weight for the trap in the Weight field of the Stroke palette. Make sure that the fill and stroke colors are the same in the Swatches palette.

5. Turn on the Overprint Stroke option in the Attributes palette.

At this point, the ellipse you pasted inside the rectangle spreads slightly, while the part of the ellipse outside the rectangle remains the same size and shape. If you want the rectangle's color to choke into the ellipse, then change the color of the nested ellipse's stroke to match the rectangle's fill color.

What happens when the object you need to trap overlaps more than one other, differently colored object? In this case, you can run into trouble. The trap you use for one background color might not be the trap you want to use for the other. You might want to spread one and choke the other, depending on the colors you're using. In these cases, you can use the same basic techniques described above for the overlapping and/or abutting objects. But, at this point, we have to urge you to save yourself some trouble and use either of InDesign's automatic trapping methods.

**Trapping Lines.** The trapping techniques above work well for filled paths, but what open paths? After all, you can't apply two different stroke properties to a single path. Instead, you clone the path and make the width of the clone larger or smaller for the spread or choke you want. One of the strokes overprints; the other line knocks out.

Follow these steps to spread an open path (see Color Figure 2).

1. Draw a rectangle and fill it with a spot color.

2. Draw a path inside the rectangle. Create another spot color and apply it to the path. Do not set this path to overprint.

3. Select the path and clone it with Step and Repeat.

4. Increase the stroke weight of this duplicate path by twice the amount of spread you need (remember, PostScript strokes grow out from their centers) and turn on the Overprint Stroke option in the Attributes palette to make the stroke overprint.

That's all there is to it. The original path knocks a hole in the background rectangle, and the clone of the path spreads to just a little bit beyond the edges of the knockout. Of course, this doesn't create a trap around the ends of the line, just the sides.

To choke the path, follow these steps (see Color Figure 2).

1. Draw a rectangle. Create a spot color and fill the rectangle with it.

2. Draw a path inside the rectangle. Create another spot color and apply it to the line. Set this path to overprint.

3. Select the path and clone it.

4. Decrease the weight of the path by twice the amount of choke you need in the Stroke palette. Turn off the Overprint Stroke option in the Attributes palette.

This time, the cloned path is narrower than the original and knocks out an area that's slightly smaller than the original path, creating a choke.

**Trapping Text.** Text is usually the element in a publication that needs trapping the most. For whatever reason, it's easier to notice poor trapping around text than around other elements. At the same time, traps that are too large distort the shapes of the characters you're trapping. It's especially a problem with small type, especially serif type.

Here's how to create a spread for text (see Color Figure 3).

1. Draw a rectangle, create a spot color ("Color 1"), and apply it to the rectangle.

2. Enter text in a text frame. Position the text frame on top of the rectangle so that the text is entirely within the area occupied by the rectangle.

3. Create a second spot color ("Color 2") and apply it to the text in the text frame.

4. While the text is still selected, display the Stroke palette. Enter the stroke weight you want (remember, it's two times the amount of trap you want) in the Weight field. Turn on the Overprint Stroke option in the Attributes palette.

The next example shows how you can choke text by making the shape the characters knock out of the background a bit smaller than the characters themselves.

1. Draw a rectangle, create a spot color ("Color 1"), and apply it to the rectangle.

2. Create a text frame. Position the text frame on top of the rectangle so that it's entirely within the rectangle.

3. Create a second spot color ("Color 2"). Select all the text in the text frame and apply "Color 2" to the fill of the text.

4. Clone the text frame using Step and Repeat with zero offsets.

5. Select the text in the duplicate frame, set its fill color to None and give it a stroke color the same as the background rectangle ("Color 1").

6. Enter the stroke weight you want for the trap in the Weight field of the Stroke palette. Turn on the Overprint Stroke option in the Attributes palette.

If text crosses color boundaries, use the techniques described earlier for trapping overlapping paths.

**Process-Color Trapping.** Process-color trapping is a bit simpler than spot-color trapping, because it's usually less critical that process-colored elements have traps (because many of these colors are built of multiple process colors, so there are shared colors—if one color shifts on press, then the other colors are still there to cover the white paper). However, it can be far harder to figure out exactly what color to make the stroke for a process-colored object. And when you're talking about trapping two process-colored graduated fills, watch out!

The main thing to keep in mind, however, is that for each of the process inks the ink percentage used in the topmost object in any stack of objects always wins—they knock out all percentages of that ink behind them, regardless of any overprinting settings.

*Unless, that is, the ink percentage is zero.* If, for example, the percentage of cyan used in the fill color of the topmost object in a stack of objects is zero, turning Overprint off makes the path knock out any other cyan in the area covered by the path. Overprinting the fill, in this case, means that the area taken up by the fill disappears from the cyan plates—the percentage of cyan in the next object in the stack shows through the area where the objects overlap. If your head is spinning at this point, just go see Color Figure 4 for a visual explanation.

Another way to think of this is to think of each ink in a process color as behaving like a separate spot ink.

**Simple Process-Color Trapping.** In process-color trapping, you've got to make your overprinting strokes different colors from either the background or foreground objects. Why? Because process colors have a way of creating new colors when you print them over each other. It's what they do best.

As in the spot-color trapping section above, we'll demonstrate process-color trapping techniques by example.

1.  Create a rectangle that's filled with "Color 1," which is specified as 20C 100M 0Y 10K.

2.  On top of this rectangle, draw an ellipse and fill it with "Color 2," which is specified as 0C 100M 50Y 0K.

3.  Select both objects and set their stroke to None.

4.  Save the file.

The ellipse needs to be trapped, or you run the risk of having cyan-colored lines appearing around the ellipse when the publication is printed—which could happen if the cyan and yellow plates aren't in good register, or if your paper stretches. Whether you spread or choke the ellipse depends on its color. If the ellipse is darker than the background rectangle, choke the ellipse. If the ellipse is a lighter color than the background rectangle, spread the ellipse. In this case, the ellipse is a lighter color, so you'll use a spread. To spread the ellipse, follow these steps.

1.  Create a new process color in the Swatches palette containing only those colors in "Color 2" having higher values than "Color 1." Quick quiz: what component colors in "Color 2" have higher values than their counterparts in "Color 1"? If you said 50Y, you're the lucky winner. Specify a new color: 0C 0M 50Y 0K (we'll call this "Color 3").

2.  Select the ellipse.

3.  Press F10 to display the Stroke palette, if it's not already visible. Enter the stroke weight you want for your stroke in the Weight field. It should be twice the width of your desired trap.

4.  Apply the color swatch "Color 3" to the stroke of the ellipse and set it to overprint.

When you print, all the areas around the ellipse have some dot value inside them, and the new colors created where the objects abut won't be too obvious. Choose Revert from the File menu to get ready for the next example.

What if the ellipse is the darker color? If it were, we'd have to choke it. To choke the ellipse, follow these steps.

1. Select the ellipse and fill it with "Color 1." Select the rectangle and fill it with "Color 2."

2. Create a new color ("Color 3") that contains only the largest color component in "Color 1." That's 100M, so "Color 3" should be specified as 0C 100M 0Y 0K.

3. Use the Weight field in the Stroke palette to specify the weight of the trap you want.

4. Set the stroke color to "Color 3."

5. Turn on the Overprint Stroke option in the Attributes palette.

When you print, the stroke you applied to the ellipse guarantees that there's no gap around the ellipse, even if you run into registration problems when you print the publication.

**Automatic Trapping**

At this point, you've read your way through the manual trapping techniques and are seriously considering hiring twenty house elves to take care of your trapping needs. But wait—InDesign includes two powerful automatic trapping methods: In-RIP trapping and InDesign built-in trapping (see Color Figure 5).

What are the differences between the two automatic trapping methods? InDesign's built-in trapping cannot do the following things (all of which can be accomplished by in-RIP trapping).

◆ Trap gradients created in InDesign.

◆ Use trap widths greater than 4 points.

◆ Be used with in-RIP separations.

◆ Be used with most OPI or DCS workflows.

◆ Create traps inside color images, or trap InDesign objects to images contained in DCS, EPS, or PDF files.

◆ Trap imported vector graphics or type within PDF or EPS files. See "Built-in Trapping and Imported Graphics," later in this chapter.

Don't let the length of the above list discourage you—InDesign's built-in trapping can take care of the trapping needs of most publications and printing processes. If, however, you see an item in the above list that is crucial to your publication, then you'd probably better use in-RIP trapping.

Of course, in-RIP trapping only works with PostScript printers that have trapping built in. All PostScript 3 devices should be able to handle this, but if you have a PostScript Level 2 printer, check with the manufacturer to see if it has this feature. In-RIP trapping also only works when you're also using in-RIP color separations. Most people don't use in-RIP separations (they separate on a host machine), so they can't use in-RIP trapping either. In that case, we recommend third-party post-process trapping software that creates traps for you.

Note that both forms of automatic trapping work best with PostScript and OpenType fonts; this is another instance where TrueType fonts may cause problems.

**Built-in Trapping and Imported Graphics.** When InDesign elements overlap an imported EPS or PDF graphic, InDesign won't be able to trap the InDesign elements properly and you can get odd trapping results. If the elements don't touch each other, or don't need to be trapped, this isn't a problem. If the InDesign object does touch the graphic, however, you can sometimes work around the problem by adjusting the frame that contains the graphic. If the InDesign elements overlap an empty area in the graphic, edit the shape of the frame containing the graphic so that it doesn't touch the elements.

Alternatively, you can copy and paste paths from Illustrator or FreeHand (or any other application capable of putting data on the system Clipboard in Illustrator format), thereby converting the paths into InDesign objects—but this will only work for very simple graphics.

**Specifying Trapping Settings.** While InDesign's default trap settings are reasonably good for most sheetfed print jobs, you will likely have to change the trap settings for different jobs or for different pages within a job (InDesign does not let you adjust the trap style for individual objects on your page). You can do all of this with the Trap Styles palette (see Figure 10-12). Note that this is different from InDesign 1.x, which hid trapping settings in the Print dialog box.

All documents start with two trap styles: Default and No Trap Style. We'll see how you can use No Trap Style later when we talk about assigning trap styles to pages. If you just want to change the trapping values for the entire document, edit Default by double-clicking on it in the Trap Styles palette. Or, to create a new trap style,

Option/Alt-click on the New Trap Style button at the bottom of the palette (or select New Trap Style from the palette menu).

The New Trap Style and the Modify Trap Style dialog boxes are functionally equivalent. Here's a quick rundown of what all these cryptic features are for.

**Trap Width.** The value you enter in the Default field sets the trap width for all inks except solid black—you set that trap width using the nearby Black field. If you're using InDesign's built-in trapping, the trapping width is never greater than four points (regardless of the value you enter in these two fields).

If you're working with a rich black (that is, a color containing other process inks in addition to black), the value you enter in the Black Width field also sets a kind of "margin" of black ink at the edges of a rich black object. This margin is known as the "holdback" or "holdback area."

The holdback area comes in handy at the edges of a rich black object. If, for example, you've placed white text over a rich black area, the holdback area prevents the non-black inks from appearing around the edges of the white characters.

FIGURE 10-12
**Trapping Settings**

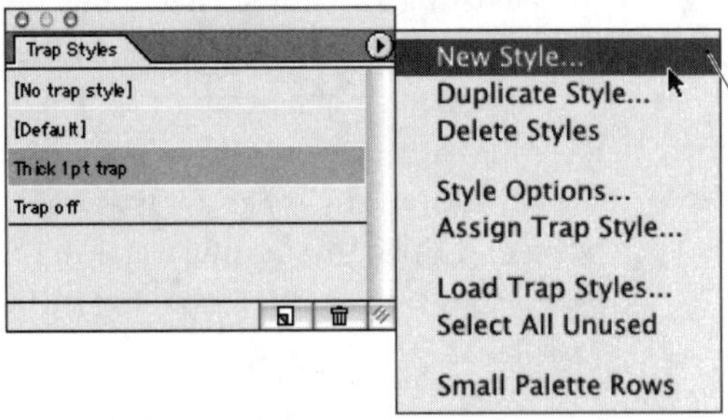

To create a trapping style, select New Style from the menu or Option/Alt-click the New Style button.

*InDesign displays the New Trap Style dialog box.*

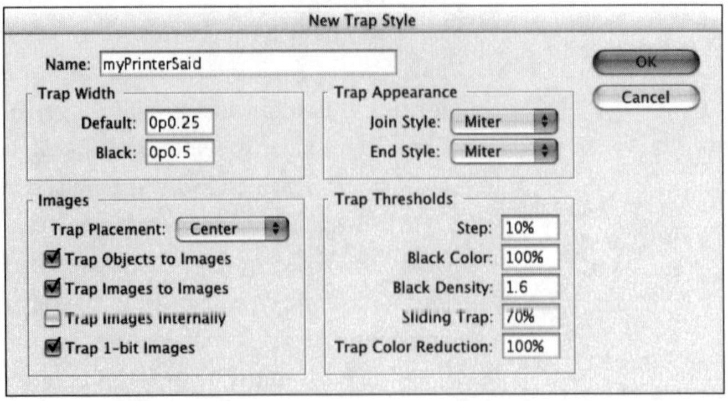

**Trap Appearance.** Those of you who *really* care about how your traps appear can adjust the look and feel of trap lines with the Join Style and End Style pop-up menus. Join Style determines how corner points in trap segments will appear (mitered, rounded, or beveled). End Style determines how the trap lines act at their end points (the default, Mitered, keeps the trap lines slightly away from each other, while Overlap lets the trap lines... well, overlap). We typically just leave both of these set to their default values.

**Trap Thresholds.** Imagine that you have two process colors in your publication. Color 1 is defined as 60C 20M 0Y 0K, and Color 2 is 65C 15M 0Y 5K. Do these two colors need to be trapped if they happen to end up next to each other on your InDesign pages? That depends on you, your publication, and your commercial printer. The fields in the Trapping Thresholds section of the New Trap Style dialog box control when and how InDesign traps the boundaries between colors in a publication.

The Step field sets the percentage of difference between each color component to trigger automatic trapping. In the above example of Color 1 and Color 2, using the default value of 10 percent in the Step Limit field means that InDesign would not trap the two colors—there's not enough difference between the inks that make up the two colors. If you lowered the value in the Step Limit field to 5 percent, InDesign would trap the objects (because the C, M, and K ink components vary by that percentage).

**Black Color.** How much black ink has to be used in a color before InDesign applies the holdback defined by the value you entered in the Black field? That depends on what you enter in the Black Color Limit field. Enter 100 percent when you want to apply a holdback to colors containing 100 percent black ink, or lower the percentage to apply a holdback to colors containing less black ink.

**Black Density.** InDesign traps colors in a publication based on their ink neutral densities (see "Editing Ink Neutral Densities," later in this chapter). Lighter colors typically spread into areas of darker colors, which usually produces a less obvious trap. You can manipulate the way that InDesign traps objects by changing the neutral densities in the Ink Manager dialog box. Or you can use the Black Density field to redefine the density InDesign thinks of as black. By default, black ink is set to an ink neutral density of 1.6.

The value you enter in the Black Density Limit field also affects InDesign's application of the Black holdback area. By reducing the value in the Black Density Limit field, you instruct InDesign to apply the holdback to inks other than black.

**Sliding Trap.** When gradients abut, the colors at the edges of the gradients vary along the border between the two gradients. You can't use a simple spread or choke for the entire length of the boundary between gradients—at some point, the trap will just become too obvious.

One way to solve this problem is to use a centerline trap—a trap that extends equally on either side of the boundary between the gradients. Another method is to use a sliding trap—which changes from a spread to a centerline trap, and then to a choke, depending on the ink neutral densities of the colors used in the gradients.

The value you enter in the Sliding Trap Limit field defines the point (or points) at which the trap switches from a spread to a centerline trap, and from a centerline trap to a choke. This value is a percentage of the difference between ink neutral densities (note that this is unlike the percentage in the Step Limit field, which is the difference between the color components making up a color). Enter zero percent to force InDesign to use a centerline trap for the entire length of the trap, or enter 100% to make InDesign apply a spread along the length of the boundary between the two gradients. Other values (such as the default 70 percent) apply sliding traps.

**Trap Color Reduction.** The value you enter in this field defines the colors InDesign creates as it builds traps. When the value in this field is 100 percent, some color combinations can result in a trapping color (or colors) that is darker than either of the original colors. To avoid this, enter a smaller value in this field. Enter zero to set the neutral density of the objects created by the trapping system to the neutral density of the darkest color (note that this doesn't necessarily mean it's the same color).

**Image Settings.** The controls in the Images section of the New Trap Style dialog box define the way that InDesign traps InDesign page items to imported graphics. Note that "image," in the context of this dialog box, means any imported graphic—not just bitmaps.

**Trap Placement.** Choose Center to apply a centerline trap (see "Sliding Trap," above) to the boundary between the InDesign object and the imported graphic. Choose Choke to extend the InDesign objects into the area inside the imported graphic. Choose Neutral Density to apply the trap based on the ink neutral density of the abutting colors. Choose Spread to spread the colors from the image into the InDesign object.

**Trap Objects to Images.** Turn this option on to apply automatic trapping to areas where InDesign objects abut imported images. InDesign uses the trapping method you chose from the Image Trap Placement pop-up menu to trap the objects (see above).

**Trap Images to Images.** This feature lets InDesign build traps where two bitmapped images abut each other.

**Trap Internal Images.** Turn this option on to apply in-RIP trapping to areas of color inside imported bitmap images. Most scanned images (photographs) don't need trapping—this option is for synthetic images (such as screen shots) containing abutting areas of flat color. Turn this option off for faster trapping.

**Trap 1-bit Images.** Turn this option on to trap bilevel (black and white) images to InDesign objects. This affects images to which you've applied colors in InDesign.

**Trapping Ranges**

If the pages in your publication have differing trapping needs, you can use trapping ranges to vary the trapping styles used to trap the publication. For instance, if one or more pages don't require trapping at all (perhaps they include only black text or objects don't overlap at all), your document will print faster if you turn off trapping for those pages. To change one or more page's trap style, select Assign Trap Style from the Trap Styles palette menu (see Figure 10-13).

In the Assign Trap Styles dialog box, select a trapping style from the Trap Style pop-up menu, then enter the page range you want to trap using the style (separate individual pages with commas and page ranges with hyphens). Make sure you click the Assign button before clicking Done, or else InDesign ignores your change. To turn off trapping for a page or range of pages, select [No Trap Style] from the Trap Style pop-up menu.

**Editing Ink Neutral Densities**

When you use either automatic trapping method, the trapping system (whether in InDesign or in a PostScript RIP) bases its trapping decisions on the inks used in abutting objects on an InDesign page. In general, the trapping system tries to spread lighter inks into darker inks. How can the system tell which inks are lighter or

FIGURE 10-13

**Assigning Trap Styles**

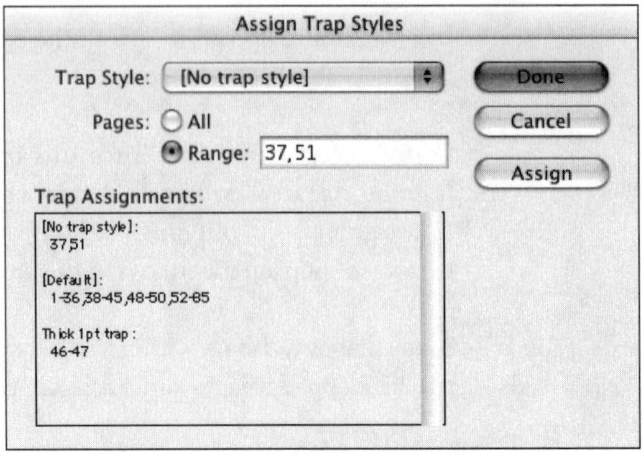

**Assign Trap Styles**

Trap Style: [No trap style]    Done

Pages: ○ All    Cancel
● Range: 37,51    Assign

Trap Assignments:

[No trap style]:
37,51

[Default]:
1-36,38-45,48-50,52-65

Thick 1pt trap :
46-47

darker? By comparing the ink *neutral density* values between the objects. A color's neutral density is sort of like "how dark would the color be if this were in grayscale."

In general, InDesign assigns ink neutral density values based on the CMYK values of the colors you've used in a publication. If you've used spot colors (inks), or have created colors using the RGB or LAB color model, InDesign uses the process color equivalent of the color.

Most of the time, this approach works pretty well. But we can think of three cases in which you might want to edit the ink neutral density values.

◆ **Varnishes.** A varnish should almost always be the lightest ink on the page, so set its ink neutral density to 0 (zero). This way, the trapping system will spread the varnish into abutting objects.

◆ **Metallic Pantone inks.** Metallic inks are more opaque than other inks, and they're also somewhat reflective. Spreading a metallic ink into an abutting area of some other color is almost certain to create an obvious trap. Set the ink neutral density of metallic inks to 1.7 (the value of black ink) or higher—that way, they will be considered the darkest ink on the page by the trapping system (and all other inks will spread into them).

◆ **Pantone fluorescent inks.** Like metallic inks, fluorescent inks are more opaque than other inks, and they're also very bright. In general, you want every other ink to spread into an area of fluorescent ink, so you set the ink neutral density to a high value. We think that 1.6 makes a good setting for fluorescent inks— that way, they'll spread into black areas, but most other inks will spread into the fluorescent ink.

◆ **Pantone pastel inks.** These are very light colors and should be treated in much the same way as you'd treat a varnish. Set the ink neutral density value to .15—approximately the same value as that of process yellow ink.

To edit the neutral density value for an ink, follow these steps.

1. Open the Ink Manager dialog box from the Swatches palette menu or the Print dialog box.

2. Select the ink you want to edit.

3. To set the ink type, choose an option from the Type pop-up menu. You use these options to declare to the trapping system that a specific ink doesn't follow the usual trapping rules. This can come in handy when you're working with certain types of spot inks: varnishes, metallic colors, fluorescent colors, and pastel colors. You can also control the inks trapping behavior by manipulating its ink neutral density, as in Step 5.

   ◆ Choose Normal for all process inks and for most spot colors.

   ◆ Choose Transparent for varnishes and very light spot inks (Pantone pastels, for example).

   ◆ Choose Opaque for very opaque inks, such as Pantone metallic or fluorescent colors.

   ◆ Choose OpaqueIgnore for inks you want to have the trapping system ignore entirely. For instance, nontransparent metallic inks or varnishes.

4. Enter a new value in the Neutral Density field. Do this only if you've set the Type pop-up menu to Normal. Use this approach if your publication contains "specialty inks" (the ink types listed in Step 4) and you need to define the ways these inks trap to each other.

5. The Trapping Sequence field offers a way for you to tell InDesign the order in which the inks will be printed (this has no effect at all on the order in which the color separations will print). While it's rare that you'd need this, the Trapping Sequence feature can be useful if you're printing multiple opaque inks. For instance, InDesign can then know to spread other inks underneath the last-printed opaque ink.

6. Click the OK button to close the Ink Manager dialog box and apply your changes.

Note that changing the neutral density values for an ink has no effect on how the color appears on screen, even when Overprint Preview is turned on. This only affects InDesign's trapping behavior.

## Color Management

When you aim at a target—and it doesn't matter whether you're aiming a rifle, a bow, a laser, or a camera—you have to make adjustments. You've got to consider the atmospheric conditions, the distance to the target, the characteristics of the target itself. Once you know what the variables are, and how they affect what you're trying to do, you've got a better chance of hitting the bullseye.

The same thing is true in color management. You need to understand the tools you have to work with, how they work together (or don't), and how they combine to produce the colors you see in the printed version of your publication.

It would be nice if we could make what we see on our screen exactly match what we'll get when we print. But we can't, for a variety of practical and physiological reasons (not to mention simple lack of time and money). That said, we must also add that we can get very close—and we can also make the relationship between the display and the printed piece more consistent and predictable.

The "device" (a printer, scanner, monitor, or printing press) is the key. Every device renders colors in a slightly different way. To adjust color in one environment so that it matches the color as seen in another environment, color management systems refer to a file containing information on the color characteristics of a device (how it displays or prints color). This file is called a "device profile." Device profiles for scanners and printers are usually created by the manufacturers who make the hardware, though quite a few come with InDesign. You've got to make monitor profiles yourself, because every monitor is different (just as several television sets from the same manufacturer can show the same image differently). The process of creating a device profile is called "characterizing" a device.

Once a device profile has been created for a device, you've got to maintain (or "calibrate") the device so that it doesn't vary from the profile. Imagesetter operators and commercial printers calibrate their equipment regularly (or should) to match industry standards.

InDesign's color management system uses device profiles approved by the International Color Consortium (ICC). If you're on the Macintosh, you can also use device profiles provided by Apple with the system-level ColorSync color management system (these profiles are also approved by the ICC).

For more on choosing device profiles, see "InDesign's Color Management Controls," later in this chapter.

**For More Information**

Color management is an enormous subject and we can only focus on one aspect of the big picture here: How color management works in InDesign. If any terminology in this section is confusing to you (like gamut, ICC profile, color engines, and rendering intents), we encourage you to go look at two other sources for a truly in-depth look at getting consistent color. First, because most of what you want to manage is probably created in Photoshop, check out a book that David wrote with Bruce Fraser: *Real World Photoshop*. Then, to really see how all this fits together, see *Real World Color Management*, by Bruce Fraser, Chris Murphy, and Fred Bunting.

**Do You Need Color Management?**

Everyone wants consistent color from original to screen to proof print to printing press, but it's worth asking yourself whether you really need it. Managing color is not as simple as turning on a checkbox, and though it's not as hard as flying an airplane, it can still cause a fair amount of rifling through medicine cabinets trying to ease the pain in your head. You may not need to worry a lot about managing color in InDesign if you can rely on color swatch books when picking solid colors, and if you can rely on color prepress professionals to deal with your color Photoshop images.

There are other instances when it's not even worth trying to get InDesign to manage your color. For example, InDesign can't manage grayscale images or spot colors (unless you convert them to process colors). Similarly, InDesign isn't really set up to color manage vector art when saved as an EPS file (it can do it, but we don't recommend it). Vector art saved as PDF or native Adobe Illustrator (.ai) files should work reasonably well.

Nevertheless, we must admit that it is particularly satisfying when you work through all the issues and achieve (as close as possible) parity among your screen, inkjet printer, and final press output. Being able to rely on your screen ("soft proofing") and desktop color printer is a great boost in efficiency, too. Plus, as the world becomes increasingly reliant on direct to plate technologies, bypassing film entirely, color management systems become increasingly important to ensure quality output. And if you want to import RGB images and let InDesign do the color separation for you at print time, you'll get better reults if color management is turned on (see Color Figure 10).

**Controlling Your Color-Viewing Environment**

If it's important to you that what you see on your screen looks as much like the printed version of your publication as possible, there are a few rules you need to follow.

◆ Use a monitor and video system capable of displaying at least 24-bit color.

◆ Characterize and calibrate your monitor with a tool like the Spyder with Optical software. If color is of critical importance to you and your publications, find a system that works with your monitor, or buy a monitor that works with the calibration system you prefer.

◆ Control the lighting around your monitor and keep it consistent when you're working. Just about everyone agrees that the fluorescent lighting used in most of our office buildings is the worst possible lighting for viewing colors. Turn it off, if you can, and rely on incandescent lighting (desk lamps with one sort of bulb or another) to light your work area. If you can't turn it off, try getting some "full spectrum" (or "amber") fluorescent tubes to install above your monitor. These also reduce eye strain.

◆ Control the lighting of the area where you'll be viewing your color proofs. Ideally, you'd have a room or small booth equipped with "daylight" (or 5,000-degree Kelvin) lamps—but few of us can afford the money or space required.

Why is lighting important? Basically, the temperature of the light affects what a color "objectively" looks like. You can't assume ideal viewing conditions, but you have to work in them to be able to do consistent work.

**Is What You See Anything like What You'll Get?**

One of the simplest rules for getting the color you expect is also one of the least technologically advanced: Any time you're working with ink, refer to printed samples, rather than looking at the colors on your screen. Remember that, unlike the paper you'll be printing on, your screen is backlit, so it displays colors very differently from what they'll look like when printed.

If you're using uncoated paper, look at samples of the ink (spot color) or ink mix (process color) printed on uncoated stock. If you're using coated paper, look at examples printed on coated paper. If you're using a colored paper, try to find an example of the ink printed on a colored paper—though these examples are much harder to find (if it's a big enough job, your printer might be willing to make a "draw down" for you by mixing the ink and scraping it on the paper by hand).

Pantone makes a line of swatch books showing their libraries of spot and process colors (including process color equivalents of the spot colors); they're printed on both coated and uncoated stocks, and, although they're kind of expensive, they're not as expensive as pulling a job off of a press because you didn't like the press check. They're downright cheap if you consider what they must cost to print.

However, we don't recommend you use Pantone spot colors (the ones you find in the Pantone spot color library) to specify a process color. The Pantone Matching System is a spot-color specifying system, and the colors don't convert to process colors particularly well because you can't make any given hue just using process colors (see the discussion earlier in this chapter).

While Pantone also makes a swatch book with a spectrum full of process colors, we tend to like the one made by Trumatch even more; it's just easier to use for some reason.

Don't assume that color printers will automatically produce an accurate simulation of what the colors in your publication are going to look like when they're printed by your commercial printer. To do that, you'll have to do some work—you'll have to run test pages and adjust device profiles. And, at the same time, bear in mind that most color printers print using something akin to the process-color method. Your spot colors will be converted to process colors during printing. Some of the six- and seven-color inkjet printers can produce good matches for most spot inks.

Note, however, that the color proofs you print on a color inkjet printer cannot show you the way that your pages will print on a printing press. In particular, they can't show you trapping problems. For that, you need to use one of the color proofing processes (such as Chromalin or Press Match) to create your proofs from the film you've gotten out of your imagesetter. Imagesetting service bureaus frequently offer color proofing as part of their business. Some of these proofing processes can give you a proof on the paper you're intending to use, or can give you transparent overlays that you can place on top of your selected paper to get an idea of what your publication will look like when printed. If you're printing direct to plate or direct to press, then there won't be any film from which to burn proofs and you have to be all the more careful when setting up your files.

**When Color Management Is Turned Off**   InDesign's color management is turned off by default (we dicuss how to turn it on in the next section). However, the program can still do some basic color management when it needs to. For example, if you import an RGB image and print color separations, InDesign will convert the RGB to CMYK (which is one of the prime uses of color management). The result may look only adequate because InDesign is making two assumptions: that the RGB image is based on the Adobe RGB (1998) profile and the CMYK ink behavior is based on the U.S. Web Coated (SWOP) v2 profile. The farther from these descriptions your images or press, the worse the quality will be.

Of course, when InDesign is not called to specifically do color conversions like this, it ignores the image space. That is, if you import CMYK images and color management it turned off, then InDesign will simply pass those CMYK values to the printer; it won't try to mess with them.

## InDesign's Color Management Controls

You can control how color appears in InDesign in two places: The Color Settings dialog box (under the Edit menu), and the Proof Setup dialog box (under the View menu). This is very different than earlier versions; it works much more like Illustrator and Photoshop now. Because proofing relies entirely on how you've set up Color Settings, we'll start with the former and then cover proofing later. You can use the Color Settings dialog box to choose the color management engine you want to use, and to set up the device profiles for your monitor, your separations printer, and your composite printer.

**Application Color Settings**

The choices you make in the Color Settings dialog box form the basis for how InDesign displays and prints color (see Figure 10-14). These controls all match the similarly-named features in Adobe Photoshop, though the meanings are sometimes subtly different.

**Enable Color Management.** Use the Enable Color Management option to turn color management on or off. If you're not planning to print color separations or color composite pages, you can turn InDesign's color management features off—you don't need them, and they do slow the program down. Note that when color management is on, it's on for all documents; when it's off, it's off for all documents. This is an application-wide setting, and is not saved with your documents.

**Settings.** InDesign ships with a handful of preset setups for the Color Settings dialog box, available from the Settings pop-up menu. We can't imagine why you'd want to use most of these (like Emulate

FIGURE 10-14

**Color Settings
Dialog Box**

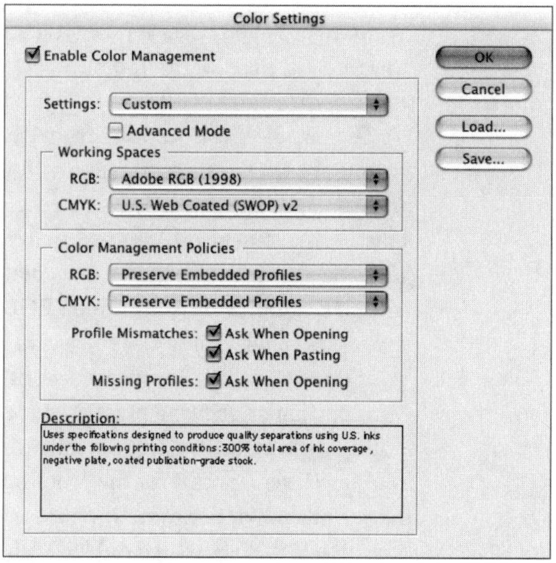

Acrobat 4). Most of these just control the CMYK document working space (the default definition for your document's CMYK colors). We usually either just pick U.S. Prepress Defaults (because we live in the United States) or ignore this menu altogether and just customize the dialog box with our own settings.

The real power of the Settings pop-up menu isn't what ships with InDesign, but rather the fact that you can save your own settings to disk and then recall them quickly later.

**Monitor profile.** While you could specify your monitor profile in earlier versions of InDesign, now InDesign is smart enough to pull this information from the default operating system monitor profile. The software that you use to characterize your monitor generally makes the profile it generates the default monitor profile automatically. If you don't have a hardware calibration system, like Spyder with OptiCal, you can try to eyeball it using ColorSync (on the Mac) or Adobe Gamma (which was installed along with InDesign for Windows).

**Working Spaces.** Perhaps the most important features of the Color Settings dialog box are the two Working Spaces pop-up menus, which control InDesign's default color profiles for RGB and CMYK colors. Remember that an RGB value doesn't mean anything because red, green, and blue phosphors are different on different devices. Cyan, magenta, yellow, and black inks can also be radically different depending on location, paper stock, press conditions, and so on.

So RGB and CMYK colors are all just a bunch of numbers. Profiles assign color meaning to the numbers: such-and-such CMYK value *on this particular device*.

The profiles you choose from the CMYK and RGB pop-up menus are the profiles InDesign will use for any objects you create in InDesign, and for any imported graphics that did not include a color management profile (and that you have not applied a profile to using the Image Color Settings dialog box). Although we almost always recommend using Adobe RGB (1998) for the RGB working space, the choice of a CMYK working space depends entirely on your print workflow. In a perfect world, you'd have a color profile for your particular printing press or output device, with your particular paper stock, and so on. But in reality, you can typically get away with picking either a profile for the proofing system you'll be using (if you have a profile) or use something close. For most of our print jobs we just pick U.S. Web Coated or U.S. Web Uncoated. ("Web" here refers to a Web press, as opposed to a sheetfed press, and has nothing to do with the World Wide Web.)

Note that your imported graphics don't have to share the same working space with your document; InDesign is smart enough to handle different spaces at the same time.

If you're looking for a particular profile that you know you've installed in the operating system correctly, but doesn't appear here, try turning on the Advanced Mode checkbox (see "Advanced Color Settings," later in this section).

**Color Management Policies.** InDesign assigns the default working spaces to each new document you create while color management is turned on. However, what should InDesign do when color management is turned on and you open a document that was created when color management was turned off (so no profile was associated with the document)? What if you open a document made by someone else who used a different working space? You can tell InDesign what to do in these cases with the Color Management Policies section of the Color Settings dialog box.

We suggest leaving these set to the default values most of the time—the RGB and CMYK pop-up menus should be set to Preserve Embedded Profiles, and all three Profile Mismatches and Missing Profiles checkboxes should be turned on. In this arrangement, all documents that are already color managed stay that way, and you're asked what to do when you open a document which doesn't contain working spaces or which has a different working space than the current application defaults. This is safe and practical.

However, there may be times when you want to change these policies. For instance, if you need to open 20 InDesign files created in Japan using the Japan Standard CMYK working space and you want to force them into the U.S. Sheetfed Coated working space, you can set the CMYK policy to Convert to Working Space and turn off the Profile Mismatches Ask When Opening checkbox. Now, when you open the documents, InDesign just converts them all. (Actually, it'll display an alert first, but you can turn on the Don't Show Again checkbox and then the rest of the documents should open smoothly.) Once you open those files, however, don't forget to switch the policies back to the defaults, so you don't accidentally screw up other documents.

Note that setting the RGB or CMYK policies to Off simply means ignore the embedded profiles. This is a silly thing to do, as it strips the document colors of any meaning. If you really don't want to use color management, then just turn the whole color management system off in the Color Settings dialog box rather than select Off.

**Advanced Color Settings**

While the color management options we've described are enough for many workflows, you can get even more tweaky by turning on the Advanced Mode checkbox (see Figure 10-15). First, when Advanced Mode is turned on you can select any color profile installed in your operating system for your working spaces (as opposed to only the recommended Adobe profiles). Next, you can select an alternate color management engine, adjust the default rendering intent, and choose whether or not to use black point compensation.

**Engine.** Color management engines (the actual software at the heart of the system that converts one color into another) are made by a variety of manufacturers—InDesign comes with a few: the Adobe CMS and either the Microsoft ICM (on Windows) or Apple ColorSync (on the Mac). Mac users will notice separate entries for the Apple CMM and for Apple ColorSync. Apple CMM means that the Apple CMM will always be used; Apple ColorSync uses whatever engine is set in the ColorSync control panel or System Preference. You may even have other third-party engines available. Ultimately, it's very unlikely that you would ever see a difference between any of these. However, unless you have a really good reason to swtich, you should just use the Adobe CMS.

**Intent.** What happens when the color management system encounters a color that is outside of the gamut of the selected printing device? The color management system must change the color to a

FIGURE 10-15
**Advanced
Color Settings**

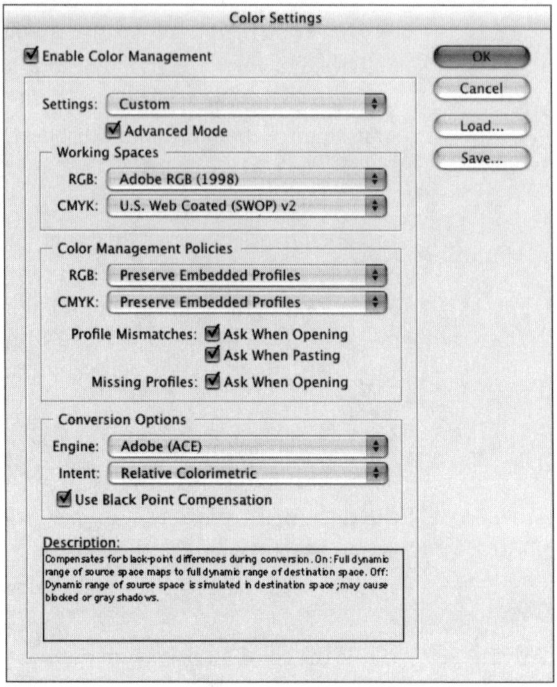

Color Settings

☑ Enable Color Management

OK

Settings: | Custom |
☑ Advanced Mode

Cancel
Load...
Save...

Working Spaces
RGB: | Adobe RGB (1998) |
CMYK: | U.S. Web Coated (SWOP) v2 |

Color Management Policies
RGB: | Preserve Embedded Profiles |
CMYK: | Preserve Embedded Profiles |

Profile Mismatches: ☑ Ask When Opening
☑ Ask When Pasting
Missing Profiles: ☑ Ask When Opening

Conversion Options
Engine: | Adobe (ACE) |
Intent: | Relative Colorimetric |
☑ Use Black Point Compensation

Description:
Compensates for black-point differences during conversion. On: Full dynamic range of source space maps to full dynamic range of destination space. Off: Dynamic range of source space is simulated in destination space; may cause blocked or gray shadows.

color that's inside the printer's gamut. *How* it does that is the topic of the Intent pop-up menu. Intent is shorthand for *rendering intent*.

When you choose either Relative Colorimetric (which is the default) or Absolute Colorimetric, the out-of-gamut colors are moved to the nearest edge of the color gamut—also called gamut clipping—which means that differences between out-of-gamut colors can disappear (*very* red and *very, very* red both become the same in-gamut CMYK red). When this happens, you'll see an effect similar to posterization in the more saturated areas of images. The Perceptual rendering intent squeezes all the document's colors so that out-of-gamut colors are brought into the color gamut in a way that maintains a distinction between the colors. The Saturation rendering intent, on the other hand, moves all colors toward the edge of the color gamut, resulting in more saturated color.

In general, Relative Colorimetric is best for solid colors and synthetic images (like images made in Illustrator or FreeHand), and Perceptual is best for scanned images. Unfortunately, InDesign uses this rendering intent both for colors built in InDesign and for imported images (unless you specifically override it, which we discuss in "Applying Device Profiles to Images," below). However, for most documents and images—especially those already in CMYK mode—Relative Colorimetric probably makes the most sense. On the other hand, if you use a lot of RGB images with saturated out-of-gamut colors, and you're trying to match these colors with swatches built in InDesign, you might want to use Perceptual instead. If you want more intense color in business graphics (such as charts and graphs), you might try choosing Saturation.

**Use Black Point Compensation.** The Use Black Point Compensation option, when turned on, maps the black of the source profile to the black of the target profile. We usually think of black as being "just black," but of course black on different devices appears differently (for instance, solid black on newsprint is much more gray than solid black on glossy sheetfed stock). We generally recommend leaving this turned on, ensuring that the entire dynamic range of the output device is used.

**Changing Document Spaces**

By default the document working space is whatever Color Settings was set to when you first created the document. If you later change Color Settings, the application's default working space will be different than your document's space; that's no big deal because InDesign always uses the document space if there is one.

What if you want to change the document working space? For example, you thought you were going to print on coated stock but later found you had to cut your budget and switch to uncoated stock? You can add or change a document's working space profiles using the Assign Profiles and the Convert to Profile features in the Edit menu.

Assign Profiles lets you tag your document with another set of RGB and/or CMYK profiles, or even remove the document profile entirely (see Figure 10-16). Changing the document profiles with Assign Profiles is like saying, "The colors in this document now mean something else, because cyan now looks like this, magenta looks like this, and so on." Accordingly, the colors on screen may change, but the actual color definitions don't.

Convert to Profile is the opposite: It actually converts the colors in your document to a new profile, changing the color definitions to maintain the look of the colors (see Figure 10-17). That means a 100-percent cyan will end up as something like 96-percent cyan, 5-percent magenta (or something else, depending on what profile you're converting to). We encourage you to be very careful when using Convert to Profile; it can really mess up your documents, or it can be a lifesaver if you really know what it's doing.

Note that Convert to Profile is the only good way to find out what your document space currently is (it's listed at the top of the dialog box).

FIGURE 10-16
**Assign Profiles**

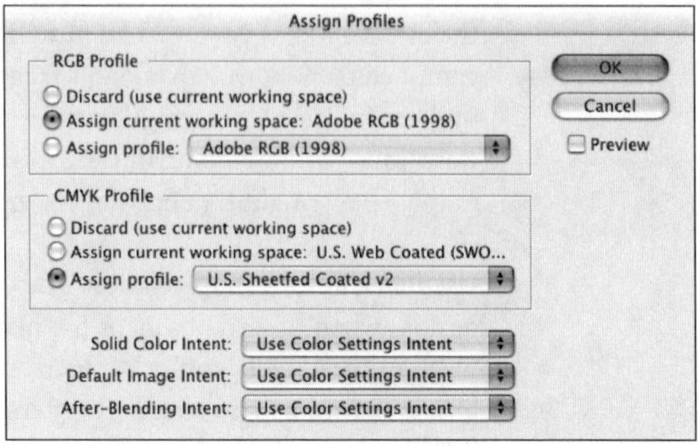

Assign Profiles

RGB Profile

○ Discard (use current working space)
● Assign current working space: Adobe RGB (1998)
○ Assign profile:  Adobe RGB (1998)  ⬍

CMYK Profile

○ Discard (use current working space)
○ Assign current working space: U.S. Web Coated (SWO...
● Assign profile:  U.S. Sheetfed Coated v2  ⬍

Solid Color Intent:  Use Color Settings Intent  ⬍
Default Image Intent:  Use Color Settings Intent  ⬍
After-Blending Intent:  Use Color Settings Intent  ⬍

OK
Cancel
☐ Preview

FIGURE 10-17
**Convert to Profile**

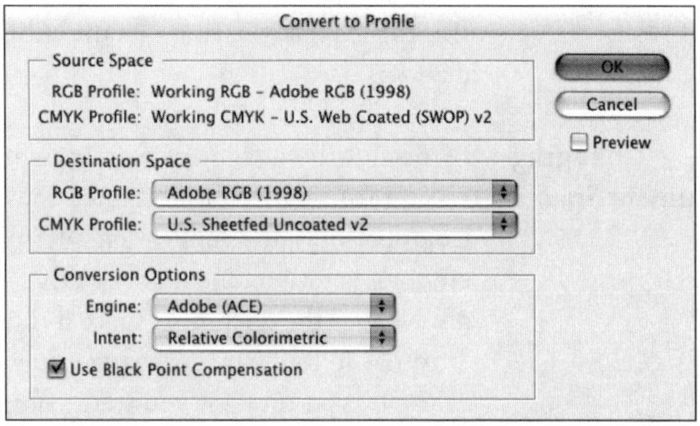

Convert to Profile

Source Space

RGB Profile:  Working RGB – Adobe RGB (1998)
CMYK Profile:  Working CMYK – U.S. Web Coated (SWOP) v2

Destination Space

RGB Profile:  Adobe RGB (1998)  ⬍
CMYK Profile:  U.S. Sheetfed Uncoated v2  ⬍

Conversion Options

Engine:  Adobe (ACE)  ⬍
Intent:  Relative Colorimetric  ⬍
☑ Use Black Point Compensation

OK
Cancel
☐ Preview

**Applying Device Profiles to Images**

When you save an image from Adobe Photoshop, by default the program embeds a color profile that describes the image's color space (see *Real World Photoshop* for more on Photoshop's behavior). InDesign recognizes that profile (if color management is turned on) when you place the graphic on your page. However, you can adjust this behavior if you turn on the Show Import Options checkbox in the Place dialog box, and then click on the Color Settings tab of the Image Import Options dialog box (see Figure 10-18).

The three options here are: whether or not to color manage this graphic, what profile to apply, and what rendering intent to use when InDesign needs to convert the colors to a different profile space. Generally, you should leave the Profile pop-up menu set to Use Embedded Profile (if one is embedded), but if you're sure that the wrong profile was embedded then feel free to choose the correct one. Note that this is like using Assign Profile in Photoshop; it doesn't change the data, it just changes the meaning of the data. If the image has no embedded profile, you can assign one here, or leave the Profile pop-up menu set to Use Document Default, which assigns the document's RGB or CMYK working space. If you have any idea

FIGURE 10-18

**Applying a Profile
at Import**

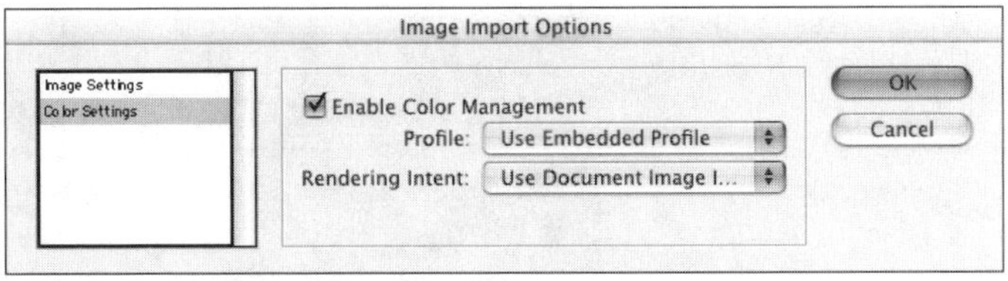

of what the profile should be, it's best to choose it here; selecting Use Document Default can lead to images changing color if you assign a different document profile.

If your InDesign document is set to Relative Colorimetric rendering intent and you're placing an RGB image that has a large, saturated color gamut, you might consider selecting Perceptual from the Intent pop-up menu here. That way, this particular image will avoid the gamut-clipping behavior. For most images, however, using the default value of Use Document Image Intent is reasonable.

Whatever you choose upon placing the image, you can always override it by selecting the image and choosing the Image Color Settings option on the Graphic submenu of the context menu (or choose the corresponding option from the Object menu).

**Soft-Proofing Controls**

You probably want to get some sense of what your pages are going to look like before you commit to a $50,000 print run. Increasingly, proofing is being done not on traditional color proofing system, but rather on desktop inkjet printers and on screen. Proofing images on screen is called soft-proofing, and the quality of soft-proofing in InDesign is limited only by the accuracy of the profiles involved.

The Proof Colors command on the View menu lets you turn soft-proofing on and off. But it's in the Proof Setup submenu that you can control what the proof is showing you. Note that the settings you make in Proof Setup are specific to the window that's in the foreground, not the document itself. This means you can create several views of the same page (by choosing New Window from the Window menu) and apply different soft-proofing settings to each view, letting you see how the page will work in different output scenarios. However, note that turning on Proof Colors slows down document redraw, so while it's good to look at, it's not particularly fun to work on your document when this is on.

The three items in the Proof Setup submenu are Document CMYK, Working CMYK, and Custom. We typically just use Custom, which displays the Proof Setup dialog box (see Figure 10-19), which gives us more control over the soft-proof (though not as much as Photoshop offers). First, choose the profile of the device you're trying to emulate. Then, choose whether to simulate Paper White and Ink Black.

FIGURE 10-19

**Soft-Proofing**

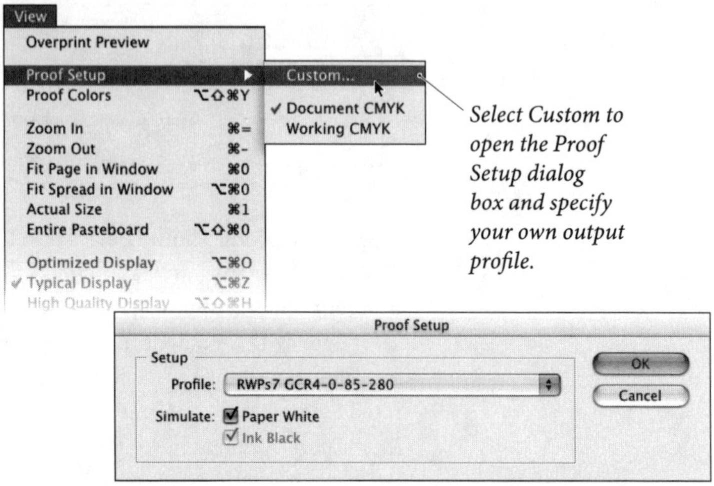

View

Overprint Preview

Proof Setup                    ▶      Custom...
Proof Colors            ⌥⇧⌘Y
                                    ✓ Document CMYK
Zoom In                   ⌘=         Working CMYK
Zoom Out                  ⌘-
Fit Page in Window        ⌘0
Fit Spread in Window     ⌥⌘0
Actual Size               ⌘1
Entire Pasteboard        ⌥⇧⌘0

Optimized Display        ⌥⌘O
✓ Typical Display         ⌥⌘Z
High Quality Display     ⌥⇧⌘H

*Select Custom to
open the Proof
Setup dialog
box and specify
your own output
profile.*

Proof Setup

Setup

Profile:  RWPs7 GCR4-0-85-280

Simulate: ☑ Paper White
          ☑ Ink Black

OK

Cancel

These two checkboxes control the rendering of the document's colors from the proofing space to the monitor. When Paper White and Ink Black are turned off, InDesign does a relative colorimetric rendering, mapping the white of the proof device's paper to monitor white and the black of the device's black ink to monitor black. This isn't particularly useful; after all, for a soft-proof you're trying to see what the real paper's white and ink's blacks will look like.

Instead, we almost always turn on the Paper White checkbox (which automatically also turns on the Ink Black checkbox). This way, the monitor simulates the paper's white (which is often duller than monitor white), and you can see the compressed dynamic range of print. If you're simulating a low-dynamic-range process—like newsprint, or inkjet on uncoated paper—turning on Ink Black (or Paper White) gives you a much better idea of the actual color range you'll get in print.

Unfortunately, the effect of simulating a compressed dynamic range is so dramatic that it feels like it ruins the document's colors. It's a good idea to put the document in Preview mode (press W while not editing text), hide your palettes (press Tab), then select Proof Colors from the View menu but before actually letting go of the mouse button, close your eyes for a few seconds. When you open your eyes, your brain can readjust its own internal white point, giving you a better sense of what the image really will look like when it comes off the printer.

It's worth noting again that you'll never get an exact match between screen and final printed output. However, like any proofing system, the key is not in getting a perfect match, but rather in getting pretty dang close, and then learning the *relationship* between screen and printed piece. The more you do this (and the more accurate your profiles are), the more accurate you'll get at predicting final color.

**Color Management in Output**

None of this color management stuff is relevant if you can't get your final design to print well. Fortunately, you can perform color conversions from your document space to a selected profile when you print your document or export it to PDF or EPS.

It's important to remember that when color management is turned on, InDesign will convert the colors in your document and embedded images (when it can) to the output space. If the output profile is the same as the document profile, then of course it doesn't change anything. However, if your graphics have embedded profiles different than the document space, InDesign will attempt to color manage that data, even if it means changing CMYK data to other CMYK values. If you are used to a workflow in which you import CMYK images and you absolutely don't want that data to change at print time, consider turning off color management before you print (there's no way to turn it off once you're in the Print dialog box).

**Print dialog box.** When color management is on, InDesign activates the features in the Color Management tab of the Print dialog box (see Figure 10-20). The key to managing color is to specify a source space and a target space, so the color management engine knows where the color is coming from (what the color is supposed to look like) and where the color is going (how that device images color, so it can convert the colors properly).

You have two choices for a source space: Document (the document working space) or Proof (the profile you chose in the Custom Proof Setup dialog box, or the document CMYK working space, if you haven't used Custom Proof Setup). The Proof option lets you print your file to a composite printer, like a desktop inkjet, and make it simulate the CMYK output you've been soft-proofing—that is, it gives you a hard copy of your soft-proofed document. When you choose Proof, you can also select a rendering intent to tell InDesign how to convert your document colors that are out of the printer's gamut.

The target profiles you can choose for a print space (the space of the print device) depend on whether you have chosen an RGB or a CMYK space from the Color pop-up menu in the Output tab of the Print dialog box. If you're printing to an inkjet printer, you should probably choose Composite RGB and then pick the RGB profile for that device.

FIGURE 10-20

**Color Management in the Print Dialog Box**

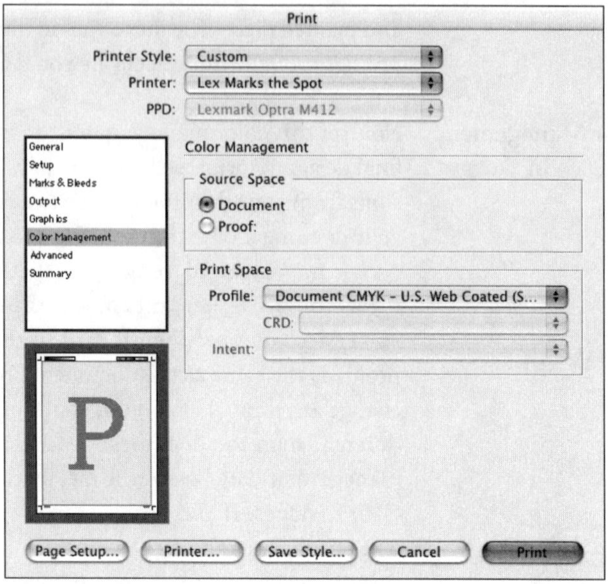

When you print, InDesign compares your target print space to the document space and the profiles applied to or embedded in graphics; if they're all the same, then it doesn't do any color conversion. Whenever the profiles differ, InDesign runs the colors through the color management engine to maintain visual consistency of the colors.

**Use Device Independent Color When Printing.** Okay. This is where things get a bit theoretical for us, because we admit we have never worked with a workflow that relied on the PostScript RIP to separate and color manage our files (it's a workflow that Adobe thinks is cool, but few people take advantage of). If you're using "in-RIP separations" (a feature of some PostScript Level 2 and PostScript 3 RIPs), you can have the printer create the separations for you using color rendering dictionaries (CRDs)—these are essentially the same thing as separation profiles.

When you want to use in-RIP separations, you do not turn on the Separations option in the Color panel of InDesign's Print dialog box—instead you choose either Composite CMYK or InRIP Separations from the Color pop-up menu in the Output tab of the Print dialog box. Then switch to the Color Management tab, choose PostScript Color Management from the Profile pop-up menu, and choose a profile for the printer in the CRD pop-up menu (or better yet, just leave this set to Default). The RIP uses the default CRD (or the CRD you've downloaded) to determine how to separate the publication. We recommend you ignore this option and stick with more traditional color management workflows.

**Export as PDF.** You can tell InDesign whether to color manage your exported PDF files in the Advanced tab of the Export PDF dialog box (see Figure 10-21). If you don't want InDesign to convert any colors (if you want all the document and image color data left as is) then either turn off color management before exporting, or select Leave Unchanged from the Color pop-up menu in the Advanced tab.

If you're exporting the PDF for primarily on-screen viewing, choose RGB from the Color pop-up menu and then choose an RGB profile—the sRGB profile is probably the most useful, as it purports to define the "average" monitor. If you're exporting for print and you do want to color manage the document, then choose CMYK from the Color pop-up menu, choose your final output device in the Profile pop-up menu, and turn on the Include ICC Profiles checkbox.

**Export as EPS.** There is no color management interface in the Export EPS dialog box; InDesign simply color manages your document—converting all imported images (at least the ones that it can, like TIFF and .PSD files) to the document working space—when you save as EPS. This makes us crazy, so we usually turn color management off before saving files as EPS.

FIGURE 10-21
**Color Management in the Export PDF Dialog Box**

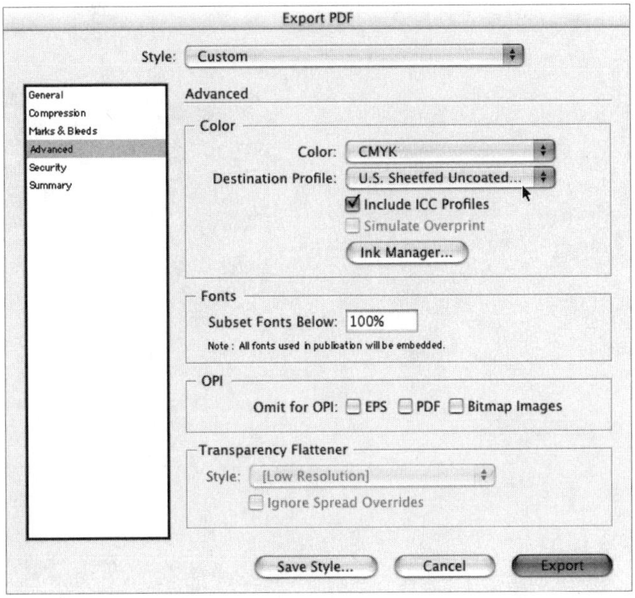

# The Color "Done"

As you work with commercial printing, always remember that you're at the mercy of a series of photochemical and mechanical processes—from your imagesetter through the printing press—that, in many ways, haven't changed since 1900 (if that recently). Temperature, humidity, and ambient static electricity play large roles in the process, and the people who operate these systems are at least skilled craftspeople; at best, artists. Ask them as many questions as they'll answer, set your job up the way they want it, and then sit back and watch your job come off the press.

# Printing

Printing is an ancient art, and has been invented and reinvented many times. You can print by rolling a carved cylinder over a sheet of wet clay, as the Mesopotamians did. Or you can smear a carved block of wood with ink and then press the block into a sheet of paper, as the Chinese started doing in the 8th or 9th century. With grease, water, and ink, even a slab of limestone can learn to transfer an image to paper, as Alois Senefelder of Munich found in 1798 (thereby inventing lithography).

In the fifteenth century, Gutenberg (and possibly others) came up with cast, moveable type—which, in turn, changed printing from a craft into an industry. Scribes the world over lamented the decline in the quality of written materials. The romance novel followed closely on the heels of this technological advance.

Printing—the ability to make dozens, hundreds, thousands, millions of copies of an image—flourished. For whatever reason, we humans will go to great lengths to get our pictures, text, and advertising into the hands of our willing or unwilling audience. And, in spite of the encroachments of the Web, printing is still the best way to do that.

Adobe completely revamped the printing interface for InDesign in this version, so getting your pages to print is easier and faster than ever before.

# The InDesign Print Dialog Box

When you press Command-P/Ctrl-P or choose Print Book from the Book palette (see Chapter 8, "Long Documents"), InDesign displays the Print dialog box. There are so many features packed into this dialog box that Adobe had to break it up into eight different tabs, each listed along the left side of the dialog box: General, Setup, Marks & Bleeds, Output, Graphics, Color Management, Advanced, and Summary (see Figure 11-1).

Even if you're just printing to a lowly desktop printer, it's worth at least glimpsing at each of these tabs. Fortunately, you can use keyboard shortcuts to navigate among them: Command/Ctrl-Down Arrow jumps to the next tab, Command/Ctrl-Up Arrow jumps to the previous tab, and holding down the Command/Ctrl key while pressing a number from 1 to 8 skips to the respective tab number (1 for General, 2 for Setup, and so on). We'll cover each of these tabs, in order, below.

**Printers, Postscript Files, and PPDs**

Before you go anywhere in the Print dialog box, you've got to make one or two important decisions. First, you must choose from the options on the Printer pop-up menu, which lists the printers you have installed on your computer. When you choose a printer, InDesign looks to the printer driver to see what PPD (PostScript Printer Description) file is associated with that printer, and it displays it—grayed out—in the PPD pop-up menu. In the case of a non-PostScript device, InDesign just leaves this pop-up menu blank.

If you instead want to print a PostScript file directly to disk rather than to a device (also called making a "PostScript dump"), choose PostScript File from the Printer pop-up menu. In this case, you must also pick the PPD file that describes your final output device or choose Device Independent. You can typically use device-independent PostScript files—also called ".sep files" or "prepress files"—for output through imposition and trapping systems.

Writing PostScript to disk offers some advantages (you can change the PostScript with a word processor to learn about InDesign's PostScript, fix printing problems, add special design effects, or just goof around). However, most output providers now prefer receiving PDF files over PostScript files. Some companies don't even accept PostScript files anymore, except from clients that they know will create them properly (because it's difficult to make changes to your document once it's written as PostScript). We discuss exporting PDF files in Chapter 7, "Importing and Exporting."

FIGURE 11-1

**The Print Dialog Box**

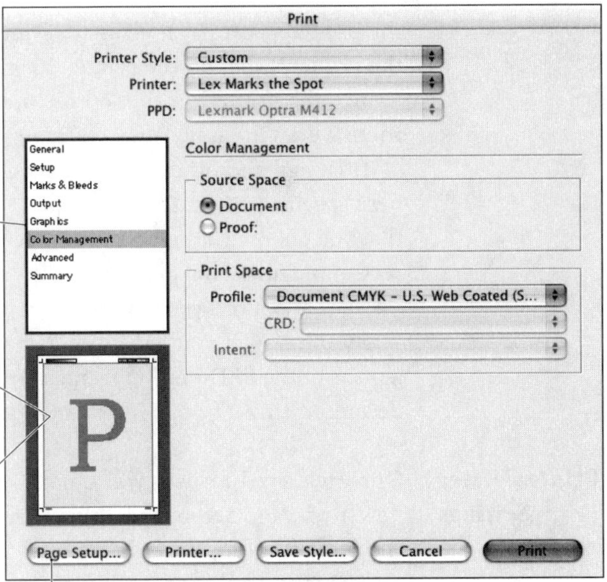

*Hold down Command or Ctrl and press 2 to jump to the Setup panel, 3 for the third panel, and so on.*

*Click once or twice on the Preview to see more information about your print job.*

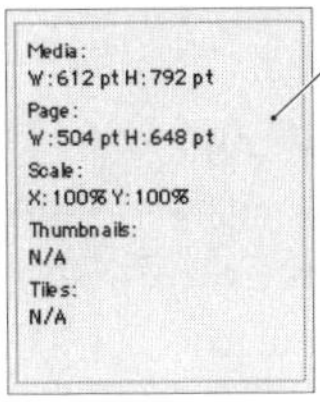

*Click Page Setup to open the printer driver's print options. In general, you should avoid using the printer driver dialog boxes.*

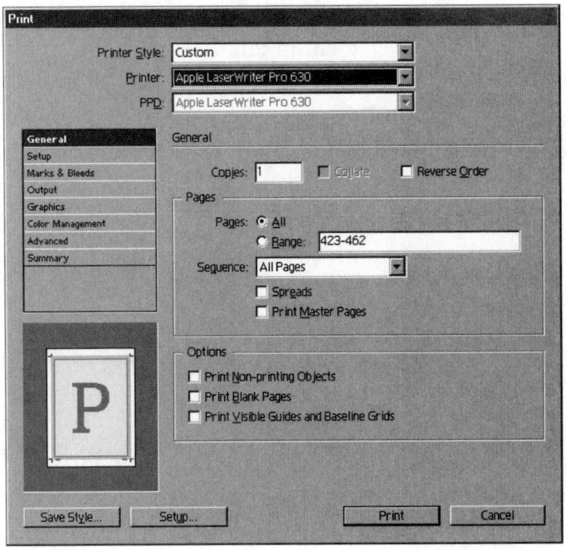

Note that PPDs are not, and should not be confused with, printer drivers. Printer drivers are pieces of software that direct information from your system and applications to a hardware port—usually, your computer's printer port or network connection. PPDs work in conjunction with printer drivers to give applications information about the printer (what paper sizes are available? what's the resolution of the printer? what do the printer error messages mean?) and to customize the printer's operation for the application (what PostScript routine does the application use to render halftones?).

InDesign and other applications use PPDs to optimize printing for a specific printer. If you are specifying a PPD file, it's important that you choose the right one, or else your pages may not print correctly (and might not print at all). The settings you choose here determine what options you have in the rest of the Print dialog box.

By the way, if you have installed a PPD in OS X and it doesn't appear in the PPD pop-up menu, it may be a compressed PPD. Try decompressing it using Stuffit Expander first.

## Printer Driver Settings

Our eagle-eyed readers will quickly find a Setup button (in Windows) or Page Setup and Printer buttons (on the Macintosh) at the bottom of the Print dialog box. These are doorways into your operating system's printer drivers. At print time, InDesign interacts with whatever printer driver you're using. However, there are very few instances when you'd need to click these buttons to change the printer driver settings. In most cases, the settings are duplicated somewhere in InDesign's Print dialog box, and it's always better to set it within this dialog box than in the driver.

However, if you know of an option in the printer driver that InDesign doesn't handle, click the appropriate button. For example, many inkjet printers require you to specify resolution, quality, and color adjustments in their own drivers. Similarly, some PostScript printers offer options like toner density, paper tray handling, and so on, which also require a trip to the printer driver dialog box.

Note that in some rare cases you may get really weird results when applying both printer driver settings and Print dialog box settings (like when trying to do color separations at the same time as telling the driver to print multiple document pages per printed page).

## Postscript Versus Non-Postscript

While InDesign can print to non-PostScript printers reasonably well, it's really designed for PostScript devices. PostScript is a page-description language—a collection of commands that PostScript devices understand. When you tell InDesign to print a page, it writes a computer program in PostScript describing the page, and sends that program to the printer. The printer (or imagesetter, or platesetter), which has a PostScript interpreter (called a RIP) inside it or attached to it, interprets the PostScript and puts marks on the paper or film.

When InDesign detects that your printer doesn't have a RIP (based on the driver you're using), it grays out the Print dialog box features that don't work on non-PostScript devices, such as color separations and the transparency Flattener (transparency effects print fine on these devices, but you don't need the Flattener to create them; see "Printing Transparency," later in this chapter).

**Print Preview**    InDesign displays a preview of the way your page fits on the selected paper size in the lower-left corner of the Print dialog box. This preview does not include a preview of the elements on your pages, unlike the print preview features found in Word, Excel, Illustrator, or FreeHand. The previews, however, do provide feedback that can save you from printing pages in the wrong orientation or printing pages that won't fit on the paper.

InDesign displays additional information "behind" the preview icon. Click once on the preview and you can see data such as the paper size, the page size, how many tiles will print (see "Tile" in "Setup," later in this chapter), and so on. Click again, and InDesign shows you how your page will print relative to the paper path through the printer. For laser printers and other printers with fixed paper sizes, this isn't very helpful, but it's great when printing to a roll-fed imagesetter or platesetter.

# General

The General tab of the Print dialog box contains the lowest common denominators of printing features: what pages do you want to print, how many copies do you want, and how do you want them to come out of the printer (see Figure 11-2).

**Copies**    Enter the number of copies of the page you want to print in the Copies field. You can print up to 9999 copies of your publication.

**Reverse Order**    When you print a multi-page document, do you want the first page to come out first or last? Turning on the Reverse Order checkbox tells InDesign to print the last page first, then print "backwards" to the first page. You'll want to turn this on if your pages come out of the laser printer face up.

**Collate**    When you turn on the Collate option, InDesign prints the range of pages you've specified, in order, for each copy of the publication you print. This makes for much slower printing. When you print multiple

FIGURE 11-2

**The General Panel
of the Print Dialog Box**

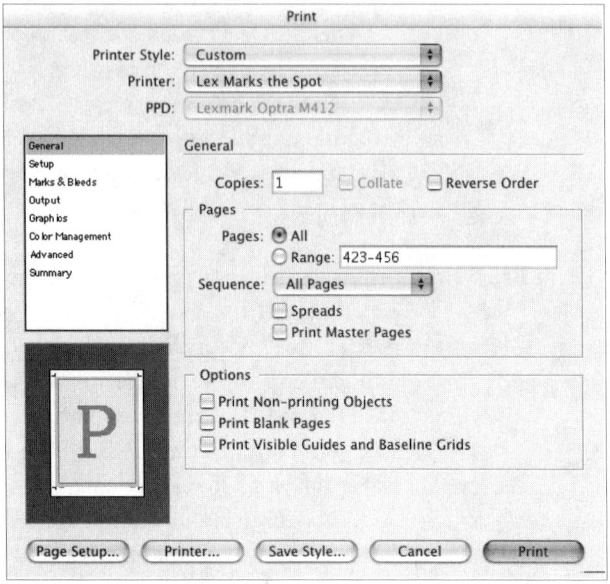

copies of a page, your printer only needs to process each page once (and then prints multiple copies of the page using the same image); when you turn on the Collate option, your printer must process each page once for every copy of the print job.

**Page Ranges**  Turn on the All Pages option to print all of the pages in the publication. To print a range of pages, turn on the Ranges option. Enter the page range in the Range field as shown in Table 11-1.

You can mix and match page ranges. To print pages one, three, six through ten, and 20, for example, you'd enter "1,3,6-10,20." The pages and ranges you specify must be in order (you couldn't, for example, print page 20 before printing page six). Specifying "1,5,5,9" means print page 1, then two copies of page 5, and then page 9. If you want to print from page 10 to the end of the document, just type "10-". Or, to print from the beginning of the file up to (and including) page 10, type "-10".

If you've used the Page Numbering and Section feature, then printing specific page ranges gets even more complicated. For example, let's say your first section uses roman numerals and is 5 pages long. To print the first six pages, you type "i-6" (you can't type "1-6" because there is no page called "1"—the first page is called "i"). However, you can change this behavior: If you select Absolute Numbering in the View pop-up menu of the General tab of the Preferences dialog box, then you should type "1-6" because the range now refers to *absolute* page numbering ("the first through the sixth page").

| | To print: | Enter: | Example: |
|---|---|---|---|
| **TABLE 11-1**<br>**Printing Page Ranges** | A continuous range of pages | first page - last page | 12-21 |
| | Up to a specific page | -last page | -5 |
| | From a page to the end of the document | first page - | 5- |
| | Non-contiguous pages | page, page | 1, 3 |
| | Mixed page ranges | | -3, 6-9, 12, 15- |

**Sequence**    To print even and odd pages, turn on the Both Pages option; to print even pages, turn on the Even Pages Only option; and to print odd pages, turn on the Odd Pages Only. These options affect all page ranges, including page ranges you've entered in the Ranges field. The only time we've used this pop-up menu is when we've printed double-sided documents on a laser printer (print just the odd pages, then flip the pages, put them back in the printer, and print the even pages). If you've turned on the Reader's Spreads option, these options will be unavailable.

**Spreads**    When you turn on the Spreads option, InDesign tries to print each spread in the publication on a single sheet of paper (or other output media). If the spread is larger than the selected paper size, turn on the Scale to Fit option in the Scale and Fit panel of the Print dialog box and/or change the paper orientation. This is also called "readers spreads." Note that this is not the same as printer spreads, which are a form of imposition, printing the first and last page together, and so on. Fortunately, you can get good printer spreads out of InDesign using a plug-in such as InBooklet (from www.alap.com) or the free script that Ole wrote (see Chapter 12, "Scripting," for more on where to find scripts, or see http://share.studio.adobe.com).

**Print Master Pages**    Sometimes you need to print your master pages instead of your document pages. No problem: Just turn on the Print Master Pages checkbox. There's no page ranges possible here; it just prints all the master pages in the document.

**Print Non-Printing Objects**    When you turn on the Print Non-printing Objects checkbox, InDesign prints every object on your pages, whether or not the Nonprinting checkbox is turned on or off in the Attributes palette. However, this feature does not print objects on hidden (and therefore non-printing) layers.

**Print Blank Pages**    What happens when you print a three-page document that has nothing on page two? By default, only pages one and three print out. If you want the blank page two to print, too, you'd better turn on the Print Blank Pages checkbox.

**Print Visible Guides and Baseline Grids**    When you turn the Print Visible Guides and Baseline Grids checkbox on, all visible margin guides, baseline grid guides, and page guides print out (but not the document grid). We find this particularly helpful when designing templates for others to use.

# Setup

When we talk about page size, we're talking about the page size you've defined for your publication using the New Document or Document Setup dialog boxes. This page size should be the same as the page size of the printed piece you intend to produce. "Paper size," on the other hand, means the size of the paper or film you're printing on. There can be a big difference between these two sizes. You can tell InDesign the paper size in the Setup tab of the Print dialog box, as well as how you want the page to appear on that paper (see Figure 11-3).

**Paper Size**    PPDs contain information about the paper sizes that a printer can handle, and this information then shows up in the Paper Size pop-up menu. When you specify a non-PostScript printer, Paper Size changes to Defined by Driver, and you'll have to handle the paper size in the printer driver dialog box. Once again, the paper size doesn't have to be the same as your page size; if you're printing page marks (like crop marks), then the paper size will need to be larger. In the case of printers that image larger sheets of film, we usually set Paper Size to Custom, and then leave the Width and Height fields set to Auto (so InDesign figures out the proper imaging area for us).

**Offset**    The Offset feature controls the placement of your document on the paper, film, or plate. The printer's default paper offset, even when set to zero, is almost always large enough so that you don't have to worry about changing the value of Offset here. However, if you need the page to image farther from the paper edge, change this value.

**Gap**    The Gap setting, which is really only relevant for roll-fed printers, determines the amount of blank space between each page of the document as it prints out. Some output providers that print to film like to set this to about 2p, so they can cut the pages apart more easily. In most cases, you can just ignore this setting.

FIGURE 11-3

The Setup Panel
of the Print Dialog Box

FIGURE 11-3

The Setup Panel
of the Print Dialog Box

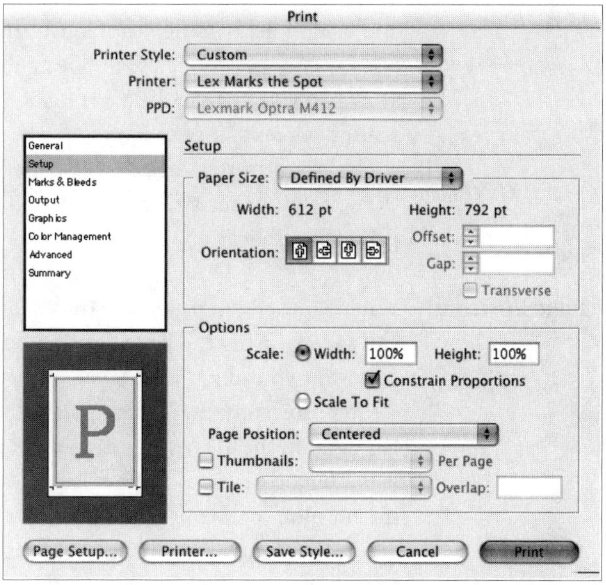

**Orientation** You can control the rotation of your page on the paper using the Orientation setting. The four choices (each rotated another 90 degrees) are indicated with tiny icons, but we find it easier to watch the preview page in the lower-left corner of the dialog box.

**Transverse** The Transverse setting is like Orientation, but is used for roll-fed imagesetters and platesetters when the Paper Size is set to Custom. When you turn on Transverse, the width of the paper is placed along the length of the imagesetter's paper roll, which can save paper or film. The best way to get a feel for the Transverse command is to click the Preview icon twice (to see the page versus the paper path) then turn on and off this checkbox. Of course, you have to first select an appropriate PPD.

**Scale** You can scale the output of your pages, from as small as one percent to as large as 1000 percent of their actual size. You can specify a scaling percentage yourself, or ask InDesign to fit the page to the size of the paper. When you use large percentages, watch the print preview to see that the enlarged page will fit on the paper you've selected.

If you're printing using a commercial printing process that distorts the printed images (flexography, for example, typically stretches the image axis that's parallel to the rotation of the printing cylinder), you can compensate for the distortion by entering different values in the Width and Height fields. To do this, turn off the Constrain Proportions option, then enter the percentages you want in the Width and Height fields. When the Constrain Proportions option is turned on, any changes you make in one field are reflected in the other.

When you turn on the Scale to Fit option, InDesign calculates the scaling percentage necessary to fit the page (plus any printer's marks you selected in the Page Marks panel of the Print dialog box) onto the selected paper size, and uses that scaling percentage when you print the publication.

**Page Position**  When you select a paper size that is larger than your document, you can specify using the Page Position pop-up menu where on the page you want your document to sit. You've got four choices: Upper Left, Center Horizontally, Center Vertically, and Centered. Upper Left is the default; the other three are self-explanatory. We find this control a matter of personal preference most of the time, though it's not uncommon for the printer's internal margins (the area of the paper where the printer simply cannot lay down toner or ink) to clip off the top or left part of your page. In this case, just change the page position to Centered and try printing again.

**Thumbnails**  Thumbnails are great when you're trying to print out an overview of your document. For instance, you can print nine pages on a single piece of paper—three across and three down—by turning on the Thumbnails checkbox and then choosing 3x3 from the Per Page pop-up menu. Note that on PostScript printers it takes as long to print this one sheet as it would to print all nine pages individually, so plan your time accordingly.

**Tile**  If your pages just won't fit on your paper, you've got to resort to tiling and (horror of horrors) tape, wax, or glue. InDesign offers three ways to tile documents—Automatic, Auto Justified, and Manual.

**Automatic Tiling.** When you choose this option, InDesign starts the tile at the upper-left corner of the page, and prints as much of the page as it can given the paper size. Then it starts the next tile, with an overlap as specified in the Overlap field. It goes across the page, then moves down the page by the height of the paper you're printing on (again allowing for overlap), and then goes across the page again.

If you click once on the page preview, InDesign tells you how many tiles will be required to print each page. If you find that it's producing *lots* of tiles per page, try reducing the overlap. If you're just tiling together a proof, a slight reduction in the scaling percentage could save you a lot of time with scissors and tape.

**Auto Justified Tiling.** The Auto Justified Tiling option lays out the pieces of your page on the paper so that there's no extra white space to the right or underneath the page image (as you typically get with Automatic tiling). When you use this option, the Overlap field is meaningless; InDesign is actually figuring the overlap amount itself.

**Manual Tiling.** When you choose Manual tiling, InDesign only prints one tile per document page, using the zero point on the ruler as the upper-left corner of the tile. To print successive tiles, you have to move the zero point and print again. We find manual tiling much more useful than automatic tiling—automatic tiling always seems to split the tiles right in the middle of an important text block, so you can't read it. Or, worse, splits a large image or other tinted area—have you ever tried cutting and pasting to get the halftone dots in a photograph to line up? With manual tiling, you can ensure that items that you want to be able to proof are positioned so they're easy to see.

**Tiling: Just Say No.** Now it's time for pure, unadulterated (no adults were used), talk-radio-style opinion. Any time anyone tells us that they plan to tile a publication, our sense of honesty and fair play forces us to ask them why they want to do that. Is it a masochistic streak they've had since childhood? A profound sense of personal inferiority? Something genetic?

If you can't find some way to print your publication without tiling, then use a copy camera or other photographic process to enlarge it to the size you want, rather than printing tiles and then trying to paste the printed tiles together. If you don't know if such a service is available in your area, get out the Yellow Pages. Even if you have to send the publication across the country to get it blown up to the size you want, do it. Sure—these services do cost money. But what's your time—or your sanity—worth?

## Marks & Bleeds

When you print your publication, you can choose to include (or exclude) a number of printer's marks—crop marks, registration marks, and other information (see Figure 11-4). The preview window displays the effect (given the current page and paper sizes) of your choice of printer's marks options, though they're usually too small to see well.

**All Printer's Marks**    Turn on the All Printer's Marks option when you want to print all of the printer's marks and page information. This is usually more than you need; for instance if you don't have any objects bleeding off the page, then why bother with the Bleed Marks?

**Crop Marks**    Turn on the Crop Marks option to print lines outside the area of your page that define the area of the page (these are also called "trim marks"). Of course, if your paper size is not larger than your page size, InDesign won't (can't) print your crop marks.

**Bleed Marks**    Turn on the Bleed Marks option to print lines outside the area of your page that define the area of the bleed. Like crop marks, if your paper size is not larger than your page size, InDesign won't print your bleed marks. We almost always turn this option off, even when bleeding objects off the page; in our experience, it doesn't offer any useful information, and it can cause confusion.

**Registration Marks**    When you turn on the Registration Marks option, InDesign prints little targets around the edge of your page for your commercial printer to use when they're lining up, or registering, your color separations for printing. If your paper size is smaller than your page size, InDesign won't print the registration marks.

**Color Bars**    When you turn on the Color Bars option, InDesign prints small squares of color outside the bleed area of your printed page. Your

FIGURE 11-4
**The Marks & Bleeds Panel of the Print Dialog Box**

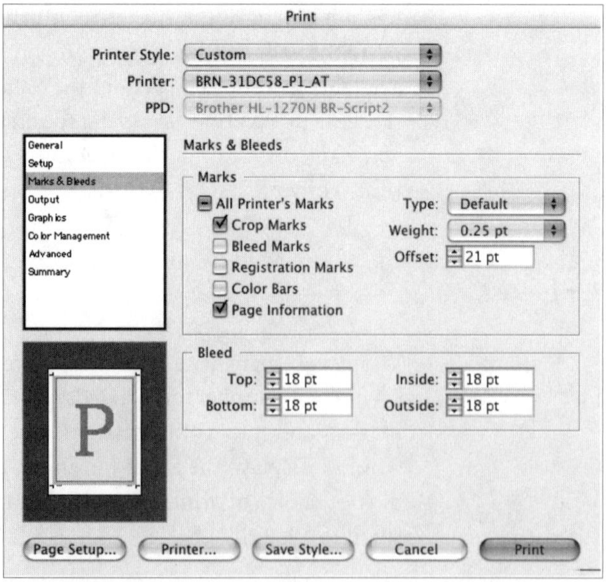

commercial printer can use these samples to adjust their press as they print the publication. It's worth checking with your printer to find out if they really want these before turning on this checkbox.

**Page Information**     Turn on the Page Information option to print the file name and date of your publication on each printed page. In color-separations InDesign also adds the name of the color plate. This makes it easy to tell which of several printed versions is the most current. It can also make it easier for your commercial printer to tell which pieces of film in a stack of separations go together (it's easy for you to tell, but put yourself in their shoes for a minute). We almost always leave this turned on (as long as the paper size is larger than the page size).

**Type**     Now here's an intriguing option—a pop-up menu offering only "Default" as a choice. The idea is that developers will be able to add different printer's marks at some point. We haven't seen any yet (apart from the specialized Japanese marks in InDesign-J).

**Weight**     You can change the thickness of the page marks by choosing from among three options in the Weight pop-up menu: .125 pt, .25 pt, and .5 pt. We're pretty happy with the default weight, .25 pt.

**Offset**     The Offset feature determines how far from the edge of the page the page marks should sit. The default value of six points seems a little tight to us. We don't operate a two-ton paper cutter at a bindery, but if we did, we'd sure wish people increased the space between page and trim marks (and registration marks) to at least 12 points.

**Bleed**     The values you enter in the Bleed fields set the real boundary of the printed page. When the value in the Bleed field is zero, InDesign neatly clips off any page elements extending beyond the edges of the page. This leaves little room for error in trimming the resulting printed pages—usually, when you want a page element to bleed off of a page, you should allow at least 24 points of bleed to compensate for inaccuracies in printing and trimming. If objects bleed off the page to the pasteboard, you must change these Bleed values in order for the object to still bleed upon printing.

## Output

Do you want to print a composite version of your publication, or do you want to print separations? If you want to print separations, which inks to you want to print? Those are among the questions you answer using the Output tab of the Print dialog box (see Figure 11-5).

**Composite Versus Separations**

If you've only used black and white in your document, you can pretty much ignore the Output tab. However, for those of us who create color documents, the most important setting here is the Color pop-up menu, with which you can tell InDesign to print composite color or color separations. Which of these you should choose depends on your printer and the output you're trying to achieve. Desktop inkjet printers should generally be considered RGB devices, so you should send composite RGB data to them. Color PostScript printers usually do a better job with composite CMYK data. If you choose Composite CMYK, InDesign converts all your RGB data (including any RGB TIFF files) into CMYK at print time. You can use any of the composite choices when printing to a black-and-white desktop laser printer.

Composite CMYK is also useful for workflows in which the separations will be performed by a RIP, even if that RIP is running as software on another machine. However, in most of these instances, it makes more sense to create a PDF file, a device-independent PostScript file, or—for the adventurous—a device-dependent PostScript file using In-RIP separations, especially if you are using trapping (trapping is not supported in CMYK composite output). Choosing In-RIP Separations from the Color pop-up menu instructs InDesign to create a special type of composite CMYK file which will

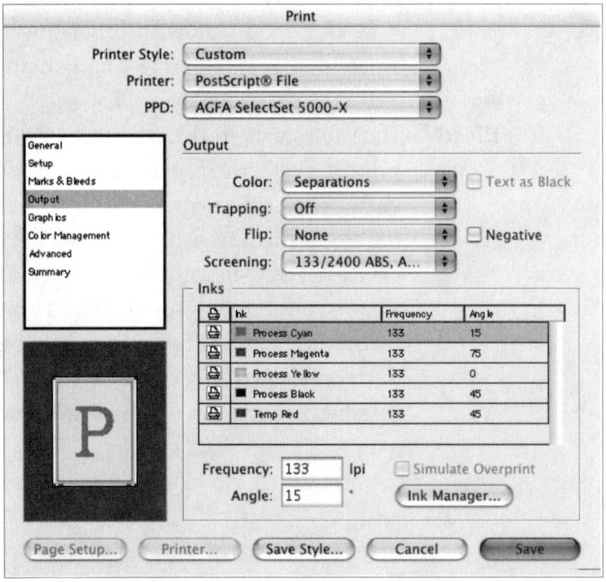

FIGURE 11-5

**The Output Panel of the Print Dialog Box**

only print properly on a PostScript 3 output device and some newer PostScript Level 2 devices.

You can also tell InDesign to separate each of your pages into four plates (or more, in the case of spot colors) by choosing Separation from the Color pop-up menu. If you turn on the Separations or In-RIP Separations options, InDesign activates the Inks list and its associated controls (the Flip, Frequency, Angle, Trapping settings, and so on).

**Text As Black**    One problem with printing proofs on a desktop laser printer is that sometimes it's difficult to read colored text because it appears as a tint. Similarly, when you want to fax a black-and-white version of your document, screened text just looks icky. If you turn on the Text as Black checkbox, InDesign ensures all your text appears as solid black—except for text that is already set to solid white, Paper color, or None.

**Trapping**    The Trapping pop-up menu controls whether InDesign applies automatic trapping to your documents. Choose one of the following trapping options from the Trapping pop-up menu.

◆ **Off.** Use this option if you're done all of your trapping manually (using InDesign's fills and strokes) or if you plan to separate and trap the publication using a post-processing program.

◆ **Application Built-In.** Choose Application Built-In when you want InDesign to trap your publication as it's sent to the printer (or to disk).

◆ **Adobe In-RIP.** Turn this option on when you want to leave trapping up to the RIP in your printer or imagesetter. This feature, which makes us rather nervous, only works on PostScript 3 and some PostScript Level 2 printers.

We cover trapping in greater detail in Chapter 10, "Color").

**Flip and Negative**    InDesign can mirror pages at print time if you choose Horizontal, Vertical, or Horizontal & Vertical from the Flip pop-up menu. Flipping an image is used mainly for creating either wrong- or right-reading film from imagesetters, or film with emulsion side up or down. This is often handled in the imagesetter or platesetter, so be careful before you go changing this setting. The same thing goes for the Negative checkbox, which inverts the entire page so that everything that is set to 100-percent black becomes zero-percent black (effectively white). Never make assumptions about what your output provider wants; what you think will help might actually hinder (and cost you money in the long run).

**Screening**   What halftone screen frequency (in lines per inch) and screen angle do you want to use to print your publication? If you selected Composite Gray in the Color pop-up menu, you can choose either the printer's default (which is defined by the PPD you selected) or you can choose Custom and then enter your own values in the Frequency and Angle fields.

When you're printing separations, you'll see more choices on the Screening pop-up menu, and the values shown in the Frequency and Angle fields change as you select inks in the Inks list. Where the heck are these choices and values coming from? They're coming from the PPD. Every PPD contains a list of screen frequencies and screen angles optimized to avoid moiré patterns on the specific PostScript device described by the PPD. Because of the way that PostScript halftoning (or any digital halftoning, for that matter) works, a PostScript RIP cannot perfectly "hit" just any halftone screen.

On PostScript Level 1 devices, the screen angle and screen frequency you'd get would sometimes fail to match the frequency and angle you specified. This often resulted in serious output problems and severe moiré patterns. PPDs list combinations of screen angles known to be safe for a given printer at a screen frequency and angle.

While the need for these optimized screen angles has diminished somewhat with newer versions of PostScript, we strongly advise you to stick with them when you're printing separations.

To override the optimized screen settings for an ink, select the ink in the Inks list and then enter new values in the Frequency and Angle fields. Again, we don't recommend this, but you might have a very good reason for doing so that we simply haven't thought of yet (like perhaps you've lost your mind).

The optimized screen angles only cover the process inks, however. When your publication includes spot inks, InDesign sets the screen angle of every spot ink to 45 degrees.

For spot-color work—especially where you're overlaying tints of two spot colors or using duotones from Photoshop based on two spot inks—you need to specify the screen angles appropriately. Here's how to set them.

◆ If the spot inks *never* interact, set the screen angle for the inks to 45 degrees (because a 45-degree halftone screen is the least obvious to the eye).

◆ If you're creating lots of two-ink tint builds, or using duotones, you have a few choices, and two (somewhat contradictory) goals. You want both colors to print as close as possible to 45 degrees (especially the dominant, or darker, color), and you want as much separation between the angles as possible (the greater the separation between angles—45 is the maximum possible—the less patterning is visible where the screens interact). Table 11-2 lists some options.

◆ If you're printing with two spot inks and the spot colors don't overprint any process inks, use the default screen angles for Magenta and Cyan from the optimized screen you've selected.

Note that even if you set specific screen frequencies and angles for every color, you may not get what you ask for. Most imagesetters and platesetters these days strip out all screening settings and replace them with their own unless you (or your output provider) turns off this process. We've been caught by this several times, when we've chosen low-frequency screens in order to create a special effect, only to find our instructions ignored and the normal 133 lpi halftone appear. Very annoying.

**TABLE 11-2**
**Screen Angles for**
**Spot Color Work**

| Subordinate: | Dominant: | Notes: |
|---|---|---|
| 15 | 45 | Traditional. Only a 30-degree separation, but neither angle is very obvious on its own. |
| 0 | 45 | Avoids patterning. Ideally, the ink printed at zero degrees is a very light color—otherwise, the horizontal bands of halftone dots will be too obvious. |
| 22.5 | 67.5 | The complete compromise. Both angles are more obvious than 45 degrees, but less obvious than 0, and you get the full 45-degree separation to avoid patterning. |
| 75 | 30 | The dominant color screen is slightly less obvious than the subordinate screen. Full 45-degree separation. |

**Inks**   When you turn on the Separations option, InDesign activates the Inks list. In this list, you'll see at least the four process inks (yes, they'll appear even if you aren't using process colors in your publication), plus any spot inks you've defined. When you select an ink in the Inks list, InDesign displays the halftone screen properties for that ink in the Frequency and Angle fields (see "Screening," above).

You can tell InDesign not to print one or more inks from this list by clicking the printer icon that's to the left of the ink name in the Inks list. You can also turn on or off all the inks by Option/Alt-clicking. Don't worry about inks that aren't used in your publication—InDesign will not generate a blank separation for them. If, for example, your publication uses only black ink and a spot ink, InDesign will not create separations for Cyan, Magenta, and Yellow, even though those inks appear in the Inks list.

**Simulate Overprint**   As we discussed in Chapter 10, "Color," you can set various objects to overprint using the Attributes palette. However, most composite printers (like laser printers and inkjets) don't support overprinting. Fortunately, you can simulate overprinting on these output devices by turning on the Simulate Overprint checkbox. Because this can change color definitions (spot colors get converted to process, for example), you *don't* want to turn this on for anything other than proofing your files on composite printers.

**Ink Manager**   The Ink Manager manages how colors trap with each other and how spot color interact (for instance, you can use the Ink Manager to alias one spot color to another). We cover the Ink Manager in Chapter 10, "Color."

# Graphics

The options in the Graphics tab control the way that InDesign prints the fonts and graphics in your publication (see Figure 11-6).

**Send Data**   The Send Data pop-up menu affects what InDesign does with bitmaps in TIFF, JPEG, and other explicitly bitmapped file formats. It has no effect on images inside imported EPS or PDF graphics.

Do you want to print that 30-megabyte color scan every time you proof a document on your laser printer? Probably not. The Send Image Data pop-up menu gives you four options to control what InDesign does with images when you print: All, Optimized Subsampling, Proxy, and None, each of which is described below.

**All**   Use this option when you want InDesign to send all of the image data from the image file to the printer. We recommend that you always use this option when printing the final copies of your pages.

**Optimized**   This option tells InDesign to only send as much information from
**Subsampling**   the image as is necessary to produce the best quality on the given output device using the current settings. It reduces the amount of data that has to be passed over the network and imaged by the printer. It can speed up printing immensely.

How InDesign pares down the data depends on whether the image is color/grayscale or black and white.

◆ **Color/Grayscale images.** As we mentioned in Chapter 7, "Importing and Exporting," there's no reason for the resolution of grayscale and color images (in pixels per inch) to exceed two times the halftone screen frequency (in lines per inch). When you choose Optimized Subsampling from the Send Image Data pop-up menu, InDesign reduces the resolution of grayscale and color images to match the halftone screen frequency you've selected (in the Output tab of the Print dialog box). If you've set up a 75-line screen (for instance), InDesign won't send more than 150 dots per inch of image resolution. Note that InDesign does not change the resolution of the images in your publication—it just reduces the amount of data that's sent to the printer.

FIGURE 11-6
**The Graphics Panel**
**of the Print Dialog Box**

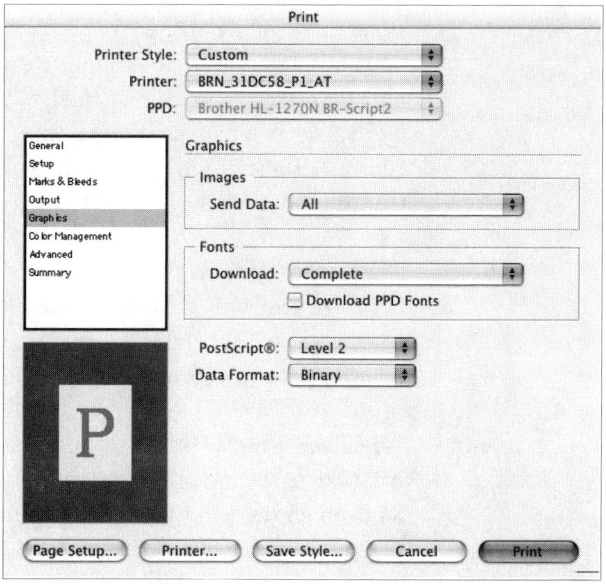

◆ **Black-and-white (bi-level) images.** When you're printing bi-level, black-and-white images, and have selected Optimized Subsampling from the Send Image Data pop-up menu, InDesign matches the images it sends to the resolution of the output device. So if you've got a 600-pixels per inch black-and-white TIFF, and you're printing on a 300-dpi laser printer, InDesign reduces the resolution of the image to 300 pixels per inch before sending it to the printer. For those who really want to know, InDesign gets the printer's resolution from the DefaultResolution keyword in the PPD.

The real value of the Optimized setting lies in printing laser proof copies of jobs that are destined for high-resolution (hence high halftone screen frequency) output. If you're producing a document that will be printed with a 133-lpi screen, for instance, you may be working with images that have resolutions of 250 or even 300 ppi. But for proofing on a 600-dpi laser printer (which has a 85-lpi default screen frequency), you only need 106 dpi—maximum. By subsampling to this lower resolution, InDesign is sending *less than one fifth* of the information over the wire. Obviously, this can save you a lot of time. With high-resolution line art, InDesign might send only a sixteenth of the data.

Printing an image using the Optimized Subsampling option produces a more detailed printed image than using the Low Resolution option, but doesn't take as long to print or transmit as the full-resolution version of the image.

While Optimized Subsampling might sound like the universal cure for perfect (speedy, high quality) printing, it isn't. Subsampling, by its nature, blurs and distorts images, especially in areas of high contrast. Therefore, we think you should use this option for proof printing, but not for printing the final copies of your pages.

**Proxy**    Choose Proxy from the Send Image Data pop-up menu to have InDesign send only the low-resolution preview images it displays on your screen to the printer. Again, this is an option to use when you're printing proof copies of your pages, not for final output.

**None**    When you print with the Proof Print option turned on, InDesign prints all of the imported graphics in your publication as boxes with Xs through them. As you'd expect, this makes it print faster. Proof printing is great when you're copy-editing the text of a publication—why wait for the graphics to print?

Note that you can speed things up a bit, without completely eliminating the graphics, by using the Proxy or Optimized Subsampling options on the Send Image Data pop-up menu. Also, note that you can turn off the printing of a particular type of imported graphic using the Omit EPS/PDF/Bitmap Images options in the Advanced tab of the Print dialog box.

**Font Downloading**

One of the best ways to speed up InDesign's printing is to manage dowloaded fonts sensibly. You can save many hours over the course of a day, week, or month by downloading fonts to your printer in advance, and by understanding how InDesign handles font downloading.

The basic concept is pretty simple: Fonts can be either "resident" (which means that they're stored in your printer's memory or on a hard drive attached to the printer) or "downloadable" (which means they're stored somewhere on your system or network).

When you print, InDesign checks the printer PPD to see if the fonts are available on the printer. If the font is available, InDesign sends a reference to the font, but does not send the font itself, which means that the text will be printed in the font available on the printer.

What happens when a font is not available in the printer's memory or on its hard drive? That depends on the option you've chosen in the Font Downloading section of the Graphics tab of the Print dialog box.

When you turn on the None option, you're directing InDesign to refrain from including any fonts in the PostScript it's sending to the printer (or to disk). If text in your publication has been formatted using fonts that are not resident on the printer, that text will be printed using the printer's default font (usually Courier).

When you choose the Complete option, InDesign checks the state of the Download PPD Fonts option. If this option is on, InDesign sends all of the fonts used in the publication to the printer's memory. If the option is turned off, InDesign downloads all of the fonts used in the publication that are not listed in the PPD (PPDs contain lists of fonts available on a given make and model printer, plus any you've added by editing the PPD). InDesign downloads the fonts once for each page that's printed. As you'd expect, this increases the amount of time it takes to send the job to your printer.

To decrease the amount of your printer's memory that's taken up by downloaded fonts, or decrease the amount of time it takes InDesign to send the fonts to your printer, turn on the Subset option.

When you do this, InDesign sends only those characters required to print the publication. This can speed up printing tremendously.

**Postscript Level**    Adobe would love it if everyone had PostScript 3 devices. Not only would they make tons of money from licensing fees, but their software could also take advantage of all the cool features in PostScript 3 RIPs. However, currently most people only have PostScript Level 2 devices. (Please don't ask us why "PostScript 3" omits the "Level" moniker. We can only assume that Adobe's marketing strategists have their reasons.) In most cases, InDesign reads the PostScript level from the PPD, so you don't have to think about this. However, if you're making a device-independent PostScript file you will need to choose "Level 2" or "Level 3". (Here Adobe *does* use "Level." We guess consistency isn't really a human trait.) If you have trouble printing to a PostScript 3 device, you might consider changing this to Level 2; that might change the PostScript enough to get it to print.

**Data Format**    The Data Format feature controls how bitmapped images (like TIFF and JPEG) are sent to the printer. While sending the information in ASCII format is more reliable over some older networks, binary is almost always fine and has the benefit of creating a much smaller PostScript file (the images are half the size of ASCII). We usually use binary unless we're sending files to an output provider that we know uses a PC- or UNIX-based system for output.

# Color Management

The features in the Color Management tab of the Print dialog box are grayed out until you turn on Color Management in the Color Settings dialog box. We discuss color management, including all these Print dialog box settings, in Chapter 10, "Color."

# Advanced

We're not sure what makes this tab more "advanced" than the others, but it's where you specify how InDesign should print gradients (blends), images in an OPI workflow, and objects that have transparency settings (see Figure 11-7).

**OPI Image Replacement**    When you're printing through an OPI server, you can direct the server to replace the low-resolution images you've used to lay out

FIGURE 11-7
**The Advanced Panel
of the Print Dialog Box**

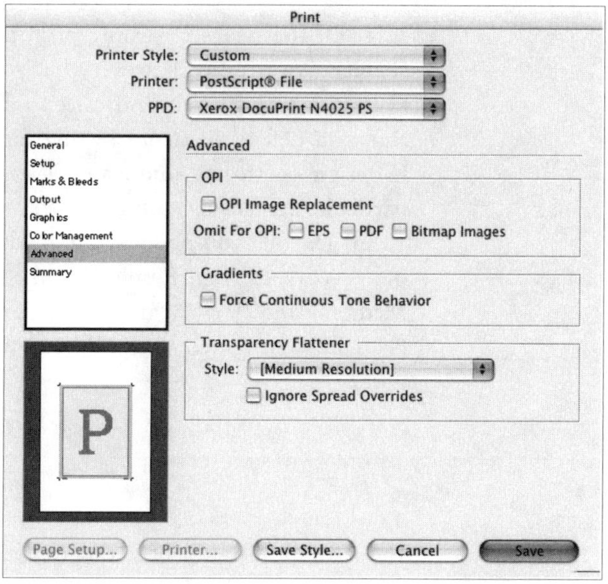

your document with the high-resolution images you've stored on the server. To do this, turn off the OPI Image Replacement option and turn on the appropriate Omit for OPI checkboxes. This omits the images from the PostScript output, leaving only the OPI link information in their place.

Note that you can specify which types of images you want to replace with OPI comments: EPS, PDF, or Bitmap Images. When you turn on the EPS option, you're telling InDesign not to print any EPS graphics in the file, but if PDF and Bitmap Images are still turned on then the program will include that image data at print time.

When you turn on OPI Image Replacement, InDesign acts as an OPI server at print time, replacing the low-resolution OPI proxy images with the high-resolution versions. InDesign needs access to the server or drive containing the files for this to work. To retain OPI image links to images stored inside imported EPS graphics, make sure that you turn on the Read Embedded OPI Image Links option in the EPS Import Options dialog box.

**Gradient Options**

Turn on the Force Continuous Tone Behavior when you're printing to a dye-sublimation color printer or a color laser printer. This option creates better-looking gradients on those (rare) devices. Note that this does not help with gradients on printers that create halftones, and so it should not be used for final output.

**Transparency
Flattener**

We hate to give you the runaround, but if you're reading this hoping to learn all about how the flattener works, you're out of luck. We cover all the issues regarding printing transparency later in this chapter. We will say, however, that you can use the Transparency Flattener section of the Advanced tab of the Print dialog box to choose a default Flattener setting for your print job, and to tell InDesign whether to ignore any Flattener settings you've applied to particular spreads in your document with the Pages palette.

In general, you should use Medium Resolution when printing proofs and High Resolution when printing final artwork. But "Medium" and "High" can mean different things depending on the Flattener settings, so you still need to go read that other section. Sorry.

## Summary

The last tab of the Print dialog box, Summary, simply lists all the various settings in all the tabs in one long text list. We think this is perhaps the silliest of all features in the Print dialog box; it's just harder and more time-consuming to read through this unformatted list of settings than it is to skip through each of the tabs. However, it's nice that you can click the Save Summary button to save this list to disk as a text file. If you're writing PostScript to disk to send to someone else, it's a good idea to include this summary along with it, so they know how you set up the dialog box (and can check to see if you did anything inappropriate). You can also use this saved summary as a log of what you did to later refer to if something prints in an unexpected fashion.

## Printer Styles

We don't know about you, but we find we print a typical InDesign publication (at least) three different ways. We print a proof copy on our laser printer, a color proof on a color printer, and then we print our final copies on an imagesetter. In the first two instances, we print composites; when we print to an imagesetter, we typically print color separations. You might think that for each type of printing we have to claw our way through the settings in the Print dialog box. Instead, we save our Print dialog box settings in a *printer style*—which means that switching from proof to final printing is as easy as selecting the appropriate printer style.

Printer styles are like paragraph styles—they're bundles of attributes that can be applied in a single action. All of the attributes in the

Print dialog box and in the printer driver dialog boxes are included in a printer style.

**Creating a Printer Style**

It's easy to create a printer style; just set up the Print dialog box with the options the way you want them, click the Save Style button at the bottom of the dialog box, and then give the style a name. You can then go ahead and print, or just cancel out of the Print dialog box (if you just wanted to set up the style without printing).

InDesign also has a second method for making printer styles, though we find it slightly more cumbersome.

1. Choose Define from the Printer Styles submenu of the File menu. InDesign displays the Define Printer Styles dialog box (see Figure 11-8).

2. Click the New button. InDesign displays the Print dialog box, except with one difference: there's a Name field at the top.

3. Enter a name for the printer style in the Name field, then set up the dialog box with the settings you want, and click the OK button. InDesign returns you to the Define Printer Styles dialog box and adds the new printer style to the list of available printer styles.

To print using the settings in a printer style, you can choose the style from the Printer Style pop-up menu in the Print dialog box. Or, even easier, just choose the printer style name from the Printer Styles submenu of the File menu. InDesign displays the Print dialog box. Click the Print button (or the Save button, if you're printing to disk), and InDesign prints the specified pages.

To print without displaying the Print dialog box, hold down Shift as you choose the printer style name from the Printer Styles submenu.

**Managing Printer Styles**

You can use the Define Printer Styles dialog box to add printer styles, delete printer styles, rename printer styles, edit printer styles, or import or export printer styles.

◆ To create a new printer style that is based on an existing printer style, open the Define Printer Styles dialog box, select a printer style, and then click the New button. Enter a name for your new printer style, then modify the settings in the panels of the Print dialog box. Note that this does not link the two printer styles—changes made to the "parent" printer style will not affect any printer styles you've based on it. It is, however, a little less

**FIGURE 11-8**
**Creating a Printer Style**

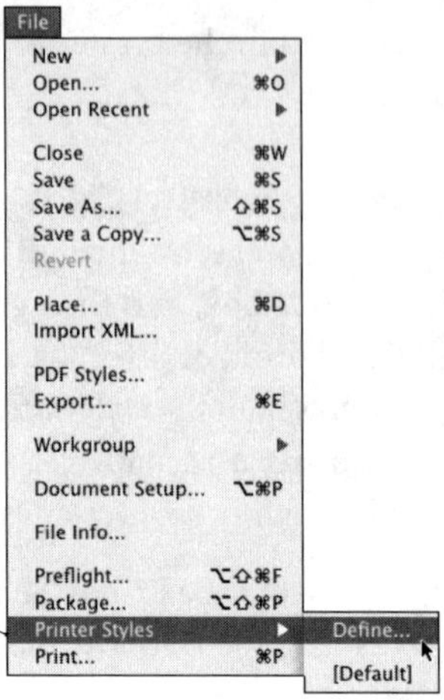

*Choose Define from the*
*Printer Styles submenu of*
*the File menu.*

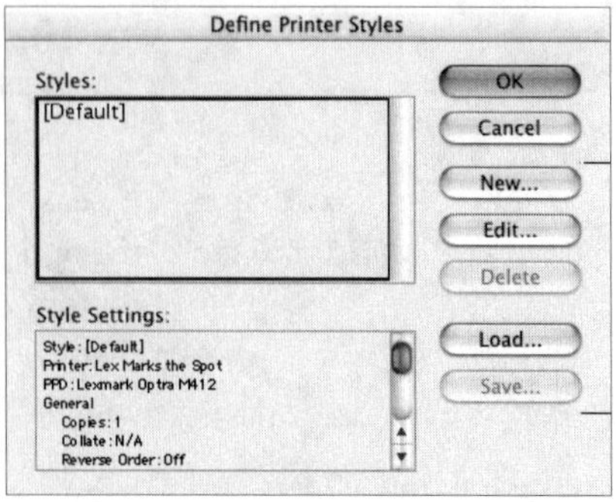

*InDesign displays the Define Printer Styles*
*dialog box. Click the New button.*

*Enter a name for the new printer style and*
*set up the Print dialog box the way you want it.*

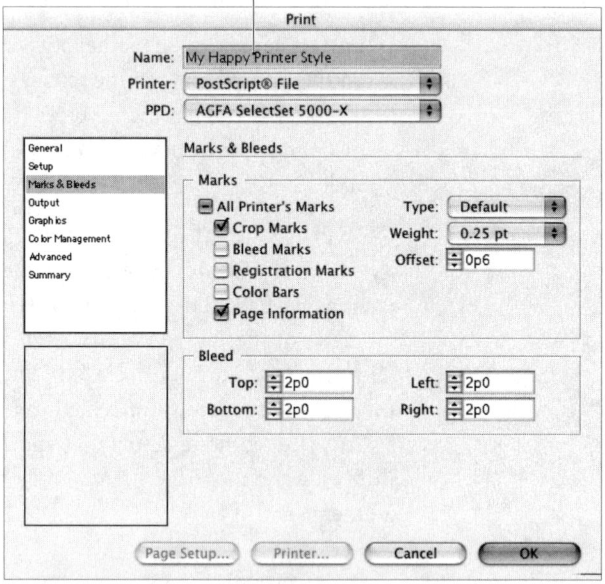

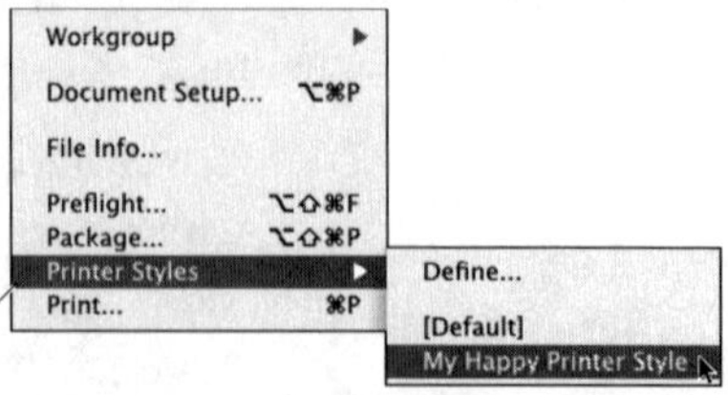

*InDesign adds the new printer*
*style to the list of available styles.*
*To print using the printer style,*
*choose the style name here...*

*...or hold down Shift if you want to print*
*without displaying the Print dialog box.*

tedious than working your way through all of the printing controls just to change a single setting.

◆ To delete a printer style, select the printer style name and click the Delete button.

◆ To export a printer style, select one or more style names and click the Save button. Specify a file name and location for the printer styles document and click the OK button.

◆ To import a printer style or set of printer styles, open the Define Printer Styles dialog box and click the Load button. Locate and select a printer styles document (or an InDesign publication containing printer styles), then click the OK button. If the printer styles you're importing already exist in the publication, InDesign will create copies of the styles (InDesign will append a number—usually "1"—to the duplicate printer styles).

◆ To edit a printer style, select the printer style name in the Define Printer Styles dialog box, then click the Edit button. InDesign displays the Print dialog box. Make the changes and click the OK button

## Printing Transparency

Two of the most important figures in the desktop publishing revolution—Tim Gill (founder of Quark, Inc.) and John Warnock (co-founder of Adobe, Inc.)—each had a blind spot that led to a tragedy of unparalleled proportions. Well, maybe not quite that strong (they both retired quite happily in recent years). But the blind spots did have interesting results that caused their companies difficulties.

Tim Gill didn't believe that HTML was worth much attention, and Quark suffered by being late to supporting the Web. John Warnock didn't believe transparency was important and so it took PostScript 20 years to support it. Everyone knows that vector transparency is important to designers, but because PostScript couldn't print it, programs couldn't support it.

But wait, you say, some programs have had transparency features for many years! Photoshop supported transparency because it only had to worry about pixels, not vector artwork. The transparency features of every other program (including Illustrator, FreeHand, and so on) worked by faking the effects at print time, "flattening" the transparent objects into a form that PostScript could handle.

In recent years, transparency has finally made its way into PostScript 3 by way of the PDF 1.4 specification (PostScript 3, version 3015 or later, to be precise). RIPs that support PDF 1.4 directly can print transparency without any chicanery. Unfortunately, as we write this, the vast majority of RIPs—especially RIPs suited for high-resolution imagesetters and platesetters—support only PostScript Level 2. So most of the time programs like Illustrator and InDesign are still forced to flatten files that include drop shadows, feathering, or any other cool transparency effects.

**The Flattener**    Adobe's technology for turning transparent objects into a form suitable for older RIPs is called "the flattener." (David is pleased to have finally found a word that more or less rhymes with his last name.) The flattener works by breaking up transparent objects into smaller non-transparent objects. It has three basic methods to do this. (Note that the flattener works the same in Illustrator 10, Acrobat 5, and InDesign 2.)

◆ **Divide and conquer.** If you have a 50-percent transparent magenta square partially over a cyan square, the flattener splits this into three objects: where the two overlapped it creates a rectangle made of cyan and magenta; where they didn't overlap, it makes two L-shaped objects, one cyan the other magenta.

◆ **Clip it up.** Let's say you have a 20-percent transparent picture partially overlapping that cyan square (or vice versa, a partially-transparent cyan square overlapping a picture). The flattener splits the picture into two (or more) pieces by drawing invisible frames (clipping paths) and putting pieces of the picture into them. The part of the picture that is inside the square gets cyan added to it to finish the effect.

◆ **Rasterize.** When all else fails, and InDesign realizes that it'll take too long to use the previous two methods (too long to flatten means the file will probably also take way too long to print), it punts and just turns the whole thing into a bitmapped picture (converting vectors into bitmaps is called rasterizing).

Again, all of this is done behind the scenes and only at print time (or when you export the file as an EPS or an Acrobat 4 PDF file, both of which also use the flattener). In most cases, you'd never know that InDesign was doing any of this if we hadn't told you, because the results are extremely clean. In some cases, primarily when InDesign ends up rasterizing part of your page, you may find the results only fine, okay, or (rarely) unacceptable.

**Transparency Tricks**

Okay, here comes our "with power comes responsibility" talk. Transparency is all about accepting compromise, and if you can't deal with compromise then you might consider avoiding transparency altogether. The first compromise is time versus quality: The better quality, the more time your files will take to print (or export). The next compromise is that if you want to play with transparency (or your clients want to, and you've agreed to print their documents), you need to pay attention to how your document is created and be prepared to proof the final results carefully.

Here's a few things you should pay attention to when messing with transparency.

◆ Transparency comes in all sorts of forms. If you use the Drop Shadow or Feather feature, you're introducing transparency. So does importing a native Photoshop, Illustrator, or PDF document which includes any transparenct object. If the page icon in the Pages palette has a checkerboard in it, you can bet that the flattener will kick in.

◆ If you're going to use transparent objects in Adobe Illustrator (including transparent brushes, most filters, drop shadows, and so on), make sure you're using version 9.02 or later (you should probably just use version 10 or later). Also, we suggest saving files in the native .ai format, the Acrobat 5 PDF format, or use .eps compatible with Illustrator 9 or 10 (not earlier versions). This way InDesign handles flattening at print time instead of you worrying about Illustrator getting it right.

◆ If you're importing Illustrator documents that include images and use transparency effects, it's probably a good idea to embed the images in the Illustrator file itself rather than relying on linking to the file on disk.

◆ Set the Transparency Blend Space (in the Edit menu) to CMYK rather than RGB, and—if you've turned on color management— use Convert to Profile to convert the document working space to your final output space.

◆ Spot colors offer a number of opportunities for problems, especially the flattener converting spot colors to process colors (or worse, converting part of an object to process color and leaving the rest of the object a spot color). Fortunately, this typically only happens when you use fancy transparency modes (like Color, Saturation, Difference, and so on) or when you have spot color gradients involved with transparency.

◆ The flattener must work with high-resolution images on disk, which means that DCS files and an OPI workflow—both of which rely on importing low-resolution images that get swapped out with high-resolution later—are out. (Of course, if you have DCS or OPI images that are not involved with transparency then you can still use them.) Adobe's documentation says that EPS duotones are also a no-no, but we haven't run into any problems with them.

◆ It's better not to mix overprint settings (like Overprint Stroke or Overprint Fill in the Attributes palette) with transparency. For example, if you're using transparency anyway, then consider using the Multiply blend mode rather than turning on Overprint Fill.

◆ Most PostScript RIPs can handle the flattener tricks just fine, but we have encountered some RIPs that cause problems. For example, because Scitex (now part of Creo) RIPs rely on separating continuous tone imagery from linework (vector) images, you can get some very bad results, especially where text interacts with transparent objects. Creo says they're working on a fix for this, but be extra careful when perusing your output if you (or your output provider) are using this sort of RIP.

◆ In fact, it would behoove you to always look over your final output carefully. Look for spot colors that were converted to process, overprinting instructions that were ignored, vector objects that were rasterized in unpleasant ways, unintentionally rasterized type, and text or strokes that became heavier.

**Flattener Styles**    As we said earlier, flattening is a matter of compromise. Fortunately, you have a say in the matter, by selecting among various flattener styles. Each flattener style is a collection of flattening choices, such as how hard should InDesign try before giving up and rasterizing the artwork.

InDesign ships with three predefined flattener styles: Low Resolution, Medium Resolution, and High Resolution. You can mentally replace the word "resolution" with "quality." You should typically use Low or Medium when printing to a desktop laser printer and High when printing to an imagesetter or platesetter (see "Applying Flattener Styles," below).

Occasionally we find a need to create our own flattener style. For example, if you're doing a lot of proofs on a black-and-white desktop laser printer, you could probably get away with making a "Very

Low" style, which may print faster than Low Resolution with "good enough" quality. Or, if you're getting unacceptably slow printing, PostScript errors, or poor quality on an imagesetter with the High Resolution style, you might want to create a custom style that works better for you.

To make a custom flattener style, select Transparency Flattener Styles from the Edit menu (see Figure 11-9). While you cannot edit the default styles, you can base a new one on a default style by selecting the style then clicking the New button, which opens the Transparency Flattener Style dialog box. Beyond the name of the style (pick whatever you want), there are six controls here.

**Raster/Vector Balance.** The Raster/Vector Balance slider is a graphic representation of the quality/speed compromise. Push the slider all the way to the left and InDesign rasterizes everything on the page (we can't think of any good reason to do this). Push the slider all the

FIGURE 11-9
**Creating a Flattener Style**

*To define a flattener style, select Transparency Flattener Styles from the Edit menu.*

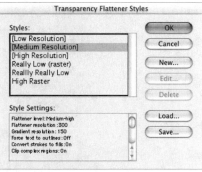

*To base a new style on an existing style, select a style and click the New button.*

*Enter a name for the flattener style. (Something more descriptive than this one would be good.)*

way to the right and InDesign tries its best to maintain every vector in the document, even if that means taking a long time to flatten and a long time to print. As left-leaning as we tend to be, we always prefer pushing this to the far right when printing on imagesetters. However, on a complex page, this creates so many clipping paths that your file might not print at all. In that case, you'd need to take it down a notch. On desktop PostScript printers, we'd set this even lower.

**Flattener Resolution.** When InDesign ends up rasterizing a vector object, it looks to the Flattener Resolution setting in order to find the appropriate resolution. The Low Resolution flattener style uses a flattener resolution of 288 ppi (pixels per inch), which will look very slightly jagged on a desktop laser printer. The High Resolution flattener style uses 1200 ppi. If you were printing on newsprint, you could easily get away with creating a flattener style that used 800 ppi. If you're printing on glossy stock for an coffee table book, you could probably raise this to 1600 ppi.

The flattener resolution also acts as an "upper boundary" when imported bitmapped images are involved with transparency. For example, let's say you import a 300 ppi image, put transparent text over it, and then print using the Low Resolution flattener style. InDesign resamples the image down to 288 ppi. However, if you use the High Resolution flattener style, InDesign will not upsample the image to 1200 (that would be crazy).

**Gradient Resolution.** Sometimes objects get rasterized no matter what happens—for instance, soft drop shadows or feather effects. The gradient resolution determines the appropriate resolution for these sorts of raster effects. The Gradient Resolution setting in the Low Resolution flattener style defaults to 144 ppi, even though you typically don't need more than 100 ppi on any desktop printer. You generally don't need more than 200 ppi for high-resolution output. (After all, you need resolution to capture detail in an image, and these "images" have no detail).

InDesign may upsample your bitmapped images if they're involved with a transparent areas of the page and they're lower resolution than the Gradient Resolution setting. For example, if you import a 72 ppi image (like a JPEG saved from a Web site) and change its transparency setting, the flattener upsamples the image to the gradient resolution. Unfortunately, if you import a 200 ppi TIFF image (which is very reasonable for most printed artwork today), set its transparency, and print it using the High Resolution flattener style, InDesign also upsamples it to 300 ppi—causing slower printing and possibly image degradation. (InDesign uses "nearest neighbor" interpolation, which results in a pretty clunky images.)

**Force Text to Outlines.** When text gets involved with transparency (either it is transparent or something transparent is on top of it), the type almost always gets turned into paths which act as clipping paths. This slows down printing a bit, and sometimes that text appears heavier than the equivalent characters that aren't converted to outlines, especially on lower-resolution printers. If, for example, you had an image that was partially transparent on top of half a column of text, the text under the image might appear like it was very slightly more bold than the rest of the text. One answer would be to create a flattener style in which the Force Text to Outlines option was turned on and apply that to this particular spread (we discuss applying flattener styles below). This way, all the text on that spread gets converted to outlines. The page prints even slower, but is more consistent. This is rarely a problem when imagesetting or platesetting, however, so we usually just ignore this feature.

**Convert Strokes to Outlines.** The problem with type "heavying up" is also an issue around thin lines. The flattener converts lines that are involved with transparency effects into very thin boxes. These boxes may appear thicker, however, than equal lines that don't have any transparency effects. Turning this feature on ensures that InDesign converts all the lines in the document, making them more visually equal. Again, this is rarely an issue on high-resolution printers.

**Clip Complex Regions.** When InDesign does resort to rasterizing vectors, it usually does so in rectangular areas, called "atomic regions" (sort of like the smallest regions the flattener deals with). The problem with this lies along the line between a rasterized area and an area drawn with vectors—in many cases, the step from raster to vector is visually obvious (sometimes called "stitching"), which sort of ruins the whole point. When you turn on the Clip Complex Regions checkbox, however, InDesign works extra hard to keep the transitions between raster and vector occur only along the edges of objects. The result is a better-looking page that is more complex and prints more slowly (or not at all). Ah, compromises.

**Applying Flattener Styles**    After reading all of this, don't you wish you had a PDF 1.4-aware PostScript 3 device that can print transparency effects without flattening? Until you have one, however, you'd better know about how to apply these flattener styles.

You can set the flattener style to either the whole document (the "default style") or specific page spreads (a "local style"). To apply a default style at print time, choose it from the Transparency Flattener Style pop-up menu in the Advanced tab of the Print dialog box. You can also set the default style in the Advanced tabs of the Export as PDF and Export as EPS dialog boxes, as well as the Export as SVG dialog box (if you click More Options).

To apply a local flattener style, select one or more page spreads in the Pages palette and select from among the choices in the Spread Flattening menu in the Pages palette menu: Default, None (Ignore Transparency), or Custom. If you choose None, InDesign prints this spread without any transparency effects. You might use this as a troubleshooting technique if your page isn't printing properly: if you turn off transparency for the spread and it then prints, then it's likely a transparency-related print issue.

Choosing Custom opens the Transparency Flattener Style dialog box. We assume there's a good reason that there's no way to select one of the flattener styles you've already built, but we can't imagine what that reason would be. Perhaps Adobe just wants to give you something to look forward to in future versions of the program.

If you (or some nefarious client) has applied flattener styles to spreads and at print time you want to override them all with the default style, you can turn on the Ignore Spread Overrides checkbox in the Print dialog box.

## Preparing an InDesign File for Imagesetting

We've listened long and carefully to the grievances of imagesetting service bureau customers and operators. We've heard about how this designer is suing that service bureau for messing up a job, and we've heard imagesetter operators talking about how stupid their clients are and how they have to make changes to the files of most of the jobs that come in. We've listened long enough, and we have only one thing to say: Cut it out! All of you!

There's no reason that this relationship has to be an adversarial one. We don't mean to sound harsh. We just think that we can all cooperate, to everyone's benefit.

Designers: You have to learn the technical chops if you want to play. That's just the way it is. The technical challenges are no greater than those you mastered when you learned how to use a waxer, an X-Acto knife, or a copy camera.

Your responsibility to your imagesetting service bureau is to set your file up so that it has a reasonable chance of printing and to communicate to your service bureau exactly how it is you want your publication printed (or, if you're delivering a PostScript file or PDF, to make sure that the settings in the file are correct).

Service bureau folks, you've got to spell out the limits of your responsibility. If you don't think you should be fixing people's files, don't do it. If you do think it's your responsibility, tell your customer up front you'll fix the files, and tell them what you'll charge for your time. And if you get customers who know what they're doing, give them a discount. This will encourage everyone else.

Okay, back to the book.

**Sending Your File**    You have three basic choices in transporting your document to an output provider: sending the file itself, sending a PostScript dump, or sending an Acrobat PDF version of the document. While our preference has always been to send PostScript dumps or PDF files, many printers and service bureaus want the file itself. It's a question of who is in control of the final output: us or them.

When we send the InDesign file off to be printed on someone else's system, we don't know whether their fonts are different, whether they'll forget to set up registration marks, and so on. If you send them a PDF file, you can be reasonably sure that the file will print correctly. If you send a PostScript file (and you know what you're doing), you put yourself in the driver's seat. The only things that can go wrong are related to film handling and processing—the wrong film's used, the film's scratched, or the film's been processed incorrectly.

However, no matter what you're going to send to your output provider, you have to be dead certain you've thought of everything before it goes, because it's difficult to change things after that. For instance, make sure that any linked graphics in the publication are up to date, and that any embedded graphics are what you want them to be. If you're printing PostScript, make sure the Print dialog box is set up correctly: What screening? Is tiling off? Do you need separations or composite color? What inks to print? Do you want spot colors or process colors? Your output provider should be able to help you make most of these decisions, and perhaps even give you the appropriate PPD file.

Fortunately, the Preflight feature helps with some of this. And, if you're going to send the InDesign file itself, then you should plan on using the Package feature. We discuss both of these in the next section.

## Preflight and Package

Are all systems "go?" Do you know the number of kilometers, meters, and centimeters it'll take to get your publication safely in orbit around Mars? Or is it miles, feet, and inches?

**Preflight**

To make sure that your publication is really ready for "prime time," you should use the Preflight plug-in (choose Preflight from the File menu or press Command-Option-Shift-F/Ctrl-Alt-Shift-F). When you do this, InDesign examines the publication for missing fonts, lost image links, and other conditions that might cause you problems and/or embarrassment when you take your publication to an imagesetting service bureau for printing. After it's done analyzing the publication, it displays the results in the Preflight dialog box (see Figure 11-10).

As we get along in years (David never thought he'd be saying that), we wish you could change the font size in the Preflight dialog box; it's very tiny. But it's worth taking a few minutes to squint and read everything in the Summary tab: How many fonts are used? How many images? Any in RGB that should have been CMYK? Are there spot colors that you didn't expect?

Near the bottom of the summary is a cryptic line labeled Non Opaque Objects on Page. Warning: This means this page includes transparency! If an object became partially transparent without you realizing it (maybe a colleague snuck in last night and "accidentally" changed your file), it's worth catching that now.

Even better than reading this dialog box is saving all the information to disk by clicking the Report button and then reading this exported text file in your favorite word processor using whatever font size you want.

Of course, as helpful as Preflight is, it's nowhere near as good as third-party preflighting systems such as Markzware's Flightcheck (which can also check other file formats, like QuarkXPress and Illustrator files). But we'll let our output provider buy Flightcheck, and we'll pre-preflight our documents within InDesign.

**Package**

Once your publication has successfully passed the preflight check, you can assemble all of the files needed to print the publication using the Package plug-in (this is similar to QuarkXPress' "Collect for Output" feature, or PageMaker's "Save For Service Provider" plug-in). InDesign also creates a report containing detailed information about your document, including fonts and pictures you used. Then

FIGURE 11-10

**Preflight Testing a Publication**

*The Summary panel gives you a quick look at the status of the preflight check. If anything is amiss, you'll see it reported here.*

*Choose Preflight from the File menu. InDesign displays the Preflight dialog box.*

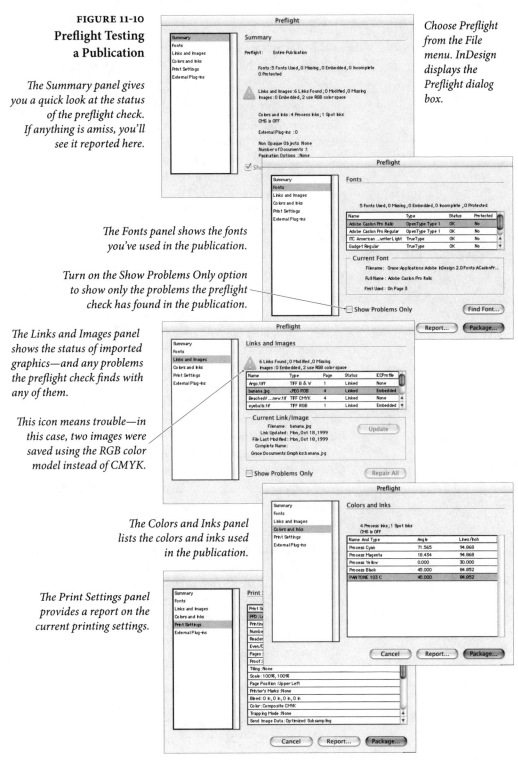

*The Fonts panel shows the fonts you've used in the publication.*

*Turn on the Show Problems Only option to show only the problems the preflight check has found in the publication.*

*The Links and Images panel shows the status of imported graphics—and any problems the preflight check finds with any of them.*

*This icon means trouble—in this case, two images were saved using the RGB color model instead of CMYK.*

*The Colors and Inks panel lists the colors and inks used in the publication.*

*The Print Settings panel provides a report on the current printing settings.*

all you have to do is get the folder to your output provider by modem, messenger, or carrier pigeon.

To "package" a publication, follow these steps (see Figure 11-11).

1. Choose Package from the File menu (or press Command-Option-Shift-P/Ctrl-Alt-Shift-P). InDesign runs a preflight check on the publication and then displays the Printing Instructions dialog box. You can also get here by clicking Package from the Preflight dialog box or Package Book from the Book palette menu. If the preflight came up with any possible problems (such as an RGB image), you have the choice to view the Preflight info before proceeding.

2. Enter contact information in the Printing Instructions dialog box—this information will appear in the final text report that InDesign adds to the package you're creating.

3. Click the Continue button. InDesign displays the Create Package Folder dialog box. Set the options you want and enter a name for the folder that will contain the packaged publication.

   When you turn on the Copy Fonts or Copy Linked Graphics options, InDesign copies the files to the folder you specify. The Update Graphic Links in Package option tells InDesign to set the links for non-embedded images to the images in the packaged folder (rather than leaving them linked to the original files). It's pretty rare that you'd want to turn this off. When you turn on the Use Document Hyphenation Exceptions Only option, InDesign flags this document so that it won't reflow when someone else opens or edits it on a machine that may have different dictionaries and hyphenation settings. We generally turn this on when sending the file to an output provider.

4. Click the Package button. InDesign creates the folder and copies the publication and the files you specified into it. If the Copy Fonts option was turned on, InDesign also alerts you that copying fonts may be a violation of your rights. Adobe fonts can be copied to send to an output provider, but some font vendors don't allow this (though we've never heard of anyone being taken to court for this).

When you send this folder full of files to your printer or service bureau, make sure you remind them that there is a file called Instructions.txt in there that they should read. In fact, we sometimes rename this file "READ ME.txt" to make it stand out better.

**FIGURE 11-11**

**Packaging a Publication for Remote Printing**

*When you choose Package from the File menu (or click the Package button in the Preflight dialog box), InDesign displays the Printing Instructions dialog box.*

*Enter your contact information and any notes you want to include in the fields; these instructions will be saved as a text file.*

*After you click the Continue button, InDesign displays the Create Package Folder dialog box.*

*Enter a name and location for the package (the publication file and any other files you choose to copy).*

*Choose the files you want to copy to the package folder.*

*You can go back to the Printing Instructions dialog box by clicking here.*

*If you're copying fonts, InDesign displays this message.*

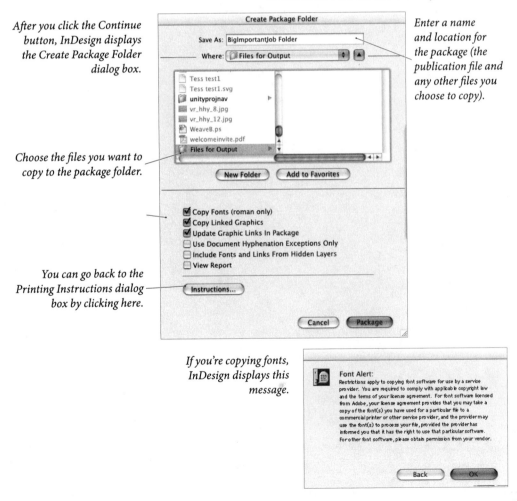

Of course, if you're working on really large files with hundreds of megabytes of images, you need to be careful with the Package feature so that you don't run out of hard disk space.

## All the News That Prints to Fit

Printing is all about thinking ahead. From the time you press Command-Shift-N/Ctrl-Shift-N to create a new publication, you really should be thinking "How the heck are we going to print this thing?" By the end of the production process, you'll be tired, cranky, and less able to deal with any problems that come up—so make your decisions about paper size, color selection, and graphic file types as early as you can.

# Scripting

CHAPTER 12

Most of the time, we tell a program (an application, a plug-in, or our system software) what to do by manipulating the program's user interface—we click, drag, and type. Scripting is a way of telling a program to perform the same tasks and accomplish the same things. The difference is that, with scripting, we don't have to click the buttons, type the characters, or choose the menu items. The script does it for you. Scripting is what computing is supposed to be *about*: having your computer take over boring, repetitive tasks so that you can spend more time playing *EverQuest*. Er, we mean, concentrating on your creative work.

Scripting also gives you the ability to add the features you need to InDesign *now*, rather than waiting for Adobe to give them to you. Even better than that, scripting gives you a way to customize InDesign to match your publications and habits to a degree that Adobe is *never* going to provide.

We're convinced that the reason many people have not taken up scripting is that they're scared. They think scripting is difficult, and is only for people with advanced computer science degrees. And they tell themselves that they're too "intuitive" and "artistic" to master the minimal analytical skills required to write a script.

Ole says: "Look. I'm practically a high school dropout, and my background is in illustration, not computer science. I have never taken a single class on programming. As a rebellious teenager I did my best to ignore the sciences and to panic at the sight of even simple equations (in psychoanalytical terms this makes sense: my father was a high school algebra teacher).

"I got over it. These days, I write scripts. You can, too."

## System Requirements

What do you need to write and run scripts for InDesign? Two things:

◆ The standard scripting system for your computer.

◆ The InDesign scripting documentation and example scripts.

**Macintosh**    On the Macintosh, all you need is AppleScript. You almost certainly already have it installed, but in case you don't, it comes on the Mac installation CD. If you can't find your installation CD, you can download AppleScript directly from Apple (http://www.apple.com/applescript). What's the easiest way to tell if it's installed? Search for a file named "Script Editor" (this is the application you use to write and run AppleScripts). If you can't find it, you'll have to install it from the CD.

A number of alternative script editors are available—and, if you're planning to do serious scripting, we strongly recommend you take a look at the amazing Script Debugger, from Late Night Software (http://www.latenightsw.com).

If you want to build user interfaces for your AppleScripts, you'll probably want to get FaceSpan (http://www.facespan.com). You can also check out AppleScript Studio (use the same Apple URL as above), but it's quite a bit harder to learn than FaceSpan (and, at the time of this writing, it's rather buggy).

**Windows**    On the Windows side, you've got a number of options. There are (at least) three slightly different scripting systems claiming to be the system standard: Visual Basic Script (VBScript), Visual Basic for Applications (VBA), and Visual Basic (VB). As footnotes to the above, you'll also find Visual Basic .NET and Visual Basic 5 Control Creation Edition. They're all from Microsoft, and they're all variants of the Basic programming language. Almost all of them work.

**The Cheapest Option: VBScript.** Get the Windows Scripting Host if you don't already have it. To find out if the Windows Scripting Host is installed on your machine, search for "wscript.exe." If you find this program, your machine is equipped with the Windows Scripting Host and can run VBScripts; if not, go to http://msdn.microsoft.com/scripting/ and download and install the program. Once it's installed, you can write scripts using your word processor or text editor.

This approach, while inexpensive, has a few drawbacks.

◆ The example scripts on your InDesign CD and in the Scripting Guide PDF were written using Visual Basic, not VBScript, and there are a number of differences between the scripting methods. You will not be able to use most of the scripting examples without modifying them.

◆ Troubleshooting (debugging) VBScripts can be difficult. You're not in a sophisticated programming environment (as you would be if you were using Visual Basic), and you can't step through the lines of your script. All you can do is run the script and then note any error messages that appear.

◆ It's hard to build user interfaces in VBScript.

**Also Free: VB5 CCE.** As we write this, the Visual Basic 5.0 Control Creation Edition is still available for free download from Microsoft, at: http://msdn.microsoft.com/vbasic/downloads/tools/cce/default.asp. It tends to move around, though, so this URL might not be valid by the time you read this. If not, a quick Google search should yield another page download location.

VB5 CCE is an almost-complete version of Visual Basic 5.0, and works very well for scripting InDesign. Its advantages are the same as those listed for Visual Basic 6.0, below. It is easily better than VBScript, unless your primary need is to embed scripts in web pages.

**Something You Might Already Own: VBA.** If you own Microsoft Excel, Microsoft Word, Microsoft Access, or Visio, you already own a copy of VBA. If you plan to write scripts to move data from these programs to InDesign (Access for database publishing, for example), you might want to simply write VBA scripts to control InDesign from inside these programs. The disadvantages are similar to those of VBScript—you won't be able to use the examples from the Scripting Guide verbatim; you'll have a harder time troubleshooting your scripts; and you'll have a harder time building user interfaces than you would in Visual Basic.

**Not Quite Free, But Worth Every Penny (If You Can Still Find It for Sale): Visual Basic 6.** The true claimant to the title of "Windows Scripting Standard" is Visual Basic, and it's an 800-pound gorilla of a contender. Visual Basic is a complete programming environment capable of building applications of the size and complexity of InDesign itself. C++ programmers reading that last assertion might scoff—let them. They've got their jobs and esoteric knowledge to protect, after all. But the truth is that Microsoft has improved the lowly and ancient programming language Basic to the point that it can hold its own with the most modern, object-oriented languages.

All of the Windows scripting examples on the InDesign CD were written in Visual Basic. This means it's easy to base your scripts on the examples—you can copy the examples right out of the PDF and paste them into Visual Basic subroutines. It's easy to construct dialog boxes and other user interface items in Visual Basic, and the environment offers powerful debugging tools.

**A Non-Starter: VB.NET.** Wait. We take back everything we said earlier. The newest version of Visual Basic—VB.NET—is a tremendous step backwards in performance, ease of use, and ease of learning. We could rant for hours (and have) about how messed up VB.NET is (at least from the standpoint of a scripter), but we'll pass, because InDesign scripting is not compatible with VB.NET anyway.

**If You Cannot Run the Visual Basic Scripts:** It's probably because your system lacks the required Visual Basic resources. Go check out http://support.microsoft.com/support/downloads/ and search for the file "VBRUN60.EXE" (We'd give you an exact URL, but Microsoft keeps moving the file around). Download and install this package—it contains everything you need to get the scripts working on your system.

## Learning About InDesign Scripting

Once you've gathered and installed the software you need to start scripting, you need to learn about how InDesign implements scripting. You're in luck—you'll find the *Adobe InDesign Scripting Guide* in the Scripting folder inside the Adobe Technical Information folder on your InDesign CD. This is a PDF file that contains an introduction to scripting, reference chapters for AppleScript and Visual Basic, and dozens of scripting examples (it's more than 600 pages long). We don't ordinarily refer people to other documentation, but we'll make an exception in this case because Ole wrote it, and you can think of it as an enormous appendix to this book.

In addition, you'll find 13 example scripts in the same folder. Even if you don't intend to write scripts of your own, you might find something useful in the example scripts:

◆ **AddGuides.** Draws guides around the currently selected object or objects. This script shows you how to get positioning information back from InDesign, and how to create ruler guides.

◆ **AddPoints.** Adds points to a path: each point is added at the midpoint of each line segment in a path. This script demonstrates simple Bezier math and path and point manipulations.

◆ **BoxCharacters.** Draws boxes around characters tagged with a specific character style. This script shows you how to implement a Find/Change feature in a script, and how to get page coordinates from text objects.

◆ **CreateCharacterStyle.** When you create a character style in InDesign by basing the style on the selected text, InDesign records only those attributes that differ from the default formatting of the surrounding text. While this is a powerful and flexible way of working with character styles, it's also different from the way that other applications (like QuarkXPress and FrameMaker) work. In those applications, character styles apply every formatting attribute. The CreateCharacterStyle script creates a new character style based on the selected text and defines every formatting attribute.

◆ **CropMarks.** Draws crop and registration marks around the selected object or objects. Like AddGuides, this script shows how to create new objects around existing objects.

◆ **ExportAllStories.** Exports all of the stories in a document to a specified folder using the file format of your choice (RTF, tagged text, or text only). Shows how to traverse all stories in a document and how to export text.

◆ **ExtractParagraphs.** Creates a text frame in a new document and fills it with a sorted list of all paragraphs of a given paragraph style in the active document. Shows how to use InDesign's Find/Change features to search for a paragraph style. Useful when you need to collect all of the text formatted using a specific paragraph style. It's similar to the Table of Contents feature.

◆ **Neon.** Creates a simple "glow" effect by duplicating the selected path or paths. Each copy of the path is slightly smaller than the original, and slightly lighter. The final duplicate path is a white hairline. The resulting group of paths is something like an Illustrator blend.

◆ **PathEffects.** If you've used Illustrator, you've probably played with the path effects "Bloat" and "Punk." This script includes those path effects, as well as a few others. If you want to learn about scripting InDesign paths, path points, and control handles, this is a good place to start.

◆ **RandomFill.** Draws a number of rectangles, ellipses, or polygons and pastes them inside the selected path. You can control the object type, size, color, and stroke weight. This is a great script for quickly generating a random background for your publications.

◆ **SelectObjects.** Selects all of the objects on a spread that belong to a specific object type (or set of types). This script is only slightly useful by itself, but it shows you how to traverse the objects on a spread to find objects based on their type or content. As such, it's a great starting point for any graphic "search and replace" operation you might want to implement. Want to make sure that all of the graphics in your publication are scaled to the same percentage or use the same color management profile? Modify this script (as shown later in this chapter).

◆ **SortParagraphs.** Alphabetically sorts the paragraphs in the selection. Shows how to sort text using a simple "bubble sort" algorithm, and how to move text in an InDesign story.

◆ **TabUtilities.** This script automates two tasks: setting a right tab stop at the right margin of a paragraph, and setting a left tab at the current cursor position. Select some text in a single-column text frame, then click the Tab at Right button to set a tab stop at the right edge of the text column (this will also remove any existing tab stops in the paragraph). Click the Tab at Cursor button to set a left tab at the current cursor position.

You'll find newer versions of these scripts at Adobe Studio Exchange (http://share.studio.adobe.com), where you'll also find a number of other useful scripts (some by Ole, some by other folks).

# Thinking About Scripting

Because scripting is a great tool for automating large, repetitive tasks, many of us think that that's *all* it's good for. But there's far more to scripting than that. Scripting is also good at little things—operations that might save you only a few seconds a day, but can make your work easier or more precise.

By "little things," we means scripts that save you only a few mouse clicks, drags, or key presses at a time. It's these tiny tasks, repeated dozens, hundreds, or even thousands of times day by day, that add up to fatigue, irritation, and repetitive motion injuries. When you take a common task that involves some number of actions and replace it with a simple double-click or keystroke (all it takes to run a script), you reduce the difficulty and complexity of your work.

Scripting, which many of us think of as being somehow *opposed* to the creative process, can be a powerful creative tool. We often imagine effects we'd like to use in a publication layout that would be difficult to accomplish by hand. When there's time, we turn to scripting for help. Frequently, in the course of working on a script, we'll find a variation on the effect that leads us in an entirely new creative direction. Scripting gives us time to experiment—and we think experimentation has a lot to do with creativity.

What we're getting at here is that scripting is what you make of it, and how you think about it. If you only think of scripting as something applicable to massive projects, you're missing out on many of the benefits—and most of the fun.

# Using the Script Label and Scripts Palettes

InDesign includes two scripting-related plug-ins: the Scripts palette and the Script Label palette. The Scripts palette gives you a way to run scripts without leaving InDesign, and significantly speeds script execution; the Script Label palette gives you a way to enter text into the Label property of a page item (for example a text frame, a rectangle, or an ellipse).

If you do not see these palettes, or if your Scripts palette is titled "Script," rather than "Scripts," you need to update your copy of InDesign to version 2.0.1 or higher. It's available for free download from adobe.com.

The Scripts palette (see Figure 12-1) displays the scripts (or aliases/shortcuts to scripts, or folders) stored inside the Scripts folder inside your InDesign application folder. This folder is not created when you install the plug-in, so you'll have to create it yourself. In general, we think it's better to store your scripts somewhere else, and place aliases (on the Mac OS) or shortcuts (in Windows) in this folder. Why? We've accidentally deleted all of our scripts by re-installing InDesign more than once. It's painful.

To run a script, double-click the script in the Scripts palette. To edit a script, hold down Option/Alt and double-click the script. InDesign will open the script in your script editor. To delete scripts from the Scripts palette, open the Scripts folder on your hard drive and move the scripts to another location (or delete them).

*To run a script, double-click the script name in the Scripts palette.*

*"Install" scripts in the Scripts palette by adding them to the Scripts folder in your InDesign application folder. (Create this folder if it does not already exist.)*

The Script Label palette (see Figure 12-2) has only one purpose—it gives you a way to enter text into the label of an object. Once you work with scripting for a bit, you'll realize how useful the label property of a page item is. When your script is looking through the objects in a document, it can be difficult to find the object you're looking for. By attaching a label to an object, we make finding the object a great deal easier.

But labels are useful in a wide variety of other ways, as well. An object's label can store up to 32 Kb of text, so you could actually store quite complex scripts (which are just text, after all) inside an object. Or a label could contain an XML representation of the object.

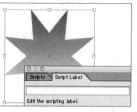

*Display the Script Label palette.*

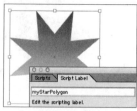

*Enter a label for the object. Adding the label does not change the object in any visible way.*

# Getting Started

For your first script, try the "Hello World" examples in the *Scripting Guide*. They're short, they show you how to create a new document, create a new text frame, add text to the text frame, and apply formatting to that text. After that, start thinking about what you'd like to do with scripting. Is there some task you do in InDesign every day that's driving you crazy?

Wait—we've got one! When you want to get an object or series of objects *out* of a frame you've pasted them into, you end up doing a lot of selecting, cutting, and pasting. A script that could remove all of the objects from a frame (while maintaining the positions they occupied in the frame) would save you time and trouble. Right? Let's go!

**Applescript**    This script assumes you have an object selected, and that the object contains at least one other object or group. The script will not ungroup a group as it processes the objects. To create the script, follow these steps (see Figure 12-3).

1. Start the AppleScript Script Editor and InDesign.

2. Enter the following text (note that ¬ indicates a long line—do not enter a line break in the Script Editor).

```
--CutContents
--An InDesign 2.0 script.
set done to false
tell application "InDesign 2.0.2"
 activate
 set mySelection to selection
 if (count mySelection) = 1 then
    set myPageItem to item 1 of mySelection
    repeat while done is false
       if class of myPageItem is not group and ¬
       (count page items of myPageItem) is greater than 0 then
          set myItem to page item 1 of myPageItem
          copy geometric bounds of myItem to myBounds
          set myX to item 2 of myBounds
          set myY to item 1 of myBounds
          select myItem
          cut
          paste
          set myPageItem to item 1 of selection
          tell myPageItem to move to {myX, myY}
       else
          set done to true
       end if
    end repeat
 end if
end tell
```

3. Switch to InDesign. Select a path that contains one or more objects.

4. Switch back to the Script Editor and run the script. InDesign will remove each nested object inside the frame and paste it into the same position as it occupied while inside the frame.

**FIGURE 12-3**
**Cut Contents Script**
**(Applescript Version)**

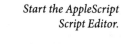

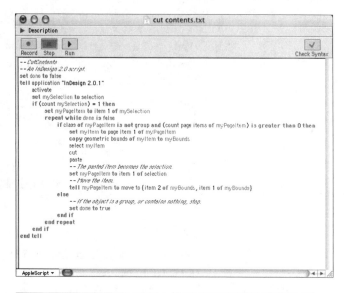

*Start the AppleScript Script Editor.*

*Enter AppleScript (don't worry about the indents or formatting—the Script Editor takes care of it for you).*

*Once you've tested the script, save a compiled version and put it (or an alias to it) in the Scripts folder. That way, you can run it from the Scripts palette inside InDesign.*

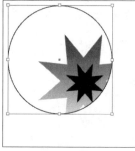

*Once you've entered a script, select an object you've pasted other objects into.*

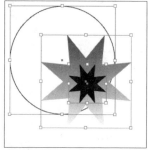

*Run the script (click the Run button in the Script Editor), and InDesign will "un-nest" the objects while retaining their original positions.*

**Visual Basic**

To create this script, follow these steps (see Figure 12-4). These are the same steps as you take to create any Visual Basic script, but we'll repeat them here as a reminder.

1. Start InDesign and Visual Basic.

2. In Visual Basic, create a new project. Choose "Standard EXE" as your project template.

**FIGURE 12-4**

**Cut Contents Script (Visual Basic Version)**

*Start Visual Basic and choose New Project from the File menu. Choose Standard EXE.*

*Click the OK button.*

*Visual Basic creates a new project and displays a blank form.*

*Choose References from the Project menu. Visual Basic displays the References dialog box.*

*Turn on the Adobe InDesign 2.0 Type Library option and click OK to close the dialog box.*

*Click the Command Button tool.*

*Draw a new command button on the form, then double-click the button.*

*Visual Basic displays the Code window.*

*Enter the code for the button (between the "Private Sub" and "End Sub" lines).*

*To run your script, choose Start from the Run menu (or press F5), then click the button. The result will be the same as that shown in the AppleScript example.*

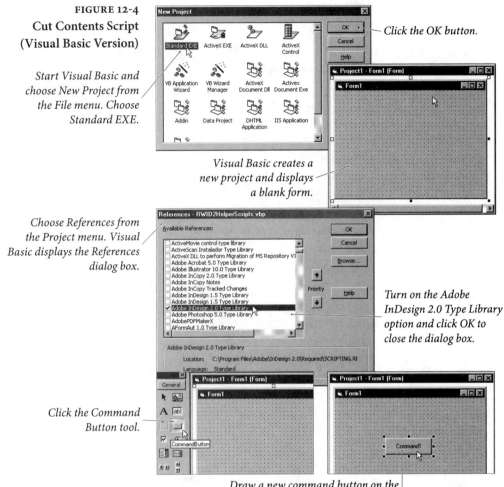

```vb
Private Sub Command1_Click()
Dim myInDesign As InDesign.Application
Set myInDesign = CreateObject("InDesign.Application.2.0")
myDone = False
Set mySelection = myInDesign.Selection
If mySelection.Count = 1 Then
    Set myPageItem = mySelection.Item(1)
    Do While myDone = False
        If TypeName(myPageItem) <> "Group" And myPageItem.PageItems.Count > 0 Then
            Set myItem = myPageItem.PageItems.Item(1)
            myBounds = myItem.GeometricBounds
            myInDesign.Select myItem, False
            myInDesign.Cut
            myInDesign.Paste
            Set myPageItem = myInDesign.Selection.Item(1)
            myPageItem.Move Array(myBounds(1), myBounds(0))
        Else
            myDone = True
        End If
    Loop
End If
End Sub
```

3. Choose References from the Project menu. Visual Basic displays the References dialog box. Turn on the Adobe InDesign 2.0 Type Library option (in the Available References list), then click the OK button to add this reference to your project.

   If you can't see an entry for the Adobe InDesign 2.0 Type Library in the list, click the Browse button. Visual Basic displays the Add Reference dialog box. Locate and select the file "Scripting.rpln" in the Required folder inside your InDesign folder. Click the Open button. When Visual Basic returns you to the References dialog box, the Adobe InDesign 2.0 Type Library option should appear in the Available References list.

4. Create a new form by choosing Add Form from the Project menu. Visual Basic displays the Add Form dialog box. Select the standard form template ("Form") and click the Open button. Visual Basic creates a new, blank form.

5. Add a button to the form by selecting the CommandButton tool and then drag the tool in the form.

6. Double-click the button to display the Code window. Enter the following text (between the line beginning with "Private Sub" and the line containing "End Sub" that Visual Basic will already have entered for you).

```
Dim myInDesign As InDesign.Application
Set myInDesign = CreateObject("InDesign.Application.2.0")
myDone = False
Set mySelection = myInDesign.Selection
If mySelection.Count = 1 Then
 Set myPageItem = mySelection.Item(1)
 Do While myDone = False
    If TypeName(myPageItem) <> "Group" And
    myPageItem.PageItems.Count > 0 Then
       Set myItem = myPageItem.PageItems.Item(1)
       myBounds = myItem.GeometricBounds
       myInDesign.Select myItem, False
       myInDesign.Cut
       myInDesign.Paste
       Set myPageItem = myInDesign.Selection.Item(1)
       myPageItem.Move Array(myBounds(1), myBounds(0))
    Else
       myDone = True
    End If
 Loop
End If
```

Now you're ready to test your new script. Go to InDesign and select a path that has another path or group pasted inside it. Return to Visual Basic and click the Run button. Visual Basic displays the form. Click the button you created in Step 5. If everything's working properly, the script should extract the objects inside the selected path.

This example script contains very little error checking code—so you'll get an error from Visual Basic if the script encounters a condition it's not prepared for. The script will fail if no publication is open, for example.

Why did we leave out error checking? It can make the script a lot longer, slower, and harder to read. For examples of proper (which is not to say foolproof) error checking, refer to the example scripts on your InDesign CD.

## More Fun with Scripting

We'll limit ourselves to just two more scripting examples, because we want to finish this book sometime this decade.

**Automatically Creating Style-to-Tag Mappings**

If you've looked through Chapter 7, "Importing and Exporting," you probably noticed the section on mapping paragraph styles to XML tags. It's a very powerful method of converting your existing InDesign documents to an XML workflow.

If your documents contain a large number of styles, and if those styles contain spaces, you probably groaned aloud thinking about the amount of work you'd have to put in to map all of your paragraph styles to tags.

Automating this process is exactly the sort of thing that scripting is very good at. The following are two example scripts (one for each platform). The script creates tags that match each paragraph style in the document, replacing invalid characters in the style names as it does so. The script then associates each paragraph style with the corresponding tag.

**AppleScript.** Follow the steps shown earlier in this chapter, and enter the AppleScript shown below. Note that ¬ indicates a long line in this layout—do not enter a line break in the Script Editor.

```
tell application "InDesign 2.0.2"
 set myDocument to active document
 tell myDocument
   repeat with myCounter from 1 to (count paragraph styles)
     set myParagraphStyle to paragraph style myCounter
     set myStyleName to name of myParagraphStyle
     if myStyleName is not "[No paragraph style]" then
```

```
    --Replace spaces. Search for other characters if necessary.
    set myStyleName to my myReplaceCharacters ¬
    (myStyleName, " ", "_")
    set myTag to make XML Tag with properties {name:myStyleName}
    --Map styles to tags
    set myMap to make XML export map with properties ¬
    {markup tag:myTag, mapped paragraph style:myParagraphStyle}
    --To map tags to styles, remove the comment from the
    --following line and comment out the line above.
    --set myMap to make XML import map with properties ¬
    {markup tag:myTag, mapped paragraph style:myParagraphStyle}
        end if
    end repeat
    --Apply the mapping specified above.
    auto Tag
  end tell
end tell
on myReplaceCharacters(myString, mySearchString, myReplaceString)
 set AppleScript's text item delimiters to the mySearchString
 set the myList to every text item of myString
 set AppleScript's text item delimiters to the myReplaceString
 set myString to the myList as string
 set AppleScript's text item delimiters to ""
 return myString
end myReplaceCharacters
```

**Visual Basic.** Follow the steps shown earlier in this chapter for creating a Visual Basic script, and enter the code shown below.

```
Rem MapStylesToTags
Dim myInDesign As InDesign.Application
Set myInDesign = CreateObject("InDesign.Application.2.0")
Set myDocument = myInDesign.ActiveDocument
For myStyleCounter = 1 To myDocument.ParaStyles.Count
 Set myParaStyle = myDocument.ParaStyles.Item(myStyleCounter)
 myStyleName = myParaStyle.Name
 If myStyleName <> "[No paragraph style]" Then
    myStyleName = Replace(myStyleName, " ", "_")
    Set myXMLTag = myDocument.XMLTags.Add(myStyleName)
    Set myMap = myDocument.XMLExportMaps.Add(myParaStyle, myXMLTag)
    Rem To map XML tags to styles, comment the line above
    Rem and uncomment the following line.
    'Set myMap = myDocument.XMLImportMaps.Add(myXMLTag, myParaStyle)
 End If
Next
myDocument.AutoTag
```

**Drawing NINAs**    Have you ever played with a Spirograph? Or been fascinated by one of the geometric patterns created by M. C. Escher? Both authors admit a fondness (well, more like an obsession) for geometric art. While writing this book, we stumbled across a very interesting web site: http://www.washington.edu/bibsys/mattf/nina/. Matt Freedman, at the University of Washington, invented (or is it "discovered"?) a very nifty new algorithm for drawing shapes he's named NINAs (NINA being an acronym for "Nina Is Not An Acronym"). NINAs are fascinating shapes, and we had to see if we could write InDesign scripts that make use of the NINA algorithm. Figure 12-5 shows some of our results.

Note: This script involves a small amount of trigonometry—so we've had to add some handlers (subroutines) to the AppleScript section, because AppleScript has no built-in trigonometric functions. In addition, you should note that the Visual Basic functions return values in radians, rather than degrees, and that InDesign's vertical axis is upside down relative to traditional geometric plotting.

**Applescript**  Again, follow the steps shown for creating an AppleScript earlier in this chapter. Note that ¬ indicates a long line in this layout—do not enter a line break in the Script Editor. Note, too, that this AppleScript can be very slow. If you have an AppleScript extension that supports sine and cosine functions, you could use those functions to improve script performance. In the meantime, experiment with fairly low values for the "myNumberOfLines" variable.

```
set myList to {}
set myNumberOfLines to 128
set a_pulse to 33
set b_pulse to 37
set myLength to 6
repeat with myCounter from 0 to (myNumberOfLines * 2)
 --Note: the "*(180/pi)" part converts radians to degrees,
 --as the sine/cosine handlers expect degrees as their input.
 set myAValue to ((-2 * pi * a_pulse * myCounter) / myNumberOfLines)¬
 * (180 / pi)
 set myBValue to ((-2 * pi * b_pulse * myCounter) / myNumberOfLines)¬
 * (180 / pi)
 set myASine to my sine_of(myAValue)
 set myACosine to my cosine_of(myAValue)
 set myBSine to my sine_of(myBValue)
 set myBCosine to my cosine_of(myBValue)
 set myX to (myACosine + myBCosine) * myLength
 set myY to (myASine + myBSine) * myLength
 copy {myX, myY} to end of myList
end repeat

tell application "InDesign 2.0.2"
 set myDocument to active document
 tell page 1 of myDocument
    set myGraphicLine to make graphic line
    set entire path of path 1 of myGraphicLine to myList
 end tell
end tell
```

```
--Sine and Cosine routines from Apple's
--Essential Subroutines collection.
on sine_of(x)
 repeat until x ≥ 0 and x < 360
    if x is greater than or equal to 360 then
       set x to x - 360
    end if
    if x < 0 then
       set x to x + 360
    end if
 end repeat
 --convert from degrees to radians
 set x to x * (2 * pi) / 360
 set answer to 0
 set numerator to x
 set denominator to 1
 set factor to -(x ^ 2)
 repeat with i from 3 to 40 by 2
    set answer to answer + numerator / denominator
    set numerator to numerator * factor
    set denominator to denominator * i * (i - 1)
 end repeat
 return answer
end sine_of

on cosine_of(x)
 repeat until x ≥ 0 and x < 360
    if x ≥ 360 then
       set x to x - 360
    end if
    if x < 0 then
       set x to x + 360
    end if
 end repeat
 --convert from degrees to radians
 set x to x * (2 * pi) / 360
 set answer to 0
 set numerator to 1
 set denominator to 1
 set factor to - (x ^ 2)
 repeat with i from 2 to 40 by 2
    set answer to answer + numerator / denominator
    set numerator to numerator * factor
    set denominator to denominator * i * (i - 1)
 end repeat
 return answer
end cosine_of
```

**Visual Basic**    Follow the steps shown for creating a Visual Basic script earlier in this chapter (as usual, "¬" indicates a line break in this layout; do not break the line or type the character).

```
Rem Draw NINA
Rem For more on NINA, see:
Rem http://www.washington.edu/bibsys/mattf/nina/index.html
Dim myInDesign As InDesign.Application
Set myInDesign = CreateObject("InDesign.Application.2.0")
Set myDocument = myInDesign.ActiveDocument
Set myPage = myInDesign.ActiveWindow.ActiveSpread
pi = 3.14159265358979
Rem myNumberOfLines sets the number of line segments in the NINA.
myNumberOfLines = 194
Rem Experiment with a_pulse and b_pulse to create different NINAs.
Rem Total of the a_pulse and b_pulse values must not exceed
Rem myNumberOfLines
a_pulse = 67
b_pulse = 90
Rem The "radius" of the NINA is roughly 2 x myLength.
myLength = 6
ReDim myArray(myNumberOfLines - 1)
Rem Fill in an array with point locations.
For myCounter = 0 To (myNumberOfLines - 1)
 cur_x = (Cos((-2 * pi * a_pulse * myCounter) / myNumberOfLines) + ¬
Cos((-2 * pi * b_pulse * myCounter) / myNumberOfLines)) * myLength
 cur_y = (Sin((-2 * pi * a_pulse * myCounter) / myNumberOfLines) +
Sin((-2 * pi * b_pulse * myCounter) / myNumberOfLines)) * myLength ¬
 myArray(myCounter) = Array(cur_x, cur_y)
Next
Set myLine = myPage.Lines.Add
Rem Move the line a bit to clear up page "ownership" issues.
myLine.Move , Array("1p", "1p")
Rem Set the points on the path to the array generated by the loop.
myLine.Paths.Item(1).EntirePath = myArray
Rem Label the NINA with the a_pulse and b_pulse settings.
myLine.Label = "number_of_lines = " & CStr(myNumberOfLines) & ¬
", a_pulse = " & CStr(a_pulse) & ", b_pulse = " & CStr(b_pulse)
myLine.Paths.Item(1).PathType = idClosed
```

**Testing the NINA Drawing Script**

To test the NINA drawing script, move InDesign's ruler zero point to the point at which you want to locate the center of the shape, then run the script (we recommend setting the publication's measurement system to points before running the script). If all goes well, InDesign will draw a NINA. We urge you to experiment with the settings in the script—the number of different types of shapes you can draw is truly endless. Even very slight changes to the settings can produce wildly differing results. Figure 12-5 shows some of our NINAs.

This is a good script to add a user interface to—all you need is a dialog box containing four text fields (to set the myNumberOfLines, a_pulse, b_pulse, and myLength variables) and OK/Cancel buttons.

**FIGURE 12-5**
**Various NINAs**

## End Script

Scripting is all about *user empowerment*. Don't just sit around telling yourself that the reason you're working late is that InDesign can't do something you'd like it to do. Sure, there are things in every program we'd like the manufacturer to fix, but, with InDesign's scripting architecture, we've finally been given the tools we need to *fix them ourselves*.

By urging you to take up scripting, we're urging you to take control of InDesign, your publications, your work, and your life. We know you can do it!

# INDEX